Nikāya Buddhism and Early Chan

Oxford Centre for Buddhist Studies Monographs
Series Editor: Richard Gombrich, Oxford Centre for Buddhist Studies

The Oxford Centre for Buddhist Studies promotes teaching and research into all Buddhist traditions, as found in texts and in societies, and is equally open to the study of Buddhism by methods associated with the humanities (philology, philosophy, history) and the social sciences (anthropology, sociology, politics). It insists only on using sources in their original languages and on aiming at the highest scholarly standards.

Published in the series from Equinox Publishing Ltd:

Buddhist Monks and the Politics of Lanka's Civil War: Ethnoreligious Nationalism of the Sinhala Saṅgha and Peacemaking in Sri Lanka, 1995–2010
Suren Raghavan

Chinese Buddhism Today
Yu-Shuang Yao and Richard Gombrich

Dudjom Rinpoche's Vajrakīlaya Works: A Study in Authoring, Compiling, and Editing Texts in the Tibetan Revelatory Tradition
Cathy Cantwell (with a chapter by Robert Mayer)

How Buddhism Acquired a Soul on the Way to China
Jungnok Park

Sermon of One Hundred Days: Part One
Venerable Seongcheol
Edited by Linda Covill
Translated by Hwang Soon-Il

What the Buddha Thought
Richard Gombrich

Nikāya Buddhism and Early Chan

A Different Meditative Paradigm

Grzegorz Polak

equinox

SHEFFIELD UK BRISTOL CT

Published by Equinox Publishing Ltd.
UK: Office 415, The Workstation, 15 Paternoster Row, Sheffield,
South Yorkshire S1 2BX
USA: ISD, 70 Enterprise Drive, Bristol, CT 06010

www.equinoxpub.com

First published 2024

British Library Cataloguing-in-Publication Data
A catalogue record for this book is available from the British Library.

ISBN-13	978 1 80050 424 0	(hardback)
	978 1 80050 425 7	(paperback)
	978 1 80050 426 4	(ePDF)
	978 1 80050 511 7	(ePub)

Library of Congress Cataloging-in-Publication Data
Names: Polak, Grzegorz, author.
Title: Nikāya Buddhism and early Chan : a different meditative paradigm / Grzegorz Polak.
Description: Bristol : Equinox Publishing Ltd, 2024. | Series: Oxford centre for Buddhist studies monographs | Includes bibliographical references and index. | Summary: "This book is the first detailed comparative study of the philosophical and meditative concepts of Nikāya Buddhism and early Chan"-- Provided by publisher.
Identifiers: LCCN 2023046536 (print) | LCCN 2023046537 (ebook) | ISBN 9781800504240 (hardback) | ISBN 9781800504257 (paperback) | ISBN 9781800504264 (pdf) | ISBN 978180505117 (epub)
Subjects: LCSH: Meditation--Buddhism. | Theravāda Buddhism--Doctrines. | Zen Buddhism--Doctrines.
Classification: LCC BQ5612 .P65 2024 (print) | LCC BQ5612 (ebook) | DDC 294.3/4435--dc23/eng/20231026
LC record available at https://lccn.loc.gov/2023046536
LC ebook record available at https://lccn.loc.gov/2023046537

Typeset by S.J.I. Services, New Delhi, India

CONTENTS

Acknowledgements vii
Abbreviations ix
Notes on references to the source texts xi

Introduction 1

1 The wrong and the right forms of meditation 28

2 Calm and insight, concentration and wisdom 85

3 The world of experience 132

4 Meditative cessation as a process of cognitive deconstruction 168

5 Can there be a methodless meditation? 228

6 Meditation as an extension of a specific way of life 265

7 Calming the mind through awareness 297

8 Beyond method 319

Conclusions 356

Bibliography 368
Index 382

ACKNOWLEDGEMENTS

I would like to express my gratitude to the following people who in various ways have contributed to the creation and publication of this book: Richard Gombrich, Krzysztof Kosior, Weijen Teng, Lin Chenkuo, Michael Hunt, Christopher J. Frackiewicz, my brother Paweł and my parents. I would also like to thank the creators of the following electronic tools and databases which proved to be very useful during the preparation of this book: Digital Pāli Reader, Digital Pāḷi Dictionary and CBETA Online Reader. Some parts of this book elaborate and build upon the ideas which have appeared in a different form in my book *Wczesny Buddyzm a Chan. Medytacja i wyzwolenie*, published by Księgarnia Akademicka in 2020.

This book contains the results of the research projects which have received funding from the following research grants:

- *Philosophical ideas of early Buddhism: A critical reconstruction through an interdisciplinary approach*, Research Project No. 2018/31/B/HS1/01324 financed by the National Science Center (NCN) in Poland.
- *Chan Buddhism in relation to early Buddhism: A reassessment based on new results of research of early Buddhist literature*, Sheng Yen Education Foundation Grant for Visiting Scholars from Abroad, National Chengchi University in Taipei (NCCU).
- 「禪宗」與「早期佛教」的禪修方法和哲學思想之比較研究 (*Chan and Early Buddhism: A Comparative Study of Meditative Methods and Philosophical Ideas*), Chung-Hwa Institute of Buddhist Studies Research Grant, Dharma Drum Mountain, Taiwan.

The cover design of this book is inspired by the following passages:

- "No activity of the mind whatsoever, the mind-ground as if empty space, the sun of wisdom naturally appears, like the sun emerging when the clouds open up". *Baizhang Huaihai chanshi guanglu* (X69, no. 1323, p. 7c12).
- "Luminous, bhikkhus, is this mind and it is released from the adventitious defilements". *Pabhassara-sutta, Aṅguttara Nikāya* (AN 1.50/i.10).

ABBREVIATIONS

AN	*Aṅguttara Nikāya*
B	*Dazangjing bubian* 大藏經補編
c.	Chinese
CBETA	Chinese Buddhist Electronic Text Association
Dhp	*Dhammapada*
Dhs	*Dhammasaṅgaṇī*
DN	*Dīgha Nikāya*
gr.	Greek
Kd	*Khandhaka*
Iti	*Itivuttaka*
MĀ	*Zhong ahanjing* 中阿含經 (*Madhyama Āgama*)
MN	*Majjhima Nikāya*
p.	Pali
PTS	Pali Text Society
s.	Sanskrit
SĀ	*Za ahanjing* 雜阿含經 (*Saṃyukta Āgama*)
SN	*Saṃyutta Nikāya*
Snp	*Suttanipāta*
Spk	*Sāratthapakāsinī*
T	*Taishō shinshū dai zōkyō* 大正新脩大藏經 (*Taishō Tripiṭaka*)
Thag	*Theragāthā*
Thig	*Therīgāthā*
Ud	*Udāna*
Vism	*Visuddhimagga*
X	*Xuzangijng: Manji Shinsan Dainihon Zokuzōkyō* 卍新纂大日本續藏經

NOTES ON REFERENCES TO THE SOURCE TEXTS

References to the Pali texts

Numerical references to the Nikāya texts use a twofold system. A reference to the number of a text is given before the slash, while the volume number and page number(s) of the text in the PTS edition are provided after the slash. Volume numbers of the PTS edition are in roman numerals written in the lowercase form. In the case of particular texts, the numerical references to Pali texts are respectively to:

- *Aṅguttara Nikāya* – (before the slash) the number of the *nipāta* and the number of the sutta / (after the slash) the volume number and page number(s) in the PTS edition.
- *Dhammapada* – the verse number / the page number(s) in the PTS edition.
- *Dhammasaṅgaṇī* – the number of the page(s) in the Burmese Chaṭṭha Saṅgāyana edition / the number of page(s) in the PTS edition.
- *Dīgha Nikāya* – the number of the sutta / the volume number and page number(s) in the PTS edition.
- *Itivuttaka* – the number of the sutta / the page number(s) in the PTS edition.
- *Khandhaka* – the number of the chapter / the page number(s) in the PTS edition.
- *Majjhima Nikāya* – the number of the sutta / the volume number and page number(s) in the PTS edition.
- *Saṃyutta Nikāya* – the number of the *saṃyutta* and the number of the sutta / the number of the volume and number of the page(s) in the PTS edition.

- *Sāratthapakāsinī* – the number of the volume and number of page(s) in the Burmese Chaṭṭha Saṅgāyana edition / the number of the volume and number of the page(s) in the PTS edition.
- *Suttanipāta* – the number of the *vagga* and the number of the sutta / the page number(s) in the PTS edition.
- *Theragāthā* – the number of the *nipāta* and the number of the sutta / the page number(s) in the PTS edition.
- *Therīgāthā* – the number of the *nipāta* and the number of the sutta / the page number(s) in the PTS edition.
- *Udāna* – the number of the *vagga* and the number of the sutta / the number of the page(s) in the PTS edition.
- *Visuddhimagga* – the number of the volume and number of page(s) in the Burmese Chaṭṭha Saṅgāyana edition / the number of page(s) in the PTS edition / the number of the chapter and the paragraph number in Bhikkhu Ñāṇamoli's (2010) translation.

The numbering of the suttas which is used before the slash follows the numerical scheme used at https://suttacentral.net. In the case of general references to a particular sutta, the numbers after the slash refer to the range of pages in the PTS edition in which the sutta in question is found. In the case of references to a specific fragment of a particular text, the number after the slash refers to the page of the PTS edition on which this fragment is found.

All citations of Pali texts are from the *Chaṭṭha Saṅgāyana Tipiṭaka, Version 4.0* (*CST4*) published by the Vipassana Research Institute and available online at http://tipitaka.org with some occasional amendments based on the PTS and the Sinhalese Buddha Jayanti editions which are explained in the relevant fragments of the book.

References to the Chinese texts

Numbers used in the references to the *Taishō shinshū dai zōkyō* (T) refer respectively to the number of the volume, the number of the text, the page number, the letter of the register and the line number(s). For example, "T48, no. 2011, p. 379a8–14" refers to the 48th volume of the *Taishō shinshū dai zōkyō*, text no. 2011, page 379, register "a" and lines 8–14.

Numbers used in the references to the *Xuzangjing*: *Manji Shinsan Dainihon Zokuzōkyō* (X) refer respectively to the number of the volume, the number of the text, the number of the page, the letter of the register, and the line number(s). For example: "X63, no. 1224, p. 25b8–9" refers to the 63rd volume of the *Xuzangjing*: *Manji Shinsan Dainihon Zokuzōkyō*, text no. 1224, page 25, register "b" and lines 8–9.

Numbers used in the references to the *Dazangjing bubian* 大藏經補編 (B) refer respectively to the number of the volume, the number of the text, the number of the page, the letter of the register, and the line number(s). For example: "B25, no. 142, p. 67a6–7" refers to the 25th volume of the *Dazangjing bubian* 大藏經補編, text no. 142, page 67, register "a" and lines 6–7.

The citations of Chinese texts contained in the footnotes use the following scheme:

address of the citation：citation

For example: "T48, no. 2015, p. 402b3：南北宗中相敵如楚漢。" means that the fragment「南北宗中相敵如楚漢。」is contained in the 48th volume of the *Taishō shinshū dai zōkyō* 大正新脩大藏經, in the text no. 2015, on page 402, in register "b" and in line 3.

Citations of Chinese texts are from the CBETA (Chinese Buddhist Electronic Text Association) version 2022.Q4 (2023–01), available online at http://cbetaonline.cn.

The exceptions to this rule are:

- Citations of the *Xiuxin yao lun* 修心要論, which are from the critical version based on the Dunhuang manuscripts as published by McRae (1986) in his book *The Northern School and the Formation of Early Ch'an Buddhism*. As the pages containing the Chinese text of the *Xiuxin yao lun* are numbered separately from the rest of that book using Chinese numerals, the references to its particular fragments refer first to the general number of the page of the book on which they are found and then after the slash to an individual number of the page of the text itself. For the sake of comparison, numerical references are also provided to the corresponding fragments of the *Zuishangsheng lun* 最上乘論 (T48, no. 2011), which is a later edition of the same text contained in the *Taishō shinshū dai zōkyō*.
- Citations of the text *Daofan qusheng xinjue* 導凡趣聖心決, which is not contained in the CBETA. Citations are from the version of the text contained in Yamabe's (2014) *Yogācāra Influence on the Northern School of Chan Buddhism*.

A note on transcription of words and phrases from oriental languages

Pali words and phrases are usually written in italics and appear in parentheses directly after their English equivalents. A standard Roman script with diacritic marks is used, for example: "Concentration (*samādhi*) plays an important role in early Buddhism". The form in which Pali words are given usually follows the standard convention present in Pali-English dictionaries, e.g., nouns are given in their uninflected stem forms, while verbs in the third person singular of the present tense. The exceptions from this convention are instances when a Pali phrase or word are quoted in parentheses in the form in which they occur in the source text directly after their English translation which is given in quotation marks, e.g., "one of tranquil body experiences pleasure" (*passaddhakāyo sukhaṃ vedeti*).

Due to the difficulties of accurately translating some terms into English, or for the sake of clarity, they appear in their Pali forms throughout the book. This particularly refers to the term *jhāna*. For the sake of convenience and to improve the flow of the text, plural English forms of Pali terms are sometimes used. In order to clarify that they are not genuine Pali words ending with "s" (e.g., "*manas*"), the "s" in regular font is added at the end of the italicized Pali word (e.g., *jhāna*s). The titles of the Pali texts are in italics, for example: "The *Sandha-sutta* is an important early Buddhist text".

In the case of Chinese words and phrases, two systems of transcription are simultaneously being used. First, a pinyin transcription is given in italics, followed by an original inscription with the use of traditional Chinese characters. Usually, these transcriptions are found in parentheses immediately following the word or phrase which are their translations into English. For example: "mind (*xin* 心)", means that the English word "mind" corresponds to the traditional Chinese character 心, transcribed in pinyin as "*xin*".

The titles of the Chinese texts are given in pinyin in italics and in traditional Chinese characters whenever they appear for the first time in the book. The English translation of the title is provided in parentheses. Afterwards, only the pinyin is given. The same convention applies to the names of ancient Chinese Buddhist authors. The citations from Chinese texts in the footnotes are given exclusively in Chinese traditional characters.

Although both Chinese pinyin and Pali terms are given in italics, the context makes it clear whether the particular term is a Chinese pinyin or a Pali term. In rare cases where this is not obvious (e.g., when Chinese, Pali and sometimes Sanskrit equivalent terms are provided at the same time) they are distinguished by additional abbreviations being used before them (e.g., c. *zhi* 止, p. *samatha*, s. *śamatha*).

When quoting translations of Chinese and Pali fragments by other authors, I often insert relevant Chinese or Pali technical terms from the translated original texts in parentheses after English words which are their translations. These insertions are not part of the original translation which is being quoted.

INTRODUCTION

The idea of a comparative study of Nikāya Buddhism[1] and early Chan may appear surprising or even be dismissed as outright pointless if approached from the perspective of commonly held, stereotypical views about Buddhism. After all, it is pretty much taken for granted that these two traditions have relatively little in common besides sharing some fundamental tenets that are found in all Buddhist traditions. They originated in completely different cultural and historical conditions, and due to their temporal and spatial separation there was no direct contact or influence between them. However, this book will argue that the texts of both traditions contain certain similar but very unconventional ideas about meditation that are quite different from those that are commonly associated with Buddhism and were dominant through most of its history.

It has long been acknowledged that many Chan meditative ideas are unique and unusual, especially when compared to those representative of other, more mainstream traditions of Buddhism. Their unorthodox character is immediately evident upon initial reading, and some Chan authors explicitly emphasize this feature in their texts. The uniqueness of Chan ideas and their difference from mainstream Buddhism has even led some scholars in the past to question whether this tradition is quintessentially Buddhist at all.[2]

1 As it will be explained in greater detail in the course of the introduction, in this book this term refers to the doctrine found in the main four Pali Nikāyas of the *Suttapiṭaka* and the older parts of the *Khuddaka Nikāya* and not, as in Hirakawa's (1990) work, to monastic Buddhism after the initial schism into the Mahāsaṅghika and Sthavira schools.

2 E.g., Edkins (1890) and Wieger (1927).

In contrast, outside of a small circle of scholars, there has been relatively little awareness that early Nikāya texts contain many unique ideas that are very different from those found in the classical works of the fully developed Theravāda school. Rather, there has been a tendency to ignore them and see the Nikāyas as merely containing a basic version of the doctrine which was later to become that of classical Theravāda. And since the latter is very different from Chan teachings, this would effectively undermine the meaningfulness of any comparative study aiming at exploring parallels between the ideas found in Nikāya and Chan texts.

However, critical research in recent decades has produced important new results which have changed our perspective on the early Buddhist teachings contained in the Nikāyas. Although contemporary scholars of early Buddhism often strongly disagree regarding the correct interpretation of particular concepts found in these texts, a consensus seems to be emerging that later developments within the Buddhist schools, which start with the Abhidharma scriptures, represent a significant shift away from the earliest doctrine. By the time of Buddhaghosa's commentaries, the doctrinal differences are already quite fundamental. New evidence for this claim is steadily accumulating with each new critical scholarly work that is being published.

According to some of these scholarly claims, early Buddhist philosophical views regarding the nature of reality, mind and cognition may have been in many respects different from those developed by the schools of pre-Mahāyāna Indian Buddhism (i.e., the so-called Hīnayāna schools).[3] However, the most important and numerous discrepancies which exist between the Nikāyas and the later developments within both Theravāda and other mainstream forms of Buddhism concern meditation. Critical research has uncovered many features that do not fit well or are even directly at odds with the historically dominant approaches to meditation in Buddhism.[4] These unusual features mostly concern the role and nature of meditation, its position in early Buddhist soteriology, the relation between calm (*samatha*) and insight (*vipassanā*) and the character of liberating insight. Particularly problematic and controversial is the issue of the exact character of the meditative states

3 E.g., Harvey (1995), Hamilton (2000), Ronkin (2005), Gombrich (2009) and Wynne (2010; 2015b).

4 E.g., Bronkhorst (1986), Vetter (1988), Bucknell (1993), Wynne (2007), Polak (2011), Shulman (2014) and Arbel (2017).

known as the four *jhānas* and of the method of attaining them. When taken at face value, some of these unusual features appear to be similar to those present in early Chan texts. This opens up a new perspective for a more detailed examination of the similarities and parallels between Nikāya and early Chan teachings. It needs to be said here that it is not the aim of this book to provide an exhaustive comparison of various aspects of both traditions simply for comparison's sake. It is quite obvious that there exist important differences between Nikāya Buddhism and early Chan in terms of terminology as well as some of the ideas and practices and this fact does not require detailed elaboration.

Unusual features present in both Nikāya and early Chan texts

The focus of this book is on the passages in the texts of both traditions which may be read as expressing similar and at the same time very unconventional meditative and philosophical ideas. They are problematic and puzzling in the sense of being difficult to harmonize with historically dominant Buddhist ideas about meditation or even with commonsense views. These passages concern issues of central importance and pertain to the very nature of meditation and its general place in the Buddhist path. Sometimes their unconventionality does not lie in anything they positively state, but rather in the surprising absence of seemingly crucial information expected to be found in a particular context. Listed below are some of the unusual features present in the texts of both traditions which will be discussed in this book:

- One of the most puzzling features of both Nikāya and early Chan texts is the scarcity of detailed information regarding meditation techniques and objects used for attaining altered states of mind. This feature is particularly surprising, given the general emphasis on meditation *per se* in the texts of both traditions, and the fact that there is nothing in the structure of these texts that would prevent the inclusion of more detailed instructions, were this the intent of their authors.
- Several Nikāya and early Chan texts criticize certain forms of meditation while praising other ones. What is unusual is that both criticized and praised practices share the characteristic traditionally attributed to calm meditation (p. *samatha*, s. *śamatha*, c. *zhi* 止), namely that of tranquillization of thoughts and

conceptual activity. The dichotomy of wrong and right forms of meditative calm is not present to that extent in the mainstream, historically dominant model of Buddhist meditation which generally only distinguishes between calm and insight (p. *vipassanā*, s. *vipaśyanā*, c. *guan* 觀).

- Some early Chan and Nikāya texts explicitly criticize or can be read as implying a critique of an approach to meditation which involves deliberate and active implementation of a method or a technique. Furthermore, some descriptions of right meditation involve a paradoxical denial of seemingly all conceivable ways of practising it.
- Early Chan and to a lesser extent Nikāya texts contain accounts suggesting that insight or wisdom (p. *paññā*, s. *prajñā*, c. *hui* 慧) may occur naturally in the meditative state of concentration or unification (p. s. *samādhi*, c. *ding* 定). This is generally not recognized as a possibility in the historically dominant theories of Buddhist meditation which consider insight to be a separate form of practice undertaken after emergence from a concentrated state.
- The texts of both traditions contain descriptions of a special meditative state in which the most basic characteristics and elements of reality as experienced by us are said to cease. They include various mental factors but also life, death, and even the world itself. However, at the same time this state is often characterized as different from common insentience, or even as cognitive in nature.

Questions and problems discussed in this book

It needs to be emphasized here that some of the abovementioned features of Nikāya and early Chan texts are open to competing interpretations. Their unorthodox implications may sometimes be avoided, though often at a considerable cost of abstaining from their most direct reading and taking them at face value. Within this book we shall refer to several such alternative interpretations, which either try to read the unusual passages through the lens of more mainstream Buddhist views, explain them away as forms of specific rhetoric, or assume that some crucial information is absent and must be provided from other sources, such as tradition or direct teaching of a meditation teacher.

What has certainly contributed to the resistance to taking the abovementioned puzzling passages at face value is that the ideas implied by their direct reading are often so unusual that they may appear paradoxical, absurd, or even inherently impossible. If an idea is philosophical in character and concerns the nature of reality or mental functioning, it might appear to us in this way because it goes against certain commonsense or folk-psychological views that are deeply rooted in every human being. However, this is not necessarily the case with meditative ideas as our common sense hardly provides us with any preconceptions about what meditation practice is or is not. One can speak, however, about a set of general ideas about Buddhist meditation which can be found within the majority of traditions existing throughout the history of Buddhism. These ideas can be said to form a relatively coherent theoretical framework or a model, which for the purpose of this book will be labelled as the mainstream Buddhist paradigm of meditation. This paradigm involves the notion of meditation practice as a deliberate implementation of a particular technique or method, the idea that soteriological and meditative progress can be conceptualized in a relatively straightforward, linear and almost quantifiable manner as an accumulation of positive factors, and the sharp distinction between calm or concentration on the one hand and wisdom or insight on the other. Such a characteristic of course involves a certain degree of oversimplification and schematization. A more detailed and nuanced analysis of this paradigm will be undertaken in further sections of this book. In addition to being the dominant paradigm in the history of Buddhism, it has shaped our most basic convictions and preconceptions about the very nature of meditation and Buddhist practice, to the point that we consider them almost self-evident. The common denominator of the Nikāya and Chan passages, which are the focus of this book, is that they are either difficult to comprehend from the perspective of this paradigm or are downright at odds with it. Hence, they appear to us as paradoxical, absurd or even inherently impossible.

The identification of these problematic passages of the Nikāya and early Chan texts within this book only serves as a starting point for further investigation, which is philosophical in nature.[5] The unorthodox

5 It is the contention of this study that meditative ideas are ultimately specific types of philosophical ideas. Since meditation is one of the ways of cognizing reality, it should be considered within the scope of philosophical epistemology. Furthermore, as a vehicle for self-transformation and liberation, meditation is

statements contained in the texts of both traditions are very interesting because they are open to readings that challenge some of our most basic and seemingly self-evident assumptions about the nature of meditation, cognition and reality. Their very presence allows us to consider the possibility of a unique way of approaching meditation which is very different from the mainstream Buddhist paradigm.

The main objective of this book is to draw out and discuss the philosophical and meditative implications of the problematic passages of Nikāya and early Chan texts. This also involves assessing whether the ideas implied by the passages in question are philosophically plausible. One of the main goals of this book is to establish if these ideas constitute a coherent, unique paradigm of meditation, alternative to the mainstream one. An attempt will also be made to render these ideas as intelligible and comprehensible to a modern reader as possible, often by trying to express their content using modern philosophical and scientific categories and concepts.

Another objective lies in assessing how the proposed interpretation of the problematic passages works in a wider textual context of the Nikāya and Chan texts and whether it leads to solving interpretative problems or generating new ones. Below are some of the questions and problems that will be discussed in this volume:

- Can altered states of mind be attained without a meditation method in the sense of a deliberately implemented technique? If so, by what mechanism?

---

a subject matter of the philosophy of religion and philosophical soteriology. Therefore, the investigation of meditative concepts undertaken in this study is by its nature a philosophical one. Shulman (2014) emphasized a deep, vital connection between philosophy and meditation as the most important aspects of early Buddhist liberation and has suggested that Buddhist philosophy may be conceptualized as a sort of "meditative perception" (Shulman, 2014: 17). The project of philosophical investigation of early Buddhist meditative ideas and assessment of their plausibility and inner coherence has also been laid out by Wynne (2018c) in his series of Oxford lectures.

However, since this understanding of the intrinsic relation between meditation and philosophy is not commonly accepted or self-evident for the modern reader, this book will sometimes refer to meditation and philosophy separately, e.g., "philosophical and meditative ideas". This of course does not imply that the two are considered mutually exclusive. There will be also many instances where we will be discussing philosophical ideas that do not directly concern meditation, but the structure of reality, the nature of cognition or the function of language.

- How can pre-meditative elements of the Buddhist path, such as leading a particular lifestyle and maintaining a specific mindset, contribute to the attainment of altered states of mind?
- Are there forms of meditation which do not fit into the typology of calm and insight, characteristic of mainstream Buddhism?
- Can insight occur in a meditative state characterized by an absence of thoughts? If so, by what process? What concept of mind is implied by such an idea?
- Can the most basic elements of the world that we experience cease to be present in a meditative state which is not a form of insentience or unconsciousness? In what way could such cessation occur? What philosophical vision of reality is implied by this concept?
- Can awareness of thoughts, urges and feelings lead to their pacification? By what mechanism could this occur?
- Are there some crucial elements of the Buddhist path which cannot be straightforwardly practised by following instructions? If so, what contributes to their development and is there any pattern that it follows?

The purpose and value of a comparative study of Nikāya Buddhism and early Chan

One might rightly ask at this point about the very purpose of using a comparative approach in order to deal with these issues. Why not just examine Nikāya and Chan ideas separately and in their own specific textual contexts? This is, after all, how they are usually studied. For example, if one examines the ideas contained in the *Sāmaññaphala-sutta*, one usually does so in the wider context of other Nikāya texts and later Pali works such as the Abhidhamma scriptures, the Commentaries, the *Visuddhimagga* or even teachings of modern Theravāda masters. Likewise, if one studies ideas found in a particular Chan text, it is done in the context of other Chan texts or earlier Chinese texts on meditation, such as the fifth-century manuals of meditation or the works of Huisi 慧思 (515–577) and Zhiyi 智顗 (538–597).

The problem with this isolative approach is that it does not provide us with any means of making sense of the unusual features listed above. If, when studying a particular tradition in isolation and in its own specific context, we discover one of these seemingly absurd or inherently impossible elements which cannot be harmonized with the mainstream Buddhist paradigm of meditation, we are naturally inclined to either ignore it or to somehow explain it away. This is because we simply have no means of making sense of it and hence cannot even attempt to read it directly and take it at face value. For example, let us consider a situation where we are confronted with a surprising absence of meditative methods or instructions for attaining the *jhāna*s in the Nikāya texts. The Pali commentaries and treatises such as the *Visuddhimagga* do not provide a theoretical framework for making sense of this feature, and instead supplement additional information that is supposedly missing from the Nikāyas. Therefore, someone interpreting this problematic feature from their perspective is prone to assuming that the text implies a detailed meditative instruction but does not describe it explicitly. The situation in the case of Chan studies is very similar. When viewed against the context of the several fifth-century Chinese manuals of meditation or the seminal works of Zhiyi, the absence of a detailed meditative method in many of the Chan texts seems incomprehensible. Therefore, one might conclude that the Chan Buddhists were actually practising historically dominant forms of Buddhist meditation, but due to a certain ideological taboo, they were reluctant to mention it.[6]

However, the awareness that a particular unusual textual feature also occurs in the texts of another tradition, opens up the possibility of at least attempting to take it at face value and seriously considering its direct implications without resorting to *ad hoc* explanations. Instead of questioning the source text, we may begin to question the paradigm from which perspective the feature in question appears incomprehensible or absurd, and start taking into account the possibility that this feature may represent an entirely different approach to meditation. This leads to several new questions. If we are to take a problematic passage at face value and accept the idea that is implied by it, we must show that it does not lead to absurd or self-contradictory consequences. One of the basic principles of logic and the theory of argumentation is that if a premise implies an absurd conclusion, then this premise cannot be true. For example, the idea that altered states of mind could be achieved without an actively implemented meditative method appears absurd to us. Therefore, we are inclined to reject any reading of a Buddhist text which implies such an idea. How can we show that a particular idea

6 Such interpretations have been offered by Bielefeldt (1988: 96) and McRae (2005: 6).

is not absurd? We can for example start by pointing out the presence of similar ideas in the texts of other traditions. However, this is not enough in itself to remove the charge of absurdity. One may need to show that an idea in question is coherent and intelligible and that it is an integral part of a wider group of ideas, which may form a specific paradigm. Furthermore, one may need to show that this idea is plausible in the sense that it is not impossible; it provides an acceptable account of reality and that it can be explained how the authors of the text could have arrived at such an idea. Since the problematic ideas present in Nikāya and Chan texts concern meditation, an assessment of their plausibility will involve establishing whether they are psychologically possible.[7] This, in turn, may require reconstructing a specific concept of the mind which serves as a backdrop to these ideas.

If we are able to show that taking a particular statement at face value does not lead to absurd consequences, we are not bound to reject such a reading. According to the principle known as Occam's Razor, when faced with competing explanations, one should select the solution that is the simplest and requires the fewest assumptions. In this case, it means accepting the direct reading of the text, even if it disagrees with its historically dominant interpretation.

The second potential usage of a comparative approach is based on a tentative, perhaps even provocative assumption adopted for the purpose of this study that since the early Chan and Nikāya texts contain some apparent similarities and parallels, they may actually refer to a similar type or model of meditation. It might however be the case then that while both traditions in question refer to generally similar forms of meditation or contain a similar meditative paradigm, they put a different emphasis on its various aspects in their texts. One tradition may more strongly emphasize elements that are much less pronounced in the text of the other one. Nonetheless, such elements would still be present in the texts of the latter tradition. However, without the knowledge drawn from the study of the former tradition, one would simply not give these elements enough attention or be prone to ignoring them. The awareness of the existence of certain elements in the teachings of one tradition may inspire us to look for them in the texts of the other, or even make us more sensitive to noticing them upon reading the

7 Several attempts to assess whether certain key Buddhist concepts are true from the perspective of modern psychology have been made by Bronkhorst (e.g., 2012; 2023).

texts of this latter tradition. Thus, relatively obscure features which would otherwise be ignored, can be noticed. For the sake of investigation and as a form of scholarly experiment, one can also attempt to tentatively apply the understanding drawn from the study of one tradition, to some seemingly parallel but problematic and unclear aspects of the other and see the results it produces. If this approach solves some interpretive problems without generating further ones, it may be carefully pursued further and tested how it works in case of other problematic passages and contexts. It also needs to be thoroughly checked if the idea implied by such a reading is in harmony with the other ideas present in the texts of the tradition in question. However, when using this approach, it is important to maintain caution and avoid making definite conclusions too easily.

To return to our example of the absence of detailed meditative instructions in Nikāya and Chan texts: taking this feature at face value entails considering a possibility that there was really no method for attaining altered states of mind in the sense of a set of activities which would need to be deliberately performed after sitting down for meditation. Showing that this implication is not absurd may require establishing whether the idea of methodless meditation is connected to other meditative ideas, with which it forms a coherent whole. This may further require reconstructing a specific paradigm which serves as a theoretical framework for the idea in question. Such a paradigm may involve specific ideas about the mind and reality, which also may need to be reconstructed. Lastly, in order to show that the idea of attaining altered meditative states without a method is plausible, it is necessary to propose a psychological mechanism by which this process could occur. This may, for example, involve shifting the emphasis from a meditative method in a strict sense, to some other crucial factors and elements of the Buddhist path of which meditation is a culmination and extension. Much of this book will be devoted to these kinds of discussions.

Some remarks on the scope of this book

Some remarks need to be made about the scope of this book. The usage of the terms "Nikāya Buddhism" or "early Chan" is a form of convention and it needs to be emphasized that in this book they are used only with respect to the Buddhist doctrine as presented in the Nikāya and Chan texts, specifically their philosophical and meditative ideas. Other aspects of Nikāya and Chan Buddhism, such as the social and political ones, are not particularly relevant to this study. Similarly, "Nikāya Buddhism" and "early Chan" are sometimes referred to within this book as "traditions" which again is a convention adopted for the sake of convenience. However, the term tradition is used with respect to the doctrines contained in the Nikāya and Chan texts and not to their cultural or institutional aspects nor the transmission and preservation of their customs or behaviours, which are the usual hallmarks of a religious tradition.

The point of using umbrella terms such as "Nikāya Buddhism", "early Chan" or "tradition" is also to convey a meaning that the ideas being discussed are not some individual and unconnected items drawn from a jumble of entirely arbitrarily selected texts but are representative of certain wider, collective groups of interrelated texts. This implies that they possess some shared features or are different in some ways from other texts. This also allows clear limits to be set on the range of texts that will be taken into consideration. The fulfilment of this criterion is clear in the case of Nikāya Buddhism, as the Nikāyas are a well-defined corpus of texts, with relatively little controversies regarding which texts belong to it and which do not.[8] However, the texts constituting the Nikāyas are not chronologically homogeneous. Therefore, this study will only deal with the portion of the Nikāyas classified by Sujato and Brahmali (2015: 9–10) in their useful study as early, namely the first four Nikāyas, the *Suttanipāta*, the *Udāna*, the *Itivuttaka*, the *Dhammapada*, the *Theragāthā* and the *Therīgāthā*. In other words, I use the term Nikāya Buddhism with reference to the doctrine found in the early portions of the Pali Nikāyas.

While it would be naive to accept the traditional Theravāda view that the early portions of the Nikāyas are a faithful record of the words of the Buddha and his direct disciples or that they even contain a homogeneous doctrine, they nonetheless share several specific features which distinguish them from other Pali texts and are representative of a particular period of development of early Buddhist thought. Therefore, the term "Nikāya Buddhism" as used in this book is in some respects clearer, better defined and less problematic than that of "early

8 The Burmese, Sinhalese and Thai editions differ regarding the exact number of books constituting the *Khuddaka Nikāya*. The Thai edition does not include the *Peṭakopadesa* and the *Nettipakarana*, which are found in Burmese and Sinhalese editions. The *Milindapañha* is present only in the Burmese edition. However, none of these three texts are discussed in detail in this book.

Buddhism". Sometimes, in this study, the terms "early Buddhism" and "Nikāya Buddhism" are used in similar contexts and almost interchangeably which might give the impression that they are fully synonymous. This is not entirely so; my usage of the term "early Buddhist" is mostly in the context of discussing the works of other scholars who use this term. Of course, Nikāya ideas are by definition also early Buddhist ideas, since they are some of the relatively earliest Buddhist ideas in the historical sense. However, the category of early Buddhism is wider than that of Nikāya Buddhism; some early Buddhist texts such as the Chinese Āgamas or Gandhari fragments are not part of the Nikāyas. Therefore, when claims are made about the ideas in the Nikāyas or terms such as "early Buddhist idea" are used, this does not imply that there are no other early Buddhist ideas which may be chronologically earlier or even diametrically opposite to the discussed ideas in question.

Compared to Nikāya Buddhism, the meaning of the term "early Chan" is much less self-evident and more problematic, as there are no immediately obvious criteria for establishing what exactly makes a particular text an early Chan text. There is no fixed, well-defined corpus of Chan scriptures comparable to the Nikāyas which could be simply labelled as the early Chan corpus. The shared feature of several of the Chan texts discussed in this book is that they were preserved in the Dunhuang cache, but this is not the case for all of them. If one would be interested in maximal clarity, it would probably be best to make Chan tradition as a whole the subject of this comparative study. However, this would make the scope of this book too wide as the texts and ideas which are of interest for this study were mostly created in the early period of this tradition. Therefore, simply using the word "Chan" as an umbrella term for the texts and ideas which are compared with Nikāya Buddhism, would not be representative of this book's content. Furthermore, the history of Chan Buddhism spans at least fifteen hundred years and during this period the ideas of the school and ways of expressing them have undergone such profound changes that it is difficult to even establish what is their common denominator. It would be extremely naive and simply wrong to assume the homogeneity and unity of the Chan tradition as a whole and to make wide-sweeping statements referring to Chan in general.[9] Assuming homogeneity and unity

9 Cf. Poceski (2015b: 99): "we might want to reconsider the illusion of Chan homogeneity, notwithstanding its rootedness in normative views and sectarian traditions that continue to this day".

of the whole Chan tradition would be the same kind of mistake that is unfortunately being made with respect to early Indian Buddhism, where the earliest Buddhist texts are read through the lens of much later doctrinal developments.

The period of Chan history we will focus on generally corresponds to the one chosen by Poceski (2015a) in his article *Conceptions and attitudes towards contemplative practice within the early traditions of Chan Buddhism*, and to the phases of Chan development classified by McRae (2003: 13) as proto-Chan, early Chan and to some extent that of middle Chan. The texts we will consider will encompass the *Erru sixing lun* 二入四行論 (*Treatise on the two entrances and four practices*) attributed to Bodhidharma (c. *Putidamo* 菩提達摩, d. ca. 530) , the texts of the East Mountain tradition (*dongshanfamen* 東山法門) attributed to Daoxin 道信 (580–651) and Hongren 弘忍 (600–674), and those of various Chan factions which emerged during the Tang period, including the Northern school (*beizong* 北宗), the Niutou 牛頭 school, the Heze 菏澤 school, the Baotang 保唐 school and the Hongzhou 洪州 school.

The common denominator of the vast majority of these texts is that they were created during the Tang period (618–907). Therefore, the term "early Chan" as understood in this book is to a large extent synonymous with "Tang era Chan". The latter term is very clear as it involves a chronological criterion for establishing its denotation. However, as this book will also consider the work of Bodhidharma which predates the Tang period, this label would not be fully adequate. It would then probably be most precise to describe the texts discussed in this book as pre-Song Chan texts, barring few exceptions. Besides being created in the same historical period, the early Chan texts share certain common features which permit addressing them collectively. Of course, it does not mean that the early Chan doctrine is homogeneous. However, as we shall see, there are certain common motives and patterns running throughout various texts of the early Chan period. As already noted, one such significant common feature is the presence of ideas which are to a various extent at odds with the mainstream Buddhist paradigm of meditation.

In past scholarship, there was a tendency to see certain sharp demarcation lines within the history of early Chan, which were supposed to mark fundamental transitions between different versions of Chan doctrine. This view would of course preclude the possibility of any deeper unity within the early works of this school, and by extension would make collective references to early Chan as a whole quite meaningless.

However, these long-held traditional ways of classifying and evaluating developments within the Chan tradition are no longer considered adequate and tenable. This old paradigm saw the supposed transition from the gradualist teachings of the Northern school of Shenxiu 神秀 (606?–706) to the subitist teachings of the Southern school of Huineng 慧能 (638–713), and Shenhui 神會 (684–758) as a major demarcation line within Chan Buddhism. The ensuing period of the development of the so-called Southern Chan was supposedly marked by a transition from the more traditional methods of Buddhist practice to completely new, unusual forms such as paradoxical "encounter dialogues" (*jiyuan wenda* 機緣問答) and koans (*gongan* 公案).

According to the traditional paradigm of Chan studies, this was a period in which the school of Chan developed its unique character and reached full maturity. These developments were mostly connected with the flourishing of the Hongzhou school founded by Mazu Daoyi 馬祖道一 (709–788). Thanks to the discovery of the Dunhuang texts and the critical work of Chan scholars in recent decades we now know that this image is far from being true.

McRae has argued in his works that the sharp distinction between the supposedly gradualist Northern school and the subitist Southern school does not reflect the real historical situation. The distinction was supposedly part of a narrative created by Shenhui and his followers for polemic purposes. As McRae (1986: 241) puts it: "there was no Northern School until Shen-hui created the label for the purpose of his own campaign". The gradualist "Northern school" as presented by the traditional narrative should be considered "a fictitious entity" which never actually existed and there is no evidence that the supposed "conflict in question was not restricted to the minds of Shen-hui and his followers" (McRae 1986: 246).

The ideas of the real Northern school were much more nuanced and not as simplistic as those ascribed to it by its critics. As McRae (1987: 248) has noted, its meditative practices were "not exactly as Shen-hui described them, but were instead free and easy exercises in the emulation of the expansive mind of the sage". In fact, "descriptions of these practices contained warnings against the same abuses Shen-hui later descried so strongly" (McRae 1987: 248).[10]

10 McRae (1987: 249) points out "the lack of absolute originality of Shenhui's criticisms themselves within the context of the Chan tradition".

As for Shenhui himself, his teachings should be considered "extensions of, rather than radical alternatives to, Northern school doctrine" (McRae 1987: 259).[11] In a similar vein, Gómez (1987: 92) has noted that "ironically, and perhaps inconsistently, at the level of the path the differences between Shen-hui and 'Northern' Ch'an are not so clear".

This does not mean that there are no significant differences between particular ideas expressed by various Tang-era schools and factions. There surely are; however, it also appears that too often these differences were overemphasized while their similarities were overlooked. According to McRae (2023: 255), "the early Chan factions known as the Northern school, Southern school (i.e., that of Shenhui), Oxhead school, and the Baotang 保唐 and Jingzhong 淨眾 schools of Sichuan all share a common mode of discourse". The real major demarcation line was the emergence of a new form of Chan connected with the so-called encounter dialogue, which marked the transition from the early to the "classical" period. However, McRae was probably wrong in his initial attribution of this important change to Mazu Daoyi and his immediate followers from the Hongzhou school.[12] Poceski (2007: 230) has convincingly shown that the early teachings of this school should instead be seen as a "culmination of doctrinal developments within Tang Chan" and that one should be "especially wary of viewing Mazu, Baizhang, and other monks associated with the Hongzhou school as instigators of new developments that paved the way for the teachings and practices of Song Chan". The introduction of the new form of Chan, connected with the prevalence of "encounter dialogue", had in fact occurred in a much later period and the new teachings were only retrospectively attributed to the early masters of the Hongzhou school in order to give them some legitimacy.[13] Another scholar to emphasize the presence of common patterns in the texts representing various phases of early Chan was Chappell (1983: 100), who has noted that "there is a progression of

11 Also cf. McRae (2023: 253; 2001: 79–80): "There are pronounced similarities between his [Shenhui's] teachings and those of his predecessors in the Northern school".

12 E.g., see McRae (1987: 229–30).

13 McRae eventually modified his position in favour of a less radical view. He acknowledged that the famous stories involving the masters such as Mazu, who were supposed to be representatives of what he considered the classical phase of Chan, were not "accurate accounts of actual words and events, but rather retrospective recreations of how those masters must have acted, composed essentially out of whole cloth by later generations" (McRae 2001: 66–67).

common themes from Bodhidharma to Tao-hsin[14] which lends support to the classic Ch'an lineage which we find articulated for the first time by the disciples of Hung-jen".[15] In the same book, Chappell claims (1983: 101) that "the practices of Tao-hsin and his followers also bear remarkable resemblances to later Ch'an meditation practices".

Another important feature of early Chan which distinguishes it from later phases of this school is the relative richness and complexity of its philosophical and meditative ideas. Poceski (2015b: 34–35) described the Tang era as a period of "significant flourishing of the Chan school". To paraphrase a very apt title of Morten Schlütter's book (Schlütter 2008), it was only during the Song period that Chan became Chan in its more stereotypical form, commonly associated with this tradition, However, it happened at the expense of losing some of the richness of its earlier phases and starting from the Song period, Chan teachings became more limited in their scope. The doctrine of early Chan included some very original philosophical ideas about the nature of reality or the role of language, although they were not systematically presented. As we shall see, these ideas show some important similarities to those found in Nikāya texts. The richness of the doctrine of early Chan constitutes an additional argument in favour of selecting this phase of development for comparison with Nikāya Buddhism.

Between perennialism and constructivism: Necessary methodological assumptions

The approach of comparing early Chan and Nikāya Buddhism used in this book is based on an assumption that it may be possible for two traditions functioning in different historical and cultural contexts to arrive at similar ideas without direct transmission from one to the other. Despite the claims of Chan authors of an unbroken lineage connecting the school patriarchs with the Buddha himself, there are no indications in their texts that they were well-acquainted with early Buddhist discourses. Therefore, any possibility of direct textual transmission of certain ideas between early Buddhism and Chan must be ruled out. This book tentatively assumes that the apparent similarity and parallelism of certain passages may be an indication of actual similarity

14 Daoxin in pinyin transcription.
15 Hongren in pinyin transcription.

and parallelism of the ideas implied by these passages. In other words, this book assumes a possibility that Chan Buddhists may have independently arrived at quite similar ideas as the authors of Nikāya texts.

Such a possibility, although regarding a narrower range of ideas and texts, has already been considered by Gómez in his article *Proto-Mādhyamika in the Pāli Canon*. He (Gómez, 1976: 140) argues that "an extreme apophatic tendency", present in some passages from the *Aṭṭhakavagga* and the *Pārāyanavagga*, "reappears later in the literature of the Perfection of Wisdom, and, even more patently, in the *Prāsaṅgika Mādhyamika* and in the various Ch'an lines." Gómez (1976: 152–53) considers the possibility of "a continuous tradition of apophatic Buddhism", and at one point even speaks of the abovementioned tendency in the *Aṭṭhakavagga* as a sort of "proto-Mādhyamika" and "a possible Indian proto-Ch'an". Ultimately, however, he concludes that the existence of any historical connection between the *Suttanipāta*, Nāgārjuna and Chan is impossible to establish and it "would be more reasonable to discard the possibility of a one-line transmission". Nonetheless, he believes that "the *Aṭṭha*, the Mādhyamika and, perhaps, the Ch'an, represent one type of path theory" and that they all "belong to the same type of Buddhist tradition with regard to the value of views and the function of conceptual thought" (Gómez, 1976 :153).

A hypothesis that two traditions can independently arrive at very similar ideas without any direct transmission is bound to be considered very controversial or even provocative from the perspective of the currently dominant views in Buddhist studies. The dominant approach in studying Buddhism seems to be influenced by strong cultural constructivism which sees both meditative experiences and meditative ideas as products of particular historical and cultural conditions. Such an approach would make the comparative approach adopted in this study pretty much baseless, since, even if there are parallels between Nikāya and Chan texts, under this assumption they would be entirely superficial and could not be made the starting point of any further reflection. However, such a strong cultural constructivist position is an extreme view which would need to be sufficiently justified in itself and such a justification has never been offered.[16] It is worth emphasizing that,

16 Kenneth Rose (2016) offers a convincing critique of a constructivist approach in the study of mysticism. He concludes that "rather than an empirical approach to the mystical evidence, strong constructivism is more of an a priori, ideological, and dogmatic approach to the body of mystical evidence than an actual analysis of what the whole body of this evidence suggests" (Rose 2016: 31).

throughout their history, the Buddhists themselves have maintained a directly opposite stance, claiming that the Dharma is universal and not limited to particular cultural and historical conditions.

It needs to be emphasized that a strong perennialist position which would assume that exactly the same meditative states were actually attained and experienced within Nikāya Buddhism and Chan is not an absolutely necessary precondition for this study. For this comparative approach to be fruitful, it is enough to consider the possibility that the authors in both traditions may have arrived at certain similar ideas about meditation. While this possibility cannot be established *a priori*, there is also nothing that really precludes it. Ultimately, early Buddhists and Chan Buddhists operated within a similar milieu of general Buddhist ideas, which included the notions of seated meditation and altered states of mind. The very nature of meditation allows a relatively limited number of potential approaches to it. After all, how many different things can be done when sitting cross-legged? Is it really that improbable that if several individuals or groups attempt to meditate or even think about meditation in isolation from one another, some of them may independently develop similar approaches to meditation? Of course, this can only be possible if the individuals and groups in question are allowed a certain degree of experimentation and are not totally restricted by the ideological framework of a particular tradition or paradigm. While such an ideological restriction was often the case throughout the majority of Buddhist history, an examination of early Chan writings from Bodhidharma to the Tang era shows in many cases a surprisingly small or even nonexistent reliance on earlier Buddhist meditative ideas and the development of entirely new ways of speaking about meditation. Chan Buddhists were certainly open to experimentation, at the very least on a theoretical level, and therefore it is plausible that they could arrive at ideas that would be substantially different from those maintained by other Buddhist schools of their era. Why then could Chan Buddhists not arrive at similar meditative ideas or even practise similar forms of meditation as the early Buddhists? Is there some evidence or argument which precludes such a possibility? If so,

---

He also makes an interesting case for a modified perennialist approach in the study of meditation and mysticism. Also cf. Bronkhorst (2022: 13–14), who claims that "the position defended by Steven Katz and his fellow constructivists is mistaken" as it "does not take into account the complex nature of human consciousness, some of whose components are not touched (or much less touched) by the factors that are co-responsible for standard consciousness".

it has never been offered. Let us note that it seems generally accepted that some forms of what is considered calm meditation (*samatha*) in Buddhism and that involve one-pointed concentration and sensory inactivity, are also practised outside Buddhism, by the Hindu Yogins, the Jains, the Muslim Sufis in the form of *dhikr*, and Christian Orthodox Hesychasts as "Jesus prayer". It is rightly assumed that the psychological mechanism by which these practices generate altered states of consciousness is the same despite them being practised in very different cultural and social milieus. Nikāya Buddhism and early Chan are culturally much closer to one another than the abovementioned meditative and mystical traditions which are assumed to have practised similar forms of meditation. Therefore, there should be no *a priori* reasons preventing us from considering a hypothesis that they may have developed some relatively similar ideas about meditation.

Not rejecting this assumption out of hand and merely considering its possibility, in itself opens up new perspectives that are worthy of investigation. To paraphrase the famous Nikāya phrase, it is an assumption that invites us to come and examine its potential results.[17] Depending on whether this initial tentative assumption helps to solve interpretive difficulties or generates additional ones it may be pursued further or safely discarded.

On the value of comparisons with Western philosophy and cognitive science

Above, I suggested that an investigation of the unusual ideas implied in Nikāya and Chan texts involves trying to make sense of them, i.e., establishing whether they are coherent, intelligible, and plausible. Often, the problematic ideas in question are psychological or philosophical in character. In other words, they imply a particular vision of the mind and of reality. As we have previously noted, these ideas often go against commonsense, folk-psychological beliefs about mental functioning and the structure of the world. How can we assess the intelligibility and plausibility of psychological and philosophical theories? What should we evaluate them against? Our common sense cannot be a

17 E.g., SN 1.20/i.9: *sandiṭṭhiko ayaṃ dhammo akāliko ehipassiko opaneyyiko paccattaṃ veditabbo viññūhī.* "This Dhamma is directly visible, immediate, inviting one to come and see, applicable, to be personally experienced by the wise". Translation by Bodhi (2000: 98).

sufficient criterion since the relevant claims in Nikāya and Chan texts often involve very unusual states of mind. Therefore, to make sense of such ideas we shall employ a cross-cultural comparative and interdisciplinary approach which draws on Western philosophy. Engaging the philosophical problems in Nikāya and Chan texts from the point of view of modern Western philosophy may offer certain interesting fresh insights which can enrich our understanding of these problems. Modern philosophy of mind draws heavily on new developments in the natural sciences, such as brain studies, which were generally unavailable to the philosophers of previous centuries. This gives it a stronger empirical basis and provides perspectives that were not possible before.

It is interesting to consider whether the discussed ideas of early Chan and Nikāya Buddhism have any parallels in the modern philosophy of mind and whether the altered states of mind they postulate could be regarded as possible from the latter's perspective. In order to compare Eastern philosophical concepts with Western ones, one must establish a way to make them mutually intelligible. Nikāya and Chan texts do not contain direct Pali or Chinese equivalents of several key terms of modern Western philosophy such as "content", "cognitive mechanism", "phenomenon", "representation", "noumenon", "objective", "subjective" or "globally available". That, however, does not preclude that their authors had some sort of understanding of the concepts behind these terms. A case can be made that the ideas behind these terms can still be found in these Buddhist texts, although they may function in an implicit form or be expressed in idiosyncratic ways which are specific to these texts. Furthermore, comparisons with relevant developments in Western philosophy prove particularly useful when dealing with Nikāya and Chan ideas about the mind and reality which may at first appear counterintuitive or even at odds with common sense. This concerns, for example, the problematic notion that insight or wisdom can coincide with the thought-less state of *samādhi*. Someone approaching this notion from a perspective of the mainstream Buddhist model of meditation or commonsense views about psychology may be inclined to reject it out of hand due to its inconceivability. However, it so happens that many theories of the modern philosophy of mind are also highly counterintuitive and strongly challenge commonsense views which they label as "folk-psychology". The awareness that certain parallel ways of thinking about mental functioning may have appeared within the modern philosophy of mind and are considered valid may allow one to make better sense of problematic Buddhist ideas and make them more intelligible from a modern perspective.

An interdisciplinary approach using comparisons with the modern philosophy of mind and psychology has been gaining popularity in Buddhist studies. The works of authors such as Siderits (2011; 2020), Bronkhorst (2012), Coseru (2012), and Garfield (2015) can serve as examples of fruitful comparative studies of Western and Eastern philosophy. Garfield (2015: xi) aptly notes that "the concerns and methods of Buddhist philosophy and Western philosophy are sufficiently proximate to each other, sharing sufficient horizons, that they are easily mutually intelligible, but sufficiently distant from one another that each has something to learn from the other".

Of course, such an approach cannot be harmonized with a strong cultural constructivist position. From the latter perspective, any potential similarities between Western and Eastern philosophy can be disregarded as merely accidental and ultimately meaningless. A comparative and interdisciplinary perspective can bring the most meaningful results only on the assumption that there exists an objective human nature, and that both Buddhist texts and Western philosophical theories refer to some aspects of that nature, e.g., those connected with our mental functioning. The existence of human nature is considered pretty much irrefutable from the perspective of modern natural science, which has amassed gigantic supportive evidence which continues to grow. However, this claim is not universally accepted within the domain of humanities. Another tentative assumption which makes such a comparative approach potentially useful is that the meditative accounts in the Buddhist texts may not just be purely theoretical constructs but refer to actual altered states of mind. As Bronkhorst (2012: 73) has aptly put it, it involves a "working hypothesis that certain central claims of the early Buddhist texts are true" and that:

> The relevant claims in the early Buddhist texts ... concern psychological states and processes that are unusual from a commonsensical point of view. They are not, however, in conflict with any established rules of natural science or psychology. (Bronkhorst, 2012: 73)

As was the case with the idea of comparing Nikāya with Chan texts, this too is merely a working hypothesis accepted for the purpose of investigation. It is hard to see any reasons why we should reject this possibility out of hand. However, we should not fall into the opposite extreme, and automatically assume that all accounts in Nikāya and Chan texts reflect actual experiences. It might be that some of them do and some of them do not. Of course, we can agree that Nikāya and early Chan meditative ideas would be more interesting if they were indeed a faithful reflection of actual experiences. It is nonetheless possible to arrive at interesting and original ideas without basing them on personal meditative experiences. In the end, we have no absolute criterion or method for evaluating whether a particular notion is based on an actual experience or not. Ultimately, this book does not belong to the field of experimental psychology but to that of the study of ideas.

Some remarks on the methodology and potential implications of this study

It needs to be emphasized that it is not the direct aim of this book to establish what ideas and texts in the Nikāyas represent the earliest Buddhist teaching, and which ones represent a later deviation from the original doctrine.[18] The question of the genesis of the early Buddhist texts is not really the focus of this study. It is also not concerned with the early Buddhist doctrine as a whole, but with its meditative and philosophical ideas which, due to their uniqueness and originality, are difficult to harmonize with the historically dominant mainstream Buddhist paradigm. The same reservation can be made with regards to early Chan, i.e., this book is not concerned with early Chan as a whole.

It will also not be claimed that the problematic ideas in question represent the teachings of the historical Buddha. While this is quite probable,[19] establishing it beyond any doubt goes beyond the scope of this study. The focus is on the content of these ideas, regardless of who their author was. This book will also not assume that the teachings present in the Nikāyas represent a completely homogeneous doctrine.[20] Given the

18 While it is true that sometimes judgements about relative earliness of Nikāya texts are made too easily, and as Gethin (2020: 67) says, "amount to little more than intuitions and preferences", in some cases they are the only way of explaining discrepancies between Buddhist texts.

19 Convincing arguments in favour of this thesis have been offered by Gombrich (2009) and Wynne (2019a), who pointed out the idiosyncratic character and coherency of several early Buddhist ideas which suggest that they could not have been created by "committees" of multiple authors.

20 Cf. statement by Shulman (2014: 55): "No serious scholar will claim today that the texts of the Pāli canon can be seen as a reliable expression of the true words spoken by the historical Buddha. The texts are too full of contradictions,

sheer number of texts constituting the Nikāyas and the specifics of their origin, preservation, and dissemination, such an assumption could only be considered dogmatic and more typical of religious exegesis than of text-critical scholarship.[21] Since this book does not assume the doctrinal homogeneity of the Nikāyas, the meaning of one text arrived at through the process of interpretation will not be automatically generalized to the whole canon. This also entails that when interpreting a problematic text or fragment, the implications derived from other texts cannot be treated as absolutely decisive evidence in itself for a particular interpretation of the fragment in question.[22] Of course, it does not mean that these implications should be ignored; they very much can be taken into account and considered, but one must maintain caution as the texts in question may have been created by different authors or be representative of different phases of the development of the ideas of a particular author. In both these cases, generalizing the meaning of one text to other texts would not be justified and could lead us astray. Instead, particular texts or even fragments or stock passages will be allowed to stand on their own so that they may be read as directly as possible and taken at face value. At most, an attempt will be made to identify certain groups of texts expressing similar ideas.

A similar approach will be adopted towards early Chan texts. In the case of Chan studies, however, there already exists a scholarly awareness of the lack of homogeneity of Chan texts. The implications arising from reading the texts of the Hongzhou school are not necessarily relevant for the proper interpretation of, say, a text such as the *Wuxin lun*. Therefore, whenever this book makes claims about any "Nikāya ideas" or "early Chan ideas" it does not imply that the ideas in question are representative of the whole Nikāyas or all early Chan texts, but simply that such ideas occur either in some Nikāya or Chan texts.

Since this study is not attempting to provide a "genealogy" or a chronological stratification of the early Buddhist scriptures to establish their relative earliness, referring to the Āgama parallels of the analysed Nikāya texts will not be considered obligatory. This does not mean that

---

too standardized, and too repetitious to be viewed as voiced by one and the same author. At the same time, it seems no less than awkward to assume that the texts do not reflect the Buddha's words in any way".

21 See Wynne (2018b) for a detailed discussion of a distinction between these two approaches.

22 This is particularly the case with the Nikāya texts which attempt to elucidate the meaning of some other enigmatic Nikāya passages, the latter usually being basic stock formulas or lists of elements.

the Āgamas will be ignored completely, just that a potential discrepancy between the Āgama text and the Nikāya text or even a total absence of Āgama parallels to an analysed Nikāya text will not really have any significant implications for this study. It also needs to be pointed out that, despite its undisputed value, such a comparative project has certain inherent limitations, as its results only show with absolute certainty the state of the early Buddhist doctrine at the time directly preceding the schisms in the Sangha. As the history of other religions, such as Christianity, shows, many significant changes and modifications to the original doctrine occur in the period directly following the founder's death, as it is usually characterized by uncertainty and a lack of centralized control over the creation and introduction of new texts and ideas. We have no tools that would allow us to reach absolutely certain conclusions regarding the state of the doctrine in this period.

Of course, the results of this study may have important implications for understanding the historical development of the ideas and doctrines of both traditions, and some of these implications will be discussed within this book. If, for example, by our investigation we come to the conclusion that a certain idea implied by a specific text is philosophically plausible and is coherent with other ideas, then this should be taken into consideration for the purpose of establishing what was the original form of a particular doctrine. Nevertheless, it needs to be honestly said that absolute certainty regarding the exact meaning intended by the author(s) of some of the texts analysed in this book is probably unreachable, given the nature of Nikāya and early Chan sources that are the subject of this study. Their shared feature is that their teachings are not presented in an exhaustive, comprehensive and systematic way; they are often quite ambiguous and open to different interpretations, rely on the usage of metaphors, and sometimes contain apophatic or paradoxical language.

However, this does not mean that we resign ourselves to baseless speculation and conjecture, or that all interpretations of analysed texts are equally valid or probable. Lack of absolute certainty characterizes many claims of modern science as well as some of the most important aspects of our lives. There is much value in identifying the problems and weak points of historically dominant interpretations which have been all too easily taken for granted. Instead of drawing definite conclusions while ignoring evidence to the contrary, one should rather acknowledge the presence of a problem and consider alternative readings of the problematic texts in question and assess their implications. And this is exactly what this book is concerned with, as it considers a possibility of a specific reading of Nikāya and early Chan texts and assesses philosophical plausibility and coherence of the ideas arrived at through such a reading. Even if we are unable to establish with absolute certainty in the historical sense whether all Nikāya and early Chan texts analysed in this book indeed represent a similarly unorthodox paradigm of meditation, following up on this tentative hypothesis brings into awareness issues and opens up perspectives that would otherwise not be available. In the course of dealing with the questions outlined briefly in the earlier part of this chapter, one is engaging crucial problems which possess universal importance and relevance transcending the specific historical contexts of Nikāya Buddhism and early Chan. Nonetheless, I believe that the hypothesis forwarded in this book offers a good explanation of the analysed texts and allows us to make sense of their unusual features while leading to fewer interpretative difficulties than its alternatives.

The results of this study may also potentially be interesting for anyone attempting to evaluate the general place of Chan within the history of Buddhism and its level of originality. It is natural that any such assessment should take into account the relation of Chan to the earliest forms of Buddhism which are available to us, which include the doctrine present in the Nikāyas. Faure (1993) offers a summary of many such scholarly attempts which included comparisons of Chan with early forms of Indian Buddhism. The problem of most of these assessments was that they identified early Indian Buddhism with the fully developed doctrine of the pre-Mahāyāna schools of the so-called small vehicle (Hīnayāna) while failing to acknowledge the distinctiveness of the even earlier forms of Buddhist teachings preserved in the Nikāyas and the Āgamas. Taking them into account may result in a very different assessment of the place of Chan within the history of Buddhism, especially given the presence of the parallels between the Nikāya and early Chan teachings which this book will try to show.

Brief outline of contents

Chapter 1 takes as its starting point the juxtaposition of wrong and right forms of meditation present in Nikāya and early Chan texts. This juxtaposition is problematic in that both criticized and praised forms of meditation are states of mental calm and absence of thought, which raises the issue of the exact nature of their difference. It is argued that the criticized practices share a common denominator: their cultivation involves various forms of deliberate mental effort and active implementation of a meditative method. It is pointed out that such practices were prevalent in the history of Buddhism and the chapter introduces a notion of the mainstream paradigm of meditation.

Chapter 2 focuses on the early Chan and Nikāya passages which suggest that insight or wisdom may occur naturally in the meditative state of concentration or unification characterized by mental calm and the absence of thoughts. The chapter attempts to reconstruct the concept of mind implied by these accounts and discusses the issue of psychological plausibility of the notion of insight described in the texts of both traditions. The final part of the chapter reconsiders various Nikāya formulas of insight.

Chapter 3 attempts to reconstruct specific views about the nature of reality, experience and language present in Nikāya and early Chan texts. It argues that many of these texts imply an anti-realist view that the world, as we experience it, does not exist independently of our cognitive activities. The character of some of its supposedly most fundamental and objective elements and features is in fact a reflection of our cognitive structure and mental processes. The final part of the chapter considers the relation of phenomenal consciousness to noumenal reality. It argues that the former is heavily interpreted and constructed by various processes and thus its content is not a faithful reflection of the latter. It also argues that some of the constitutive features of *saṃsāra* responsible for suffering are only relevant within the sphere of phenomenal consciousness.

Chapter 4 focuses on the philosophical implications of the idea of an apophatically described meditative state in the texts of both traditions in which the most basic elements constituting the world of our experience are absent or cease. It argues that the said state of cessation need not be understood as a form of insentience but rather as a cognitive deconstruction of our ordinary consciousness through suspending various mental processes which mediate and shape our experience. Thus, such a meditative cessation may be paradoxically considered to be a form of direct cognition. The final part of the chapter explores the question of what it is like to be in such a state and the issue of its linguistic expressibility.

Chapter 5 focuses on the problem of the absence of detailed instructions regarding the methods needed for the attainment of altered states of mind in early Chan and Nikāya texts. It discusses the possibility of methodless forms of meditation and considers the psychological plausibility of such a hypothesis. It argues that in such a case, the emphasis would need to shift from the method in the strict sense to some other crucial elements of the Buddhist path. It points out the existence of fundamental differences between the *Visuddhimagga* and the Nikāyas regarding the mechanism of attainment of the *jhānas*. The final part of the chapter offers a hypothesis regarding the roles of pleasure, relaxation and motionlessness in attaining states of concentration.

Chapter 6 considers the possibility that mental calm and intense spiritual feelings characterizing altered meditative states arise as a result of a specific lifestyle and mindset and are not produced by meditation itself. It points out that various forms of mental movement are a result of psychological adaptive mechanisms which drive human behaviour. The chapter argues that the Buddhist renunciate way of life can lead to the attenuation of these mechanisms, thus removing important sources of mental movement. The final part of the chapter focuses on the significance of renunciate livelihood and right speech for removing the psychological roots of verbal thinking and mental monologue.

Chapter 7 discusses the role played by awareness as a means of pacifying the mind. The first part of the chapter presents various forms of meditative awareness of mental processes described in Nikāya and early Chan texts. It considers whether meditative awareness can be conceptualized as an active form of meditation which involves the implementation of some method. The final part of the chapter offers a hypothesis regarding the mechanism by which awareness of mental activities may lead to their pacification.

Chapter 8 argues that in the paradigm present in Nikāya and early Chan texts there are crucial meditative factors which cannot be developed by directly practising them. Rather, they must naturally occur to an individual. It is claimed in the chapter that their occurrence is not a chance event, but follows its own specific but implicit logic and is dependent on a set of various conditions, including being in a particular existential situation. The chapter discusses the significance of various paradoxes connected with meditation, such as the fact that the search for spiritual achievement can be detrimental to meditative success. The final part of the chapter analyses some differences in approach between Nikāya and early Chan texts.

The final part of this book contains a brief recapitulation of the findings of the preceding chapters together with some final remarks and conclusions.

Chapter 1

THE WRONG AND THE RIGHT FORMS OF MEDITATION

The problem of the *jhānas* in the Nikāyas

As we have briefly noted in the introduction, the unorthodox meditative ideas present in Chan texts are much more obvious and explicit than those in the Nikāyas, and there is a greater general awareness of them. Therefore, before starting a detailed comparison of these features in the texts of both traditions, we will first devote some space to a general introduction of the problem of the *jhānas* which is one of the most controversial topics of early Buddhist studies.

The image of this meditation practice which emerges from the critical study of the Nikāyas seems to be in many ways at odds with mainstream Buddhist ideas. According to the historically dominant view within Buddhism, the practice of the *jhānas* is a form of calm meditation (p. *samatha*, s. *śamatha*, c. *zhi* 止). The *jhānas* are supposed to be meditative states attained by the practice of one-pointed concentration on specific meditation objects, which are usually characterized by relative simplicity and unity. At the same time, the *jhānas* are not considered to be absolutely necessary elements of the Buddhist path. By themselves they are unable to lead the practitioner to awakening as they fail to produce insight which would lead to the destruction of ignorance and ultimate freedom from suffering. It is insight or wisdom that are considered to be the essential features of the Buddhist path, while the *jhānas* are supposedly a pre-Buddhist form of meditation shared with certain non-Buddhist sects such as Hindu yogis.[1] The *jhānas* are also said to

1 An example of this approach can be found in King (1992) and Rahula (1980: 271), with the latter claiming that "*dhyānas* or *samādhis*, are pre-Buddhist; there is nothing particularly Buddhist about them; they are not a sine qua non, not a must, for the realization of Nirvana."

possess some drawbacks as the intensely pleasant feeling accompanying these states can become a cause of attachment and eventually lead to rebirth in celestial realms which is not considered beneficial from the Buddhist perspective. This is pretty much a mainstream view on the *jhānas* shared by most Buddhist schools or traditions. It needs to be said that this view is not without its basis in the Nikāyas as there are several suttas which can be cited in support of at least some of its elements.

However, many Nikāya texts imply a very different vision of the *jhānas*. For a supposedly nonessential practice shared with non-Buddhists, the four *jhānas* occupy a surprisingly central and prominent position in many suttas as a crucial stage of the path to awakening and as an important part of the life of the Buddha himself. According to the passage in the *Mahāparinibbāna-sutta*, the Buddha entered *parinibbāna* immediately upon emerging from the state of the fourth *jhāna*.[2] In the narrative describing the practices of the Bodhisatta preceding his awakening, the *jhānas* are presented as a positive counterpart of several inefficient meditative practices. In these texts,[3] the memory of a spontaneous attainment of the first *jhāna* in the Buddha's youth proves to be a major breakthrough and is followed by the attainment of all the four *jhānas* and awakening. According to an account of the gradual path of practice present in the *Sāmaññaphala-sutta* (DN 2/i.47–86) and several other discourses possessing a similar structure,[4] destruction of the influxes and final knowledge of a bhikkhu are directly preceded by the attainment of the fourth *jhāna*, which is described as a special, purified state particularly conducive to awakening. The general impression given by these texts is that the development of the four *jhānas* is organically linked to that of the other elements of the early Buddhist path, some of which function as necessary conditions for the *jhānas*, while others depend on the *jhānas*' prior attainment.

There are several other Nikāya passages which lead to conclusions that are at odds with the mainstream approach to *jhāna*. The implications of these texts are particularly problematic from the perspective of the view that the *jhānas* are a non-essential element of the Buddhist path, shared with non-Buddhists. Below, we will provide just a few examples of such texts as, due to lack of space, this issue cannot be

---

2 DN 16/ii.156: *catutthajjhānā vuṭṭhahitvā samanantarā bhagavā parinibbāyi*.

3 MN 36/i.238–251, MN 85/ii.91–97 and MN 100/ii.210–213.

4 See Gethin (2020) for a thorough comparative study of the structure of the texts following this pattern.

expounded here in greater detail.[5] For example, according to a simile contained in the *Jhāna-saṃyutta* (SN 53.1/v.307), the one who develops the four *jhānas*, slants, slopes and inclines towards *nibbāna* just as surely and irreversibly as the river Ganges slants, slopes and inclines towards the east.[6] When read directly, the text implies that the development of the four *jhānas* is a sufficient condition for one's final liberation.[7]

Some Nikāya texts speak of the importance of *samādhi*, without mentioning the *jhānas* explicitly. The *Vijjā-sutta* (AN 10.105/v.214) contains a list of the ten elements of the Buddhist path. They consist of the

5 For a more detailed presentation of this issue, see Polak (2011: 24–28).

6 SN 53.1/v.307: *seyyathāpi, bhikkhave, gaṅgā nadī pācīnaninnā pācīnapoṇā pācīnapabbhārā; evameva kho, bhikkhave, bhikkhu cattāro jhāne bhāvento cattāro jhāne bahulīkaronto nibbānaninno hoti nibbānapoṇo nibbānapabbhāro*. Translation follows Bodhi (2000: 1762).

7 Anālayo (2020: 580) claims that the "entire *Jhāna-saṃyutta* has no parallel in other transmission lineages and can safely be considered a later addition". It might indeed be the case; however, the fact that we know of no extant parallel of a particular text or group of text by itself does not automatically imply that it is a late addition, especially since we do not have access to the texts of all early schools of Buddhism. Anālayo (2020: 581) concludes that the "tendency to add the four absorptions in this way concords with the apparent development of definitions of right concentration. In all of these cases, it seems as if, with the passing of time, in some Buddhist traditions an increasing importance had been accorded to absorption attainment as required for progress to awakening". However, this does not seem to match the general trend of development within the Therāvada school which preserved the *Jhāna-saṃyutta*, as it was a tradition in which, as Gombrich (2006: 96) rightly argues, "insight worsted concentration". Kuan (2008: 142) speaks of the "tendency to devaluate concentration, whether the formless attainments or even the *jhānas*" which is evidenced by the modifications of the Pali *Satipaṭṭhāna-suttas*. Regardless of whether the *Jhāna-saṃyutta* is a late addition or not, it may be argued that the association of the development of the four *jhānas* with the ultimate soteriological goals of early Buddhism is to some extent implied by the message of other similarly structured saṃyuttas, which associate the same soteriological outcomes with the development of the sets of factors generally considered to be uniquely Buddhist, such as the noble eightfold path and the seven factors of awakening (*bojjhaṅga*). For example, it can be argued that the last four of the *bojjhaṅgas* correspond to some key features of the four *jhānas*. It has already been suggested by Gethin (2001: 181), that the *bojjhaṅga* list "links directly into a range of ideas associated with the *jhānas* and is intended to characterize a particular variety of *jhāna*".

Ultimately, the issue of the relative earliness of the *Jhāna-saṃyutta* is not crucial from the perspective of this study, as it is concerned with specific ideas contained in the Nikāyas, and not with establishing what was the earliest doctrine of Buddhism.

traditional eight elements of the noble eightfold path and two additional ones: right knowledge and right release.[8] The texts present these elements in a causal sequence in which every immediately preceding element serves as a necessary and sufficient condition for the one that follows it and which is said to proceed from it (*pahoti*). The eighth element is constituted by right concentration (*sammāsamādhi*) which in the Nikāyas is usually defined as the four *jhānas*.[9] Therefore, the attainment of the four *jhāna*s would imply prior full development of all the preceding seven elements of the path. According to a passage found in an identical version in the two *Cetanākaraṇīya-sutta*s (AN 10.2/v.2–4 and AN 11.2/v.312–313) of the *Aṅguttara Nikāya*, it is natural for one who is concentrated (*samāhita*), that he knows and sees things as they really are (*yathābhūtaṃ jānāti passati*) and no special intention nor separate practice needs to be made in that direction.[10] Again, if this text assumes that concentration (*samādhi*) is attained through the practice of the *jhāna*s, then this implies that knowledge and vision occur almost by default for someone who has developed them. Finally, the famous verse of the *Dhammapada* states that there is no *jhāna* for one devoid of understanding (*apañña*).[11]

All the abovementioned texts share a common denominator. They suggest that the attainment of the *jhāna*s or *samādhi* either implies the

8 Bucknell (2023: 151–61), offers an interesting hypothesis that the tenfold set of factors was a result of an extension of the original eightfold set which started from right action and ended with right release. As there was an awareness that the original set consisted of eight elements, at some point the last two elements of the tenfold set were removed. However, the historically dominant version of the eightfold path, which was the result of this alteration, was substantially different from the original eightfold set.

9 E.g., in the *Vibhaṅga-sutta* (SN 45.8/v.10). Of course, we cannot be certain that in the texts where *sammāsamādhi* or *samādhi* are only mentioned in general, they imply the four *jhānas*. However, this is the view presented in several Nikāya texts, and the position of *samādhi* in these sets generally corresponds to the position of the four *jhāna*s in the *Sāmaññaphala* pattern of gradual practice.

10 AN 10.2/v.3: *samāhitassa, bhikkhave, na cetanāya karaṇīyaṃ – 'yathābhūtaṃ jānāmi passāmī'ti. dhammatā esā, bhikkhave, yaṃ samāhito yathābhūtaṃ jānāti passati.* Cf. translation by Bodhi (2012: 1341). The fact that being concentrated (*samāhita*) is preceded in this text by experiencing pleasure (*sukha*) and by the arising of rapture (*pīti*) implies that we are probably dealing here with an alternate account of the same meditative process described by the formula of the four *jhānas*.

11 Dhp 372/53: *Natthi jhānaṃ apaññassa, paññā natthi ajhāyato. Yamhijhānañcapaññāca, savenibbānasantike.*

possession of various factors traditionally considered to be exclusively Buddhist or is in itself a necessary and sometimes seemingly even sufficient condition for the attainment of liberation. This is particularly problematic from the perspective of a traditional view that the *jhāna*s are meditative states practised by non-Buddhists as it would imply that if non-Buddhists attain the four *jhāna*s, then they must also possess, or have direct access to several supposedly exclusively Buddhist factors, such as the right view, right mindfulness, *paññā* and knowledge and vision.

In all the above cases, maintaining a historically dominant, mainstream view of the *jhāna*s ultimately leads to quite unorthodox conclusions. Of course, one cannot fully exclude the possibility that the authors of these texts were simply not aware of their far-reaching implications, and that the internal logic of these passages is faulty. However, the abovementioned texts are just an example of a far wider trend in the Nikāyas. One has to accept that there exists at least a substantial stratum of early texts which imply an unorthodox vision of the *jhāna*s that is difficult to harmonize with the mainstream Buddhist view.

In comparison to the Nikāyas, Chan texts are in general much more explicit regarding their opposition to the meditative ideas of mainstream Buddhism and this fact is widely acknowledged by scholars. Of course, at the time of the creation of the Nikāya texts in question there was hardly any Buddhist mainstream to be opposed against, and even if the ideas expressed in particular texts would appear unorthodox from the perspective of later developments, there would be simply no reason for their authors to emphasize their unorthodoxy. What is at stake in the case of Chan texts is whether their opposition to the Buddhist mainstream was merely a form of rhetoric, an element of a self-created narrative about the uniqueness of the Chan lineage or if it represented an actual difference of ideas about meditative practices and experiences.

The wrong and ineffective forms of meditation in the Nikāyas

In addition to the already mentioned suttas, there are other Nikāya texts from which we can indirectly infer that the *jhāna*s possess some features that are at odds with their mainstream view. Some of these passages either directly criticize certain meditative practices or simply present them as soteriologically inefficient. Others explicitly present a dichotomy of wrong and right meditative states. In all these texts, the negatively evaluated meditative states are directly or at least implicitly juxtaposed to the positively evaluated ones.[12]

The dichotomies of negatively and positively evaluated meditative practices and states are particularly relevant for our investigation, as they occur both in the Nikāya and Chan texts. As we shall see, it is their meditative and philosophical implications that are especially interesting. First, we shall focus on the characteristics of negatively evaluated meditative states and practices in Nikāya texts and later see if they share some similarities with those presented in the scriptures of the Chan tradition.

While the accounts of the praised meditative states do not always explicitly label them as the four *jhānas*, there is relatively good evidence for at least considering the possibility that these accounts may nonetheless refer to some other aspects of the very same jhānic process. It needs to be said here that it is a typical feature of the Nikāyas to provide various alternative and mutually complementary accounts of the same soteriological elements, practices or processes without ever explicitly explaining that they possess the same reference. Thus, for example, the set of the seven factors of awakening, the account of mindfulness of breathing and the description of the four *jhānas* can be interpreted as referring to various aspects of the same meditative and soteriological process.[13] Therefore, even if the particular meditative state or practice is not explicitly referred to as the four *jhānas* in a particular passage, it still might be the case that the fragment in question refers to some aspects of the practice labelled in other places as the four *jhānas*. Of course, one needs to provide some evidence for even considering such a possibility.

We shall start by examining a very famous fragment of the *Indriyabhāvanā-sutta* (MN 152/iii.298), in which the Buddha criticizes the meditative practice of the Brahmin Pārāsariya, which is said to lead

12 The method of indirectly inferring the nature of early Buddhist *jhāna* from the characteristics of the criticized meditative practices which are juxtaposed to it in particular texts, has been first utilized to a considerable extent by Bronkhorst (1986) in his *The Two Traditions of Meditation in Ancient India*.

13 Gethin (2001: 169–72) shows the parallels between the formulas of the seven *bojjhaṅgas*, the four *jhānas*, the four *satipaṭṭhānas* and mindfulness of breathing (*ānāpānassati*). Arbel (2017: 103) argues that "the seven factors of awakening (*bojjhaṅgas*) and the four *jhānas* should be construed as parallel models of spiritual ascension". Also, cf. Kuan (2008: 70–80) for a discussion of interrelation between *ānāpānassati*, the *satipaṭṭhānas* and the *jhānas*.

to insentience, as in this state one neither sees forms with the eye nor hears sounds with the ear.[14] In contrast, the Buddha describes various forms and levels of the proper development of the sense faculties, none of which seem to involve unawareness of the sense data. What is interesting about this text is that the criticized method of meditation is characterized by isolation from sensory input. This feature is usually ascribed to the Buddhist practice of calm (*samatha*), or at least to the higher stages of it. Such a temporary insentience is said to result from an absorption by a meditative object which is so strong that it simply leaves no possibility of being aware of anything else.

According to the mainstream Buddhist view, calm meditation is also practised by non-Buddhists and in the *Indriyabhāvanā-sutta* it is indeed ascribed to a Brahmin master of meditation. What is particularly interesting, however, is that the positively evaluated state of the development of sense faculties which is juxtaposed to Pārāsariya's method, is described using the terms that are also present in the standard account of some of the *jhānas*. Its description speaks about avoiding both the repulsive (*paṭikūla*) and the un-repulsive (*appaṭikūla*) and abiding in equanimity (*upekkhaka*), mindful (*sata*) and clearly comprehending (*sampajāna*).[15] The latter three terms occur in an identical form in the description of the third *jhāna*.[16] The stock account of the

14 MN 152/iii.298: *cakkhunā rūpaṃ na passati, sotena saddaṃ na suṇāti*. Burmese Chaṭṭha Saṅgāyana version gives the Brahmin's name as Pārāsiviya, while PTS, Sinhalese and Thai versions have Pārāsariya, and the latter name is predominantly used in modern translations and scholarship. This sutta cannot be considered an entirely faithful and honest account that gives full justice to non-Buddhist ideas and practices. While inactivity of the senses is indeed a feature of meditation attested in several Brahminic texts, its role can only be understood in connection with the goal of realizing *ātman*. However, the Buddhist text conveniently omits this aspect, giving the impression that for the Brahmin Pārāsariya insentience was an aim in itself, thus making his teaching an easy target for ridicule. It would be also relatively easy for someone familiar with the Upanishadic teachings to point out the difference between a meditator in a state taught in the Upanishads and the person who is deaf and blind, since unlike the latter, the former does not think or conceptualize, while supposedly experiencing *ātman/brahman*. Also see Bronkhorst (1986: 25–26) and Wynne (2007: 105–106) for a discussion of this text and its implications.

15 MN 152/iii.301: *sace ākaṅkhati - 'paṭikūlañca appaṭikūlañca tadubhayaṃ abhinivajjetvā upekkhako vihareyyaṃ sato sampajāno'ti, upekkhako tattha viharati sato sampajāno*. Translation follows Ñāṇamoli and Bodhi (1995: 1150).

16 SN 45.8/v.8: *Pītiyā ca virāgā upekkhako ca viharati sato ca sampajāno, sukhañca kāyena paṭisaṃvedeti, yaṃ taṃ ariyā ācikkhanti: 'upekkhako satimā sukhavihārī'ti tatiyaṃ jhānaṃ upasampajja viharati*.

fourth *jhāna* speaks of the purification of mindfulness due to equanimity (*upekkhāsatipārisuddhi*), of abandoning (*pahāna*) pleasure (*sukha*) and pain (*dukkha*), as well as of the earlier subsiding (*atthaṅgama*) of mental satisfaction and dissatisfaction (*somanassadomanassa*).[17] This may correspond to avoiding both the agreeable and the disagreeable described in the *Indriyabhāvanā-sutta*. We cannot be absolutely sure whether the account of the final form of *indriyabhāvanā* implies the state that is in other places described as the third (and maybe fourth) *jhāna*, or if the states in question merely share some crucial cognitive qualities. However, even if the latter is the case, the implication of the *Indriyabhāvanā-sutta* appears to be that at least the third and the fourth *jhānas* significantly differ from the practice taught by Pārāsariya with regard to the functioning of the sense faculties and an attitude towards their input. As according to the mainstream views the latter meditation is a typical example of meditative calm (*samatha*), then the third and fourth *jhānas* must also differ, at least regarding certain features, from the mainstream forms of *samatha*.[18]

17 SN 45.8/v.8: *Sukhassa ca pahānā dukkhassa ca pahānā pubbeva somanassadomanassānaṃ atthaṅgamā adukkhamasukhaṃ upekkhāsatipārisuddhiṃ catutthaṃ jhānaṃ upasampajja viharati.*

18 Anālayo (2017b: 138) offers a different interpretation. He claims that "the exposition in MN 152 is not a criticism of deeper stages of concentration during which sensory experience is absent, but rather a criticism of attempting to deal with sensory impact during daily life by simply trying to avoid it …". However, the text does not explicitly say that Pārāsariya considered sense inactivity to be a way of avoiding sensory impact connected with daily life, or as a default mode of functioning of someone with developed faculties. While as we have noted earlier, the Buddhist sutta does not offer an entirely honest account of Brahminic ideas and practices, sense inactivity seemed to be reserved in the Upanishads for special meditative states meant to provide liberating insight into the nature of *ātman/brahman* and serve as an anticipation of the final liberation after death. The account of the final stage of Buddhist *indriyabhāvanā* which uses the terms occurring in the description of the higher *jhānas*, does not seem to refer to an attitude towards sensory experience that that can be readily adopted by a deliberate decision, but rather to a deeply altered meditative state. The sutta ends with the Buddha's exhortation to meditate (*jhāyati*), and as we shall see in the later part of this chapter, there are good reasons to believe that this verb may refer in this context to abiding in the *jhānas*. This in turn would imply that the author of the text considered the *jhānas* as a path for developing the final stage of *indriyabhāvanā*. In other texts, the ability to dwell in the latter state according to one's wish (*sace ākaṅkhati*) is granted to those who develop each of the seven *bojjhaṅgas* accompanied by one of the four *brahmavihāras* (e.g., *metta*: SN 46.54/v.115–121), the state of *samādhi*

We have already briefly noted that the narrative presenting the Bodhisatta's practices preceding his awakening contains a description of several meditative techniques deemed inefficient. The various versions of this narrative may be found in the *Ariyapariyesanā-sutta*[19] (MN 26/i.161–175), the *Mahāsaccaka-sutta* (MN 36/i.237–251), the *Saṅgarava-sutta* (MN 100/ii.209–213) and the *Bodhirājakumāra-sutta* (MN 85/ ii.90–97), with the latter text containing the most complete narrative. Amongst the meditative states considered soteriologically ineffective are the sphere of nothingness (*ākiñcaññāyatana*) and the sphere of neither perception nor non-perception (*nevasaññānāsaññāyatana*) taught respectively by Āḷāra Kālāma and Uddaka Rāmaputta.[20] According to the historically dominant interpretation, they represent the highest stages of the development of meditative calm.[21] This is also implied by their very names, which suggest that they are states characterized by the absence of ordinary mental content and by restriction of mental activity. Some further hints about the nature of the stage of nothingness may be found in the passage of the *Mahāparinibbāna-sutta* (DN 16/ ii.130) where Āḷāra Kalama is described as seated in a deep meditative state in which he does not hear a noisy caravan of carts passing close by. While the name "sphere of nothingness" is not mentioned, it might be possible that the author of the text tacitly implied that Āḷāra was practising the state that he considered to be the highest and which he

connected with *ānāpānassati* (SN 54.8/v.316–320), and the four *satipaṭṭhānas* (SN 52.1/v.293–296). Some scholars have already emphasized the connection between the *jhānas*, the *bojjhaṅgas*, *ānāpānassati*, and the *satipaṭṭhānas* (e.g., Gethin 2001, Arbel 2017, Wynne 2018d) and one can consider the possibility of these formulas being alternative and complementary conceptualizations of the same meditative process. This would provide further evidence in favour of a connection between the *jhānas* and *indriyabhāvanā*. The account in the *Indriyabhāvanā-sutta* can at least in part be read as a juxtaposition of two forms of meditation: the early Buddhist one, which is conspicuously characterized by qualities otherwise attributed to the higher *jhānas*, and the Brahminic one, connected with sensory inactivity.

19 In some editions, this discourse is entitled the *Pāsarāsi-sutta*. See Ñāṇamoli and Bodhi (1995: 1216, n. 297). For an interesting hypothesis regarding the reasons for ascribing this name to this text, see Shulman (2021: 214).

20 It is important to emphasize that from the perspective of the Bodhisatta narrative these two states are not considered "wrong" in the sense of having deleterious effects, but merely soteriologically ineffective.

21 The cessation of perception and feeling (*saññāvedayitanirodha*) is in the Theravāda tradition considered to require both calm and insight, and thus cannot be considered a form of pure calm.

taught in his school.[22] According to the Bodhisatta narrative, the states of nothingness and of neither perception nor non-perception were already known and practised in pre-Buddhist times.

So far, all these characteristics agree with the mainstream Buddhist views on calm meditation. However, in the later part of the narrative contained in the *Mahāsaccaka-sutta*, the *Saṅgarava-sutta* and the *Bodhirājakumāra-sutta*,[23] the Bodhisatta attains a breakthrough by recollecting a spontaneous attainment of the first *jhāna* from his youth and reaches a realization that this practice represents a path to awakening. This is followed by an attainment of all the four *jhāna*s and by the destruction of the influxes. Interestingly, this seems to indirectly lead to consequences which are at odds with the classical set of eight successive meditative states in which the spheres of nothingness and neither perception nor non-perception are preceded by the four *jhāna*s and the spheres of boundless space and boundless consciousness.[24] If the truthfulness of this set is implied in the narrative, then the Bodhisatta would have to be a master of the four *jhāna*s already during his training with Āḷāra and Uddaka, as the attainment of the sphere of nothingness and neither perception nor non-perception would require a prior mastery of all the four *jhāna*s. In such a case, however, why would he consider the memory of the first, somewhat imperfect *jhāna* from a distant past to be such a breakthrough? He could have easily gone back to frequent attainment of all the four *jhāna*s during his practice in the schools of Āḷāra and Uddaka.

This implies that the author of the text may not have been aware of the classical list of eight (or nine) successive concentrative states in which the four *jhāna*s are succeeded by the four formless states ending with the spheres of nothingness and neither-perception nor

---

22 Of course, it also might be the case that the account of Āḷāra's meditation in the *Mahāparinibbāna-sutta* is earlier than the one in the narrative about the Bodhisatta's path to awakening. This could mean that Āḷāra's name was retroactively inserted to the narrative. However, Wynne (2007: 8–23) raises many arguments in favour of the historical authenticity of the account in *Ariyapariyesanā-sutta*.

23 This account is not contained in the *Ariyapariyesanā-sutta*. For a discussion of this important discrepancy see Wynne (2007: 15–18) and Polak (2011: 92–104).

24 I follow Anālayo (2010; 2020) in translating *ananta* in *ākāsānañcāyatana* and in *viññāṇañcāyatana* as "boundless" and not as "infinite" as it is traditionally done (e.g., Bodhi 2012). This translation will work better in the context of interpretation of the formless states offered in Chapter 4. Also cf. definitions of *ananta* in Cone (2001: 147) and Rhys Davids and Stede (2007: 47).

non-perception. One possible explanation for this fact would be that the set in question simply did not exist at that point, and the *jhāna*s and the *āruppa*s were not yet considered to be successive stages of the same process. An analysis of the Nikāyas shows that the interrelation of the *jhāna*s and the *āruppa*s is somewhat problematic. The four *jhāna*s are often presented by themselves in their own specific context and there are also variations regarding the sequence of the *āruppas*.[25] One also cannot fail to notice that the account of the *jhāna*s and that of the *āruppa*s have a different character and focus on entirely different aspects of the states they describe. The pattern and principle of the progress through the *jhāna*s is different from that through the formless states. All this calls into consideration whether the *jhāna*s and *āruppa*s from the very beginning belonged to one joint set.[26]

Another possibility is that the author of the Bodhisatta narrative knew the set of the eight successive meditative states, but was opposed to it. Yet another possibility is that the narrative is a clumsy patchwork of various elements, created without awareness of its implications. However, we should at least tentatively consider the implications of this account, as there are no good reasons for rejecting them out of hand.

The *jhānas* and the *āruppas*

Anālayo (e.g., 2017b; 2020) holds the position that there is nothing especially problematic about the interrelation of the *jhāna*s and the *āruppa*s in the Nikāyas. In order to justify the validity of the joint set of the *jhāna*s and the *āruppa*s, he points to several examples, including the account of the Buddha's passing away in the *Mahāparinibbāna-sutta* and its parallels "where a range of sources agree that he gradually proceeded through the four absorptions and the four immaterial spheres in forward and reverse order" (Anālayo, 2020: 574). However, if anything, the latter account suggests that even agreement of various parallel versions is not an ultimate guarantee that the text in question did not undergo earlier modifications. For as Gombrich (2009: 108) has

25 See Bronkhorst (1986: 76–88) and Polak (2011: 114–26), for a discussion of that claim.

26 Some possibilities regarding the interrelation of the *jhāna*s and the *āruppa*s will be considered in Chapter 4.

pointed out, this text clearly "juxtaposes earlier and later material" and the incongruity is so blatant that it "almost stares you in the face".

The account in question shows the Buddha first attaining in traditional order the stages from the first *jhāna* to *saññāvedayitanirodha*, and then returning in reverse order to the first *jhāna*. Afterwards he goes from the first *jhāna* to the fourth, and there attains *parinibbāna*. Gombrich (2009: 108) rightly notes:

> [W]e must have in the text before us a combination of two versions of the Buddha's death. Normally one would expect the later version to come second, but in this case the content makes that impossible, so the simpler version, that with just the four *jhānas*, is likely to be the older.

However, this is hardly surprising. The agreeance of two parallel versions merely shows that at some point preceding schisms in the early Saṅgha the text in question had a particular form. If any period was particularly conducive to introducing changes in the Buddhist texts, it was an earlier period directly following the Buddha's death.[27] Making definite claims regarding this earlier form of Buddhist doctrine with absolute certainty is pretty much impossible. One can at best consider various possibilities and arguments for and against them.

Earlier, I commented on the significance of the fact that in the suttas presenting the Bodhisatta's strivings, Gotama recollects the experience of the first *jhāna* from his youth. I hypothesized that it may imply that the author of this text did not consider that during the Bodhisatta's training with Āḷāra and Uddaka he already mastered the four *jhānas*, and that this suggests that at least this text does not imply that the *jhānas* are absolutely necessary for attaining the *āruppas*. Anālayo (2020: 576) offers a different interpretation. He claims that the Buddha had experienced the first and higher *jhānas* during the training with his two teachers but did not go back to these experiences as they "would have been affected by the thrust of his overall attempt to find liberation, in the sense of being from the outset viewed in relation to this goal". According to Anālayo (2020: 576), the influence of popular Indian belief of that time that liberation requires abstaining from pleasure "could

27 That this crucial period was marked by disagreements and uncertainty regarding the basic doctrines of Buddhism is attested by texts such as the *Kosambi-sutta* (SN 12.68/ii.115–118), the *Susima-sutta* (SN 12.70/ii.119–128) or the *Mahācunda-sutta* (AN 6.46/iii.354–356). See Wynne (2019b) for a discussion of the implications of these texts.

easily have led to regarding any joy and happiness experienced during an absorption with suspicion". Conversely, due to the accidental nature of his earlier experience of the first *jhāna* it "was not accompanied by some kind of evaluation or even apprehension of its potential repercussions" and therefore could have led to "a decisive shift in perspective". If this was indeed the case, then it is not conveyed in the text itself. Also, there is nothing in the account of training with Āḷāra and Uddaka that suggests they adhered to an ideological view that one should abstain from pleasure. While the explanation offered by Anālayo is not impossible from a psychological point of view, it requires that one refrains from accepting the implications resulting from a direct reading of the narrative and instead approaches it with the assumption that it implies the impossibility of entering the states of *ākiñcaññāyatana* and *nevasaññānāsaññāyatana* without prior attainment of the four *jhāna*s.

However, I want to stress here that by acknowledging that the historically dominant, classical Buddhist view on the interrelation of the *jhāna*s and the *āruppa*s is problematic I do not reject the possibility of attaining the *āruppa*s from the base provided by the *jhāna*s. In fact, I shall consider such a possibility in greater detail in chapter 4.

Anālayo (2020: 574–75) points to the *Laṭukikopama-sutta* (MN 66/i.447–456) and its Āgama parallel (MĀ 192 at T01, no. 26, pp. 740c15–744a3) as examples of a convincing explanation for a progression from the *jhāna*s to the *āruppa*s. In both texts, the Buddha advises Udāyin (*Wutuoyi* 烏陀夷 in the Āgama parallel) to overcome (p. *samatikkamati*/c. *guodu* 過度) the fourth *jhāna* in order to attain the sphere of boundless space (c. *wuliangkong* 無量空). The overcoming of successive states ends with cessation of perception and feeling.

However, what is problematic is whether the understanding implied in this text can be automatically generalized to numerous Nikāya texts which, for example, emphasize the role of the fourth *jhāna* as the special, purified state conducive to insight but do not explicitly mention the *āruppa*s. In the Pali version, the Buddha tells Udāyin that the fourth *jhāna* is "not enough" (*analan'ti*) and hence must be overcome or transcended. It is problematic whether from the perspective of the texts following the *Sāmaññaphala* pattern or the texts containing the Bodhisatta narrative such as the *Bodhirājakumāra-sutta*, the fourth *jhāna* is "not enough" and needs to be transcended, because in these texts it was clearly enough to attain a state of mind conducive to the realization of the knowledge of the exhaustion of the influxes (*āsava*). That is of course unless we assume that these texts tacitly imply that within the fourth *jhāna* one progresses through the *āruppas* to *saññāvedayitanirodha* but do not explicitly describe it. This does not preclude the possibility that the fourth *jhāna* may be a very good basis from which the meditator may attempt to attain the *āruppas*, since the former state is often described as endowed with potency to perform various cognitive functions. However, the accounts of the nine successive states do not provide in themselves conclusive evidence that attaining the four *jhānas* is the only way of attaining the *āruppas*.

Anālayo (2020: 575) is probably right when he claims that the sphere of boundless space cannot be attained directly from an ordinary mental state of being perceptive of diversity without first unifying the mind. However, are we justified in assuming that the four *jhānas* are the only possible states of meditative unification? As we shall see in this chapter, there exists a whole range of forms of meditative concentration, which, judging from how they are described, do not necessarily seem to be modalities of the four *jhānas*. The *Gopakamoggallāna-sutta* speaks of the *jhāna* that the Buddha did not praise (*vaṇṇeti*: MN 108/iii.13), while the Bodhisatta narrative mentions breathless (*appāṇaka*) *jhāna* (e.g., MN 36/i.243). Ānanda's statement in the former text that the Buddha did not "praise every *jhāna*" (*sabbaṃ jhānaṃ vaṇṇesi*) in itself implies that there are different types of *jhāna*. It is also noteworthy that the Nikāyas sometimes speak of the wrong *samādhi* (*micchāsamādhi* e.g., AN 4.205/ii.200) which seems to be conceptualized as a different form of meditation from the four *jhānas*. A possibility that needs to be considered is that the Nikāya account of the four *jhānas* is not a description of a universal but of a specific form of meditative unification, distinguished from other such states by its particular features. This would coincide with the fact that their stock account is not just a neutral account of various mental qualities but contains strong affirmations and positive evaluations of some of these qualities from the early Buddhist point of view. This is evidenced by the words "of which the noble ones declare: he is equanimous, mindful and dwells in pleasure"[28] contained in the stock account of the third *jhāna*, or by the description of purity of mindfulness due to equanimity (*upekkhāsatipārisuddhi*) in the account of the fourth *jhāna*.[29]

---

28 E.g., SN 45.8/v.10: *yaṃ taṃ ariyā ācikkhanti – 'upekkhako satimā sukhavihārī'ti.*

29 Gethin (2001: 348) writes about "a special *jhāna*, a *jhāna* in which *paññā* plays a special role, and a *jhāna* that establishes the eight factors of the noble path in the subsequent deeds", which is connected with the seven *bojjhaṅgas*. At least

The four *jhānas* in relation to other criticized meditative practices in the Nikāyas

In addition to the sphere of nothingness and neither perception nor non-perception, the Bodhisatta narrative (with the exception of the *Ariyapariyesanā-sutta*) describes another group of meditative practices as soteriologically inefficient. These practices, labelled as strivings (*padhāna*),[30] were traditionally considered to be forms of ascetism and self-mortification, and not meditation in the strict sense. While one of them, the radical food restriction, indeed does fit this characteristic, it is not necessarily the case with the other forms of "striving" which involve quite peculiar practices. During the first practice, the Bodhisatta restrains (*abhiniggaṇhāti*),[31] crushes (*abhinippīḷeti*),[32] and scorches (*abhisantāpeti*)[33] "the mind with the mind" (*cetasā cittaṃ*), while having clenched his teeth, and pressing the tongue against the palate.[34] During the second practice, the Bodhisatta tries to enter a "breathless *jhāna*" (*appāṇaka jhāna*) by successively restraining his breaths in his nose, mouth and ears. As the result of these practices, he experiences several painful sensations, including various degrees of headache connected with hearing internal noises, the feeling of burning on the surface of the body as well as sharp pain in the abdomen.

It is easy to see why such descriptions could lead later interpreters of this account to consider the Bodhisatta's practices as forms of self-mortification. However, a critical analysis of the account of these supposed ascetic practices reveals something fascinating: they were not really forms of self-torment, but rather advanced methods of pranayama (s. *prāṇāyāma*), very similar to those present in the hatha-yoga texts.

---

the third and fourth *jhānas* as described in the *Sāmaññaphala* account clearly match these characteristics.

30 See Bronkhorst (1986: 1–17) for a discussion of this account and of its implications.

31 Cone (2001: 200) gives the following meanings for *abhiniggaṇhāti*: "hold of", "holds fast", "restrains".

32 The meanings of *abhinippīḷeti* include: "presses", "crushes", or "oppresses" (Cone 2001: 201).

33 According to Cone (2001: 220), *abhisantāpeti* may also mean "torments" or "afflicts". It literally means "to cause to burn".

34 MN 85/ii.93: *'yannūnāhaṃ dantebhidantamādhāya, jivhāya tāluṃ āhacca, cetasā cittaṃ abhiniggaṇheyyaṃ abhinippīḷeyyaṃ abhisantāpeyyan'ti. So kho ahaṃ, rājakumāra, dantebhidantamādhāya, jivhāya tāluṃ āhacca, cetasā cittaṃ abhiniggaṇhāmi abhinippīḷemi abhisantāpemi.*

Their comparison with testimonies of modern pranayama masters such as Swami Rama[35] reveals that the drastic painful sensations described in the Buddhist narrative may in fact be natural, physiological side effects of yogic practices of breath restriction.[36] For the future Buddha these practices were simply means to achieve "superhuman *dhamma*" (*uttari manussadhamma*) and the distinction of the noble knowledge and vision (*ariyañāṇadassanavisesa*), while the painful sensations were only an undesired obstacle on the path and not an aim in itself. Therefore, they do not really deserve the label of self-mortification. Even food restriction and maintaining a radical diet consisting of liquids could be explained as a means of purification of body for the purpose of enabling knowledge and vision and not as a method of self-torment. The indirect implication of this fragment of the narrative is that certain meditative practices are inefficient, while the four *jhāna*s are presented as their positive counterparts devoid of their flaws. The inefficient practices again possess some of the traditional features of calm meditation: they seem to be forms of restraining mental activity ("restraining" and "crushing" the mind), and pre-Buddhist practices (though the narrative itself is not really clear about their origin and allows an unlikely interpretation that the Bodhisatta discovered them himself by experimenting). Unlike the spheres of nothingness and neither perception nor non-perception, these practices are very well-attested in the Brahminic and Hindu texts, such as the so-called Yogic Upanishads and the *Haṭha Yoga Pradīpikā*. The question of the status of breathless meditation is a bit more problematic. While breath restraint is a typical element of Brahminic and Hindu forms of meditation, several key Buddhist mainstream sources like the *Visuddhimagga* and the *Vimuttimagga* do not mention it as a distinct meditative practice. Some Nikāya texts claim that breathing stops in the fourth *jhāna*,[37] but it is seen as a consequence of the gradual calming of bodily and mental processes and not as a technique in its own right. Of course, various

35 See Rama (2004: 26, 59–64).

36 For a more detailed analysis, see Polak (2011: 85–89).

37 E.g., DN 33/iii.266: *catuttham̩ jhānam̩ samāpannassa assāsapassāssā niruddhā honti*. Shulman (2014: 33, n. 86) finds this feature problematic and comments: "This ascetic characterization of the fourth *jhāna* is puzzling, since the regular descriptions of this state do not suggest such an extreme bodily state but 'only' that one transcends experiences of pleasure and pain". Cf. Polak (2011: 154–55) for a discussion of this problem.

forms of breath restraint are well-known in Tibetan Buddhism, but these are not the subject of this study.

In addition to the *Indriyabhāvanā-sutta* and the narrative describing the path of the Bodhisatta, there are two more important texts containing a critique of certain meditative states and practices. These are the *Sandha-sutta* (AN 11.9/v.322–326)[38] and the *Gopakamoggallāna-sutta* (MN 108/iii.7–15). In contrast to the Bodhisatta narrative, these texts explicitly juxtapose two forms of meditation: a wrong one and a right one. Interestingly, the account of the wrong form of meditation in both texts shares one particular characteristic; it is said of the practitioner whose mind is obsessed (*pariyuṭṭhita*) and overcome (*pareta*) by any of the five hindrances (*nīvaraṇa*), who harbours them within (*antaraṃ karoti*), and does not understand the escape (*nissaraṇa*) from them, that he meditates (*jhāyati*), meditates forwards (*pajjhāyati*), meditates down (*nijjhāyati*) and meditates away (*apajjhāyati*).[39] In addition, the *Sandha-sutta* describes another feature of the wrong type of meditation, which is labelled in this text as the meditation of an unruly horse (*assakhaḷuṅka*); the practitioner is said to meditate (*jhāyati*) dependent on several basic elements or qualities of the world of human experience including the four elements, the four formless states, this world and the other world and "what is seen, heard, sensed, cognized, reached, sought after, and examined by the mind".[40]

The four *jhānas* are explicitly stated to be the positive counterpart of the wrong type of meditation in the *Gopakamoggallāna-sutta*, while in the *Sandha-sutta* it is merely said that the good meditator knows how to escape from the five hindrances and does not meditate dependent on any of the already mentioned basic qualities. Compared to

38 The title of this sutta comes from a name of a bhikkhu to whom the Buddha delivers his teaching. Burmese Chaṭṭha Saṅgāyana version has his name as Saddha, while the PTS and Sinhalese versions have the name Sandha. Despite using the Chaṭṭha Saṅgāyana version for quoting the Pali text, I refer to this discourse as the *Sandha-sutta* throughout this book due to this title being predominantly used in modern translations and scholarship. See Polak (2011: 51–58) for a more detailed analysis of the *Sandha* and the *Gopakamoggallāna-suttas*.

39 MN 108/iii.14: *Idha, brāhmaṇa, ekacco kāmarāgapariyuṭṭhitena cetasā viharati kāmarāgaparetena, uppannassa ca kāmarāgassa nissaraṇaṃ yathābhūtaṃ nappajānāti; so kāmarāgaṃyeva antaraṃ karitvā jhāyati pajjhāyati nijjhāyati apajjhāyati*. Bodhi (2012: 1560) translates the four verbs as "meditates, cogitates, ponders, and ruminates".

40 AN 11.9/v.325: *yampidaṃ diṭṭhaṃ sutaṃ mutaṃ viññātaṃ pattaṃ pariyesitaṃ anuvicaritaṃ manasā, tampi nissāya jhāyati*. Translation by Bodhi (2012: 1561).

the previously analysed passages, it is much less obvious in the case of these two texts to which form of meditation known from the later Buddhist typologies they refer when they criticize certain forms of practice. However, they contain some hints which allow us to at least consider certain interpretations. We shall return to the implications of these texts in the later part of this book.

The criticized forms of meditation in early Chan texts

In the case of early Chan, we find a critique of "wrong" forms of meditation in Hongren's *Xiuxin yao lun* 修心要論 (*Treatise on the Essentials of Cultivating the Mind*).[41] Of particular interest to us is the fragment which criticizes the state labelled as *wujixin* 無記心 (lit. non registering mind).[42] The meditator is warned of the danger of falling into that state during the practice of concentration of the mind (*shexin* 攝心) which is dependent (*yuan* 緣) on external objects (*waijing* 外境),[43] is connected with a coarse state of mind (*cuxin* 麁心), and with restriction of breathing (*shaoxi* 少息). During such a practice one internally binds (*neifu* 內縛) the "True Mind" (*zhenxin* 真心). If at the time when the mind is not yet pure (*jing* 淨) one tries to observe the mind (*kanxin* 看心), then due to the inability to illuminate (*zhao* 照) the mind source (*xinyuan* 心源) with clarity and purity, one enters the state of non-registration which is equated with a defiled mind (*louxin* 漏心[44]).[45]

The distinction between positively and negatively evaluated states of calm is also present in the *Dasheng wusheng fangbian men* 大乘無生方便門 (*The Expedient Means for Attaining Birthlessness in the Mahāyāna*),[46] a text associated with the Northern school of Chan.[47] One fragment questions whether it is possible to distinguish the devious (*xie* 邪) form of

41 Translation of the title follows McRae (1986: 121).

42 McRae (1986: 128) translates *wuji xin* 無記心 as "blankness of the mind".

43 McRae (1986: 128) translates *waijing* 外境 as "sensory perceptions".

44 *Lou* 漏 in Chinese texts is usually a translation of the Sanskrit term *āśrava* (p. *āsava*).

45 McRae (1986: 430/十): 問曰，云何名無記心。答曰，諸攝心入為緣外境麁心少息。內縛真心。心未淨時，於行住坐臥中恒徵意看心。由未能了了清淨獨照心源，是名無記。亦是漏心，猶不免生死大病。 Cf. T48, no. 2011, p. 378b23–27. For a translation of the whole passage, see McRae (1986: 128).

46 Translation of the title follows Sasaki (2009: 377) and McRae (1986: 149).

47 For a translation of selected fragments of this text, see McRae (1986: 171–96). For a discussion of this text, see McRae (1986: 218–33).

concentration (*ding* 定) from the right (*zheng* 正) one. The text labels the wrong form of concentration as Hinayanist (*ersheng* 二乘) while its positive counterpart is described as the practice of a bodhisattva (*pusa* 菩薩).[48] When the Hinayanists are in the state of concentration (*zaiding* 在定), they are devoid of wisdom (*wuhui* 無慧) and do not hear (*buwen* 不聞). As a result, they cannot preach the dharma and save living beings.[49] In an earlier part of the text, it is said that the Hinayanists fear motion (*weidong* 畏動), so they extinguish (*mie* 滅) the six consciousnesses (*liushi* 六識) and realize empty serenity (*kongji* 空寂). This results in developing attachment (*tanzhe* 貪著) to *dhyāna* (*chanmei* 禪昧) and falling into a Hinayanist nirvana.[50]

In his recent publication, Eric Greene (2021: 225–27) pointed out and analysed a very interesting early Chan text entitled *Tianzhu guo Putidamo chan shi lun* 天竺國菩提達摩禪師論 (*Treatise of the Chan Master Bodhidharma of India*).[51] This text is significant for our investigation as it directly juxtaposes wrong forms of meditation with the right ones. The wrong forms of meditation are, like in the *Dasheng wusheng fangbian men*, labelled as "Lesser Vehicle" meditations and are forms of practice in which "there is something one seeks, something one sees, and something one attains". Meditation on the breath, a standard form of mainstream calm meditation, is said to be an example of such lesser method. Incorrect contemplation (*xieguan* 邪觀) is said to involve contemplating what is other (*taguan* 他觀) by "focusing on a cognitive object (*jingjie* 境界) outside yourself" (Greene, 2021: 226) and can lead to various visions of colourful lights. As Greene (2021: 227) summarizes, this text "seems to reject any meditation technique that focuses attention on an external object of cognition".

Perhaps the most extensive critique of wrong forms of meditation can be found in the writings of Shenhui, the self-proclaimed successor of Huineng. In his *Putidamo nanzong ding shifei lun* 菩提達磨南宗定是非論 (*Treatise on the Definition of the Truth regarding the Southern School*

48 T85, no. 2834, p. 1275a23–24: 是沒是邪定正定。二乘人有定無慧名邪。菩薩有定有慧名正。

49 T85, no. 2834, p. 1275a2–4: 二乘人出定。即聞在定不聞。二乘人在定無慧。不能說法亦不能度眾生。出定心散。說法無定。 For a translation of this fragment, see McRae (1986: 183).

50 T85, no. 2834, p. 1274c18–20: 畏動執不動。滅六識證空寂。涅槃有聲無聲。聲落謝不聞。不聞貪著禪味。墮二乘涅槃。 For a translation of this fragment, see McRae (1986: 182).

51 Translation of the title follows Greene (2021: 225).

of Bodhidharma),[52] we encounter a very famous criticism of meditative methods attributed to Shenxiu, the supposed rival of the Sixth Patriarch Huineng and leader of the Northern school of Chan. In a dialogue with master Chongyuan 崇遠, Shenhui states that Shenxiu teaches people to freeze the mind (*ningxin* 凝心) to enter *samādhi* (*ruding* 入定), to stop the mind (*zhuxin* 住心)[53] and observe purity (*kanjing* 看淨), to activate/arouse the mind (*qixin* 起心) and illuminate the outside (*waizhao* 外照), to concentrate the mind (*shexin* 攝心) and to realize internally (*neizheng* 內證).[54] This famous line is repeated virtually in identical form in a much later text,[55] the *Zhenzhou Linji Huizhao chanshi yulu* 鎮州臨濟慧照禪師語錄 (*Discourse Records of Chan Master Huizhao of Linji in Zhenzhou*) containing the teachings of Linji Yixuan 臨濟義玄 (d. 866).[56]

In the *Nanyang heshang wenda zazheng yi* 南陽和尚問答雜徵義 (*Dialogues on Miscellaneous Inquiries to the Reverend [Shenhui] of Nanyang*),[57] Shenhui identifies cultivation of *samādhi* (*xiuding* 修定) with what is fundamentally (*yuan* 元)[58] a deluded state of mind (*wangxin* 妄心).[59] In another fragment of the same text we read that cultivating concentration (*xiuding* 修定) and establishing concentration (*zhuding* 住定) means that one actually becomes fettered by concentration (*beidingfu* 被定縛).[60] In Shenhui's *Nanyang heshang dunjiao jietuo chan-*

---

52 Translation of the title follows McRae (2023: 72). Sasaki (2009: 405) translates it as *Treatise establishing the true and false according to the Southern school of Bodhidharma.*

53 McRae (2023: 97) translates *zhuxin* 住心 as "fix the mind".

54 B25, no. 142, p. 67a6–7: 為秀禪師教人凝心入定，住心看淨，起心外照，攝心內證。 For translations and discussions of this fragment see Bielefeldt (1988: 91), Gómez (1987: 81) and McRae (2023: 97). McRae (2023: 97, n. 144) labels this criticism as "the four pronouncements". It appears in virtually identical form in all three major texts of Shenhui discussed in this book.

55 In his book *The Linji lu and the Creation of Chan Orthodoxy*, Albert Welter (2008) suggests the relatively late origin of the currently available version of *Zhenzhou Linji Huizhao chanshi yulu* and points out numerous modifications that this text has undergone.

56 T47, no. 1985, p. 499b14–16: 祖師云：『爾若住心看靜，舉心外照、攝心內澄、凝心入定，如是之流皆是造作。

57 Afterwards, the title of this text is given in this book in a shortened form as the *Wenda zazheng yi*. Translation of the title follows McRae (2023: 129). Sasaki (2009: 403) translates it as *The priest of Nanyang's question-and-answer examination of various points of doctrine*.

58 元 may also be read as "originally". See McRae (2023: 159, n. 201).

59 B25, no. 143, p. 235a2: 今修定者，元是妄心。See McRae (2023: 158).

60 B25, no. 143, p. 236a2: 修定住定，即被定縛。See McRae (2023: 159).

men zhiliaoxing tanyu 南陽和上頓教解脱禪門直了性壇語 (*A Platform Sermon by [Shenhui], the Reverend of Nanyang on Directly Comprehending the [Buddha-]Nature according to the Chan Doctrine of Sudden Teaching and Emancipation*),[61] freezing the mind in order to enter *samādhi* is described as falling into an emptiness of non-registering (*duowujikong* 墮無記空),[62] while the four wrong forms of meditation already mentioned in the *Putidamo nanzong ding shifei lun* are collectively described as the dharma bondage of the mind (*fafuxin* 法縛心) and not mind of liberation (*jietuo* 解脫).[63]

An interesting account of the wrong methods of meditation may be found in the *Lidai fabao ji* 歷代法寶記 (*Record of the Dharma-Jewel Through the Generations*),[64] a major work of the Baotang school containing the teachings attributed to Master Wuzhu 無住 (714–774), which includes methods such as contemplation by counting breaths (*shuxiguan* 數息觀), contemplation of white bones (*baiguguan* 白骨觀), contemplation of the sun (*riguan* 日觀) and contemplation of the Buddha (*foguan* 佛觀) that are described as methods of Hīnayāna and not those of Bodhidharma.[65] In another fragment of the same text, Wuzhu singles out the contemplation of the Buddha for his criticism. He quotes *Chan men jing* 禪門經 (*Scripture on the Gate of Chan*),[66] which states that if during seated meditation one sees the Buddha with his thirty-two marks, radiating light and flying through space, then it is just one's own mind being confused (*zixin diandao* 自心顛倒) and being caught

61 Below, this title appears in a shortened form *Tanyu*. Translation of the title follows McRae (2023: 47). Sasaki (2009: 403) translates it as *The priest of Nanyang's platform sermon on direct realization of innate nature according to the Chan doctrine of emancipation through the teaching of sudden awakening*.

62 B25, no. 142, p. 21a6: 即如「凝心入定」，墮無記空。 McRae (2023: 61) translates *wujikong* as "blank emptiness".

63 B25, no. 142, p. 21a10–11:『〔凝心入定〕，住心看淨，起心外照，攝心內證』，非解脫心，亦是法縛心，不中用。Cf. translation by McRae (2023: 61).

64 Regarding the *Lidai fabao ji*, see Yanagida (1983), Adamek (2007), Adamek (2011). Translation of the title is based on Adamek (2007: 297).

65 T51, no. 2075, p. 183a11–13: 諸小乘禪及諸三昧門。不是達摩祖師宗旨。列名如後。白骨觀。數息觀。九相觀。五停觀。日觀。月觀。樓臺觀。池觀。佛觀。For a translation and discussion, see Adamek (2007: 326).

66 Translation of the title follows Greene (2021: 211). Early Chan texts often quote earlier Mahāyāna texts. As Poceski (2007: 146) points out, "the Chan sermons integrate scriptural citations and metaphors into their overall narrative structure, without explicit boundaries or markings that set the canonical excerpts apart from the teachings of the Chan teacher in question". See Poceski (2007: 144–49) for a more detailed discussion of this issue.

in the Māra's net.[67] Interestingly, all the methods criticized by Wuzhu are well-known forms of meditative calm, featuring prominently in the fifth-century Chinese manuals of meditation.[68] As Greene (2021: 210) aptly summarizes:

> Singled out for censure here are general techniques of meditation associated with both the fifth-century chan scriptures,[69] such as the white bone contemplation, and the closely related Contemplation Scriptures, such as the sun contemplation and the pond contemplation. One fifth-century chan scripture is even mentioned by name: the Chan Essentials.

An interesting critique of certain meditative practices can be found in the *Xuansha Shibei chanshi guanglu* 玄沙師備禪師廣錄 (*Extensive record of Great Teacher Xuansha Shibei*). Xuansha Shibei 玄沙師備 (835–908) criticizes meditators who "decide to focus the mind (*shexin* 凝心) and restrain thoughts (*liannian* 斂念)". Furthermore, "whenever thoughts arise (*nianqi* 念起), one after another they 'brush them away' (*pochu* 破除) – as soon as a subtle thought arises, they immediately suppress it".[70]

The texts attributed to the representatives of the Hongzhou school also contain criticisms of various forms of traditional calm meditation. In the *Chuanxin fa yao* 傳心法要 (*Essentials of the Transmission of Mind*),[71] Huangbo Xiyun 黄檗希運 (d. 850?) criticizes sentient beings for using the mind (*jiangxin* 將心) in order to seize the mind (*zhuoxin* 捉心).[72] This statement may be considered as a very apt characteristic

67 T51, no. 2075, p. 183a19–21: 佛言。坐禪見空無有物。若見於佛三十二相。種種光明。飛騰虛空。變為自在。皆是自心顛倒。繫著磨網。Cf. translations by Greene (2021: 211) and Adamek (2007: 326).

68 See Adamek (2007: 28): "The dhyana techniques disparaged in the *Lidai fabao ji* are reminiscent of the techniques found in early translations of dhyana scriptures".

69 By "chan scriptures" Greene does not mean texts of the Chan tradition tracing its lineage to Bodhidharma but early Chinese meditation scriptures.

70 X73, no. 1445, p. 15b9–11: 便擬凝心斂念。攝事歸空。閉目藏睛。終有念起。旋旋破除。細相纔生。即便遏捺。This fragment is directly quoted by Dahui 大慧 (1089–1163) in one of his letters (for translation, see Broughton and Watanabe, 2017: 221).

71 Translation of the title follows McRae (2005). The full title of this text is *Huangboshan Duanji Chanshi Chuanxin Fayao* 黃蘗山斷際禪師傳心法要.

72 T48, no. 2012A, p. 379c24–25: 但是眾生著相外求。求之轉失。使佛覓佛。將心捉心。McRae (2005: 13) translates this fragment as: "However, sentient beings are attached to characteristics and seek outside themselves. Seeking it, they lose it even more. Sending the Buddha in search of the Buddha, grasping the mind with the mind".

of the classical form of calm meditation. According to Guifeng Zongmi 圭峰宗密 (780–841), the Hongzhou school was negatively predisposed towards the classical practice of *śamatha*. In his notes on the houses of Chan embedded in the third fascicle of his sub-commentary entitled *Yuanjuejing dashu shiyi chao* 圓覺經大疏釋義鈔 (*Extracts from the Great Commentary on the Perfect Awakening Sutra*),[73] he states that the representatives of that school believed that one should not arouse (or stir, activate) the mind (*qixin* 起心) to do what is bad and cultivate good, not "use the mind (*jiangxin* 將心) to cultivate the mind (*xiuyuxin* 修於心)" and not use the mind (*yixin* 以心) to cut off the mind (*duanxin* 斷心).[74] The latter statement is very similar to the one made by Huangbo Xiyun.

According to his magnum opus on Chan, *Chanyuan zhuquanji duxu* 禪源諸詮集都序 (*Prolegomenon to the Collection of Expressions of the Chan Source*),[75] Zongmi himself considered the practice consisting of sitting in silence (*yanmo* 宴默), pressing the tongue against the palate (*shezhushange* 舌拄上腭), and concentrating the mind on one object (*xinzhuyijing* 心注一境)[76] as a lower form of Chan. To him, this practice belonged to the so-called first axiom of Chan, representative of the Northern school of Shenxiu and the Baotang school of Wuzhu.

Pressing the tongue against the palate[77] is also criticized in the relatively late *Linji yulu* together with other techniques, such as sitting leaning against the wall (*yibizuo* 倚壁坐) and being profoundly immobile

73 Translation of the title follows Broughton (2009: xiii).

74 X09, no. 245, p. 534b20–21: 謂不起心造惡修善。亦不修道。道即是心。不可將心還修於心。惡亦是心。不可以心斷心。Translation follows Broughton (2009: 185).

75 Translation of the title follows Broughton (2009: xiii).

76 T48, no. 2015, p. 402b29: 舌拄上腭心注一境。Cf. translation by Broughton (2009: 121): "[P]ress the tongue against the roof of the mouth [in order to inhibit salivation]; and have the mind concentrate on one sense object". As we have seen above, Zongmi's attribution of this method to the Northern School and the Baotang School does not seem correct, as these schools were in fact criticizing the same forms of meditations. While Zongmi's works are extremely valuable for historical purposes, they contain many such misinterpretations of the teachings of other schools of Chan. For a discussion of certain limitations of Zongmi's work, see Poceski (2007: 130).

77 Interestingly, one finds a positive evaluation of this technique in the *Chan mi yao fa jing* 禪祕要法經, an early Chinese manual of meditation, which advises the meditator to rest the tongue on the palate (*shezhue* 舌拄腭: T15, no. 613, p. 243b26).

(*shenranbudong* 湛然不動).[78] This is likened to recognizing darkness (or ignorance) as one's overlord (*wuming wei langzhu* 無明為郎主) and is considered a great error (*dacuo* 大錯).

As we have seen, criticism of certain forms of wrong meditation was a relatively common theme found in early Chan writings. It seems that the majority of criticized meditative practices can be classified as forms of calm meditation. We often encounter descriptions of the activity of concentrating the mind (e.g., *shexin* 凝心), focusing on external objects, sensory inactivity and classical calm methods like mindfulness of breathing. Of course, not all the analysed Chan authors criticized exactly the same features of meditation and therefore one should be careful when making generalizations that would apply to all of them. At this point we will only conclude that criticism of some features of what was traditionally considered calm meditation is quite prevalent in early Chan scriptures.

Positively evaluated forms of meditative calm

While both Nikāya and Chan texts criticize certain practices and states traditionally associated with calm meditation, they also praise other states connected with deep quietude and the absence of discursive thought. Interestingly, this positive appraisal of certain meditative states is often found in the same texts which contain a criticism of other forms of meditation.

As we have already noted, in the Nikāyas most of the criticized meditative states are either directly or at least implicitly juxtaposed with the four *jhāna*s, which function as their positive counterpart. It is worth emphasizing that the *jhāna*s are without doubt states of mental calm, just like their negative counterparts. According to the stock passage describing these forms of meditation, starting from the second *jhāna*, there is no more thinking (*vitakka*) and pondering (*vicāra*), and this state is even described as the "noble silence" (*ariya tuṇhībhāva*) in the *Kolita-sutta* (SN 21.1/ii.273–274).[79] While the lack of *vitakka* and *vicāra* is not

78 T47, no. 1985, p. 501a22–25: 學人不會，便即向裏作解，便即倚壁坐，舌拄上齶，湛然不動，取此為是祖門佛法也。大錯，是爾若取不動清淨境為是，爾即認他無明為郎主。Cf. translation of this fragment by Sasaki (2009: 24–25).

79 SN 21.1/ii.273: '*idha bhikkhu vitakkavicārānaṃ vūpasamā ajjhattaṃ sampasādanaṃ cetaso ekodibhāvaṃ avitakkaṃ avicāraṃ samādhijaṃ pītisukhaṃ dutiyaṃ jhānaṃ upasampajja viharati. ayaṃ vuccati ariyo tuṇhībhāvo'ti*.

explicitly mentioned in the context of the third and fourth *jhānas*, their continuous absence seems to be nonetheless implied. Furthermore, the latter two states are endowed with equanimity (*upekkhā*). In addition, the fourth *jhāna* is characterized by the absence of pleasure and pain (*adukkhamasukha*) and by the earlier subsiding of mental satisfaction and dissatisfaction (*somanassadomanassa*). All these features suggest a deep level of mental quietude, both regarding thought activities and emotional states.

Similarly, most Chan texts containing a critique of practices possessing features traditionally associated with calm meditation, at the same time contain praise of meditative states connected with an absence of thought or of other forms of mental activity.

Hongren's *Xiuxin yao lun* recommends a practice of looking (見 *jian*) at the flowing consciousness (*liudongzhishi* 流動之識), which ultimately leads to its self-cessation (*zimie* 自滅). As a result, "one's mind becomes peacefully stable (*ning* 凝), simple (*danbo* 淡泊) and pure (*jiaojie* 皎潔)".[80] In the *Tanyu*, Shenhui praises the state of true no-thought (*zhenwunian* 真無念),[81] in which one does not even make an act of intention (*zuoyi* 作意) and there is no activation/arousing of the mind (*xinwuyouqi* 心無有起).[82] In the *Lidai fabao ji*, Wuzhu describes arousing the mind (*qixin* 起心) as a defilement, while movement of thought (*dongnian* 動念) as the demons' net.[83] This implies a positive evaluation of non-movement of thought and non-arousal of the mind. And indeed, the same fragment praises a state of no-thought (*wunian* 無念) and proclaims that not arousing the mind equals seeing the Buddha. All these positively evaluated features are typical of a state of deep mental quiescence. If we can trust Zongmi's account, the Baotang school of Wuzhu aimed at extinguishing consciousness (*mieshi* 滅識) and considered arousing of

80 McRae (1986: 427/十三): 其此流動之識，颯然自滅。滅此識者，乃是滅十地菩薩眾中障惑。此識身等滅已，其心即虛凝淡泊皎潔然。Cf. T48, no. 2011, p. 379a11–13. For a translation of this passage, see McRae (1986: 130–31).

81 McRae (2023: 65) translates *wunian* as "non-thought".

82 B25, no. 142, p. 28a10: 但不作意，心無有起，是真無念。McRae (2023: 53, n. 48) translates *zuoyi* as "intentionalize" and points out that the "verb *zuo* 作 indicates the willful or intentional performance of an action". The term corresponds to Pali *manasikaroti*.

83 T51, no. 2075, p. 193b15–17: 不起即是見佛。又問和上。若此教人得否。和上云。得。起心即是塵勞。動念即是魔網。Cf. Adamek (2007: 387) for a translation of this fragment.

the mind as deluded (*qixinjiwang* 起心即妄), while the non-arousing as the real (*zhen* 真).[84]

Despite lacking details about meditative techniques, the texts connected with the Hongzhou school often contain a positive evaluation of the states of absence of thought. The *Tiansheng guangdeng lu* 天聖廣燈錄 (*Tiansheng-era Record of the extensive transmission*)[85] contains a fragment in which Mazu Daoyi states that when there is not a single thought (*wuyinian* 無一念), the root (*genben* 根本) of birth and death becomes eliminated.[86] In the same text, his direct disciple Baizhang Huaihai 百丈懷海 (749–814) considers the states of raising the mind (*juxin* 舉心) and movement of thought (*dongnian* 動念) to be a breach of the monastic discipline (*pojie* 破戒).[87] In the *Baizhang Huaihai chanshi guanglu* 百丈懷海禪師廣錄 (*The Extensive Record of Master Baizhang Huaihai*) we find Baizhang's admonitions to "not remember (*ji* 記), recollect (*yi* 憶), get caught up (*yuan* 緣) or think (*nian* 念)" and to have a mind like wood or stone (*mutou* 木石) and without any activity (*wusuoxing* 無所行).[88] In the *Chuanxin fa yao*, Huangbo Xiyun describes the movement of thought (*dongnian* 動念) as going against (*guai* 乖) the One Mind (*yixin* 一心).[89] In the ensuing passage he emphasizes that it is enough to end thinking (*xinian* 息念) and forget about mentation (*wanglü* 忘慮) for the Buddha to self-manifest (*fozixianqian* 佛自現前).[90] The absence of movement of thought and mentation is certainly a mark of a meditative state of deep calm.

---

84 X09, no. 245, p. 534a13–14: 言滅識者。即所修之道也。意謂生死輪轉。都為起心。起心即妄。不論善惡不起即真。Cf. translation by Broughton (2009: 183): "'Extinguishing consciousness' is the path practiced, meaning that all wheel turning in the rebirth process is the production of mind. The production of mind is the unreal. No matter whether good or bad, not producing [mind] is the real".

85 Translation of the title follows Sasaki (2009: 431).

86 X78, no. 1553, p. 449a2: 但無一念。即除生死根本。Cf. translation of this fragment by Poceski (2007: 161).

87 X78, no. 1553, p. 462c4–5: 但有舉心動念。盡名破戒。Cf. translation by Cleary (1978: 67).

88 X69, no. 1323, p. 7c10–12: 莫記莫憶。莫緣莫念。放捨身心。全令自在。心如木石。口無所辯。心無所行。 Translation follows Poceski (2007: 163).

89 T48, no. 2012A, p. 379c18–22. Cf. McRae (2005: 13) for a translation of this fragment.

90 T48, no. 2012A, p. 379c25–26:不知息念忘慮佛自現前。Cf. translation of this fragment by McRae (2005: 13).

As we have seen, the authors of Nikāya and early Chan texts criticize certain forms of calm meditation leading to inactivity of the mind and the senses. However, the practices they themselves preach seem to lead to quite similar results. What then exactly distinguishes the "right" forms of meditation from the criticized ones? If there indeed exists a fundamental difference between the two, it does not seem immediately self-evident. This issue has been acknowledged by several scholars, as exemplified by the following apt statement by Bielefeldt (1986: 145) about Shenhui:

> Yet for all his doubts about *dhyāna* and suspicions of *samādhi*, his description of practice still seems to suggest (though he is careful to keep this ambiguous) that no-thought, or the original, non-abiding nature of the mind, is to be discovered when thoughts have been extinguished.

This ambiguity and lack of clarity resulted in some Chan masters themselves coming under attack from non-Chan Buddhists for promoting "heterodox" and essentially non-Buddhist views on meditative practice. This was the case with Heshang Moheyan 和尚摩訶衍 during the Samye debate. As Gómez (1987: 104) points out:

> One could accuse him, as Kamalaśīla does, of proposing a meditation practice that is pure calm – that is to say, blind mental concentration. Mo-ho-yen is partly to blame for this misinterpretation, because he uses the term chan (*dhyāna*) unaware of his opponent's understanding of the word, and because he hesitates too much in his treatment of the question of "means".

Kamalaśīla's criticism is based on interpreting Moheyan's meditative teachings as referring to:

> [A] type of inactive, nonconceptual contemplation that he knows from India – the practice of pure calm (*samatha*). He insists that the practice of mental calm and concentration for their own sake is a non-Buddhist practice that does not lead to true liberation. (Gómez, 1987: 107)

The problem of distinguishing Chan meditative states from total insentience has been rightly identified by Robert Sharf (2014a: 160) as the central struggle on which the Chan tradition was weaned on. He writes:

> And repeatedly, the controversies bear on the relationship between Buddhist practice on the one hand, and the simple insentience (*wuqing*) of the physical world on the other. (Sharf, 2014a: 149)

What is the difference between wrong and right forms of meditation?

Is it therefore possible to point out any essential difference that would allow us to distinguish the right forms of meditative calm from the wrong ones in the analysed texts? For now, let us refrain from automatically assuming that all the texts of both traditions that we have analysed so far share exactly the same understanding regarding right and wrong forms of meditation. It is after all possible that the distinctions between right and wrong forms of practice present in particular texts reflect very different ideas about meditation.

A possibility that one needs to consider is that the critique of certain meditative states may be entirely rhetorical in character and undertaken for polemical reasons. Such explanations have already appeared with regard to Chan authors. According to this interpretation, certain forms of calm meditation receive criticism simply because they were advocated by the sectarian rivals of the authors of the Chan texts in question. Many internal Chan debates may have actually concerned the issues of power, legitimacy, transmission and lineage, though they were masked as polemics regarding practical aspects of meditation. That would explain why the criticized states appear outwardly similar to the meditative practices praised by the very same authors. This explanation seems to be hinted at in the already quoted Bielefeldt's (1986: 145) interpretation of Shenhui's method of meditation as a form of extinguishing thoughts.

The other hypothesis would assume ideological, but not practical and psychological grounds for the criticism of "wrong" forms of meditation. This interpretation sees the specific meditative discourse of early Chan texts as resulting from their subitism. This latter ideology is particularly prominent in the texts of the so-called Southern school of Chan, as exemplified by Huineng's verse in the *Liuzu tanjing* 六祖壇經 (*Platform Sutra of the Sixth Patriarch*).[91] It contains a criticism of another

91 The full title of the Dunhuang version of this text which is referred to in this book is *Nanzong dunjiao zuishangsheng mohe boreboluomi jing, liuzu Huineng dashi yu shaozhou dafansi shi fa tanjing* 南宗頓教最上大乘摩訶般若波羅蜜經六祖惠能大師於韶州大梵寺施法壇經 (*The Sūtra of the Perfection of Wisdom of the Supreme Vehicle of the Sudden Teaching of the Southern Tradition: The Platform Sūtra Taught by the Great Master Huineng, the Sixth Patriarch, at the Dafan Monastery in Shaozhou*: translation of the title by Schlütter, 2012: 2). It is the earliest out of the currently existing seven versions of this seminal text, though as Schlütter

verse written by Shenxiu, which states that the mind is like a clear mirror but needs to be constantly cleaned of dust (*chenai* 塵埃).[92] In his own verse, Huineng states that the Buddha's nature (*foxing* 佛性) is always clear and bright (*qingjing* 清淨), and there is no place which can be soiled by dust.[93] The concept of any difference between enlightenment and ignorance, and between the practice and its lack would therefore be a form of mistaken dualism. Thus, any idea of "practice" involving reaching enlightenment from a non-enlightened point of departure would have to be considered wrong. According to such an interpretation, the critique of meditation found in at least some Chan texts would not be directed against certain forms of meditation in themselves, but only against a particular discourse about meditation, which presents it in gradualist terms. Chan monks would therefore be practising exactly the same forms of meditation as other Buddhists, but due to ideological reasons their own texts could not contain any instructions or detailed descriptions of their meditative practices. A good example of this approach can be found in the following statement by McRae (2005: 6):

> We may be sure that trainees in Mazu's school still engaged in seated meditation (*dhyāna*), but there was a palpable taboo against even referring to this subject, let alone considering it the quintessential feature of Buddhist spiritual discipline.[94]

In a similar vein, Bielefeldt (1988: 96) writes:

> We can probably assume that, even as these masters labored to warn their disciples against fixed notions of Buddhist training, the monks were sitting with legs crossed and tongues pressed against their palates. But what they were doing had now become a family secret.

However, a careful analysis of at least some early Chan texts reveals that their rejection of particular forms of meditation may have been made on psychological and practical grounds and not merely polemical and

---

(2007: 386) points out, it is "almost certainly a product of a long evolution with elements coming together from several different Chan groups with different agendas" as attested by the internal inconsistencies of the text.

92 T48, no. 2007, p. 337c1–2: 身是菩提樹， 心如明鏡臺，時時勤拂拭， 莫使有塵埃。Cf. translations by Yampolsky (1967: 130) and Gregory (2012: 88).

93 T48, no. 2007, p. 338a7–8: 菩提本無樹， 明鏡亦無臺，佛性常清淨， 何處有塵埃？Cf. translations by Yampolsky (1967: 132) and Gregory (2012: 88).

94 Also cf. Bielefeldt (1988: 60) and Sharf (2014b: 937–38) for similar interpretations. It needs to be emphasized that Sharf merely summarizes a position of other scholars.

ideological ones. This is particularly the case with Shenhui, who of all the Chan authors has probably been the most vocal critic of the mainstream Buddhist model of meditation. In the *Wenda zazheng yi*, we find Shenhui in a very interesting discussion[95] with a certain Master Cheng 澄, who acts as an apologist for traditional, mainstream Buddhist views regarding meditative practices of calm and insight.[96] When asked by Shenhui about the method[97] for obtaining (*de* 得) a vision of (Buddha) nature (*jianxing* 見性), Master Cheng answers that one must first study how to cultivate concentration (*xiuding* 修定), and then concentration will become the cause from which wisdom will develop (*fahui* 發慧). On hearing this, Shenhui asks whether during the time of cultivation of concentration (*xiudingzhishi* 修定之時), one needs to consciously apply the mind (or make a willful act of mental intention – *zuoyi* 作意), to which Master Cheng agrees. In response, Shenhui states that if one consciously applies the mind (*zuoyi*), then it is a form of conscious (or conceptual) concentration (*shiding* 識定).[98] "How can one see the nature in this way?" – he asks rhetorically.[99] To Shenhui, the very presence of *zuoyi* seems to disqualify the classical Buddhist model of calm and insight exemplified by Cheng's method as a valid path to spiritual realization.

95 B25, no. 143, pp. 234a06–235a10.

96 Gómez (1987: 80) rightly suggests that the point of Shenhui's critique of various forms of meditation was not really an attack on gradualism from the position of subitism. As he writes, "Ch'eng's exposition of the basic elements or stages of contemplative practice is in agreement with traditional Indian and T'ien t'ai definitions: concentration (*śamatha*, *ting* or *chih*) followed by insight (*vipaśyanā*, *hui* or *kuan*)".

97 Literally *dharma* (*fa* 法).

98 The meaning of the term *shiding* 識定 is not fully clear here. It does not seem to be used by other early Chan authors. The context suggests that the term refers to some negatively evaluated form of concentration. *Shi* 識 usually corresponds to Sanskrit *vijñāna* and Pali *viññāṇa* (consciousness). As we shall see later on, *vijñāna/viññāṇa* should not be seen as entirely synonymous with the mind (p. *citta*/c. *xin* 心). In the passage we are considering, McRae (2023: 158) translates *shiding* as "conceptual concentration", but when it occurs in the *Tanyu* (B25, no. 142, p. 29a1), he renders it as "concentration of consciousness" (McRae 2023: 65). In the latter case, the context in which the term is used also seems to be negative.

99 B25, no. 143, p. 234a6–11: 上和問澄禪師修何法而得見性？澄禪師答曰：先須學坐修定。得定已後，因定發慧，〔以智慧〕故，即得見性。問曰：修定之時，豈不要須作意不？答言：是。〔問：〕既是作意，即是識定，若為得見性。See Gómez (1987: 79–80) and McRae (2023: 158–59) for translations and discussions of this fragment.

As we shall see, a negative evaluation of *zuoyi* 作意 and several other concepts referring to a conscious, active, and volitional process of meditating is a recurring pattern in several early Chan texts. Analysis of Shenhui's writings shows that his criticism is not restricted to the mainstream concept of calm, but to that of insight as well. In the *Tanyu*, he again criticizes forms of calm meditation, warning his disciples against making an act of intention to concentrate the mind (*zuoyi shexin* 作意攝心) as well as against freezing the mind to stop the mind (*ningxin zhuxin* 凝心住心).[100] However, he also advises against using the mind (*jiangxin* 將心) to directly view the mind (*zhishixin* 直視心).[101] The latter formula can be pretty much seen as a general description of some classical forms of Buddhist insight meditation.

According to Shenhui's statement in the *Wenda zazheng yi*,[102] every form of meditation involving active usage of the mind (*yongxin* 用心) and conscious mental intention (*zuoyi* 作意) is a form of forceful restraint (*tiaofu* 調伏).[103] Such are the methods of the "listeners" (*shengwen* 聲聞), i.e., the Hinayanists, and not the methods of true liberation. By cultivating concentration (*xiuding* 修定) and being stabilized in it (*zhuding* 住定), they are ultimately fettered by it (*beidingfu* 被定縛).

It seems then, that for Shenhui the major flaw of the meditative methods he criticizes does not lie in a state of mental quietude and absence of thoughts, but in the fact that they involve active, deliberate appliance of the mind, regardless of whether it occurs during the practice of calm or insight. Various terms are used throughout early Chan texts in reference to this psychological mechanism, including *zuoyi* 作意, *jiangxin* 將心, *qixin* 起心, and *yongxin* 用心. It results in the states described as *youwei* 有為 (conditioned) or *zaozuo* 造作 (fabricated). Any act of intention or conscious effort connected with meditation is

100 McRae (2023: 56) translates *zhuxin* in this context as "force it to abide", though in other places he renders it as "fix the mind" (e.g., 2023: 61).

101 B25, no. 142, p. 18a8–11: 不得凝心住〔心〕。亦不得將心直視心，墮直視住，不中用。不得垂眼向下，便墮眼住，不中用。不得作意攝心，亦不得遠看近看，皆不中用。

102 B25, no. 143, pp. 235a11–236a3: 今言用心者，為是作意，不作意？若不作意，即是聾俗無別。若言作意，即是有所得。有所得者，即是繫縛，何由可得解脫？聲聞修空住空，即被空縛。修定住定，即被定縛。Cf. translation of this fragment by Gómez (1987: 77).

103 McRae (2023: 159) translates *tiaofu* in this passage as "being fettered", but in other context he notes that it can mean "regulate and subjugate" (2023: 97, n. 146) and refers to "meditative discipline".

therefore a grave error. This has been very aptly observed by Gómez (1987: 80–81), who stated:

> He finds fault in a system that not only separates different aspects of realization, but actually seems to "confuse" some form of conscious observation or conceptual analysis with direct insight. The meditation practice attributed by Shen-hui to his opponents is not direct or immediate in the sense that it makes use of mental effort and construction (*manasikāra, tso-i*) as the means to attain insight.

The mainstream paradigm of meditation

In earlier parts of this book I sometimes referred in a very general way to historically dominant, classical or mainstream ideas about Buddhist meditation. I also hinted at the possibility that the critique of certain forms of meditative states in Chan texts may have been actually directed at some of these ideas and that the wrong forms of meditation described in both Nikāya and early Chan texts are characterized by some traditional features of calm meditation. Therefore, it is worthwhile at this point to discuss these mainstream ideas in a more detailed and systematic manner and to identify their most significant elements. This will in turn help us to evaluate how the praised and the criticized forms of practice described in the Nikāya and Chan texts relate to the mainstream Buddhist model of meditation.

A comprehensive presentation of what may be considered historically dominant, mainstream Buddhist ideas about meditation can be found in the *Visuddhimagga* (*Path of Purification*), a treatise written by Buddhaghosa during the fifth century AD in Sri Lanka. Though it is a work of the Theravāda school, its meditation theory is, in its general features, quite similar to meditative ideas found in the texts of many other Buddhist traditions. It stands out, however, for its very systematic and detailed treatment of the topic, and hence may serve as a good example of the mainstream Buddhist approach to meditation. Below, we shall focus on the ideas about calm meditation and a theory of the *jhānas* contained in Buddhaghosa's treatise, as they are particularly relevant for our investigation.

In the *Visuddhimagga*, the development (*bhāvana*) of calm (*samatha*) or of concentration (*samādhi*) is to a large extent synonymous with the practice of the *jhānas*.[104] They are developed by one-pointed concentration on a single meditation object (*ekārammaṇa*),[105] which gradually leads to suppression of the hindrances (*nīvaraṇa*) by the five positive *jhāna* factors. The *Visuddhimagga* describes forty such meditative objects (*kammaṭṭhāna*; lit. workplace), with particular emphasis on *kasiṇas*: simple artifacts representing basic, primordial universal qualities. The initial physical object of meditation is often replaced during the progress of the practice by its mental image ("the learning sign" – *uggahanimitta*)[106] which may later be transformed into the so-called counterpart sign (*paṭibhāganimitta*).[107] The latter often differs in a considerable way from the initial form of the meditative object. Its appearance marks the achievement of access concentration (*upacārasamādhi*),[108] a state preceding full absorption (*jhāna*) into a meditative object. This sign may at that stage be extended within the mind of the practitioner.[109] One can potentially achieve four subtle form (*rūpa*) *jhānas*, in which one contemplates the counterpart sign. Afterwards, one can remove the sign from the mind and enter the four formless states (*āruppas*).[110] Absorption coincides with a temporary suppression of negative mental states coupled with a relative inactivity of the mind and an experience of subtle but intense forms of rapture and pleasure. Its main drawback is that it does not produce insight or wisdom and can lead to attachment or rebirth in the *deva* realms. According to the historically dominant point of view, *jhāna* is considered a pre-Buddhist form of practice shared with non-Buddhists, while it is insight that is considered an essential feature of Buddhism, a unique discovery of the Buddha himself.

As we have noted above, relatively similar ideas on meditation may be found in other Buddhist texts. Such is the case with the *Vimuttimagga* (*Path of Liberation*) attributed to Upatissa (first or second century AD)

104 Vism i.80–369/84–372/III.1–XI.126. Strictly speaking, the development of *samādhi* involves attaining various levels of *jhāna* (or at least access concentration) through the usage of forty meditation objects. Combining the prior attainment of the *jhānas* (or access concentration) with the practice of insight is known as the vehicle of calm (*samathayāna*).

105 Vism i.81/84/III.1.

106 Vism i.122/125/IV.29–30.

107 Vism i.122/125–126/IV.31.

108 Vism i.123/126/IV.32–33.

109 Vism i.147–149/152–153/IV.126–129.

110 Vism i.320/326–340/X.1–66.

and surviving in its Chinese translation as the *Jietuo dao lun* 解脱道論. The theory of meditation presented in the *Vimuttimagga* is very similar to the one in the *Visuddhimagga*. In fact, it seems almost certain that Buddhaghosa was using Upatissa's work as a reference (though he never refers to it explicitly by its title) when writing his treatise and possibly even drawing on it, while disagreeing on minor details. The differences between the approach to *jhāna* in both texts are small and concern issues of relatively minor importance.[111] For example, the *Vimuttimagga* lists thirty-eight meditation objects, while the *Visuddhimagga* speaks about forty. One small difference concerns the counterpart sign (*bifenxiang* 彼分相 in the *Vimuttimagga*): in Upatissa's work, it is merely a mental image of the original object which can be kept in mind at will, and its appearance is not connected with access concentration.[112]

Relatively similar ideas about *jhāna* and calm meditation may also be found in several influential early Chinese manuals of meditation from the middle of the first millennium AD. As these works deal with meditation (*chan* 禪) but precede the rise to prominence of the chan school, they have been very aptly labelled by Eric Greene as "chan before Chan".[113] These include the *Chan mi yao fa jing* 禪祕要法經 (*The Five Essentials*; lit. *Scripture on the Secret Essential Methods of Chan*),[114] the *Zuochan sanmei jing* 坐禪三昧經 (*Meditation Scripture*; lit. *Dhyāna-samādhi Scripture*) translated by Kumārajīva,[115] the *Damoduoluo chan jing* 達摩多羅禪經 (*Chan Scripture of Dharmatrāta*) translated by Buddhabhadra,[116] the *Wu men chan jing yao yong fa* 五門禪經要用法 (*Five Gates*; lit. *Essential methods [drawn from] the chan scriptures [that are based on] the five gates [of meditation]*).[117] While these works differ from the *Visuddhimagga* regarding particular details of their meditative theories, their general approach to *dhyāna*/*chan* 禪 is quite similar to the Pali treatise. All these texts present *dhyāna* meditation as practised by a deliberate act of focusing on a particular meditation subject. These include the mindfulness

111 Bapat (1937: xxx) notes: "It is only on comparatively minor points that they differ".

112 For differences between the two treatises, see Bapat (1937), Crosby (1999), Anālayo (2009) and Greene (2021: 99, nn. 119–20).

113 Greene, 2021. The English translations of the titles of these texts are taken from Greene's excellent presentation (2021: 64–90).

114 T.15, no. 613.

115 T.15, no. 614.

116 T.15, no. 618.

117 T.15, no. 619.

of breathing, contemplation of impurities (especially of white bones), and recollection of the Buddha (*nianfo* 念佛). Concentration gradually leads to the attainment of the first *dhyāna*, which is marked the presence of certain psychophysical states (such as pleasure and relaxation) and by the attainment of what Greene (2021: 78) calls "confirmatory visions" (rendered in the *Five Gates* as *jingjie* 境界) and generally corresponds to *Visuddhimagga*'s *nimittas*. According to Greene, the latter feature is particularly significant in the Chinese manuals and goes beyond being merely a "sign" of meditative success, becoming a revelatory experience in itself. As Greene (2021: 75) summarizes, "comparing the *Meditation Scripture* and *Visuddhimagga*, on the one hand, with the *Chan Scripture of Dharmatrāta* on the other, there is little difference in their approaches to either the basic techniques or stages of meditation practice". Pretty much the same can be said regarding the *Five Gates* and the *Five Essentials* (cf. Greene, 2021: 77).

We have noted that in the *Visuddhimagga* the development of calm ultimately serves a higher goal of developing insight. A somewhat similar approach to meditation is also present in the works of Zhiyi, the seminal figure of the Tiantai school of Chinese Buddhism. Zhiyi's works on meditation were extremely influential in China and therefore can serve as an example of the mainstream Chinese model of conceptualizing meditation. Most of Zhiyi's methods for calming the mind follow the same pattern as those in the *Visuddhimagga* and early Chinese manuals of meditation. As Greene (2021: 115, n. 11) points out, they include techniques such as "fixing [the mind] to an object" (*xiyuan* 繫緣), and "suppressing the arising of thoughts" (*zhixin* 制心).[118] Although Zhiyi stresses the need to develop both calm (*zhi* 止) and insight (*guan* 觀) in a harmonious and balanced way, a closer look at their definitions reveals that he follows the mainstream Buddhist trend of subjugating the former to the latter. According to Zhiyi's *Xiuxi zhiguan zuochan fayao* 修習止觀坐禪法 (*Essentials of seated meditation for practicing calming and contemplation*),[119] calm is only the first gate (*chumen* 初門) of overcoming bonds (*fujie* 伏結), but insight is the right "essential" (*zhengyao* 正要) for cutting off (*duan* 斷) delusion (*hu* 惑). While calm is the supreme

118 These methods are described in the *Shi chan boluomi cidi famen* 釋禪波羅蜜次第法門 (*Elucidation of the Sequential Approach to the Perfection of Chan*), the earliest major work of Zhiyi.

119 Translation of the title follows Sasaki (2009: 421).

cause (*shengyin* 勝因) of *dhyāna samādhi*[120] (*chanding* 禪定), it is by means of insight that there is wisdom (*zhihui* 智慧).[121] Also, in Zhiyi's writings, it is ultimately wisdom that dispels the darkness of ignorance and reveals emptiness, just like the sun dispels the darkness in the sky. In the *Fajie cidi chumen* 法界次第初門 (*Sequenced Introduction to the Dharma Realm*),[122] Zhiyi states that "*dhyāna* concentration (*chanding* 禪定) is [only] the entranceway (*menhu* 門戶), a step-by-step level-by-level practice".[123] One needs insight, described by Zhiyi as "the wisdom of the eighteen emptinesses" (*shiba konghui* 十八空慧) and its illumination, as otherwise one might get stuck in the middle of *dhyana samādhi* (*chansanmei zhong* 禪三昧中) and never obtain liberation.

As the above examples show, we can speak about the presence of a shared paradigm or a model of conceptualizing meditation in various traditions and texts across the history of Buddhism.[124] We will refer to it as the mainstream paradigm of Buddhist meditation. Due to its prevalence in Buddhist presentations of meditation, some of its features appear so fundamental and obvious to us that they are rarely emphasized or singled out. Such is the case with the idea that meditation is an active deliberate implementation of a particular technique or method. In the case of calm meditation this may mean conscious activity of concentrating on a particular object, while in the case of insight it may refer to deliberate, active effort to understand certain truths or to be aware of one's experience in accordance with certain Buddhist theoretical categories. The progress in meditation comes through gradual strengthening of positive factors such as

120 A standard in scholarly works on Chinese Buddhism is to provide Sanskrit and not Pali equivalents of technical Chinese terms. Thus "*dhyāna samādhi*" and not "*jhāna samādhi*".

121 T46, no. 1915, p. 462b7–11: 若夫泥洹之法，入乃多途。論其急要，不出止觀二法。所以然者，止乃伏結之初門，觀是斷惑之正要；止則愛養心識之善資，觀則策發神解之妙術；止是禪定之勝因，觀是智慧之由藉。

122 Translation of the title follows Foulk (2021: 633).

123 T46, no. 1925, p. 689b22–26: 若菩薩始從初修自性禪。終至清淨淨禪。雖有大功德神通智慧之用。而禪定是門戶。詮次階級之法。若不善以十八空慧。照了遣蕩。或於所證諸禪三昧中。十八有法。隨滯一有。則不得無礙解脫。縱任自在。Translation following Greene (2008: 66).

124 It needs to be said, however, that Zhiyi's works contain some unorthodox and unique features and specific practices, such as that of "following one's own mental activity" (*suiziyi* 隨自意) also known as "*samādhi* of the awareness of mental activity" (*jueyisanmei* 覺意三昧), or "neither walking not sitting *samādhi*" (*feixing feizuo sanmei* 非行非坐三昧).

concentration or one-pointedness, which results from their repetition and practice. Meditation can be seen as a skill of sorts, which may or may not be mastered. This idea appears to be so basic that it does not seem to be in any need of underlining. After all, how could one meditate in any other way? However, it is by contrasting the mainstream Buddhist meditative paradigm with unusual accounts of meditation practices and states found in some Nikāya and early Chan texts, that one becomes more sharply aware of such features. That is because they are conspicuously missing in the texts of these latter two traditions or are even explicitly criticized.

The other important element of the mainstream paradigm which we can emphasize at this point is the idea of a sharp dichotomy between calm and insight meditation or between concentration and wisdom. Calm and insight are essentially different practices, almost to the point of being mutually exclusive. They cannot be practised at exactly the same time and they differ in a fundamental way regarding their methods and effects. Other features of the mainstream paradigm will become more apparent to us during the course of this book, by contrasting them with relevant ideas found in Nikāya and early Chan texts and at that point will be given a detailed analysis. It is worth emphasizing that the mainstream Buddhist meditative paradigm still greatly influences our most basic views about the meditation process and soteriology in general. Hence, those ideas that are at odds with this paradigm may appear enigmatic or even absurd to us.

What is wrong with the mainstream forms of meditation according to early Chan texts?

After having identified some of the main features of the Buddhist mainstream paradigm, we can go back to the accounts of wrong practices in early Chan and Nikāya texts. It seems relatively safe to conclude that Shenhui's critique was directed in particular against the idea of meditative practice as a deliberate activity. Was this the case with the other Chan texts we have analysed so far? It seems so, especially in the case of texts associated with those schools of Chan which traced their spiritual lineage to Huineng. In the fragment of the *Zongjing lu* 宗鏡錄 (*Records of the source-mirror*),[125] attributed to Mazu Daoyi, we read that

125 Translation of the title follows Sasaki (2009: 431).

it is not necessary to make an act of conscious intention (*zuoyi* 作意), to concentrate the mind and obtain *samādhi* (*quding* 取定), and even if one freezes the mind (*ningxin* 凝心) and collects thought (*liannian* 斂念), this is not the ultimate state (*jiujing* 究竟).[126] According to another fragment attributed to Mazu in the *Tiansheng guangdeng lu*, contemplation of emptiness (*guankong* 觀空) and entering *samādhi* (*ruding* 入定) belongs to the sphere of what is (artificially) fabricated (*zaozuo* 造作).[127]

In the *Liuzu tanjing*, we read that arousing/activating the mind (*qixin* 起心) in order to observe purity just gives rise to the illusion of purity (*jingwang* 淨妄).[128] Baizhang Huihuai states in the *Tiansheng guangdeng lu* that it is useless to "use" *samādhi* (*jiangding* 將定), in order to enter *samādhi* (*ruding* 入定), just as it is useless to use *dhyāna*, to create an ideation of *dhyāna* (*jiangchan xiangchan* 將禪想禪).[129] As we have already remarked, the *Lidai fabao ji* contains many warnings against arousing or activating the mind (*qixin* 起心).

Interestingly, similar ideas may have been expressed much earlier, though by different terminology, in the *Rudao anxin yao fangbian famen* 入道安心要方便法門 (*Essentials of the Teaching of the Expedient Means of Entering the Path and Pacifying the Mind*),[130] purported to contain the teachings of the Fourth Patriarch Daoxin. In one fragment, we find a paradoxical denial of almost all possible methods of meditation: recollection of the Buddha (*nianfo* 念佛), grasping the mind (*zhuoxin* 捉心), observing the mind (*kanxin* 看心), reckoning the mind (*jixin* 計心), reflecting (*siwei* 思惟), contemplating (*guanxing* 觀行), and scattering (*sanluan* 散亂).[131] The names of the practices seem to refer to

126 T48, no. 2016, p. 492a26–27: 汝自是金剛定。不用更作意凝心取定。縱使凝心斂念作得。亦非究竟。 Cf. Poceski (2015b: 251) and Jia (2006: 122–23) for translations of this fragment.

127 X78, no. 1553, p. 448c23–24: 師云。自性本來具足。但於善惡事上不滯。喚作修道人。取善捨惡。觀空入定。即屬造作。 Cf. translation by Poceski (2007: 161).

128 T48, no. 2007, p. 338c26–27: 不見自性本淨，起心看淨，却生淨妄，妄無處所。Cf. translation by Yampolsky (1967: 139).

129 X78, no. 1553, p. 458c18: 不用將定入定。不用將禪想禪。 Cf. translation by Cleary (1978: 44).

130 Translation of the title follows McRae (1986: 119). This text is contained in the *Lengqie shizi ji* 楞伽師資記 (*Record of the masters and disciples of the Lanka school*).

131 T85, no. 2837, p. 1287b18–20: 信曰。亦不念佛。亦不捉心。亦不看心。亦不計心。亦不思惟。亦不觀行。亦不散亂。直任運。亦不令去。亦不令住。Cf. translations by Chappell (1983: 110), McRae (1986: 143), and Van Schaik (2018: 158).

the most basic and fundamental forms of calm and insight meditation. However, their common denominator seems to be that they all involve actively "trying to do something", since ultimately even "making [it] go" (*lingqu* 令去) and "making [it] stay/stop" (*lingzhu* 令住) is advised against.[132] The real problem lies therefore in "making" or "causing" (*ling* 令) anything, i.e., the active, volitionally driven process of meditating. Instead, Daoxin suggests "just letting it be" or "allowing fate" (*renyun* 任運).[133] This fragment definitely fits the pattern of criticizing any active form of meditation.

However, it needs to be stated at this point that the same text contains meditative instructions attributed to Daoxin which are very much in line with the mainstream Buddhist paradigm. For example, in his account of "one-practice *samādhi*" (*yi xing sanmei* 一行三昧) he advocates continuously bringing the Buddha to mind (*nianfo*). He also repeats this instruction in a later part of the text. As Greene points out (2021: 212–15), what distinguishes Daoxin's account from more traditional forms of *nianfo* practice is that instead of producing a vision of the Buddha, it is supposed to culminate in a state in which there will be no object at all in mind and "the mind thinking about the Buddha will itself cease". As Greene (2021: 215) writes: "what is provided here is not a new technique of meditation but a new statement about the kind of experience that is to be taken as evidence of meditative attainment". According to Greene, the practice of "Guarding the One without moving" (*shouyibuyi* 守一不移) is another example of Daoxin's methods which is in harmony with mainstream ideas. Here, the meditator is advised to "gaze upon a single object with focused attention" and he "keeps one's attention 'tied' to it like a flighty bird kept in check by a string tied to its legs" which leads to eventual concentration of the mind.[134] As Greene (2021: 216) aptly summarizes, this is "little more than a mildly idiosyncratic summary of the basic methods of calming

132 Translation of 亦不令去。亦不令住 follows McRae (1986: 143). Van Schaik (2018: 158) translates it as "Don't try to get rid of it, Don't try to make it stay"; Chappell (1983: 110) as "Don't force anything to go. Don't force anything to stay".

133 We shall focus on this term to a much larger extent in Chapter 8.

134 T85, no. 2837, p. 1288b16–20: 守一不移者。以此淨眼。眼住意看一物。無問晝夜時。專精常不動。其心欲馳散。急手還攝來。以繩繫鳥足。欲飛還掣取。終日看不已。泯然心自定。Translation by Greene (2021: 215–16). Also, cf. translation by Chappell (1983: 210), McRae (1986: 141), and Van Schaik (2018: 165).

from Zhiyi's treatise". Therefore, we cannot generalize the meaning of one instruction from the *Rudao anxin yao fangbian famen* which rejects all forms of active meditation to the whole text. However, the text in question does not have a homogeneous structure and as McRae (1986: 119–20) has noted, may have been written after the time of Daoxin and only retrospectively attributed to him. Therefore, it may represent input from different authors and thus reflect their different ideas.

Interpretative problems are also connected with the already analysed fragment of the *Xiuxin yao lun* which warned against falling into a state of a non-registering mind connected with the concentration of a mind dependent on external objects. While at first look it appears to be a critique of the most fundamental elements of the mainstream paradigm, the same text contains an account of a technique that very much agrees with the historically dominant model. This is the practice of sun contemplation in which the meditator is advised to "imagine a single sun at a suitable distance and keep it there, moment after moment without cease"[135] which in turn will lead to the disappearance of deluded thoughts and of the notion of self. This is certainly a classical form of calm meditation, which is criticized by so many Chan texts. This raises the question of whether the fragment about a non-registering mind criticizes calm meditation in itself or merely its particular form. It is of course possible that various fragments of the *Xiuxin yao lun* were produced by various authors, since as McRae (1986: 120) suggests, the text was attributed to Hongren only retrospectively.

It is also not entirely clear whether the fragment of the *Dasheng wusheng fangbianmen* criticizing various aspects of "Hīnayāna" meditation is for certain directed against the mainstream idea of calm meditation. Some of the criticized features, like an inability to hear or a lack of wisdom during the attainment of the state, are indeed traditional features of calm meditation, present not only in "Hīnayāna" works, but also in early Chinese manuals which are undoubtedly of Mahāyāna provenance. However, several other fragments of the text criticize arousing of the mind (*qixin*) and praise its non-arousal[136] which suggests that the criticism of meditation in the *Dasheng wusheng fangbianmen* follows the same pattern as other Chan texts we have analysed.

135 McRae (1986: 432/六): 心前平視隨意遠作一日想守之念念莫住。Cf. T48, no. 2011, p. 378a29–b1. Translation by Greene (2021: 222–24). Also, cf. translation by McRae (1986: 127).

136 E.g., T85, no. 2834, p. 1273c20: 心不起心真如。

Of course, in the case of this and several other texts, there is always a possibility that we are dealing with a rhetoric, not based on any practical experiences,[137] where various fantastical claims are being made about positively evaluated meditative states. Nonetheless, despite these reservations, it can be relatively safely stated that most of the analysed Chan texts criticize meditation as a deliberate activity involving mental effort, and in particular as consciously intended concentration or focus.

Do the meditative practices criticized in the Nikāyas share a common denominator?

At this point, we must return to the problem of criticized meditative methods and states in Nikāya texts. Does the critique contained in these texts share any common denominators with the one found in Chan texts? Do the various early Buddhist fragments mentioned so far actually even criticize the same type of meditation? First, we must underline the fact that the situation of the early Buddhist authors was quite different from that of Chan Buddhists. They had no reason to attack the mainstream model of meditation as during their time there was not yet any Buddhist mainstream at all. Also, even if we assume for the sake of argument that their approach to meditation involved no notion of active, deliberate application of some method or technique, then there would be no special need for them to highlight this fact as their emphasis would be on the elements of practice that can actually be implemented. One can perhaps still speak about a certain mainstream towards which the early Buddhist authors would be opposed, but it would be a non-Buddhist one. The idea of such a mainstream was proposed by Bronkhorst (1986), who claimed that the early Buddhist practices were developed in opposition to the dominant meditative approach of Jains and Brahmins, which involved attaining states of deep inactivity of the mind, body and senses which anticipated liberation occurring after death. Therefore, if we want to contrast some of the Nikāya ideas with the later mainstream Buddhist ones, we can

137 Bronkhorst (2022: 11) points out the difficulty in assessing whether particular statements are actually based on mystical experiences: "'mystical statements', as we have seen, can be made by people who are not 'authentic mystics'. In fact, mystical statements can be made by authentic mystics, by non-mystics, and by those who may have had half-way mystical experiences".

at best say that the former are at odds or difficult to harmonize with the latter, but not that they were a direct critique of the historically dominant Buddhist paradigm.

I previously suggested that the states rejected in the early Buddhist texts possess some general features of calm meditation. But do any of the texts in question actually contain a criticism of meditation as a deliberate activity similar to the one we have identified in some Chan texts? As we have already noted, the Nikāya texts do not explicitly describe any detailed method for entering the *jhānas* nor any meditative objects to focus upon. However, from some of the discourses, we can at least infer what the *jhānas* were not according to their authors. We have already briefly mentioned the *Gopakamoggallāna-sutta* (MN 108/iii.7–15) which distinguishes two types of *jhāna* meditation, the right one and the wrong one. The four *jhānas* are described as the right type of meditation which was praised (*vaṇṇeti*) by the Buddha. Of particular interest is the description of the wrong form of meditation. Due to the fact that a meditator practising the wrong meditation has mind obsessed and overcome by the five hindrances, harbours them within, and does not understand "as it really is" (*yathābhūtaṃ*) the escape from them, he meditates (*jhāyati*), meditates forwards (*pajjhāyati*), meditates down (*nijjhāyati*), and meditates away (*apajjhāyati*).[138] This enigmatic description is certainly open to various interpretations. The verbs used to describe the improper form of meditation seem to carry a negative undertone, as if they were describing a meditative process gone astray. Interestingly, they are indeed sometimes used in a denigrative sense by monks devoted to the Dhamma towards the jhāins in the *Mahācunda-sutta* (AN 6.46/iii.355) and by the Brahmins aroused by the evil Māra Dūsī towards the Buddhist bhikkhus in the *Māratajjanīya-sutta* (MN 50/i.334),[139] though the latter story concerns the times of the former

138 MN 108/iii.14: *Idha, brāhmaṇa, ekacco kāmarāgapariyuṭṭhitena cetasā viharati kāmarāgaparetena, uppannassa ca kāmarāgassa nissaraṇaṃ yathābhūtaṃ nappajānāti; so kāmarāgaṃyeva antaraṃ karitvā jhāyati pajjhāyati nijjhāyati apajjhāyati*. This is a literal translation of the verbs based on the meaning of their prefixes. Ñāṇamoli and Bodhi (1995: 885) translate these verbs as: "meditates, premeditates, out-meditates, and mismeditates".

139 MN 50/i.334: *atha kho te, pāpima, brāhmaṇagahapatikā anvāvisiṭṭhā dūsinā mārena bhikkhū sīlavante kalyāṇadhamme akkosanti paribhāsanti rosenti vihesenti – 'ime pana muṇḍakā samaṇakā ibbhā kiṇhā bandhupādāpaccā 'jhāyinosmā jhāyinosmā'ti pattakkhandhā adhomukhā madhurakajātā jhāyanti pajjhāyanti nijjhāyanti apajjhāyanti*. Cf. translation by Ñāṇamoli and Bodhi (1995: 433).

Buddha Kakusandha and thus can hardly be considered historically authentic. It might be the case that this string of verbs does not carry any particular meaning and may have been simply a popular play on words used in India at the time the Nikāyas were created as a way of ridiculing meditators.

One possible interpretation in harmony with the traditional vision of the *jhāna*s would be that not knowing how to escape the hindrances refers to not knowing how to properly meditate in the sense of not having the required meditative skill or not applying the proper method. As a result, meditation goes astray, and although one starts by trying to meditate (*jhāyati*), one ends by falling prey to one's thoughts, as the verbs *pajjhāyati, nijjhāyati*, and *apajjhāyati* may perhaps be translated as referring to various forms of active thinking.[140] However, another hypothesis would be that the use of directional prefixes suggests that meditation is actively directed towards some goal, involving effort or seeking for a meditative success. Arbel (2017: 39) may therefore be right in pointing out that "the use of the verb from the same root, in connection to the term *jhāna* in these occurrences, indicates an active meditative practice of some kind". Therefore, similarly to the Chan texts, the reasons for condemnation of the wrong type of *jhāna* in this discourse would lie in its active, consciously controlled, goal-driven nature.

But how would that be connected with not understanding how to escape from each of the five hindrances? It is worth emphasizing that according to the sutta, the perverted meditation rendered by four variations of the verb *jhāyati* occurs due to not understanding how to escape from each of the five hindrances and having the mind obsessed and overcome by their presence. Therefore, there is a causal link between the two. One possible explanation would be that if one knows how to escape the hindrances through leading a virtuous, self-restrained lifestyle, then *jhāna* develops almost effortlessly and spontaneously after sitting down and establishing mindfulness.[141] However, if the *nīvaraṇa*s are still present, then the meditator can only attempt to suppress them by some active technique, such as concentrating on an object, thus fabricating an artificial altered psychophysical state. Seen in this way, this fragment would indeed be a critique of one of the basic ideas that would

140 In his translation of the *Aṅguttara Nikāya*, Bodhi (2012: 1560) translates them as: "cogitates, ponders or ruminates".

141 This hypothesis shall be considered in much greater detail in the later chapters of this book.

come to characterize the mainstream Buddhist meditative paradigm in later times.

Such an interpretation seems to work well in the context of the *Sandha-sutta*, which also includes the string of verbs *jhāyati*, *pajjhāyati*, *nijjhāyati*, and *apajjhāyati* in its description of the wrong form of meditation, which is labelled as that of an "unruly horse" (*khaḷuṅka*). Like in the *Gopakamoggallāna-sutta*, this meditation results from not knowing the escape from the five hindrances and having the mind overcome by them. However, as we have already noted, this text also contains additional detail, namely that the person who is similar to an unruly horse meditates dependent (*nissāya*) on the four basic elements, the four formless states, this world and the other, and whatever is seen, heard, sensed, cognized, reached, sought after, and examined by the intellect. A good meditator, likened to a thoroughbred (*ājānīya*), knows the escape from the hindrances and thus he does not meditate dependent on any of the abovementioned elements and qualities, and yet he somehow paradoxically meditates (*jhāyati ca pana*). The *deva*s led by Inda and Pajāpati praise such a meditator and express their inability to conceive of the nature of his meditation. The latter statements imply that the author of the text was well-aware of the paradoxicality of the manner of meditation which he described.

It needs to be noted that the *Sandha-sutta* does not explicitly use the term *jhāna* with regard to the two types of meditation it presents, but the corresponding verb *jhāyati*, from which the noun *jhāna* seems to be derived (Rhys Davids and Stede, 2007: 286). Usually, when the suttas speak about the four *jhāna*s, they do not explicitly use the verbal form *jhāyati*. However, this verb is sometimes used directly with reference to *jhāna* to express the activity of practising *jhāna* (e.g., DN 19/ii.237: *karuṇaṃ jhānaṃ jhāyati*). As we have seen, in the *Gopakamoggallāna-sutta* (MN 108/iii.14) the string of verbs – *jhāyati pajjhāyati nijjhāyati apajjhāyati* – is explicitly said by Ānanda to represent a sort of *jhāna* that the Buddha did not praise: *evarūpaṃ kho ... bhagavā jhānaṃ na vaṇṇesi*. In the Bodhisatta narrative, the first-person singular reflexive/middle (*attanopada*) optative (*sattamī*) form *jhāyeyyaṃ* (which due to niggahita sandhi is changed to *jhāyeyyan'ti* in the text) is used with regard to breathless (*appāṇaka*) *jhāna*.[142] In a relatively frequent stock passage (e.g., SN 43.1/iv.359) occurring at the endings of many discourses, when

142 MN 36/i.243: *tassa mayhaṃ, aggivessana, etadahosi—'yaṃnūnāhaṃ appāṇakaṃyeva jhānaṃ jhāyeyyan'ti.*

the Buddha exhorts his disciples to meditate, the second person plural imperative (*pañcamī*) form *jhāyatha* is used. That this verb most likely refers to abiding in *jhāna* and not conceptual reflection, is implied by the reference to the roots/bases of trees (*rukkhamūla*) and empty dwellings (*suññāgāra*), which are in other texts listed amongst the secluded places in which meditation in the sense of attaining altered states of mind is to take place. These two locations are also listed in the *Sandha-sutta* (together with the forest [*arañña*]) as the places in which activity rendered by the verb *jhāyati* occurs both for the bad and good meditators.

The Āgama parallel of the *Sandha-sutta*, SĀ 926 at T02, no. 99, pp. 235c27–236b11, uses terms such as *xiuchan* 修禪 (cultivate *dhyāna*), *xiuchanding* 修禪定 (lit. cultivate *dhyāna samādhi*), *chanding* 禪定 (lit. [do] *dhyāna samādhi*), *ruchan* 入禪 (enter *dhyāna*) as correspondents of *jhāyati* in the Pali text, and not, for example, *siwei* 思惟 which is sometimes used to render "brooding over" or "thinking upon". While this does not constitute decisive evidence regarding the original meaning of the verb in question, it shows that the translator of the Indian text into Chinese believed that it denoted abiding in *jhāna/dhyāna,* and not thinking or contemplating.

A possible interpretation of the *Sandha-sutta*, which is in tune with the one proposed with regards to the *Gopakamoggallāna-sutta,* would be that the practitioners who are not able to dispel the hindrances through maintaining a specific lifestyle and mindset have to resort to suppressing them by focusing on various simple elements and qualities which are used as meditative objects. Therefore, such practitioners can be described as meditating dependent on them. In contrast, for those who have already allayed the hindrances, the *jhāna*s develop naturally and they do not need to depend on artificially inducing altered states of consciousness by means of concentrating on special meditative objects. Some of the elements and qualities listed in the *Sandha-sutta* would indeed later become formal objects of meditation in their own right, as they correspond to four of the ten *kasiṇa*s and the four formless states in the *Visuddhimagga*.

One could perhaps also think of yet another interpretation, which would make all the above hypotheses wrong. On this reading, the description of the meditation of a thoroughbred, which involves not meditating in dependence on any element or quality of the world, would say nothing about meditative methods and objects as it would refer to a special state at the apex of the meditative progress, which can only be described apophatically, i.e., by way of negation. To get to that state, however, one would need to start with typical meditative methods which involve concentration on certain objects, or active forms of insight.

However, if it was indeed the point that the author of this sutta wanted to convey, then the text falls short of conveying it perfectly. The dichotomy presented in the *Sandha-sutta* seems to leave no middle ground; either the meditator knows the escape from the hindrances and meditates without dependence on anything, or due to the hindrances still present in him, he has to meditate depending on worldly qualities, and "he meditates forth, meditates down, and meditates away" which seems to imply meditative failure. The four *jhānas* are always presented in the Nikāyas as the states which arise only when the hindrances are absent. In fact, in the suttas following the *Sāmaññaphala* pattern, the process that leads to the first *jhāna* is set off by becoming aware of the absence of the hindrances (e.g., in DN 2/i.73). Of the two forms of meditation presented in the *Sandha-sutta*, this may only correspond to the *jhāna* of a thoroughbred. The latter account could perhaps be understood as complementary to the stock description of the fourth *jhāna* which does not describe what objects one does or does not experience, but merely "how" one experiences (i.e., in an equanimous way and without pleasure and pain).

Meditation and the *saṅkhāras*

The Nikāya texts do not really contain explicit warnings against actively applying the mind during meditation or against a deliberate implementation of some method in the vein of Chan texts. However, neither do they encourage such approaches in their accounts of meditative states such as the four *jhānas*. Why should therefore they contain warnings against something that is not directly encouraged anywhere in the first place? In contrast, Chan authors found their ideas regarding this aspect of meditation to be at odds with the mainstream Buddhist views that were dominant in their era so it was only natural that they were more explicit in their criticism of any active effort during meditation.

One issue that is worth examining in this context is that of the role of *saṅkhāras* in the meditative process. *Saṅkhāra* is a very difficult term to translate, and the Nikāyas hardly provide any exhaustive and comprehensive definitions of it. One can only infer the meaning of the term from the contexts in which it is used and from how it is related to other early Buddhist terms. It seems to refer to fabrication (lit. being made up together) that is connected with an act of will, the notion of selfhood and deeply rooted ignorance.[143] Therefore, it corresponds to a certain extent to Chinese terms such as *youwei* 有為, *zuoyi* 作意 or *zaozuo* 造作, which occur in the descriptions of the wrong forms of meditation contained in early Chan texts.

At least some Nikāya authors may have considered the four *jhānas* to be a *saṅkhāra*-less type of meditation. According to the *Sasaṅkhāra-sutta* (AN 4.169/ii.155–156)[144] one attains *parinibbāna* without *saṅkhāra* (*asaṅkhāraparinibbāyī*) by developing the four *jhānas*. Whether this *parinibbāna* will occur "in this life" (*diṭṭheva dhamme*) or after the breakup (*bheda*) of the body (*kāya*) depends on whether the practitioner will also be able to develop the five strengths (*bala*) and the five faculties (*indriya*). Interestingly, the sutta also describes attainment of *parinibbāna* with *saṅkhāra* (*sasaṅkhāraparinibbāyī*). In this case, instead of experiencing the *jhānas*, one dwells contemplating the foulness (*asubhānupassī*) in the body, perceiving repulsiveness (*paṭikūlasaññī*) in food, perceiving the whole world as not delightful (*anabhiratisaññī*), contemplating impermanence (*aniccānupassī*) in all the *saṅkhāras* and having a well-established (*sūpaṭṭhita*) internal perception of death (*maraṇasaññā*). Interestingly, Bodhi (2012: 534) translates *asaṅkhāraparinibbāyī* as "attains *nibbāna* without exertion", which would harmonize with the vision of the *jhānas* as spontaneous meditative practices not requiring any form of mental effort. As we have already noted, in the Bodhisatta narrative, the forceful yogic practices juxtaposed to the *jhānas* are labelled as strivings (*padhāna*), which may suggest their *saṅkhāra*-driven nature. The *jhānas*, on the contrary, do not receive such a label, which agrees with their interpretation as a *saṅkhāra*-less form of meditation. Of course, it does not imply that no forms of *saṅkhāras* are present in the earlier *jhānas* at all, as some texts claim that body *saṅkhāras* only disappear in the fourth *jhāna*.[145] However, this does not mean that *saṅkhāras* are the driving force behind the meditative progress, but rather an imperfection that must be gradually removed.

---

143 A more detailed discussion on the meaning of this term will be given in Chapter 4.

144 Cf. translation by Bodhi (2012: 533–35).

145 E.g., in the *Ariyavāsa-sutta* (AN 10.20/v.31): *kathañca, bhikkhave, bhikkhu passaddhakāyasaṅkhāro hoti? idha, bhikkhave, bhikkhu sukhassa ... catutthaṃ jhānaṃ upasampajja viharati.*

The *Paṃsudhovaka-sutta* (AN 3.101/i.253–256) is one of those relatively rare Nikāya texts that provide some unique information about the nature of right meditation which is absent from the more frequent and well-known stock formulas, such as that of the four *jhānas*. It is interesting for our investigation as it touches upon the role of *saṅkhāras* during meditation. While it does not present any dichotomy of wrong and right forms of meditation, it describes the gradual process of the purification of the mind. When the defilements (*upakkilesa*) have not yet been removed, the concentration of such a person is described as still "held down by restraint of *saṅkhāra*" (*sasaṅkhāraniggayhavāritagato*).[146] It is only when all defilements have been removed, that concentration becomes calmed, sublime, tranquil and is no longer held down by the said restraint.

While this text positively evaluates a meditative state that is not restrained by *saṅkhāras*, it acknowledges that at the initial stages of meditation the said restraint is still present. This is a somewhat different approach to what we have been analysing so far and in which there was no middle ground between right and wrong forms of meditation. It is interesting to consider whether meditating with the restraint of *saṅkhāras* is considered a necessary condition for the final, *saṅkhāra*-less state or whether it is just an unavoidable but non-essential intermediary stage, which does not in itself condition any higher states. Another intriguing question is what exactly causes concentration to become at some point peaceful and sublime. We will focus on this issue in greater detail in later chapters of this book. The term *sasaṅkhāraniggayhavāritagata* (precisely its negation) may also be found in the *Ānanda-sutta* of the *Aṅguttara Nikāya* (AN 9.37/iv.426–428), where the sublime *samādhi*, having higher knowledge as its fruit (*aññāphala*), is described as "not held down by the restraint of *saṅkhāra*" (*na sasaṅkhāraniggayhavāritagato*).[147] Furthermore, we read that this special *samādhi* is "neither bent forward nor bent away" (*na cābhinato na*

146 AN 3.101/i.255: *So hoti samādhi na ceva santo na ca paṇīto nappaṭippassaddhaladdho na ekodibhāvādhigato sasaṅkhāraniggayhavāritagato*. Bodhi (2012: 336) translates *sasaṅkhāraniggayhavāritagato* as "reined in and checked by forcefully suppressing [the defilements]". In the note to this translation (2012: 1669, n. 560) he states that he interprets *sasaṅkhāra* as "forceful" (lit. "with exertion").

147 AN 9.37/iv.428: *yāyaṃ, bhagini, samādhi na cābhinato na cāpanato na ca sasaṅkhāraniggayhavāritagato, vimuttattā ṭhito, ṭhitattā santusito, santusitattā no paritassati. ayaṃ, bhagini, samādhi aññāphalo vutto bhagavatā'ti*. Cf. translation by Bodhi (2012: 402).

cāpanato). This last line may remind us of Daoxin's warning against making [the mind] go or making it stay, or Shenhui's statement that making [the mind] come or making it go is a disease.[148] An almost identical description is contained in the *Sakalika-sutta* (SN 1.38/i.27–29), where a visiting celestial being (*deva*) uses it to describe the mental state of the Buddha who is experiencing painful feelings due to being hurt in his foot by a splinter.[149] The *deva* describes the Buddha's *samādhi* as well-developed (*subhāvita*), his mind as well-released (*suvimutta*), neither bent forward nor bent away and not held down by the restraint of *saṅkhāra*. In all the above-mentioned texts, the usage of the term *saṅkhāra* seems to imply that the right form of Buddhist meditation does not involve any form of forceful effort and is not an artificially induced state created and maintained through the activity of will.

While the term *saṅkhāra* is not used in the Bodhisatta narrative, a similar notion seems to be conveyed by the description of practice in which Gotama is trying to restrain (*abhiniggaṇhāti*), crush (*abhinippīḷeti*) and scorch (*abhisantāpeti*) "the mind with the mind" (*cetasā cittaṃ*). The abovementioned terms and the simile of a strong man who would grab and restrain, crush and destroy a weaker man, suggest a forceful nature of this technique. The words used here sound similar to Zongmi's statement that the Hongzhou school was against using the mind (*yixin* 以心) to cut off the mind (*duanxin* 斷心)[150] and Huangbo Xiyun's critique of using the mind (*jiangxin* 將心) in order to constrict the mind (*zhuoxin* 捉心).[151] Interestingly, the Bodhisatta's practice is accompanied by gritting teeth and by pressing the tongue against the palate.[152] To anyone acquainted with early Chan texts, these descriptions may appear familiar. We have already seen that pressing the tongue against the palate formed an integral element of the meditation technique criticized in Zongmi's texts and in the *Linji yulu*.

It needs to be said, however, that sometimes the latter practice is presented in a positive context, as a sort of last resort to be used to deal with unskilful thoughts if all other methods fail, as is the case in the

148 B25, no. 142, p. 31a9: 去來皆是病。

149 SN 1.38/i.28: *passa samādhiṃ subhāvitaṃ cittañca suvimuttaṃ, na cābhinataṃ na cāpanataṃ na ca sasaṅkhāraniggayhavāritagataṃ*. For a translation, cf. Bodhi (2000: 117).

150 X09, no. 245, p. 534b20. Translation follows Broughton (2009: 185).

151 T48, no. 2012A, p. 379c25. Cf. McRae (2005: 13) for a translation.

152 MN 85/ii.93: *So kho ahaṃ, rājakumāra, dantebhidantamādhāya, jivhāya tāluṃ āhacca, cetasā cittaṃ abhiniggaṇhāmi abhinippīḷemi abhisantāpemi*.

Vitakkasaṇṭhāna-sutta (MN 20/i.120–121). This feature also returns in Changlu Zongze's and Dogen's meditation instructions (see Bielefeldt, 1988: 180).

The critique of meditative insentience found in the *Indriyabhāvanā-sutta* has of course its parallels in Chan texts such as the *Dasheng wusheng fangbian men* where such insentience forms an integral element of Hinayanist *dhyāna*, in which one does not hear sounds, and in the account of the state of non-registering (*wuji* 無記) found in the texts of Hongren and Shenhui. It needs to be emphasized that such a critique is by no means exclusive to Chan and early Buddhism. According to mainstream Buddhist ideas about meditation, insentience is a feature of calm meditation, but the latter is not considered a goal in itself, but merely a tool for development of insight. From the perspective of the mainstream paradigm, the point of texts such as the *Indriyabhāvanā-sutta* is a warning about treating calm meditation as an end in itself.

What is controversial and problematic from the perspective of mainstream paradigm in the texts we have analysed, is that they imply a possibility of a form of deep meditative calm and absence of thoughts which does not entail insentience and mental stasis. This seems to be the implication of the juxtaposition of Pārāsariya's meditation with a state described in the same terms as the third *jhāna* in the *Indriyabhāvanā-sutta*. Of course, temporary insentience is from a psychological angle a natural consequence of deep absorption into a meditative object. After all, it is exactly this absorption which provides mental calm by suppressing thoughts and emotions in the same way as it suppresses sense impressions. The absorption into a meditation object is simply so strong that it leaves no room for any other phenomena to be conscious of. But can there be a state of mental calm and absence of thoughts not attained by deliberate one-pointed-concentration and not involving mental stasis and sensory inactivity? Exactly such a state seems to be indirectly implied by some Nikāya and Chan texts.

Were the four *jhānas* a pre-Buddhist practice?

The textual evidence examined in this chapter suggests that the four *jhānas* may have been at some point understood quite differently than in the later course of Buddhist history. They may have differed in some important respects from what we have labelled as the mainstream Buddhist form of calm meditation. Further evidence to that extent will be discussed in the course of the next chapters. Such an interpretation would, however, challenge the traditionally accepted view that the four *jhānas* were a type of practice, which is well-attested in the texts of the non-Buddhists such as Yogis and the Jains. But does it follow from this that the four *jhānas* were a uniquely Buddhist practice which did not exist before the times of the Buddha? This issue is not obvious. Drawing on his analysis of the account of the Buddha's teachers and of the *Laṭukikopama-sutta* and its Āgama parallel, Anālayo (2020: 575) comes to the following conclusion:

> The description offered in the passages translated above, with its clear indication that the immaterial spheres build on previous mastery of the four absorptions, in turn implies that the future Buddha's apprenticeship under Āḷāra Kālāma and Uddaka Rāmaputta is yet another instance where the early Buddhist texts point to the four absorptions as a pre-Buddhist practice, as their mastery would have been required in order to attain the third and fourth immaterial spheres.

However, an unqualified assertion that attaining the last two *āruppas* implies prior mastery of the *jhānas* is problematic. We have already discussed the implications of the Buddha's recollection of the first *jhāna* and the possibility of attaining *āruppas* without the *jhānas*. Even were we to accept Anālayo's hypothesis about the Buddha's recollection, we would still need to explain the accounts in the *Bhayabherava* (MN 4/i.16–24), *Dvedhāvitakka* (MN 19/i.114–118) and *Upakkilesa* (MN 128/iii.152–162) *suttas* which portray the Bodhisatta as unable to enter the *jhānas* straightaway, instead having to first learn how to remove various mental defilements. Would this be the case if he mastered the four *jhānas* under Āḷāra and Uddaka? Of course, we cannot be sure if all these accounts have the same author and are coherent.

Anālayo (2020: 571–72) points out three Nikāya texts which ascribe the practice of the *jhānas* or at least knowledge of them to non-Buddhists: the *Agañña-sutta* (DN 27/iii.80–98), the *Cūḷasakuludāyi-sutta* (MN 79/ii.30–39) and the *Brahmajāla-sutta* (DN 1/i.1–46), and analyses their Āgama parallels. The historical value of these texts as a source of knowledge about actual ideas and practices of the non-Buddhists in the times of the Buddha is debatable. The history of the world as presented in the *Agañña-sutta* is entirely at odds with what we know from science, thus making the reliability of its historical account dubious. Rather than being a description of the actual ideas and practices of historical non-Buddhist thinkers and sects (as is the case with the account found in the *Sāmaññaphala-sutta* at DN 2/i.52–59), the *Brahmajāla-sutta* seems to be more of a discussion of various conceivable forms of views regarding selected issues. Many of the variations of the sixty-two views are arrived at somewhat mechanically by listing specific misinterpretations of each of the successive meditative attainments from the lists of the *āruppa*s and the *jhāna*s as particular instances of wrong views.[153] According to the account in the *Cūḷasakuludāyi-sutta*, the wandering ascetics (*paribbājaka*) belonging to Udāyin's circle expressed familiarity with the state of the third *jhāna* after hearing it being described by the Buddha but were shocked by the very notion of a state surpassing it, i.e., the fourth *jhāna*. An account in similar vein may be found in the *Nigaṇṭhanāṭaputta-sutta* of the *Citta-saṃyutta* (SN 41.8/iv.297–300) with an Āgama parallel SĀ 574 at T02, no. 99, pp. 152b28–153a2. The latter text describes Nigaṇṭha Nāṭaputta's (c. *Nijian Ruotizi* 尼犍若提子) shock at the very possibility of the second *jhāna* (i.e., *samādhi* without *vitakka* and *vicāra: wujue wuguan sanmei* 無覺無觀三昧). According to the text, the leader of the Jains supposedly believed that the second *jhāna* is as impossible as catching wind in a net or stopping the current of Ganges with one's own fist. Commenting on this text, Bronkhorst (1986:83) points out that "the leader of the Jainas is depicted as considering impossible the very aim of Jaina meditation".

The value of the *Cūḷasakuludāyi-sutta* and the *Nigaṇṭhanāṭaputta-sutta* as accounts of actual historical pre-Buddhist views and practices is debatable. Similarly to the already discussed *Indriyabhāvanā-sutta*, they are representative of a more widespread Nikāya pattern of presenting non-Buddhists, their views and reactions to Buddhist teachings in a relatively crude, exaggerated way. This, of course, serves a rhetorical purpose, as the Buddha's own teachings may then be favorably contrasted with the obviously flawed ideas of non-Buddhists.

Sometimes the authors of early Buddhist texts go so far in attributing the practices traditionally considered uniquely Buddhist to non-Buddhists, that one must wonder whether they were fully aware of the implications of the texts they created. For example, according to the *Saṃyukta Āgama* text (SĀ 713 at T02, no. 99, p. 191a17–c14), similarly

153 Interestingly, the phrase "*samaṇa*s and Brahmins" (*samaṇabrāhmaṇā*) used in the *Brahmajāla-sutta* with respect to the adherents of each of the sixty-two views is not always a clear indicator in the Nikāyas that its referents are non-Buddhists. Sometimes it evidently functions as a designation of Buddhists, as several texts ascribe to *samaṇa*s and Brahmins the development of factors which serve as a conceptualization of the final stages of the Buddhist path (e.g., the five *indriya*s: SN 48.6/v.76–77, or the four noble truths: SN 56.5/v.416–417).

to the Buddha, non-Buddhists (*waiidao* 外道) teach their disciples to remove (*duan* 斷) the five hindrances (*wugai* 五蓋), well establish the four *smṛtyupasthānas* (*si nianchu* 四念處), and cultivate the seven factors of awakening (*qi juefen* 七覺分).[154] Attribution of the factors of awakening and especially of the *smṛtyupasthānas* to non-Buddhists is quite problematic, as these sets represent conceptualizations of the final meditative stages of the path to awakening, with *smṛtyupasthāna* traditionally considered to be an exclusively Buddhist practice. The Nikāya parallel of this text, the *Pariyāya-sutta* (SN 46.52/v.107–111) only describes non-Buddhist wanderers (*paribbājaka*) as teaching abandoning the hindrances (*nīvaraṇa*) and developing correctly the seven factors of awakening (*bojjhaṅga*) and does not mention the four *satipaṭṭhāna*s. However, this is not really at odds with the message of the Āgama text, as the Nikāyas contain many statements about the vital interconnection of the *satipaṭṭhāna*s and the *bojjhaṅga*s. The core of the *dhammānupassanā* is constituted by the abandonment of the hindrances and the development of the *bojjhaṅga*s. According to the passage in the *Kuṇḍaliya-sutta* (SN 46.6/v.73), when the four *satipaṭṭhāna*s are developed and cultivated (*bhāvita bahulīkata*), they fulfil (*paripūreti*) the seven *bojjhaṅga*s. The implications of the *Pariyāya-sutta* were uncomfortable enough for the author of its commentary, the *Sāratthapakāsinī* (Spk iii.204–205/iii.168–169), to attempt to explain away the problem by claiming that the *paribbājaka*s only adopted these teachings after hearing the Buddha preach them.[155]

It is therefore often difficult to assess whether a particular presentation of non-Buddhist views merely serves as a rhetorical device for introducing some Buddhist teaching or indeed reflects historical truth. This could only be established with certainty by comparisons with other sources describing non-Buddhist teachings in question, and preferably their own texts from roughly the same period in which the Nikāyas were created. Thus, we may know that Pārāsariya's method of cultivating the senses reflects to a certain extent historical Brahmin meditative practices as described in some of the Upanishads. On the other hand, the *Nigaṇṭhanāṭaputta-sutta* probably offers a poor representation of Jain ideas about meditation, since as Bronkhorst (1986) has shown, its message is at odds with some of Jain meditative texts. However, we do not have access to any non-Buddhist accounts of the

154 T02, no. 99, p. 191a25–27: 我等亦復為諸弟子說斷五蓋 – – 覆心、慧力羸，善住四念處，修七覺分。

155 See Gethin (2001: 180, n. 163) and Bodhi (2000: 1909, n. 98) for a discussion of this feature.

meditative practices of the group of Udāyin's *paribbājakas* or anonymous *samaṇas* and Brahmins from the *Brahmajāla-sutta* who supposedly knew about some of the *jhānas*. Thus, while these texts are very valuable in that they inform us about the ideas held by their early Buddhist authors and the rhetoric employed by them, they cannot be considered decisive evidence in support of the claim that the four *jhānas* (or some of them) were practised prior to the times of the Buddha. As Gethin (2001: 347) aptly points out: "we do not have any clear evidence of the *jhāna* meditations prior to their appearance in early Buddhist texts—the *jhānas* surface first in Buddhist writings" and "all we know is that they [the four *jhānas*] first become explicit in and are a central feature of early Buddhist texts" (Gethin, 2001: 348).

However, even if the accounts such as that in the *Cūḷasakuludāyi-sutta* were true in the historical sense, their implications would not be particularly problematic from the perspective of the argument forwarded in this book. I believe that there is nothing inherently impossible about meditative states corresponding to at least some of the *jhānas* being known and practised before the time of the Buddha (though certainly these states were not described in non-Buddhist teachings using exactly the same scheme and terminology as in the Nikāyas).[156] Even if it had been the case, it would have little bearing on the plausibility of the hypothesis forwarded in this book as this hypothesis does not rest on the claim that the Buddha discovered the *jhānas*. What is problematic from the perspective of this book, given so much evidence to the contrary, is the automatic and unproblematic assumption that all Nikāya texts imply that the four *jhānas* are a classical type of calm meditation practised by active one-pointed concentration on meditation objects, leading to insentience and mental stasis and not allowing simultaneous occurrence of any form of liberating insight. This would make them the same type of yogic states as those that are mentioned in texts such as the *Katha Upaniṣad*, the *Bṛhadāraṇyaka Upaniṣad*, or the so-called Yogic Upanishads.

While an analysis of the non-Buddhist texts does not show any meditative concepts directly paralleling the four *jhānas*, it needs to be said that our textual sources regarding this issue are limited to the surviving Hindu and Jain sources. The image arising from these sources may fail to reflect the true state of the non-Buddhist teachings in the times

156 This agrees with Gethin's (2001: 346) position that "we have to acknowledge that we really have no idea what the Buddha borrowed from the pre-existing nascent 'yogic' tradition of India".

of the Buddha. These teachings may have been much richer and more diverse than it is now acknowledged, as the region of Greater Magadha[157] in which they originated was probably a scene of a creative circulation and interchange of ideas between various *samaṇa* and Brahmin thinkers and spiritual seekers. Āḷāra and Uddaka may have been representatives of some original meditative movements based in Greater Magadha which could have influenced the Buddha's teaching. Let us emphasize the fact that according to the Nikāya narrative, the freshly awakened Buddha considered them capable of quickly understanding his message. We cannot know if this reflects the historical truth, but it might suggest some affinity between the earliest Buddhist and pre-Buddhist teachings. In the following chapters I will consider an alternative interpretation of the *āruppas* in light of which the Buddha's high opinion of his teachers may seem more understandable. However, history is written by the victors and even if there were some pre-Buddhist groups practising and teaching states corresponding to at least some of the Nikāya *jhānas*, their doctrines seem to be irreversibly lost to us.

Uncertainties and question marks

Some of our reasoning regarding the meditative practices in the Nikāyas were based on the implications of the Bodhisatta narrative, which indirectly juxtaposes the *jhānas* with other meditative practices and states. However, in this case one can also consider different hypotheses. One possibility is that some elements of the narrative (either the memory of the first *jhāna*, account of the strivings, or the names of the states taught by the teachers) have been artificially introduced to the original text for some purpose and the author of this insertion failed to notice the problems to which it led.[158] It might be that the original account contained the description of training with Āḷāra and Uddaka, but not the memory of the first *jhāna*. It also might be that the original account

157 To use Bronkhorst's (2007) term. Wynne (2023) has recently suggested that Buddhism started in the region of Kosala, where there may have functioned unorthodox Brahminic seekers and thinkers who were developing innovative ideas.

158 For such a hypothesis, see Wolf (2022), whose analysis of the three similes which compare the necessity of physical and mental seclusion to attain enlightenment to a man who wants to light a fire leads to the conclusion that the account of the strivings is an addition to the original account containing the aforesaid similes and the recollection of the first *jhāna*.

only contained the names of the two teachers, but the states of nothingness and neither perception nor non-perception were only ascribed to them at a later date, perhaps to show that calm meditation in itself is inefficient. In both cases, in a hypothetical original form of the text there would be no discrepancy with the mainstream views. There is also something peculiar about the fact that Uddaka would teach a state representing a direct refinement and progression with regard to Āḷāra's sphere of nothingness. Would not Āḷāra be aware that there is another teacher who challenges his notion that the stage of nothingness represents the apex of meditative development? It just seems too convenient for a compiler of the sutta to ascribe meditative states to the Buddha's teachers in such a way. Or alternatively, the ascription of the names of the states to their respective teachers is correct, but the set in which the stage of neither perception nor non-perception is preceded directly by the stage of nothingness is a later invention. Yet another possibility is that it is not obligatory but only optional to attain the four *jhānas* before the *āruppas*, and that there is a possibility to develop the latter states without entering the *jhānas* first.[159]

I have commented earlier on the difficulty of ascertaining whether all analysed Chan critiques of meditative states are based on the same principle or are directed against the same meditative paradigm. A somewhat similar difficulty may also be mentioned regarding the criticisms found in the Nikāya. We have seen that the Bodhisatta narrative juxtaposes the four *jhānas* with the sphere of nothingness and sphere of neither perception nor non-perception on the one hand, and with the quasi hatha-yogic methods described as *padhāna* (strivings) on the other. But can we be certain that these two types of meditation represent the same general model and have a common denominator?[160] The simple fact that the Bodhisatta starts the practices described as

159 Exactly this has been suggested by Thanissaro (2012: 216), who points to the set of the eight liberations/releases (*vimokkha*: e.g., DN 33/iii.260), in which the four *āruppas* and *saññāvedayitanirodha* are not preceded by the four *jhānas*. Thanissaro believes that the first three releases preceding the *āruppas* are not synonymous with the four *jhānas*, but "provide an alternative route to the formless attainments", which furthermore explains how "the Buddha, prior to his awakening, was able to reach the formless attainments when studying under Āḷāra Kālāma and Uddaka Rāmaputta, without at the same time passing through the four jhānas" (Thanissaro, 2012: 216).

160 Wynne (2007: 97) believes that Bronkhorst's (1986) idea of the main stream of meditation which was supposed to encompass both the meditative methods of Āḷāra and Uddaka and painful strivings (*padhāna*) involves a conflation of

strivings only after having left Āḷāra and Uddaka implies that attaining the meditation states taught by the two teachers did not involve these radical methods. While the practices described as the strivings are very well-attested in the Brahminic and later Hindu scriptures, such is not the case with the names of states taught by the two teachers. Could it be that they represented an entirely different type of meditation?

All these above considerations serve as an example of difficulties in establishing with absolute certainty the issues of relative earliness, authenticity, and evolution of early Buddhist ideas. Nonetheless, what matters to our investigation is that when taken at their face value, at least some of the Nikāya and Chan texts that we have analysed so far appear to criticize meditative features which are typical of the mainstream Buddhist paradigm, while at the same time proclaiming a different form of meditative calm attained in some other way. This generates several new questions which need to be considered, especially concerning the very plausibility of an idea of a special form of meditation which does not fit into the classical scheme of calm and insight and cannot be strictly classified as either of these.

So far, we have noted that this meditation possesses some features of classical *samatha*, though it differs from it by the method of its attainment. This raises questions regarding its connection with other fundamental qualities of Buddhist meditation, particularly that of insight. One also needs to examine whether an idea of a meditation practice which leads to states of mental and emotional quietude, but purportedly does so without any form of deliberate technique or method such as active concentration, is psychologically and practically plausible. If the attainment of these states of quietude was not meant to be a chance event devoid of any regularity, then this means that there are some necessary conditions and factors that make it possible. What then would be the nature of these conditions and factors? Are there any patterns or regularities connected with the attainment of such a state? What kind of philosophy of mind does it imply? And finally, are these ideas coherent enough and differ from the mainstream ones to such an extent that we can talk about the presence of an entirely unique meditative paradigm? Does the assumption of a presence of such a paradigm in Nikāya and Chan texts help to solve some interpretive problems or does it generate new ones? These problems will be considered in the next chapters.

---

evidence from different texts and forms of meditation which are not really closely connected.

Chapter 2

CALM AND INSIGHT, CONCENTRATION AND WISDOM

The problematic interrelation of calm and insight in the Buddhist mainstream

In the previous chapter I briefly noted that Shenhui's criticism was not only directed against mainstream Buddhist calm meditation but against insight as well, as both forms of meditation require a conscious, deliberate application of the mind expressed by terms such as *zuoyi* 作意 or *jiangxin* 將心. For Shenhui, however, this was not the only flaw of the mainstream paradigm. To him, the very classical model of an interrelation between calm/*samādhi* and insight/wisdom was problematic too.

Particularly relevant to this problem is the following fragment contained in the *Tanyu*.[1] It describes a situation in which one first freezes the mind and enters *samādhi*, which Shenhui negatively evaluates as falling into non-registering emptiness (*wujikong* 無記空). Subsequently, after having left a state of concentration (*chuding yihou* 出定已後), one arouses/activates the mind (*qixin* 起心) and [conceptually] discriminates (*fenbie* 分別) that what is conditioned (*youwei* 有為) in the world. As a sort of commentary to this approach, Shenhui ironically asks: "And this is called wisdom!?" He claims that according to the sutras (*jingzhong* 經中) this is a state of deluded mind (*wangxin* 妄心). According to him, those who believe that in the state of wisdom (*hui* 慧) there can be no simultaneous presence of concentration, and conversely, that in the state of concentration there is no wisdom, have still not transcended

1 B25, no. 142, p. 21a6–10: 即如「凝心入定」，墮無記空。出定已後，起心分別一切世間有為，喚此為慧！經中名為妄心。此則慧時則無定，定時則無慧。如是解者，皆不離煩。Cf. McRae (2023: 61) for a translation and discussion of this fragment.

afflictions (*buli fannao* 不離煩惱). It is worth emphasizing that what is criticized in this fragment is a fundamental mainstream Buddhist notion regarding the interrelation of calm and insight, or of concentration and wisdom, namely that one must first attain a state of concentration and then leave it to practise insight by using conceptual analysis or discrimination (*fenbie* in Shenhui's text). Therefore, concentration and wisdom cannot occur at the same time; when one is present, the other is not.

Shenhui's criticism touches on an important point. Despite its prevalence in the history of Buddhism, the mainstream paradigm of calm and insight is in fact riddled with many fundamental difficulties. In particular, the mutual relation between these two forms of meditation is very problematic. Again, we shall refer to Buddhaghosa's presentation as a good example of the mainstream paradigmatic approach to the interrelation of calm and insight. According to the model of the vehicle of calm (*samathayāna*) presented in the *Visuddhimagga*,[2] a meditator must first develop one of the four *jhāna*s. Then, he should leave the attained *jhāna* and return to an ordinary state of consciousness. Next, he should make the *jhāna* state from which he has just emerged the object of his practice of insight. He should conceptually analyse the mental and material constituents of that state and realize that they are self-less. This constitutes just the first in a long list of stages of development of insight, known as "the purification of view" (*diṭṭhivisuddhi*). It is not mandatory to attain the *jhāna*s at all before undertaking the practice of insight, as one can instead use the so-called vehicle of insight (*vipassanāyāna*) where the meditator simply analyses the mental and material constituents of his current, ordinary state.[3] However, using *jhāna* as an object of insight has an important benefit. Due to the refinement of this state, the number of mental and material factors which constitute it is relatively small and thus easier to analyse during insight practice. When, on the other hand, a meditator attempts to analyse the ordinary state of consciousness, he may be overwhelmed by a great multitude of mental factors. Therefore, a practitioner of dry insight is advised to start by analysing material factors, as the mental ones will become clear as a

2 Vism ii.222/587/XVIII.3: *taṃ sampādetukāmena samathayānikena tāva ṭhapetvā nevasaññāṇāsaññāyatanaṃ avasesarūpārūpāvacarajjhānānaṃ aññatarato vuṭṭhāya vitakkādīni jhānaṅgāni, taṃsampayuttā ca dhammā lakkhaṇarasādivasena pariggahetabbā. pariggahetvā sabbampetaṃ ārammaṇābhimukhaṃ namanato namanaṭṭhena nāmanti vavatthapetabbaṃ.*

3 Vism ii.222–223/588/XVIII.5.

consequence. The one who uses the vehicle of calm, starts by analysing mental factors of a particular *jhāna*.

The idea of combining the attainment of *jhāna* with the practice of insight as presented in the *Visuddhimagga* leads to some serious problems which need to be considered. The reason why the meditator has to leave the attained *jhāna* in order to practise insight lies in the fact that while in the state of meditative absorption his mind is unable to undertake the practice of insight in the sense of an active, conceptual analysis. But if the meditator analyses *jhāna* after having emerged from it, it means that instead of simply being aware of his present state he merely contemplates his memory of a state which already belongs to the past. This in turn entails that he is not actually aware of his present state in the here and now as it is constituted (at least on the mental level) by the very act of contemplating the past *jhāna* that he had attained. Furthermore, the meditator is not actually using the qualities of calm and concentration connected with the achieved *jhāna* for his practice of insight, because after having emerged from absorption these qualities are simply not present, or are greatly diminished. To use the abhidhammic terminology, the positive mental factors which constitute a particular jhānic state, such as concentration or equanimity, are not present or are greatly diminished after returning to an ordinary state of consciousness. Therefore, regardless of whether one has reached the first *jhāna*, the fourth *jhāna* or the sphere of boundless consciousness (which still counts as a form of the fourth *jhāna* and possesses its factors in Buddhaghosa's treatise), it will have very little or no bearing on the quality of calm and concentration with which one will practise insight. In Buddhaghosa's system, the whole justification for achieving higher stages of concentration does not lie in their superior quality of calm and concentration which could later be used in insight practice but in the relative simplicity of the mental factors which constitute them, since as we have already noted, they are to serve as an object of insight.

It is noteworthy that while in the late nineteenth and early twentieth century the Theravāda Buddhists were using classical Pali texts as a source of inspiration for the development of their meditative techniques,[4] they would often stray away in many respects from the classical paradigm presented in the *Visuddhimagga*. While the latter model involved a great deal of active conceptual analysis and the application of a variety of doctrinal Buddhist categories, the most popular

4 For a discussion of the origins of the modern *vipassanā* movement, see Davis (2003), Davis (2004), Braun (2013).

modern forms of insight practice taught by masters such as Mahasi, Sunlun, Goenka or U Ba Khin often stressed the need for passive, bare, and non-conceptual awareness.[5] Some elements of such practice would probably not even be considered "insight" from the standpoint of a classical mainstream Buddhist paradigm as they actually resemble, to a certain extent, the practice of non-conceptual and bare contemplation of thoughts taught by Heshang Moheyan, which was taken by his adversaries in the Samye debate to be a form of calm. It is also noteworthy that the *samathayāna* model of combining *jhāna* with insight was pretty much abandoned in most popular modern Theravāda approaches in favour of dry insight. Instead, several leading figures of Burmese and Thai meditation lineages were issuing stern warnings about the dangers and relative uselessness of higher stages of absorption.[6] It needs to be said, however, that the concept of *jhāna* to which they were referring was inherited from the fully developed classical Theravāda theory of meditation, and thus not necessarily representative of the Nikāya texts we are considering in this book. Why was the classical model of the vehicle of calm pretty much abandoned in the most popular forms of modern Theravādin meditative practice?

There are good reasons to suspect that the reluctance of modern Theravadins to combine *jhāna* with insight was based on practical reasons, and was not just motivated, as Sharf (2014b) would have it, by the desire to simplify the practice in order to make it more accessible for the masses. Due to the problems that we have discussed above, it seems likely that the *samathayāna* model in the *Visuddhimagga* was simply very difficult or perhaps even impossible to implement in real-life practice. So, why was such a convoluted model developed in the first place? It needs to be remembered that treatises such as Buddhaghosa's work were not really meant to be practical manuals for practitioners, but rather exegetical texts. This was actually the supposed historical reason for writing the *Visuddhimagga*, as this treatise was meant to provide proof of Buddhaghosa's mastery of the Theravada doctrine which would convince the Mahāvihāra monks to give him access to the local commentaries he was interested in. By that time, attaining *jhāna*s or arahantship was considered a thing of the past, pretty much impossible for practitioners of that era. This corresponds with Sharf's (1995: 241) observation that most of the classical passages on meditations neither

5 This fact has been noted by Sharf (2014b: 952–953; 2015: 473).

6 E.g., Kornfield (1996: 42, 260), Mahasi (1980: 5).

describe the actual experiences of their authors, nor are they even instructions intended to be put into use by anyone.[7] The reasons for the inherent difficulties of the classical model may lie in the fact that it had to be based on scriptural sources which often contained discrepancies and originated in different periods. Most of the problems related to the fact that these source texts contained different notions of *jhāna* meditation, which in turn reflected various stages of the evolution of this concept. Harmonizing these often incoherent ideas was therefore a hard or even an impossible task, and this had bearing on the final shape of the classical model of the vehicle of calm.

The terms *samatha* and *vipassanā* occur relatively rarely in the Nikāyas, which is especially striking if we consider the significance these concepts obtained in later literature. We sometimes find different pairs of terms which have been traditionally considered pretty much synonymous to that of *samatha-vipassanā*, such as that of *jhāna* and *paññā*.

This has led some scholars to question the very presence of the historically dominant model of calm and insight in early Buddhist scriptures. For example, Bhikkhu Sujato (2012a: 159) has claimed that: "The Buddha never divided the themes of meditation into two classes: *samatha* and *vipassanā*. Nor did he divide meditators into two classes: the *samatha* practitioners and the *vipassanā* practitioners." In his book *A History of Mindfulness: How Insight Worsted Tranquility in the Satipatthana sutta*, Sujato (2012b: 137) writes: "The early texts never classify the various meditation themes into either *samatha* or *vipassanā*. They are not two different kinds of meditation; rather, they are qualities of the mind that should be developed."

According to Sujato, the commonly held idea that *vipassanā* is virtually synonymous with mindfulness and *satipaṭṭhāna* also has no basis in the Nikāyas and can be probably traced back to the modern *vipassanā* movement (2012b: 1–2).

Jhāna and insight

We have already briefly noted some Nikāya fragments which, unlike later models, suggest a close, almost intrinsic relationship between

7 It needs to be said, however, that unlike the instructions for the seven last purifications, the ones for developing the *jhānas* with the help of the forty subjects of meditation are often very practical in character.

these two elements. The famous fragment of the *Dhammapada* paints a somewhat similar picture to the Chan texts, as it states that there is no *jhāna* for one devoid of understanding/wisdom (*paññā*), and no *paññā* for one devoid of *jhāna*.[8] According to the *Cetanākaraṇīya-sutta* (AN 11.2/v.312–313), it belongs to the natural order of things (*dhammatā*) that one who is concentrated will possess knowledge and vision of things as they really are, and no additional act of intention is necessary for it to arise.[9] The *Vijjā-sutta* (AN 10.105/v.214) states that "for one of right *samādhi*, right knowledge (*sammāñāṇa*) proceeds (*pahoti*)".[10]

There are numerous Nikāya texts which contain quite different visions of the interrelation of insight and *jhāna*, some of which are similar to the classical model and probably served as its textual basis. One has to agree with Schmithausen's (1981: 240) statement that the Nikāyas contain "various, even conflicting views or theories of Liberating Insight (and Enlightenment)". In his typology of calm-insight soteriologies, Wynne (2018a: 94–95) distinguishes five main types of the interrelation between calm and insight, ranging from that of pure insight to pure meditation, with three additional models which involve some sort of a soteriological cooperation of these two qualities.

These models seem to be based on different understandings of *jhāna*. The model that is present in the *Sāmaññaphala-sutta* (and numerous texts which follow its pattern of a gradual path), as well as in some of the texts describing the Buddha's path to awakening (i.e., MN 4/i.17–24, MN 19/i.114–118, MN 36/i.238–251, MN 85/ii.91–97, MN 100/ii.210–213), places final insight after the attainment of the fourth *jhāna*, when the mind is said to be "concentrated, purified, bright, unblemished, rid of imperfection, malleable, wieldy, steady, and attained to imperturbability" (*samāhite citte parisuddhe pariyodāte anaṅgaṇe vigatūpakkilese mudubhūte kammaniye ṭhite āneñjappatte*).[11] Then the practitioner is said to turn (*abhininnāmeti*)[12] the mind towards knowledge of the exhaustion

8 Dhp 372/53: *natthi jhānaṃ apaññassa, paññā natthi ajhāyato. yamhi jhānañca paññā ca, sa ve nibbānasantike.*

9 AN 11.2/v.313: *Samāhitassa, bhikkhave, na cetanāya karaṇīyaṃ: 'yathābhūtaṃ jānāmi passāmī'ti. Dhammatā esā, bhikkhave, yaṃ samāhito yathābhūtaṃ jānāti passati.* Cf. translation by Bodhi (2012: 1555).

10 AN 10.105/v.214: *sammāsamādhissa sammāñāṇaṃ pahoti.* Cf. translation by Bodhi (2012: 1486).

11 E.g., MN 27/i.83. Translation follows Ñāṇamoli and Bodhi (1995: 276).

12 The suttas from the *Dīgha Nikāya* use two verbs: *abhinīharati abhininnāmeti* to describe the act of directing the mind towards various forms of knowledge.

(*khayañāṇā*) of the influxes (*āsava*), which involves prior penetration of the four noble truths. In addition, the suttas from the *Dīgha Nikāya* describe an earlier form of insight, when a bhikkhu directs his mind towards knowledge and vision (*ñāṇadassana*), which is constituted by an act in which one understands (*pajānāti*) the impermanent nature of one's body and the way consciousness (*viññāṇa*) is bound to it. It is worth emphasizing that in this model of insight, the fourth *jhāna* is a very special, distinguished state of the highest purification of the mind.[13] While the narrative does not explicitly say that the state of the concentrated and purified mind used for attaining various insights is still that of the fourth *jhāna*, it seems to be implied as no mention is made of emerging from it. Such an interpretation has been offered by Shulman (2014: 21, n. 45), who points out that the usage of the phrase *so evaṃ samāhite cite* ("when his mind is thus concentrated") in the account of directing the mind to higher knowledges immediately after description of the fourth *jhāna*, suggests that the meditator has not left this state.[14]

Such an interpretation is of course pretty much impossible to harmonize with the mainstream notion of the fourth *jhāna* as a state of deep one-pointed absorption into a *nimitta* of a particular meditation object and by extension of almost total unawareness of anything else. As such qualities preclude the possibility of practising insight in a classical sense, it seems reasonable that the later models assumed the necessity of prior emergence from the state of *jhāna*. But does the Nikāya stock description of the fourth *jhāna* really give the impression of a state of deep one-pointed absorption and mental stasis? Very interesting comments questioning the traditional interpretation of the third and fourth *jhānas* have been offered by Gombrich (2004: 134):

> I know this is controversial, but it seems to me that the third and fourth *jhānas* are thus quite unlike the second. I suppose that one can be "aware and cognisant" without being aware of anything in particular: the terms "aware and cognisant" could perhaps be described as a state of receptivity, of potential rather than actual thought. But I find this an unsatisfying argument. One has to ask whether a real meditator would or would not notice a flashing light or a loud noise in his vicinity. The natural explanation of the text, in my view, is that

13 On the significance and special status of the fourth *jhāna*, see Shulman (2014: 18).

14 Shulman (2014: 23, n. 53) rightly points out that the texts are "thoroughly unambiguous" regarding the fact that wisdom arises in the fourth *jhāna* and not in some related *samādhi* state.

> in the third and fourth *jhāna* he would, but in the second he would not. If that is correct, this description of the *jhāna* describes (and prescribes) two quite different cognitive states, and the later tradition has falsified the *jhāna* by classifying them as the quintessence of the concentrated, calming kind of meditation, ignoring the other – and indeed higher – element.

In another place, Gombrich (2006: 115) notes that "the four *jhāna* contain elements from both of what were later formulated as two sides: for example, the *jhāna* are themselves assigned to *samādhi*, but the third and fourth *jhāna* include *sati*, awareness".

One indeed finds terms such as *upekkhaka* (equanimously looking), *sata* (mindful), and *sampajāna* (fully comprehending) in the stock description of the third *jhāna*, and *upekkhāsatipārisuddhi* (purification of mindfulness due to equanimity) in that of the fourth one. Were one to read these texts without prior knowledge of their historically dominant interpretation, it is highly doubtful whether one would consider the *jhānas* to be the states of frozen one-pointedness and stasis of the mind that they were later claimed to be. This has not escaped the attention of some scholars. Wynne (2007: 123) has suggested that:

> Words expressing the inculcation of awareness e.g., *sati, sampajāno, upekkhā* are mistranslated or understood as particular factors of the meditative states. ... They give the misleading impression that the third and fourth *jhāna* are heightened states of meditative awareness characterized by some sort of indescribable inner calm. But these terms have quite distinct meanings in the early Buddhist texts: they refer to a particular way of perceiving sense objects.[15]

Arbel (2017: 160) writes in a similar vein:

> As we have seen in the previous chapter, the fourth *jhāna* can be characterized as complete openness to the influx of experience, free from grasping and any type of reactivity (mental or physical, latent or obvious). I have showed that in the fourth *jhāna*, the manifold of sensuous impressions is perceived by non-reactive (*upekkhā*) lucid and vivid

15 Also cf. Wynne (2015a: 56): "To be 'mindful and fully aware' in the third stage indicates the resumption of sensory experience and objective consciousness, even if there is no indication that the ability to verbalize has returned. The meditator would instead seem to have entered a more vivid form of transitive consciousness, one devoid of conceptualization that usually arises in the process of cognitive conditioning. In the fourth stage this state is taken much deeper, or completely purified, with all cognitive and affective responses to experience fading away, so the mental construction of primary experience apparently all but ceases."

> awareness (*sati*), free from any hindrances and mental faculties that obstruct a clear perception of phenomena.

In his more recent article, Wynne (2018a: 103) has stated that:

> [O]ur argument is against interpreting the fourth *jhāna* as a state of inner concentration, and against interpreting insight or understanding as knowledge of a particular object. We instead argue that Kaccāna's philosophy suggests mindfulness as bare cognition or (passive awareness), and that just this is meant by the expression *upekhāsati-pārisuddhi* (in the fourth *jhāna*). Hence the fourth *jhāna* was originally understood to be quite different from the concentrative ideal of trying to confine the mind within a box.

Shulman (2014: 22) notes that while the mind in the *jhāna*s is "in an unusual, serenely deep, and quiet mode of operation", these states are "evidently cognitive". In another place (Shulman, 2014: 32) he states that the fourth *jhāna* "has moved beyond some forms of rational thinking but is nevertheless a cognitive state in which there still is room for certain restricted forms of understanding".[16] And indeed, in his interpretation of the key insight, the "meditative perception" according to the scheme of the four noble truths occurs in the fourth *jhāna*.

Thanissaro (2012: 214–215) also argues against the standard interpretation of the *jhāna*s as states characterized by unawareness of sensory input. He points to an account in the *Pārājikapāḷi* of the Vinaya (PTS iii.109), which he reads as a confirmation that it is possible to hear sounds during formless attainments. The account speaks of Moggallāna's claim that he heard the sounds made by bull elephants (*nāga*) emerging from the river Sappinikā and trumpeting, after he attained (*samāpanna*) an imperturbable (*āneñja*) *samādhi* on its bank. The Buddha confirms the veracity (*sacca*) of Moggallāna's claim, while making an interesting qualification that his *samādhi* was not pure (*aparisudhha*). Although Thanissaro interprets *āneñja samādhi* as a reference to the *āruppa*s, the term *āneñjapatta* is in the *Sāmaññaphala* account (e.g., DN 2/i.76) one of the epithets of the elevated state of the mind directly after the attainment of the fourth *jhāna*. Of course, this Vinaya account does not in itself constitute definite evidence in favour of the claim that

16 Jianxun Shi (2022: 302) argues that "the original concept of *jhāna* should contain insight meditation" since the verb *jhāyati* from which it is derived means "contemplate" or "think upon". She further points to the fact that "it is rendered into Chinese as 禪思, which can be interpreted as 'to meditate and contemplate' or 'to meditate through contemplation'".

the four *jhānas* are universally considered in the early Buddhist texts to be states in which one hears sounds, as it would assume the homogeneity of the early Buddhist canon. Nonetheless, it shows that some early Buddhist authors thought in this way.

In Bronkhorst's (2012: 132) theory, the fourth *jhāna* is a state in which the practitioner brings about the ultimate psychological transformation of a human being and no additional, post-*jhāna* insight practice is needed.[17]

Such an interpretation is, however, by no means a consensus amongst modern scholars. Amongst the most prominent proponents of the more traditional approach to the higher *jhānas* as forms of meditative absorption we can count Anālayo (e.g., 2017b). Amongst contemporary Buddhist meditation masters, such a position is held by Ajahn Brahm.[18]

It is possible to read the *Mahātaṇhāsaṅkhaya-sutta* (MN 38/i.256–271) in a way that provides support for such a vision of the *jhāna*. After the account of the fourth *jhāna*, we immediately read that the meditator dwells with each of the six senses registering its respective objects, with mindfulness of the body established (*upaṭṭhitakāyasati*), and with a non-measuring mind (*appamāṇacetasa*). He is said to dwell having abandoned both compliance and opposition (*anurodhavirodhavippahīna*), and whatever feeling (*vedanā*) he feels, he does not delight in it (*nābhinandati*), does not welcome it (*nābhivadati*), and "remains not being bound to it" (*nājjhosāya tiṭṭhati*).[19] Read in such a way, the message of the sutta seems to describe the same state as the *Indriyabhāvanā-sutta*, just by using different terms. Of course, such a reading assumes that the lack of an explicit statement about emerging from the fourth *jhāna* implies that the meditator is still in this state. Or, it might mean that some essential qualities of the fourth *jhāna* (understood strictly as a state of seated meditation) get extended onto a post-jhānic state of functioning. A similar message may be conveyed by the *Venāgapura-sutta* (AN 3.63/i.180–185), in which the Buddha describes how he attains the four *jhānas*. Immediately after the description of the fourth *jhāna* he claims that when he is in such a state (*evaṃbhūta*), then whether he is walking,

17 Also cf. Bronkhorst (2019: 9), where he states that "destruction of the influxes takes place in a state of deep absorption".

18 Brahm (2006: 178): "one cannot gain deep insight while experiencing *jhāna*. This is because the *jhāna* states are too still for the mental activity of contemplation to occur".

19 MN 38/i.270–271. Cf. translation by Ñāṇamoli and Bodhi (1995: 360).

standing, sitting or lying down, his state is heavenly (*dibba*). Again, this implies the extension of some qualities of *jhāna* into more ordinary activities.

Another relevant passage concerning the relation of the fourth *jhāna* to final insight may be found in the *Upakkilesa-sutta* (MN 128/iii.162) where the Buddha recollects meditative states which led to his awakening. He describes his meditative progress in terms of successive stages of *samādhi* characterized by the presence or absence of certain factors, such as *vitakka*, *vicāra*, *sati*, or *uppekhā*. While he does not resort to the stock *jhāna* formula, and in fact does not even use the term *jhāna* at all, his description clearly implies the four *jhāna*s. The last stage is described as *samādhi* endowed with *upekkhā*, which seems to correspond to the fourth *jhāna*. It is worth emphasizing that, immediately after describing this state, the Buddha says that there arose for him knowledge and vision (*ñāṇadassana*) that his release of mind (*cetovimutti*) is unshakable (*akuppa*), and that it is his last birth (*antima jāti*) and there is now no further becoming/being (*punabbhava*). Of course, one may attempt to argue that some additional insight practice is implied here, but nothing in the text itself suggests it.

Various models of calm and insight in the Nikāyas

According to Wynne's typology, the account in the *Anupada-sutta* (MN 111/iii.25–29) represents a different type of calm-insight model compared to the one analysed above. Compared to the *Sāmaññaphala* model, we find several differences. The text contains a classical account of nine meditative stages, in which the four *jhāna*s are succeeded by the four formless states and cessation of perception and feeling. A major difference lies in the fact that the fourth *jhāna* is no longer distinguished as a special, purified state; now it is merely an intermediary stage between the third *jhāna* and the sphere of boundless space. No mention is made of a concentrated, purified, and malleable mind. Furthermore, some form of insight accompanies each one of the first seven meditative stages, as the mental states present therein are "successively analysed".[20] The idea of defining the factors constituting particular meditative states is quite close to the concept of insight present in the *Visuddhimagga*. It has

20 MN 111/iii.25: *tyāssa dhammā anupadavavatthitā honti*. Cf. translation by Ñāṇamoli and Bodhi (1995: 901).

an even more direct parallel in Buddhaghosa's account of reviewing (*paccavekkhana*)[21] which is actually not a form of insight in the sense of leading to liberating knowledge, but is a key factor in developing successive stages of concentration. Through reviewing, one realizes that some of the factors of a meditative stage which has just been attained are gross (*oḷārika*), which in turns allows one to let go of attachment to this stage and progress to a higher level of meditative absorption.

There is, however, one significant difference between the model of insight in the *Anupada-sutta* and the concepts of reviewing and insight in the *Visuddhimagga*. In the latter text, one has to emerge from the attained meditative state to either review it or make it the object of one's insight. In the *Anupada-sutta*, insight occurs within the meditative state, with the exception of the sphere of neither perception nor non-perception and cessation of perception and feeling.[22] In the case of the two latter states, one emerges from them in a mindful way and contemplates (*samanupassati*) "the states that had passed, ceased, and changed" (*ye dhammā atītā niruddhā vipariṇatā*).[23]

In texts such as the *Jhāna-sutta* (AN 9.36/iv.422–426) and the *Aṭṭhakanāgara-sutta* (MN 52/i.349–353), the conditioned nature of the *jhānas* becomes the object of insight. In the former sutta, after attainment of any of the four *jhānas* and the first three *āruppas*, one regards (*samanupassati*) whatever element there is connected to any of the five *khandhas* as impermanent (*anicca*), painful (*dukkha*), void (*suñña*) and not-self (*anattā*), among other labels. As a result, his mind is being turned away (*paṭivāreti*)[24] from these phenomena (*dhamma*) and he "focuses" (*upasaṃharati*) on the deathless property (*amata dhātu*) which

21 E.g., Vism i.150/155/IV.136–138.

22 According to Anālayo's (2017b: 123) interpretation of the *Anupada-sutta*, "contemplation of the impermanent nature of the mental constituents of an absorption takes place before or on emerging from the attainment" and not within it. Anālayo bases this reading on an assumption that "awareness of these mental qualities arising and disappearing while being in an absorption is impossible, because the very presence of these qualities is required for there to be an absorption in the first place and for it to continue being a state of absorption" (Amālayo, 2017b: 121).

23 Translation by Ñāṇamoli and Bodhi (1995: 901).

24 I am grateful to Richard Gombrich for pointing out that although the Chaṭṭha Saṅgāyana and PTS versions have *paṭivāpeti*, it seems impossible to provide a plausible etymology of this term. Gombrich suggests emending *paṭivāpeti* to *paṭivāreti*, which would fit better in this context. Interestingly, the Thai edition has *patiṭṭhāpeti* while the Cambodian one has *paṭipādeti*. This may be a hint that

leads to liberation. In the *Aṭṭhakanāgara-sutta*, one attains any of the first seven of the classical list of the nine successive meditative states and discriminates/reflects (*paṭisañcikkhati*) that the attained *jhāna* is made up/constructed (*abhisaṅkhata*), and volitionally intended/planned (*abhisañcetayita*).[25] Then he understands (*pajānāti*) that such a state is impermanent and subject to cessation (*nirodhadhamma*). The model of insight in these two texts is not very much different from that in the *Visuddhimagga*, with the exception that the two Nikāya texts do not explicitly say anything about emerging from the meditative states in question in order to practise insight.

The model of insight in the suttas which follow the *Sāmaññaphala* pattern is fundamentally different from the one present in the *Anupada*, *Jhāna* and *Aṭṭhakanāgara-sutta*s. Most importantly, the two models appear to be based on a different understanding of the *jhāna*s, and in particular of the fourth *jhāna*. In the former model it is a purified, elevated state of mind which is a necessary condition for insight to occur. In the latter, there is not anything special about the fourth *jhāna*, and there is no mention of the concentrated, pliant and purified mind, while the meditative states themselves (and especially their imperfections) become an object of insight. It is possible that the model of insight in the *Anupada*, *Jhāna* and *Aṭṭhakanāgara-sutta*s appeared in correlation with some fundamental change of understanding of the *jhāna*s. In the previous chapter, we saw that there are at least some Nikāya texts which imply a vision of the *jhāna*s that is quite different from the mainstream

---

some corruption of the original text occurred during the transmission so that there was uncertainty concerning the verb used in this fragment.

25 In these two latter terms we perhaps find the closest parallel to the Chan notions of *zuoyi*, *zaozuo* or *youwei*. However, their ascription to the *jhāna*s seems to be in conflict with the already mentioned *Sasaṅkhāra-sutta* (AN 4.169/i.155) which claimed that one attains *parinibbāna* without *saṅkhāra* (*asaṅkhāraparinibbāyī*) exactly by developing the four *jhāna*s. It might be the case that the very idea of criticizing anything that is made up/constructed (*abhisaṅkhata*), and volitionally intended/planned (*abhisañcetayita*), may be earlier than its particular application in this text. While the text presents the *jhāna*s as "intended", would not the same be the case with the practice of insight rendered by terms such as *paṭisañcikkhati* in this text? Should not it (the act of insight) therefore become an object of insight itself? This is part of a wider problem with any notion of active, consciously applied and intended form of practising insight. Such an active practice of insight is an important part of what constitutes an individual at a given moment, and thus should not be excluded from being the object of insight itself (see Polak 2016: 97). However, this problem is rarely acknowledged in classical approaches to insight practice.

Buddhist one. In this view, the *jhāna*s are not concentrative practices leading to mental stasis and sensory inactivity, while the fourth *jhāna* is a state that is especially conducive to insight. If at some point the *jhāna*s started to be understood in a similar way as in the historically dominant Buddhist paradigm, then this made it difficult to explain how their achievement related to the development of insight. One possible answer was to postulate that the *jhāna*s themselves would become the objects of insight practice. The *Visuddhimagga* refined this theory by introducing the notion of practising insight only after emergence from the meditative state, which harmonizes with the vision of the *jhāna*s as states of deep mental absorption into a meditation object which do not allow for any other mental activity, such as insight, to occur. However, due to its inherent problems and psychological implausibility, the model proved to be difficult to implement in practice. Therefore, it did not become an element of the meditative practices of the majority of leading modern Theravāda meditation masters.

As a summary, we may say that there are at least some Nikāya texts which seem to imply that, in addition to being states of deep mental calm, the *jhāna*s also possessed some features that are usually connected with insight. Whether being in a state such as the fourth *jhāna* was seen as a sufficient condition for liberating insight to occur, or merely a necessary one with the presence of some additional factors still needed, is an open issue.

The union of *samādhi* and wisdom in Chan texts

Can a similar view regarding the relation of calm and insight, or *samādhi* and wisdom, be found in early Chan texts? As we have briefly noted, Shenhui considered the mainstream Buddhist belief that *samādhi* (*ding*) cannot simultaneously coexist with wisdom (*hui*) to be mistaken. This implies that for him wisdom and *samādhi* can coexist at the same time within one meditative state. Furthermore, Shenhui believed that *ding* and *hui* are deeply interrelated and ultimately share the same nature. In the *Tanyu*, he states that "concentration does not differ from wisdom, and wisdom does not differ from concentration, just as a lamp and its light cannot be separated".[26] Further on, he proclaims that *ding*

26 B25, no. 142, p. 25a2–3: 定不異慧，慧不異定，如世間燈光不相去離。Translation by McRae (2023: 63).

and *hui* are cultivated in combination (*shuangxiu* 雙修) and cannot be separated.[27]

The idea of a coexistence of concentration and wisdom is a very common theme of many Chan texts representing various time periods. It is perhaps most strongly emphasized in the *Liuzu tanjing*. In one of the fragments of this text,[28] Huineng states that his teaching takes *samādhi* and wisdom as its basis (*ben* 本). He warns his listeners against being deluded (*mi* 迷) and saying that wisdom (*hui* 惠)[29] and *samādhi* (*ding*定) are different (*bie* 別) from one another, since wisdom is the function (*yong* 用) of *samādhi*, while *samādhi* is the substance (*ti* 體) of wisdom. Most importantly, both qualities coexist simultaneously, and at the time of wisdom, *samādhi* exists in wisdom, while at the time of *samādhi*, wisdom exists in *samādhi*.

Immediately afterwards, he cautions against considering *samādhi* and wisdom as temporally distinct, either in the form of the mainstream Buddhist view that first there is *samādhi* (*xianding* 先定) and then wisdom develops (*fahui* 發惠) or that the development of *samādhi* is preceded by wisdom.[30] Interestingly, the relation between *samādhi* and wisdom in the *Liuzu tanjing* does not appear to be fully symmetrical. We have already mentioned the formulation that wisdom is the function of *samādhi*, while the latter is in turn the essence of wisdom. This is elucidated further by the simile of a lamp (*deng* 燈) and its light (*guang* 光): "If there is a lamp there is light; if there is no lamp there is no light".[31]

One cannot avoid the impression that the lamp is more essential than its light, since it functions as its necessary condition. This would imply

27 B25, no. 142, p. 25a8: 此即定慧雙修，不相去離。

28 T48, no. 2007, p. 338b6–9: 善知識！我此法門，以定惠為本。第一勿迷，言惠定別，定惠體一不二。即定是惠體，即惠是定用。即惠之時定在惠，即定之時惠在定。Cf. translations by Yampolsky (1967: 135) and Gregory (2012: 95–96).

29 Instead of using 慧 to render "wisdom", many Dunhuang manuscripts of Chan texts (e.g., the *Lengqie shizi ji*, the *Xiuxin yao lun*, the *Liuzu tanjing* and the *Lidai fabao ji*) use its homonym *hui* 惠, which literally means "kindness" (McRae 2023: 158, n. 196).

30 T48, no. 2007, p. 338b10–11: 莫言先定發惠，先惠發定，定惠各別。Cf. translations by Yampolsky (1967: 135) and Gregory (2012: 97).

31 T48, no. 2007, p. 338b26–29: 善知識！定惠猶如何等？如燈光，有燈即有光，無燈即無光。燈是光之體，光是燈之用。名即有二，體無兩般。此定惠法，亦復如是。Translation by Yampolsky (1967: 137). Also cf. translation by Gregory (2012: 96).

that *samādhi* is actually more essential than wisdom, which would be at odds with the mainstream Buddhist paradigm. It is unclear whether the author of the simile was aware of this implication. A similar understanding of the relation between wisdom and *samādhi* is present in Dazhu Huihai's 大珠慧海 (fl. 8th c.) *Zhufang menren canwen yulu* 諸方門人參問語錄 (*Record of questions asked by disciples from everywhere*),[32] a second fascicle of the *Dunwu rudao yaomen lun* 頓悟入道要門論 (*Treatise on the essentials for entering the Way through sudden awakening*).[33] Dazhu repeats Huineng's assertion that *samādhi* is the essence, while wisdom is its function. In addition, Dazhu states that wisdom arises from *samādhi* (*congdingqihui* 從定起慧), while the latter "returns" from wisdom (*conghuiguiding* 從慧歸定). *Samādhi* and wisdom are of one substance, just as the water and the waves (*rushuiyubo* 如水與波).[34]

Some peculiar passages in the texts associated with Shenhui may be read as implying that wisdom may actually precede concentration, or that the latter consists in the ability to maintain a non-reactive attitude (lit. non-activated mind, *buqixin*) towards one's own acts of discrimination (*fenbie*). For example, in the *Tanyu*, he claims that discriminating well (*shan fenbie* 善分別) the four basic colours in the world is wisdom, but not activating [the mind] in consequence of this discrimination (*busui fenbieqi* 不隨分別起) is concentration.[35] In another passage of the same text, he claims that when all the sensory faculties (*zhugen* 諸根) discriminate well, it is fundamental wisdom (*benhui* 本慧), and if one does not follow this discrimination with an activation of the mind, it is a fundamental *samādhi.*[36]

The idea of a meditative state simultaneously possessing qualities of *samādhi* and wisdom, as well as those of calm and insight, may well go back to the earliest period of Chan. The state described in the *Erru sixing lun* attributed to Bodhidharma, may perhaps be interpreted in such a manner.[37] Initially, the qualities connected with calm seem to be more evident: according to the text, one abides in a frozen state

---

32 Translation of the title follows Sasaki (2009: 430).

33 Translation of the title follows Sasaki (2009: 379).

34 X63, no. 1224, p. 29b19–20: 從定起慧。從慧歸定。如水與波一體。Cf. translation by Blofeld (1962: 128).

35 B25, no. 142, p. 21a5–6: 善分別世間青黃赤白，是慧。不隨分別起，是定。Translation follows McRae (2023: 61).

36 B25, no. 142, p. 24a10: 如是諸根善分別，是本慧。不隨分別起，是本定。Translation follows McRae (2023: 63).

37 This text appears in CBETA as *Putidamo dashi lüebian dasheng rudao sixing guan* 菩提達磨大師略辨大乘入道四行觀.

(*ningzhu* 凝住) firmly abiding without moving (*jianzhubuyi* 堅住不移). However, qualities that seem to be connected with insight can also be distinguished – one is said to abandon what is deluded (*shewang* 捨妄) and return to the real (*guizhen* 歸真) while being in deep harmony (*mingfu* 冥符) with the principle (*li* 理).[38] Some of the descriptions may lead to an impression that the state is connected with sensory inactivity. However, it is rather an apophatically described state of an elimination of various dualisms. The presence of "substantial components of both concentration and insight" in Hongren's meditation techniques has been noted by McRae (2003: 43). As he writes,

> Hongren's instructions to concentrate on the movement of the discriminatory mind imply both cessation – in that it is expected that the mind's movement will eventually stop in the course of one's practice – and understanding – in that the cause of that cessation is said to be a "wind of wisdom".

In another fragment of the *Xiuxin yao lun*, Hongren speaks about the wisdom of serene illumination (*jizhaozhi* 寂照智) which is born when one is possessed of right mindfulness (*zhengnian* 正念), and in turn leads to the exhaustive attainment of dharma nature (*dafaxing* 達法性).[39] The notion of serene illumination also occurs in the *Dasheng wusheng fangbianmen* which speaks about "serenely illuminating, illuminating serenity" (*jizhao zhaoji* 寂照照寂). The serenity spoken about in this text is clearly not the mental stasis typical of the higher stages of mainstream calm meditation as it is said to be "serene but always functioning" (*jierchangyong* 寂而常用).[40] We have already seen in the preceding chapter that this text contains an idea of the coexistence of *sāmadhi* and wisdom in the state of the bodhisattva's *samādhi*.[41] In the same text, we read that the non-movement of the mind (*xinbudong* 心不動), which is usually a feature connected with calm, is in itself *samādhi* (*ding* 定), wisdom/knowledge (*zhi* 智) and principle (*li* 理).[42] The idea of calm and

38 X63, no. 1217, p. 1a22–24: 若也捨妄歸真。凝住壁觀。無自無他。凡聖等一堅住不移。更不隨文教。此即與理冥符無有分別。寂然無為名之理入。Cf. translation by Broughton (1999: 9).

39 McRae (1986: 435/五): 正念具故寂照智生。寂照智生故窮達法性。Cf. T48, no. 2011, p. 377c16–17. For a translation of this passage, see McRae (1986: 124–25).

40 T85, no. 2834, p. 1274b6–7: 寂而常用。用而常寂。即用即寂。離相名寂。寂照照寂。Cf. translation by McRae (1986: 178).

41 T85, no. 2834, p. 1275a23–24.

42 T85, no. 2834, p. 1274b25–26: 問是沒是不動　答心不動心不動是定是智是理。Cf. translation by McRae (1986: 180): "The motionlessness of the mind is

insight, and of *samādhi* and wisdom coexisting in the same state would reappear in the Song period teachings of silent illumination (*mozhao* 默照), where silence (*mo* 默) represents the aspect of calm, while illumination (*zhao* 照) that of insight.

What kind of insight is implied in early Chan and Nikāya texts?

Admittedly, the Nikāya and Chan texts we have analysed do not present the issue of an interrelation between calm and insight, or *samādhi* and concentration, in exactly the same manner. They do, however, share some general ideas, most importantly concerning the strong presence of features traditionally associated with insight and wisdom within the positively evaluated states of mental calm and concentration. As we have seen, this largely goes against the mainstream Buddhist ideas regarding this matter. Therefore, the very presence of such unorthodox features immediately raises some interesting questions which should be considered. These questions are philosophically interesting in themselves, regardless of their particular historical context. One such question concerns the way in which insight or wisdom could occur in, or coincide with, a state of deep mental calm and the absence of thoughts.[43] The second question relates to the way such insight could be triggered. We have already discussed the texts which criticize any forms of meditation practice that involve conscious application of the mind or acts of intention. But how could one initiate insight, without resolving to an act of intention or a decision? The very notion of the presence of the features connected with insight in a state of deep meditative calm, a presence that would not be caused by a special, deliberately implemented practice, is very problematic from the point of the mainstream Buddhist meditative paradigm.

After all, as Henepola Gunaratana has noted, "insight cannot be practiced while absorbed in *jhāna*, since insight meditation requires investigation and observation, which are impossible when the mind is immersed in one-pointed absorption" (Gunaratana 1985: 151). Paul Griffiths has aptly summarized the historically dominant concept of

---

meditation, is wisdom, is the absolute (li)". In this text, McRae translates *zhi* 智 as "wisdom", and *hui* 慧 as "sagacity".

43 A similar question has been raised by Shulman (2014: 40): "Once again, the question of whether any form of knowledge is possible in deep *samādhi* – in the fourth *jhāna* and especially in cessation – is not one that is easily answered".

insight in Buddhism: "Wisdom is a type of ... discursive knowledge and vision. The means used to achieve this kind of conscious awareness is a continuous attempt to internalize the categories of Buddhist metaphysics" (Griffiths, 1981: 613).

None of this should be possible in the traditionally understood meditative states of deep calm and absence of thoughts.

I have suggested that even though the right form of calm in the Nikāya and early Chan texts we have analysed so far was not a state of blankness or insentience, it was purported to be a state free from conceptual thought and possibly from any active, volitional activity. However, the presence of these latter features is required in the traditionally understood insight practice. Would such a form of non-conceptual, thought-free insight/wisdom be possible from a psychological point of view? Such an idea is not only at odds with the traditional paradigm of Buddhist meditation but with commonsense stereotypical views about human psychology as well. Have we therefore not come upon a purely theoretical construct which could never function on a practical level? Such a hypothesis would be in agreeance with the kind of approach in Chan studies which suggests that the formulations about meditation in the texts of this school should be rather read as polemical or rhetorical statements than as practical or psychological ones. As Sharf aptly sums up, according to this approach, early Chan "was merely a meta-discourse that had little effect on practice and technique per se"[44] and "is not distinguished by forms of monastic practice and meditation technique so much as by its mythology, doctrine, and literary style".[45]

Let us at this point return to the early Chan texts in search of some additional details and hints regarding the cognitive nature of insight or wisdom that they postulate. In the *Xiuxin yao lun*, Hongren states that once deluded thought (*wangnian* 妄念) no longer arises and the possessive mind ceases (*wosuoxinmie* 我所心滅), then there is a natural (*ziran* 自然) realization of understanding (*zhengjie* 證解).[46] According

44 Sharf (2014b: 952). It is worth emphasizing that this is not the position held by Sharf himself, as he claims (Sharf 2014b; 2015) that the Chan masters introduced certain new simplified techniques of meditation.

45 Sharf (2014b: 938).

46 McRae (1986: 437/三): 妄念不生我所心滅自然證解。Cf. T48, no. 2011, p. 377c3–4. Cf. translation by McRae (1986: 124): "[W]ithout generating false thoughts or the illusion of personal possession. Enlightenment will thus occur of itself".

to a very well-known fragment of the same text, when the clouds of deluded thoughts (*wangnianyun* 妄念雲) are exhausted (*jin* 盡), the sun of wisdom (*huiri* 惠日) will appear.[47] Another passage of the *Xiuxin yao lun* speaks about the natural (*ziran* 自然) manifestation (*xianxian* 顯現) of the dharma sun of nirvana (*niepan fari* 涅槃法日), which occurs when deluded thoughts are no longer generated.[48] The notion of the sun of wisdom (*huiri* 慧日) reappears in the *Baizhang Huaihai chanshi guanglu* where it is said it will naturally appear (*zixian* 自現), when the mind has no activity whatsoever (*wusuoxing* 無所行) and its ground (*xindi* 心地) is like an empty space (*kong* 空).[49] In the *Tanyu*, Shenhui delivers the following words:

> Non-abiding (*wuzhu* 無住) is quiescence (*jijing* 寂靜), and the essence (*ti* 體) of quiescence is called concentration. The natural (*ziran* 自然) knowledge (*zhi* 智) that occurs on the basis (*shang* 上) of this essence, whereby one can cognize (*zhi* 知) the inherently quiescent essence, is called wisdom (*hui* 慧).[50]

Similarly, the *Wenda zazheng yi* contains Shenhui's statement that the knowledge of *prajñā* (*bore zhi* 般若智), which is able to cognize (*neng-zhi* 能知), occurs naturally (*zi* 自) upon the fundamentally empty and serene essence (*benkongji ti* 本空寂體).[51]

---

47 McRae (1986: 434/六): 妄念雲盡惠日即現。Cf. T48, no. 2011, p. 378a4. For a translation of this passage, see McRae (1986: 125).

48 McRae (1986: 438/二): 妄念不生。涅槃法日自然顯現。Cf. T48, no. 2011, p. 377b2. For a translation of this passage, see McRae (1986: 122). Interestingly, this symbolism reappears in the following line from the *Lidai fabao ji*: "Like the roiling of thick clouds and the sun of bright wisdom, the veil of karma will suddenly roll back. Cut back delusory conceptualization by emptying the mind, tranquilly not moving" (tr. Adamek, 2007: 402). T51, no. 2075, p. 195c8–9: 卷重雲而朗惠日。業障頓祛。廓妄相以定心。寂然不動。

49 X69, no. 1323, p. 7c12: 心無所行。心地若空。慧日自現。如雲開日出。Translation follows Poceski (2007: 163).

50 B25, no. 142, p. 19a7–9: 無住是寂靜。寂靜體即名為定。從體上有自然智，能知本寂靜體，名為慧。Translation follows McRae (2023: 57–58), with very slight changes of terminology and addition of several original Chinese terms in parentheses. To distinguish between the terms 智 and 慧 in Shenhui's texts, which are both usually translated as "wisdom", I have decided to render 智 as knowledge and 慧 as wisdom, instead of McRae's respective rendering as wisdom and sagacity. According to Soothill and Hodous (2014: 120, 134), Chinese 智 was often used to render Sanskrit *jñāna* (knowledge), while 慧 usually stood for *prajñā* (Soothill and Hodous, 2014: 432).

51 B25, no. 143, p. 227a7–11. Cf. translation by McRae (2023: 153).

All these passages consider the manifestation of wisdom to be simply an almost automatic, spontaneous effect of the quiescing of the mind and the absence of deluded thinking. They seem to imply that there is no need for undertaking any additional insight practice understood as some sort of deliberate mental activity. We have already noted that according to the historically dominant Buddhist paradigm, such a thing should not even be possible, since the absence of thought also prevents the possibility of any active, conceptual form of insight. However, it seems that we are dealing in this case with an entirely different understanding of calm and insight and of their mutual relation.

Similar notions occur in several later Chan texts. In the *Chuanxin fa yao*, Huangbo Xiyun states that sentient beings do not understand that with the ending of thought (*xinian* 息念) and forgetting of mentation (*wanglü* 忘慮) the Buddha will self-manifest.[52] When presenting the beliefs of the Heze school in the *Chanyuan zhuquanji duxu*, Zongmi speaks of quiet illumination (*jizhao* 寂照) which manifests before (*xianqian* 現前) the meditator once mental afflictions are exhausted and the processes of arising and cessation have ceased (*shengmiemieyi* 生滅滅已).[53] We are therefore dealing with an entirely unique kind of insight, an insight that is not the result of any deliberate practice involving active analysis or applying traditional Buddhist conceptual categories to one's experience. This notion is very aptly summed up by Bielefeldt (1986: 139):

> Hence meditation leads to wisdom not in the usual sense that it prepares the mind to undertake the discipline of prajñā but in the sense that it uncovers a preexistent prajñā, inherent to the mind. Thus it is possible to speak of the calm of meditation, if not as an end in itself, at least as a sufficient condition for that end.

One could perhaps claim that such concepts simply stem from the ideology of subitism, since the traditional relation of calm and insight implies a certain graduality, as one first develops calm and insight afterwards. However, Gómez has pointed out that this concept also possesses several practical and psychological implications. Apart from the question of gradual cultivation versus sudden enlightenment (Gómez, 1987: 101), there is also that of the immediacy of access. Gómez (1987:

52 T48, no. 2012A, p. 379c25–26: 不知息念忘慮佛自現前。Cf. translation by McRae (2005: 13).

53 T48, no. 2015, p. 403a9–10: 煩惱盡時生死即絕。生滅滅已。寂照現前應用無窮。名之為佛。Cf. translation by Broughton (2009: 88).

97) distinguishes two fundamentally different approaches regarding that matter, namely "access to the nonconceptual through mental effort and cultivation" and "direct access to the nonconceptual". Those two different approaches correspond to two radically different concepts of calm and insight. The first approach implies the necessity of mental cultivation involving cooperation of calm and insight, while in the second one, they "are automatically included in nonconceptual thought" (Gómez, 1987: 97).

In the case of Nikāya texts, there are far fewer statements that can be interpreted as implying a concept of spontaneous insight resulting almost automatically from a concentrated mind. Nonetheless, there are such fragments. The most explicit formulations of this idea can be found in the already mentioned two *Cetanākaraṇīya-sutta*s found in an almost identical form in the collections of tens (AN 10.2/v.2–4) and elevens (11.2/v.312–313) of the *Aṅguttara Nikāya*. Both these texts contain a statement that one who is concentrated (*samāhita*) "does not need to make an intention" (*na cetanāya karaṇīyaṃ*) to know and see as it really is (*yathābhūtaṃ*), as it is natural and expected that the one who is concentrated will know and see things as they are.[54] Taken at face value, this fragment explicitly states that knowing and seeing (which is a synonym of insight) is not an intentionally driven activity, but almost a natural by-product of concentration.

The *Sekha-sutta* (MN 53/i.353–359) is another text that can be read as implying a similar concept of insight. The sutta contains a simile of a hen (*kukkuṭī*) whose eggs had been properly covered, warmed and incubated. The text emphasizes that even though the hen "would not arouse wish/intention" (*na ... icchā uppajjeyya*) for the hatching of chicks, it nonetheless happens on its own accord. Likewise, a practitioner who is possessed of virtue (*sīlasampanna*), guards the senses, is moderate in eating food and devoted to wakefulness, and who naturally enters the four *jhāna*s without difficulty (*akicchalābhī*) and without trouble (*akasiralābhī*), is said to be capable of "breaking out" (*abhinibbhidā*) and of awakening (*sambodhi*). While it is not stated explicitly that a practitioner does not have to make a wish in order to "break out", such a meaning seems to be implied by the simile used in the sutta. This reading is supported by the fact that when the text later describes entering and

54 AN 10.2/v.3: *samāhitassa, bhikkhave, na cetanāya karaṇīyaṃ – 'yathābhūtaṃ jānāmi passāmī'ti. dhammatā esā, bhikkhave, yaṃ samāhito yathābhūtaṃ jānāti passati*. Translation follows Bodhi (2012: 1341).

abiding in the influx-less mind-release and wisdom-release by "realizing for oneself with higher knowledge in the visible state of things" (*diṭṭheva dhamme sayaṃ abhiññā sacchikatvā*), it is described as a "breaking out" similar to that of chicks from their shells.

No specific practice of insight is explicitly mentioned as one of the conditions for "breaking out", and the account of practices ends with the four *jhānas*. The text then seems to imply that awakening and *abhiññā* are entirely resultant from earlier conditions such as perfection of virtue and mastery of the *jhānas*. It is also noteworthy that the *Sekha-sutta* describes this realization of the higher knowledge of the influx-less mind-release and wisdom-release as occurring due to (*āgamma*) unsurpassed (*anuttara*) purity of mindfulness owing to equanimity (*upekkhāsatipārisuddhi*).[55] This is a clear reference to the fourth *jhāna*, as the latter term always occurs in the stock account of that meditative state. In a way, this text follows the model of insight contained in the suttas following the *Sāmaññaphala* pattern, but instead of a reference to a concentrated and malleable mind, we find a direct reference to *upekkhāsatipārisuddhi*. This is hardly a discrepancy, as it could be pretty much assumed that the former description did also refer to the qualities of mind connected with the fourth *jhāna*. What is even more important is that the *Sekha-sutta* does not contain any formula which could be read as pertaining to insight as a consciously undertaken and deliberately implemented practice, as is the case with the phrase *cittaṃ abhinīharati abhininnāmeti* ("bends and directs the mind") found in the texts that follow the *Sāmaññaphala* pattern.

Another Nikāya text worth mentioning in this context is the *Samādhi-sutta* (SN 35.99/v.312–313). It contains an exhortation to develop concentration (*samādhi*) and an explanation that the one who is concentrated understands as it really is (*yathābhūtaṃ pajānāti*) the impermanence of the six sense bases (*saḷāyatana*). Initially, this text can be seen as simply expressing the mainstream concept of a relation between calm and insight; first one develops concentration to later use it for insight. However, when read directly, the text implies that "understanding how it is" actually occurs in the state of *samādhi* which in turn implies that this is almost a natural effect of being concentrated.

55 MN 53/i.357–358: *sa kho so, mahānāma, ariyasāvako imaṃyeva anuttaraṃ upekkhāsatipārisuddhiṃ āgamma āsavānaṃ khayā anāsavaṃ cetovimuttiṃ paññāvimuttiṃ diṭṭheva dhamme sayaṃ abhiññā sacchikatvā upasampajja viharati.* Cf. translation by Ñāṇamoli and Bodhi (1995: 464).

The luminous mind

In early Chan texts, the idea of spontaneous insight or wisdom occurring in a state free from conceptual thought is closely connected to a very specific concept of the mind. This concept assumes the existence of a deep, basic layer of the mind endowed with the inherent ability for insight. This layer, however, is usually obscured by the presence of conscious thoughts and other mental defilements which prevent the occurrence of insight.

The exact terms used to express this concept may slightly differ depending on a particular text, but there are general similarities. Thus, the *Rudao anxin yao fangbian famen* speaks about "mind nature" (*xinxing* 心性), which is originally (*benlai* 本來) always pure (*changqingjing* 常清淨), but the sentient beings are not enlightened to it.[56] The *Xiuxin yao lun* contains several statements about the "true mind" (*zhenxin* 真心) or "pure mind possessed by all sentient beings" but which is "simply being covered by the layered clouds of discriminative thinking, false thoughts, and ascriptive views", and one's own mind which is known to be inherently pure (*zixin benlai qingjing* 自心本來清淨).[57] The latter description has been repeated in an identical form by Zongmi, who speaks about one's practice being based "on having all-at-once awakened to the realization that one's own mind is from the outset pure, that the depravities have never existed, that the nature of the wisdom (*zhixing* 智性) without influxes (*lou* 漏) is from the outset complete (*benzijuzu* 本自具足), that this mind is Buddha and that they are ultimately without difference".[58] Huangbo Xiyun describes it in the *Chuanxin fa yao* as originally pure and bright (*benlaiqingjingjiaojiao* 本來清淨皎皎).[59] As already noted, Daoxin has used the term "mind-nature" (*xinxing* 心性). The terms "mind" (*xin* 心) and "nature" (*xing* 性) are often used as near-synonyms and many early Chan texts simply speak about "the nature" (*xing*). The *Erru sixing lun* is chronologically the earliest Chan

---

56 T85, no. 2837, p. 1287b26–27: 眾生不悟心性本來常清淨。Cf. translations by Chappell (1983: 110–11) and Van Schaik (2018: 158).

57 McRae (1986: 438–39/一-二): 一切眾生清淨之心亦復如是。只為攀緣妄念煩惱諸見黑雲所覆。但能凝然守心。妄念不生。涅槃法自然顯現。故知自心本來清淨。Cf. T48, no. 2011, p. 377a29–b3. Translation by McRae (1986: 122).

58 T48, no. 2015, p. 399b16–18: 若頓悟自心本來清淨。元無煩惱。無漏智性本自具足。此心即佛。畢竟無異。Translation by Broughton (2009: 103).

59 T48, no. 2012A, p. 383c13: 本來清淨皎皎地。Cf. translation by McRae (2005: 39).

text to speak about living beings possessing the same true nature (*tongyizhenxing* 同一真性), which is covered by the incoming external dust of deluded ideations (*wangxiang* 妄想) so that it cannot manifest (*xian* 顯).[60]

This idea makes its comeback in an almost identical form in the *Liuzu tanjing* which speaks about originally pure human nature (*renxing* 人性) and deluded thoughts (*wangnian* 妄念), which obscure (*gaifu* 蓋覆) "thusness" (*zhenru* 真如).[61] The message conveyed by this fragment seems to be surprisingly close to Shenxiu's verse which is criticized in the early part of this text and which states that one should constantly remove dust from the clear mirror of the mind. This shows that the texts considered to represent "Southern Chan" were not free from ideas that could be classified as gradualist. In the *Wenda zazheng yi*, the supposed subitist Shenhui uses a metaphor of purifying gold which has gradualist implications.[62] He insists on the necessity of distinguishing afflictions from dharma nature as fundamentally different. Dharma nature is like gold (*jin* 金), while afflictions are like the admixture of slag/gangue (*kuang* 鑛). They can be separated by successive smelting processes, and as a result gold will become a hundred times brighter, while slag will turn into gray dust (*huitu* 灰土). Shenhui quotes the *Nirvana-sutra* in support of the claim that afflictions do not belong to original nature and are merely incoming dust (*kechen* 客塵). In the *Tanyu*, Shenhui refers to the "original essence" (*benti* 本體),[63] and speaks about "the mind that is empty and serene in its inherent nature" (*zixing kongji xin* 自性空寂心)[64] and "the pure inherent mind" (*zi ben qingjing xin* 自本清淨心).[65]

Similar ideas can be found in Nikāya texts, although the formulas expressing them are less frequent and prevalent than in Chan literature. The famous statement in the *Pabhassara-sutta* (AN 1.49–1.50/i.10), about the luminous mind (*pabhassara citta*) which is defiled by the adventitious defilements (*upakkilesa*) but may become released (*vippamutta*)

60 X63, no. 1217, p. 1a21–22: 深信含生同一真性。但為客塵妄想所覆不能顯了。Cf. translations by McRae (1986: 103) and Broughton (1999: 9).

61 T48, no. 2007, p. 338c25–26: 若言看淨，人性本淨，為妄念故，蓋覆真如。Cf. translation by Yampolsky (1967: 139).

62 B25, no. 143, pp. 216a11–217a8. Cf. McRae (2023: 143) and Gómez (1987: 76), for translations and discussions of this fragment.

63 E.g., B25, no. 142, p. 21a5.

64 B25, no. 142, p. 19a1. Translation by McRae (2023: 56).

65 B25, no. 142, p. 17a6. Translation by McRae (2023: 55).

from them,[66] can be considered almost a direct antecedent of parallel expressions in Chan texts. The *Paṃsudhovaka-sutta* (AN 3.101/i.253–256) compares the mind to gold (*jātarūpa*) which contains impurities/defilements (*upakkilesa*). After their gradual removal which occurs in several stages, the gold becomes luminous (*pabhassara*) and malleable (*mudu*).[67] This is a metaphor for the mind, which becomes capable of various forms of *abhiññā* (super knowledge) once it has been made free from defilements. The terms luminous (*pabhassara*) and malleable (*mudu*) are in fact directly used with reference to the mind in other texts, such as the *Nimitta-sutta* (AN 3.102/i.256–258), when it is said that a developed mind "becomes malleable, wieldy, and luminous, not brittle but properly concentrated (*sammā samādhiyati*) for the destruction of the influxes".[68] According to the *Paṃsudhovaka-sutta*, the lowest defilements have the nature of misconduct, but all the subtle defilements are said to be thoughts (*vitakka*), with the subtlest being thoughts of the dhamma (*dhammavitakka*).

The *Vattha-sutta* (MN 7/i.36–40) compares cleansing the mind from its defilements to a cloth (*vattha*) which had been defiled (*saṃkiliṭṭha*) and stained (*malaggahita*), but has become clean and bright thanks to clean water, or to gold (*jātarūpa*) which has become bright and clear owing to the furnace (*ukkāmukha*).[69]

It is worthwhile to consider the philosophical implications of the abovementioned similes. The metaphors of purifying gold from impurities and of cleansing cloth from its stains suggest that purity is an original, default state of mind. Pali term *āsava* also may be read as implying that the fundamental negative factors binding one to *saṃsāra* are not inherent to the mind, but are "inflowings" (which is the literal meaning of *āsava*). This implies that the process of the development of the mind is not so much about directly enhancing certain positive factors, but

66 AN 1.49–1.50/i.10: *'pabhassaramidaṃ, bhikkhave, cittaṃ. tañca kho āgantukehi upakkilesehi upakkiliṭṭhan'ti. 'pabhassaramidaṃ, bhikkhave, cittaṃ. tañca kho āgantukehi upakkilesehi vippamuttan'ti.*

67 AN 3.101/i.254: *Taṃ hoti jātarūpaṃ dhantaṃ sandhantaṃ niddhantaṃ niddhantakasāvaṃ, mudu ca hoti kammaniyañca pabhassarañca, na ca pabhaṅgu, sammā upeti kammāya.*

68 AN 3.102/i.257 *taṃ hoti cittaṃ muduñca kammaniyañca pabhassarañca, na ca pabhaṅgu, sammā samādhiyati āsavānaṃ khayāya.* Translation by Bodhi (2012: 339).

69 MN 7/i.38: *Seyyathāpi, bhikkhave, vatthaṃ saṅkiliṭṭhaṃ malaggahitaṃ acchodakaṃ āgamma parisuddhaṃ hoti pariyodātaṃ, ukkāmukhaṃ vā panāgamma jātarūpaṃ parisuddhaṃ hoti pariyodātaṃ.*

about eliminating negative ones. From this perspective, states such as insight or concentration (*samādhi*) could be seen as a direct consequence of a lack of distraction, rather than as a new quality to be generated as an outcome of the conscious effort of trying to understand or concentrate. Quite the contrary, any form of conscious effort is in fact a subtle form of thought, even if it is a thought of dharma itself. According to the *Paṃsudhovaka-sutta*, as long as there are thoughts of *dhamma*, *samādhi* is still "held down by restraint of *saṅkhāra*" (*sasaṅkhāraniggayhavāritagato*),[70] which as we have seen implies the notion of conscious effort. It is worth emphasizing that the mere absence of thought is not in itself a sufficient condition for the occurrence of insight. Mainstream forms of calm meditation also lead to the absence of thinking, and yet they become the subject of criticism in certain Nikāya and Chan texts. Their flaw seems to lie in the fact that mental calm and the absence of thought are achieved due to active concentration and, as a result, the fundamental layer of the mind becomes suppressed.

Is spontaneous insight coinciding with the state of absence of thought psychologically plausible?

As we have seen, several Chan and Nikāya texts can be read as implying an idea of a spontaneous insight which occurs in a unified state of absence of thought and is not the result of an additional deliberate mental act. Regardless of whether this was the meaning intended by the authors of all the texts we have analysed and whether or not it was based on personal meditative experiences, this idea is very interesting philosophically due to its originality. Its presence in Chan and Nikāya texts inspires further questions about its psychological plausibility. That is because it is at odds with not only mainstream Buddhist concepts but also our commonly held notions about mental functioning.

The last decades have seen a spectacular development of cognitive science and philosophy of mind. As opposed to the more "humanistic" branches of psychology, these disciplines are to a much larger extent rooted in natural sciences: neurology, evolutional biology, genetics and artificial intelligence research. Cognitive science is interested in the issues connected with human consciousness, cognition, selfhood, and subjectivity, and so is Buddhism. Both Buddhism and contemporary

70 AN 3.101/i.255: *So hoti samādhi na ceva santo na ca paṇīto nappaṭippassaddhaladdho na ekodibhāvādhigato sasaṅkhāraniggayhavāritagato.*

philosophy of mind question many commonly held, stereotypical views regarding human psychology. According to evolutionary biologists, human mental functioning has hardly changed since the times of the Buddha. Therefore, the results of modern science should also be relevant for assessing and making better sense of the claims contained in Nikāya and Chan texts. It will be interesting to examine whether the philosophical implications of ancient Buddhist texts can be considered plausible from the perspective of the contemporary philosophy of mind.

As we have noted, many theories of the modern philosophy of mind are at odds with commonsense or the so-called folk-psychological intuitive attitudes about the way the human mind works. Most importantly, they challenge the popular notion that consciousness is the actual locus of creating ideas, performing acts of will, active cognizing, i.e., activities traditionally constitutive of human agency and subjectivity. Siderits (2020: 199) aptly notes that there is now wide consensus in cognitive science regarding the idea that not all mental states are conscious.[71] According to these new developments, thoughts, ideas and insights do not actually originate or get produced by consciousness. They may eventually become conscious (often suddenly and unexpectedly) but are a result of several non-conscious cognitive processes, often occurring in a modular and parallel way. The non-conscious nature of actual cognitive processing can in fact be inferred based on observing our everyday behaviour, the way we think, solve problems and arrive at new ideas. One striking example of this truth is the well-known phenomenon of "sleeping on it" which is described in the following way by Carruthers in his book *The Centered Mind*:

> Consider the phenomenon of "sleeping on it". It is a familiar occurrence in daily life that one's reflective reasoning about some problem has become stuck – one is unable to see a way to a solution. So one lays the problem aside, either literally going to sleep for the night or occupying oneself with other tasks. But then sometimes after an interval the solution suddenly and unexpectedly emerges into consciousness. It is natural to think that one must have continued reasoning about the problem, unconsciously, in the interim. (Carruthers 2015: 176)

71 Also cf. Solms (2021: 78), who states that "the scientific evidence showing that we are unaware of most of what we perceive and learn is now overwhelming. Perception and memory are not inherently conscious brain functions. In this respect, common sense was wrong. It turns out that everything your mind does (except one thing, as we shall see) can be done pretty well unconsciously".

Carruthers (2015: 177) also considers cases when a solution of a problem "emerges fully formed into consciousness without any prior attention to the problem". Benjamin Libet, one of the pioneers of research on unconscious cognitive processes, points out the significance of the unconscious for creativity:

> Creativity in general is almost certainly a function of unconscious or at least semiconscious mental processes. There are many anecdotal reports by great scientists of ideas for imaginative hypotheses of solutions to problems, which consciously appeared only after some period of unconscious incubation. (Libet 2004: 96)

Such was the case with Henri Poincaré, who, as Libet (2004: 96) notes, "was puzzled about how to solve a particularly difficult mathematical problem and, after some conscious mulling over the problem, he gave up on it. On a later trip to Lyon, the entire solution 'popped' into his consciousness just as he stepped off the bus. Clearly, a great deal of unconscious yet creative thinking had gone on to produce that solution."

The peculiar nature of this phenomenon, and the fact that it is at odds with the commonsense idea that it is "consciousness" that thinks, has led people in past centuries to attribute this type of insight to some kind of supernatural inspiration, be it divine or devious, implying that some supernatural agent puts certain ideas inside the human mind.

However, this mechanism does not merely apply to such special situations like moments of illumination. In fact, every thought, decision and impulse that becomes conscious is a result of prior mental operations at a non-conscious level. As Carruthers (2015: 173) sums up, "thoughts and images enter our minds and interrupt our reflections unbidden, seemingly appearing out of nowhere ... Ideas that appear seemingly from nowhere are really a result of unconscious decisions that resolve conflicts over the direction of attention or concerning what actions to rehearse".

Even such seemingly trivial mental events such as shifting our conscious attention to a new stimulus, such as an unexpected sound, are actually a result of evaluation and selection of competing stimuli which occurs on a non-conscious level, even though at the conscious level there is no knowledge of real reasons for the shift of attention. As Carruthers (2015: 237) points out, when a person suddenly becomes aware of the sound of one's own name in a crowded, noisy room, it is a result of an unconscious decision to shift the attention to the sound, but neither the decision nor the reasons why it was taken become conscious. The only thing the person is aware of is the sudden sound of one's own name.

Exactly the same mechanism applies to acts of conscious will and decision making. As S. M. Kosslyn (Libet, 2004: x) summarizes Libet's influential hypothesis, "being conscious of having made a decision might be best thought of as a result of brain processes that actually do the work, rather than as part of the causal chain of events leading up to a decision". Wegner (2002) claims that a consciously experienced feeling of volition is an epiphenomenon, lacking direct causative power which he ascribes to unconscious processes. In other words, at some moment one has the feeling of having taken a decision, but the actual processes that had led to its taking have already occurred on an unconscious level.[72]

What is the role of consciousness, then? While it is not that of actual cognizing in the sense of processing certain information, producing thoughts, solving cognitive problems and decision making, it is nonetheless very important. According to Baars and Franklin's (2007: 958) theory of "global workspace", consciousness makes information that was local and restricted to just one module, globally broadcast[73] to unconscious processors/modules throughout the whole cognitive system. Thus, the initial idea or impulse to act can be reflected upon, modified or rejected. In other words, information that is conscious becomes accessible to many different modules, including those

72 Unlike Bronkhorst (2012: 208–209), I do not believe that Wegner's hypothesis is seriously challenged by the role of conscious experience of pleasure and pain in our lives, or that its acceptance would make these conscious states irrelevant. By becoming conscious, pleasure and pain become globally available, including to those centres or modules which evaluate our potential courses of action and undertake decisions. Once they undertake (unconsciously) a decision, it is manifested as phenomenal conscious will within our phenomenal self-model (to use Metzinger's [2009] term) so that the combination of self-less processes may conceive of itself as a unified entity who is taking this decision (i.e., its agent and owner). Furthermore, consciousness and its contents strongly influence our decision making, although not directly, but by providing data based on which further decisions are taken. Thus, it can be said to be indirectly causally efficacious, and not just be a redundant epiphenomenon. The phenomenal feeling of conscious will in itself is often not synonymous with actually undertaking a particular act – by becoming conscious, it can then be further evaluated and eventually acted upon or not.

73 For various definitions of global availability/broadcasting see Metzinger (2003: 31), Siderits (2011: 325), and Carruthers (2015: 2).

responsible for speech, memory and movement. And indeed, what we are aware of, we can also remember, express through the medium of words and body movements, or introspect.

Contrary to commonly held views, thinking in the sense of solving cognitive problems does not happen through conscious thoughts, i.e., mental words through which we silently talk to ourselves.[74] Such thoughts may, however, carry with them the results of actual problem solving which occurs on a non-conscious level. Mercier and Sperber (2011) suggest that the role of conscious verbal thinking lies in rehearsing potential social situations which may require us to communicate verbally by speech.

Let us now return to the issue of meditative insight. We have mentioned Libet's view that creative insights sometimes occur in the most unexpected moments and that the generative phase of creativity is connected with a lack of conscious thinking about the problem, though usually such conscious thinking was necessary to initiate this phase at some point. Commenting on the same issue, Carruthers (2015: 169) has noted that "the generative phase of creativity results from decreased or defocused top-down attentional control" and that "alcohol increases creativity, sleepiness increases creativity; and being in a good or relaxed mood improves creativity". Bagassi and Macchi (2016: 58) suggest that "during incubation, when an overall spreading activation of implicit, unconscious knowledge is under way, in the absence of any form of conscious control, relevance constraint allows multilayered thinking to discover the solution".

It seems then, that the most crucial factors connected with the generative phase of creativity are the lack of active, problem directed conscious-thinking, absence of focused attentional control and relaxation accompanied by pleasure. All these features are to a various extent present in the meditative texts of Nikāya Buddhism and early Chan as characteristics of the proper form of meditation.[75]

---

74 Cf. Dijksterhuis et al. (2005: 81): "First of all, and strictly speaking, conscious thought does not exist. Thought when defined as producing meaningful associative consciousness, happens unconsciously. One may be aware of some elements of the thought process or one may be aware of a product of a thought process, but one is not aware of thought itself".

75 The texts of both traditions differ regarding the prominence of these particular factors. While the Nikāya texts speak more about bodily pleasure and rapture, Chan scriptures place more emphasis on lack of focused attentional control.

All these considerations about creativity and unconscious processing are highly relevant in the context of our discussion of Chan and Nikāya notions of insight. In light of these developments within the philosophy of mind and cognitive science, the idea of spontaneous insight occurring in a thought-less state without the need for a deliberate mental act does not seem inherently contradictory but in fact appears psychologically plausible. Furthermore, we have already noted some inherent difficulties connected with certain features of the mainstream paradigm of calm and insight which may suggest their psychological implausibility. Not only then is the idea of spontaneous insight occurring in a thought-less state of calm possible from a psychological point of view, it may be actually more plausible than the one present in the mainstream paradigm.

The no-mind

Certain Chan texts do not merely limit themselves to general statements about the original, pure and bright mind. Some contain statements which can be read as pertaining to a non-conscious and thought-less but creative layer of the mind. The concept of no-mind (*wuxin* 無心), or strictly speaking *wuxinxin* 無心心 (lit. "the mind of no-mind" i.e., the mind characterized by the quality of "no-mind", or "mind-less mind") is especially interesting in the context of our discussion and deserves particular attention. Probably the first usage of this term can be traced back to the writings of Sengzhao 僧肇 (374?–414) from the fourth century AD, long before the supposed introduction of Chan into China. According to Sengzhao, the mind of the saint reacts unerringly to all circumstances despite being "without knowing" (*wuzhi* 無知). In another place of the *Zhaolun* 肇論 (*The treatises of Zhao*), he explains that *wuxin* does not actually mean the absence of the mind, but simply the existence of "the mind of no-mind" (*wuxinxin* 無心心).[76] Sharf (2014a: 149) rightly notes that "while Sengzhao's writings are not always clear, ... there is little evidence that *wuxin* was understood as unconsciousness or insentience".

76 T45, no. 1858, p. 154b19–25: 難曰：聖心雖無知，然其應會之道不差。是以可應者應之，不可應者存之。然則聖心有時而生、有時而滅。可得然乎？答曰：生滅者，生滅心也。聖人無心，生滅焉起？然非無心，但是無心心耳。Cf. translation by Robinson (1976: 219).

Somewhat similar ideas are found in a much later *Wuxin lun* 無心論 (*Treatise on No-Mind*), a text attributed to Bodhidharma, but historically representative of the views of the Niutou school.[77] The treatise is similar to other works of that school, like the *Jueguan lun* 絕觀論 (*Treatise on Transcendence of Cognition*),[78] in that it contains paradoxical language and what McRae (1986: 42) describes as "extensive use of negation". The author of the *Wuxin lun* was most likely familiar with the above-mentioned writings of Seng Zhao as he also uses the term *wuxin xin*.[79] Initially, the term "no-mind" may suggest ordinary mindlessness, a sort of state similar to that of inanimate objects. However, the author of the *Wuxin lun* explains that "the mind of no-mind" (*wuxin xin* 無心心) is different from the trees and rocks (*butongmushi* 不同木石).[80] App (1995: 95, n. 119) comments that the expression *wuxin xin* "emphasizes that no-mind is not a simple absence of mind, thus contradicting interpretations of *wuxin* that equate it with simple absentmindedness or thoughtlessness". Quite the contrary, as despite being in the state of *wuxin xin* one is still able to see, hear, and feel and know[81] and to understand the real characteristics (*shixiang* 實相) of all the dharmas, one's threefold body is at ease (*zizai* 自在), and able to react (*yingyong* 應用) without obstruction (*wufang* 無妨). Therefore, the non-mind paradoxically turns out to be the "true mind" (*zhenxin* 真心).[82] From the commonsense point of view this fragment may appear meaningless or be considered a typical example of religious hyperbole and paradoxical language. However, when approached from the perspective of modern cognitive science and the philosophy of mind, it could in fact be read as referring to the type of concepts we have been discussing above. No-mind could therefore denote a sort of "cognitive unconscious", a spontaneous and creative layer of the mind, capable of operating without the mediation

77 See Adamek (2007: 409, n. 21).

78 Translation of the title follows Adamek (2007: 409, n. 21).

79 Cf. App (1995: 78).

80 T85, no. 2831, p. 1269c10: 答曰。而我無心心不同木石。App (1995: 95) translates this line as "Our mindless mind is not identical with trees or rocks".

81 T85, no. 2831, p. 1269a29–b1: 我雖無心能見能聞能覺能知。Cf. translation by App (1995: 95): "Though I have no mind, I can very well see and hear and feel and know".

82 T85, no. 2831, p. 1269c12–16: 雖復無心自然能作種種變現。而我無心亦復如是。雖復無心善能覺了諸法實相具真般若三身自在應用無妨。故寶積經云。以無心意而現行。豈同木石乎。夫無心者即真心也。Cf. translation by App (1995: 96–98).

of conscious thoughts. Of course, we cannot be certain whether this was the actual intention of the author of *Wuxin lun*, or whether the idea of *wuxin xin* is simply an example of a specific rhetoric of the Niutou school and was meant to convey a Buddhist concept that there is no fixed subject (I/self) of cognition.

The concept of no-thought (*wunian* 無念) was also not understood as referring to a comatose blank state but implied retaining sensory activity. In the *Tanyu*, Shenhui claims that if one sees (*jian* 見) no-thought, then although entirely possessing seeing, hearing, sensing and cognition (*jianwenjuezhi* 見聞覺知), one will be constantly empty and serene.[83] In other place, he claims that, seeing no-thought equals the six senses being without defilement (*wuran* 無染).[84]

A similar reading may be offered for the fragment of the *Lidai fabao ji* in which Wuzhu states that no-thought (*wunian* 無念) is mental brilliance (*congming* 聰明), while thinking (*younian* 有念) is dullness (*andun* 暗鈍).[85] This would harmonize with the already discussed concepts of unconscious creativity and of the limited role of conscious verbal thoughts. Of course, just as in the case of *Wuxin lun*, we might be dealing here with a specific form of paradoxical rhetoric of which the author of the *Lidai fabao ji* seems to be particularly fond, and which involves reinterpreting various concepts in a very specific way. In the case of such a reading, the concept of *wunian* would be pretty much devoid of any actual psychological meaning.

Interestingly, the term *wuxin* also appears in the *Rudao anxin yao fangbian famen*. The text speaks about the body of Dharma nature (*faxingshen* 法性身), which is able to manifest (*xian* 現) all sorts of phenomena but makes them arise (*qizuo* 起作) in a no-mind (*wuxin* 無心) way. This is then compared to a crystal mirror (*polijing* 頗梨鏡) hanging in the hall, which is also able to reflect all kinds of images, despite being of "no-mind" (*wuxin*).[86] In this text, *wuxin* seems to refer to a mode of

---

83 B25, no. 142, p. 23a1–2: 若見無念者，雖具見聞覺知，而常空寂. Cf. translation by McRae (2023: 61). I read 見聞覺知 as corresponding to the tetrad of *diṭṭha, suta, muta, viññāta*, instead of McRae's rendering as "perceptive functions are operating".

84 B25, no. 142, p. 91a8.

85 T51, no. 2075, p. 192a1: 無念即聰明。有念是暗鈍。Translation by Adamek (2007: 377).

86 T85, no. 2837, p. 1287b2–3: 而法性身。無心起作。如頗梨鏡懸在高堂。一切像悉於中現。鏡亦無心。能現種種。Cf. Chappell (1983: 109) and Van Schaik (2018: 156) for translations of this fragment. The metaphor of the mirror of

functioning which does not require conscious intention but is efficient and unimpeded in its reactions to circumstances. The metaphors of inanimate objects that nonetheless are able to respond to changes in the environment and perform certain functions are also used in the *Wuxin lun*, which compares *wuxin xin* with "a celestial drum (*tiangu* 天鼓) which, though just lying there without mind, by itself emits various wondrous teachings" and with a "wish-fulfilling gem (*yizhu* 意珠) that, though also without mind, is by nature able to produce a variety of different apparitions".[87] It seems that the usage of these particular metaphors by the authors of the *Wuxin lun* and *Rudao anxin yao fangbian famen* is meant to convey a notion of efficient functioning and responding to the environment without the need for conscious intention or being phenomenally conscious. Such a notion is of course very much in harmony with some trends in modern philosophy of mind.

Another very interesting fragment which deserves our attention may be found in the *Xiuxin yao lun*, where Hongren proclaims that true learning occurs through an unconditioned, spontaneous (*wuwei* 無為) mind, but ultimately nothing is learned (*jingwusuoxue* 竟無所學).[88] This seemingly paradoxical statement agrees with the important notions of implicit learning and tacit knowledge present in contemporary cognitive science.[89] However, the explanation of this statement offered immediately afterwards in the *Xiuxin yao lun* does not directly support such a reading, nor does it really help to clarify the meaning of the fragment.[90]

---

the mind was more prevalent in Chinese thought as evidenced by the notion of *dayuan jingzhi* 大圓鏡智 (great perfect mirror wisdom) as found in Xuanzang's 玄奘 (602–664) *Cheng weishi lun* 成唯識論.

87 T85, no. 2831, p. 1269c11–13: 譬如天鼓。雖復無心自然出種種妙法教化眾生。又如如意珠。雖復無心自然能作種種變現。而我無心亦復如是。Translation by App (1995: 95–96).

88 McRae (1986: 433/七): 無為心中學得者此是真學。雖言真學竟無所學。Cf. T48, no. 2011, p. 378a7–8. Cf. translation by McRae (1986: 126): "True learning is that which is learned by the inactive (or unconditioned, *wu-wei*) mind, which never ceases correct mindfulness. Although this is called 'true learning', ultimately there is nothing to be learned".

89 These concepts were first popularized by Reber (1996) in his book *Implicit Learning and Tacit Knowledge: An Essay on the Cognitive Unconscious*.

90 McRae (1986: 433/七): 何以故。我及涅槃二皆空故。更無二無一。故無所學。Cf. T48, no. 2011, p. 378a8–10. McRae (1986: 126) translates it as: "Why is this? Because the self and nirvana are both nonsubstantial, they are neither different nor the same. Therefore, the essential principle of [the words] 'nothing to be learned' is true".

The abovementioned fragments can all be read as expressions of an original concept of the mind which agrees in some important respects with recent developments in cognitive science. If this was indeed the meaning intended by the authors of these texts, then it was at odds with the commonsense beliefs regarding human psychology and contained many seemingly paradoxical elements. Therefore, it was necessary for Chan authors to develop a new language and terminology to express this new and difficult concept. It has to be said, however, that the fragments we have been analysing so far do not contain a uniform terminology. Texts associated with the Niutou school, such as the *Jueguan lun* and the *Wuxin lun*, use the term "no-mind" (*wuxin*), with reference to the mode of cognition not requiring the mediation of a conscious, discriminating mind. Thus, the *Jueguan lun* identifies having a thought with having a mind (*younianjiyouxin* 有念即有心), and the latter is considered synonymous with violating the Way (*youxinjiguaidao* 有心即乖道).[91] The other texts, however, try to maintain a distinction between negatively evaluated conscious, volitional thinking (*nian* 念) and a positively evaluated mind (*xin* 心) in the more general sense. In these texts, thought is not identified with the mind as it is merely its specific product resultant from its arousing or activation (*qi* 起).

Such an interpretation also allows us to better understand the difference between a positively evaluated state of mental calm and absence of thought on the one hand and mere insentience or mindlessness on the other. It seems that for Chan authors, lack of activation or movement of the mind was by no means synonymous with a state of mental stasis akin to a coma. Quite the contrary, it meant that the mind was functioning in its natural state, and its inherent intelligence was not inhibited by the presence of conscious thought. On the other hand, the criticized methods of calm meditation were supposed to lead to the blockage of mental activity by active, forceful suppression. From the point of view of Chan authors this was synonymous with the obstruction of the original pure mind and of its inherent wisdom. It is possible to show antecedents of this view in the early Buddhist texts. The Nikāyas criticize the forceful methods used by the Bodhisatta to "restrain the mind with the mind" and the meditative insentience taught by the brahmin Pārāsariya.

---

91 B18, no. 101, p. 693a16–b2: 問曰、若非心念、當何以念。答曰、有念即有心、有心即乖道。無念即無心、無心即真道。Cf. translation by McRae (1983: 211–12).

If this was indeed the philosophical backdrop of Chan meditative ideas, then it makes the constant criticisms of "activation" or arousing of the mind (*qixin*) present in Chan texts more understandable. While we have already noted several such fragments, they are much more ubiquitous in Tang period Chan literature. For example, the *Liuzu tanjing* redefines "seating" (*zuo* 坐) as a lack of activation of thought (*shangnianbuqi* 上念不起) with regard to all external objects (*jingjie* 境界).[92] Furthermore, this helps explain why the lack of mental activation could be considered an aim in itself. The *Dasheng wusheng fangbian men* contains a statement that the lack of mental activation (*xinbuqixin* 心不起心) is synonymous with the mind achieving true thusness (s. *tathātā*, c. *zhenru* 真如).[93] According to another fragment of the same text, the very lack of movement of the mind is in itself not merely equal to *samādhi* but to wisdom as well.[94] In yet another place we read that, when in reference to the eye seeing a shape (*yanjianse* 眼見色) there is no arousing of the mind (*xinbuqi* 心不起), it is a fundamental wisdom (*genbenzhi* 根本智). The text later describes this form of cognition as "spontaneous seeing" (*jianzizai* 見自在), which is synonymous with obtaining wisdom/knowledge (*dezhi* 得智).[95] Such notions can be seen as paralleling, to a certain extent, the idea of a released way of the functioning of the senses implied by the *Indriyabhāvanā-sutta* and the *Mahātaṇhāsaṅkhāya-sutta*.

Revisiting the Nikāya formulations of insight

At this point, it is worthwhile to return to the Nikāya formulations of liberating insight. While we have pointed out certain early Buddhist fragments which can be read as implying the notion of spontaneous insight in the state of deep mental calm, it needs to be said that there are many formulas which when taken at face value appear to express

---

92 T48, no. 2007, p. 339a3–5: 何名坐禪？此法門中，一切無礙，外於一切境界上念不起為坐。Cf. translation by Yampolsky (1967: 140).

93 T85, no. 2834, p. 1273c20: 心不起心真如。Cf. translation by McRae (1986: 174): "If the mind does not activate, the mind is suchlike".

94 T85, no. 2834, p. 1274b25–26: 問是沒是不動　答心不動心不動是定是智是理。Cf. translation by McRae (1986: 180): "The motionlessness of the mind is meditation, is wisdom, is the absolute (*li*)".

95 T85, no. 2834, p. 1275b20–21: 眼見色心不起是根本智。見自在是後得智。Cf. translation by McRae (1986: 185).

the notion of insight as a separate, deliberate mental activity undertaken after an attainment of a concentrated state. Among the terms that express this notion are: "understands as it really is" (*yathābhūtaṃ pajānāti*), "directs and bends the mind towards knowledge and vision" (*ñāṇadassanāya cittaṃ abhinīharati abhininnāmeti*) (e.g., DN 2/i.76), "reflects" (*paṭisañcikkhati*) that something is made up/constructed (*abhisaṅkhata*) and willed (*abhisañcetayita*: e.g., MN 52/i.350) or "regards/ contemplates (*samanupassati*) something as impermanent" (e.g., AN 9.36/iv.423). When read directly, these formulas may be interpreted as presenting insight as a form of deliberate mental activity undertaken after an attainment of a meditative state, but also expressing in various ways the content of the supposed liberating insight. This content may be constituted by an understanding (*pajānāti*) that one's consciousness (*viññāṇa*) is bound up with the body which is impermanent and conditioned in various ways (e.g., DN 2/i.76),[96] or by an understanding of how it really is (*yathābhūtaṃ pajānāti*) the nature of suffering, its origin, cessation and way leading to cessation, or of the influxes (*āsava*) in an analogous fourfold way (DN 2/i.93–84). The content of insight may also consist of the understanding of a constructed and intentioned character of a particular meditative state,[97] or of the contemplation of the impermanence, not-self nature and suffering characterizing its factors (*dhamma*).[98]

Such formulas are more frequent than the ones that may be read as pertaining to spontaneous insight. However, according to Wynne (2018a: 77), "the apparent ubiquity of calm and insight in early Buddhist discourses is an illusion ... created by a very small number of teachings repeated again and again in the canonical Suttas" while "all calm-insight soteriologies are based on the same model of mind, derived from the early Upaniṣads, which was not found in the earliest phase of Buddhist activity". Wynne (2018a: 87) also suggests that in some vitally

96 DN 2/i.76: *so evaṃ pajānāti – 'ayaṃ kho me kāyo rūpī cātumahābhūtiko mātāpettikasambhavo odanakummāsūpacayo aniccucchādana-parimaddana-bhedana-viddhaṃsana-dhammo; idañca pana me viññāṇaṃ ettha sitaṃ ettha paṭibaddhan'ti.*

97 MN 52/i.350: *idampi paṭhamaṃ jhānaṃ abhisaṅkhataṃ abhisañcetayitaṃ. yaṃ kho pana kiñci abhisaṅkhataṃ abhisañcetayitaṃ tadaniccaṃ nirodhadhamman'ti pajānāti.*

98 AN 9.36/iv.423: *bhikkhu ... paṭhamaṃ jhānaṃ upasampajja viharati. so yadeva tattha hoti rūpagataṃ vedanāgataṃ saññāgataṃ saṅkhāragataṃ viññāṇagataṃ, te dhamme aniccato dukkhato rogato gaṇḍato sallato aghato ābādhato parato palokato suññato anattato samanupassati.*

important early teachings the practice of non-conceptual mindfulness understood as bare cognition occupied the decisive stages of the path rather than calm-insight practices.

Regardless of whether this was indeed the case, it is interesting from a philosophical point of view to consider various possible interpretations of the abovementioned formulas. The first, probably most straightforward possibility, is that the formulas intend to convey a certain instruction which needs to be implemented, i.e., they tell the practitioners that they should perform a deliberate conscious act of directing their mind to some truth or reflecting on it. Not only do these instructions tell the meditators that they should undertake a practice of some sort of deliberate, conscious understanding or reflection but they also instruct them regarding what truth exactly should be contemplated or reflected upon.

According to the second interpretation, the formulas of the content of liberating insight are phenomenological accounts which express from a first-person subjective perspective what is experienced by the meditators, i.e., the content of their experiences, e.g., the knowledge of a constructed character of a particular state, consciousness of impermanence of a certain mental factor, or the understanding of the four noble truths. In other words, a formula may convey that at the moment of insight one suddenly becomes aware of the four noble truths which present themselves to consciousness. What is uncertain is whether the formulas are direct accounts of the contents of the mind of a meditator or merely their approximations. Another difference between the first and second interpretation is that, according to the former, a meditator proactively generates and applies a certain understanding, while according to the latter, this understanding emerges in the mind by itself. What is somewhat problematic with the first and second interpretation is that the various Nikāya formulas of supposed insight practice and their purported content are essentially different from one another. This would imply that liberation can occur through various alternative forms of insight and result in different realizations.

The third interpretation is the least straightforward, as it assumes that the formulas are neither normative instructions nor first-person phenomenological descriptions, but functional accounts which focus on the role and effect of a performed cognitive act. In order to better explain the idea of functional explanation, let us consider the following example. Suppose one is trying to understand some practical mathematical formula or a theorem. What are the criteria for establishing that one has successfully understood it? According to a functional perspective, it is not any internal, introspectable feeling of having understood, but rather the practical ability to solve a particular mathematical equation. The actual cognitive process of understanding may occur unconsciously and may not have anything to do with conscious attempts to understand a particular formula. Such an interpretation is connected with a particular understanding of the cognitive nature of liberating insight. It draws on the already mentioned developments in cognitive science and philosophy of mind. Particularly relevant for this case is the following hypothesis by Hassin:

> It seems that the processes that yield insights do not require conscious awareness. ... These findings seem to suggest that insights tend to pop up in awareness without prior conscious evidence for their formation. (Hassin 2005: 204)

Hassin (2005: 205–15) claims that in a series of studies and experiments he was able to establish together with his colleagues the existence of insights which occur not only in the absence of conscious awareness of the processes that lead to them, but also in the absence of the conscious awareness of the insights themselves. If we tentatively apply Hassin's concept of unconscious insight to the ideas found in the Nikāyas, then this would imply that there was no explicit content of liberating insight, as it was tacit. When discussing possible conceptualizations of the highest goal in early Buddhism, Bronkhorst (2019: 3) makes a distinction between intellectual knowledge, mystical insight resulting from absorption, and psychological transformation. The textual evidence we have been considering so far does not seem to support the first option. But what about the latter two? If we understand insight in the common sense as resulting in declarative, explicit knowledge, then these two alternatives are indeed, as Bronkhorst claims, difficult or impossible to harmonize. However, if we understand insight along the lines of Hassin's concept, then it no longer needs to be seen as being at odds with the idea of psychological transformation.

In such a case, we could however still expect that there would be a new transformed way of cognizing and functioning resulting from the insight, which could be reflected upon.[99] It also does not preclude that immediately after this transformation there may have been an awareness that some irreversible change has occurred. Therefore, if there was

99 Cf. Shulman (2014: 40): "The possibility remains that a full verbal account of the events is part of the post-meditation process of reflection".

liberating knowledge, it was tacit knowledge resultant from implicit learning, if we were to use the terms introduced by Reber (1996).

By reflecting upon one's new form of mental functioning one could reach certain conclusions about the nature of insight which had occurred earlier. The formulas of insight would therefore represent different attempts at expressing the same psychological mechanism. By their very nature they would be merely imperfect verbal approximations of what was realized during the insight, reflecting intellectual, historical and social conditions of northeastern India in the middle of the millennium BC as well as the specific psychological features of the persons who created them. It is possible that these post-hoc, verbally expressed approximations of the nature of transformation that had occurred were confused at some point in Buddhist history with the actual transformative cognitive act. This would result in identifying liberating insight with an act of deliberate, conscious maintenance of a certain discursive Buddhist truth. The concept of such an insight would of course be psychologically implausible, in the sense that it could not produce any significant psychological transformation. That is not to say that deliberate acts of consciously thinking some Buddhist truths are not very useful at the earlier stages of practice, i.e., that of the right effort. We shall return to this issue in Chapter 6.

The value of such an interpretation lies in the fact that it allows one to see seemingly irreconcilable differences between different forms of insight, as merely different approximations of the same transformative cognitive event. It also harmonizes with the insistence on the ineffability of the ultimate truth found in many places in the Nikāyas. Such an interpretation also makes the early Buddhist position similar to the one found in Chan texts. It needs to be honestly said, however, that such an interpretation cannot be proven with certainty and is only a possibility that can be considered.

We have briefly commented on the connection between the fourth *jhāna* and insight in several Nikāya texts. What needs to be considered is whether the attainment of this state according to these texts[100] would be a sufficient condition for the occurrence of insight in the sense of a fundamental inner transformation resulting in a different mode of cognizing and functioning. The view of the fourth *jhāna* as a sufficient

100 E.g., the suttas following a *Sāmaññaphala* pattern. As we have already noted, this position cannot be generalized to the whole Nikāyas, as there are several texts that do not ascribe any special status to the fourth *jhāna*.

condition for liberating insight must be clearly distinguished from the view that such an insight is merely possible in the state of the fourth *jhāna* or that the latter state is very conducive to such insight. The Nikāya texts in themselves do not provide enough evidence in this regard. However, from the perspective of cognitive science, any fundamental change of mental functioning such as Buddhist liberating insight would need to be correlated with certain changes in the brain. These changes would probably need to be structural, were they to be permanent. The occurrence of such changes may not follow simple rules and may be dependent on various factors. Therefore, it is conceivable that there would not be a direct and simple overlap between achievement of the fourth *jhāna* and transforming insight.[101] The standard Nikāya account might be just a reflection of one specific personal experience of life-transforming insight (perhaps of the Buddha himself). We shall return to the question of irregularity and implicit logic of insight in Chapter 8.

The liberating insight spoken about in the Nikāya texts is supposed to result in permanent psychological transformation of a human being. According to the formula of the four noble truths, this occurs by an elimination of craving/thirst (*taṇhā*) which is the cause of our suffering (*dukkha*). So far, we have only argued in favour of the possibility of transformative insight occurring spontaneously within a deep meditative state such as the fourth *jhāna* without the need for any active and deliberately undertaken form of conceptual analysis. However, this does not explain what psychological mechanism causes the elimination of desire. Historically dominant Buddhist interpretation is that seeing reality in its raw, naked form as impermanent (*anicca*),

101 That is, unless the transition from the third to the fourth *jhāna* was in itself a result of some fundamental but tacit transformative insight. Some features of this state, such as abandoning (*pahāna*) of pleasure (*sukha*) and pain (*dukkha*), subsiding (*atthaṅgama*) of mental satisfaction and dissatisfaction (*somanassa-domanassa*) and purity of mindfulness by equanimity could be interpreted as indications that some fundamental transformation has already occurred. In light of such an understanding, the subsequent acts of "directing" the mind towards various knowledges, including knowledge of the destruction of the influxes, would not be active cognitive transformative processes, but would be merely revealing the knowledge resultant of the processes that had already occurred. Bronkhorst (2012: 160) explains the mechanism leading to the disappearance of pleasure in the fourth *jhāna* in the context of his theory of tension; what causes us to feel pleasure is a decrease of tension. This reduction reaches its maximum level in the third *jhāna* and stabilizes itself, which in turns causes one to stop experiencing pleasure as there is no further decrease of tension.

full of suffering (*dukkha*) and not-self (*anattā*) results in disenchantment (*nibbida*) towards it, which further causes exhaustion of craving (*taṇhākkhaya*) and dispassion (*virāga*). This concept has its Nikāya basis in the texts such as the already mentioned *Jhāna-sutta* (AN 9.36/iv.422–426). In the *Visuddhimagga* (e.g., Vism ii.276/639/XXI.1) it is elaborated further into several stages of insight-knowledge concerning the negative aspects of conditioned experience, such as the knowledge of the contemplation of dissolution (*bhaṅgānupassanā-ñāṇa*), the knowledge of fearsome appearance (*bhayatūpaṭṭhāna-ñāṇa*) or the knowledge of contemplation of danger (*ādīnavānupassanā-ñāṇa*).

Bronkhorst (2012; 2019; 2023) has offered an alternative hypothesis regarding the psychological mechanism by which desire (or craving, depending on the translation of *taṇhā*) may be eliminated. Bronkhorst (2019: 4) believes that even mystical insight involving less interpreted awareness "will leave the person essentially as she was before" and "cannot be claimed to destroy attachments and put an end to suffering" which in the Nikāyas corresponds to the exhaustion of the influxes (*āsava*). We suffer and desire because of having particular habits, compulsions and addictions. These result from unconscious mental contents, so-called "knots" in the implicit system and in particular from emotional memory traces and associated urges. Only through their alteration or disentanglement can the *āsava*s be destroyed, and our personality permanently changed. However, in an ordinary state of awareness we have no direct access to these unconscious contents. Such access may only be provided in the state of deep absorption (Bronkhorst 2023: 12), especially the fourth *jhāna* which can bring hidden memories to consciousness. Drawing on Freudian psychoanalysis and recent research on mechanisms of memory, Bronkhorst suggests that activating (i.e., making conscious) the memory traces lying at the base of "our automatized emotionally charged responses" opens the possibility of modifying these responses into a form that will no longer bring about our suffering (e.g., responses such as desire, hate or fear). The key mechanism here is that of "memory reconsolidation"; once a memory trace is activated (i.e., made conscious) during absorption, this opens up a window of reconsolidation, when the trace is labile and may be even permanently erased, freeing us from an important source of suffering (Bronkhorst 2023: 9). A key condition for this is that of "mismatch or prediction error", i.e., that activated memory is not met with the expected response to which we have been conditioned in the past (e.g., desire towards some object). Thus, the old, automatized reaction that used to cause our suffering can be removed together with the associated memory trace which will result in having a neutral attitude to this kind of stimulus from now on.

What makes the fourth *jhāna* particularly conducive to this process is that, according to Bronkhorst (2012), it is a state of low bodily tension and strong concentration which allows the hidden memory trace to manifest, and that it is a state of equanimity which enables "prediction error", i.e., non-emotional reaction to the stimulus as opposed to an emotional one, typical of our previous, conditioned responses (Bronkhorst 2023: 14). According to Bronkhorst (2012: 149), another very important feature of *jhāna* state which makes it crucial for psychological transformation is the specific type of pleasure it brings. We shall return to this issue in Chapter 4.

Bronkhorst's theory certainly represents the most detailed, in-depth attempt at explaining the mechanism of psychological transformation in early Buddhism so far, which furthermore appears plausible from a scientific point of view. It comes at a price, however, as it entails an acceptance of a claim that "the early Buddhist tradition preserves materials that it does not always understand" (Bronkhorst 2019: 14). Many Nikāya concepts of central importance play no role whatsoever in Bronkhorst's theory. These include the transformative value of insights into impermanence, self-lessness and dependent origination, none of which appear to be directly influencing the process proposed by Bronkhorst. Of course, it is possible that all these elements represent later additions to the Nikāyas, absent in the earliest doctrine or functioning in purely theoretical, non-transformative contexts. However, there seems to be no evidence for such a claim. Another issue is the exact procedure by which one is supposed to use the jhānic state to reveal the unconscious knots/emotional memory traces. Does Bronkhorst's hypothesis assume that at some point while being in the fourth *jhāna* one intentionally directs attention to particular problematic memories, thereby volitionally initiating this process? It may be possible, given the presence of the already mentioned statements about the practitioner bending and directing the mind towards the knowledge of exhaustion of the influxes. Bronkhorst (2012: 134) describes it as follows: "Urges will announce themselves as feelings if and when the mind, in this concentrated state, imagines an object or event related to them and thus activates the relevant trace unit ... He repeats the process with respect to all of his urges, one after the other". Would the deeply altered state of fourth *jhāna* still allow undertaking such volitionally initiated activities as deliberate imagining? This also seems to imply the presence of active thinking which would be needed to direct the whole process, similarly to psychoanalysis. Or is the process more passive and the *āsavas* just spontaneously manifest in consciousness and one simply becomes aware of them in an equanimous manner?

The latter interpretation would not be at odds with the notion of spontaneous, tacit transformative insight I have proposed. I have pointed to eureka moments as paradigmatic examples of unconscious insights. However, for eureka moments to occur, a certain amount of conscious occupation with the cognitive problem that needs to be solved is required beforehand. The functional significance of information being made conscious lies in making it globally accessible throughout the cognitive system to various modules which will work upon it but would otherwise have no access to it. The same can be the case with influxes as understood by Bronkhorst. As long as they are unconscious, the modules responsible for analysing, learning and implementing changes simply have no access to them and therefore cannot do anything about them. The process of destroying the influxes need not be conceptualized as requiring any conscious, deliberate effort or method, as it is exactly by not following through on the impulses that their underlying sources are disentangled. It is doubtful that a practitioner in the state of the fourth *jhāna* would need to make an intention or an effort in order to try to bring the "knots" to consciousness or even be able to volitionally do so. Becoming aware of the impulses but not acting upon them may correspond to what in the Nikāyas is expressed through the noun *upekkhā* or the verb *upekkhati*, which may mean "to look on (without involvement or reaction or action)".[102] As Wynne (2007: 107) has convincingly shown, *upekkhā* is not some neither pleasant nor painful feeling, but "means to be aware of something and indifferent to it". Such understanding implies a passive nature of *upekkhā*; it is not an attitude one can actively maintain.

Bronkhorst (2019: 11) brings attention to research about body memory which focuses on "the role the body plays in maintaining and giving expression to the accumulated habits and compulsions that make up what we are". According to the stock passage found in the *Sāmaññaphala-sutta* (DN 2/i.75–76), in the fourth *jhāna* the meditator is said to sit "having pervaded (*pharitvā*) the body (*kāya*) with a clear and bright mind" (*parisuddhena cetasā pariyodātena*), so that no spot of

102 Cone (2001: 488).

the whole body is left unpervaded. The text seems to consider "pervading with the clear and bright mind" as synonymous to "pervading with equanimity".[103] The influxes would then manifest against the backdrop of somatic sensations. Such an understanding would be in harmony with Wynne's (2018a) interpretation of *upekkhāsatipārisuddhi* as bare cognition, i.e., passive awareness of the sensory and somatic roots of experience. This form of equanimous cognition would correspond to *kāyagatāsati*, i.e., mindfulness "gone" to the body (MN 119/iii.94). It needs to be underlined here, though, that several Nikāya texts give an impression that at the earlier, pre-jhānic stages of the practice, mindfulness is an active process which involves a strong conceptual component.

Although the general mechanism of psychological transformation proposed by Bronkhorst seems to be very plausible, one has to wonder whether in the Nikāya context it would involve dealing with many different suppressed urges and desires similar to the ones discussed by Freud, which are specific to a particular person and representative of their unique personal experiences. For example, in the fourth *jhāna*, would one be confronted with various repressed memories such as those of being sexually abused in childhood, or other painful events which gave rise to some automatisms? If this was the case, then the Nikāyas failed to preserve that meaning, unless we assume that *sati* in the third and the fourth *jhāna* should be literally understood as memory and not mindfulness.[104] The Nikāyas rather give the impression that the *āsavas* represent some very basic psychological mechanism universal to all humans, expressed by terms such as sensuality (*kāma*), grasping (*upādāna*), or becoming (*bhava*). Due to its fundamental character, in normal states of consciousness it is probably obscured by more gross mental states. In the state such as the fourth *jhāna*, it could perhaps be laid bare and thus made available to various modules responsible for learning and implementing changes into memory and behaviour. If the destructive nature of this mechanism could become evident, the modules would perhaps be able to respond by nipping it in the bud,

103 This reading is also supported by an analysis of the *Dhātuvibhaṅga-sutta* (MN 140/iii.238–247) and its parallel MĀ 162 at T01, no. 26, pp. 690a20–692b2. Cf. Polak (2022: 135–36).

104 Or that the notion of "knowledge of remembrance of one's previous lives" (*pubbenivāsānussatiñāṇa*) is actually a warped representation of such memories. However, there is hardly any evidence in the Nikāyas which would allow one to seriously consider such a possibility.

just as one automatically draws back one's hand when touching a hot object. I shall return to this problem in Chapter 4, where I will attempt to formulate a theory of transformative insight which would harmonize some of Bronkhorst's key insights with the Nikāya concepts of not-self and cessation.

Finally, it needs to be said that the Chan notion of the "originally pure mind" is not entirely in harmony with the contemporary concept of a "cognitive unconscious". In the case of the former, the mere absence of thoughts reveals a perfect, enlightened mind. The latter, while capable of quick and complex cognitive operations, is still characterized by many features that result from its evolution and would be negatively evaluated from the Buddhist point of view, such as desire or various cognitive biases.[105] Some intuitions found in Chan texts may be therefore considered to be somewhat one-sided and underdeveloped from a philosophical point of view. What also differentiates the Chan approach from the Nikāyas is the general lack of consideration of the transformative effects of meditative wisdom. Chan texts simply emphasize the existence of wisdom in a concentrated state, but hardly offer any details about its function. This is just one example of a more general feature of the texts of this tradition, namely that unlike the Nikāyas they do not purport to provide exhaustive and comprehensive accounts of the whole path to liberation, but instead focus on its particular features. As we shall see in the following chapters, Chan can be seen more as a discourse directed against various limitations and forms of one-sidedness connected with the mainstream paradigm of meditation.

105 Bronkhorst (2019: 11) rightly notes that "this implicit system has aspects that are less attractive. Even so-called healthy people have ingrained habits and compulsions, even addictions, in the face of which they are quite helpless".

Chapter 3

THE WORLD OF EXPERIENCE

Antirealism in early Chan texts[1]

In several Chan texts the issue of activation or arousal (*qi* 起) of the mind is not merely presented in psychological terms as it also seems to possess profound ontological and soteriological consequences. In Shenhui's *Wenda zazheng yi*, we find a statement that it is only due to the arousal of the mind (*xinqi* 心起) that birth and death (*shengmie* 生滅) follow.[2] In other place, Shenhui proclaims that, what is called characteristics (*xiang* 相)[3] is actually a deluded mind (*wangxin* 妄心).[4]

The notion that even the most fundamental elements of reality as we experience them are dependent on various mental factors is present in several early Chan texts. According to the *Dasheng kaixin xianxing dunwu zhenzong lun* 大乘開心顯性頓悟真宗論 (*Treatise on the True Principle of Opening the Mind and Manifesting the [Buddha]-nature in Sudden Enlightenment [according to] the Mahāyana*),[5] seeing, hearing, knowing and the four elements all possess intrinsic-nature (lit. self-nature *zixing* 自性 s. *svabhāva*), which originates from the deluded mind (*wangxin* 妄心).[6] In the already mentioned fragment of the *Lidai fabao ji*, Wuzhu

1 This chapter contains certain claims that have already appeared, though not in an identical form, in Polak (2023a) and Polak (2023b).

2 B25, no. 143, p. 237a4: 只由心起故，遂有生滅。McRae (2023: 161) renders *shengmie* as "generation and extinction".

3 I.e., various worldly features and qualities (s. *lakṣaṇa/nimitta*).

4 B25, no. 142, p. 28a11: 所言『相』者，並是妄心。

5 Translation of the title follows McRae (1987: 239). As McRae (1987: 239) has noted, this text was connected with the Northern School of Chan, but also contains Shenhui's influence.

6 T85, no. 2835, p. 1278b21–23問曰。云何自性　答曰。見聞覺知四大及一切法等各有自性　問曰。自性從何而生　答曰。從妄心生。For a translation of this fragment, see McRae (1987: 242–43).

claims that arousing the mind (*qixin* 起心) is precisely birth and death (*shengsi* 生死).[7] In other fragments of the same text, we read that "thinking (*younian* 有念) is birth and death",[8] while a "verbal explanation (*yanshuo* 言說) is the origin of the three Worlds (*sanjieben* 三界本)", flux and change (*bianyi* 變異).[9] According to Zongmi's *Yuanjuejing dashu shiyi chao*, the representatives of the Baotang school considered "all wheel turning in the rebirth process" (i.e., *saṃsāra*: *shengsilunzhuan* 生死輪轉) to be arousing/activation of the mind (*qixin* 起心), which in itself is deluded (*wang* 妄).[10] Heshang Moheyan's statement that "the root of the wheel of birth and death in the world is the discriminating mind" is also noteworthy in this context.[11] It shows far reaching similarities to the position of the Baotang school and is almost identical to the statements of Wuzhu in the *Lidai fabao ji*.

Very similar ideas are contained in the texts connected with the Honghzhou school. In the *Tiansheng guangdeng lu*, Mazu proclaims that one thought of deluded ideation (*yinianwangxiang* 一念妄想) is the root of birth, death and of the three realms of existence (*sanjieshengsigenben* 三界生死根本).[12] In the *Baizhang huaihai chanshi guanglu* we read that none of the dharmas (*fa* 法) arise by themselves (*buzisheng* 不自生), but they all exist (*you* 有) due to one thought of deluded ideation (*yinianwangxiang* 一念妄想) which wrongly grasps the characteristics of things (*quxiang* 取相).[13]

Some of the above statements could be read as implying idealist metaphysics. However, such a position clearly cannot be generalized to all early Chan texts. Let us consider, for example, the following statement attributed to Mazu in the *Zongjing lu*:

> Whenever you perceive external forms, they are all perception of the mind. The mind, however, does not exist in and of itself: it is because

7 T51, no. 2075, p. 193b15: 起心即是生死。Translation follows Adamek (2007: 387).

8 T51, no. 2075, p. 191c29: 有念是生死。

9 T51, no. 2075, p. 191c21–23: 和上說云。非是涅槃經。此並是言說。言說三界本。真實滅苦因。言說即變異。真是離文字。For a translation of this and the abovementioned passage, see Adamek (2007: 377).

10 X09, no. 245, p. 534a13–14: 意謂生死輪轉。都為起心。起心即妄。For translation see Broughton (2009: 183).

11 Cf. Gómez (1983: 107–108).

12 X78, no. 1553, p. 449a1–2: 一念妄想。即是三界生死根本。

13 X69, no. 1323, p. 8a1–2: 但了諸法不自生。皆從自己一念妄想顛倒取相而有。Cf. translation by Poceski (2007: 162).

> of external forms that there is mind. The forms do not exist of themselves: it is because of mind that there are forms.[14]

Mazu's statement cannot be interpreted as straightforward idealism, since the mind does not exist in and of itself (*xinbuzixin* 心不自心) but is said to exist "because of forms" (*yinsegu* 因色故). It is therefore safer to characterize the position of the Chan authors as antirealist in a very general sense. According to this type of philosophy, it is impossible to speak of the world in total independence of the individual who experiences it. The character of some of its most fundamental elements and features is dependent on our cognitive structure and mental processes.

Of course, these notions are by no means an original creation of early Chan authors, as they are mostly derived from earlier Mahāyāna sutras which they often quote, and to various extents reflect the ideas of Madhyamaka, Yogācāra and Tathāgatagarbha. Nonetheless, their mode of presentation in Chan texts displays some features that are specific to this school.

The world of human experience: antirealism in early Buddhist texts

Chan meditative ideas are grounded in an entirely different philosophy than that of classical Theravāda. According to the latter school's doctrine there exist objective, ultimate (*paramattha*) irreducible components of reality, i.e., the *dhammas*. The objective structure of reality can be adequately represented in language, and there is hardly any explicit awareness of its limits within Theravāda. Even *nibbāna* is a dhamma which can be taken by the mind as an object.

However, as recent critical research by several scholars has shown,[15] there exists at least a substantial stratum of Nikāya texts which contain views of a very different kind. It needs to be said that, similarly to Chan texts, the Nikāyas do not contain a systematic, exhaustive and direct presentation of philosophical doctrines. Nonetheless, early Buddhist soteriological statements are grounded in philosophical ideas which can be inferred and reconstructed.

Of particular importance for understanding these ideas is a very specific notion of the world (*loka*) present in the Nikāyas. According to

14 T48, no. 2016, p. 418c9–10: 凡所見色。皆是見心。心不自心。因色故心。色不自色。因心故色. Translation follows Poceski (2015b: 205).

15 E.g., Hamilton (2000), Ronkin (2005), Gombrich (2009), Wynne (2010).

the *Rohitassa-sutta* (SN 2.26/i.61), the world may be found in the body (*kaḷevara*) endowed with perception (*sasaññī*) and intellect (*samanaka*). According to the interpretation of this passage given in another Nikāya text, the *Lokantagamana-sutta* (SN 35.116/iv.93), the world (*loka*) in the Noble One's (*ariya*) Discipline (*vinaya*) is that "in the world" (*lokasmiṃ*) by which one is a "perceiver of the world (*lokasaññī*), a conceiver of the world (*lokamānī*)".[16] The same text later explains that it is through each of the six senses that one comes to perceive the world and conceive of the world which implies that they constitute the world of our experience. Indeed, a similar message can be found in other texts, such as the *Lokapañhā-sutta* (SN 35.82/iv.52) and the *Palokadhamma-sutta* (SN 35.84/iv.53), which identify the world with that which disintegrates (*lujjati*), namely the six senses and their respective phenomena, consciousnesses, contacts and feelings.

Commenting on the philosophical implications of the *Rohitassa-sutta*, Gombrich (2006: 94) points out that the "term *lokasaññi* does not tell us whether there really is a world 'out there' or not". The point of these texts seems to be that the only way in which the world is given to us is through our apperception and sensory modalities, and talking about any world in total independence of the individual experiencing it through the means of a specific cognitive apparatus is not possible. Indeed, this seems to be the message of the *Samiddhilokapañhā-sutta* (SN 35.68/iv.39–40) which claims that the world (*loka*) or the concept of the world (*lokapaññatti*) exists only when there are the six sense bases.[17] This could be classified as an anti-realist position in the sense defined by Siderits (2016: 28) as taking "the very notion of a way that the world is independently of our cognitive activity to be devoid of meaning". In other words, our very notion of the world is dependent on the specific structure of our cognition. Thus, as Coseru (2012: 67) notes, this world of experience is not "an independent domain of physical entities and relations, but rather the 'phenomenal world of perception' (*lokasaṃjñā*) that depends on the conceptual and proliferating activities of the mind". From this perspective, it is not possible to postulate an objective world consisting of objects in the three-dimensional space, which would be external to us and fully independent of our cognition.

16 Translation by Bodhi (2000: 1190).

17 Cf. Shulman's (2014: 70) statement that: "The world of the *Samiddhilokapañhasutta* is heavily dependent on subjectivity; indeed, it appears to be the world of subjectivity itself. Where the structural elements of perception – the senses, their objects, consciousness and the cognized – exist, that is where there is a world."

According to the *Sabba-sutta* (SN 35.23/iv.15), the "all" (*sabba*) is constituted by our senses and their objects, and it is not possible to declare (*paññapeti*) another "all". This could be read as a denial of the very possibility of conceiving of any hypothetical external and objective world independent of our cognitive architecture. That is because the very notions of object, space, externality or even the world itself are only meaningful within the sphere of our lived experience.[18]

Wynne (2015b) makes a strong point for an antirealist reading of several key Nikāya texts. According to his (2015b: 213) interpretation, a number of early discourses imply that a "world of experience is a cognitive construction" and that "thought cannot transcend its limits ... and attain an objective picture of reality". However, the abovementioned statements do not in themselves imply that the mind-independent objective reality does not exist or that the world is created *ex nihilo* by the mind. In other words, we are not dealing here with idealism, as it was conceived of in Western philosophy.[19]

It is interesting that the *Samiddhilokapañhā-sutta* uses the terms "world" and "concept (*paññatti*) of the world" almost as if they were synonyms.[20] The term *paññatti* carries with it a meaning of a designation, notion, or name. Therefore, this text may imply the meaninglessness of the notion of the world as independent not only from our cognitive activity, but of our language as well. Even if we try to talk or think about the mind-independent, objective world in itself, we are ultimately forced to do so by using linguistic concepts (*paññatti*). This message seems to be even more strongly emphasized in the Āgama parallels of the Pali texts containing the idea of the world (*loka*). When enumerating what comes to be reckoned as the world (*rushijianshu* 入世間數), the SĀ 234 at T02, no. 99, pp. 56c12–57a15 lists the following elements: *shijianjue* 世間覺 (which literally means "world-awareness"

18 As we shall see, this does not preclude the possibility of the existence of mind-independent, noumenal correlate of our experience which could perhaps be labelled as "objective reality". However, the latter cannot be conceived of as an external spatiotemporal world of objects and their relations similar to that postulated by Western classical physics, but is totally inconceivable.

19 Wynne (2015b: 222–23) rightly notes that "no idealistic step is taken to say that cognitive construction is all there is, and thus that the world consists of mind only", and that "[a]lthough this is not a philosophy of realism since it assumes that the reality of space-time does not extend beyond a person's cognitive conditioning, this does not imply an idealist understanding" (Wynne, 2010: 156).

20 Gombrich (2006: 116) pointed out that when a string of terms is used in the Nikāyas, it usually implies their near synonymity.

and may correspond to Pali *lokamānī*), *shijian ming* 世間名 (lit. world-name), *shijian yanci* 世間言辭 (lit. world-words) and *shijian yushuo* (世間語說 lit. world speech).[21] The three latter terms are connected with language and may perhaps correspond to Pali *terms*, such as *samaññā* (designation), *nirutti* (common way of speaking), *vohārā* (verbal expression), and *paññatti* (concept) found throughout the Nikāyas. Therefore, the message of these early Buddhist texts may be seen as similar to that of the already mentioned statement by Wuzhu that verbal explanation (*yanshuo* 言說) is the origin of the three Worlds (*sanjieben* 三界本).[22]

The problem of cessation in the Nikāyas

An even bigger argument in favour of a subjective and phenomenal interpretation of the Nikāya notion of the world as well as of the various elements that constitute it (e.g., the *khandhas* and the *āyatanas*) is presented by several statements about the necessity of their ending or cessation. In addition to speaking about the presence of the world in the human body, the *Rohitassa-sutta* also speaks about its cessation (*lokanirodha*) and the path leading to it. According to the *Loka-sutta* (AN 4.23/ii.23–24), the *Tathāgata* is fully awakened (*abhisambuddha*) to the cessation of the world; furthermore, it is said that this cessation has been realized (*sacchikata*) by him.

Several statements in the Nikāyas claim that the noble eightfold path is a way (*paṭipadā*) leading to the cessation (*nirodhagāmī*) of each of the five aggregates. (e.g., SN 22.56–57/iii.58–65). The *Kāmaguṇa-sutta* (SN 35.117/iv.97–101) speaks about a sphere (*āyatana*), where each of the six senses and their respective perceptions (*saññā*) cease (*nirujjhati*). Another example of cessationist teaching may be found in the *Udāna-sutta* (SN 22.55/iii.55–58) which contains the following line: "It might not be, and it might not be for me; it will not be, [and] it will not be for me".[23] The following part of the sutta makes it clear that the line refers to the five aggregates, as one is supposed to understand that each of them "will cease to be" (*vibhavissati*). This implies the possibility of

21 T02, no. 99, p. 56c28–29: 若世間、世間名、世間覺、世間言辭、世間語說，此等皆入世間數。

22 T51, no. 2075, p. 191c21–23.

23 SN 22.55/iii.56: *'no cassaṃ, no ca me siyā, nābhavissa, na me bhavissatī'ti.* Translation by Bodhi (2000: 892).

realizing a state where the aggregates "will not be" for the practitioner, i.e., that of their cessation.

The historically dominant way of explaining this cessation was by placing it after the death of an awakened person. This, however, inevitably results in an annihilationist interpretation of final liberation as a post-mortem destruction of the objective constituents of a human being, which was a position that the Nikāya authors were at pains to distance themselves from (e.g., AN 8.11/iv.174–179, MN 22/i.130–142).

However, there are some texts that directly state or at least imply that such a cessation may paradoxically occur in a special meditative state during the life of an individual. According to the *Kaccānagotta-sutta* (SN 12.15/ii.16–17) it is possible to see the cessation of the world as it is (*yathābhūtaṃ*), through right understanding (*sammappaññā*). In the *Channovāda-sutta* (MN 144/iii.263–266), Channa states that it is through seeing and directly knowing cessation in each of the six sense bases, that he considers them not to be his self. According to the above-mentioned *Kāmaguṇa-sutta* (SN 35.117/iv.97–101), the sphere in which each of the six senses and their respective perceptions cease, should be "experienced/known (*veditabba*)".[24] This seems to imply experiential, direct knowledge attained by living through that state, as *post-mortem* cessation may only be known speculatively.[25]

Several texts describe cessation or non-presence of particular *khandhas*. In the *Vimokkha-sutta*, the Buddha proclaims:

> By the extinction of perception and consciousness,
> By the cessation and appeasement of feelings:
> It is thus, friend, that I know for beings –
> Emancipation, release, seclusion.[26]

The Buddha's statement clearly implies that the state of cessation (*nirodha*) and extinction (*saṅkhaya*) mentioned in the text is attainable during life, and not after death, since he claims that he knows it (*jānāti*).

---

24 SN 35.117/iv.98: *se āyatane veditabbe yattha cakkhu ca nirujjhati, rūpasaññā ca nirujjhati.*

25 While these statements could also be read as referring to momentary cessations which occur with great frequency in every moment of existence, it needs to be said that such a doctrine only developed in the later classical Theravāda and does not seem to be present in the Nikāyas.

26 SN 1.2/i.2: *saññāviññāṇasaṅkhayā, vedanānaṃ nirodhā upasamā – evaṃ khvāhaṃ, āvuso, jānāmi sattānaṃ nimokkhaṃ pamokkhaṃ vivekan'ti.* Translation by Bodhi (2000: 90).

In the *Udayamāṇavapucchā* of the *Pārāyanavagga* (Snp 5.13/214–215), we read that for one who is living mindfully in such a way that he is not seeking delight in feeling internally and externally, consciousness (*viññāṇa*) is stopped (*uparujjhati*).[27] In the *Poṭṭhapāda-sutta* (DN 9/i.178–203) we find a description of a state at the apex of the meditative progress in which perceptions (*saññā*) cease (*nirujjhati*) "due to neither intending nor constructing" (*acetayato anabhisaṅkharoto*).[28] The *Kalahavivāda-sutta* (Snp 4.11/862–877) contains an account of a meditative state in which all possible modes of perception are denied, form (*rūpa*) is said to vanish (*vibhoti*) and contacts (*phassa*) do not touch.[29] Of course, as its very name implies, the meditative state of *saññāvedayitanirodha* is characterized by the cessation of feeling and perception.

The apophatic state beyond dichotomies in the early Chan texts

A notion of the immediate ending of the world of *saṃsāra*, with its dichotomies of life and death by turning off the mental activities that make its experience possible, may also be found in early Chan texts.

According to the *Dasheng kaixin xianxing dunwu zhenzong lun*, non-activation of the mind (*xinbuqi* 心不起) equals transcendence or separation (*li* 離) from the empirical reality of intrinsic-natures (*zixing* 自性) (i.e., four elements and perceptive capacities)[30] and is tantamount to true nature (*zhenxing* 真性), which is a permanent state of purity devoid of characteristics (*changwuxiangqingjing* 常無相清淨).[31] Shenhui speaks of the state of awakening in which one does not consciously apply the mind (*mozuoyi* 莫作意) and in which being and non-being (*youwu* 有無) are both eliminated (*shuangqian* 雙遣).[32] In the *Tiansheng guangdeng lu*, Mazu proclaims:

27 Snp 5.13/215: *ajjhattañca bahiddhā ca, vedanaṃ nābhinandato. evaṃ satassa carato, viññāṇaṃ uparujjhatī'ti*. Translation of *uparujjhati* follows Cone (2001: 468). Bodhi (2017: 342) translates it as "ceases".

28 It is noteworthy that the terms *ceteti* and *abhisaṅkharoti* correspond to a certain extent to Chinese *zuoyi* 作意 and *zaozuo* 造作, which occur in Chan texts.

29 Cf. translation by Bodhi (2017: 306).

30 T85, no. 2835, p. 1278b23–24: 又問曰。云何離自性　答曰。心不起即離。

31 T85, no. 2835, p. 1278b20: 問曰。云何真性　答曰。不起心常無相清淨。For a translation of this and the abovementioned passage, see McRae (1987: 242–43).

32 B25, no. 142, p. 32a1: 有無雙遣，境智俱亡。莫作意即自性菩提。Cf. translation by McRae (2023: 69).

> Just put an end (*jin* 盡) to all mental conceptions (*xinliang* 心量) in the three realms. If there is not a single thought (*wuyinian* 無一念), then one eliminates the root of birth and death (*shengsigenben* 生死根本), and obtains the unexcelled treasury of the Dharma king.[33]

In a similar vein, Wuzhu proclaims in the *Lidai fabao ji* that no-thought (*wunian* 無念) equals no-birth (*wusheng* 無生) and no-death (*wusi* 無死).[34] Freedom from birth and death is synonymous with release from *saṃsāra*, and thus represents the ultimate liberation in Buddhism. In another fragment of the same text, it is said that no-thought equals the negation of the most basic categories of ordinary experience such as "that" (*bi* 彼) and "this" (*ci* 此). In this state there is also no Buddha (*fo* 佛) and no sentient beings (*zhongsheng* 眾生).[35] Wuzhu's statements are examples of using an apophatic and paradoxical language to refer to the ultimate state. Such descriptions are much more frequent in Chan texts and go back to the earliest period of that tradition.

Already in Bodhidharma's *Erru sixing lun* we read that during wall-contemplation (*biguan* 壁觀), "self and other, common man (*fan* 凡), and sage (*sheng* 聖), are identical".[36] Apophatic descriptions are particularly prevalent in the texts of the Hongzhou school. In the *Zongjing lu*, Mazu's teacher, Nanyue Huairang 南嶽懷讓 (677–744) engages in a series of apophatic negations to describe the ultimate state:

> If one conforms to the Way, then there are no beginning (*shi* 始) and end (*zhong* 終), no creation (*cheng* 成) and destruction (*huai* 壞), no coalescing (*ju* 聚), and scattering (*san* 散), no longness and shortness, no quietude (*jing* 靜) and disturbance (*luan* 亂), no urgency (*ji* 急) and postponement (*huan* 緩).[37]

Huirang remains consistent in his apophatic approach and even cataphatic labels traditionally associated with original, pure mind-nature are negated. In a similar vein, Baizhang states that originally (*benlai* 本

33 X78, no. 1553, p. 449a1–3: 但盡三界心量。一念妄想。即是三界生死根本。但無一念。即除生死根本。即得法王無上珍寶。Translation by Poceski (2007: 161).

34 T51, no. 2075, p. 192b3–4: 無念即無生。無念即無死。Cf. translation by Adamek (2007: 380).

35 T51, no. 2075, p. 192a1–2: 無念即無彼。無念即無此。無念即無佛。無念無眾生。Cf. translation by Adamek (2007: 377).

36 X63, no. 1217, p. 1a22–23: 無自無他。凡聖等一堅住不移。Translation by Broughton (1999: 9).

37 T48, no. 2016, p. 940b11–13: 若契此道。無始無終。不成不壞。不聚不散。不長不短。不靜不亂。不急不緩。Translation by Poceski (2015b: 254).

來), the intrinsic nature (*benyouzhixing* 本有之性) is neither mundane (*fan* 凡), nor holy/saint (聖 *sheng*), neither impure (*gou* 垢) nor pure (*jing* 淨).[38] Numerous apophatic descriptions may also be found in the *Chuanxin fa yao*. In one of the passages of this text, in addition to negating the abovementioned pair of dichotomies, Huangbo goes as far as to say that the fundamental essence (*benti* 本體) is "without delusion and without enlightenment" (*wumiwuwu* 無迷無悟), as well as "without people and without Buddhas" (*wurenyiwufo* 無人亦無佛).[39]

Philosophical implications of the apophatic teachings

The statements in the Nikāyas which speak about the possibility of cessation of the world, the *khandha*s and the *āyatana*s, in a special state during life, are very interesting philosophically. The same is the case with early Chan passages describing the ending of the three realms or birth and death as being concurrent with the absence of thought. We have already considered their antirealist implications. But what concepts of mind and of a human being are implied by these passages?

The sets of the *khandha*s and the six sense bases were traditionally seen in Theravāda Buddhism as objective constituents of a human being. Furthermore, the historically dominant view was that the set of the five *khandha*s is an exhaustive account of a person, in the sense that a person can be reduced to the set of the five aggregates.[40] However, such an interpretation is undermined by the very possibility of the cessation of these elements during a special meditative state without ensuing total annihilation or insentience of a human individual. Instead, this seems to imply their subjective and phenomenal and not fully objective and mind-independent nature.[41]

After all, when Nikāya texts, such as the *Kalahavivāda-sutta* (Snp 4.11/170), speak about the vanishment of form (*rūpa*) or in the case of the *Kāmaguṇa-sutta* (SN 35.117/iv.100) about the cessation of the six

38 X69, no. 1323, p. 8a3–4: 又本有之性。不可名目。本來不是凡不是聖。不是垢淨。Translation by Cheng Chien (1993: 103).

39 T48, no. 2012A, p. 383c14–15: 無漏無為無迷無悟。了了見無一物。亦無人亦無佛。Translation by McRae (2005: 39).

40 This view goes back to the *Vajīra-sutta* (SN 5.10/i.296) and is later elaborated in works such as the *Milindapañha* and the *Visuddhimagga*.

41 Cf. Wynne (2019a: 138): "the cessation of 'phenomena' is not an early Buddhist way of talking about death, and must refer to mental or experiential phenomena".

sense bases, they certainly do not presume that a meditator's body disappears as well, since it is implied that it can still be seen from a third-person perspective. As we have seen above, some texts speak about the temporary meditative cessation or absence of the so-called mental aggregates such as *viññāṇa* or *saññā*, and yet this often does not result in insentience but a mode of cognition which is not conceptualized in terms of the *khandhas*.

What are then the *āyatanas* and the *khandhas*? Instead of being objective biological sense organs, the six senses of the *saḷāyatana* set may correspond to the basic sensory modalities understood in a phenomenal and qualitative sense, which enable us to have particular phenomenal experiences (e.g., a visual or an olfactory experience). In order to elucidate what I mean by phenomenal sensory modalities, let us consider the following example. To have a visual experience of a red cube, our mind must beforehand be capable of visually experiencing redness, shape and three-dimensional space, regardless of whether a biological sense receives any stimulus or not. In his famous paper, Nagel (1974) considered the question of "what it means to be a bat" to emphasize our inability to even imagine a qualitative or "what it is like" character of the phenomenal experience connected with a bat's sense of echolocation, regardless of whether we understand its mechanism on a physical level. If we were to express this problem by referring to the concept of sensory modality, we could say that we cannot imagine what it is like to be a bat, because we lack the qualitative phenomenal modality connected with the sense of echolocation. The individual sensory modalities are also unique in the sense that they cannot be reduced to one another – for instance, the modality of seeing cannot be reduced to that of smelling. In contrast, the sense data and the senses, as understood in natural sciences, are ultimately reducible to the same basic physical principles, be they particles or waves. If we were to use Kantian terminology, phenomenal sensory modalities would be labelled as *aprioric*, meaning that they represent the very potential to have a particular qualitative phenomenal experience, before it even occurs.

Another interesting issue to consider in that context is that of the interrelation between the concepts of the senses from the *saḷāyatana* set and the *indriyas* in the Nikāyas. Initially, one could be tempted to consider these two concepts as nearly synonymous as they both refer to the senses such as the eye or the ear. However, an analysis of how these terms are used in particular texts shows some fundamental differences.

Unlike the *āyatanas*, the *indriyas* are never said to become a subject of cessation. In fact, some accounts of the attainment of cessation in the Nikāyas contain information that in this state the *indriyas* are very pure (*vippasanna*).[42] The contexts in which both terms are used are different. *Indriyas* seem to correspond to biological senses understood in a functional way, as faculties that enable receiving stimuli from the external environment. The senses from the *saḷāyatana* set represent qualitative and phenomenal modalities connected with the individual senses from a first-person, subjective perspective. Thus, one can imagine a hypothetical situation where the six sense bases cease,[43] while the faculties (*indriya*) continue their functioning in an uninterrupted way.

On the nature of the aggregates

Somewhat similar considerations can be made regarding the nature and status of the aggregates. The fact that they can cease within certain meditative states without ensuing the disappearance of the body as seen from the third-person perspective or total shutdown of cognitive functions is a strong argument for understanding them as various aspects of our subjective phenomenal experience. Furthermore, there are several Nikāya texts which imply that the set of the *khandhas* is not an exhaustive account of an individual, i.e., that there are non-*khandha* elements within a human being. When read directly, some of these texts strongly imply that within a human being there exists a dichotomy of the aggregates and their counterpart. The latter may cling to the aggregates, wrongly regard them as self, but also become disenchanted with them and eventually abandon or even destroy them. As is the case with many other teachings in the Nikāyas, the dichotomy in question is illustrated with the help of various vivid similes. In some cases, the vehicles of the similes (i.e., persons, animals and objects) are explicitly said to correspond to the aggregates and the human being; in others, this relation is clearly implied.

Thus, the relation between the aggregates and the individual are illustrated by the dichotomies of:

---

42 MN 44/i.296: *yo cāyaṃ bhikkhu saññāvedayitanirodhaṃ samāpanno ... āyu na parikkhīṇo, usmā avūpasantā, indriyāni vippasannāni.*

43 Cessation of the six *āyatanas* (*saḷāyatananirodha*) is explicitly mentioned in the SN 35.117/iv.100, while no such claims are made about the *indriyas*.

- the burden and its bearer (SN 22.22/iii.26).
- the turtle and the anthill from which it is to be thrown out (MN 23/i.143–145).[44]
- the post and the dog that is tied to it and runs obsessively around it (SN 22.99–100/iii.149–152).
- the faithful effigy of a human being and the painter who created it (SN 22.100/ iii.151–152).
- the facial reflection in the mirror or in a bowl of water and the young person who develops grasping towards it (SN 22.83/ iii.105–106).
- the sand-castles and the children who create them, play with them, but ultimately may destroy them (SN 23.2/iii.189–190).
- the dirty soiled cloth and a blind man who considers it white and beautiful but may lose desire for it due to his eyesight being restored (MN 75/i.502–513).
- the plants growing on the bank of the river and the man carried by the current who tries in vain to hold onto them, only to see them break (SN 22.93/iii.137–139).
- the murderer and the householder who is murdered by him due to failing to see the former for what he really is (SN 22.85/ iii.110–115).
- the branches carried by some people in Jeta's grove and the observers of this situation who may mistakenly think themselves to be these branches (MN 22/iii.130–142 and SN 22.33–34/ iii.34).

It is important to note that unlike the famous chariot metaphor used in the *Vajīra-sutta*, these similes do not convey the message that a human being is a conglomeration of various self-less elements. Their main point is that instead of identifying with the aggregates, one should abandon them or even destroy them. Of course, this is not synonymous with the historically dominant Buddhist interpretation that the human being can be reduced to a combination of the *khandhas*. However, as several scholars have already suggested, the set of the aggregates was not originally meant to serve as an exhaustive, comprehensive analysis of a human being.[45] Instead, the *khandha* formula was rather a way of

44 In case of this simile, the anthill is said to be the designation of the body (*kāya*), and not of the individual as a whole.

45 These scholars include Gethin (1986), Hamilton (1996; 2000), Wynne (2009; 2010), Shulman (2014) and Davis (2016).

conceptualizing various aspects and elements of a subjective, first-person experience of the world, a sort of a phenomenological perspective from within (Davis 2016: 140). The aggregates are those aspects of our experience of the world and of ourselves in it that are introspectable, reportable in speech or possible to be stored in memory. To use the terms of modern cognitive science, the aggregates seem to refer to various aspects of those of our mental states that are "access-conscious", i.e., whose content is globally accessible/broadcast to various cognitive systems or modules. It is generally accepted that global accessibility of a particular content is correlated with it being phenomenally conscious (Carruthers 2015), though the issue of whether phenomenal consciousness may be reduced to access consciousness is the subject of intense debates in modern philosophy of mind.

As we have already observed, the naive realist position that we are aware of the things as they really are independently of the mediating activity of our cognitive processing is not harmonizable with the early Buddhist teaching. Quite the contrary, the way in which the objects that we experience appear to us is dependent on the specific functioning of our cognitive system and reflects its structure. What I am subjectively aware of (while attending to my experience, introspecting it, verbally reporting on it, or recollecting it) when I look at my hand is, therefore, not the hypothetical objective hand "as it really is" externally to us, entirely independent of our cognitive processes.[46]

The position of the Nikāya and early Chan texts certainly cannot be harmonized with physicalism. However, it does not preclude a possibility of the third-person perspective on perception, which would focus on several stages of representing the original sensory stimulus: first in the sense organ itself, then in the neural pathways and finally in the brain. Of course, the Nikāya (as well as Chan) texts do not show any

46 It needs to be emphasized that this position is not synonymous with the philosophical view that we only cognize our subjective representations and not the external objects. As we have noted, the position of the Nikāyas (and early Chan texts as well) is that it is impossible to speak of the external, quasi-physical world independent of our cognitive apparatus. Therefore, the very idea of a dichotomy of the external objects and their internal mental representations does not even arise in the Nikāyas. From their perspective, we simply cognize the objects together with their properties and not their inner representations. However, in the Nikāyas, an object (e.g., a visual object [*rūpa*], such as a tree or a mountain) does not belong to the hypothetical sphere of the mind-independent reality, but to that of the world of the lived experience.

awareness of the fact that conscious states are correlated with certain neural states. However, even if they did, it could not be meaningfully said from their perspective that the awareness of a certain object is in fact a state of the brain. One could only speak about correlation of the first-person awareness of an object with the fact of the brain forming its neural representation which is available from the third-person perspective.

It seems possible that the aggregates were not meant to denote all aspects of our first-person experience, but only those related to our experience of ourselves (i.e., how we appear to ourselves). In the Nikāyas the aggregates are never defined as the world, while the six sense bases are. The *Puppha-sutta* (SN 22.94/iii.138) describes each of the aggregates as "a world-*dhamma* within the world" (*loke lokadhammo*),[47] but not as the world itself. This may imply that the Nikāya notion of the world (*loka*) may possess wider denotation than that of the aggregates.[48] According to such an interpretation, *rūpa* from the *khandha* set would not correspond to all corporeal aspects of our phenomenal experience but only those connected with our body. In other words, a distant tree experienced from a first-person perspective would not be classified as *rūpakkhandha*, but our hand would. One of the main features of the aggregates is that they are prone to be misinterpreted as "self", and it does not seem probable that one could regard a tree or a mountain in such a way.

All these considerations are essential for properly understanding the nature of the aggregates and of the notion of mistakenly seeing them as self. If the aggregates refer to various aspects of our first-person awareness of the world, then they cannot be an exhaustive account of what a human being really is. That is because there are many crucial aspects of a human being that are not experienceable in this way. These latter aspects can be observed from the third-person perspective (e.g., various brain processes that are observable through the medium of modern scientific devices) or inferred (e.g., we have to assume the existence of various cognitive processes which are unavailable to our introspection and which result in the so-called eureka moments). Furthermore,

---

47 Wynne (2015b: 226) believes that this line implies a phenomenal and not-objective vision of both the aggregates and the world.

48 Interestingly, the Āgama parallel to the *Rohitassa-sutta*, SĀ 1307 at T02, no. 99, p. 359a10–b21, defines the world (*shijian* 世間) as the five aggregates of clinging (*wushouyin* 五受陰).

it seems that we have no first-person access through introspection to many important processes which constitute us. All this implies that some essential elements of the human being cannot be conceptualized in terms of the aggregates. As modern philosophy of mind and cognitive science tell us, the actual cognitive processes responsible for our intelligence and agency are not directly introspectable. Libet (2004) and Wegner (2002) argue that even our subjectively experienced feeling of volition and agency is an epiphenomenon devoid of direct causal efficacy and is merely correlated with an unconscious neural process responsible for our acts of decision which is temporally prior to it.

Another issue worth considering is that the first-person experience of ourselves conceptualized in terms of the aggregates may not only be limited, but may also be cognitively distorted. In other words, the way in which we experience ourselves may not be reflective of the true state of things. For example, it seems plausible that our first-person introspectable experience of ourselves is structured in such a way that it involves the notion of selfhood from the very beginning. While we are actually a conglomerate of self-less processes, we appear to ourselves through our introspection as conscious selves, separated by firm boundaries from the external environment. The *Sakkāya-sutta* (SN 22.105/iii.159) defines all five aggregates of grasping as personal identity (*sakkāya*), while the *Anta-sutta* (SN 22.103/iii.58) as a portion/ side of personality (*sakkāyanta*). The inherently deceitful nature of the aggregates may be implied by the similes in the *Pheṇapiṇḍūpama-sutta* (SN 22.95/iii.140–143) which liken the *khandhas* to insubstantial, illusory phenomena. For example, *saññā* is compared to a mirage (*marīcikā*) in the last month of the summer season, while *viññāṇa* to an illusion (*māyā*) conjured by a magician (*māyākāra*) at the crossroads.

In light of these considerations, the already mentioned dichotomous *khandha* similes make much more sense. The counterpart of the aggregates, symbolized by various vehicles (e.g., the bearer of the burden, the painter, the children etc.) represents human being as a whole, while the *khandhas* correspond to the various aspects of the first-person consciousness of oneself. According to such a reading, the main point of the similes would be that we should not identify[49] with various aspects of

49 Cf. Wynne (2010: 113): "It would seem, then, that the teaching addresses the problem of personal identity by questioning the identification with phenomenal being". Also cf. Shulman (2014: 63): "the main aim of the *anatta* doctrine is not to advance a general understanding regarding the selflessness of all things

our first-person phenomenal experience, and in particular with those phenomena which serve as our own phenomenal self-representation.

To put it somewhat differently, the message of these similes is not: "within you, who actually are just a conglomerate of the five aggregates which is conventionally called a person, there is no ontic entity called 'the self'". Rather, they say: "you are not the phenomena which you experience, and which you believed to be yourself, and you should not identify with them". The point is, therefore, not only that the aggregates are not our "self" in the sense of a stable ontic entity, but that they are simply not ourselves, i.e., we are not them.[50]

It is important that this reading shifts the locus of agency and active cognitive operations to the counterpart of the aggregates. It is this non-*khandha* part of a human being which identifies with the aggregates but can also stop seeing them as self and eventually abandon them. The *anattā* teaching in the Nikāyas seems to be addressed directly to this counterpart of the *khandha*s, as it contains an exhortation to not see them as self, or to abandon and destroy them. This, in turn, indirectly implies that this counterpart possesses the cognitive capacity to understand this teaching and implement the results of this understanding into its actions.

Of course, such an understanding of the aggregates cannot be harmonized with their historically dominant interpretation as the active selfless processes responsible for our cognition and functioning in the world. As we have already commented, we have no first-person introspective access to the key processes responsible for our cognition, decision making and functioning. The *khandha*s, however, correspond to the various aspects of our first-person introspectable and verbally reportable consciousness. There is hardly any evidence in the Nikāyas for interpreting the aggregates as the active processes which actually "do" something.[51]

... but rather to show that they are selfless in the sense of being 'not-my-self' or 'not-I'".

50 Of course, there are also Nikāya texts that criticize the notion of the self in the ontic sense, as a sort of monadic entity, agent of action and subject of experience (e.g., DN 15/iii.66–67, MN 2/i.8). The two meanings may be seen as complementary and not mutually exclusive. Wynne (2010: 113) rightly notes that texts play on the flexibility in the term *ātman/attan*, using it first in the sense derived from the reflexive pronoun (where it denotes a person's phenomenal identity), and second in the more philosophical sense of intrinsic identity.

51 See Polak (2023b: 676–80) for a more detailed argumentation in favour of this claim.

Mind and consciousness

Are there any aspects of human cognition, and of human being in general, which are not conceptualized in terms of the *khandhas* in the Nikāyas? A case can be made that the concept of *citta/cetas*[52] is often used in a way that implies its distinction from the aggregates. Gombrich (2006: 112) has very aptly observed that originally "*citta/ceto* is not one of the five aggregates (*khandha*), but a general term for mind or thought". There are texts which speak about the possibility of *citta/cetas* being separated from the *khandhas*. The already mentioned *Jhāna-sutta* and the *Mahāmālukya-sutta* (MN 64/i.432–437) speak about the mind being turned away (*paṭivāreti*) from the phenomena (*dhamma*) that are connected with (*gata*) each of the particular *khandhas* (e.g., *rūpagata*, *vedanāgata* etc.). This would imply that at least for the author of these texts, *citta* was not synonymous with the aggregates. According to the *Vāhana-sutta* (AN 10.8/v.151–152), the *Tathāgata* has escaped (*nissaṭa*), is disentangled (*visaṃyutta*), and released (*vippamutta*) from the ten things which include the five aggregates and dwells with an unrestricted (*vimariyādīkata*) mind (*cetas*).[53] This seems to imply some distinction between *cetas* and the aggregates. In the *Dutiyasikkhattaya-sutta* (AN 3.90/i.235–236) we encounter the following passage:

> For one freed by craving's destruction,
> with the cessation of consciousness
> the release of the mind
> is like the extinguishing of a lamp[54]

---

52 The terms *citta* and *ceto/cetas* are to a large degree synonymous. Cone (2010: 162) comments that *cetas* is "often not to be distinguished from *citta*". Commenting on the relation between *citta* and *cetas*, Rhys Davids and Stede (2007: 268) write: "there is no cogent evidence of a clear separation of their respective fields of meaning; a few cases indicate the role of *cetas* as seat of *citta*, whereas most of them show no distinction. There are cpds. having both *citta°* & *ceto°* in identical meanings (see e.g. *cittasamādhi* & *ceto°*), others show a preference for either one or the other".

53 AN 10.8/v.151–152: *dasahi kho, vāhana, dhammehi tathāgato nissaṭo visaṃyutto vippamutto vimariyādīkatena cetasā viharati. katamehi dasahi? rūpena kho, vāhana, tathāgato nissaṭo visaṃyutto vippamutto vimariyādīkatena cetasā viharati, vedanāya kho, vāhana ... pe ... saññāya kho, vāhana... saṅkhārehi kho, vāhana... viññāṇena kho, vāhana tathāgato nissaṭo visaṃyutto vippamutto vimariyādīkatena cetasā viharati.* Translation by Bodhi (2012: 1440).

54 N 3.90/i.236: *viññāṇassa nirodhena, taṇhākkhayavimuttino. pajjotasseva nibbānaṃ, vimokkho hoti cetaso.* Translation follows Bodhi (2012: 322).

According to this text, a cessation (*nirodha*) of consciousness (*viññāṇa*) is somehow connected with the fact of the mind (*cetas*) being released (*vimokkha*).[55] This fragment therefore implies that *citta/cetas* and *viññāṇa* may not possess the same denotation, as the former can continue while the latter undergoes cessation. This is at odds with the fully developed position of Theravāda Buddhism,[56] according to which the mind is pretty much synonymous with consciousness (*viññāṇa*). Although some texts in the Nikāyas indeed may be read as supporting the latter interpretation (e.g., SN 12.61/ii.94–95), in general the terms *citta/cetas* and *viññāṇa* occur in their own specific contexts and are not used interchangeably. This suggests that a conscious effort has been made by the authors of the Nikāyas to maintain the distinction between the two, which furthermore implies that they did not consider them synonymous.

The terms *citta/cetas* are used in the context of describing the mind as performing a particular function, for example being directed (*abhininnāmeti*) to the personal realization (*sacchikiriyā*) of particular "super-knowledge" (*abhiññā*), such as that of the exhaustion of the influxes.[57] *Citta* may also be described with various epithets denoting its cognitive potency for performing certain functions. For example, it may be described as unified (*samāhita*), malleable (*mudubhūta*), workable (*kammaniya*). Other epithets describe the presence or absence of various cognitive imperfections typical of the ordinary state of mind, which hinder *citta*'s cognitive potency. Thus, *citta* may be without defilement (*vigatūpakkilesa*) and free from blemish (*anaṅgaṇa*) or purified (*parisuddha*: e.g., MN 27/i.182). The terms *citta/cetas* do not seem to be used in the context of describing the first-person content of experience or its "what it is like" qualitative phenomenal character. We often find the descriptions of the release of the mind (*cetovimutti*), but never of its cessation (*nirodha*). *Citta* also does not feature in the schemes of dependent origination and, by extension, in those of dependent cessation.

---

55 The Āgama parallel SĀ 816 at T02, no. 99, p. 210a6–22 agrees to a large extent with the Pali verse, but makes no reference to cessation of consciousness. It describes the mind obtaining liberation (*xin de jietuo* 心得解脫), but it connects it with establishing right mindfulness in an un-forgetful way (*zhengnian bu wangzhu* 正念不忘住) which the Pali version does not mention. Also, it has a line about breaking up of the body and ending life (*shen huai er mingzhong* 身壞而命終) before describing nirvana being like an extinguished lamp.

56 Cf. Heim (2013: 385), Dhs 18/10, Vism ii.28/452/XIV.82.

57 E.g., in AN 3.101/i.254–256.

In contrast, *viññāṇa* is not presented as the mental faculty which performs insights or can be directed to certain tasks. It is never said to be concentrated, while this term is very often used with reference to *citta* (e.g., MN 27/i.182: *so evaṃ samāhite cite...*). It is however described in terms that suggest first-person, phenomenal consciousness,[58] for it is through *viññāṇa* that one is conscious of (*vijānāti*) basic gustatory qualities, like those of bitter and sweet (SN 22.79/iii.87–91) or sensory qualities of pleasure and pain (MN 140/iii.238–247). Also, *viññāṇa* is closely related to the six sense bases (*saḷāyatana*), as each sense has a corresponding sense-consciousness (e.g., *cakkhuviññāṇa*). Thus, the reading of *viññāṇa* as phenomenal qualitative consciousness harmonizes with the hypothesis that the six sense bases are phenomenal sensory modalities. *Viññāṇa* also occurs in its own specific soteriological context: the fact of *viññāṇa* being established (*patiṭṭhita*) is a negatively evaluated precondition to the descent (*avakkanti*) of name and form and eventually rebirth,[59] while its non-establishment is a condition for liberation. Conversely, the fact of *citta* being stable (*ṭhita*) is said to result from its release (*vimutti* – e.g., SN 22.45/iii.45).[60] *Viññāṇa* is also quite frequently

58 It needs to be emphasized, though, that the early Buddhist *viññāṇa* should not be conceived of as a phenomenal consciousness in a strong sense associated with phenomenal realism where it is understood as a special inner space of the mind containing qualia which are absent from the physical sphere. It is rather understood in a weak sense simply as consciousness whose content has a specific phenomenal structure which is spatiotemporal and related to particular sensory modalities, and finds expression in our verbal reports about colours, shapes, sounds etc.

59 E.g., SN 12.64/ii.101: *yattha patiṭṭhitaṃ viññāṇaṃ virūḷhaṃ, atthi tattha nāmarūpassa avakkanti.*

60 One peculiar passage where *viññāṇa* appears to be described with the epithets usually reserved for *citta* may be found in the three suttas of the *Khandhasaṃyutta*: SN 22.53–55/iii.53–58. The passage starts by describing *viññāṇa*, which due to abandoning passion (*rāga*) for all the *khandhas* "has cut off the basis" (*vocchijjatārammaṇaṃ*) and therefore is unestablished (*appatiṭṭhita*) and not undergoing growth (*avirūḷha*). The descriptions of the absence of *ārammaṇa*, its un-establishment and non-growth belong to the typical *viññāṇa* soteriological context. However, in the second part of the passage in question, there follows a sequence of descriptions which in other contexts (e.g., SN 22.45/iii.44–45) are either used with reference to *citta* (i.e., *vimutta*, *ṭhita*), or to a liberated person (*na paritassati, paccattaññeva parinibbāyati*). The unusual element unique to the three suttas in question and connecting the descriptions which usually belong to the different contexts of *viññāṇa* and *citta* is the phrase *anabhisaṅkhaccavimuttaṃ*. *Abhisaṅkhacca* appears to be an absolutive (*pubbakiriyā*) of *abhisaṅkharoti* (make up, fabricate), and

said to undergo cessation, while as we have already noted, this is never the case with *citta*.

The notion of distinction of the mind in the functional sense and consciousness in the phenomenal sense is very interesting philosophically. Throughout most of the history of philosophy, both Western and Eastern, it was generally assumed that the mind and consciousness are the same thing, or in other words, that consciousness is the mental faculty which cognizes reality, performs volitional acts, or thinks thoughts. It is also an intuitive view, representative of the common-sense approach of the majority of ordinary people. This may raise the question of philosophical coherence and the plausibility of a position which distinguishes the mind from consciousness. However, such positions are very prevalent in modern cognitive science and philosophy of mind. As we have already noted in the previous chapter, according to these theories (e.g., Carruthers 2015), consciousness is correlated with global availability of a certain set of data. The role of information becoming conscious would therefore lie in making a set of information globally available throughout the cognitive system. Cognitive operations in the sense of actively processing data, solving problems, generating insights and undertaking decisions are often performed unconsciously by multiple modules which operate in a parallel, simultaneous way. This relation may be compared to that between the internal hardware components of a computer (e.g., hard drive, processor, RAM memory) which perform active computing operations and are controlled by software, and the external monitor which merely passively displays the input it receives from the internal hardware.

The distinction between conscious content available from a first-person perspective and the mind in the sense of a faculty capable of actively generating certain forms of knowledge is particularly relevant for a discussion of differences between *citta* and the *khandhas*, and particularly *viññāṇa*. It seems that the Nikāya notions of the six sense bases and the *khandhas*, including *viññāṇa*, correspond to some extent to the phenomenal and globally accessible aspects of our consciousness.[61] On

thus *anabhisaṅkhaccavimuttaṃ* would literally mean "not having fabricated – released". Though the grammar of the passage creates an impression that all descriptions refer to *viññāṇā*, the structure of the passage may actually result from an amalgamation of descriptions which originally appeared in their own unique contexts and referred to different things.

61 Bodhi (2000: 1122) considers the sets of the *saḷāyatanas* and the *khandhas* to be alternative schemes of phenomenological classification.

the other hand, the Nikāya concept of *citta* may be seen as corresponding to the contemporary concept of the mind in a functional sense, i.e., defined in the context of its functions and operations.

What does it mean to regard the aggregates as self?

Metzinger's (2009) theory of a phenomenal self-model (PSM) is particularly relevant from the perspective of our study, as it may be harmonized with some important aspects of the *khandha* and the not-self teachings found in the Nikāyas. Metzinger believes that the organism creates through the medium of its neural system a model of the external world and of us in it. The PSM is "a distinct and coherent pattern of neural activity that allows you to integrate parts of the world into an inner image of yourself as a whole" (Metzinger 2009: 115). Metzinger (2009: 6) claims that "our conscious model of reality is a low-dimensional projection of the inconceivably richer physical reality surrounding and sustaining us". Our conscious experience of reality is metaphorically labelled by Metzinger as an "Ego-tunnel" due to its relatively narrow, limiting character and because it includes "the phenomenal Self" or "Ego", which is an internal image of ourselves. As Metzinger explains, we live in this tunnel lacking direct contact with external reality. However, we are not aware of this fact since the PSM is "transparent" to us, which means that we do not recognize that it is merely a representation or a model. The Ego is the content of the PSM at a particular moment and consists of bodily sensations, emotional states, perceptions, memories, acts of will and thoughts (2009: 8). The evolutionary role of the PSM lies in the fact that it allows the organism to represent and conceive of itself as a whole or a person and develop a sense of ownership and agency.

There are certainly differences between Metzinger's approach and the worldview found in the Nikāya and Chan texts. The former is based on a naturalist view, which assumes that natural sciences such as physics and biology provide a true picture of objective reality. In Metzinger's theory, the statements about conscious experience, the PSM and the brain seem to refer to one continuum of reality conceived of in naturalist terms.[62] As we have seen, Nikāya and early Chan views may neither

62 E.g., "Conscious experience can thus be seen as a special global property of the overall neural dynamics of your brain" (Metzinger, 2009: 29).

be harmonized with physicalism, nor do they allow us to meaningfully speak of the world that we experience as an internal representation of some external objective world. However, this worldview allows making statements about correlation between certain propositions representing first- and third-person person approaches to the world. Thus, it could be meaningfully said that our first-person awareness of a tree is correlated with a certain activation pattern in the brain serving as a neural representation of an external tree.

However, there are some very important parallels between Metzinger's theory and the notions found in the Nikāyas. According to Metzinger, the organism identifies not with itself as it really is, but with its internal representation of itself, the so-called phenomenal self-model. In the Nikāyas, seeing the aggregates in terms of "I am this" (*esohamasmi*) means that one identifies with various aspects and elements of one's first-person conscious experience of oneself. And as we have noted, the image provided by this form of experience is inherently distorted, limited and misses several crucial aspects of ourselves which are not available to our introspection. Thus, although as human beings we are much more, we identify with our phenomenal consciousness and conceive of ourselves as conscious-selves governing our bodies. This seems to correspond to what in the Nikāyas is conceptualized as seeing each of the aggregates as *attā*. There are also more sophisticated formulas, conceptualizing the development of the self-view in terms of mis-identification with *viññāṇa* (MN 38/i.258) or *vedanā* (DN 15/iii.66–67).

Why is it a bad thing? Firstly, because it is simply incorrect. Identifying oneself with the *khandha*s means that one wrongly attributes agency to something that is devoid of it. As we have already noted, the dominant trend within modern philosophy of mind is that phenomenal consciousness is correlated with a certain subset of data being made globally available to various modules of the implicit cognitive system. Let us once again refer to the computer analogy. Suppose that the units of internal hardware would run on a software that would allow them to gather data, make inferences based on it and implement the results of this learning into their functioning. However, this software would have no direct access to most of its own operations, but only to a monitor connected to the hardware and displaying its output in form of images (perhaps this access would be through a camera registering the changes on a monitor and sending data to the computer). Of course, not all data processed by hardware and software would find its way into images displayed on a monitor. This software would "observe" that its own operations are correlated with changes of display on a monitor, since whenever any computational procedure is initiated, some change of display occurs. Not having direct access to the units of internal hardware, it would inevitably make an inference that the monitor is the active unit of the whole system and all its operations originate from it, and that its own identity (i.e., of the computer) is that of the monitor. Therefore, this computer would start to mistakenly "think" that it is in fact the monitor. In Nikāya terms this would correspond to a to a belief that we are actually the *khandha*s, and more specifically *viññāṇa*, which governs the body, experiences various states and performs acts of will. This notion seems to be conveyed in the passage of the *Mahātaṇhāsaṅkhaya-sutta* (MN 38/i.258), where misguided Sāti proclaims that it is *viññāṇa* which speaks (*vada*, i.e., is an agent of actions) and feels (*vedeyya*, i.e., is the subject of experience). We shall focus on other negative consequences of identifying with the aggregates later on in this book.

Mind, aggregates and consciousness in early Chan texts

While the concept of the aggregates is not particularly prominent in Chan texts, nonetheless some of them contain the idea of their non-fundamental character and of their distinction from the mind. From the Mahāyāna perspective, this notion is not problematic, as it agrees with the basic philosophical tenets of this branch of Buddhism. For example, at the beginning of the *Xiuxin yao lun*, when asked about how to know that one's own mind is inherently pure, Hongren favourably quotes the fragment of the *Shidijing lun* 十地經論 (*Treatise on the Ten Stages Sutra*)[63] which states that the adamantine Buddha Nature (*jingang foxing* 金剛佛性) exists in the bodies of human beings but is covered by the black clouds of the five aggregates (*wuyin* 五陰).[64] The *Liuzu tanjing* contains a statement that the Mahāprajñāpāramitā uses great wisdom (*da zhihui* 大智惠) to destroy (*dapo* 打破) the passions and troubles of the five aggregates (*wuyin fannao chenlao* 五陰煩惱塵勞).[65] The *Baizhang chanshi*

63 This text is a Chinese translation of Vasubandhu's *Daśabhūmikasūutra śāstra*.

64 McRae (1986: 439/一): 十地經云。眾生身中有金剛佛性。猶如日輪體明圓滿廣大無邊。只為五陰黑雲之所覆。Cf. T48, no. 2011, p. 377a24–26. For a translation of this passage, see McRae (1986: 121–22).

65 T48, no. 2007, p. 340a16–18: 摩訶般若波羅蜜，最尊、最上、第一，無住、無去、無來。三世諸佛從中出，將大智惠到彼岸，打破五陰煩惱塵勞。Cf. translation by Yampolsky (1967: 148).

guanglu speaks of intrinsic nature (*benyouzhixing* 本有之性) which is identified with the mind that is free (*qixin zizai* 其心自在). In addition to several other worldly qualities, it is said to be ultimately dissociated from the aggregates (*yun* 蘊) as well as the *āyatanas* (*ru* 入).[66] Shenhui states in the *Wenda zazheng yi*, the Buddha-nature (*foxing* 佛性) is not the aggregates (*yin* 蔭), realms and *āyatanas*.[67]

The notion of consciousness being different from the mind, and the possibility of the former undergoing cessation while the latter continues its functioning, is also discussed in some Chan texts. In the *Xiuxin yao lun*, we find a unique account of the meditative practice of watching the movements of one's own consciousness (*shi* 識) which will ultimately cease by itself (*zimie* 自滅). This, however, does not result in insentience, but in the mind (*xin* 心) becoming simple (*danbo* 淡泊), clear (*jiaojie* 皎潔) and stable.[68] As we have already noted, according to Zongmi's *Yuanjuejing dashu shiyi chao*, the Baotang school taught extinguishing or cessation of consciousness (*mieshi* 滅識). However, this was not synonymous with cessation of the mind but merely its non-arousal (*buqi* 不起) which was considered to be "real" (*zhen* 真).[69] While there may not be an absolutely perfect correspondence between the Pali concepts of *citta* and *viññāṇa* and Chinese notions of *xin* 心 and *shi* 識 respectively, there is nonetheless some similarity of the idea in general.

Both above-mentioned texts use the term *mie* 滅, which in the Chinese translations of Indian Buddhist literature was generally used to translate Sanskrit *nirodha* (cessation). It needs to be said that most Chan texts do not use *mie* 滅 in reference to the meditative states they describe, instead using other apophatic descriptions such as *wunian* 無念 (no-thought). However, for the purpose of convenience, when discussing the philosophical implications of the notion of a meditative, apophatically described state characterized by the absence of basic elements of our ordinary experience, I will be using the term "cessation" in reference to both Chan and Nikāya texts. This of course involves a

66 X69, no. 1323, p. 8a7–8: 其心自在。畢竟不與諸妄虛幻塵勞蘊界生死諸入和合。For a translation, see Cheng Chien (1993: 103).

67 B25, no. 143, p. 220a10: 佛性者，非蔭界入.

68 McRae (1986: 427/十三): 其此流動之識颯然自滅。滅此識者乃是滅十地菩薩眾中障惑。此識滅已其心即虛凝寂淡泊皎潔泰然。Cf. T48, no. 2011, p. 379a11–13. For a translation of this passage, see McRae (1986: 130–31).

69 X09, no. 245, p. 534a13–14: 言滅識者。即所修之道也。意謂生死輪。都為起心。起心即妄。不論善惡不起即真。Cf. translation by Broughton (2009: 183).

tentative assumption that the states described in the texts of both traditions have a similar nature. I have already commented on the impossibility of reaching absolute certainty regarding such issues. Therefore, our philosophical considerations of the implications of the apophatic accounts present in texts of both traditions will have to involve a certain amount of speculation.

Subjective phenomenal experience and objective reality

So far in our investigation I have only briefly remarked on the fact that the aspects and elements of our first-person experience, such as the aggregates, also possess a representational nature. Drawing on Metzinger's theory, I have considered the possibility of phenomenal content playing a representational role in order to create a virtual image of reality and of ourselves in it. The very concept of something subjective, phenomenal and representational implies a notion of something that is objective and mind-independent. It is simply impossible to explain the functioning of the world and of us in it, if we only take into account the phenomenal elements that are available introspectively from the first-person perspective, as they do not form any coherent picture. Therefore, we naturally infer and assume that there are some crucial elements that are not given to us subjectively as phenomena and that are crucial for explaining the functioning of the world. These elements must somehow be correlated with the contents of our first-person experience of the world.

The exact status of these non-subjective aspects is another issue and varies according to a particular philosophical position. The answers may include: commonsense external world of bodies and persons, physical reality of spatiotemporal objects postulated by natural sciences, or hypothetical noumena which are unimaginable from our perspective. Even idealist and purely phenomenalist positions such as that of George Berkeley need to assume aspects (even if they are phenomenal) that are unavailable from an ordinary individual subjective perspective, in the form of God's mind. Regardless of whether they are phenomenal or not, they are certainly not access-conscious, as they are not available to introspection, direct verbalization or memory of one's experience. These globally inaccessible aspects cannot be described from a first-person perspective, and apparently there is nothing that is like for us to have them, or at least one is unable to talk about experiencing them.

This opens up the issue of how the contents of our first-person phenomenal experience are related to their hypothetical noumenal correlates. Are they their direct and faithful mental copies or are they different, and if so, then to what extent? In the course of its history, philosophy has offered various answers regarding these questions, ranging from the assumption of their relative similarity, to that of total inconceivability of the objective correlates of our experiences.

Recent developments within the philosophy of mind and cognitive science provide some new evidence regarding this crucial issue. Several researchers suggest that even seemingly basic elements of our subjective experience are heavily constructed and do not accurately reflect the nature of the hypothetical objective reality. One of the more important relevant concepts which appear in recent research is that of predictive coding or predictive processing. It turns out that our cognitive systems create models of reality based on already stored memories in order to predict incoming sensory input. According to Laukkonen and Slagter (2021: 199), this concept "recharacterizes organisms as fundamentally anticipatory – as continuously inferring or predicting the outside world based on prior experience". Instead of treating every stimulus as if it was something new and fresh, the organism just compares its predictions to new stimuli and only further processes those stimuli that do not match the predictions. The remaining data used to generate our supposed experience of the present is actually generated from the memory traces. This is done to minimize information processing which is time and energy consuming.

Solms (2021: 143) aptly summarizes this notion:

> Why treat everything in the world as if you'd never encountered it before? Instead, what the brain does is propagate inwards only that portion of the incoming information which does not match its expectations. That is why perception is nowadays sometimes described as 'fantasy' and 'controlled hallucination'.

As Solms suggests (2021: 144), "[w]hat appear in consciousness are not the raw sensory signals transmitted from the periphery, but rather predictive inferences derived from memory traces of such signals and their consequences".

This is particularly the case with our experience of time. Apparently, the sense of the present moment that we have is merely a mental construct based on processing and synthesizing various sets of data from the senses, each of which may have been received at a different time preceding them being consciously experienced. Metzinger (2009: 37–38) writes that "the temporal inwardness of the conscious Now is an illusion. There is no immediate contact with reality" and that "we are never in touch with the present". What we experience as the present moment actually already belongs to the past. Buonomano (2017: 216) notes that "while the unconscious brain continuously samples and processes information about events unfolding in time, consciousness itself is generated in a highly discontinuous manner". It seems that while the brain processes its input continuously, it only sends a finished narrative into consciousness from time to time at certain "junctures", in "fits and starts". However, we have no conscious awareness of these gaps or of the delay of our experience with respect to objective events. Buonomano (2017: 219) also points out that there is evidence that "the later sensory events can alter our conscious perception of the earlier events". For example, the meaning of the first word in some sentences may be fully determined only based on the context provided by the following words. However, if the sentence is spoken in a normal uninterrupted way, we are immediately consciously aware of the correct meaning of the word in question, and do not need to hear the following words to determine its meaning.

According to Marchetti (2014: 11–12), spatial aspects of our experience are also a result of a mental reconstruction based on synthesizing disconnected data from different senses into a unified image of a three-dimensional space with us in it. The spatiotemporal aspects of our experience are therefore not a faithful reflection of the structure of objective reality. One can perhaps raise a point that the structure of our experience agrees relatively well with that of classical physics, with the exception of the so-called qualia (e.g., colours, tastes) which are supposedly only present in our minds. Similar to our phenomenal experience, classical Newtonian physics is also based on the notion of distinct objects moving and entering causal relations in a three-dimensional, absolute space and of the steady, objective flow of time. This image of reality is however being challenged by the developments in physics roughly starting from the late nineteenth century. For example, the implications of Einstein's theory of relativity led to a revision of the classical concepts of time and space. Einsteinian special relativity theory implies a vision of a static, four-dimensional universe where time is just one of the dimensions. As Price (1997: 15) sums up, according to such a view "present has no special objective status, instead being perspectival in the way that the notion of here is. And I'll take it for granted that there is no objective flow of time". According to Jammer (2002: 160), "the relations 'earlier', 'simultaneous with', and 'later' are merely geometrical relations in the static four-dimensional space-time, and the terms 'past', 'present', and 'future' have no objective reality". Buonomano (2017: 11) labels this stance as "eternalist" as opposed to the commonsense, intuitive presentist stance, which contends that only the present is real. The upshot of this is of course that "our perception of the flow of time must be an illusion" and that it "must be relegated to some sort of trick of the conscious mind" (Buonomano 2017: 13).

Causation, and in particular the idea of causal asymmetry (i.e., the view that cause-effect relations always seem to be aligned from past to future and not future to past), is another of the commonsense notions which are being challenged by results of modern physics. As Price (1997: 266) argues, "causation and physical dependence are importantly anthropocentric notions" while "the asymmetry of causation is a projection of our own temporal asymmetry as agents in the world" (Price 1997: 264). Things get even stranger with more recent developments in physics. Glattfelder (2019: 273) writes:

> The amalgamation of information theory, black hole thermodynamics, and string theory is hinting at a radical ontology: The universe is a hologram. In other words, our three-dimensional reality is an illusion created by the information content encoded on a two-dimensional area.

It needs to be emphasized that none of these theories question the notion of objective reality in itself. They only challenge the commonsense image of it, which is to a large extent similar to that of classical physics. In other words, objective reality cannot be conceived of as consisting of objects in three-dimensional space engaged in causal relations which occur during an objective flow of time. Objective reality cannot even be said meaningfully to be external to us, as the notions of inner and outer are specific to our experience and should not be applied beyond it. It does not mean, however, that there is no noumenal, objective correlate of what we experience from the first-person perspective. We can agree with Tartaglia (2017: 311), when he claims that:

> [T]here is nothing we can cogently say about this independent existence, except that (1) it is transcendent (it is not accurately characterized as belonging to the world of objective space and time, though its existence is responsible for our finding this world), and that (2) it exists.

In order to illustrate the extent to which the world of our experience may differ from the hypothetical noumenal reality, let us consider an example of a movie being played from a digital file on a screen. When the movie is played using some software and hardware, we can experience movements, colourful images and a steady progression of a plot from the beginning of a movie to its ending. But the digital file that contains the movie consists just of bytes, i.e., units of digital information. In contrast, our first-person phenomenal experience and the world of Newtonian physics are still similar to a significant extent, just as an analogue movie bears some similarity to the tape from which it is being played.

To a considerable degree, these developments lend support to Kant's idea that time, space, substantiality and causality are not features of the things in themselves but are a priori forms which the mind applies to experience.[70] It might be the case that the fact that classical physics has a particular structure and uses particular concepts is only because it is a reflection of the structure of our experience. Seen from this perspective, it could not be seen as a faithful image of the true nature of the hypothetical objective reality, but a useful instrumental model which allows us to foresee certain events or to efficiently manipulate reality.[71] Of course, in order for it to be possible, there must exist some sort of correlation between the elements of classical physics and the objective reality. However, on the micro level of quantum physics and on the macro level of relativity theory, classical physics starts to fail. Hence, one can agree with Tartaglia (2017: 303) when he claims that "we drew up our physical conception of the world on the basis of (phenomenal) conscious experience", and that the independent reality of our experiences is not to be found in the world described by science (Tartaglia 2017: 311). Hypothetical species endowed with different sensory modalities to ours would likely create an entirely different form of physics which would perhaps not even be based on a notion of distinct bodies causally interacting in a three-dimensional space.

All this is very important from the point of view of our investigation, as it gives a new perspective on Nikāya and early Chan statements, such as Mazu Daoyi's claim of one deluded thought being the root of three realms of existence[72] or Ānanda's proclamation that "the world

70 For a Kantian reading of the Nikāyas, see Hamilton (1999).

71 Such instrumentalist interpretation of physics has already been offered in the nineteenth century by Ernst Mach.

72 X78, no. 1553, p. 449a1–2.

in the human body is that by which we perceive and conceive of the world".[73] From this perspective they do not appear to be merely forms of a rhetorical hyperbole and can be said to be philosophically plausible. It needs to be said that the issue of potential objective correlates of the phenomenal content of our experience is not discussed explicitly in Nikāya and Chan texts. As we shall see, they do, however, imply certain views regarding that matter. It needs to be emphasized that the view which allows the possibility of noumenal objective correlates of the elements of phenomenal consciousness is not in itself at odds with the antirealist position we have inferred from the texts of both traditions. The latter position assumes that the world as we experience it owes some of its structural features to the workings of our cognitive processes and that the notion of the world independent of our cognitive activity is devoid of meaning. An antirealist position can be harmonized with an assumption that there is an objective correlate of our phenomenal experience, but it is entirely different from it, or it is even inconceivable from our perspective.

Phenomenal consciousness, language, life and death

Certain specific features that characterize our first-person phenomenal experience are especially significant from the soteriological point of view of Buddhism. Particularly relevant in this context is the following passage from the *Mahānidāna-sutta* (DN 15/ii.63–64):

> It is to this extent (*ettāvatā*), Ánanda, that one can be born, age, and die, pass away and re-arise, to this extent that there is a pathway for designation, to this extent that there is a pathway for language, to this extent that there is a pathway for description, to this extent that there is a sphere for understanding (*paññāvacaraṃ*), to this extent that the round turns for describing this state of being, that is, when there is mentality-materiality together with consciousness (*nāmarūpaṃ saha viññāṇena*).[74]

73 SN 35.116/iv.93.

74 DN 15/II 63–64: *ettāvatā kho, ānanda, jāyetha vā jīyetha vā mīyetha vā cavetha vā upapajjetha vā. ettāvatā adhivacanapatho, ettāvatā niruttipatho, ettāvatā paññattipatho, ettāvatā paññāvacaraṃ, ettāvatā vaṭṭaṃ vattati itthattaṃ paññāpanāya yadidaṃ nāmarūpaṃ saha viññāṇena aññamaññapaccayatā pavattati.* Translation follows Bodhi (2007: 66), with "*paññāvacaraṃ*" translated as "sphere of understanding" instead of Bodhi's rendering as "sphere of wisdom". There are good reasons to believe that the term *paññā* did not possess in the Nikāyas such

The complex of *nāmarūpa* and *viññāṇa* seems to represent one of the earlier ways in which Nikāya authors tried to express the notion of a whole range of phenomenal experience. According to certain texts this complex can be considered pretty much synonymous with the five *khandhas* (e.g, MN 9/i.153, SN 12.2/ii.3–4). Anālayo (2017a: 803) comments that the "range of *nāma-rūpa* – as the conceptual and apparitional aspects of an object ... encompasses the whole gamut of what is present to consciousness" and "appears to represent the entire field of experience available to consciousness".

Therefore, the above passage of the *Mahānidāna-sutta* seems to convey a notion that dying and being reborn is only possible in the sphere of *nāmarūpa* and *viññāṇa*, i.e., that of phenomenal consciousness. This makes particular sense in the light of our considerations about the relation of objective reality to the world of our experience. One can meaningfully speak about dying or being born only with reference to a particular living being in relation to other beings and objects within a certain spatiotemporal framework. Let us suppose that, as modern physics imply, there would be no objective flow of time, no causal asymmetry and no distinct three-dimensional objects separate from each other. Then, it would be simply impossible to meaningfully speak about dying or being born. Interestingly, this conclusion agrees with the tenor of the comments made by Einstein in a letter to a family of his deceased friend, Michele Besso. He wrote:

> Now he has departed a little ahead of me from this quaint world. This means nothing. For us faithful physicists, the separation between past, present, and future has only the meaning of an illusion, though a persistent one.[75]

When stating that death "means nothing" Einstein is not writing from an ordinary perspective of our worldly experience, but from the ultimate perspective of what he considered to be objective reality. And indeed, death can only mean something in the phenomenal world of our experience characterized by temporality, spatiality, substantiality and asymmetrical causal relations.

The idea that the very notions of being born and dying are dependent on the particular structure of our mental processes and not

---

lofty, unequivocally positive meaning as it did in the later forms of Buddhism, and that it originally referred to a linguistically mediated, and thus imperfect, form of knowledge.

75 *Albert Einstein, Michele Besso Correspondance, 1903–1955* (Paris: Hermann, 1972), 537–38. Cited in Jammer (2002: 161).

reflective of hypothetical objective reality harmonizes with several paradoxical statements found in early Chan texts. We have already brought to attention Shenhui's claim that birth and death (or arising and cessation: *shengmie* 生滅) follow the arousal of the mind (*xinqi* 心起)[76] and Wuzhu's statements equating birth and death (*shengsi* 生死) with the arousal of the mind (*qixin* 起心)[77] and thinking (*younian* 有念).[78] Interpreted from a traditional Buddhist perspective, these claims could mean that due to mental acts one generates karma which causes future rebirth. However, in light of our recent considerations, these statements gain a much more literal meaning.

The already mentioned fragment of the *Mahānidāna-sutta* is also interesting for the fact that it states that one can be born and die only to an extent that there is a pathway for designation (*adhivacanapatha*), a pathway for language (*niruttipatha*), a pathway for concept (*paññattipatha*), and a range for understanding (*paññāvacara*). One way of interpreting the message of this fragment is that the range of phenomenal experience (i.e., *nāma-rūpa*) is coextensive with the range of verbal expressibility. We have already noted that in the modern philosophy of mind, the fact of a state being phenomenally conscious pretty much correlates with its content being globally available, which includes availability to the modules responsible for speech. Indeed, what we are conscious of, we can speak about, both aloud and through inner speech. Some Nikāya texts seem to display an awareness of the connection of phenomenal consciousness with verbal expressibility. This seems to be expressed by the notion of *saññā*. Thus, the *Nibbedhika-sutta* (AN 6.63/iii.410–417) contains a line that *saññā* has verbal expression (*vohāra*) as its result. Other texts inform us of an intricate relation between *saññā* and *vitakka* – the latter usually referring to verbal thoughts used in internal monologue. According to the passage in the *Madhupiṇḍika-sutta* (MN 18/i.112), what one perceives (*yaṃ sañjānāti*), one also thinks about (*taṃ vitakketi*).

The second potential implication of the *Mahānidāna-sutta* is also significant. Co-extensiveness of the range of language (as expressed by the terms *nirutti*, *paññatti*, *vocara*) and understanding (*paññā*) with that of phenomenal consciousness (i.e., *nāmarūpa*) and with the possibility of being born and dying could imply that language and conceptuality

76 B25, no. 143, p. 237a4.
77 T51, no. 2075, p. 193b15: 起心即是生死。
78 T51, no. 2075, p. 191c29: 有念是生死。

are somehow a contributing factor to those features of our subjective experience which make *saṃsāra* possible.[79] As we have already noted, such a claim occurs in an explicit form in some early Chan texts. In the *Lidai fabao ji*, Wuzhu states that verbal explanation (*yanshuo* 言說) is the origin of the three Worlds and flux and change.[80]

The idea of the constitutional role played by language in our experience of the world seems to also be conveyed by the passage found in an identical form in the *Addhā-sutta* (Iti 63/54) and the *Samiddhi-sutta* (SN 1.20/i.18) which states that beings (*satta*) perceive in terms of what can be declared/expressed (*akkheyyasaññī*), and thus are established (*patiṭṭhita*) in the expressible (*akkheyya*). Perceiving in terms of what can be declared/expressed could be interpreted as referring to the fact that the structure of our phenomenal consciousness reflects that of our language. Being established (*patiṭṭhita*), which is referred to in this passage, probably has negative connotations. In the Nikāyas, the generation of the *saṃsāric* existence characterized by the notions of birth and death is often connected with the process of the establishment of consciousness.[81] Thus, experiencing the world through the lens of language would result in the maintenance of *saṃsāra*. The power of language is attested by the *Nāma-sutta* (SN 1.61/i.39) which states that name "conquers all" (*sabbaṃ addhabhavi*) and has everything under its power so that no being is free from conditioning by a name.[82]

Of all the five aggregates, *saññā* is the one that is particularly connected with language. While the term *saññā* is usually translated as perception or apperception, it may be said that it refers to our conscious experience with the emphasis on the aspect of the linguistic expressibility of its content. Commenting on the role of *saññā*, Gombrich (2009: 149) has aptly noted that "we have to express our cognitions through language, using *saññā*, but that imposes on experiences linguistic categories which cannot do justice to its fluidity" and that application of language to one's experience implied in the notion of *saññā* has been considered problematic by the Buddha himself (Gombrich, 2009: 150).

79 A similar point has already been made by Wynne (2010: 155), who writes: "Indeed, the equating of the two latter concepts ('existence' and 'time') with those of 'articulation', 'designation' and 'understanding' indicates the understanding that space-time is only conceptually real."

80 T51, no. 2075, p. 191c21–23. Translation follows Adamek (2007: 377).

81 E.g., SN 12.64/ii.101: *yattha patiṭṭhitaṃ viññāṇaṃ virūḷhaṃ, atthi tattha nāmarūpassa avakkanti.*

82 Cf. Levman (2017a: 37), for translation and discussion of this passage.

In some Nikāya texts the notion of *saññā* is closely connected with that of *papañca*. The latter term carries with it the connotations of some cognitive distortion connected with the process of conceptual proliferation and expansion. Gombrich (2009: 150) translates *papañca* as "conceptualizing".[83] Hamilton (1996: 56) has suggested that the denominative verb *papañceti* should be translated as "one causes to become manifold" and that *papañca* causes "seeing things as manifold" and to "attributing independent existence to them, and to oneself as perceiver".[84] The *Madhupiṇḍika-sutta* (MN 18/i.111–112) speaks of *papañcasaññāsaṅkhā*, while in the *Aṭṭhakavagga*, *saññā* is said to condition the arising of *papañcasaṅkhā* (lit. proliferation-name: Snp 4.11/170).[85] The *Adantāgutta-sutta* (SN 35.94/iv.71) speaks of *papañcasaññā*. All these terms seem to refer to the same negatively evaluated cognitive process entangling human beings in the net of suffering. Among the meanings of the word *saṅkhā* we find "name", "word", "definition", "number", "calculation" or "estimating". Therefore, it can be said that it has very strong linguistic connotations. It seems then, that the compound *papañcasaññāsaṅkhā* refers to a form of consciousness or perception (*saññā*) which is a result of some sort of negatively evaluated proliferation (*papañca*) that may concern some elements of language (*saṅkhā*). Wynne (2010: 131) has translated it as "conceptual diffuseness or proliferation" while Levman (2017a: 28), rather literally, as "proliferation-perception-naming".

In exactly what way can language influence our conscious experience? By comparing language with the world of our ordinary experience we note a high degree of isomorphism. Nouns correspond to beings and objects, verbs to activities, and adjectives to qualities. The most natural and simple conclusion would be that the structure of language is simply a faithful reflection of the objective reality. However, it may also be the other way around: the content of our ordinary consciousness may have been processed to possess a particular structure exactly in order for us to be able to express it linguistically. We are, after all, social beings, and communicating by the medium of language is crucial for our survival. Starting from the twentieth century, there has been an important trend in Western thought which attributes great importance

83 Cf. Gombrich (2009: 150): "The very act of conceptualizing, the Buddha held thus involves some inaccuracy. His term for it was *papañca*".

84 Hamilton (1996: 57).

85 The term also occurs in Snp 4.14/179 but without connection to *saññā*.

to the role in which our language shapes our perception of the world. Summing up the relevant results of recent research in psychology and cognitive science, Bronkhorst (2016: 15) notes that "experiments show that language influences perception already at pre-conscious and non-linguistic levels" and that "there are good reasons to think that language plays an important role in the construction of our experience of the world" (Bronkhorst, 2022: 6).

Language involves manifoldness and diversity of names, which are sharply delineated from one another. Therefore, if our consciousness of the world is dependent on the structure of the language that we use, then we are bound to cognize it as consisting of separate entities which are separated from other entities by rigid boundaries, and which are the vehicles of certain qualities and agents or objects of actions. As Hamilton (2000: 76; original emphasis) notes, "each more clearly defined and identified aspect of what one is experiencing is separated from others. What one is doing in the process … *making manifold and naming* what one is experiencing".

Such a reading works well in the context of the already noted fragment of the *Samiddhilokapañhā-sutta* (SN 35.68/iv.39–40) which seems to equate the world (*loka*) with the concept of the world (*lokapaññatti*), and the fragment of SĀ 234 which spoke about world-name, world-words, world-language as being pretty much synonymous with the notion of the world. It also harmonizes with the already mentioned statement by Wuzhu in the *Lidai fabao ji*, that verbal explanation (*yanshuo* 言說) is the origin of the three Worlds (*sanjieben* 三界本).

However, we should be wary of overestimating the level of creative power attested to language in the Nikāyas, as it certainly does not reach the extreme of linguistic relativism connected with Sapir (1929) and Whorf (1940). There does not seem to be enough evidence in favour of the thesis that learning and using a particular language instead of some other one has a dramatic effect on our cognition. It is doubtful if the structure of our consciousness would fundamentally change, were we to speak a different language or never learn to use language at all. It is rather that we are able to create, learn and use languages at all, because our mind is beforehand already primed for it due to some of its innate features. The very same features of our mind that make the mastery of language possible, probably also contribute to a certain degree to the specific structure of our phenomenal consciousness.[86]

86 Cf. Bronkhorst (2022: 6), for a discussion of this problem.

Chapter 4

MEDITATIVE CESSATION AS A PROCESS OF COGNITIVE DECONSTRUCTION

Is meditative cessation a form of simple insentience?[1]

As we have seen in the previous chapter, both the Nikāya and early Chan texts suggest that the structure of the world as we experience it is heavily dependent on various elements of our cognitive architecture. The content of our ordinary conscious experience is not a faithful reflection of the hypothetical noumenal, mind-independent reality. However, the same texts speak about the possibility of cessation or ending of such a world of experience which occurs in a special meditative state and has fundamental soteriological significance.

The very notion of such a state is very interesting philosophically and inspires many questions which we will consider in the course of this chapter. By what mechanism does it occur? How can it be conducive to the realization of the most important goals of the Buddhist path, such as psychological transformation, vision of reality in its true form and liberation from *saṃsāra*? What is it like to be in such a state, or in other words, what is its first-person content? Does the very possibility of meditative cessation have some implications for the question of our identity?

The first impulse may be to conceive of the mechanism of such a cessation as simply becoming unaware of the elements that are said to cease. Such temporary insentience may be accomplished in deep states of meditative calm, where either one is so strongly absorbed into a meditation object that one is unaware of anything else, or the mind

1 This chapter contains certain claims that have already appeared, though not in an identical form, in Polak (2023a) and Polak (2023c).

and the senses enter into a state of temporary stasis resulting in mental and sensory inactivity.

Some Chan authors were aware of the possibility of interpreting apophatic accounts of meditative states as accounts of mere insentience or annihilation. For example, when commenting on Bodhidharma's teachings, Zongmi emphasizes in the *Chanyuan zhuquanji duxu* that although in the highest state one cuts off all thoughts (*juezhunian* 絕諸念), it is not an annihilation (*duanmie* 斷滅).[2] When Shenhui considers in the *Wenda zazheng yi* the possibility of a state in which one does not generate acts of intention (*zuoyi*), he rhetorically asks whether it does not differ (*wubie* 無別) from that of a "deaf fool" (*longsu* 聾俗).[3]

The paradoxical nature of this specific form of insentience which is connected with the highest meditative state is explored in the *Dasheng wusheng fangbianmen*. The text speaks about "not seeing even one thing" (*yiwubujian* 一物不見). Initially, this appears to imply ordinary insentience. However, according to the text it actually results from a very specific way of viewing (*kan* 看), which is without any obstruction (*zhangai* 障礙) or constriction (*jiansuo* 卷縮), and which involves "unfolding" (*shuzhan* 舒展) of the body and mind, and "viewing afar" (*yuankan* 遠看) with an "extensive release" (*fangkuang* 放曠).[4] In a similar vein, Shenhui states in the *Wenda zazheng yi* that to see "no thing" (*wuwu* 無物) is the true and constant seeing.[5]

It is clear that we are not dealing here with the type of insentience which is resultant of absorption into a meditation object during the higher stages of classical forms of calm meditation. The epithets used in the text describe a mode of viewing that is radically different from a one-pointed, exclusive concentration which characterizes mainstream forms of meditative calm. This is confirmed by another fragment of the *Dasheng wusheng fangbianmen* which claims that when the six sense faculties (*liugen* 六根) are pure (*qingjing* 清淨) and unimpeded (*lizhang* 離障), they do not perceive their respective sense

2 T48, no. 2015, p. 405b5–6: 問諸緣絕時有斷滅否。答雖絕諸念亦不斷滅。See translation by Broughton (2009: 138).

3 B25, no. 143, pp. 235a11–236a1: 若不作意，即是聾俗無別。Translation by McRae (2023: 159).

4 T85, no. 2834, p. 1273c6–9: 一物不見　和。看淨細細看。即用淨心眼無邊無涯除遠看　和言。問無障礙看　和問見何物　答。一物不見和向前遠看。Cf. translation by McRae (1986: 172–73).

5 B25, no. 143, p. 232a7: 見無物即是真見常見。See McRae (2023: 157) for a translation and discussion of this passage.

characteristics (*liugenxiang* 六根相), which is synonymous with liberation (*jietuo* 解脫).[6]

The *Tiansheng guangdeng lu* attributes a seemingly paradoxical statement to Baizhang in which he claims that hearing nothing (*wuyiqiewen* 無一切聞) while not being without hearing (lit. not non-hearing, *yiwuwuwen* 亦無無聞), is called the right hearing (*zhengwen* 正聞).[7]

It is impossible for us to ascertain whether all these accounts actually refer to genuine meditative experiences during which one experiences reality in such a way, that all its basic elements, such as "things" (*wu* 物) or characteristics (*xiang* 相), are absent. It is possible that some or even all these paradoxical apophatic accounts were just a form of literary genre meant to discuss and illustrate certain philosophical tenets of Mahāyāna. It is after all relatively easy to develop a style of writing that relies on the usage of paradox and denial, and to create apophatic descriptions without basing them on personal meditative experiences.[8] One other possibility is that the statements about "not seeing a thing" or "seeing nothing" are highly metaphoric, and refer to a mode of experiencing where the objects are still experienced, but without desire and conceit, and as a result they are not substantialized or reified. In other words, the content of a meditator's experience is not radically different from that of an ordinary person; it is only the emotional reaction to it that differs. Such may be the intended meaning of a fragment of the *Dunwu rudao yaomen lun* which attributes to Dazhu a claim that "seeing by seeing nothing" (*jianwusuojian* 見無所見) is the right seeing (*zhengjian* 正見). Achieving such a vision is synonymous with seeing by the means of the "eye of the Buddha" (*foyan* 佛眼).[9] However, the text later explains that it is a mode of perception where at the time of seeing all forms (*jianyiqiese* 見一切色) one does not arouse defilements (*ran* 染) or love and hate (*aizeng* 愛憎).

---

6 T85, no. 2834, p. 1273c16–18: 如是乃至六根清淨。六根離障。一切無礙是即解脫。不見六根相。For translation, see McRae (1986: 174).

7 X78, no. 1553, p. 461b1–2: 無一切聞。亦無無聞。名正聞。Cf. translation by Cleary (1978: 59).

8 Cf. Bronkhorst's (2022: 1–2) claim that "the philosophical developments within Buddhism can well be accounted for without assuming any kind of extraordinary experience whatsoever".

9 X63, no. 1223, p. 19a16–18: 問。云何是正見。答。見無所見。即名正見。問。云何名見無所見。答。見一切色時不起染著。不染著者。不起愛憎心。即名見無所見也。若得見無所見時。即名佛眼。Cf. translation by Blofeld (1962: 51).

We need to clearly articulate different philosophical implications resulting from the two possible ways of reading such accounts. According to one interpretation, although from the third-person perspective the sense organ of a meditator reacts to the stimulus in the same way as that of an ordinary person, the resultant first-person conscious content is entirely different. What was experienced as an object by an ordinary person, is experienced in an entirely different, unspecified way by a meditator. This could be labelled as a strong interpretation.

According to a weak interpretation, the first-person content experienced by the meditator is not substantially different from that of an ordinary person; it merely does not arouse emotional responses and wrong views of substantiality. In such a case, labelling this type of vision as "not seeing anything" or "seeing nothing" must be considered a type of rhetorical hyperbole. It is the "strong" interpretation that is particularly interesting from the philosophical perspective, and we shall be considering its implications and plausibility, regardless of whether it is in harmony with the meaning intended by the authors of the fragments in question.

Some accounts of meditative cessation in the Nikāyas also imply that it was not conceived of as a state of total mental stasis and insentience. For example, although the attainment of cessation (*nirodhasamāpatti*) involves stopping of perception and feeling, a meditator is nonetheless capable of some sort of cognitive functioning, as the stock description account of that state mentions that "having seen with understanding, his influxes are utterly exhausted" (e.g., MN 26/i.175).[10] Shulman (2014: 33–34) has noted the presence of several ambiguous features of this state which make it questionable whether it was originally understood as simple form of unconsciousness. He rightly notes that the notion of stilling of perception and feeling does not preclude the possibility of "a conscious state that is beyond these types of cognition but which still maintains a degree of awareness" and that "transcendence of *saññā* ('perceptions') does not inevitably demand that no form of consciousness can still operate". Daniel M. Stuart (2013: 43) considered the possibility that the notion of *saññāvedayitanirodha* was "one of the earliest ways that Buddhist practitioners attempted to make sense of the ineffable liberatory experience".

10 MN 26/i.175: *puna caparaṃ, bhikkhave, bhikkhu sabbaso nevasaññānāsaññāyatanaṃ samatikkamma saññāvedayitanirodhaṃ upasampajja viharati, paññāya cassa disvā āsavā parikkhīṇā honti*. Of course, the passage does not explicitly state that "seeing with *paññā*" occurs exactly in the state of cessation.

Similarly, when read directly, the already mentioned fragment of the *Udayamāṇavapucchā* (Snp 5.13/512) implies that the stopping (*uparujjhati*) of consciousness coincides with a particular mode of behaving mindfully, which would make it a cognitive state. In the meditative state described in the *Sandha-sutta*, perceptions (*saññā*) towards all conceivable objects are said to have vanished (*vibhūta*), and yet the meditator is still somehow meditating (*jhāyati ca pana*).[11] In the *Kalahavivāda-sutta*, all possible modes of perception are being denied, but nonetheless the text insists that the meditator is not impercipient or unconscious (*asaññī*).[12]

Cessation as direct cognition

The above considerations are very relevant for the issue of the mechanism of the arising of the meditative state of cessation described in early Chan and Nikāya texts. They suggest that the special type of unconsciousness described in these texts would not come about through suppressing sense impressions and inactivating the whole mind. It would also not be a selective type of insentience when one is unaware of the world due to being completely absorbed in some truth or a meditative object.[13]

In my recent paper (Polak 2023a) I have hypothesized that such a form of cessation could perhaps involve a gradual suspension of higher-level constructive processes responsible for several key features of our phenomenal consciousness.[14] This may correspond to what in early Chan texts is expressed by the already mentioned statements about the

11 AN 11.9/v.325.

12 Snp 4.11/170.

13 There are reports among modern meditators of attaining at least temporary states of cessation of phenomenal consciousness, not through *samatha* type of meditation, but in the course of what could either be classified as "open monitoring" or "non-dual" types of meditation which to some extent correspond to *vipassanā*. See Laukkonen at al. (2023), Davis and Vago (2013), and Warren (2013). Of course, we cannot know whether "cessations" described in these reports are the same states as those in the Nikāya and Chan texts.

14 A very interesting hypothesis in a somewhat similar vein has been proposed by Laukkonen et al. (2023: 73, 78) who explain meditative cessation of consciousness as "the logical result of progressively reducing abstract predictive processing in the brain". They also hypothesize that there may occur a reduction of neural integration which leads to "unbinding of the elements of experience that bind together a coherent consciousness" and as the result to unconsciousness.

absence of the arousal/activation of the mind (*qixin* 起心), and about the elimination of thoughts (*nian* 念) and ideations (*xiang* 想). By analogy, in case of the Nikāyas, this would entail turning off the cognitive processes described by verbs such as *sañjānāti*, *abhisaṅkharoti* or *papañceti* and the resultant elements and features of experience rendered by the terms *saññā*, *saṅkhāra/saṅkhata* and *papañca*, respectively. The cessation of the level of experience conceptualized in terms of the *khandhas* in the Nikāyas would thus occur not due to their removal or by being unconscious of them, but due to the suspension of the processes that made them possible in the first place.[15]

I have also suggested (Polak 2023a) that this type of unique cessation of consciousness could coincide with the sense faculties still working and remaining sensitive and the mind operating in a way that does not lead to a generation of globally available content. In the preceding chapters I have referred to recent developments in philosophy of mind and cognitive science which suggest that most of our cognition occurs in exactly that way. Dietrich (2003: 237) suggests that higher-level associative processes could be turned off, without ensuing inactivity of the lower-level ones.[16]

It is noteworthy in this context that in the Nikāya discussion of the attainment of cessation (MN 43/i.296), the faculties (*indriya*) are said to be very clear (*vippasanna*).[17] Interestingly, some Nikāya passages imply

15 Cf. a hypothesis by Laukkonen et al. (2023: 77) that "unbinding or disintegrating of these aggregates play a role in the gradual breakdown of functional connectivity, information integration, and associated consciousness". However, this does not seem to imply deconstruction of the *khandhas* themselves but only their mutual unbinding.

16 Laukkonen et al. (2023: 79) note an "additional challenge to conducting research on cessation" which is constituted by "the discrepancy between phenomenological absence and the absence of processing at a physiological level". In other words, brain monitoring of subjects supposedly undergoing cessation reveals that phenomenological absence of consciousness is not correlated with the total absence of processing within the brain as the latter "may continue to respond to stimuli even though they are not registered consciously". However, this feature is only challenging when cessation is understood in line with the *Visuddhimagga* as a state of total mental stasis. The possibility of information processing at the physiological level harmonizes with our interpretation of cessation.

17 Commenting on that line, Shulman (2014: 34, n. 88) notes that: "these bright faculties imply some level of consciousness". In her entry on the meaning of *indriya*, Cone (2001: 376) notes that "the serenity of the senses is perceptible to others".

a belief that a state of consciousness manifests on the face of a person, and may be immediately discerned by outside observers.[18] This was the case with the newly awakened Buddha, whose clear features (*vippasanna indriya*) and very bright and clear (*parisuddha pariyodāta*) skin complexion (*chavivaṇṇa*) were noted by Ājīvaka Upaka (MN 85/ii.93). If a person in the state of *saññāvedayitanirodha* is said to have very clear faculties, then this implies a certain form of sentience and not a dead-like state of total insentience.

Therefore, it might be the case that the senses of a person in the state of meditative cessation still receive their input, and it is represented further up the neural system. However, due to suspension of higher associative processes, this input would perhaps no longer be organized into the familiar mode of phenomenal presentation known from our everyday experience. Were one to use Kant's terminology, this could correspond to the sense input not being organized by the forms of sensuality (ger. *Sinnlichkeit*) and categories of understanding (ger. *Verstand*), which make our experience into what it is. One could therefore still speak of some form of cognizing reality. I have already commented on how several key features of our ordinary phenomenal consciousness are not a reflection of objective reality, but of the specific structure and functioning of our cognitive apparatus. Therefore, their deconstruction would entail a cessation of the ordinary world of human experience. This may perhaps be the meaning of the Buddha's instruction in the *Māluṅkyaputta-sutta* (SN 35.95/iv.72–76) and in the *Bāhiya-sutta* (Ud 1.10/6–9). In these two texts the Buddha gives Māluṅkyaputta and Bāhiya, respectively, an instruction to the effect that "regarding things seen ... in the seen there will be merely the seen".[19] An analogous exhortation is repeated regarding the heard, sensed and cognized. The Buddha then claims that as the result:

> [Y]ou will not be "by that". When you are not "by that" (*na tena*), then you will not be "therein" (*na tattha*). When, you are not "therein", then you will be neither here (*nevidha*) nor beyond (*na huraṃ*) nor in between the two (*na ubhayamantarena*). This itself is the end of suffering.[20]

18 Cf. Wittgenstein's (2007: 40e.) comment in the *Zettel*, that consciousness "is in the face".

19 SN 35.95/iv.73: *ettha ca te, mālukyaputta, diṭṭhasutamutaviññātabbesu dhammesu diṭṭhe diṭṭhamattaṃ bhavissati.*

20 SN 35.95/iv.73: *tato tvaṃ, mālukyaputta, na tena. yato tvaṃ, mālukyaputta, na tena; tato tvaṃ, mālukyaputta, na tattha. yato tvaṃ, mālukyaputta, na tattha; tato tvaṃ,*

One way of reading the text is by putting the emphasis on "you" (*tvaṃ*) and its absence in all potential situations. Therefore, this would be in harmony with the traditionally understood not-self teaching, in the meaning of the self not being present within a state described in this text. However, an alternative reading may place the focus on the absence of "that", "therein", "here", "beyond" and "between the two". These terms could be interpreted as referring to the most basic categories characterizing our phenomenal existence, and in particular spatiality. The postulate of the seen in the seen, etc., could therefore be read as an account of bare, unmediated cognition of reality.[21] According to such a reading, an act of direct cognition would be synonymous with the deconstruction of the world of our experience together with its most basic categories.

Instead of considering cessation as a state of mental stasis, it can therefore be conceptualized as a state of direct, relatively unprocessed cognition which remains as faithful to perceived reality as possible. Perhaps this is implied by the passage in the *Mūlapariyāya-sutta* (MN 1/i.1–6) which claims that instead of perceiving (*sañjānāti*) various elements of reality, an awakened being directly knows it (*abhijānāti*) as it really is. According to the *Paramaṭṭhaka-sutta* (Snp 4.5/156–157), not even a subtlest *saññā* is fabricated (*pakappita*) with respect to what is seen, heard and sensed by a perfect meditator described in the text.[22] This also does not imply insentience, but rather that the sensory input (i.e., the seen, the heard etc.) is not "translated" into an interpreted, verbally expressible form of consciousness (*saññā*).

In the earlier part of this chapter, I have briefly mentioned developments in the philosophy of mind and cognitive science which suggest that the generation of ordinary phenomenal consciousness involves temporal delay and its content does not keep up with the physical "now" of our senses and the external environment. If every occurrence of ordinary consciousness involves a delay with respect to the present and generation of knowledge whose content is not representative of the true current state of things, then it cannot fulfill the Nikāya criteria which demand seeing things as they really are (*yathābhūtaṃ*) in the

---

mālukyaputta, nevidha, na huraṃ, na ubhayamantarena. esevanto dukkhassā'ti. This and the previous passage are translated by Bodhi (2000: 1175–76).

21 For such an interpretation see Wynne (2018a).

22 Snp 4.5/157: *tassīdha diṭṭhe va sute mute vā, pakappitā natthi aṇūpi saññā. Muta* can be understood as meaning either "sensed" or "thought".

visible state of things (*diṭṭhadhamma*). Elsewhere (Polak 2023a), I have suggested that the state of perfect mindfulness could therefore not coincide with the arising of such a form of consciousness.[23] This, perhaps, is the meaning of a line in the *Udayamāṇavapucchā* (Snp 5.13/215) about a particular way of "living mindful" (*satassa carato*) with respect to feelings, which causes consciousness (*viññāṇa*) to be stopped (*uparujjhati*). Regardless of whether this was the intended meaning of this fragment, the notion of perfect mindfulness coinciding with the stopping of consciousness does not seem so absurd in the light of our considerations in this chapter. If cessation occurs by turning off forms of cognitive operations such as predictive processing which are responsible for the heavily interpreted character of our phenomenal consciousness, then the remaining, more basic cognitive processes may continue their operations unhindered.

Why does consciousness arise?

According to the developments in the modern cognitive science and the philosophy of mind we have been considering in the preceding two chapters and contrary to commonsense, intuitive views, it is not consciousness that actively thinks, solves cognitive problems or undertakes decisions. Oakley and Halligan (2017: 2) summarize this position, by stating that "'consciousness' although temporally congruent involves no executive, causal, or controlling relationship with any of the familiar psychological processes conventionally attributed to it". We have reviewed the evidence suggesting that the actual processes responsible for our agency, active cognitive processing and creativity occur through multiple parallel unconscious activities which are not phenomenal in nature. As Solms (2021: 78, 224) aptly points out, pretty much everything the mind does can be done well unconsciously, in the form of algorithmic processing. Therefore, it should at least be theoretically possible to temporarily function without ordinary consciousness (in the sense of access consciousness) and without falling at the same time into total insentience and mental stasis. Establishing whether this is indeed the case, is important in the context of our considerations of

23 Cf. Laukkonen et al. (2023: 73): "[I]f awareness rests only in the now, even very basic structures of ordinary cognition should logically fall away, including conceptualization, self-awareness and time perception".

the possibility of meditative cessation of ordinary conscious experience coinciding with maintaining some form of cognizance and sentience. Of course, this concerns only our wakeful state, as it is commonplace that we experience a gap in our conscious experience which corresponds to the time-interval of deep sleep. However, we do not experience such gaps during wakefulness which may give the impression that consciousness is a constant and inherent feature of our wakeful state. The question that we will now consider is whether the organism needs to uninterruptedly maintain such a form of consciousness.

In order to deal with this problem, we must first consider the question of why exactly does consciousness arise? In the preceding two chapters we have already hinted at its functional role as a "global workspace" which makes certain content available throughout the modules of the cognitive system allowing them to access it simultaneously. This usually implies that this data is introspectable, reportable in speech and available to short-term, working memory and potentially integrable to long-term memory. The fact of certain data being globally accessible is correlated with the fact of us being conscious of it in the common sense of the word. An interesting hypothesis regarding the cause of the arising of consciousness has been recently offered by Solms. According to his theory (Solms 2021: 220–23) human organisms prefer to resort to automatic, non-conscious forms of processing, as they are highly precise, fast and minimize uncertainty. That is due to the general tendency of all self-organizing systems within the universe to minimize free-energy, which in thermodynamic terms is correlated with entropy, while in information-theoretic ones with surprisal and uncertainty (Solms 2019: 5). However, we do not live in stable and fully predictable environments. On the contrary, we often meet situations where our automatic and fast algorithmic patterns stored in our memories are not enough to efficiently deal with a new situation which challenges our functional and structural integrity and ability to maintain homeostasis. According to Solms (2019: 13), the evolutionary role of consciousness lies in the fact that it "guides the behavior of self-organizing systems as they negotiate situations beyond the bounds of their preferred states". This is possible, because in Solms's view consciousness is fundamentally a feeling; feeling is the constitutive feature of every consciousness, while its cognitive and volitional aspects are not as basic and essential. Feelings, with their affective valence, serve as a sort of a compass, which "enables us to determine in the heat of the moment whether one course of action is better or worse than another"

(Solms 2021: 101). The feeling of pleasure is a signal that our actions are moving us towards the desired goal of restoring homeostasis and minimizing free energy, entropy and uncertainty, while the opposite is the case with the feelings of pain and stress.

Is conscious experience generated continuously during wakeful states?

What is particularly important in our context is that according to Solms (2021: 221–26), the arising of consciousness is not a desired state of an organism as it is correlated with uncertainty. The preferred state is in fact that of the absence of consciousness, where automatic unconscious processes may efficiently maintain homeostasis as well as the functional and structural integrity of the organism. Of course, it needs to be emphasized that this is not tantamount to a coma-like state, since unconscious processes are very much capable of quite complex cognitive operations. Solms (2021: 222–26) even goes as far as to figuratively label the state to which the organism aspires as "zombiedom" since it involves no consciousness and, by extension, feelings.

If Solms's hypothesis is correct, then it would imply that ordinary, access consciousness is not an essential feature of our every wakeful state and a necessary condition of being sentient and cognizant. However, when we introspect our inner state or review our memories, it seems that such consciousness is present all the time, save for the periods of deep sleep. We do not experience any moments of absence of consciousness. How can we account for this fact?

In the preceding chapter we have considered the results of the research which showed that our consciousness does not keep up with the events occurring in the physical reality. As Metzinger (2009: 37), has aptly noted, "we are never in touch with the present" due to the simple fact that "neural information processing itself takes time". What we are experiencing as the present is actually the past (Metzinger, 2009: 38). Buonomano (2017: 73) summarizes the state of neurological research by claiming that "[c]onsciousness is a delayed account of not only what is happening in the external world, but of what is happening in the unconscious brain".

However, consciousness is not merely temporally delayed with respect to physical reality. As Van Rullen and Koch (2003: 207) have pointed out, the commonsense and intuitive notion that consciousness involves a "continuous translation of the external world into explicit perception .... cannot satisfactorily account for a large body of psychophysical data". If various sensory stimuli are separated by a small enough margin which is measured in milliseconds, they will be consciously registered as if they occurred simultaneously. For example, if the sound source is separated from us by a large enough distance, visual and auditory signals (i.e., light reflected from it and soundwaves generated by it) reach us at a slightly different time, with the auditory signal being delayed with respect to the visual one. However due to the processing in the brain, we perceive its image and voice in perfect correlation (Buonomano 2017: 218). Buonomano (2017: 217) points out that our brain tends to delete certain information that it considers unnecessary, e.g., the visual frames that occur during eye movements. It has been calculated that as a result of this editing, our conscious record of reality is missing a full hour of visual information every day! All this means that the subjective, psychological time of our consciousness is not isomorphic to the objective, physical time. This in turn implies that the processed data correlated with our conscious experience is not generated continuously in physical time by the unconscious brain. While the latter is uninterruptedly processing information, it only sends "a polished narrative" into consciousness at "critical junctures", at "fits and starts" (Buonomano 2017: 217, 220).

Therefore, from the perspective of physical time, there are moments or whole time-intervals when the data that is correlated with our conscious experience is not generated at all. As Madl et al. (2011) put it, "[h]umans can only have a single conscious content at a time, and there are short breaks between these periods of consciousness".

Why do we experience our consciousness as continuous?

We experience and remember our consciousness as a continuous stream because the periods of physical time during which the brain does not generate data correlated with our conscious experience are not reflected in our memory record in the form of blank moments or periods of darkness. Though consciousness is generated intermittently during particular timeframes of physical time, these originally discrete intervals of consciousness are integrated into memory one after another without any breaks between them. One may perhaps compare this mechanism to the usage of a voice recording app; we usually have an option to pause our recording without the need to stop the record completely, and afterwards we may resume it. This will result in a continuous sound record without any periods of silence. If we could intermittently pause the recording and very quickly resume it with high enough frequency, then afterwards when playing the recorded sound file in question, we would not be able to notice any discontinuities. Something of a similar nature occurs during our conscious life. However, the analogy to the sound recording device is not perfect, as it illustrates only the delayed and discrete character of our consciousness but not its highly processed nature. It also assumes that there is something like the objective flow of physical time, and as we have already commented, modern physicists consider it to be an illusion. The current dominant approach in physics is that of eternalism, i.e., the view that the past and the future exist, while the present is not absolute, but relative to a particular observer. Therefore, a better metaphor would perhaps be that of a digital file of a movie, where all the scenes are already encrypted in the form of a digital code, and of an editing software which would cut some fragments of the original movie and heavily edit them using various effects and filters, and then play the resultant movie in real time.

All this goes against one of our most basic intuitions that consciousness is a sort of phenomenal stream that is continuously flowing, in the sense that at every moment of time, there occurs some form of qualitative phenomenal consciousness connected with the unique feeling of there being something that it is like to experience qualia. The assumption at the basis of this idea is that there exists a distinct inner space in which this qualitative experience takes place. It might be perhaps compared to a cinema room in which a movie is continuously playing, regardless of whether anyone is watching it or taking notes from it. Similarly, it is natural to assume that phenomenal consciousness is always present, regardless of whether we attend to it or store its content into our memory.

We believe our consciousness to be a continuous stream because this is how it appears to us when we actively attend to it (in the sense of introspecting our mental states) and when we recollect our conscious experiences. However, our introspection and memory may be misguiding us regarding the nature of our inner life.

According to a very interesting hypothesis by Blackmore (2017: 70–71), every act of deliberately attending to our mental life, which can be described as a form of asking "what am I conscious of now", results in a construction of "a temporary unity of a set of thoughts and perceptions" which "is linked to a representation of self as a continuing observer". As Blackmore (2017: 67) sums up, "looking into consciousness reveals only what it is like when we are looking into it – and most of the time we are not. So introspecting on our own minds is thwarted by the very fact of introspecting". On such an account, we have no way of knowing what our consciousness is like during the moments we are not attending to it. In fact, from this perspective, the very conception of consciousness which exists by itself, independently of being attended to or introspected, is meaningless. Blackmore (2017: 72) suggests that:

> [C]onsciousness appears as a stream only when we reflect on it as such. The rest of the time, multiple parallel processes carry on, sometimes interacting with each other, often not. When we ask 'What am I conscious of now?' or 'What is it like being me now?' some are gathered together and the answer appears stream-like.

Recollection may be equally unreliable, due to its reconstructive, rather than faithful storage-retrieval mechanism.[24] Therefore, any theory of consciousness that is based on introspection and recollection may in fact only be addressing relatively rare moments in our lives.

We are considering the possibility of (dis)continuity of consciousness during ordinary wakeful mental life due to its relevance for understanding the nature of apophatically described states of meditative unconsciousness in Nikāya and early Chan texts. It might be the case that these meditative cessations share some common denominator with the states that occur much more regularly during our wakeful lives. It might be just that the former represent the extreme end of a certain spectrum regarding the presence (or absence) of some feature(s) which might be present to a different extent in ordinary forms of consciousness.

How is the presence of ordinary consciousness connected to the experience of psychological time?

If consciousness is not continuous, but discrete, and is generated "in fits and starts", then it might be the case that the quantity or frequency

24 See Garfield (2015) and Siderits (2011) for a reviewal of the arguments in the debate in ancient Buddhist philosophy regarding the role of memory in cognizing one's own consciousness.

of such discrete episodes may not be constant across different time intervals. In other words, the quantity or "density" of occurrences of consciousness during two different time-intervals connected with the same duration of physical time may be significantly different. Would this difference result in their different evaluation from the first-person perspective? We have good reasons to suspect that it would be the case. We have already noted the existence of a certain affinity between consciousness and memory. Ultimately, what we consider to be our consciousness is correlated with the data that became available to our memory. It does not mean that the content of every conscious act is integrated into long-term memory, as it is obviously not the case, but rather that every instance of access consciousness is correlated with the availability of its content for working or short-term memory. According to Carruthers (2015: 12), "working memory is the system within which reflective thinking takes place, and in which the stream of consciousness occurs more generally". Dietrich (2004: 749) sums up the dominant position in cognitive science regarding this issue in the following way:

> The view emerging from the cognitive and neuroscientific literature is that memory contains the content of consciousness ... Put another way, our immediate conscious working experience of the here and now is made possible by the sustained buffering of information in working memory.

This would imply that the data correlated with every content of consciousness has to at least be held for some relatively short amount of time in working memory, and may or may not be potentially integrated into long-term memory.

The interval of physical time connected with the relatively smaller number of occurrences of consciousness would therefore also leave relatively fewer memory traces compared to another interval lasting the same amount of physical time but involving the greater number of occurrences of consciousness. How would this weigh on a subjective perception of these time intervals? I would suggest that it would particularly impact our evaluation of the duration of psychological time connected with these intervals. As we have already noted, subjective estimations of psychological time connected with two intervals lasting the same amount of physical time may differ significantly. It is commonplace that we perceive various events or experiences as involving different speeds or durations of psychological time. There seems to exist a correlation between the perceived duration of psychological time, the level of affective valence (ranging between pleasure and displeasure) and the sense of self-consciousness. For example, when we are bored, we experience what may be called chronostasis – the sensation that time is standing still (Buonomano 2017: 58). Such experiences are connected with an enhanced sense of self-awareness understood as the opposite to forgetting about oneself. They are also perceived as generally unpleasant. On the opposite end of the spectrum, we find states where time flies fast, such as those when we are engaged in an absorbing activity or experience. It is commonplace that such states are subjectively experienced as being pleasant. Time flies when you're having fun, goes the saying. During such moments, one also tends to forget about oneself to a considerable extent, focusing instead on the absorbing activity or experience. Therefore, it can be said that such states are characterized by an attenuation of the sense of self-consciousness. The pleasant states of being absorbed into an activity or experience are often labelled as "flow"[25] in psychological literature (e.g., Csikszentmihalyi 1996; 2013). What is it exactly that makes these states pleasant? Certainly, due to being absorbed, we tend to forget about many of our everyday worries. However, this does not seem to be the only reason for the pleasant nature of the flow states.

Bronkhorst (2012: 147) has suggested that we experience the states of absorption as pleasant due to the fact that they involve a reduction of bodily tension. This might indeed be the case, since relaxation is universally considered to be pleasant, while tension to be unpleasant. Tensing up increases the experience of pain, while relaxation decreases it. But this still leaves the question of explaining the connection between absorption, pleasure and the remaining features of these states, namely shorter duration of psychological time and the attenuation of the sense of self-consciousness. Does there exist some shared basic quality underlying all these features, or will we have to resign ourselves to merely stating the fact of their correlation?

Let us start by considering the question of the mechanism underlying the sense of psychological time. We tend to evaluate the relative duration of particular experiences retrospectively. This does not imply that we can only evaluate duration of the whole period connected with

25 As Mattes (2022) rightly points out, the psychological literature uses the term "flow" to denote a number of related but often distinct concepts. In this book we are not interested in flow in the sense of the balance between skill and demands or goals, as it is discussed in positive psychology.

a particular experience (e.g., that of flow) and only after this experience has ended completely. Even while being engaged in an absorbing activity, we from time to time break out from self-forgetfulness and consciously attend to our inner state and evaluate the speed and duration of psychological time connected with the directly preceding interval. As Buonomano (2017: 60) notes, "Retrospectively, the duration of ... activities are estimated in part based on the number of events stored in memory". We have suggested that only the content connected with the occurrences of consciousness may be integrated into memory, and that the "density" of these occurrences varies across different states. If there are relatively few instances of ordinary access consciousness characterized by global availability of its content, then there will be relatively little to store in memory. Therefore, someone recollecting such a state will retroactively estimate it as involving a relatively short duration of psychological time as compared to average states spanning the same interval of physical time.

The same basic mechanism seems to underlie the differences between levels of self-consciousness across various states. Every instant of ordinary, reportable consciousness seems to involve a basic sense of self-consciousness. We do not mean here a well-developed autobiographical sense of identity or an Ego, but the very "thin" sense of agency and of the ownership of the body as well as the feeling of being a subject of experience connected with every ordinary act of consciousness. Certainly, whenever we attend to our consciousness, we find it to be self-consciousness. Although during altered states of consciousness, we may find the usually rigid boundaries that separate us from other beings or objects diminished or expanded, or we may even lose the sense of Ego or conceit, we nonetheless cannot experience a fully self-less state through an act of deliberate, conscious introspection. Therefore, the lesser the number of occurrences of consciousness during a particular time-interval, the more attenuated the sense of selfhood will be when we retrospectively assess it.

Cessation as an extreme case of the flow state

It therefore seems that the states of flow or absorption involve a relatively low number of occurrences of ordinary consciousness in relation to the interval of physical time during which a particular flow state takes place. However, the frequency of these occurrences is still high enough to maintain the delusion of continuity of consciousness. But what would happen if this frequency was reduced to such an extent that for a relatively long period of physical time there would be no generation of consciousness in the access sense? As a result, we would not be able to form any conscious memories connected with this time interval and would subjectively experience an abrupt break between our last conscious state preceding that interval and the one immediately occurring afterwards. It is not that the period of absence of consciousness would be somehow stored in memory, as it is impossible due to the very nature of consciousness and memory. It is just that the delusion of continuity of consciousness would be broken, and we could not fail to realize the stark discontinuity between two moments of our consciousness. For example, we could notice that the surrounding objects are in different positions compared to the ones observed during the preceding moment of consciousness. Interestingly, cases of such spontaneous "cessations" occurring in the midst of everyday activities may be found in modern literature on meditation. Jeff Warren's (2013) paper contains some first-person accounts by meditators from Shinzen Young's group participating in an experiment conducted by David Vago.[26] Some of the more experienced meditators would sometimes experience episodes which they described as "cessations", "gone moments" or "annihilations". Their common denominator was that that there was nothing that it was like to be in these states, as they involved a temporary complete absence of conscious experience. Another interesting feature is that these cessations were not connected with formal sessions of calm meditation, as the practitioners from this group engaged in the Mahasi-style form of *vipassanā* meditation. The "cessations" were relatively short, frequent and unexpected, often occurring during everyday activities but without hindering their efficiency, which is the testimony to the possibility of remaining sentient, cognizant and engaged in the world without being conscious in the ordinary sense of the word.

Can the absence of consciousness be pleasurable?

But why would the absence of consciousness be connected to pleasure? At the first look such a claim may appear to be self-contradictory. After all,

26 See Davis and Vago (2013), who describe two meditators in Young's group "having a temporary experience of cessation while in the scanner environment".

if there is no conscious experience then how can there be any pleasure? However, let us remind ourselves of Solms's (2021: 221–22) claims that consciousness is in fact undesirable from the perspective of the organism and that the latter aspires to a state of homeostasis in which all its needs are taken care of in an automatic way by unconscious algorithmic processes; a state in which we would "feel nothing". Since consciousness is supposed to be a mechanism which "comes to the rescue" (Solms 2021: 220) in situations of uncertainty, then maintaining it may put some strain on the resources of the organism. This could be correlated with tension, described by Bronkhorst as characterizing the states being at the opposite end of the spectrum to those connected with absorption. According to our hypothesis, these states would involve an intensified sense of self-consciousness. If the state of the absence of consciousness is desirable from the perspective of organism, then perhaps it may be connected with some very fundamental somatic sense of comfort or ease, which is not reportable, introspectable or storable in memory and therefore cannot be considered conscious. This would correspond to Bronkhorst's idea of a decrease in bodily tension as a feature of absorption. As within current cognitive science and philosophy of mind there is so much talk about unconscious cognitive processes, then perhaps we should also not reject the possibility of unconscious emotion out of hand. The "possibility of affect that is neither accessible to introspection nor phenomenally present" and yet strongly influences our behaviour is considered by Garfield (2015: 125–26). Damasio (1999) believes that our conscious feelings are mental experiences of "emotions" understood as the unconscious bodily neural responses to stimuli. As we have noted, even the states of flow do not involve continuous absence of instances of introspectable consciousness, but rather the decreased rate of their occurrence. Perhaps during the moments of introspectable consciousness which intermittently arise during the flow states, one can explicitly acknowledge being in a generally pleasant state, without being able to exactly pinpoint what is the cause of this pleasure. That is because the very act of introspectively attending to one's inner state is at odds with what made it pleasurable in the first place.

Qixin, *zuoyi* and the discontinuity of consciousness

So far in our discussion we have been mainly referring to modern psychological concepts. Is it possible to establish some connection of this theory to the ideas found in the Nikāya and early Chan texts? It needs to be said that Chan texts in general do not put as much emphasis on the issues of suffering and the release from it through psychological transformation as the Nikāya texts. This may be a reflection of a more general tenor within Mahāyāna scriptures. We have also already commented that, unlike the Nikāyas, Chan texts cannot be seen as comprehensive and exhaustive accounts of all the aspects of the soteriological process. Instead, they mostly focus on certain specific issues, especially those with respect to which their approach differs from mainstream Buddhism. However, the notions that the ordinary form of consciousness is not a continuous, but rather intermittent feature of our wakeful state, and that its absence is not tantamount to lack of cognizance, sentience and engagement in the world, are very much present in the early Chan writings. A case can be made that terms such as *qixin* 起心, *zuoyi* 作意 and *younian* 有念 refer to various features of the ordinary form of consciousness. As we have already commented in the earlier chapters, the mental acts referred to by these terms receive an unequivocally negative evaluation in early Chan. Most importantly, however, they are not portrayed as obligatory, default features of every wakeful state; quite the contrary, they are seen as optional acts in which one may or may not engage in. As we have already commented, *qixin* 起心 may be translated as meaning arousal, arising or "activation" of the mind. The literal understanding of *qi* 起 as rising, harmonizes with the idea that ordinary consciousness occurs in a discrete way and is intermittently generated by the mind in a more general, fundamental sense (*xin* 心) which may remain in a preferable, basic and "unarisen" state (*xin buqi* 心不起). The latter term seems to refer to the same notion of the mind as the term *wuxin* (no-mind), which, as we have seen, does not imply insentience and non-cognizance, but non-conscious, non-conceptual and spontaneous (*wuwei* 無為) form of functioning. The term *zuoyi*, which is often used in close connection with *qixin*, literally means "making mentation", and refers to conscious acts of intention or attention and corresponds to Pali *manasikaroti*. Both the notions of intention *yi* 意, and "making" or "doing" *zuo* 作 may be interpreted as referring to some basic sense of agency contributing to the fact that ordinary consciousness is a self-consciousness. If we read *zuoyi* in line with *manasikaroti* as referring to "conscious attending", then this harmonizes with Blackmore's hypothesis that an act of attending to one's own mental life is in fact constitutive of every occurrence of ordinary, introspectable consciousness.

To summarize, there is in Chan texts the notion that what we call ordinary consciousness is not a constant and obligatory feature of our wakeful state, and that its absence does not entail absence of sentience and cognizance but is in fact a desirable state. The concept of *qixin* also has some other significant implications which we will discuss later on.

Conscious experience as *dukkha*

The psychological theory that we are considering appears to have more direct correlations with the ideas contained in the Nikāyas. In particular, this concerns the notion that the occurrence of ordinary consciousness may be somehow connected with stress, while its absence with pleasure. In the preceding chapter, I have suggested that the concept of the five *khandhas* was used in early Buddhism to refer to various aspects of first-person consciousness of oneself in the world, consciousness whose content matches the criteria of what is described in modern cognitive science as global availability. We have also seen that the *khandhas* can cease without ensuing insentience of the mind (*citta/cetas*) in the general sense. Most importantly, however, the *khandhas* are described as *dukkha*, both individually[27] and collectively as the whole set.[28] According to the *Kaḷāra-sutta* (SN 12.32/ii.53), "whatever is felt/experienced (*vedayitaṃ*) is [included] within suffering".[29] The term *vedayita* is closely related etymologically to *vedanā* and can be read as referring to ordinary conscious experience with a particular emphasis on the aspect of its affective valence. This may be seen as paralleling Solms's notion that feeling is the constitutive feature of every act of consciousness.

The notion that the *khandhas* and *vedayita* are *dukkha* is very radical and counterintuitive and has therefore usually not been taken literally in the sense that every ordinary conscious experience is painful or stressful. Instead, it was usually read in a more general, abstract and figurative way as referring to the fact that permanent satisfaction is not to be found in conditioned existence, or that suffering is unavoidable in the ultimate sense. However, our tentative psychological theory allows us to take these radical Nikāya claims at face value and read

---

27 E.g., SN 22.16/ii.22.

28 SN 56.11/v.421 famously proclaims that "briefly speaking, the five aggregates connected with grasping are *dukkha*".

29 SN 12.32/ii.53: *'yaṃ kiñci vedayitaṃ taṃ dukkhasmi'n'ti.*

them as implying that ordinary conscious experience involves some discomfort or strain on a fundamental, somatic level. It also allows us to make sense of the seemingly paradoxical statement of Sāriputta in the *Nibbānasukha-sutta* (AN 9.34/iv.415) that pleasure (*sukha*) lies in the fact of "nothing being experienced" (*natthi vedayitaṃ*).[30] If the presence of consciousness puts some strain on an organism, then its absence may result in some form of deep relief, ease or comfort (*sukha*), though in this case it could not be introspectively attended to, reported in speech or stored in memory. It also harmonizes with our tentative hypothesis that the lower the frequency of occurrences of ordinary consciousness during a particular time-interval, the more pleasurable it is considered, such as in the cases of flow. It also allows for a more direct reading of the message of the *Bhāra-sutta* (SN 22.22/iii.26), that the aggregates are a burden (*bhāra*) carried by an individual. In light of our interpretation, it would mean that every instant of ordinary conscious experience is burdensome for the human organism.

Self-consciousness, *saṅkhāras* and tension

I have offered a tentative hypothesis that the presence of self-consciousness may be correlated with unpleasantness and the presence of tension or strain. As we have already seen in the previous chapter, some degree of self-consciousness may be implied by the notion of the aggregates, as evidenced by the fact that they are collectively defined as "personal identity" (*sakkāya*: SN 22.105/iii.159), or the side of personal identity (*sakkāyanta*: SN 22.103/iii.158). However, we have not yet considered any Nikāya concepts that would specifically imply the connection between self-consciousness and tension or strain. A case can be made that such a connection is implied in the notion of *saṅkhāras*.

Of all the terms constituting the set of the five aggregates, *saṅkhāra* probably has the most unclear meaning. Etymologically, the word refers to "that which is made up together" and implies the notion of fabrication. In Chapter 1, we reviewed certain Nikāya texts which referred to this term in the context of criticized or imperfect meditative practices involving deliberate mental effort or restraint. We have come upon

30 See Polak (2023c) for a more detailed discussion of this claim and its implications.

the terms *sasaṅkhāraparinibbāyī*[31] and *sasaṅkhāraniggayhavāritagata*,[32] containing an element "*sasaṅkhāra*" which Bodhi (2012: 1669, n. 560) interprets as "forceful" (lit. "with exertion"). The *Sasaṅkhāra-sutta* (AN 4.169/ii.155–156) sees the four *jhānas* as a practice leading to the attainment of *nibbāna* without *sāṅkhāra*, which would therefore imply that they do not involve forceful effort. According to the interpretation of the four *jhānas* partially laid out in Chapters 1 and 2, they indeed do not involve forceful concentration. The description of calming bodily and mental *saṅkhāra* may be found in the account of the *ānāpānāssati* practice, which is beyond doubt an alternative but complementary account of the practice described elsewhere as the four *jhānas* (e.g., SN 54.1/ v.310–312). In the abovementioned texts, *saṅkhāra* does not literally mean "tension", but refers to conscious effort and exertion. However, forcefulness of exertion connected with concentration during meditation certainly involves generation of a certain degree of tension.

The verb *abhisaṅkharoti* is quite often paired with *ceteti*[33] whose meanings include "to intend", "be intent upon", or "strive mentally for".[34] Such pairings in the Nikāyas sometimes imply a certain degree of synonymity of the terms forming it. This would suggest that the notion of *saṅkhāra* may carry some connotations of volition or intention. And indeed, if one makes an effort or forcefully exerts oneself then this implies an exercise of volition, and not a spontaneous activity. Intention may in turn be seen as a basic form of agency or selfhood. Another piece of evidence regarding the connection of *saṅkhāras* with self-consciousness may be found in the *Parileyya-sutta* (SN 22.81/iii.94–99). The text analyses various forms of regarding (*samanupassati*) each of the aggregates as self. Every form of this regarding (*samanupassanā*) is described as a *saṅkhāra*. For example, regarding the self as possessing *rūpa* is said to be a *saṅkhāra*.[35] The idea of the self possessing *rūpa* may relate to the feeling of the ownership of one's body which is a good example of a very basic form of self-consciousness.

Thus, the notion of *saṅkhāra* carries with it the notion of a certain degree of selfhood and effort, in addition to that of fabrication. The Nikāyas give the impression that the particular *khandhas* cannot

31 AN 4.169/ii.155–156.

32 AN 3.101/i.255.

33 E.g., DN 9/i.184: *so na ceva ceteti, na ca abhisaṅkharoti.*

34 Cone (2010: 167).

35 SN 22.81/iii.97: *api ca kho rūpavantaṃ attānaṃ samanupassati. yā kho pana sā, bhikkhave, samanupassanā saṅkhāro so.*

be separated from one another, and refer to the same first-person conscious experience, though they emphasize its different aspects. Certain Nikāya fragments actually use the term *saṅkhāra* in reference to ordinary experience in general. A good example of this approach may be found in the Buddha's last exhortation that the *saṅkhāras* are liable to dissolution (*vayadhamma*),[36] and the passage in the *Dhammapada* to the effect that all *saṅkhāras* are stressful.[37] *Saṅkhāras* are also directly connected with ignorance (*avijjā*), which precedes and conditions them in the scheme of *paṭiccasamuppāda*. As we have noted earlier, *saṅkhāra* is a feature of every ordinary conscious experience. This implies that every conscious experience carries with it some modicum of self-consciousness, fabrication, ignorance and tension connected with effort, and is inherently uncomfortable, which agrees with our hypothesis.[38]

At this point, some important correlations start to become apparent to us. On the one end of the spectrum, we have states of psychological discomfort, which are correlated with a subjective feeling of a slow passage of time, the presence of ordinary self-consciousness whose content is globally available, bodily tension and volitional effort. They correspond to the states described in the Nikāyas in terms of the five *khandhas*, *vedayita*, or *saṅkhāras* in general. In the early Chan texts, such states are described as: those of the arousing of the mind (*qixin*), made up (*zaozuo*), involving acts of volitional intention (*zuoyi*), presence of thought (*younian*), and conditioned (*youwei*).

As we move towards the opposite end of the spectrum, we find states of pleasure (or at least absence of displeasure), correlated with the subjective feeling of fast passage of time, relative attenuation of ordinary self-consciousness, as well as of bodily tension and volitional effort. These are the states labeled as flow in modern psychology.

On the very end of this side of the spectrum are the states of an uninterrupted absence of ordinary consciousness, correlated with total timelessness and lack of discomfort. They cannot be directly recollected, integrated into memory, are ineffable and opaque to

36 DN 16/ii.156.

37 Dhp 278/40: *'sabbe saṅkhārā dukkhā'ti, yadā paññāya passati.*

38 In my recent article (Polak 2023c: 16), I have suggested that this implies that every instance of generation of ordinary consciousness involves misguided striving and trying to become something different from what one really is (due to mistaken identification with one's consciousness) and that such consciousness is not something obligatory, and it is possible for it not to arise.

self-reflective introspection. They may, however, involve deep comfort on a somatic level. In the Nikāyas, such states are expressed in terms of cessation (*nirodha*) of the *khandhas*, *vedayita*, the *āyatanas* or of calming of *saṅkhāras*. This cessation reaches its climax in apophatically described states such as the *nirodhasamāpatti*, but may already attain a very high level in the fourth *jhāna*. In early Chan terms, these states are described as: non-arousal of the mind (*xinbuqi*), spontaneous and non-conditioned (*wuwei*), no-thought (*wunian*), original pure mind (*benlai qingjing xin*), or no-mind (*wuxin*).

Pleasure, craving, and its removal

In Chapter 2, we referred to some elements of Bronkhorst's theory of the transformative role of absorption in the removal of craving. We have, however, not yet considered one of his hypotheses which will be very relevant in the context of our present discussion. As we have already mentioned, Bronkhorst suggested that the real source of pleasure lies in the states of reduced bodily tension, such as absorption. Bronkhorst (2012: 144–45) asks a very pertinent question:

> If absorption brings pleasure without effort (no bodily tension needs to be generated to make it possible), why should anyone bother to search for pleasure in any other way? Why is this most efficient method to obtain satisfaction systematically ignored?

According to Bronkhorst, the answer lies in the fact that our memory traces cannot record the state of absorption itself, but the associated objects and situations.[39] However, the source of pleasure does not lie in these objects and situations but in the state of absorption itself, i.e., that of reduced bodily tension. Bronkhorst (2012: 147) aptly summarizes:

> This means that many of the aims we pursue in life, guided as we are by our memory traces, are fundamentally misguided. We strive to repeat situations connected with earlier experiences of satisfaction where these situations were not the real cause of satisfaction.

In other words, we look for pleasure in external objects and situations, while its source lies in a specific state of our body which may be obtained without pursuing them. This is just one of several cases

39 This is in harmony with our hypothesis that what actually makes a state pleasant is the relative absence of the type of consciousness whose content may be stored in memory.

showing the unreliability of conscious introspection as means of self-knowledge.[40] The reoccurring notion which we repeatedly discuss in this book is that some key causes of our behaviour and conscious states actually lie beyond consciousness, and do not originate from within it.

How can the automatic pattern of seeking pleasure in objects and situations associated in memory with the state of low tension be corrected? As we have already noted in Chapter 2, Bronkhorst's theory assumes that in the higher *jhāna*s this misguided memory trace may be laid bare and "activated" for a potential "reconsolidation" (i.e., replacement of the old pattern by a new one). One needs to activate this memory trace in the state of low bodily tension and equanimity, so that a usual stimulus is not met with a usual reaction pattern stored in memory which in turn results in what may be called a "mismatch" or a "prediction error". In the higher *jhāna*s, bodily tension is reduced to a minimum which generates an experience of pleasure or a lack of pleasure and pain.[41] This, however, is not associated with any object or external situation, as according to Bronkhorst (2012: 144), early Buddhist absorption is not directed at any object. The latter claim is in agreement with our conclusions in the first chapter about the nature of *jhāna* meditation. The resultant "prediction error" allows the reconsolidation of an old memory trace into a new form. From now on, the practitioner (or "patient" in Bronkhorst's theory) will automatically know not to strive for external objects and situations in search of pleasure. Thus, the problem of craving is eliminated.

Interestingly, there are some Nikāya texts which directly support Bronkhorst's hypothesis, though he does not discuss them. For example, in the relatively rarely discussed passage of the *Cūḷadukkhakkhandha-sutta* (MN 14/i.92), the Buddha proclaims that it was only after he attained *pīti* (rapture) and *sukha* (pleasure) that are apart from sensual pleasures (*kāma*) and apart from unskillful states, or achieved even more peaceful (*santatara*) states, that he recognized that he no longer turns back (*āvattati*) to sensuality. This statement clearly implies the *jhāna*s.[42]

40 See Garfield (2015) and Blackmore (2017) for elaborations of this idea.

41 According to Bronkhorst (2012: 160), pleasure is a reaction to a reduction of bodily tension. Once it has dropped to a minimum and stabilized itself, there occurs an absence of pleasure and pain, i.e., the state of the fourth *jhāna*.

42 The significance of this text is discussed by Arbel (2017: 60–63).

Cessation and psychological transformation: Putting the pieces together

In Chapter 2, we noted that despite its undisputable value, Bronkhorst's theory does not acknowledge several prominent elements of early Buddhist doctrine, such as the concepts of not-self, cessation or dependent co-arising. It might be, of course, that they do not belong to the same conceptual stratum of the early Buddhist teaching as the notions of the four *jhāna*s and that of the resultant exhaustion of craving. I believe, however, that these concepts may be harmonized. In the earlier part of this chapter, I have suggested that considerations about the connection of cessation with absorption may bring us closer to understanding the psychological mechanism of self-transformation which is the goal of Buddhism. At this point, we have almost all the necessary elements which we can start to piece together.

In the preceding two chapters, I have suggested that active cognitive operations in the sense of processing data, making evaluations and inferences, reaching new ideas and decisions do not originate from within consciousness. As we have noted, one of the key meanings of the notion of seeing the aggregates as the self is that we identify ourselves with our own image available to us through first-person consciousness. This means identifying with merely a small subset of data within our cognitive architecture, which is available to introspection, is reportable and storable in memory. As we have seen, it is not a truthful image of what we really are and carries with it a significant degree of distortion. However, this allows us to conceive of ourselves as unified entities, appropriate our actions and better protect our own integrity and autonomy from the external environment. I have also suggested that ordinary access consciousness is not a constant and obligatory mode of our being in the world. Apparently, from the evolutionary standpoint it was meant to be a tool for dealing with novel situations, which require breaking away from automatic but efficient cognitive patterns and recruiting wider mental resources in order to navigate ourselves through uncertain conditions. We have also established the existence of a correlation between this type of consciousness and the presence of strain and displeasure.

When an organism (by means of its cognitive processes) identifies itself with its own image available to it through first-person consciousness (which in Nikāya terms corresponds to the *khandha*s and *vedayita*), it will consider the presence of conscious experience to be tantamount to one's own presence, while its absence will be perceived as synonymous with one's own annihilation. Therefore, it will attempt to prolong what it considers to be its own existence by continuously generating and maintaining this form of consciousness. But according to our hypothesis, the latter's presence is inevitably correlated with a certain level of strain or discomfort. Therefore, despite acting in what it perceives to be its best interest, the organism inflicts stress and suffering upon oneself.

How can this error be undone? Perhaps if one were able to attain a prolonged and continuous meditative state of cessation of ordinary conscious experience while remaining sentient and cognizant, this would result in the already mentioned mismatch or a prediction error. The organism would be free from stress and tension, but at the same time, that which it considers to be its identity, i.e., consciousness, would be absent. As a result, it could experientially come to an understanding that, ultimately, it (i.e., the organism) is not its own consciousness. In Nikāya terms, this would mean ceasing to identify with the aggregates. As a result, it would stop constantly and unnecessarily generating ordinary conscious experience and bringing suffering upon oneself. It is probable that from that point on, consciousness would return to its original role of a tool reserved for special circumstances. During states of idleness, one would naturally remain in a pleasant and relaxed state akin to flow.

There is yet another very important aspect of this process. In the preceding chapter, we have mentioned that the structure of phenomenal consciousness does not reflect that of noumenal reality. Ordinary access consciousness is a phenomenal consciousness, in the basic sense that its content has a qualitative, phenomenal structure. Time, space, causality and substantiality may very much be specific aprioric features of our phenomenal experience. Therefore, as the *Mahānidāna-sutta* proclaimed, one can be born, die and reborn only within this structure, which in Nikāya terms can be expressed as a combination of *viññāṇa* and *nāma-rūpa*. The latter pair clearly represents phenomenal consciousness and its contents and roughly corresponds to the aggregates. Similarly, early Chan texts speak of the arousal of the mind (*qixin*), thought (*nian*) or ideation (*xiang*) as giving rise to the three realms, or birth and death (*shengsi*, i.e., *saṃsāra*).

Let us again refer to an analogy with the process of displaying a digital movie. It is only within the movie which is displayed on some device that there are turns of action, people dying, falling in love, etc. It makes no sense to speak of such things with respect to the digital file of the movie as it merely consists of digits. In a similar manner, being born, ageing, dying, desiring and clinging may be meaningfully spoken only with respect to spatiotemporal reality of entities connected by causal relations and these notions may have no relevance within the noumenal, mind-independent sphere which is a correlate of our phenomenal experience. It seems likely then, that the process of mistakenly considering objects and situations as sources of pleasure described by Bronkhorst would not be possible without phenomenal consciousness which allows their very presentation in such a form. Several Nikāya texts emphasize contact (*phassa*) between the sense, sense object and sense consciousness as the crucial element of the cognitive chain without which desire could not arise. For example, the passage of the *Kalahavivāda-sutta* (4.11/169–170) states that desire (*chanda*) is dependent on the notions of pleasant/agreeable (*sāta*) and unpleasant/disagreeable (*asāta*). In order to remove them, it advises to develop a meditative state in which form/object (*rūpa*) is vanished and thus "contacts do not touch" (*na phusanti phassā*). It makes sense that desire can only arise dependent on a contact between the subject and the potential object of desire. However, what is implied here is that the notion of an object (*rūpa*), and hence the very possibility of contact is not a feature of objective reality but of a specific mode of consciousness dependent upon a particular way of functioning of cognitive apparatus (especially that of *saññā*). Experiencing radical cognitive deconstruction of that type of consciousness could contribute to a fundamental disenchantment with all that is phenomenal, and thus extinguish desire.

A different interesting hypothesis regarding the transformative role of cessation has been proposed by Laukkonen et al. (2023: 78). They suggest that cessation may lead to a sort of "reset of the precision-weighting landscape at levels of the brain's functional hierarchy that maintain temporally deep (abstract) beliefs about the world and self" which would result "in an experience of the present moment that is less conditioned by past beliefs" and "a sense of clarity and freshness, as if everything is new or as if 'seen for the first time'".

The second *Gaddulabaddha-sutta* contains a statement (SN 22.100/iii.152) that an uninstructed ordinary man produces or brings into existence (*abhinibbatteti*) the five aggregates. Historically, such statements would usually be given an ontological interpretation; through *kamma*, one generates certain psychophysical elements within objective reality which are to become the building blocks of a future existence. Hence, we would be dealing in such a case with an ontological understanding of causation. However, according to our interpretation, generation of the aggregates may only refer to a generation of a specific type of experience. This represents a shift from the ontological to the epistemological perspective.[43] Such an interpretation also necessitates an epistemological reinterpretation of the concept of dependent origination. Popular interpretation of dependent origination would see it as a description of the fundamental features of objective reality and especially of the fact that all things or processes in the world are dependent on one another. However, as Gombrich (2009: 142) rightly argues, the teaching of dependent origination neither deals with the macrocosm nor conveys a message that all phenomena are interrelated. Similar interpretation has been offered by Shulman (2008: 306), who stated that "the 12 links are an explanation of mental conditioning, an analysis of subjective existence. They do not deal directly with the manner in which all things exist".[44]

In light of our considerations, *paṭiccasamuppāda* could be read as an account of how the generation of ordinary phenomenal consciousness (*viññāṇa*) brings with it the presence of the individual world of experience, the only world in which one can be born and die, as these notions are not relevant within noumenal reality.

One of the problems with harmonizing the teaching of dependent origination with other elements of early Buddhist soteriology lies in explaining how insight into *paṭiccasamuppāda* may be integrated into the meditative practice and not be considered a result of merely theoretical speculation. A potentially promising way of solving this issue has been offered by Laukkonen et al. (2023: 64) who suggest that upon emergence from cessation "one is exposed experientially to the progressive reconstitution of the mind" which represents a direct realization of the principle of dependent origination. This interpretation is in harmony with the one we have proposed above; by experiencing arising of *viññāṇa* after the period of its absence, one directly realizes that phenomenal consciousness together with its contents is not an essential, constant feature of our being in the world, but is "dependently arisen" which also entails that we are not it.

43 This point has also been made by Wynne (2010: 138–50), who speaks of "cognitive conditioning".

44 Also cf. Shulman's (2008: 307) suggestion that this teaching is "saying absolutely nothing about existence per se" and it does not say that "things depend on other things, or even that everything is conditioned" (Shulman, 2008: 310).

The understanding that the arising of ordinary phenomenal consciousness is a source of suffering goes against one of the most basic intuitions that something which is natural and innate cannot be bad for us. However, this intuition may be wrong from an evolutionary standpoint. That which is innate and natural in us is simply that which proved to make us more efficient in the evolutionary race and was therefore selected for. There is no contradiction in the fact that a trait which makes us evolutionary efficient could at the same time make us genuinely unhappy. In fact, it may even be expected. Being in a state of almost constant unhappiness makes one dissatisfied with one's own state and forces one to strive for something else, thus increasing one's competitiveness. Being ultimately happy makes one unwilling to compete and prone to idleness. If for a moment we suspend our scepticism, and just for the sake of the argument assume that the people considered to be saints or arahants by various religious traditions had really reached ultimate happiness, we will also notice that they rarely had children, meaning that they did not pass on their genes. Thus, being in a state of constant happiness is not a trait that would be selected by evolution.

The *āruppas* and *saññāvedayitanirodha* as states of cognitive deconstruction of ordinary experience

So far, we have been considering a hypothesis that the apophatic state described in Nikāya and early Chan texts may occur by turning off cognitive processes which are responsible for the generation of ordinary consciousness. It is only natural to expect that such a deep level of deconstruction would not occur all at once, but gradually in stages. As hypothesized in the directly preceding parts of this chapter, one aspect of this process would involve a general reduction of the occurrences of consciousness. However, there may also be another aspect, namely, a gradual deconstruction of various features of phenomenal consciousness, resulting in its increasingly attenuated state. These two aspects may perhaps complement one another in bringing about a state of total cessation. An interesting hypothesis regarding a potential neural mechanism of attaining states of absorption and absence of higher level, processed forms of consciousness, has been offered by Dietrich (2003; 2004). He (2003: 232) suggests that: '[T]he frontal cortex utilizes ... highly processed information to enable still higher cognitive functions such as a self-construct, self-reflective consciousness, complex social function, abstract thinking, planning, willed action, working memory, focused attention and temporal integration'.

According to Dietrich it is the transient deregulation of the prefrontal cortex, i.e., hypofrontality, "that enables the temporary suppression of the analytical and meta-conscious capacities of the explicit system". Dietrich believes that hypofrontality occurs in the states of flow, i.e., those of absorption. We have already considered Bronkhorst's (2012: 132) hypothesis concerning the soteriological necessity of absorption in early Buddhism. Bronkhorst sees the four *jhāna*s as forms of gradual attainment and intensification of absorption. As such, they may constitute the basis for a more complete form of cessation of ordinary consciousness which finds its culmination in *saññāvedayitanirodha.* Laukkonen et al. (2023: 77) hypothesize that initial reduction of hierarchically deep predictive processes may occur in the *jhāna*s, which would be a step towards "the final deconstruction/disintegration of phenomenology as such (i.e., awareness)", which occurs during cessation.

The problem with such an interpretation is that the stock account of the higher *jhāna*s hardly mentions anything regarding their first-person content. Instead, it focuses on how one is aware (e.g., mindfully, clearly comprehending, or equanimously). At best, the account of the fourth *jhāna* could perhaps be read as involving some apophatic elements, as the meditator is said to abandon the dichotomy of pleasure and pain. Thus, if we rely solely on the Nikāya stock accounts, it is difficult to posit any underlying principle of the mechanism of progression from the *jhāna*s towards the state of final cessation such as *saññāvedayitanirodha.*

A plausible account of the gradual deconstruction of consciousness may be found in the stock account of the list of successive meditative states known as the *āruppa*s. In Chapter 1, we examined evidence suggesting that the idea that the attainment of the *āruppa*s must obligatorily be preceded by that of the four *jhāna*s appears to be at odds with certain Nikāya texts. I have suggested that entering the sphere of boundless space from the level of the fourth *jhāna* may have been one, but not the only way of attaining the *āruppa*s. I have also considered the possibility that the forms of meditation taught in the *samaṇa* circles of the Greater Magadha may not have only been limited to those representative of Brahminic yoga as depicted in the *Katha* or the *Bṛhadāraṇyaka Upaniṣad* and involving one-pointed concentration and stopping of the mind and the senses. According to the historically dominant interpretation within Buddhism, the *āruppa*s were considered to be exactly this type of meditation.[45] However, such was also the interpretation of the *jhāna*s, and we have seen how problematic that is.

Below we shall consider an alternative interpretation of the *āruppa*s as an account of a gradual cognitive deconstruction of our phenomenal consciousness ending in its total cessation. The description of the sphere of boundless space can be interpreted as an account of the state in which conceptual constructive processes responsible for our experience of corporeality and our awareness of multiplicity of external objects become turned off. The stock account of this state does not explicitly mention becoming unaware of sensory stimuli but speaks of overcoming (*samatikkama*) the *saññā*s of form or shape (*rūpasaññā*), "settling down of *saññā*s of resistance and not paying attention to *saññā*s of diversity" (*paṭighasaññānaṃ atthaṅgamā nānattasaññānaṃ amanasikārā*: e.g., in MN 26/i.174). Were someone to express the simple fact that in a particular state one does not register stimuli coming from the senses, this would be a rather peculiar and complicated way to do it. But perhaps something else was meant here? I have already commented that at least in some Nikāya texts, *saññā* represents an interpreted and conceptually mediated form of consciousness. The three forms of *saññā* mentioned in the account may therefore represent aspects of conceptually mediated consciousness (i.e., corporeality, diversification/multiplicity and resistance) which are not representative of the structure of objective reality but are imposed by our minds on the raw data coming from the senses. We have already noted the significance of the passage in the *Kalahavivāda-sutta* (Snp 4.11/170) which implies that *rūpa* is a form of *papañcasaṅkhā* (lit. proliferation-name) which has its cause (*nidāna*) in *saññā*, which seems to suggest that it is conceptually constructed and not objectively real. Thus, by transcending (*samatikkama*) the conceptual processes which lead to its construction, it would be deconstructed.

Therefore, the content of this state need not necessarily be constituted by some abstract inner sphere representing another cosmic realm of existence, as *ākāsānañcāyatana* is traditionally understood, but may simply be the same reality we normally perceive, just experienced without the medium of certain higher-order constructive processes. Perhaps the world in this state would appear to be devoid of fixed

45 An example of this traditional interpretation may be found in Bucknell (2023: 211), who states that "transition from *jhāna* 4 to *āruppa* 1 entails the cessation of all perceptions of sensory inputs from the physical world".

shapes, rigid barriers and multiple distinct objects. What is apophatically described as lack of diversity may correspond to what is cataphatically presented as a state of oneness. Thus, the stock account of the sphere of the boundless space could be an idiosyncratic, apophatic account of an altered state of consciousness known from many mystical and meditative traditions where the practitioners experience a lack of barriers which normally separate them from the world. Thus, true to its name, it would be a state of "bound-less space".[46] Interestingly, a similar idea may have been conveyed in the Chan text *Dasheng wusheng fangbianmen*, which states that until thoughts (and by extension concepts) are present, there is no "pervading" (*bian* 遍), but once there is transcendence of thoughts (*linian* 離念), there is also pervading.[47] The text compares this pervading to empty space (*xukong* 虛空), which also pervades everywhere. Falling away of limiting concepts such as "I", "You" or "that" would entail the dissolving of borders between seemingly independent entities which would result in their mutual pervading.[48] We have already mentioned another relevant fragment of this text which spoke about specific ways of viewing (*kan* 看) and "viewing afar" (*yuankan* 遠看), which is connected with an "extensive release" (*fangkuang* 放曠) and results in "not seeing even one thing" (*yiwubujian* 一物不見).[49]

The sphere of boundless consciousness could perhaps be interpreted as a state of removing from our experience the basic category of space, which as we earlier suggested is not actually a feature of noumenal

46 Another possible interpretation to consider is that in the sphere of boundless space, one indeed somehow removes the typical sensory content, and is left with pure space as an aprioric structural phenomenological feature of consciousness. The latter may be seen as corresponding to Kant's space as an aprioric form of sensuality. In other words, due to absence of non-structural content, the structural content becomes evident. Cf. Costines et al. (2021: 18) for a discussion of "cognitive phenomenology of structural features of phenomenology".

47 T85, no. 2834, p. 1274a6–7: 無心則等虛空無所不遍。有念即不遍。離念即遍。For translation, see McRae (1986: 175–76).

48 Cf. Bronkhorst (2022: 3), who claims that reducing or suppressing the mental concepts that are responsible for our sense of self would result in that we would "no longer feel separate from others, that there would be no felt boundaries between us and others, easily interpreted as a sense of unity".

49 T85, no. 2834, p. 1273c6–9: 一物不見　和。看淨細細看。即用淨心眼無邊無涯除遠看　和言。問無障礙看　和問見何物　答。一物不見和向前遠看。Cf. translation by McRae (1986: 172–73).

reality but of our minds (in the Kantian sense of an apriorical form of sensuality). The sphere of nothingness may represent a stage at which the subjective category of substantiality, which normally allows us to see the world as consisting of objects or entities, is turned off, resulting in an impossibility to perceive even a single "thing", therefore resulting in a state best characterized by the statement "there is nothing", which would however not indicate mental blankness but just a state whose content is impossible to conceive of from the perspective of ordinary experience.

The sphere of neither perception nor non-perception would not be a state in which one is close to falling into sensory inactivity, but one in which the last remaining features of our conceptually mediated and interpreted phenomenal consciousness would be on the verge of being turned off. As suggested earlier, cessation would be a state in which all constructing processes come to an end which translates to total stopping of phenomenal consciousness. However, this would not imply coma, but a state in which the mind and the senses work in a globally unavailable way. Therefore, insight in the sense of a psychological transformation would be possible, though it would be entirely ineffable. As we have noted, cessation of phenomenal consciousness would also imply cessation of the most basic features characterizing our experience, including time, space, birth and death.

It is interesting that an interpretation in a somewhat similar vein has already been suggested by Hamilton, but she couched it in relatively vague terms, thus making this very provocative thesis difficult for readers to notice. Referring to the sphere of nothingness, Hamilton (2000: 155) writes:

> In the process of achieving what is referred to in this context as the complete "cessation of making manifold" – that is its "normal" uncontrolled way of operating – "form" characteristics are as it were transcended, or "seen through" first. In descriptions of the meditative exercises, this level of experience is referred to as "the plane of no-thing" ... the meditator is learning to suspend, so to speak, the operating of his cognitive apparatus in the usual making manifold (thing-like) way.

When commenting on the phrase *indriyāni vippasannāni* found in the discussion on attainment of cessation in the *Mahāvedalla-sutta* (MN 43/i.296), Hamilton (2000: 77) claims that someone in such a state (i.e., cessation) has "purified his senses" and that "apperception with 'purified senses' is nevertheless a feature of insight". Furthermore, she describes the person who has attained cessation as someone who "has transcended normal mental activities – that is, one who has stopped making manifold". Interestingly she does not explicitly use the term "cessation", though the context makes it clear that she is referring to it. Such an understanding of cessation is in harmony with the interpretation offered in this book.

Above, I have suggested a particular way of interpreting the account of the *āruppas* such as the sphere of boundless space and suggested that similar descriptions may be found in meditative and mystical literature. Below, we shall analyse one such a description. It is found in Sheng Yen's account of the progress through the higher stages of silent illumination (*mozhao* 默照) practice in his book *Hoofprint of the Ox: Principles of the Chan Buddhist Path as Taught by a Modern Chinese Master*. Sheng Yen (2001: 155–57) writes:

> The sense of physical embodiment will dissolve into a transparent awareness, and you will experience an expansive state of mind in which the external environment itself becomes your "body". With this vanishing of bodily boundaries, you will enter into the second stage of silent illumination practice.
>
> ... The transition to the second level of the second stage is marked by an actual experience of boundless oneness between self and the environment. The limited self expands and merges indistinguishably with the universe. Although events and objects in the inner and outer environments are still fully present, nothing interferes with anything else, since external environment is actually you. Just as the physical body ceases to be a burden in the first stage, in the second stage the external environment ceases to be an impediment. One's awareness penetrates right through objects in the immediate environment, without being impeded by their presence. Time passes quickly, and there is just total openness of mind and the clarity of infinite space. Everything is you.
>
> ... A third kind of experience that may arise at this deeper level of oneness is that of emptiness, or voidness. Although this sounds like the emptiness of no-self and self-nature that we identify with enlightenment, it is not the same. This is an experience of a pure vastness of space in which nothing at all seems to exist. It may seem that self and object no longer exist, that this is an experience of no-mind; but actually this "nothingness" is itself still conditioned by a subtle sense of selfhood and object.

I have allowed myself to quote Sheng Yen in such detail as his account is highly relevant for our discussion. His descriptions pretty much agree with our reading of the first three or maybe even four *āruppas*. He even uses the term "nothingness" in the account of the last stage. Of course, Sheng Yen himself did not consider these descriptions to be accounts of the formless states, as he has inherited from the classical Buddhist tradition their stereotypical understanding as "Hinayanist" yogic states of sensory inactivity and stasis. However, if our study proves anything, it is that the historically dominant understandings of meditative states described in ancient Buddhist texts are problematic. What matters are the actual characteristics of a state in question. Two texts may use the same label or term, but actually refer to entirely different states. Such is the case with the understanding of the four *jhānas* in some Nikāya texts and in the *Visuddhimagga*. On the other hand, even when using different labels or terms, different texts may in fact refer to a very similar state. Furthermore, what makes Sheng Yen's account valuable is that it seems to be based on actual experiences of the meditators, as historical Chan literature on silent illumination does not provide any such detailed accounts. Accounts similar to those of Sheng Yen have also been given by other modern meditators practising different forms of meditation[50] as well as by those experimenting with psychedelic substances. That the sense of ownership and bodily boundary is subjective and prone to manipulation is proven by several cognitive illusions such as the Rubber-Hand Illusion, the Full-Body Illusion, and the Enfacement Illusion which "rely on multisensory (e.g. visuo-tactile) stimulation to induce transient yet striking changes in body ownership, body identification, and self-face recognition" (Allen and Tsakiris 2019: 35). Lastly, Sheng Yen is a Chan master, albeit a modern one, which makes his account relevant to our study.

The *āruppas* can therefore be interpreted as the gradual process of simplification of cognition by the suspension of subjective categories which normally construct and mediate our experience, to the point in which the latter becomes totally unimaginable from our perspective.[51]

---

50 E.g., Dambrun (2016) reports that the meditators practising the experience of "body scanning" reduced the salience of body boundaries which is correlated with mindfulness-induced selflessness.

51 Attwood (2022) offers a different interpretation of the progress through the *āruppas*, focusing on the account in the *Cūḷasuññata-sutta* (MN 121/iii.103–109). He sees it in terms of an increasing inattention to sensory experience culminating in its total absence, while remaining in a state of contentless awareness. In this interpretation, meditative "end of the world (*lokassa anto*)" is synonymous with subjective and temporary state of not being aware of the world due

It needs to be honestly acknowledged that whether this was indeed the meaning intended by the authors of the *āruppa* accounts is impossible for us to establish with absolute certainty. It also needs to be emphasized that the above reading only takes into account the basic stock formula of the *āruppas* and *saññāvedayitanirodha*. There are several other Nikāya texts which attempt to expand on this basic formula and offer some additional information. However, in accordance with the methodological assumptions laid down in the introduction to this book, I refrain from generalizing the message of these texts to the basic formulas. There are good reasons to suspect that many of the early Buddhist concepts quickly became enigmas to their readers (or rather listeners), who were as confused about them as we are. Several Nikāya texts can be seen as a testimony to the attempts to elucidate their meaning. If there is some original stratum of the Nikāyas, it probably consists of the bare stock passages, lists of elements and some forms of verse.

Reinterpreting *saññāvedayitanirodha*

This interpretation of the *āruppas* and of *saññāvedayitanirodha* is very different from the one I have suggested in my earlier book (Polak 2011). Following Bronkhorst (1986), I then claimed that they were forms of yogic practice and an external intrusion, alien to the original Buddhist doctrine. However, several reasons have made me reconsider this position. Firstly, it was the awareness that the accounts of these states can be interpreted in a way that agrees with the notion of cognitive deconstruction of the conceptual features of our phenomenal consciousness which is implied by several other apophatic texts. Secondly, I realized that their traditional understanding as "hardcore" yogic forms of meditation in the sense of mental stasis and insentience which I took for granted is far from certain. What is most problematic is that the yogic texts that are available to us do not actually mention some of these states. In contrast, the forms of meditation undertaken

to not attending to sensory experience. On such a reading, these meditative experiences cannot be a source of any justified claims regarding the ontological status of the world, which continues unchanged when the meditator is subjectively unaware of its existence. "End of the world" understood in such a way is of course not exclusive to Buddhism, as states of meditative insentience may be also found in other religions and mystical doctrines; they are merely interpreted differently according to a particular religious ideology.

by the Bodhisatta and described as strivings (*padhāna*) or the practice of the brahmin Pārāsariya are very prominent in yogic literature. The argument is really simple: had the list of the *āruppas* represented the true and only order of higher stages of yogic meditation, then such a list should have been explicitly mentioned by the yogic texts. And yet it is not. Wynne (2007: 24–44) has convincingly shown the presence of certain interesting parallels of the element (*dhātu*) and formless meditations in the Nikāyas with the stages of the early Brahminic cosmogonies. However, these texts or other yogic scriptures do not really contain detailed accounts of the specific features of the states such as the sphere of boundless space that we have focused on, or of the other *āruppas*. I have no problem with accepting the fact that the notion of the *āruppas* may have originated in the Brahminic circles and be derived from certain cosmogonic beliefs. What is problematic is the assumption that in the form of the stock passage found in the Nikāyas they represent the type of meditation characterized by features traditionally associated with Hindu yoga – one-pointed concentration, sensory inactivity, and mental stasis. The Brahminic movement may have been much more diverse and included different forms of meditation and mysticism. Or, Brahminic cosmogonic lists may have been appropriated and creatively reinterpreted by other spiritual seekers, such as Āḷāra and Uddaka, whose religious affiliation is unclear, and who may have represented an intermediary position between the Brahmins and the *samaṇas*, drawing on the ideas of both groups.[52] To refer to Stace's (1961: 61) distinction they may have represented a type of more extravertive mysticism as opposed to the introvertive form associated with the classical Brahminic and Hindu texts.

In my earlier interpretation, I also pointed out that the Nikāya concept of cessation shares some crucial features with the highest forms of meditation known in many texts of the Yoga tradition and characterized by insentience and similarity to a dead person. However, what matters to our investigation is that just as some scholars have already noted (e.g., Hamilton 2000, Shulman 2014, Stuart 2013), the bare stock description of *saññāvedayitanirodha* does not mention these features explicitly and is open to different interpretations. They are indeed ascribed to this name in the Nikāyas, but in the texts that are

52 Gethin (2001: 347) rightly points out that "the relationship of the Brahmanical tradition to the emerging 'yogic' tradition is hardly clear cut. No doubt everybody was borrowing ideas and practices from everybody else".

elaborations and interpretations of the basic account. Of course, the term "cessation of perception and feeling" can be interpreted in terms of suppression and absence of all mental activity which would make it identical to the highest state mentioned in yogic scriptures. But as we have seen, there is also a possibility of interpreting it as merely cessation of phenomenal consciousness in the sense of globally available content which in itself does not entail mental stasis and insentience.

The very terms *saññāvedayitanirodha* or *nirodhasamāpatti* appear relatively seldom in the Nikāyas given their meditative status, and their Chinese correspondents (e.g., *xiangshoumie* 想受滅, *miejinding* 滅盡定) occur even less frequently in the Āgamas, although there are many texts where it would have been very fitting for them to appear, had the authors of these texts really wanted it. The implication must be that they apparently either did not know these names at all, or knew them, but were opposed to the concept behind them. But this does not mean that the general notion of the apophatically described meditative state characterized by an absence of elements and features of ordinary phenomenal experiences and standing at the apex of a meditative path is in itself a foreign or late element in the Nikāyas. *Saññāvedayitanirodha* may have been just one of several names applied to this state which were circulating among various, often geographically isolated groups of early Buddhist reciters. For some reason, this name eventually gained prominence within the Theravāda tradition at the expense of other ones and ultimately became associated with several meanings which may not have belonged to its original notion. These included a vision of *saññāvedayitanirodha* as a comatose state characterized by total insentience and absence of any mental activity and very similar to meditative states practised by the Hindu Yogins.[53] Such an evolution may have occurred due to misunderstanding of some of the paradoxical features of cessation. Cognitive deconstruction of phenomenal consciousness may have been misinterpreted as simple insentience. The paradoxical freedom from death due to the irrelevance of this notion beyond the sphere of phenomenal consciousness may have led to the concept that one cannot physically die during *nirodhasamāpatti* as evidenced by the story in the *Māratajjanīya-sutta* (MN 50/i.333) where the Venerable Sañjīva survived cremation while being in this meditative state. However, due to total mental and sensory stasis connected with this state, this new vision of *saññāvedayitanirodha* could not be harmonized

53 Cf. Polak (2011: 161–62).

with any notion of liberating insight or psychological transformation. In the *Visuddhimagga* it merely plays the role of a special achievement confirming mastery of *samatha* and *vipassanā* but is devoid of any soteriological function which is a far cry from the position of this state in the Nikāyas.

Nonetheless, it seems plausible that the early Buddhist ideas we have been discussing were reached by reflection on meditative experience of gradual deconstruction of phenomenal experience. By experiencing how features such as conceptuality, spatiality and temporality cease one by one without ensuing insentience, one could come to a conclusion that they are cognitively conditioned and do not have an objectively real nature. The notion that the aggregates or the six sense bases are not the self, could have been reached as a result of directly living through their cessation. It is difficult to conceive of how such ideas could have been reached otherwise, as the evolution of Indian thought up to this point does not seem to provide a necessary basis for the emergence of such concepts.

Ultimately, it remains unclear whether the four *jhāna*s were directly connected to the *āruppa*s and the apophatic state of cessation discussed in this chapter. The descriptions in the Nikāyas are simply not exhaustive enough to settle this problem. As we have seen, there are many possibilities that can be taken into consideration.[54] It might be the case that at some period the four *jhāna*s constituted a basic, obligatory path to liberation, while cessation was a special, optional achievement. It is interesting in this context to consider the question of why the Buddha's teachers were unable to progress from the highest formless states to

54 Shulman (2014: 36–39) considers a possibility that while the Buddha's initial version of doctrine focused on the liberating event occurring in the fourth *jhāna*, during the long course of his teaching career he may have reached some new understandings about even more profoundly calm and quiet meditative states, of which *saññāvedayitanirodha* was an example. Shulman does not see these teachings as "being in dissonance with each other" but rather as signs of "vitality and strength while different theories and approaches resonate and complement each other" (Shulman 2014: 39). In another paper (Shulman 2017), he reflects on the possibility of "polyvalent soteriologies" functioning in the early Buddhist Saṅgha which may have corresponded to more than one answer regarding the ultimate truth. Gethin (2020: 64) considers non-Buddhist origins of cessation and suggests that "the inclusion of cessation in the scheme of the path is best understood as part of an inclusivist strategy whereby meditation attainments regarded by non-Buddhist wanderers as the goal of the religious life are accommodated within an overall Buddhist scheme of the path".

the attainment of cessation, and why was the Buddha so certain that they would be very good recipients of his teaching. One hypothesis that can be taken into consideration, but cannot be proved beyond doubt, is that attaining the *āruppas* using the basis constituted by the Buddhist *jhānas* creates a qualitative difference enabling the progression to cessation as opposed to attaining them by some other means.

This notion may have been conveyed in the *Pārāyanavagga*. Wynne (2007: 66–93) shows how in the dialogues with Upasīva (Snp 5.6/205–207), Udaya (Snp 5.13/214–215) and Posāla (Snp 5.14/215–216), the Buddha discusses what seem to be formless, cessation-like states, expressed by words and phrases such as "nothingness" (*ākiñcañña*), "seeing 'there is nothing'" (*natthi kiñcīti passato*), "one for who perception of form has vanished" (*vibhūtarūpasaññissa*) and "consciousness coming to a stop" (*viññāṇaṃ uparujjhatī*). However, as Wynne points out, in his answers to the questions of the young Brahmins, the Buddha seems to suggest combining these states with qualities typical of the third and fourth *jhānas* such as "being purified by equanimity and mindfulness" (*upekkhāsatisaṃsuddhaṃ*) or "observing nothingness mindfully" (*ākiñcaññaṃ pekkhamāno satimā*). The accounts of the *āruppas* describe "what" the meditators are aware of (though in an apophatic manner, i.e., by saying what they are not aware of), while the *jhānas* describe "how" they are aware (e.g., mindfully, equanimously, clearly comprehending). It seems plausible that the two may be combined in various ways. Perhaps it was the combination of the *āruppas* with the equanimity of the higher *jhānas* and the resultant elimination of craving (if we accept Bronkhorst's theory) which allowed one to know that the fetter (*saṃyojana*) of enjoyment (*nandi*) is the origin of nothingness (*ākiñcañña-sambhava*), and thus shut down the last vestige of phenomenal consciousness and achieve its total cessation.

A similar problem occurs in early Chan texts. While they speak in apophatic terms about the ultimate state, it is not entirely clear how it is related to more basic, mundane accounts of meditation such as descriptions of meditative awareness of thoughts found in the texts of Shenhui, Zongmi or Moheyan and often labelled as no-thought (*wunian* 無念).

What is it like to be in a state of cessation?

If we conceive of cessation as the stopping of higher-order mental processes which mediate and construct our phenomenal experience, what will remain after the latter's deconstruction? To paraphrase the title of Nagel's (1974) famous article, what is it like to be in a state of cessation? If cessation involves phenomenal consciousness, does it not mean that it will result in a zombie-like blankness, the light of awareness going out and the theatre of our consciousness turning dark? Does it not ultimately mean that "we" will simply disappear?[55] One of the biggest benefits of these considerations about the nature of cessation is that it gives us an opportunity to rethink our intuitive concept of consciousness and its relation to what we actually are.

I have suggested that the cognitive mechanism of cessation may have to do with deconstruction of higher forms of cognitive processing, while retaining sentience and engagement in the world. One is therefore naturally inclined to speculate that as a result of such a deconstruction there will be some unique inner perspective, a flow of phenomenal qualia, a sort of a "movie" playing in our minds, just different from the one that is ordinarily played in them. Perhaps there would simply be none of the features which represent a cognitive distortion such as verbal thoughts, memories, conceit or the feeling of being a separate observer. There would still be a stream of phenomenal consciousness consisting of qualia, just of a different character, representative of an awakened, totally self-less and ineffable state of consciousness. However, such a perspective may be deceiving. The very possibility of imagining such a state implies the presence of self-consciousness. Imagining the inner "feel" or a first-person content of a state which would be truly devoid of self-consciousness and ineffable is inherently contradictory. Were one to trust the Buddha (as presented in the Nikāyas) on this issue, one should rather resign from any attempts at imagining such a state or talking about it. After all, according to the *Acinteyya-sutta* (AN 4.77/ ii.80) the *visaya* (range/object/scope) of both the *jhāna* and the Buddha is said to be unthinkable (*acinteyya*). Therefore, Sharf (2018: 828) is probably right in claiming that elimination of factors which "attend upon and shape conscious experience ... does not result in a more luminous or transparent state of pure consciousness, so much as in the progressive attenuation of consciousness itself".

Very valuable and pertinent reflections regarding this issue are contained in an article by Costines et al. (2021). It is centred around a conversation with an expert meditator in the Karma Kagyu Mahamudra tradition, Tilmann Lhündrup Borghardt, and discusses the issue of a

55 Similar questions are considered by Polak (2023a) and Bronkhorst (2022: 7).

pure, contentless state of consciousness as a form of minimal phenomenal experience using Metzinger's terminology. While considering the possibility of a truly self-less state, the authors (Costines et al. 2021: 3) acknowledge a key paradox to which we have referred in the earlier part of the chapter:

> During such a selfless state, perceptual or memory data are supposedly not available for phenomenal representation or cannot be integrated into autobiographical memory, as this requires a phenomenal self-model. If accessible data have been either minimized or eliminated from representational space or phenomenal representation, then how can they be experienced and reported as "emptied reference?"

Authors arrive at an inevitable conclusion that "[s]ince the knowledge that one has been in a selfless state cannot be integrated into the autobiographical self-model", the "memories of it are necessarily post-hoc confabulations" (Costines et al. 2021: 15). When describing his own first-person experiences of what he labels as "absolute emptiness", Borghardt claims that "there are no memory traces" and that "the only thing we have is the consequences".[56] However, he insists that this state is still an experience or a form of consciousness, due to its results, such as disappearance of fear of non-existence, the lack of time orientation, and feeling extremely refreshed.[57] This agrees with our hypothesis in Chapter 2 about the implicit nature of insight which only manifests through its observable effects. As the authors suggest, one can realize having been in such a state either through an inference based on its observable effects or due to "an experienced discontinuity of experiencing or the lack of memory of the experiential content" (Costines et al. 2021: 17). Thus, there can be no answer to the question of what it is like to be in that state. In face of this evidence, the authors ask a very pertinent question whether this state represents any experience at all, or whether its phenomenal properties simply cannot be integrated into memory (Costines et al. 2021: 16).

The latter option assumes that it is possible for a state to have phenomenal properties, but not be integrated into memory or be acknowledged in a self-reflective way. There seems to be no way in which we

56 Costines et al. (2021: 12–14).

57 This characteristic evokes Nikāya descriptions of observable effects of meditation such as having "very clear faculties" (*vippasannāni indriyāni*) and "very pure and very bright facial color" (*parisuddho mukhavaṇṇo pariyodāto*: e.g., SN 28.1/iii.235).

can verify the correctness of that assumption. Hypothetically, every process or aspect of the universe may be conscious, but if we cannot attend to it, store it in memory or talk about it, then from a functional perspective it is undistinguishable from an unconscious one.[58]

According to the view assumed in the paper by Costines et al. (2021), phenomenal consciousness exists in an absolute, independent sense, and its content may or may not be stored in the memory. But perhaps we should consider a different perspective? What we believe to be our phenomenal consciousness may just correspond to the content of our memory. Some data processed within our minds may get integrated into working and then long-term memory, which makes it possible to speak about it, attend to it or recollect it. However, from this point of view, it makes no sense to speak about any data prior to it being integrated into memory as being phenomenally conscious or not. The very notion of a distinct, special "representational space" in which qualitative experience takes place may be a result of an illicit hypostatization.

Let us at this point briefly return to the enigmatic passage in the *Udayamāṇavapucchā* (Snp 5.13/215) which spoke of living mindfully in such a way that consciousness is stopped. I have already suggested that due to its temporary delay and distortion, ordinary phenomenal consciousness could not coincide with the perfect mindfulness faithfully keeping up with the knife-edge present. We need to make a qualification on this statement. Zahavi (2005: 56) has noted that "had our perception been restricted to being conscious of that which exists right now, it would have been impossible to perceive anything with temporal extension and duration". And indeed, as we have already discussed, perceiving duration can only be possible with respect to a certain time-interval that has already passed. This requires at least a momentary act of consciously attending to the passage of time, which is of course tantamount to mindfulness losing contact with the present. It is tempting to imagine such a hypothetical form of perfect mindfulness which would involve experiencing an uninterrupted sequence of quickly changing impermanent self-less sensations (e.g., at moment t1 there would be sensation s1, at moment t2 sensation s2, etc.) where there simply would not be any occasion for ordinary consciousness to emerge. However, this still assumes that there is a distinct phenomenal

58 Cf. Naccache (2018) for a criticism of a notion of a phenomenal consciousness which is not correlated with access consciousness or whose content "overflows" it.

inner space in which such an experience occurs or a specific stream of conscious data. This, however, is merely a result of imagining this experience from the perspective of ordinary consciousness, and we have no way of self-reflectively experiencing what it would be like to experience such a state without interrupting it by our act of attending to it. There might just as well not be any phenomenal inner space or a stream of consciousness. The perfect mindfulness cannot therefore be but non-reflective. This, perhaps, explains why in the *ānāpānassati* formula, only in the first two of the sixteen stages the meditator is said to know/understand (*pajānāti*) that he breathes in and out, a fact to which we shall return in the conclusion of this book.

Ultimately, considering the problem of cessation allows us to rethink the question of our identity. If, like so many philosophers in the past, we identify ourselves with our consciousness or a conscious self inhabiting an inner phenomenal space, then we cannot see cessation of such a consciousness as anything but our temporary annihilation as well. Seen from this point of view, the perspective of cessation of consciousness considered in this chapter cannot be seen as anything but dreadful. However, that in us, what fears annihilation, asks about its own identity, forms beliefs and plans, and strives for liberation is neither consciousness nor any conscious self. All the abovementioned attitudes and activities originate outside consciousness in some non-conscious modules, who only function as if they were a conscious self.

In the earlier part of this book, I sometimes referred to a popular claim within modern philosophy of mind that phenomenal consciousness is correlated with the fact of global availability of its content, i.e., that what we are phenomenally conscious of, is also available to introspection, reflection, memory, verbal report, motor control and long-term planning. But perhaps we should attempt to look at this issue from another perspective. There are many processes that constitute us and a lot of cognitive data which is being processed in parallel at the same time within us. For certain evolutionary reasons connected with our fitness and efficiency, a small fragment of that data becomes available to some of our faculties, e.g., those of memory and speech. Only this may directly become part of our explicit, declarable knowledge. We conceive of this as our consciousness and we place our identity in it. This small element of cognitive architecture became very prominent in humans, probably due to the demands of social life, which involve verbal interactions and long-term planning. Global availability is crucial for efficiently rehearsing these tasks. But this is just a small part of what we are, and we are so much more than that. We can probably agree with Garfield (2015: 209), when he writes:

> [T]o be a person, from a Buddhist perspective, is to be a continuum of multiple, interacting sensory, motor and cognitive states and processes. Some of these are first-order intentional states and processes; some higher-order and some non-intentional. Some are introspectible; some are not.

It is here that our considerations about the discontinuity of ordinary consciousness during our wakeful states become particularly relevant. As we have seen, even in ordinary states, consciousness is generated intermittently and there are time intervals during which the brain does not process any data in a globally available way. Were we our consciousness, or a conscious self, this would imply that during considerable periods of time we simply do not exist but arise and cease with varying frequency. This of course constitutes a *reductio* of the view that we are our consciousness.[59] From this perspective, the state of the absence of ordinary conscious experience cannot be considered special or supermundane; it is in fact our default state, but we just do not know it. It is the arising of consciousness, which is a special event, but even during its occurrence unconscious bodily processes which constitute us are still continuously working. Meditative cessation merely represents an extreme end of the spectrum of ordinary wakeful states, in which the number of occurrences of conscious experience gets maximally reduced. The fact that at some moment, no data is made available to introspection, report or memory does not mean that we stop existing or that our cognition, sentience and engagement in the world cease. It is not really the case that something that actually exists is eliminated. Rather, the generation of a highly processed and distorted form of knowledge ceases. To use Bodhidharma's words, one simply abandons delusion (*shewang* 捨妄) and thus returns to the real (*guizhen* 歸真).[60]

These conclusions go against certain scholarly views which suggest that the Nikāyas imply the existence of a special consciousness which after stopping of the personality factors may exist timelessly beyond any worldly phenomenon in an unsupported, unconstructed, infinite and radiant form (Harvey 1995: 201–203) or which could be conscious

---

59 This type of argument often occurs in the Nikāyas in the context of the not-self teaching, where the aggregates are said to be *anattā* due to being impermanent (*anicca*).

60 X63, no. 1217, p. 1a22.

of nothing but its own consciousness-of (Nizamis 2012: 177). Despite the great value of these studies[61] in showing the limitations of the historically dominant reductionist interpretation of *anattā* teachings, I believe that the assumption of a special type of pure or transcendental *viññāṇa* as an ultimate state which is identified with *nibbāna* is problematic. The main Nikāya source for the notion of such a special consciousness is the famous line contained in the *Kevaṭṭa-sutta* (DN 11/i.211–223) which speaks about *viññāṇa* which is "non-manifesting, boundless and everywhere luminous" (*anidassanam anantaṃ sabbato pabhaṃ*), and where long and short, subtle and gross, beautiful and foul, and *nāma-rūpa* are stopped (*uparujjhati*) without remainder. And yet, the very next line proclaims that this stopping occurs "by means of cessation of consciousness" (*viññāṇassa nirodhena*), an expression we already discussed in the *Dutiyasikkhattaya-sutta* (AN 3.90/i.235–236) in connection with the release of the mind.[62] It is noteworthy in this context that according to Borghardt's report (Costines et al. 2021), one can distinguish two closely connected states representing the very apex of meditative achievement, which are labelled by the authors as "absolute emptiness" and "minimal emptiness" respectively. While it is impossible to describe what it is to be like in the former state, the latter is characterized by "feeling of consciousness *per se*" and phenomenal quality of luminosity. It might be therefore the case that luminous *viññāṇa* represents the last vestige of phenomenality before its total deconstruction and entry into a fully apophatic state of cessation.[63]

Ineffability in Nikāya and early Chan texts

In the earlier part of this chapter, I suggested that the content of the state of cessation cannot be integrated into the structure of our declarative long-term memory and is opaque to introspection and verbal report. I have also commented on the affinity between various conceptual categories which are suspended during this state and the structure

61 See also Albahari (2007) and Ñāṇananda (2016) for somewhat similar positions.

62 See Polak (2022) for a more detailed argumentation against the notion of a special consciousness in the Nikāyas.

63 It needs to be pointed out, however, that in case of Borghardt's report, the order of attainment of these states is reversed compared to the *Kevaṭṭa-sutta*, with experience of luminosity appearing as an afterglow after emerging from absolute emptiness.

of our imagination. Due to the extent to which these categories shape our ordinary experience of the world, we could not even conceive of the state resulting from their absence.[64] It is only possible to refer to the ultimate state in a negative, apophatic way by pointing out the features of our ordinary experience which are absent in it. Such is the general tenor of both Chan and Nikāya texts, which focus on the ineffability of the highest meditative state.

Strong emphasis on the ineffable nature of insight is already present in the texts connected with the East Mountain tradition. The Fourth Patriarch Daoxin speaks in the *Rudao anxin yao fangbian famen*, about knowledge that does not distinguish between objects (*wusuobiezhi* 無所別知), as similar to the one possessed by grass and trees (*caomu* 草木), but states using paradoxical language that "to know there is nothing to know is the wisdom to know everything (*yiqiezhi* 一切智)".[65] According to Hongren's statement in the *Xiuxin yao lun*, true learning occurs through the non-conditioned, spontaneous (*wuwei* 無為) mind and though it is called true learning, ultimately nothing is learned (*jingwusuoxue* 竟無所學).[66] When describing the final stage of meditative practice, during which the mind becomes calm and bright after the cessation of consciousness, Hongren claims that at this point "it is impossible to say more" (*gengbunengshuo* 更不能說).[67] Statements such as these highlight the paradoxical and implicit nature of the highest state of realization.

Ineffability is also strongly emphasized by Wuzhu in the *Lidai fabao ji*. When asked about the *Nirvana-sutra*, he states that this text is merely verbal explanations (*yanshuo* 言說), while "the real transcends texts

64 Cf. Bronkhorst (2022: 3): "Standard consciousness presents us with a picture of reality many of whose elements we recognize. Recognition is re-cognition, which is to say that associated memory images play a role in our perceptions. If the connection with those memory images were to be interrupted, we would then experience a world that we do not recognize and might interpret as being a different reality."

65 T85, no. 2837, p. 1287b12–13: 猶如草木無所別知之無知。乃名一切智。Translation by Chappell (1983: 110). Cf. translation by Van Schaik (2018: 157).

66 McRae (1986: 433/七): 無為心中學得者此是真學。雖言真學竟無所學。Cf. T48, no. 2011, p. 378a7–8. For a translation of this passage, see McRae (1986: 125–26).

67 McRae (1986: 427/十三): 此識滅已其心即虛凝寂淡泊皎潔泰然。吾更不能說其形狀。Cf. T48, no. 2011, p. 379a12–14. For a translation, see McRae (1986: 131).

and characters" (*zhenshiliwenzi* 真是離文字).[68] In another fragment, he states that dharma cannot be verbally expressed (*yanxuan* 言宣).[69]

The ineffable and non-discriminative nature of the ultimate state was also emphasized by the representatives of the Hongzhou school. Baizhang states in the *Tiansheng guangdeng lu* that the nature of wisdom (*zhixing* 智性) is neither known by wisdom (*bushizhizhi* 不是智知) nor cognized by consciousness (*bushishishi* 不是識識), transcends all thinking and measuring (*juesiliang* 絕思量), while speculation and conjecture are gone forever (*cunduoyongwang* 忖度永亡).[70] In another passage, he speaks about the deep and indistinct (*mingmeng* 冥朦) nature of wisdom (*zhihui* 智惠), which is difficult to verbalize (*nanshuo* 難說) and which cannot be compared with anything (*wukebiyu* 無可比喻).[71]

The *Chuanxin fa yao*, attributed to Baizhang's direct disciple, Huangbo Xiyun, contains several statements in a similar vein. According to Huangbo, this state can be neither cognized by wisdom (*bukeyizhihuishi* 不可以智慧識) nor can it be grasped through words and language (*bukeyiyanyuqu* 不可以言語取).[72] The position of the Hongzhou school is aptly summed up by Poceski (2007: 165), who writes: "[A]dopting a classic Mahāyāna perspective, the records of Mazu and his disciples deem ultimate reality to be 'inconceivable' (*buke siyi*), transcending conceptual constructs and verbal expressions".

Ineffability is also strongly emphasized in Nikāya texts, though in a slightly different way than in Chan writings. The already mentioned *Acinteyya-sutta* (AN 4.77/ii.80) explicitly states that the *visaya* (range/object/scope/characteristic) of both the Buddha and the *jhāna* are unthinkable (*acinteyya*) and must not be thought of (*na cintetabba*).[73] The *Sandha-sutta* concludes with praise offered by the *devas* to the meditator

---

68 T51, no. 2075, p. 191c21–23: 和上說云。非是涅槃經。此並是言說。言說三界本。真實滅苦因。言說即變異。真是離文字。Translation by Adamek (2007: 377).

69 T51, no. 2075, p. 192a14: 和上即為說法。諸法寂滅相。不可以言宣。Cf. translation by Adamek (2007: 378).

70 X78, no. 1553, p. 458c21–23: 智性自如如。非因所置。亦名體結。亦名體集。不是智知。不是識識。絕思量處。凝寂體盡。忖度永亡。Cf. translation by Cleary (1978: 44).

71 X78, no. 1553, p. 458a9: 智惠冥朦難說。無可比喻。Cf. translation by Cleary (1978: 39).

72 T48, no. 2012A, p. 381a26–27: 不可覓不可求。不可以智慧識。不可以言語取。Cf. translation by McRae (2005: 22).

73 AN 4.77/ii.80: *Jhāyissa, bhikkhave, jhānavisayo acinteyyo, na cintetabbo; yaṃ cintento ummādassa vighātassa bhāgī assa.*

due to the fact that they cannot fathom his inner state. The text states: "We ourselves do not understand, what you meditate (*jhāyasī*) in dependence on".[74] Both these texts emphasize the inconceivability of *jhāna*, which also implies that it is not simply an ordinary form of calm meditation attained by focusing on typical meditation objects, as the authors of the later treatises have no problems conceptualizing the inner content of such a state.

As Wynne (2010: 157) has pointed out, in early Buddhism "reality is ultimately ineffable, as is the state of the person who realizes it by escaping his cognitive conditioning". According to Wynne (2015b: 222), nirvana as "the dissolution of construction, is necessarily ineffable since it consists of cognitive deconstruction, and thus transcends language".

There are many suttas which stress the ineffability of the state of a liberated person. In the *Khema-sutta* (SN 44.1/iv.374–380) and the *Aggivaccha-sutta* (MN 72/i.483–489), we read that any of the aggregates "by which one describing the *Tathāgata* might describe (*paññāpeti*) him, has been abandoned by the *Tathāgata*, cut off at the root, made like a palm stump, obliterated so that it is no more subject to future arising",[75] which makes him "released from reckoning" (*saṅkhāyavimutto*) in terms of any particular aggregate. He is said to be "deep, immeasurable (*appameyyo*), hard to fathom like the great ocean".[76] This can perhaps mean that the state of *Tathāgata* is unfathomable from the perspective of ordinary first-person consciousness. This fully agrees with our interpretation of the first-person content of cessation as unimaginable from the point of ordinary consciousness. Whether the statements about each of the aggregates being abandoned (*pahīna*) or obliterated (*anabhāvaṅkata*) imply that the *Tathāgata* no longer experiences in terms of the *khandhas* at all, is difficult to ascertain.

A somewhat similar statement, but regarding the issue of describability in terms of the six sense bases, is contained in the *Phagguna-sutta*

74 AN 11.9/v.325: *Evaṃ jhāyiñca pana, saddha, bhadraṃ purisājānīyaṃ saindā devā sabrahmakā sapajāpatikā ārakāva namassanti: Namo te purisājañña, namo te purisuttama; Yassa te nābhijānāma, yampi nissāya jhāyasī'ti*. Translation by Bodhi (2012: 1563).

75 SN 44.1/iv.376: *yena rūpe tathāgataṃ paññāpayamāno paññāpeyya taṃ rūpaṃ tathāgatassa pahīnaṃ ucchinnamūlaṃ tālāvatthukataṃ anabhāvaṅkataṃ āyatiṃ anuppādadhammaṃ*. Translation by Bodhi (2000: 1381).

76 SN 44.1/iv.376: *rūpasaṅkhāyavimutto kho, mahārāja, tathāgato gambhīro appameyyo duppariyogāho – seyyathāpi mahāsamuddo*. Translation by Bodhi (2000: 1381).

(SN 35.83/iv.52–53) where it is said that one cannot describe (*paññāpeti*) the Buddhas of the past by means of any of the six senses.

The message of these texts is in harmony with what we have observed so far. The aggregates and the six senses represent alternative but complementary schemes of describing various modes of ordinary first-person conscious experience. Both texts emphasize a link between such an experience and linguistic describability. Since awakened persons transcend the former, this entails the ineffability of their status. The *Khema-sutta* connects this fact with the meaninglessness of the four questions regarding the status of the *Tathāgata* after his death. They are said to "not apply" (*na upeti*). What exactly makes these questions unanswerable? While scholars such as Collins (1982: 132–33) have suggested that their problematic nature lies merely in the fact that they use personal referring terms, this does not seem to fully explain the problem.

Much more plausible are the explanations offered by Hamilton and Wynne. Hamilton (2000: 174) has noted that the questions "are meaningful within a conceptual framework which assumes that space and time are transcendentally real" and that "if space and time are not transcendentally real, the questions are in effect unanswerable". Wynne (2010: 154–55) has pointed out that the questions are based on one more fundamental feature which is relevant with regards to our phenomenal experience but not to objective reality, namely that of existence. This explanation is very much in tune with our hypothesis that one can only meaningfully speak about dying with reference to entities that exist in a spatiotemporal world. The approach which removes features such as spatiotemporality, substantiality, existence and causality from noumenal reality and sees them as "forms" of our cognitive apparatus may be labelled as a Kantian one. The questions regarding the *Tathāgata*'s status after death constitute just four of the ten undeclarable points (*avyākata*). It is noteworthy in this context that four of the remaining six points concern the spatial and temporal infinity of the world and agree quite well with two Kantian antinomies. Kant considered all statements about the ultimate nature of the world as a whole (i.e., that it is finite or infinite in spatiotemporal terms) to be based on unjustified hypostatization of qualities of our phenomenal experiences (i.e., time and space) into a mind-independent reality. It seems likely that this was also the reason why these questions are considered unanswerable in the early Buddhist texts.

Therefore, the first-person cognitive content of a person in a state of the specific cessation we are considering, would not be constituted by the familiar and linguistically expressible reality of bodies and objects. The historically dominant Theravādin view that the ultimate vision of reality is constituted by momentary *dhammas* appearing and ceasing with enormous speed would need to be considered equally inadequate. For the *dhammas* are still conceived of as entities which occupy spatio-temporal reality and enter into causal relations. As Smith (2015: 156) rightly points out, postulating processes in place of objects also does not really change much with regards to the issue of effability, as they "[c]an be individuated from each other by their characteristics ... manifest a difference between essential and accidental properties responsible for their arising, persistence, and eventual demise". There is also nothing apophatic or linguistically inexpressible about either the *dhammas* or the processes.

If the state of cessation indeed involved going beyond the fundamental categories of being and non-being or dying and being reborn, then this would give us further clues regarding its potential soteriological role. For someone who has "touched by means of his body" (*kāyena phusitvā*) the state of such a cessation, the metaphysical views based on the categories that have been transcended lose their significance. Such a person will no longer grasp not only the Self-view, but also other metaphysical views, including the ones constituting the ten "undeclarable positions" (*avyākata*). Grasping or clinging (*upādāna*) to views is considered in the early Buddhist texts to be one of the most important sources of suffering. Those who are free from views would therefore significantly reduce their suffering.

The two perspectives of describing cessation

So far, I have been hypothesizing that the supposedly basic elements of our phenomenal experience, such as space, time, substantiality and causality, are cognitively conditioned and thus are not the features of mind-independent reality. I have also noted that the vision of the world present in classical physics cannot be considered a faithful image of such reality. Wynne (2015b: 231) is certainly right when he claims that "the bodies, brains, individual beings, objects, matter, the world – are merely ideas or concepts which can therefore be stopped, rendering the Tathāgata actually immeasurable and really lacking a body and consciousness". Yet, drawing on the modern philosophy of mind I have often been contrasting first-person passive phenomenal consciousness in the sense of globally broadcast content with active unconscious processes that occur in the brain. Even in the case of the Nikāyas, I have made a somewhat analogous distinction between the *khandhas* or the *āyatanas* on the one hand, and the body (*kāya*), sense faculties (*indriya*) and the mind (*citta/cetas*) on the other. I have also suggested that cessation may be conceptualized as a process where the basic cognitive processes in the brain continue while their conceptual elaboration ceases, or analogously where the *khandhas* and the *āyatanas* cease, but *kāya*, *indriyas* and *citta* remain active. I also considered the possibility that the generation of phenomenal consciousness is synonymous with creation of the subjective world of experience with its notions of life and death.

But is there not a serious contradiction in this way of thinking? The concepts of cognitive science and the very notions of "body", "brain" or "sense faculties" are certainly dependent on the categories of time and space, are linguistically expressible, and thus belong to what in the Buddhist texts is called the sphere of life and death. Therefore, they seem to be dependent on the structural features of the very phenomenal consciousness which is said to cease. Does it therefore make any sense to say that cessation of existence, birth, death, and the sense bases can be correlated with functioning of globally unavailable cognitive processes and the activity of their neural correlates?

Such an apparent contradiction is, however, unavoidable. We are touching here on a very important and subtle problem connected with any attempt of talking about the apophatic states, namely that of the different perspectives of description. The accounts of the body, senses or the mind of a person in a state of cessation can only be made from a hypothetical third-person perspective of someone whose cognition is still very much mediated by the basic conceptual categories of our experience. As we have noted in the preceding chapter, the concepts of natural science such as those of "the brain" and "the body" are ultimately not representative of the structure of mind-independent, objective reality, but rather imperfect models or approximations based on our first-person experience of the world which serve instrumental purposes. As we have observed, from the first-person perspective of someone in a state of cessation, even concepts such as those of the body, mind, or sense-faculties do not apply. Which perspective of these two is true, then? We have a natural tendency to assume that the perspective of a person in an apophatic state is altered, hence we speak about "altered states of consciousness". This would imply that something special has occurred in such practitioners, but the objective world around them continues as usual. However, in light of what we have said in this chapter, we should rather consider an entirely different perspective: it is our ordinary reality which is an alteration of an original state.[77] A person in an apophatic state of cessation merely stops the artificial construction of the subjective world of experience and thus returns to that which is real.[78]

Thus, we find in the Nikāyas a tenuous coexistence of the two entirely different perspectives of describing a person who is in the ultimate state. Some Nikāya texts seem to display an awareness of this paradox. This might be the case with the *Sandha-sutta* which describes the first-person perspective of a "meditator compared to a thoroughbred" in an entirely apophatic way (i.e., in negative terms) while at the same time contains the *devas*' admission that they are unable to fathom his internal state. The text thus juxtaposes the first-person apophatic perspective of cessation with the third-person account of that state from the perspective of those who still cognize in a conceptually mediated fashion. A similar perspectival incompatibility seems to be conveyed by the statements about Māra failing to find the consciousness of a liberated person.[79] From the perspective of cessation, it is meaningless to speak about passing away at a particular point of space and time, while Māra represents an ordinary unawakened perspective which is spatiotemporally limited. Similarly, a concluding passage of the *Brahmajāla-sutta* claims that:

> The body (*kāyo*) of the *Tathāgatha* remains (*tiṭṭhati*), bhikkhus, but its connection with "being" has been severed (*ucchinnabhavanettiko*). As long as his body remains, gods and men will see him; when the body breaks up, after life has been exhausted, gods and men will not see him.[80]

---

77 Such a perspective of looking at mystical experiences is considered by Bronkhorst (2022: 12–13).

78 This again harmonizes with the already mentioned Bodhidharma's statement in the *Erru sixing lun* that the person in the state of wall contemplation abandons delusion (*shewang* 捨妄) and returns to the real (*guizhen* 歸真).

79 SN 22.87/iii.124 and SN 4.23/i.122. Wynne (2022: 110) suggests that these accounts may have originated as a reworking of an earlier teaching found in MN 22/i.140, where the *devas* including Inda and Brahma cannot discover where the *viññāṇa* of the *Tathāgata* is established. The latter text clearly represents the same perspective as the *Sandha-sutta*.

80 DN 1/i.46. Translation by Wynne (2018a: 79).

In his interpretation of this fragment, Wynne (2018a: 80) has underlined the "somatic implications of his [the Buddha's] liberated condition". This may indeed be the case, but it is also possible to read the passage as an expression of the coexistence of the two perspectives of description. The connection with "being" or "becoming" (*bhava*) may be interpreted as that in us which generates our phenomenal consciousness with its reality of space, time and substance, as one can meaningfully speak about "being" or "becoming" only with reference to someone or something at a certain point of time and space. The statement about the *Tathāgata*'s body being seen by gods and men may express the third-person perspective of those in whom "the connection with being" has not yet been severed. Or, perhaps, we are reading too much into this text, as it is merely stating the obvious: since after the breakup of the Buddha's body he will no longer undergo rebirth, the gods (*devas*) and men will no longer see him!

The famous simile of the lotus flower contained in several Nikāya texts (e.g., SN 22.94/i.138–140, AN 4.36/ii.37–39, AN 10.81/v.151–152) may perhaps also be read as an illustration of this paradoxical coexistence of two perspectives within an awakened person. The "inner", first-person apophatic perspective of the *Tathāgata* is that of a lotus flower which rises up above the water and stands unsoiled by it,[81] while at the same time from the perspective of third-person, conceptually mediated cognition, the *Tathāgata* is very much a part of the spatiotemporal world of human experience, just as the lower part of the lotus is immersed in water.

Who is the *Tathāgata*, then? Exactly what notion is conveyed by that term? Gombrich (2009: 151–52) points out that the Buddhist tradition lost the original meaning of that unusual word and argues that it may have meant "the one who is like that". According to Gombrich (2009: 151), when the Buddha was referring to himself in that way, it was "tantamount to saying that there are no words to describe his state; he can only point to it". On the one hand, he is described as "the highest type of person, the supreme person who has achieved the supreme"[82] (*uttamapurisa paramapurisa*), and there are many passages referring to the

81 E.g., AN 4.36/ii.39: *seyyathāpi, brāhmaṇa, uppalaṃ vā padumaṃ vā puṇḍarīkaṃ vā udake jātaṃ udake saṃvaḍḍhaṃ udakā accuggamma tiṭṭhati anupalittaṃ udakena.* Translation by Bodhi (2012: 426).

82 E.g., SN 22.86/iii.118: *yo so, āvuso, tathāgato uttamapuriso paramapuriso paramapattipatto.*

body of the *Tathāgata*.[83] One also encounters statements referring to the *Tathāgata* in the sense of a particular person (i.e., historical Buddha) who may or may not entertain certain thoughts or wishes. For example, it is said that a particular thought does not occur to the *Tathāgata*,[84] or that the *Tathāgata* may be wishing (*ākaṅkhamāna*) to remain (*tiṭṭhati*) alive for an eon (*kappa*). Such statements are particularly frequent in the *Mahāparinibbāna-sutta* and may not reflect the original meaning of this word, but rather its understanding by the author of this relatively late text.

On the other hand, we find a more apophatic usage of this term. The *Tathāgata* is said to be beyond measure (*appameyya*), cannot be defined (*paññāpeti*) in terms of any of the five *khandhas*, is dissociated and released (*visaṃyutta vippamutta*) from any of them, and all logically possible statements regarding his existence after death which constitute the so-called tetralemma are considered equally improper. The *Tathāgata* is said to be "not apprehended as real and actual here in this very life"[85] by the unawakened monks such as Yamaka and Anurādha, which makes it improper for them to define (*paññapeti*) him apart from the tetralemma. *Tathāgata* should not be regarded as identical to any of the five aggregates or as being within them (e.g., in consciousness: *viññāṇasmiṃ*). But he should neither be regarded as being outside of (*aññatra*) them. Therefore, any hypotheses suggesting that the term *Tathāgata* ultimately refers to a special form of pure consciousness which can exist beyond the aggregates are problematic. More probable is that the term *Tathāgata* denotes a noumenal correlate of the five *khandhas*, i.e., that what a person ultimately is, when not experienced through the lens of various cognitive processes which mediate our ordinary experience. As we have suggested, the *khandhas* are various aspects of the first-person experience of ourselves within the world. However, the way we appear to ourselves (i.e., as the *khandhas*) is dependent on the particular functioning of the cognitive apparatus and on the processes labelled in Pali as *sañjānāti*, *papañceti*, *abhisaṅkharoti* or *maññati*. Were these processes to stop, how would we experience ourselves from the first-person perspective? The question is ultimately

83 E.g., DN 16/ ii.100: *seyyathāpi, ānanda, jajjarasakaṭaṃ veṭhamissakena yāpeti, evameva kho, ānanda, veṭhamissakena maññe tathāgatassa kāyo yāpeti.*

84 DN 16/ii.100: *tathāgatassa kho, ānanda, na evaṃ hoti.*

85 E.g., SN 22.86/iii.118: *diṭṭheva dhamme saccato thetato tathāgate anupalabbhiyamāne.*

meaningless, since as we have considered, the very notion of *khandha*-less experience is not conceivable. However, if the *khandhas* fall away, one may simply be what one ultimately is, without generating any form of mediated knowledge. Rather than experiencing the *Tathāgata*, one simply is the *Tathāgata*.

Perhaps the notion of the *Tathāgata* was also meant to somehow convey the paradoxical idea of the interweaving within a liberated person of the two ultimately incompatible perspectives we have been discussing above. On a purely semantic level, the concept is inherently incoherent. However, its usage may have played an important role from a pragmatic point of view. It may have served as an important soteriological ideal, an antidote to the allure of the annihilationist position to which the Buddhist position was always so prone, and as a uniquely Buddhist way of conveying the notion of sanctity of a liberated person.

Apophatic and cataphatic language

The above discussion shows the difficulties and paradoxes inherent in any attempt to cataphatically describe ultimate reality and the state of a liberated person. In light of these problems, one can appreciate the pragmatic focus on the issues of suffering and its destruction to the point of excluding anything else, that is prevalent in the majority of the Nikāyas. This approach certainly did not arise due to philosophical obscurantism but rather from a surprisingly profound awareness of the limitations of language and expressibility, and of the dangers connected with breaching them. As Wynne (2019a: 141) rightly points out, the Buddha's metaphysical reticence stemmed from the understanding that truth cannot be conceptualized. Improper, metaphysical usage of language is met with various forms of stern warning, including: *na upeti* (does not apply, lit. does not approach),[86] *tadakallaṃ* (it is not fitting),[87] *mā hevaṃ, āvuso* (do not [speak] thus, friend)[88] or *accayāsi pañhaṃ* (you overstep [the range] of question).[89] Therefore, it can be said that the

86 MN 72/i.486: *Upapajjatīti kho, vaccha, na upeti.*

87 DN 15/ii.68: *'na hoti tathāgato paraṃ maraṇā itissa diṭṭhī'ti, tadakallaṃ.*

88 AN 4.173/ii.261: *Channaṃ, āvuso, phassāyatanānaṃ asesavirāganirodhā atthaññaṃ kiñcī'ti? "Mā hevaṃ, āvuso".*

89 SN 23.1/iii.189: *Accayāsi, rādha, pañhaṃ, nāsakkhi pañhassa pariyantaṃ gahetuṃ.*

Buddha, as presented in the Nikāyas, clearly shows a preference for the apophatic approach.[90]

Some Chan texts contain surprisingly sophisticated reflections on apophatic language and its usage which mirror to a considerable extent the early Buddhist ones. In the *Wenda zazheng yi*, Shenhui points out that no-thought cannot be said (*buyan* 不言) to be either existent (*you* 有) or non-existent (*wu* 無). Even if one uses the latter two terms with respect to no-thought, they do not correspond to their "worldly" (*shijian* 同世) usages.[91] Therefore, it cannot be verbalized (*bukeshuo* 不可說). Though Shenhui admits that he himself speaks about no-thought, he explains that he does so only in response to a direct question (*weiduiwengu* 為對問故). If there were no questions, then no words would ultimately be spoken at all (*zhongwuyanshuo* 終無言說).[92]

Very rich and interesting speculations about the role of apophatic language may be found in the texts of Baizhang Huaihai.[93] In the *Tiansheng guangdeng lu*[94] he makes a distinction between the apophatic and cataphatic usage of language in Chan texts. Apophatic statements such as "no practice and no realization" (*wuxiuwuzheng* 無修無證) and "neither mind nor the Buddha" (*feixinfeifo* 非心非佛) are described by Baizhang as "concealing words" (*zheyu* 遮語) and "oxymorons" (*niyuyu* 逆喻語). Although both cataphatic and apophatic statements are the Buddha's teachings (*foshuo* 佛說), Baizhang prefers the latter ones, as they are "words of definitive teaching" (*liaoyijaioyu* 了義教語), "living words" (*shengyu* 生語) and "words outside the teachings of the three vehicles" (*sanshengjiaowaiyu* 三乘教外語).

Despite his preference for apophatic language, Baizhang is ultimately aware of the general limitations of language as a medium of communication. This is confirmed by the following statement of the *Tiansheng guangdeng lu*:

> If [the Buddha] would not want to speak at the beginning, living beings could not expect liberation. If he would have wanted to speak, living beings would follow his words and create interpretations. Little

90 Cf. Gombrich (2009: 151): "Exegetes do not like an apophatic description: it gives them nothing to get their teeth into. But the Buddha certainly did".

91 B25, no. 143, p. 230a2–5.

92 B25, no. 143, p. 231a1–2: 今言說者，為對問故。若不對問，終無言說。Cf. Gómez (1987: 84), and McRae (2023: 155) for translations of this fragment.

93 See Poceski (2007: 166–68) for a discussion of Baizhang's views on language.

94 X78, no. 1553, p. 457c7–15. Cf. Cleary (1978: 37–38) for a translation of this fragment.

> benefit, many disadvantages. Therefore [the Buddha] has said: "I would rather not teach Dharma but quickly enter Nirvana".[95]

Ultimately, there are only pragmatic criteria for assessing the veracity or falsity of statements. All verbal teachings (*yiqieyanjiao* 一切言教) are simply means for curing disease (*zhibing* 治病). Since there are various diseases, there are also different "medicine-teachings" (*yaoyibutong* 藥亦不同): apophatic ones and cataphatic ones. Therefore, Baizhang states, one sometimes says that there is a Buddha, and sometimes that there is not. The words that cure disease are the true ones (*shiyuzhibing* 實語治病). If the sickness (*bing* 病) gets better (*chai* 瘥), then every word leading to that goal is a true one. If the sickness does not get better, then every word is a false or a deluded one (*wangyu* 妄語). Even seemingly true words are ultimately false if they give rise to views (*shengjian* 生見), and seemingly false words are true if they succeed in cutting off delusions (*diandao* 顛倒) of living beings.[96]

As we have seen, just as in the case of the Nikāyas, the reluctance of Chan authors to provide detailed descriptions of ultimate reality or phenomenological accounts of higher meditative states was not a result of their obscurantism. This reluctance was well-grounded philosophically and stemmed from the conviction that in higher meditative states cognition occurs in a non-discriminatory form, without the medium of conceptual categories of language, and its results cannot be expressed verbally.[97]

95 X78, no. 1553, p. 458a13–15: 始欲不說。眾生無解脫之期。始欲說之。眾生又隨語生解。益少損多。故云我寧不說法。疾入於涅槃。Cf. translation by Cleary (1978: 40).

96 X78, no. 1553, p. 463a22–b4. Cf. translation by Poceski (2007: 165).

97 Cf. Poceski (2007: 216): "Classical Chan records do not provide comprehensive and nuanced depictions of the realm of reality and the experience of awakening, especially when compared with the texts of scholastic traditions such as Huayan and Tiantai. Both ultimate reality and the experience of awakening are indescribable and beyond the sphere of conceptualization".

Chapter 5

CAN THERE BE A METHODLESS MEDITATION?

The problem of the absence of descriptions of meditative methods

So far we have analysed several texts of both traditions which can be read as a criticisms of the notion of meditation as an active implementation of a technique. We are, however, still faced with perhaps the most important problem, namely, how can one find oneself in the positively evaluated meditative states described in Nikāya and Chan texts. But when searching for detailed meditative instructions in these texts, we encounter a silence, which is surprising given how much emphasis they put on meditation in general. This has not escaped scholarly attention, as evidenced by the following statement made by Gethin (2004: 202):

> Another curious fact, given the centrality of meditation practice to early Buddhism, is that so little is said about how to actually set about meditation practice. ... Just what the would-be meditator has to do to get from sitting down cross-legged to the *jhānas* and beyond is not at all clear.

In the case of Chan texts, this surprising silence has already been noted by Guifeng Zongmi, who has pointed out that although these texts have much to say about the "principle of Chan" (*chanli* 禪理), they nonetheless say very little about the practice of meditation (*chanxing* 禪行).[1] Bielefeldt (1988: 65) rightly notes that, "throughout the classic age of the school – the late T'ang, Five Dynasties, and early Sung – we find

1 T48, no. 2015, p. 399a24: 然今所集諸家述作。多談禪理少談禪行。Translation by Broughton (1999: 102): "However, the writings of the various houses herein collected speak mostly of the principle of Chan, while saying little of the practice of Chan".

very little discussion of the actual methods of Ch'an practice". Sharf (2014b: 933) has commented in a similar vein that:

> it may then come as a surprise to learn just how little is known about the meditation techniques associated with the 'founders' of this tradition – the masters associated with the nascent (or proto-) Chan lineages of the seventh and eighth centuries.

What could be the reason for this surprising reticence regarding what is, after all, a topic of great importance? As Bielefeldt (1988: 60), has remarked, one possible answer could be that:

> Meditation school had little to offer on the subject of contemplative technique beyond what was already available to the Buddhist community in the many Indian and Chinese treatises.

In other words, the uniqueness of the Chan school would not lie in practice of meditation but in its specific discourse about meditation. We have already noted McRae's (2005: 6) claim that the representatives of the Hongzhou school practised seated meditation but there was a "palpable taboo against even referring to this subject". In a similar vein, Sharf (2014b: 937) considers the possibility of an existence of a "rhetorical taboo against prescribing, or even discussing specific techniques". Such a taboo would supposedly stem from the ideological background of Chan, namely the doctrine of the inherent Buddha-nature and sudden enlightenment. Any notion of a meditative practice and of a goal to be achieved through such practice would thus imply gradualism and be at odds with the abovementioned ideology. Therefore, as Sharf (2014b: 938) aptly summarizes this position: "early Chan is not distinguished by forms of monastic practice and meditation technique so much as by its mythology, doctrine and literary style" and "early Chan was more about innovations in doctrine and rhetorical style than about innovations in technique".[2]

The idea that criticism coming from Chan authors was directed at meditation in itself, can be immediately dismissed as ungrounded, at least with reference to the Tang material we are dealing with. We have already seen in an earlier section that all the Chan texts which contain a critique of certain meditative practices are at the same time praising states which can also be described as meditative or contemplative in nature. Even the texts of the Niutou, Baotang and Hongzhou schools

2 It needs to be emphasized this is not Sharf's own position, which is more nuanced.

that were stereotypically considered to be radically subitist and critical of any notions of spiritual practice, contain general affirmations of meditation and highlight its significance in the life of a Chan monk.

Do Nikāyas imply transmission of meditative instructions outside the texts?

In the case of Nikāya texts one cannot postulate the existence of any rhetorical or ideological taboo against discussing meditation, as there are simply no grounds for it. One possible explanation for the lack of explicit meditative instructions has been suggested by Gethin (2004: 202–203), who stated that "the reason why the earlier texts fail to reveal very much about just how to practice meditation is not because they are uninterested in such matters, or think they are unimportant, but rather precisely the opposite: they are too important to write down" and that "the relative absence of specific instruction in the earlier texts perhaps should be understood in the light of something that is clear in the later texts: namely a view that the effective practice of meditation requires the personal instruction of a teacher".

This has, however, led Gethin (2004: 203) to the conclusion that "as historians of religion we must conclude that the earliest techniques of Buddhist meditation are lost to us". It might be the case that Gethin's hypothesis is true. After all, it implicitly assumes what seems to be one of the commonly accepted truths about meditation, namely that it can only be practised by implementing a particular method or a technique. As I have proposed, this is a central notion of what may be labelled as the mainstream Buddhist paradigm of meditation. According to that reasoning, even if there are no explicit mentions about the method of attaining the *jhāna*s in the Nikāyas, it must be assumed that there was one and that it is implied in the text. Gethin suggested that the effective practice of the *jhāna*s would require the personal instruction of a teacher. This would certainly agree with the way in which meditation is practised in modern times. Such a notion is also present in Buddhaghosa's *Visuddhimagga* where the disciple receives his meditative object from an experienced meditative teacher, the so-called "good friend" (*kalyāṇa-mitta*), who bases his choice on the student's particular psychological type. The meditative progress occurs through a series of crucial stages, each of which requires the proper application of a particular set of instructions. One needs to know how to prepare a meditation object, how to apprehend it, how to extend the sign during the first *jhāna*, how to review *jhāna* after emerging from it, and how to remove the *nimitta* in order to progress to the formless states. There are also several pitfalls connected with certain crucial stages in meditation and the advice of a teacher is essential to avoid falling into them. All these things can be learned from an experienced teacher, just as one learns other skills, like playing an instrument or driving a vehicle. In other words, meditation is a difficult skill in its own right, which requires very specific know-how. If this is indeed the way in which meditation is developed, then one will not progress very far without careful step-by-step guidance from a teacher, which may be required for quite long periods of time.

However, the assumption that the Nikāyas imply a notion of special meditative teachings transmitted from master to pupil in the course of a long, direct guidance is problematic. Such a model of a contemplative life is not really emphasized in the Nikāyas. Early Buddhist texts do not give a strong impression of some meditative doctrine which was supposed to be conveyed outside of the Buddha's teaching, or that there was a division in his doctrine where meditative instructions were not to be memorized and disseminated further as suttas but discussed in esoteric settings. Quite the contrary, in the passage of the *Mahāparinibbāna-sutta* (DN 16/ii.100), the Buddha emphatically states that his Dhamma has been proclaimed without making distinction at any esoteric (*antara*) and exoteric (*bāhira*) teaching, and that none of his teachings are "in closed fist of the teacher" (*ācariyamuṭṭhi*).[3] After the Buddha's departure it is not any person, but the Dhamma and the Vinaya which are to be considered the teacher (*satthar*). Every individual bhikkhu is ultimately on his own, as he is to live as an island to himself (*attadīpa*), having no other refuge but the Dhamma.[4]

The early texts present small groups of "good friends", i.e., bhikkhus who are peers and at a similar level of development, who live harmoniously together "like milk and water" (*khīrodakībhūta*) and support each other. Such a model is presented in the *Cūḷagosinga-sutta* (MN 31/i.205–211) of the *Majjhima Nikāya*.[5] An alternative was to wander

3 DN 16/ii.100: *desito, ānanda, mayā dhammo anantaraṃ abāhiraṃ karitvā. natthānanda, tathāgatassa dhammesu ācariyamuṭṭhi.*

4 DN 16/ii 100.

5 MN 31/i.207: *Taggha mayaṃ, bhante, samaggā sammodamānā avivadamānā khīrodakībhūtā aññamaññaṃ piyacakkhūhi sampassantā viharāmā'ti.* Translation by Ñāṇamoli and Bodhi (1995: 302): "Surely, venerable sir, we are living in

alone, which was considered a noble mode of living and compared in the *Khaggavisāṇa-sutta* of the *Suttanipāta* (Snp 1.3/8) to that of a king renouncing a conquered kingdom.[6] It is quite telling that after some time, the term good friend started to signify a meditation teacher while at the beginning it seemed to be taken quite literally.

Of course, all this does not mean that we should go to the opposite extreme and fully accept the radical thesis that from the moment of entering the Sangha the early Buddhist practitioners were entirely on their own in their meditation practice. There was certainly an initial period when one was receiving a general introduction to the Buddha's teaching and practice. Even at the higher stages of development, consultations with other monks or the Buddha himself certainly did take place.[7] The Vinaya speaks of a period of dependence (*nissaya*) where a young bhikkhu lives with a preceptor (*upajjhāya*) or a teacher (*ācariya*). However, the Vinaya focuses on the role of these mentor figures in teaching the novices about the most basic practicalities of daily renunciate life and not advanced meditation techniques. Furthermore, rules of the Vinaya such as these were not even present from the very beginning of the Sangha but were introduced as an answer to special circumstances.

Ultimately, the assumption that the Nikāya accounts of the *jhāna*s imply a notion of a specific technique or meditative method which is to be learned from a spiritual teacher, is based on an understanding of meditation as a specific skill that can be learned, and later deliberately used. From this perspective, either one knows or does not know

---

concord, with mutual appreciation, without disputing, blending like milk and water, viewing each other with kindly eyes".

6 Snp 1.3/8: *No ce labhetha nipakaṃ sahāyaṃ, Saddhiṃ caraṃ sādhuvihāridhīraṃ; Rājāva raṭṭhaṃ vijitaṃ pahāya, Eko care khaggavisāṇakappo*. I have amended the last line based on the PTS and the Sinhalese Buddha Jayanti editions, as the Chaṭṭha Saṅgāyana edition has *eko care mātaṅgaraññeva nāgo*. Translation by Bodhi (2017: 163): "But if one does not find a judicious companion, a fellow wanderer, of good behavior, resolute, like a king who has abandoned a conquered realm, one should live alone like a rhinoceros horn".

7 An example of such a consultation may be found in the *Upakkilesa-sutta* (MN 128/iii.152–162). It is noteworthy that the consultation with the Buddha is presented as a rather special, spontaneous occurrence, while the standard mode of living of the bhikkhus in the sutta is that of "good friends" living in harmony like "milk and water". The "consultation" regarding more advanced stages of meditation occurs during an unexpected visit by the Buddha and is not initiated by the bhikkhus themselves.

how to meditate. However, in Chapter 1 we discussed several Chan and Nikāya texts which could be read as criticisms of the historically dominant Buddhist model of meditation. The very same texts also contained accounts of what they considered to be right forms of meditation. Can there be an entirely unique paradigm of meditation, different from the mainstream one? Perhaps in light of this paradigm the surprising lack of detailed meditative instructions in the Nikāya and Chan texts would make better sense?

In Chapter 1, we briefly summarized some of the features of the mainstream paradigm as exemplified by the account of meditation in Buddhaghosa's *Visuddhimagga*. In order to ascertain to what extent the early Buddhist meditative ideas differ from the mainstream ones, we shall now more closely examine the nature of the differences between the Nikāya and the *Visuddhimagga* model of *jhāna* practice.

Nikāya *jhāna* vs the *Visuddhimagga jhāna*

A careful comparison of Buddhaghosa's account of the process of attaining the four *jhānas* with the one given in the Nikāyas reveals the presence of several fundamental differences. Bucknell, who has conducted a thorough comparative study of the two *jhāna* accounts in question, concludes that the one in the *Visuddhimagga* "is a fundamentally different version which is in serious conflict with the Nikāya account" (Bucknell, 1993: 403). In the *Visuddhimagga*, the essential method of achieving *jhāna* is that of a one-pointed concentration on a single object with the exclusion of everything else from the field of attention. Buddhaghosa uses several terms to emphasize the centrality of this notion. *Samādhi* is putting (*ādhāna*) or placing (*ṭhapana*) the mind (*citta*) and mental concomitants (*cetasika*) properly and equally (*samaṃ sammā*) on a single object (*ekārammaṇa*).[8] This object for concentration usually has the form of a gross physical artefact (e.g., a *kasiṇa*) at the earliest stage, but with the progress of meditation one should concentrate (lit. "bring together": *samannāharati*) on its mental image (*nimitta*, lit. sign). When this image becomes as vivid with closed eyes as they were open, it is called *uggahanimitta* (the learning sign).[9] In the case of certain meditation objects, it may be later transformed into a *paṭibhāganimitta* (the

8 Vism i.81/84/III.3.
9 Vism i.122/125/IV.28–29.

counterpart sign),[10] which is vastly changed and devoid of any flaws that may have been present in the learning sign.

Vitakka has a manifestation (*paccupaṭṭhāna*) of bringing (*ānayana*) the mind to its object, which should be "struck with it" (*vitakkāhata*). The characteristic (*lakkhaṇa*) of *vitakka* is that it functions as the fixation (*abhiniropana*) of the mind (*citta*) to its meditative object (*ārammaṇa*). Its function (*rasa*) is that of striking (*āhanana*) and threshing (*pariyāhanana*) the object. The mental factor of *vicāra* manifests as binding (*anuppabandhana*) the mind with the object in a more continued, sustained (*anumajjana*) manner, which is its characteristic.[11] The *Visuddhimagga* contains a very detailed discussion of various meditation objects, with particular emphasis on the ten *kasiṇas*. *Kasiṇas* are artifacts which represent various elementary qualities and serve as the focus of concentration. According to the *Visuddhimagga*, it is by virtue of meditating (*upanijjhāna*)[12] on a particular object that *jhāna* may be considered *jhāna* at all.

One cannot fail to notice the emphasis on the process of concentrating and fixating the mind on an object in Buddhaghosa's treatise, as attested by the presence of a significant number of technical terms referring to this mental act. Much attention is also devoted to the description of the meditation objects as evidenced by the account of the forty *kammaṭṭhānas* (meditation objects), and the theory of *uggahanimitta* and *paṭibhāganimitta*.

It is striking that all these crucial concepts are either completely absent in the Nikāyas or are used in a different context. *Vitakka* and *vicāra* do not seem to have the technical meaning they possess in the *Visuddhimagga* but rather refer to ordinary verbal thinking (*vitakka*) and examination/pondering (*vicāra*) which may be either negatively or positively evaluated.

It is noteworthy in this context that Zhiyi, despite generally being a proponent of ideas that can be considered representative of the mainstream paradigm of Buddhist meditation, had a somewhat different understanding of *vitarka* from Buddhaghosa. In Zhiyi's texts, *jue* 覺 corresponds to Pali *vitakka*. In his *Shi chan boluomi cidi famen* 釋禪波羅蜜次第法門 (*Elucidation of the Sequential Approach to the Perfection of Chan*),[13]

10 Vism i.109/117/IV.31.

11 A detailed description of *vitakka* and *vicāra* is found at Vism i.138/142/IV.88.

12 Vism i.145/150/IV.119.

13 Translation of the title follows Greene (2021: 114).

one of the definitions given for *jue* is *jingwu* 驚悟. Wang Huei-hsin (2001: 173) comments that it "literally means 'amazement and enlightenment'" and refers to "the amazement one experiences when one obtains the meritorious qualities of the First Dhyāna".[14] Such an understanding seems relatively close to the Nikāya one, while the one contained in the *Visuddhimagga* must be seen as a radical departure from it. It is very difficult to make a case for understanding *vitakka* and *vicāra* in the Nikāyas as referring to focusing and sustaining of the mind,[15] as their etymological meanings and overall usage in the early discourses are very different. Drawing on earlier research by Stuart-Fox (1989), Bucknell (1993: 397) comments that *vitakka-vicara* simply denotes the normal flow of thought, the stream of imagery and verbalizing.[16]

From an etymological point of view *vitakka* denotes an ordinary type of thinking, and this is exactly the meaning it possesses in the majority of Nikāya contexts. It is difficult to understand why that exact term would be chosen to express the idea of a mental act of focusing on a meditative object. The problem lies in finding a common denominator for these two apparently very different mental functions which would justify labelling them both as *vitakka*. One compromise hypothesis could be that while *vitakka* is a thought, it is a type of thought specific to meditative context, which occurs as a reaction to a situation when meditative mindfulness has become lost, and the mind has wandered away. Then, a *vitakka* appears, carrying with it the realization that the mind has wandered away, and this in itself marks the reestablishment of mindfulness.[17] While such an interpretation of *vitakka* could work

14 T46, no. 1916, p. 511b14: 復次覺名驚悟。行者得初禪。For a detailed discussion of this fragment and of Zhiyi's analysis of *dhyāna* factors, see Wang (2001: 174–75).

15 Cf. Stuart-Fox (1989), Bucknell (1993) and Polak (2011: 137–42) for a more detailed discussion of the differences in the usage of *vitakka* and *vicāra* between the Nikāyas and the *Visuddhimagga*.

16 In a similar vein, Arbel (2017: 73) sees "the existence of *vitakka* and *vicāra* in the first *jhāna* as wholesome 'residues' of a previous development of wholesome thoughts". Anālayo (2017b: 127) offers a different interpretation: "In sum, it seems that *vitakka* as a factor of the first absorption need not be taken to imply that thinking and reflection continue while one is in the actual attainment".

17 Establishing mindfulness need not be conceptualized as a conscious act requiring mental effort, as if flexing some imaginary attentional muscle. According to research by Wallach et al. (2010) and Carruthers (2015), the mechanism of attention is unconsciously driven, while globally available consciousness is passive. In other words, becoming aware of particular data

even in the context of the early stages of traditionally understood concentration meditation, it cannot be harmonized with the vision of the first *jhāna* as a very deep stage of absorption which does not allow any form of thought. The etymology of *vicāra* is much more unclear, as the term seems to be derived from the verb *carati* which refers to moving about, wandering and motion. In some texts the term *pavicarati* is used in the sense of mental examination or exploration.[18] It is interesting to consider the possibility of whether *vicāra* was originally used merely as an epithet of *vitakka*, in the sense of "a wandering thought" and due to a misunderstanding, it became considered as a term denoting a distinct mental factor in its own right. Rhys Davids and Stede (2007: 620) have speculated that both terms "were once used to denote one & the same thing: just thought, thinking, only in an emphatic way (as they are also semantically synonymous) and that one has to take them as one expression ... without being able to state their difference". It almost never appears on its own in the Nikāyas. This is in stark contrast with *vitakka*, which occurs very frequently in isolation from *vicāra*.

However, in none of the texts outside the *jhāna* stock passages does *vicāra* have anything to do with the mental act of sustained binding of the

results from a competition between various unconscious modules processing different information and some unconscious selective mechanism choosing which of these data will be globally broadcast, i.e., made conscious. The idea that being attentive or mindful is in its entirety a conscious act performed by our awareness can no longer be considered adequate. Therefore, it is not consciousness which can or cannot successfully attend to some data or be mindful. From the perspective of this cognitive model, the loss of mindfulness would result from the module responsible for attending to the data towards which mindfulness was originally supposed to be directed, losing competition for the access to consciousness to some other modules which process different data, such as memories or external stimuli. What is it then that brings mindfulness back? Some other unconscious module which is responsible for metacognition, i.e., monitoring current contents of consciousness, generates a thought carrying with it a realization that mindfulness has been lost. This thought breaks up the conscious occupation with the data currently present in awareness and primes the unconscious selective mechanism to again allow globally broadcasting the data towards which mindfulness was supposed to be directed, thus re-establishing it.

18 E.g., SN 46.3/v.68: *yasmiṃ samaye, bhikkhave, bhikkhu tathā sato viharanto taṃ dhammaṃ paññāya pavicinati pavicarati parivīmaṃsamāpajjati, dhammavicayasambojjhaṅgo tasmiṃ samaye bhikkhuno āraddho hoti*: "While he discriminates that Dhamma with wisdom, examines it, makes an investigation of it, his energy is aroused without slackening". Translation by Bodhi (2000: 1571).

mind to its object, i.e., the role that is ascribed to it in the *Visuddhimagga*. Interesting conclusions regarding the meaning of *vitakka* and *vicāra* in the context of the first *jhāna* can be drawn from the *Saṅgārava-sutta* (AN 3.60/i.1168–173). This unusual text discusses the four methods for reading the thoughts of other people. The third method is said to consist of hearing the sound of the diffusion of thought (*vitakkavipphārasadda*) "of one who is thinking and examining" (*vitakkayato vicārayato*) [some matter]".[19] The terms *vitakka* and *vicāra* are used in tandem, like in the account of the first *jhāna*, and yet there is no doubt that they refer here to an ordinary mental activity of thinking and examination. The fourth method is described as encompassing with one's own mind (*cetas*) the mind of a person who has attained (*samāpanna*) *samādhi* that is without *vitakka* and *vicāra*, so that one understands: "This person's mental *saṅkhāras* are so directed (*paṇihitā*) that immediately afterward he will think (*vitakkessati*) this *vitakka*".[20]

The text seems to refer to one of the higher *jhānas*, since they are states of *samādhi* devoid of *vitakka* and *vicāra*. This is explicitly the case with the second *jhāna*, while it seems to be implied for the third and the fourth. The logic of this passage seems to be that while *vitakka* is absent from the mind of a person in a state of *samādhi*, it will appear after emerging from that state. Direct juxtaposition of precisely this type of *jhāna*, to what appears to be a post-jhānic ordinary state of mind, with the focus on whether *vitakka* is present or absent in any of these states, implies that, at least for the author of this text, *vitakka* in both cases referred to the same type of mental phenomenon, i.e., thinking. Otherwise, their juxtaposition would make little sense, and there would be little reason for excluding the first *jhāna* from the states juxtaposed to ordinary state of consciousness. Of course, we cannot be certain whether this understanding of *vitakka* was shared by the author of the original *jhāna* formula.

Furthermore, one can easily find several terms in the Nikāyas which would probably serve better than *vitakka* to express the idea of an active process of applying or directing the mind towards an object. Terms

19 AN 3.60/i.171: *api ca kho vitakkayato vicārayato vitakkavipphārasaddaṃ sutvā ādisati – 'evampi te mano, itthampi te mano, itipi te cittan'ti. so bahuṃ cepi ādisati tatheva taṃ hoti, no aññathā*. Translation following Bodhi (2012: 264).

20 AN 3.60/i.171: *api ca kho avitakkaṃ avicāraṃ samādhiṃ samāpannassa cetasā ceto paricca pajānāti – 'yathā imassa bhoto manosaṅkhārā paṇihitā imassa cittassa anantarā amuṃ nāma vitakkaṃ vitakkessatī'ti*. Translation following Bodhi (2012: 264).

such as *paṇidahati* (to put forth, put down to, apply, direct), *paggaṇhāti* (exert), *padahati* (strive), *abhinīharati* (to direct to, to apply to), and *abhininnāmeti* (to bend towards, to turn), readily come to mind in this regard. However, it needs to be said that these terms are used in the Nikāya in their own contexts and not with reference to the method of attaining the first *jhāna*. The terms *uggahanimitta* and *paṭibhāganimitta* do not appear at all in the Nikāyas, while the term *nimitta* has several meanings but not that of a meditative object in the sense described in the *Visuddhimagga*.[21] The same holds true of *ārammaṇa*. Technical terms used in the *Visuddhimagga* to describe the act of one-pointed concentration, like *abhiniropana, upanijjhāna, samannāharati, vaḍḍhana, ādhāna, samādhāna*, are not used at all in the context of *jhāna* in the Nikāyas. While the list of the ten *kasiṇas* does appear in a couple of places, they are never discussed in connection with the attainment of the *jhānas*.[22]

Vitakka and *vicāra* are attributed no positive role whatsoever in the Nikāya account of meditation and judging from their disappearance from the second *jhāna* onwards they were probably considered to be an imperfect remnant of the ordinary state of consciousness. Most probably they are thoughts connected with the *dhamma*, mentioned in the *Paṃsudhovaka-sutta* (AN 3.101/i.253–256), the relatively subtle impurities that must give way before further progress. In part they may represent wholesome mental verbalization being a reaction to the removal of the hindrances and attainment of *jhāna*, as suggested by Zhiyi.[23] This interpretation may be supported by the fact that unification (*ekodibhāva*) of the mind (*cetas*) becomes present only at the stage of the second *jhāna*, once *vitakka* and *vicāra* have disappeared, as if their presence was a factor of distraction. Taking *vitakka* to refer to the process of "fixing attention" leads to a somewhat awkward result for Buddhaghosa, as it has to make a reappearance at the higher levels of concentration, since the formless spheres (*āruppa*) must be "hit with *vitakka*" (*vitakkāhatā kātabbā*).[24]

21 Bucknell (1993: 390) has commented that "such details as the *uggaha*- and *paṭibhāga-nimittas*, and *upacāra*-and *appanāsamādhi* are nowhere explicitly mentioned in the Nikāyas". See also Polak (2011: 131–36) for a more detailed argumentation in support of this claim.

22 See Polak (2011: 105–113) for a more detailed discussion of this subject.

23 T46, no. 1916, p. 511b14.

24 Vism i.321/327–328/X.9: *so taṃ kasiṇugghāṭimākāsanimittaṃ 'ākāso ākāso'ti punappunaṃ āvajjeti, takkāhataṃ vitakkāhataṃ karoti.*

The factor of one-pointedness (*cittassekaggatā*) is not even present in the standard Nikāya account.[25] Bucknell (1993: 389) comments that "the *jhāna* 1 of the Nikaya account is a rather preliminary stage in which mental onepointedness has not yet been established. The condition attained by the meditator who has mastered *appanāsamādhi* cannot be identical with the stage which the Nikāyas call 'the first *jhāna*'".

These are all very significant discrepancies. As we have seen, some essential characteristics of *jhāna* from the *Visuddhimagga* are completely absent from the Nikāyas. This particularly concerns the technical terms referring to the method and object of meditation. Stripped of these crucial features, the *jhāna*s as presented in the suttas no longer fit the mainstream Buddhist image of *samatha* meditation practice. Gethin (2004: 202) has commented that "if one set off into the forest with only a copy of the *Sāmaññaphala-sutta* as one's guide, it is doubtful that one would make very much progress in one's meditation practice". Indeed, this sutta contains no information about the act of concentrating and the object of concentration, which should be considered the most essential features of the mainstream concept of *jhāna*. Viewed from the perspective of the historically dominant paradigm, the Nikāya account of the *jhāna*s must be considered incomplete.

Can meditation be methodless?

Before accepting this conclusion, we should perhaps temporarily leave aside our implicit assumptions concerning the very nature of meditation and attempt to take these texts at face value and read them directly without assuming that some crucial information is missing.[26] Since the early Buddhist and Chan texts do not describe a meditative method in the sense of specific activities that need to be performed during meditation, then maybe we should tentatively consider the possibility that there really was none. From the perspective of the mainstream paradigm this would only be conceivable if these texts did not speak about any altered state of mind that could be achieved. Then, meditating

25 As Bucknell (2023: 208) points out, its occurrence in the Nikāyas is limited to the *Mahāvedalla-sutta* (MN 43/i.291–298) and the *Anupada-sutta* (MN 111/iii.24–29), "both of which are recognizably late".

26 A similar methodological approach regarding the question of the technique of attaining the *jhāna*s was suggested by Wynne (2018d) in one of his Oxford lectures.

without any technique would just result in remaining in a relatively ordinary state of consciousness. However, both the Nikāya and early Chan texts mention a very unusual, altered state of mind characterized by peace and tranquility which is free from movement of thoughts and conceptual elements and potentially capable of producing insight. As we have seen in the previous chapter, the highest levels of this type of meditation may involve such a radical cognitive deconstruction of ordinary experience that the resulting first-person content could only be described in a negative, apophatic manner. If there really was no method, why can an ordinary person not just sit down and get into that state? Real-life experience shows that if such persons sit down without doing anything, their minds will just be flooded with various types of thoughts and no altered psychophysical state will be reached. Another possible answer would be that the latter could occur by a chance and be a totally random event, a sort of psychological mutation happening by itself and unconditioned by any other factors. Accepting such a hypothesis makes any further exploration and explanation pretty much impossible. However, this interpretation is fundamentally at odds with at least the Nikāya sources which strongly emphasize the dependence of meditation on other elements of the Buddhist path.

But perhaps in the case of Nikāya and Chan texts we are dealing with an entirely different understanding of meditation. Several arguments can be raised in favour of the claim that at least some Nikāya and early Chan meditative ideas represent a unique paradigm, different from the mainstream Buddhist one. As we noted in the first part of this book, some Chan and Nikāya texts distinguish between two types of meditative calm and absence of thought: the right and the wrong one. The wrong form of meditative calm shares many features with the classic form of *samatha*, while the right form displays a number of very specific features that distinguish it from the mainstream forms of Buddhist meditation. Considering the very existence of a different, unorthodox paradigm of meditation is philosophically interesting in itself regardless of its historical significance in the context of Nikāya and Chan studies.

Can one therefore attain profoundly changed states of consciousness without a method in the sense of a deliberately implemented set of activities involving a particular skill? Dealing with this problem involves a serious explanative difficulty. The meditator must find himself in a thought-less state of calm that is free from mental defilements but cannot do so by means of conscious restraint, suppression, one-pointed focus on an object, or any other conceivable method at all. But even if there was no method in the mainstream sense, perhaps there was at least some sort of psychological mechanism by which the altered psychophysical state was to occur, a mechanism that had its own regularities and patterns that perhaps can be reconstructed. It might also be that in the meditative paradigm we are considering, the emphasis simply shifts from the method in the traditional sense to some other elements of the Buddhist path. One should then attempt to identify these elements and offer a psychologically plausible explanation of the way in which they contribute to the attainment of the altered meditative state.

The notion of a strict exclusive dichotomy between a method in a very strong sense and no method at all may involve a certain degree of oversimplification. However, proceeding with a tentative, working assumption of the absence of method in certain Nikāya and early Chan texts will allow us to identify and emphasize these hypothetical elements of the Buddhist path which cannot be conceptualized as meditative methods in the strict sense, but which contribute to the occurrence of an altered state of mind as its necessary, or perhaps in some cases, even sufficient conditions. As we shall see, it will be possible to further classify these elements into different groups and explain in detail the psychological mechanism by which they help to produce a meditative state. This may even lead to the re-appreciation of the role of these factors in the meditative systems which we have so far broadly classified as representing the mainstream paradigm.

Affirmation of methodlessness in Chan texts

The notion of the absence of a meditative method is very radical, as it goes against the mainstream Buddhist approach. So far, we have inferred the presence of this notion in the Nikāya and early Chan texts mostly in an indirect way, from their criticisms of forms of meditation which involved a method, and from the lack of positive accounts of what could be considered a meditative method. But there are also texts that explicitly emphasize the absence of a method in the sense of any active practice. This is particularly the case with the Chan school, whose scriptures often affirm the paradoxical nature of a methodless meditation.

In the *Dasheng kaixin xianxing dunwu zhenzong lun*, we find a question regarding the dharma/method (*fa* 法) that should be viewed (*kan* 看), and the dharma that must be realized (*zheng* 證) through cultivation (*xiu* 修). The answer contains a paradoxical phrase:

> You should not view a single dharma, and neither you should have any seeking (*qiu* 求). You should not realize a single dharma, and neither you should have any subsequent [attainment]. You should not become enlightened (*wu* 悟) to a single dharma, and neither is there any Way (*dao* 道) that can be cultivated (*xiu* 修). That is bodhi (*puti* 菩提).[27]

Several paradoxical statements concerning the methodless and effortless nature of true meditation are contained in the *Jueguan lun*. At the very beginning of this text, Yuanmen 緣門 asks the question: "What is it to pacify the mind (*anxin* 安心)?" Ruli 入理 replies:

> You should not posit a mind, nor should you attempt to pacify it (lit. force to pacify, *qiangan* 強安) – this may be called 'pacified' (*keweian* 可謂安).[28]

This passage seems to suggest that any effort to meditate in fact distances us from true meditation. This is confirmed by the passage in which the answer to the question "What should I do?" is "You should do nothing".[29]

In the *Dunwu rudao yaomen lun*, Dazhu Huihai expresses himself in a similarly paradoxical way. In response to the question about the Buddha's practice (*foxing* 佛行), he states that not practising any practice (*buxingyiqiexing* 不行一切行) is called the Buddha practice, the right practice and the holy practice.[30]

There are many more passages in the early Chan texts which convey a similar message. It seems that the theme of "no method" appears already in Bodhidharma's *Erru sixing lun*, where, despite the emphasis on meditation in the form of "being in a frozen state of wall

27 T85, no. 2835, p. 1278b15–16: 一法不看亦無有求。一 法不證亦無有後。一法不悟亦無道可修。即是菩提。Translation follows McRae (1987: 242), with *dao* 道 translated as "the Way" instead of McRae's rendering as "enlightenment".

28 B18, no. 101, p. 693a12–13: 答曰、汝不須立心、亦不須強安。可謂安矣。Translation by McRae (1983: 211).

29 B18, no. 101, p. 693b12: 問曰、若為時是。答曰、不為時是。Translation by McRae (1983: 213).

30 X63, no. 1223, p. 19a12–13: 問。云何行佛行。答。不行一切行。即名佛行。亦名正行。亦名聖行。Cf. translation by Blofeld (1962: 50).

contemplation" (*ningzhubiguan* 凝住壁觀), no method of its practising is given, unless we are to read *biguan* 壁觀 as meaning literally staring at a wall and *jianzhubuyi* 堅住不移 as referring to remaining in a motionless position.[31] The ambiguous character of this fragment has been noted by McRae (2003: 31), who asks the question: "Does this refer to some kind of yogic absorption, some kind of forced mental extinction or tranquilization?".

The presence of the term *wuwei* 無為 in the line that follows[32] in combination with the lack of an explicit description of any method may be significant here. In Chinese Buddhist texts, *wuwei* may correspond to the Sanskrit term *asaṃskṛta* and the Pali term *asaṅkhata*. In this context, it can mean "unconditioned" or "non-willed". The term *wuwei* of course has a much longer and richer history in China outside of Buddhism, and can also be translated as "non-active", "passive", "laissez-faire" or "spontaneous".[33] McRae (1986: 30) and Broughton (1999: 9) translate it as "inactive", but it is unlikely that *wuwei* would denote inactivity of the type of mental and bodily stasis and insentience connected with the higher stages of calm meditation. Of course, in the case of such a short and enigmatic text we can only speculate about the possibility of a particular meaning without reaching absolute certainty. The term *wuwei* also appears in the descriptions of meditation found in the later Chan texts. The *Xiuxin yao lun* states that if one wishes to attain Buddhahood quickly in this body, then one should *wuwei shou zhenxin* 無為守真心,[34] which can literally mean "maintain the real mind while doing nothing" or "spontaneously/non-actively maintain the real mind". The text also states that the essence (*ti* 體) of nirvana is serene extinction (*jimie* 寂滅), which is an unconditioned/spontaneous peaceful bliss (*wuweianle* 無為安樂).[35]

---

31 X63, no. 1217, p. 1a22–23: 凝住壁觀。無自無他。凡聖等一堅住不移。See McRae (1986: 103) and Broughton (1999: 9) for translations.

32 X63, no. 1217, p. 1a24: 寂然無為名之理入。

33 Soothill and Hodous (2014: 380).

34 McRae (1986: 434/六): 若願自身早成佛者，會是無為守真心。Cf. T48, no. 2011, p. 377c22–23. McRae (1986: 125) translates 無為守真心 as "do nothing except to maintain awareness of the True Mind". As he explains (McRae, 1986: 317, n. 73), "In Ch'an texts the term *wu-wei* often has the connotation of 'not doing anything'".

35 McRae (1986: 435/五): 涅槃者體是寂滅無為安樂。Cf. T48, no. 2011, p. 377c14–15. McRae (1986: 124) translates it as "The essence of what is called nirvana is serene extinction. It is unconditioned and pleasant".

The *Rudao anxin yao fangbian famen* which contains teachings attributed to Daoxin is of particular interest to us in this context, as several of its passages may be interpreted as directly emphasizing the absence of method. We have already mentioned one passage in this text in which all possible methods of meditation including remembrance of the Buddha, observing the mind, and grasping the mind are directly rejected. According to this fragment, one should neither make it "go" nor make it "stop".[36] In another passage near the end of this text, we find a paradoxical description of the method (*fa* 法), which is a "non-method" (*wufa* 無法), and a methodless method (*wufazhifa* 無法之法). It is a method that cannot be practised (lit. "intentionally done": *wuzuo* 無作) but is paradoxically a method of true reality (*zhenshifa* 真實法).[37]

As we already noted in Chapter 1, both seminal texts of the East Mountain Chan mentioned above also contain accounts of what can be very much considered typical, active forms of concentrative and mindfulness meditation. Therefore, they should either not be classified as representing the extreme position of no-method at all, or these texts are not homogeneous and in fact contain an input of various authors who may have had diametrically opposite ideas. This is particularly the case with the *Rudao anxin yao fangbian famen* which contains statements about meditation that may be considered antecedents of many later similarly paradoxical descriptions associated with the "Southern" and "subitist" schools, i.e., Niutou, Heze, Baotang, and Hongzhou.

It is particularly noteworthy that some formulations from Daoxin's text reappear almost verbatim in scriptures of the Hongzhou school. Such is the case with the phrases *wufazhifa* 無法之法 which appears in

---

36 T85, no. 2837, p. 1287b18–20. For translations, see McRae (1986: 143) and Van Schaik (2018: 158).

37 T85, no. 2837, p. 1289a26–27: 法應如是。此是作法。法本無法。無法之法。始名為 法。法則無作。夫無作之法。真實法也。Chappell (1983: 120) translates this fragment as: "This is our method of cultivation. The basis of our method is no-method. The method of no-method was from the beginning called the method. This method is therefore not to be cultivated. Thus the method of non-cultivation is the method of true reality". Van Schaik (2018: 178) does not translate 法 in this context as "method", but as "dharma": "The dharma should be like this – that is how the dharma is created. Yet the dharma is originally non-dharma. Only dharma that is not dharma can be called 'dharma'. Thus the dharma cannot be created. The true dharma jewel is the dharma which has never been created." Sheng Yen's (2008) understanding of 無法之法 is expressed by a title of his book *The Method of No-Method*.

the *Zongjing lu*[38] and *renyun* 任運 which appears in the *Chuanxin fa yao*, in the *Tiansheng guangdeng lu*, and is also attributed to the Hongzhou school in the texts of Zongmi. The most straightforward explanation of this fact would be that the Hongzhou authors were simply influenced by the teachings of the Fourth Patriarch. The other possibility is that these ideas were foreign to Daoxin himself but began to circulate at the time of writing the *Lengqie shiziji* and were retroactively attributed to him. However, Bodhidharma's *Erru sixing lun* already contained paradoxical formulations about meditation, so it is also plausible that Daoxin was continuing a certain tradition.

The emphasis on the methodlessness of meditation becomes more marked in the texts of the schools tracing their lineage to Huineng. Starting from the *Liuzu tanjing*, several authors including Shenhui and Zongmi preach the concept of no-thought (*wunian* 無念).[39] For Wuzhu, no-thought (*wunian* 無念) is synonymous with no-practice (*wuxing* 無行) and no-contemplation (*wuguan* 無觀).[40] Wuzhu's predecessor, Venerable Kim (also known as Wuxiang 無相, 684–762), taught the triad of "no-recollection, no-thought, and 'do not be deluded'" (*wuyi wunian mowang* 無憶無念莫妄).[41] Paradoxical expressions implying the methodless nature of meditation are also contained in several texts of the Hongzhou school. According to the *Mazu Daoyi chanshi guanglu* 馬祖道一禪師廣錄 (*The extensive record of Chan master Mazu Daoyi*), "not cultivating and not sitting (*buxiu buzuo* 不脩不坐) is the *Tathāgata*'s pure meditation (*qingjingchan* 清淨禪)".[42] In the *Tiansheng guangdeng lu*, Baizhang states in a similar vein that "neither movement nor meditation" (*budongbuchan* 不動不禪) is a meditation of the *Tathāgata* (*rulaichan* 如來禪), which transcends (*li* 離) generating meditative apperceptions (*chanxiang* 禪想).[43]

Rejection of active meditation methods requiring effort and deliberate application of the mind can only make sense in the context of the

38 T48, no. 2016, p. 498a14–15: 無法之法。是名真法。

39 Broughton (2009) translates *wunian* as "no mindfulness", while the majority of translators render it as "no thought".

40 T51, no. 2075, p. 192b12.

41 T51, no. 2075, p. 189a15. Translation by Adamek (2007: 338).

42 X69, no. 1321, p. 3b23: 不脩不坐。即是如來清淨禪。Translation by Poceski (2007: 136).

43 X78, no. 1553, p. 460a4–5: 不動不禪是如來禪。離生禪想。Cf. translation by Cleary (1978: 51): "Unmoved, not meditating, this is the meditation of those who come to realize thusness; it has nothing to do with producing meditational perceptions".

concept of the mind we have been reconstructing in the previous chapters. This concept implies that any consciously driven mental effort to meditate involves a disruption of the more basic level of the mind with its inherent intelligence and capability for insight. It also leads to the generation of fabricated, conceptually mediated states of consciousness marked by the typical dichotomies that characterize our ordinary experience. Any form of meditation which involves even a subtle form of actively trying to do anything, be it concentrating or even trying to be aware, is subject to a negative assessment. Achieving a thought-less state through traditional mainstream methods is considered useless because one thought is used to suppress all the other ones along with the basic, non-conceptual layer of the mind. The concept of meditation we are trying to reconstruct can therefore be characterized as negative in nature. It does not involve actively producing an entirely new mental state or a new quality, but merely reveals the already existing state. Based on what we have noted in previous chapters, such a notion of meditation can be considered psychologically plausible.

Methodlessness in the Nikāyas

As we have already noted, Nikāya descriptions of the four *jhāna*s do not contain any explicit, detailed information about meditation method or objects to meditate on. However, in contract to the scriptures of the Chan school, the majority of Nikāya texts do not explicitly state or emphasize the fact that the *jhāna*s are attained without methods or meditative objects. This can of course be potentially considered as an argument against ascribing the notion of methodlessness to the early Buddhist texts. However, we must emphasize the fact that the Nikāya authors were in a radically different situation than the writers of Chan texts. The latter were operating in the milieu where there already existed very strong mainstream ideas about meditation which of course involved a notion of actively applied methods. Therefore, it was only natural for the Chan Buddhists to somehow refer to these ideas, especially when their own ones were diametrically different.

However, in the times when the Nikāyas were created, there was not yet any Buddhist mainstream. If the early Buddhist teachings did not contain the notion of an active method of meditation, then there was simply no reason to emphasize that fact as was the case with other ideas not held by the early Buddhists. Why should a particular school or tradition underline the fact that it does not preach certain ideas? Of course, in the era in which the Nikāyas were created there were meditating non-Buddhists that had different views on meditation, but a simple quantitative analysis of the fragments presenting the non-Buddhist teachings in early Buddhist scriptures shows relatively little prominence of meditation. In the vast majority of cases nothing is said about the meditative ideas of the *samaṇas* and Brahmins that appear in the Nikāyas. Therefore, there would be no need for the Nikāya authors to highlight the notion of methodlessness, as they would simply focus on the positive elements of their teachings, i.e., those which can be actively practised, such as the right effort.

An example of a paradoxical denial of any active meditative method may be found in the *Oghataraṇa-sutta* (SN 1.1/i.1), where the Buddha states that he has crossed the flood "by not halting (*appatiṭṭhaṃ*) ... and by not straining (*anāyūhaṃ*)".[44] Such is also the case with the already mentioned *Sandha-sutta*[45] where a practitioner does not meditate based upon any of the known worldly qualities or elements, and yet paradoxically, as the text emphasizes, he still meditates.

Particularly interesting in this context is the meditative teaching contained in the *Bhikkhunupassaya-sutta* (SN 47.10/v.154–157).[46] This discourse is interesting in that it is one of those relatively few Nikāya texts containing unique information not found in any ordinary stock passages concerning meditation. It describes a situation when during the practice of *satipaṭṭhāna* meditation, there arises either a burning passion (*pariḷāha*) in the body, sluggishness (*līnatta*) in the mind, or the mind becomes distracted (*vikkhipati*) externally. As an antidote, the Buddha suggests that the mind should be directed (*paṇidahitabba*) towards an inspiring/gladdening feature (*pasādanīya nimitta*). This results in arising in succession of a series of positive states, starting from gladness (*pāmojja*), through rapture (*pīti*), being tranquil (*passaddha*), pleasure (*sukha*), up to concentration (*samādhi*). Once the mind has become concentrated, it should no longer be directed towards a gladdening feature, so the meditator withdraws it (*paṭisaṃharati*), "neither thinks nor examines" (*na ca vitakketi na ca vicāreti*) and is internally mindful while feeling pleasure.[47] This description may be read as

44 SN 1.1/i.1: *'appatiṭṭhaṃ khvāhaṃ, āvuso, anāyūhaṃ oghamatarin'ti*. Translation by Bodhi (2000: 89).

45 AN 11.9/v.322–326.

46 For a translation of this text, see Bodhi (2000: 1638–40).

47 SN 47.10/v.156.

implying a state which in other places is labelled as the third *jhāna*, since the latter is also characterized by the absence of *vitakka* and *vicāra*, as well as by the presence of mindfulness and pleasure. What is worth emphasizing is that this text presents directing the mind to a particular object as merely an optional and temporary measure, and not a basic method of meditation. This is in contrast to the mainstream approach, as exemplified by *kasiṇa* meditation in the *Visuddhimagga*, where the physical artifact and later its mental *nimitta*s are the objects of focus from the onset of meditation until the stage of the fourth *jhāna*. Instead, the sutta praises the development through non-directing (*appaṇidhāya bhāvanā*) where the mind is unconstricted/uncontracted (*asaṅkhitta*), released (*vimutta*) and undirected (*appaṇihita*).[48] This is really a significant difference in comparison with the mainstream approach.

It is interesting that this text discusses such a state of mind in connection with *satipaṭṭhāna* practice. The Buddha describes the meditative progress discussed in the sutta as "successively loftier stages of distinction" (*uḷāraṃ pubbenāparaṃ visesaṃ*).[49]

One may notice that in this book we have not devoted much attention to the four *satipaṭṭhāna*s, one of the most well-known practices associated with early Buddhism and frequently presented in the Nikāyas. However, as stated in the introduction, this book is not intended to be an exhaustive study of all early Buddhist ideas, nor does it intend to make general, conclusive statements about early Buddhism as a whole.

Kuan's (2008: 132–38) analysis and summary of research by other scholars show that the *satipaṭṭhāna* teaching may have been formulated relatively late compared to some other elements of early Buddhist teaching. This does not in itself imply that the *satipaṭṭhāna*s are "inauthentic". However, if we optimistically assume that this teaching was indeed created by the Buddha himself, then it happened in the final period of his life. The *satipaṭṭhāna* formulations are absent from the *Aṭṭhakavagga* and the *Pārāyanavagga*, which are considered to be amongst the oldest parts of the Nikāyas. They are also not contained in the presentation of the gradual path of practice in the suttas following the *Sāmaññaphala* pattern (with the exception of the *Dantabhūmi-sutta*

---

48 SN 47.10/v.156–157: *Kathañcānanda, appaṇidhāya bhāvanā hoti? Bahiddhā, ānanda, bhikkhu cittaṃ appaṇidhāya 'appaṇihitaṃ me bahiddhā cittan'ti pajānāti. Atha pacchāpure 'asaṅkhittaṃ vimuttaṃ appaṇihitan'ti pajānāti. Atha ca pana 'kāye kāyānupassī viharāmi ātāpī sampajāno satimā sukhamasmī'ti pajānāti.*

49 Translation follows Bodhi (2000: 1638).

[MN 125/iii.129–137], the peculiar structure of which seems to be a result of a later modification). It seems unlikely (though not impossible) that a formula developed during the final phase of the Buddha's life would refer to some completely new practice, different from the ones mentioned in the relatively older formulations. In Chapter 1, I emphasized the specific feature of the Nikāyas, namely, that many seemingly different formulas are in fact mutually complementary accounts of the same elements of the early Buddhist path. One should therefore expect that the *satipaṭṭhāna* formula is a specific alternative conceptualization of the soteriological process already covered by some other Nikāya teachings. As such, at least some of its elements correspond to the same meditative aspects which are covered by the formula of the four *jhānas*, to which we have devoted so much attention.

For example, the only common element of the *dhammānupassanā* occurring in all Nikāya and Āgama versions of the *Satipaṭṭhāna* discourses are the seven *bojjhaṅgas* (see Kuan, 2008: 169), which as we have seen, may be conceived of as an alternative, complementary account of the jhānic process. In the final part of this book we will also devote some space to the practice of *ānāpānassati* (mindfulness of breathing), the account of which displays a somewhat similar fourfold structure to the *satipaṭṭhāna* formula, and some Nikāya texts explicitly discuss this correlation (e.g., SN 54.13/v.328–333). Therefore, to the extent that this book discusses these teachings it also deals with the *satipaṭṭhānas*. However, I will not attempt to establish what was the general meaning of the *satipaṭṭhāna* formula and what was its evolution. This topic lies beyond the scope of this study.

The term *appaṇihita* (undirected) also occurs as part of the set of three *samādhis*: *animitta*, *appaṇihita* and *suññata* (e.g., in the *Suññatasamādhi-sutta* SN 43.4/iv.360 and in the *Saṅgīti-sutta* DN 33.6/iii.219). The three terms most probably do not refer to three distinct forms of unification, but rather to the three complementary aspects of the same state.[50] It would make sense, since *samādhi* having no *nimitta*[51] (object/

---

50 This may be an example of the feature of the Nikāyas noted by Gombrich (2006: 116), that the terms forming one string are usually near synonyms.

51 One of the definitions of the method of attaining *animitta cetosamādhi* mentions not applying attention to all *nimittas* (SN 40.9/iv.268–269: *sabbanimittānaṃ amanasikārā animittaṃ cetosamādhiṃ upasampajja viharati*). This does not necessarily imply sensory inactivity. It could refer to a mode of cognition when a normal perception which focuses only on the main, substantial characteristics of things (*nimitta*) has been suspended. This could be synonymous with the

feature/theme) would imply it being empty (*suñña*) of anything towards which the mind can be directed, thus making it undirected (*appaṇihita*). Bronkhorst (2012: 144–45, 201) interprets signlessness (*animitta*) as objectlessness. He (2012: 144) has commented that: "The absorption referred to in the Buddhist texts is not directed at an object. The texts use a special expression: 'signless-absorption-of-mind'".[52]

Arbel is another early Buddhist scholar[53] who challenges the historically dominant view of the *jhāna*s as concentrative practices. She writes: "[T]here is no support in the Nikāyas for the view that entering the first *jhāna* is the outcome of one-pointed concentration and absorption into a specific meditation object" (Arbel, 2017: 46). Regarding the method of *jhāna*, Arbel (2017: 157) has stated: "[T]he four *jhāna*s should not be conceived as meditative techniques at all. They are not concentration exercises that one can choose to practice".

Effortlessness of meditation in Chan texts

As we have already noted, in the paradigm we are trying to reconstruct, applying any form of conscious effort in order to meditate is either

suspension of conceptuality/apperception (*saññā*), since the latter is a mode of consciousness which focuses on major characteristics of things that allow to identify them as belonging to a particular class at the expense of ignoring many other aspects. If we were to refer to the example of the so-called "duck-rabbit", *animitta* mode of perception would consist of looking at this image in such a way, so as not to pick up characteristic features of duck or rabbit at the expense of other ones. The term *nimitta* may also refer to a meditative method in specific contexts. Ñāṇamoli and Bodhi (1995: 1206) comment that in the context of the *Vitakkasaṇṭhāna-sutta* (MN 20/i.118–122), *nimitta* may refer to "practical methods of removing the distracting thoughts". *Animitta* would thus mean "methodless", though it is doubtful that this was the meaning intended by the authors of Nikāya texts in which this term is used.

52 In another fragment of the same work, Bronkhorst (2012: 145) writes: "What is the absorption referred to in the Buddhist texts directed at? The answer is that absorption can but is not obliged to have an object. Like attention, of which it is a more intense variant, absorption can occur without being directed at anything in particular".

53 Also cf. Polak (2011: 206): "In other words, there was no distinct 'method' of 'practicing' *jhāna*. One should simply sit down and find oneself in this state ... One was not starting any new type of practice when he was sitting down to attain *jhāna*". Also, Wynne (2018d) has suggested in one of his Oxford lectures that the *jhāna*s may not have required concentrative practices at all but were stages of spiritual progress achieved through practising bare cognition.

unconditionally rejected or considered a transient imperfection of meditation. Not only does meditative effort not bring about the desired meditative state, but in fact it prevents its occurrence.[54] Chan texts in particular often contain direct warnings against using effort during meditation and emphasize the effortless quality of the true meditative state.

The *Chuanxin fa yao* contains a statement of Huangbo Xinyun that the highest state cannot be arrived at through effort (*feigongyongdao* 非功用到).[55] The *Zuochan ming* 坐禪銘 (*Inscription on Sitting Meditation*)[56] included in the *Zimen jingxun* 緇門警訓 (*Admonishments for monastics*)[57] and attributed to Mazu's disciple, Ehu Dayi 鵝湖大義 (746–818) contains a statement advising the meditator to sit quietly without effort (*jingzuobuyonggong* 靜坐不用工).[58] Although Chan texts usually lack any detailed positive instructions regarding meditative methods, they nonetheless stress the necessity of relaxing the body, almost as if this was the only thing that can actually be practised during meditation. Thus, Daoxin advises to "relax the body and loosen the limbs" (*fangshenzongti* 放身縱體) in the *Rudao anxin yao fangbian famen*.[59] The *Dasheng wusheng fangbian men* warns against "constricting" (*juansuo* 卷縮) the body and the mind, suggesting instead that one should unfold them (*shuzhan* 舒展).[60] The *Dasheng kaixin xianxing dunwu zhenzong lun* states that "If you let go of body and mind (*zongfangshenxin* 縱放身心), their defects will be evaporated".[61] A similar instruction is offered by Baizhang in the *Baizhang Huaihai chanshi guanglu*, where he suggests to release and let go of the body and mind (*fangsheshenxin* 放捨身心), causing them to

54 Sharf (2014b: 950) has rightly noted the following paradox: "How is it possible that any 'conditioned' (*saṃskṛta*) religious discipline – whether ritual practice, meditation, asceticism, ethical action, textual study, or what have you – could bring about an 'unconditioned' (*asaṃskṛta*) state such as *nirvāṇa*?"

55 T48, no. 2012A, p. 381a27–28: 不可以境物會。不可以功用到。Cf. translation by McRae (2005: 21–22).

56 Translation of the title follows Poceski (2015b: 101).

57 Translation of the title follows Schlütter (2008: 258).

58 T48, no. 2023, p. 1048c12. Cf. translation by Poceski (2015a: 102).

59 T85, no. 2837, p. 1289a10–11. Translation follows Chappell (1983: 119) and Van Schaik (2018: 177).

60 T85, no. 2834, p. 1273c5: 莫卷縮身心舒展身心。For translation, see McRae (1986: 172).

61 T85, no. 2835, p. 1278a21: 縱放身心虛豁其壞。Translation by McRae (1987: 241).

be completely at ease (*zizai* 自在).[62] The *Lidai fabao ji* describes Wuzhu's and Venerable Kim's form of meditation as simply "sitting in vacuity" (*kongxianzuo* 空閑坐) or "sitting in idleness" (*xianzuo* 閑坐),[63] which on the one hand suggests a relaxed, effortless manner of sitting, while on the other, points to the lack of any definite method of meditation in the Baotang school. When the East Mountain texts of Hongren and Daoxin describe the proper mode of looking at the mind, they use expressions suggesting gentleness and relaxation. The *Xiuxin yao lun* speaks of "gently quieting the mind" (*huanhuanjingxin* 緩緩靜心)[64] while the *Rudao anxin yao fangbian famen* mentions "slowly collecting the mind" (*xuxulianxin* 徐徐斂心).[65]

The latter text is also remarkable in that it strongly emphasizes the spontaneous nature of true concentration. It says that "when you give it the opportunity mind becomes peaceful and clear all by itself" (*xinzianjing* 心自安淨),[66] and that the "mind spontaneously becomes lucid and pure" (*xinzimingjing* 心自明淨).[67]

As we have already pointed out, in the paradigm we are trying to reconstruct, concentration is neither an activity nor a method that can be implemented. One does not concentrate the mind to eliminate thoughts. The order is entirely different. When defilements, thoughts, strivings and efforts drop away or are eliminated by development of virtue, the mind becomes concentrated or rather, unified of its own accord. This assumes that concentration or unification is a natural and inherent quality of the mind which is however prevented by movement

62 X69, no. 1323, p. 7c11: 放捨身心。全令自在。Cf. translation by Poceski (2007: 163).

63 E.g., T51, no. 2075, p. 187a10–11, where other monks criticize Wuzhu for "sitting in vacuity": 山中無住禪師不行禮懺念誦空閑坐云。Also, T51, no. 2075, p. 187a15–16, where Wuxiang recounts how he used to sit in vacuity during his learning period: 汝向後吾在學地時。飯不及喫。只空閑坐。 Translations of these phrases follow Adamek (2007).

64 McRae (1986: 427/十三). Cf. T48, no. 2011, p. 379a5. Translation follows McRae (1986: 130).

65 T85, no. 2837, p. 1289a13. Cf. translation by Chappell (1983: 119) and Van Schaik (2018: 177).

66 T85, no. 2837, p. 1289a8: 令其得便。心自安淨。Translation by Van Schaik (2018: 177). Chappell (1983: 118) translates it as: "Now, having attained this, the mind spontaneously becomes calm and pure".

67 T85, no. 2837, p. 1287b20–21: 獨一清淨。究竟處心自明淨。Translation by Chappell (1983: 110). Van Schaik (2018: 158) translates this fragment as: "In solitude and peace, the mind will of itself become luminous and clear".

of thought. One may say that it is a negative understanding of concentration, where a lack of distraction and scatteration is in itself a unification. This is exactly the message of the *Liuzu tanjing* which states that if internally there is no confusion (*neibuluan* 内不亂), then this in itself equals concentration (*ding* 定).[68] In the *Tanyu*, Shenhui claims that the "self-nature of the mind is concentration".[69]

The mechanism of absorption in the *Visuddhimagga*

Can a similar notion of effortless, spontaneous concentration also be found in the Nikāyas? In order to better understand the specifics of the early Buddhist approach, let us juxtapose it with the account of attainment of the *jhāna*s as presented in the *Visuddhimagga*.

The *Visuddhimagga* attempts to provide a detailed exegesis of the standard account of the four *jhāna*s contained in the Nikāyas. According to this definition, one attains the first *jhāna* "being separated from sensuality, separated from unskillful *dhamma*s" (*vivicceva kāmehi vivicca akusalehi dhammehi*).[70] The first *jhāna* is attained when the five hindrances (*nīvaraṇa*): sense desire (*kāmacchanda*), ill-will (*byāpāda*), sloth and torpor (*thinamiddha*), restlessness and worry (*uddhaccakukkucca*) and doubts (*vicikicchā*) are gone. The *Visuddhimagga* understands the phrase *vivicceva kāmehi* as being separated from the objects of sense desires (*vatthukāma*), such as charming shapes. This type of separation is further described as "bodily separation" (*kāyaviveka*).[71] While Buddhaghosa does not state it explicitly, this suggests that during absorption one is simply unaware of the external objects. Unawareness of the sense input is after all a typical feature of the traditional form of calm meditation, where meditators are completely absorbed in meditation objects to the point of excluding anything else. Bodily separation is, however, just one aspect of the process of entering *jhāna*.

According to the *Visuddhimagga*, one attains *jhāna* through the mechanism of suppression (*vikkhambhana*) of the five hindrances. One fragment of this text explains that being separated from sensuality is

68 T48, no. 2007, p. 339a6: 内不亂曰定。Cf. translation by Yampolsky (1967: 140): "inwardly to be unconfused is meditation".

69 B25, no. 142, p. 29a1: 心自性定. Translation by McRae (2023: 65).

70 E.g., SN 45.8/v.10.

71 Vism i.136/140/IV.83.

actually separation by suppression (*vikkhambhanaviveka*)[72] of sensual desire, the first of the hindrances, while being separated from unskilful *dhammas* refers to separation by suppression of the five hindrances in general. Another key fragment explains that this suppression is effectuated by the five *jhāna* factors (*jhānaṅga*): *vitakka*, *vicāra*, *pīti*, *sukha* and *cittassekaggatā*.[73] As we have already noted, *vitakka* and *vicāra* are terms used to denote the active process of concentrating on a meditative object. *Vitakka* fixes (*abhiniropeti*) the mind on an object while *vicāra* keeps it bound to it (*anuppabandhati*).[74] Rapture causes gladdening (*pīṇana*) of the mind, while pleasure performs the role of intensifying (*upabrūhana*) the mental states that are associated with it. The final factor, the one-pointedness of mind (*cittassekaggatā*), causes the mind together with the remaining associated (*sampayutta*) *dhammas* to be collected/centred (*ādhiyati*) on an object characterized by unity (*ekatta*).[75] The hindrances are supposed to be the contrary opposites of the *jhāna* factors (*jhānaṅgapaccanīkāni*). The *jhāna* factors are in opposition to (*paṭipakkha*) the hindrances, they are eliminating them (*viddhaṃsaka*) and abolishing them (*vighātaka*).[76]

Spontaneous entry into *jhāna* in the Nikāyas

However, when we turn to the Nikāyas we find an entirely different account of entering the *jhānas*. The order of some stages of this process is almost reversed. According to the account of the gradual path to liberation contained in several discourses following the model of the *Sāmaññaphala-sutta* (DN 2/i.47–86), it is actually due to realizing (*samanupassati*), that the hindrances have been abandoned (*pahīna*), that joy (*pāmojja*) is born (*jāyati*) in a meditator. What follows next is like a cascade, where each positive state naturally, spontaneously and effortlessly triggers a successive one. For one who is joyful (*pamudita*) rapture (*pīti*) is born (*jāyati*), which makes the body (*kāya*) calm down

72 Vism i.137/141/IV.87.

73 Vism i.137/141/IV.86.

74 Vism i.138/142/IV.88.

75 Vism i.142/146/IV.106.

76 Vism i.137/141//IV.86: *nīvaraṇāni hi jhānaṅgapaccanīkāni, tesaṃ jhānaṅgāneva paṭipakkhāni viddhaṃsakāni vighātakānīti vuttaṃ hoti. tathā hi samādhi kāmacchandassa paṭipakkho, pīti byāpādassa, vitakko thinamiddhassa, sukhaṃ uddhaccakukkuccassa, vicāro vicikicchāyāti peṭake vuttaṃ.*

(*passambhati*). One of tranquil body (*passaddhakāya*) "feels pleasure" (*sukhaṃ vedeti*). Concentration is not presented as a volitional activity or a form of mental effort of holding an object in mind, but is a result of feeling pleasure, since "the mind of one who feels pleasure becomes concentrated" (*sukhino cittaṃ samādhiyati*).[77]

The ensuing similes compare this process to a suffering sick person (*purisa ābādhika*) feeling joy and happiness after regaining health, or to a slave (*dāsa*) rejoicing after being released from bondage.[78]

We again find several fundamental differences regarding the process of attaining *jhāna* between the *Visuddhimagga* and the Nikāya account. In the Nikāya account, there is no mention of bodily seclusion from the sense objects or of the suppression and elimination of the hindrances by the *jhāna* factors. Quite the contrary, it is due to realization that the hindrances are no longer present that one experiences rapture and pleasure, two of the supposed *jhāna* factors. It therefore follows that they cannot play any role in suppressing the hindrances, as they themselves appear only after the latter are gone. Stuart-Fox (1989: 99) rightly notes that "it is never explicitly stated in the Tipitaka that each of the five *jhāna* factors is instrumental in overcoming a specific hindrance" and that some of the matchings of particular *jhāna* factors with specific hindrances "are quite inappropriate" (Stuart-Fox, 1989: 100).

The sequence of gradually arising positive mental states is also present in both versions of the *Cetanākaraṇīya-sutta* (AN 10.2/v.2–4 and AN 11.2/v.312–313). These texts in particular emphasize the spontaneous and natural character of their progress, explicitly stating that the meditator possessing a positive state occupying an earlier position in the sequence "need not make an act of intention" (*na cetanāya karaṇīyaṃ*) to obtain the next one. Thus, for one who feels pleasure (*sukhī*), there is no need to make an intention "let my mind be concentrated" (*'cittaṃ me samādhiyatū'ti*). It is a natural state of things (*dhammatā*) that the mind of one feeling pleasure will become unified.[79]

Let us emphasize that the abovementioned Nikāya accounts differ significantly from the *Visuddhimagga* regarding the place and role of rapture and pleasure in the attainment of *jhāna*. In the *Visuddhimagga*,

---

77 DN 2/i.73: *tassime pañca nīvaraṇe pahīne attani samanupassato pāmojjaṃ jāyati, pamuditassa pīti jāyati, pītimanassa kāyo passambhati, passaddhakāyo sukhaṃ vedeti, sukhino cittaṃ samādhiyati*. Cf. Jianxun Shi (2022: 177–80), for a discussion of this sequence.

78 DN 2/i.72.

79 AN 10.2/v.3: *dhammatā esā, bhikkhave, yaṃ sukhino cittaṃ samādhiyati*.

pīti and *sukha* are said to arise due to success of the undertaking (*payogasampatti*) of directing the mind onto its meditative object and keeping it bound to it, and achieved through its (i.e., the mind's) non-distraction (*avikkhepa*).[80] *Pīti* is the contentment (*tuṭṭhi*) due to obtaining of desired object (*ārammaṇa*), while *sukha* is the experiencing (*anubhavana*) of its taste once it has been obtained.[81] The main mechanism behind the meditative progress is the intensifying concentration on a meditation object, while *pīti* and *sukha* are positive reactions to the success of this effort and together with the other three *jhāna* factors suppress the five hindrances. In contrast, direct reading of the Nikāya account suggests that it is the abandonment of the hindrances and the resultant joy (*pāmojja*), that are the key factors which set off the entire process, in turn causing the arising of rapture, bodily calm, pleasure and eventually *samādhi*. As to the abandonment of the hindrances, it is not accomplished by their suppression through concentrative absorption, but by a pre-meditative virtuous way of life. The mechanism driving the whole process is therefore entirely different.

It is worthwhile to briefly consider the philosophical implications of these ideas and their plausibility. The idea of concentration as a passive, spontaneous state is definitely at odds with the understanding of this word in modern languages, such as English. The verb "to concentrate" carries with it the notion of a deliberate mental activity involving conscious effort and tension, as if one was flexing a mental muscle of sorts. Concentration is an act that we can perform and depends on our volition. We are often told to concentrate on our tasks or on some stimuli. In the Nikāyas, the meaning of *samādhi* would perhaps better correspond to that of a unification in the negative sense of non-distraction and non-scatteration. The notion of a spontaneous entry into *jhāna* and of a passive nature of concentration implies a very specific concept of mind as its implicit basis. Let us note that *samādhi* in the Nikāyas represents a potency for a successful cognitive act, and not the act itself. In the stock passage describing the state after the attainment of the fourth *jhāna*, it is said that the mind is already unified (*samāhita*) even before being directed to any of the so-called higher knowledges. This is not how the word "concentration" is used in modern English as it already implies that one is concentrated on something in particular. It makes little sense to speak of concentration as a state of potency.

80 Vism i.142/146/IV.106.
81 Vism i.140/145/IV.100.

The modern understanding of concentration would rather correspond to what in the Nikāyas is labelled as directing (*abhininnāmeti*) the mind towards any of the higher knowledges. The early discourses imply a concept of a mind inherently endowed with the capacity for calm and insight. These positive qualities are, however, obscured by the presence of distracting thoughts, hindrances and defilements. Once the latter have been removed, the inherent features of the mind will be able to manifest themselves. This interpretation is in agreeance with the *Pabhassara-sutta*'s (AN 1.49–1.50/i.10) vision of the luminous mind which can be freed from incoming defilements and the *Paṃsudhovaka-sutta*'s (AN 3.101/i.253–256) account of the mind which like gold may be cleansed of its impurities, becoming workable and pliant. Let us note that according to these similes, one does not add or create any new positive quality as one merely restores the original state which had been sullied by something external. Such is also the case with the five similes explaining the abandonment of the hindrances (*nīvaraṇappahāna*) in the suttas from the *Sāmaññaphala* group (e.g., in DN 2/i.71–73). All five similes (recovery from illness, release from slavery, release from prison, a man lost in wilderness getting back to safety, paying off one's debt) describe a man becoming freed from a temporary misfortune and restored to an original state. This vision is of course very much in tune with the Chan concept of the original pure mind.

How can pleasure be conducive to concentration?

Particularly interesting from a philosophical point of view is the very often repeated Nikāya statement that in "one who feels pleasure, the mind becomes unified (or concentrated)" (*sukhino cittaṃ samādhiyati*). Is it psychologically plausible? Certainly, it is not the case that someone who feels pleasure concentrates in the modern sense of the word, which involves active focus. However, if we take *samādhi* to mean non-distraction, it becomes possible to offer a hypothesis explaining its dependence on feeling pleasure. The search for pleasure is one of the strongest motivating factors of our psychology. Not feeling pleasure results in non-satisfaction with one's own state and in efforts to change it by seeking external forms of pleasure. This generates all sorts of mental activities which are the opposite of mental unification. If someone experiences intense pleasure from enjoying a particular object, it usually coincides with naturally giving this pleasant sensation one's full attention. It is therefore a type of concentration, though it does not meet the criteria of *samādhi* spoken about in the Nikāyas. For as we have already noted, being in a state of *samādhi* implies a potency to perform a successful cognitive act, while the English word concentration refers to a state of already being concentrated on something in particular. Perhaps this is why in the *Bhikkhunupassaya-sutta*, a bhikkhu who has temporarily directed his mind to a gladdening feature is told to withdraw it from such a feature once the purpose of this action has been accomplished. The type of pleasure spoken about in the Nikāyas should, therefore, not be derived from enjoying any particular object. But how would such pleasure arise? According to the stock passage describing the sequence of successively arising positive factors, "it is natural that one whose body is tranquil (*passaddhakāyo*) feels pleasure (*sukhaṃ vediyati*)". The verb *passambhati* (calm down, allay) is also used with reference to the *saṅkhāras*.[82] We have already observed that the latter term may imply the qualities of effort and conscious control and indirectly that of tension. It is commonplace that bodily tension is unpleasant, while its lack could result in feeling pleasure. This harmonizes with Bronkhorst's (2012: 163) claim that "discharge of bodily tension is experienced as pleasure". The experience of orgasm can be considered a good example of this phenomenon.

It is noteworthy in that context that in the abovementioned Nikāya stock sequence of successive positive states, calming of the body is said to occur naturally in one who feels bliss or rapture in his mind (*pītimana*). Just as it is the case with orgasm, it seems plausible that a strong experience of bliss could bring about a discharge of bodily tension, i.e., calming down of *saṅkhāras*. Bliss itself is said to result from feeling gladness (*pamojja*), which in turn is said to occur for a virtuous (*sīlavant/sīlasampanna*) practitioner who does not feel remorse (*avippaṭisāra*). The psychological link between the development of virtue and the feeling of gladness is presented in greater detail in the scheme of gradual training contained in the suttas following the *Sāmāññaphala* pattern. There, gladness is said to arise from realizing that the five hindrances have

82 E.g., MN 118/iii.82: "I will breathe in calming down bodily *saṅkhāra*" ('*passambhayaṃ kāyasaṅkhāraṃ assasissāmī'ti sikkhati*). The order in the *ānāpānassati* formula is reversed compared to the *Sāmaññaphala* account as the calming down of bodily *saṅkhāra* precedes experiencing *pīti*. This does not necessarily imply discrepancy between the two accounts, but the mutual feedback and conditioning between the two states in question.

been abandoned in oneself.[83] It hardly needs further explanation why finding oneself in a state free from sensual desire, ill-will, restlessness and worry, sloth and torpor and doubts will result in feeling joy, though it needs to be said that the five similes given in the text are very well-thought-out and fulfil that task admirably. All the five *nivāraṇas* are in themselves states involving certain amount of psychological suffering and therefore their absence is bound to arouse positive emotional reactions.

As a conclusion, we can say that the notion of spontaneous and passive attainment of *samādhi* has basis in certain Nikāya texts and appears to be plausible from a psychological point of view. A somewhat similar interpretation was offered by Vetter (1988: xxv), who claimed that when a monk who perfected his moral conduct and mindfulness "seeks out a lonely place and sits down quietly, he only needs to remove a few traces of interference before he almost effortlessly enters the first stage of *dhyāna*".

All the new developments present in the *Visuddhimagga*, such as the technical concepts of *vitakka-vicāra* as forms of mental focus, the introduction of the concepts of *uggahanimitta* and *paṭibhāganimitta* and the notion of suppression of the hindrances and their destruction by the *jhāna* factors can probably be best explained as efforts to reinterpret the first *jhāna* as a deep state of concentrative meditation, which originally it was not.[84]

The spontaneous and effortless nature of the first *jhāna* seems to be implied in the account of the Buddha's recollection of the first attainment of that state in his youth. It occurred when his "father the Sakyan was working" and he was "seated in the cool shade of rose-apple tree"

83 DN 2/i.73: *pañca nīvaraṇe pahīne attani samanupassato pāmojjaṃ jāyati*.

84 This does not imply that the first *jhāna* is in any way an easy state to achieve (i.e., that it is synonymous to the so-called "*jhāna* light" in the discourse of modern practitioners). The fact that certain meditative states are not a state of deep *samādhi* does not automatically translate into their easiness. As it is argued in this book, the absence of the hindrances, seclusion from sensuality and the presence of *pīti* and *sukha* which characterize this state are an extension and fruition of a radically transformed way of life and require a fulfilment of several crucial factors. Therefore, one can agree with Anālayo's (2017b: 126) claim made in the context of his interpretation of the *Upakkilesa-sutta* that the first *jhāna* is difficult to achieve, but not necessarily with his assumption that this in itself implies a considerable level of concentration, at least in the more modern sense of one-pointedness.

(*sītāya jambucchāyāya nisinno*).[85] No meditative method or any form of activity is mentioned. What follows is simply a standard, stock account of the first *jhāna*. Bronkhorst (1986: 16) aptly notes that "one cannot fail to be struck by the relaxed and friendly atmosphere which emanates from this passage".

As we have already noted, Chan texts emphasize the need for relaxation of the body in their meditative accounts, almost as if it was the only method that one can truly implement. In light of our considerations, it has significant importance for attaining a concentrated state of mind and a thought-less state which is of particular interest for Chan authors. In Chapter 2 we also mentioned research data highlighted by Carruthers (2015) to the effect that relaxation is one of the conditions for creativity. In Chapter 4 we have hypothesized that there exists a correlation between the lack of tension (i.e., relaxation) and absorption.

Relaxation should not be seen as being at odds or incompatible with maintaining an immobile, erect seated meditative position. The latter feature is emphasized both in early Chan and Nikāya texts. The already mentioned *Zuochan ming* advises meditators to sit straight and upright (*zhengzuo duanran* 正坐端然) as Mount Tai.[86] The *Chuanxin fa yao* contains Huangbo's words about "sitting calmly upright" (*anranduanzuo* 安然端坐).[87] Despite its seeming antinomianism and rejection of many traditional monastic rules and practices, the Baotang school put emphasis on the practice of constant sitting. Wuxiang and Wuzhu are repeatedly described in the *Lidai fabao ji* as "sitting in vacuity" (*kongxian zuo* 空閑坐) or "sitting in idleness" (*xianzuo* 閑坐). The already mentioned fragment of the *Erru sixing lun* claims that one should abide in a frozen/coagulated state (*ningzhu* 凝住) of wall contemplation, firmly abiding without moving (*jianzhubuyi* 堅住不移).[88] During the Song era, Caodong master, Tiantong Rujing 天童如淨 (1163–1228) used the phrase *zhiguan dazuo* (只管打坐: lit. minding just sitting) as a description of silent illumination (*mozhao* 默照) meditation.

While the Nikāya account of gradual training lacks information about meditative objects and methods, it explicitly describes

85 MN 85/ii.93: *Tassa mayhaṃ, rājakumāra, etadahosi: 'abhijānāmi kho panāhaṃ pitu sakkassa kammante sītāya jambucchāyāya nisinno vivicceva kāmehi vivicca akusalehi dhammehi savitakkaṃ savicāraṃ vivekajaṃ pītisukhaṃ paṭhamaṃ jhānaṃ upasampajja viharitā.*

86 T48, no. 2023, p. 1048c1: 正坐端然如泰山。Cf. Poceski (2015a: 102).

87 T48, no. 2012A, p. 384a17: 安然端坐任運不拘。

88 X63, no. 1217, p. 1a22–23. Cf. translation by Broughton (1999: 9).

a meditator sitting down while "having bent the legs cross-wise" (*pallaṅkaṃ ābhujitvā*) and having set the body erect/upright (*ujuṃ*).[89] In the passage of the *Cūḷadukkhakkhandha-sutta* (MN 14/i.94), the Buddha claims that he is able (*pahoti*) to abide (*viharati*) even for seven days and nights without moving/stirring (*aniñjamāna*) his body while feeling exclusively pleasure (*ekantasukha*).[90] It is not explicitly said that he does so in a sitting position, but this seems to be pretty much implied.

Bronkhorst (1986: 59) considered motionlessness of the body to be one of the key features of the non-Buddhist main stream of meditation, together with motionlessness of mind, breathlessness, and inactivity of sense organs, of which early Buddhist meditation ideas were in many ways the opposite. However, as we have seen, it was also a quintessential aspect of early Buddhist and Chan meditation.

This is significant. Despite so much emphasis on relaxation, there is still an insistence on meditators adopting a straight sitting position, and not for example that of comfortably lying down. Of course, as often explained by many modern meditative teachers, too much relaxation may simply lead to one falling asleep, thus defeating the very purpose of meditation. Keeping the posture straight is supposed to prevent that from happening. However, it might be the case that beside this rather obvious meaning, insistence on a straight, immobile meditative position had an additional, deeper purpose.

There is now much research in cognitive science about the key role that bodily sensations play in developing and maintaining the most basic phenomenal sense of selfhood and body ownership (e.g., Allen and Tsakiris 2019). This process occurs through the so-called multisensory integration of various types of stimuli connected with the body: visual, visceral, tactile and proprioceptive (i.e., those arriving from receptors in muscles, tendons and joints detecting position and movement of the body). According to Wittmann and Meissner (2019: 64), "the mental self is created by the continuous visceral and proprioceptive input from the body". When this multisensory integration produces results that do not match with the predictions of the cognitive system, this may result in an altered feeling of bodily ownership or bodily borders (as in the cases of Rubber-Hand Illusion or Full Body Illusion).

---

89 E.g., AN 4.198/ii.210: *so pacchābhattaṃ piṇḍapātapaṭikkanto nisīdati pallaṅkaṃ ābhujitvā ujuṃ kāyaṃ paṇidhāya parimukhaṃ satiṃ upaṭṭhapetvā.*

90 MN 14/i.94: *ahaṃ kho, āvuso nigaṇṭhā, pahomi aniñjamāno kāyena, abhāsamāno vācaṃ, ekaṃ rattindivaṃ ekantasukhaṃ paṭisaṃvedī viharituṃ.*

As stated by Solms (2021), when there is no change in a stimulus for a prolonged period of time and it becomes completely monotonous, it has a tendency to vanish from consciousness. As he explains, this is because the stimulus "becomes 100 per cent predictable and therefore carries no information" (Solms, 2021: 224).

All this may show the potential significance of maintaining a strictly immobile position for attaining altered states of consciousness.[91] Due to the lack of any variation in tactile and proprioceptive stimuli, they may at some point begin to vanish from awareness, resulting in a predictive mismatch, which in turn will generate changes in the sense of selfhood and an altered state of mind. Khalsa and Feinstein (2019: 159–60) report on specially induced conditions of attenuation of the proprioceptive, exteroceptive and tactile stimuli by motionlessly floating in a pool filled with Epsom salt. It was said to "respite the daily barrage of external triggers, reducing the occurrence of exteroceptively triggered body predictions". This in turn would lead to reduction of anxiety, increased relaxation and importantly, heightened interoceptive awareness. The latter feature seems to parallel that of the Nikāya *jhāna*s, as the meditator is said to abide having pervaded (*pharati*) the body (*kāya*) with various qualities characteristic of the particular *jhāna*s (e.g., *pīti* and *sukha*, or very bright and pure mind [*cetas*]). This is described as a form of developing mindfulness directed to the body (*kāyagātasati*: MN 119/ iii.92–94).

Radical and prolonged lack of movements, while maintaining alertness, may also gradually lead to what is called a deafferentation of the motor areas of the brain cortex. According to Stephane et al. (2021), both overt and inner speech depend on common neural resources and are correlated with activation of the same areas within the frontal motor cortex and the Broca area. According to Hertrich et al. (2016), within the general motor area there lies a supplementary motor area which is a superordinate control region for speech and language processing. This region is further divided into the posterior part responsible for purely motor-related functions and the anterior part responsible for higher-order cognitive processing which include context integration and the use of inner speech mechanisms during language encoding. If these areas could undergo deafferentation due to prolonged immobility while in the state of alertness, this could cause deconstruction of some aspects of our consciousness connected with language and

91 I am grateful to Clifford Saron for a remark pointing to such a possibility.

conceptuality without inducing the state of sleep. This would potentially result in a deeply altered state of consciousness.

In the preceding chapter, we considered a hypothesis that consciousness does not arise in a continuous way and that the states of flow or absorption may owe their special character to a relatively lesser number of occurrences of ordinary consciousness. It is noteworthy in this context that the states of flow, skilful acting or absorption are considered forms of natural, spontaneous concentration. Could it therefore be the case that the stronger the state of concentration is, the relatively lesser number of occurrences of ordinary consciousness it involves?

We have also considered Solms's (2021) idea that the arising of consciousness was meant to be a tool for preserving homeostasis and reducing uncertainty in special, challenging situations. Perhaps then, we can consider a hypothesis that a natural form of concentration (in the sense of non-distraction) arises when the needs of the organism are met through automatic patterns and it perceives its situation as that of certainty and homeostasis, so that it does not need to generate consciousness in order to deal with a novel situation that challenges its integrity. Remaining for an extended amount of time in an immobile position, and the resultant attenuation of the stimuli, could perhaps be interpreted by an organism as a state of relative certainty and therefore result in a natural state of concentration.

However, were such a hypothesis true, it would put a new light on the mechanism of meditative concentration. For it would follow from it that the actual deep mechanisms responsible for concentration lie beyond consciousness. The intuitive understanding of concentration as a deliberate, volitional act of "concentrating" originating from within consciousness itself could no longer be considered adequate. It would be equally inadequate to conceptualize concentration in phenomenological terms as a state in which the inner space of consciousness is continuously filled with one particular phenomenal quality (e.g., a *nimitta* of a *kasiṇa*) as opposed to an ordinary state of consciousness, where there is a constant flux of consciously experienced phenomena. The increasing level of concentration would rather need to be conceptualized as being correlated with a gradual decrease in the relative number of occurrences of ordinary, access consciousness. This would harmonize with the notion that the state of total cessation (*nirodha*) of consciousness represents at the same time a maximal level of concentration possible, a notion that is surprisingly at harmony with the position this state occupied in the traditional list of Buddhist meditative stages.

Given the above considerations, it seems plausible that bodily relaxation connected with prolonged, motionless, upright seated posture could positively contribute to attaining altered states of mind. It is also significant that these two features do not fall under the category of volitionally controlled, active meditative methods criticized in Nikāya and early Chan texts and conceptualized as involving *saṅkhāras*, or arousal of the mind (*qixin*), as they may be conceived of as forms of "non-doing". However, it is highly problematic whether they could induce such states by themselves. As long as the sources of mental movement are present, consciousness will be flooded by intruding thoughts, feelings and volitions, nullifying any effect that motionless posture and relaxation may bring, or even preventing the latter. The five hindrances (*nīvaraṇa*) can all be understood as states of dissatisfaction with one's current situation and as forms of reaching out for some quality which is not present at a given moment. Thus, their presence would be correlated with the intensification of conscious activity. If one could somehow diminish the presence of the *nīvaraṇas*, it could be expected that such a person would effortlessly fall into a natural state of non-distraction, i.e., concentration. But can these sources of mental movement be pacified without resorting to the active, volitional process of concentration? This question will be discussed in the next three chapters.

Chapter 6

MEDITATION AS AN EXTENSION OF A SPECIFIC WAY OF LIFE

In the previous chapter I suggested that even if according to at least some Nikāya and Chan texts there was no meditative method in the traditional sense, there may have been some other psychological mechanism by which the altered psychophysical states were to occur. This would be tantamount to the shift of emphasis from the method itself, to some other crucial factors which would be the necessary or perhaps even sufficient conditions for attaining the meditative state which was the goal of a spiritual path. As we have seen, the *Sāmaññaphala* account of the gradual arising of concentration starts from joy resulting from the absence of the hindrances. The understanding that the removal of the hindrances is a necessary and almost sufficient condition for the development of concentration, certainly agrees well with the idea of *samādhi* as an inherent quality of the mind which is, however, obstructed by the defilements or "clouds of deluded thoughts" and which is present in Nikāya texts such as the *Pabhassara* and the *Paṃsudhovaka-suttas*, as well as several Chan scriptures. Their removal would therefore result in a passive and spontaneous arising of a unified state of mind. We are thus dealing with a notion of some negatively evaluated psychological mechanisms and factors which prevent the attainment of the meditative state.

This, however, leads to another question, namely that of how these mechanisms and factors are exactly to be removed. In the mainstream paradigm they were supposed to be temporarily suppressed by the act of one-pointed concentration on a meditative object which would in turn facilitate insight. As we have seen, such a mechanism is not postulated in the paradigm we are trying to reconstruct based on Nikāya and Chan texts.

Intense spiritual feelings arising from a pre-meditative virtuous lifestyle in the Nikāyas

Some valuable hints regarding the removal of the mental factors which prevent the arising of an altered psychophysical state are provided in the account of gradual training following the pattern of the *Sāmaññaphala-sutta*. In it, we find a relatively detailed, straightforward description of practice starting from the decision to leave the household life and become a bhikkhu, up to destruction of the influxes (*āsava*) and final knowledge. This account is by no means limited to the *Sāmaññaphala-sutta*, as it occurs in a similar form in several suttas from the *Dīgha Nikāya*, the *Majjhima Nikāya* and the *Aṅguttara Nikāya*. Its prevalence in the Nikāyas[1] may be a testimony to its significance in the early period of the dissemination of Buddhist teachings. The sequence of the successive stages of practice in this account corresponds in general to the elements of the noble eightfold path but the *Sāmaññaphala* account is more detailed and far less schematic.

While as Gethin (2004: 202) has noted, the account does not offer any specific instructions for meditation, it has much to say about the way of life and the state of mind that the bhikkhu is to develop before sitting down to attain *jhāna*. It is also not really an account of a settled monastic way of life, as in that period bhikkhus were still wandering mendicants, living solitarily or in small groups and without any fixed residence. This is evident by a long list of potential locations into which a bhikkhu is to withdraw for the purpose of entering *jhāna*; it includes a forest, mountain cave, cemetery and open space, but not a cell of a monastery. As we shall see later, this is quite significant.

In the account of the gradual training, we find detailed instructions for the development of virtue (*sīla*) with much emphasis on the necessity of right speech, sense restraint, mindfulness and full comprehension. However, what is particularly striking in that account are the descriptions of the mental states of the bhikkhu resultant from the implementation of the successive steps of training. Thus, a bhikkhu who is endowed (*samannāgata*) with the "aggregate" of virtue (*sīlakkhandha*)

---

1 Apart from several suttas of the *Dīgha* and *Majjhima Nikāya* it can even be found in the *Attantapa-sutta* (AN 4.198/ii.205–211) of the *Aṅguttara Nikāya*, and most of it reappears in the *Upāli-sutta* (AN 10.99/v.201–209). A detailed comparative analysis of this account may be found in Gethin (2020) and in Bucknell (2023: 83–105), who labels it as the "stepwise training".

experiences internal (*ajjhatta*) faultless pleasure (*anavajjasukha*).[2] When endowed with the sense faculty restraint (*indriyasaṃvara*), he is said to experience internal untainted pleasure (*abyāsekasukha*)· Furthermore, the bhikkhu is described as being content (*santuṭṭha*).

Thus, even before a bhikkhu sits down to enter *jhāna* he is described several times as experiencing very positive spiritual feelings which result from his way of living. Let us note that the Pali word *sukha* used to describe the feeling connected with perfection of virtue and sense restraint is exactly the same term as the one used in the description of the first three *jhānas*. That this *sukha* is not a common, ordinary type of pleasure can be deduced from the fact that it is described either as faultless (*anavajja*) or untainted (*abyāseka*). Therefore, it needs to be emphasized that at this stage a bhikkhu experiences a saintly type of bliss and contentment directly as the result of his way of life and mindset, and not by meditation.[3] This does not seem to be emphasized or even acknowledged enough, both in the mainstream Buddhist texts and especially in modern stereotypical approaches to Buddhist practice, which see meditative absorption as the main source of arising of pleasure on a spiritual path. We can only suspect that this idea was so far removed from the expectations and experiences of the vast majority of both exegetes and practitioners of Buddhism that it was simply conveniently neglected.

If we are to take the message of the *Sāmaññaphala-sutta* seriously, we should accept that the actual practice in the sense of a deliberate performance of certain activities occurs to a large extent, if not entirely, prior to seated meditation proper. The latter should be seen more as a fruition and extension of a specific way of life and mindset. An even more significant conclusion, which would be especially surprising to modern meditators, is that one perhaps should not even think seriously about attaining the *jhānas* if one does not have a prior experience of the type of blameless, saintly pleasure and contentment described in the *Sāmaññaphala-sutta*. After all, when a practitioner sits down to meditate, he does so endowed with the "aggregate" of noble virtue (*ariya sīlakkhandha*), noble sense faculty restraint (*ariya indriyasaṃvara*), noble mindfulness and comprehension (*ariya satisampajañña*) as well as

---

2 DN 2/i.70: *so iminā ariyena sīlakkhandhena samannāgato ajjhattaṃ anavajjasukhaṃ paṭisaṃvedeti*.

3 The significance of pre-meditative happiness and contentedness as laying the foundation for the *jhānas* is acknowledged by Anālayo (2017b: 135–36).

noble contentment (*ariya santuṭṭha*). This is particularly at odds with the modern approach to meditation which pretty much sees meditation as a skill that can be mastered in itself. We have already mentioned Gethin's (2004: 202) comment to the effect that the *Sāmaññaphala-sutta* is not a very good guide for making substantial progress in meditative practice. That certainly would be the case were we to understand the early Buddhist *jhāna* as a mainstream form of calm meditation. However, perhaps if one were to really live the teachings of the text and experience the saintly feelings described in it, then the meditative progress would be much more spontaneous and easy.

An important conclusion which emerges from the direct reading of the *Sāmaññaphala-sutta* is that leading a particular lifestyle and having a specific mindset may by itself produce intense spiritual feelings. Thus, it is not necessary to assume that at least in the case of the first *jhāna*, *pīti* and *sukha* are produced due to successful concentration on a meditative object. Perhaps we should also consider the possibility that the hindrances are already abandoned to a large extent before one even sits down with crossed legs to meditate in order to attain an altered state of mind.[4]

The account which follows after a description of sitting down in a meditative position, uses absolutive (*pubbakiriya*) verb forms to state that the meditator "having abandoned" (*pahāya*) each of the five hindrances, cleanses (*parisodheti*) the mind from them. This may be read as implying that most of the work regarding the removal of the hindrances has already been accomplished, and the meditator now simply keeps his mind clean by preventing their reappearance. However, if that is the case, then one may ask why the insistence on the *jhāna*s occurring only after having assumed a meditative position? Why do they not arise naturally during everyday activities? I have already suggested a hypothesis regarding the significance of motionless and relaxed sitting position in the previous chapter. Furthermore, one can hypothesize that sitting down to meditate introduces a significant psychological change in the situation of a bhikkhu which is crucial for the attainment of *jhāna*. He no longer needs to engage in any social interactions, make any decision or plans, or initiate in a consciously controlled manner any actions. Using Nikāya terms, this could be described as a state in which

4 This qualification is important, as some forms of pre-jhānic practice can definitely be labelled as meditation, though they are not directly connected with the attainment of altered states of mind.

the presence of all kinds of thoughts (*vitakka*), intentions (*saṅkappa*) and *saṅkhāras* has been greatly attenuated. And as we have seen, several Nikāya texts present meditative progress as correlated with their diminishment or absence. A bhikkhu seating down to meditate has thus the possibility to fully realize the extent to which the hindrances have already been eliminated in him and perhaps actively remove their last fleeting remnants through practices connected with right effort and right mindfulness as opposed to suppressing them through an active process of concentration. We also need to take into account the simple fact that the early Buddhist bhikkhus were probably spending much of their time in a seated position anyway, as they simply had nothing else to do, especially after returning from begging for alms. Therefore, assuming a seated position did not necessarily mean that one would start a completely new type of practice compared to what one was doing before. Right effort and right mindfulness which were certainly well inculcated at this point could be continued but intensified and brought to a new level.

The notion that intense positive spiritual feelings arise due to a virtuous way of life is also contained in the *Vattha-sutta* (MN 7/i.36–40). This text compares the mind which has been defiled (*saṃkiliṭṭha*) to a defiled and stained cloth (*vattha saṃkiliṭṭha malaggahita*).[5] The sutta lists sixteen defilements, with most of them representing forms of malicious attitudes towards others, such as ill-will, avarice and anger. The set can be seen as corresponding to the first and mostly second of the five hindrances. The latter part of the text speaks of the possibility of such a cloth becoming clean and bright (*parisuddha pariyodāta*) due to washing it with clean water, and of gold (*jātarūpa*), becoming bright and clear in the furnace (*ukkāmukha*).[6] While the similes are not explicitly said to represent the process of cleansing the mind, this seems to be pretty much implied by the text. The *Vattha-sutta* suggests that the actual process of cleansing occurs before meditation proper as the practitioner first abandons (*pajahati*) each of the sixteen defilements, then obtains the quality of *aveccapasāda* towards the Buddha, Dhamma and Saṅgha, which Ñāṇamoli and Bodhi (1995: 118) translate as "unwavering confidence". Interestingly, according to Rhys Davids and Stede (2007: 446), other meanings of *pasāda* include "joy", "satisfaction" and "having a

5 See Ñāṇamoli and Bodhi (1995: 118–22) for a translation of this sutta.

6 MN 7/i.38: *Seyyathāpi, bhikkhave, vatthaṃ saṅkiliṭṭhaṃ malaggahitaṃ acchodakaṃ āgamma parisuddhaṃ hoti pariyodātaṃ, ukkāmukhaṃ vā panāgamma jātarūpaṃ parisuddhaṃ hoti pariyodātaṃ*.

happy or a good mind". The latter reading would support the interpretation that according to the Nikāyas, the virtuous way of life can by itself generate intensely pleasant spiritual feelings. The arising of *aveccapasāda* is said to bring about gladness (*pāmojja*) connected with the Dhamma (*dhammūpasaṃhita*) which sets off the already mentioned standard cascade of *pāmojja-pīti-passadhi-sukha-samādhi*. The text then describes the practitioner as dwelling having pervaded all directions "by means of a mind without measure" (*appamāṇena cetasā*), endowed with the four holy abidings (*brahmavihāra*): *mettā*, *karuṇā*, *muditā* and *upekhā*.[7]

There are many more texts connecting a virtuous and restrained way of life with the experience of pleasurable saintly feelings. The *Pamādavihārī-sutta* (SN 35.97/iv.77–79) states that if one is dwelling diligently (*appamādavihārī*), it means the mind is not getting soiled (*na byāsiñcati*) among the sense objects. As a result, gladness is born, which sets off the familiar sequence of rapture, tranquility, pleasure and concentration, which in case of this sutta ends in the *dhammas* becoming manifest (*pātubhavati*).[8]

The *Sukhasomanassa-sutta* (AN 6.78/iii.433) contains a statement that a bhikkhu delighting (*rāma*) in the Dhamma, development, abandoning, solitude, non-affliction, and non-proliferation, "dwells in abundant pleasure and satisfaction in this life" (*diṭṭheva dhamme sukhasomanassabahulo viharati*).[9] Similarly, the *Dukkha-sutta* (AN 6.75/iii.429) states that a monk who cultivates noble thoughts and perceptions of renunciation, good will and harmlessness "lives in pleasure in this very life" (*diṭṭheva dhamme sukhaṃ viharati*), "without trouble, tribulation and fever" (*avighātaṃ anupāyāsaṃ apariḷāhaṃ*).[10]

Significance of a virtuous way of life and mindset in Chan texts

In Chan texts, we will not find as much emphasis on the necessity of living a particular lifestyle. Many texts dealing with meditation hardly

7 MN 7/i.38: *So mettāsahagatena cetasā ekaṃ disaṃ pharitvā viharati, tathā dutiyaṃ, tathā tatiyaṃ, tathā catutthaṃ. Iti uddhamadho tiriyaṃ sabbadhi sabbattatāya sabbāvantaṃ lokaṃ mettāsahagatena cetasā vipulena mahaggatena appamāṇena averena abyāpajjena pharitvā viharati.*

8 Cf. translation by Bodhi (2000: 1180).

9 Cf. translation by Bodhi (2012: 974).

10 Cf. translation by Bodhi (2012: 973).

have anything to say about virtue and morality. This may lead one to the conclusion that these texts allow the possibility of practising meditation straightaway by total beginners without fulfilling any prior moral requirements. This is not true, however. Unlike the Nikāyas, Chan texts do not even purport to be comprehensive and systematic accounts of the whole practical Buddhist path. Several texts, such as the *Rudao anxin yao fangbian famen*, appear to be non-homogenous compilations of various meditative teachings and may never have been intended in such form by the Chan masters they are attributed to. However, as Poceski (2007: 131) suggests, "Chan doctrines and practices cannot be divorced from the religious mores and institutional ethos of Tang monasticism". Both McRae[11] and Poceski[12] have pointed out that in the Northern school of Chan there was a particularly strong insistence on maintaining the precepts as a basic prerequisite for meditation practice. While a stereotypical interpretation would see various branches of Southern Chan as somewhat neglectful of morality due to it being connected with the notion of gradualism, this was not the case. Despite supposedly being a staunch proponent of subitism, Shenhui provides in the *Wenda zazheng yi* several similes illustrating the need for putting effort at least at a certain stage of the path. He states that one will never obtain water from an underground source unless one makes an effort (*shigong* 施功) drilling for it, and a jewel (*bao* 寶) will never be clear and thus deserve its name, unless one polishes it.[13] In the *Tanyu*, he proclaims that studying and attaining the unsurpassable *bodhi* without purifying (*jing* 淨) the three types of action and without maintaining abstinence (*zhaijie* 齋戒) is impossible.[14] In the *Dunwu rudao yaomen*

11 McRae (1986: 228): "The Northern School has a reputation in modern studies for being closely associated with Vinaya School centers, and several of its works imply an advocacy of strict maintenance of the precepts. At one point the Wu fang-pien advocates that the precepts should be maintained without transgression 'even in the face of death'".

12 Poceski (2015a: 86): "Furthermore, according to Northern school texts, the observance of moral precepts, including monastic regulations, is a basic prerequisite for meditation practice".

13 B25, no. 143, p. 221a3–4: 猶如地下有水，若不施功掘鑿 ，終不能得。亦如摩尼之寶，若不磨治，終不明淨。以不明淨故，謂言非寶。See Gomez (1987: 87) and McRae (2023: 146–47) for translations of this fragment.

14 B25, no. 142, p. 11a7–8: 知識，學無上菩提，不淨三業，不持齋戒，言其得者，無有是處。Translation by McRae (2023: 50).

lun Dazhu proclaims that discipline (*jie* 戒) involves undefiled (*wuran* 無染) purity (*qingjing* 清淨).[15]

It is worth emphasizing that the similes used by Shenhui do not present gradual practice as an accumulation of positive factors, creation of a new quality, adding something or generation of "merit". Instead, they speak of revealing something that has already existed (water and jewel) by removing impurities or things that prevented it from manifesting in its natural pure state.

As Poceski (2007: 197–203) convincingly shows, the view that the Hongzhou school rejected gradual cultivation is completely wrong and is based on misrepresentation and oversimplification of the school's doctrine present in Zongmi's texts. In the *Tiansheng guangdeng lu*, we find a statement attributed to Baizhang which compares cultivation to washing (*huan* 浣) a dirty cloth (*gouyi* 垢衣). The cloth is what was "originally existing" (*benyou* 本有), while the dirt is from the outside (*wailai* 外來).[16] This simile is reminiscent of the ones found both in Shenhui's writings and the Nikāya texts. In fact, as Poceski (2007: 204) has rightly pointed out, it is very similar to the simile of a cloth given in the already mentioned *Vattha-sutta*.

However, probably the most interesting and original Chan account emphasizing the importance of a pre-meditative way of life and mindset is found in the historically earliest work of the school – Bodhidharma's *Erru sixing lun*. The second part of this short text[17] focuses on the so-called "entry of practice" (*xingru* 行入), which consists of the four practices: the practice of retribution for enmity (*baoyuanxing* 報冤行), the practice of following, or accepting circumstances (*suiyuanxing* 隨緣行), the practice of seeking nothing (*wusuoqiuxing* 無所求行)[18] and the practice of accordance with the Dharma (*chengfaxing* 稱法行). The common feature of all the four "practices" is that they do not consist of mechanical

15 X63, no. 1223, p. 19c4: 問。其義云何是戒・定・慧。答。清淨無染是戒。Cf. Blofeld (1962: 54) for a translation.

16 X78, no. 1553, p. 458c4: 亦云。合與磨 學。今似浣 垢衣。今是本有。垢是外來。 See Poceski (2007: 203–204) for a translation and discussion of this fragment.

17 X63, no. 1217, p. 1a24–24.

18 While the translations of the names of the remaining practices are mostly based on McRae (1986: 103–104), in case of the third practice I opt for a more direct translation of 無所求行 than McRae, who translates it as the "absence of craving". Broughton (1999: 10) and Van Schaik (2018: 126) translate it as "the practice of having nothing to be sought" and "the practice of not seeking", respectively.

performance of any traditionally understood religious activities or application of any particular set of rules but rather are about maintaining a specific mindset. This mindset in turn arises from the understanding of fundamental Buddhist truths, and the text describes in detail the ruminations that probably should be internalized by the practitioner or, alternatively, are just expressions of such a mindset.

It is worth emphasizing that the practices are not about quantitative accumulation of any merit or positive factors but are mostly aimed at coming to terms with life's circumstances and developing peaceful acceptance of whatever occurs through understanding. Of all Chan material, this text probably comes closest in spirit to early Buddhist texts such as the *Sāmaññaphala-sutta*. What is particularly striking is that just like the Nikāyas, some parts of the *Erru sixing lun* can be read as an account of sublime spiritual mental states developing because of leading a particular lifestyle and having a specific mindset and not due to meditation proper. Thus, in the description of the first practice we find the term *ganxin* 甘心,[19] which can be read as referring to a sort of contentedness connected with peaceful self-resignation or with coming to terms with seemingly painful occurrences in life. The practice of seeking nothing is perhaps the most interesting from the perspective of our study. According to McRae's (1986: 104) translation, someone who develops this attitude "pacifies his mind in inactivity" (*anxin wuwei* 安心無為) and accepts whatever happens to him (lit. "[allows his] form to be transformed in accordance with fate" *xingyuanyunzhuan* 形隨運轉).[20] As we have already noted, *wuwei* does not mean inactivity in the sense of mental stasis, but lack of conscious control or reactivity which implies spontaneity and passivity.[21] Therefore, the whole line may mean that the practitioner passively and with peace of mind accepts whatever happens to him. To reinforce this message, the author of the text then quotes some unidentified sutra,[22] which states that "seeking nothing is joy" (*wuqiujile* 無求即樂).

The most interesting aspect of this account is that one is said to experience elevated spiritual feelings due to leading a specific way of life and maintaining a specific mindset. This agrees well with the model

19 X63, no. 1217, p. 1b5–6: 甘心甘受都無冤訴。McRae (1986: 103) translates 甘心甘受 as "patiently and contentedly"; Broughton (1999: 10) as "With satisfaction I will bear and accept it".

20 X63, no. 1217, p. 1b13–14: 安心無為形隨運轉。萬有斯空無所願樂。

21 See Soothill and Hodous (2014: 380).

22 See Broughton (1999: 123, n. 6) and Van Schaik (2018: 225, n. 38).

we are trying to reconstruct, since it does not involve generating these sublime feelings directly through meditative concentration.

Removal of thoughts through right effort

As we have noted, both Chan and Nikāya texts put emphasis on the attainment of a thought-less state during meditation. According to some of the texts we have analysed (e.g., the *Paṃsudhovaka-sutta*, the *Xiuxin yao lun*) thoughts obstruct the fundamental layer of the mind, preventing the occurrence of spontaneous insight. We have also emphasized that in the paradigm we are considering, one cannot suppress thoughts through any meditative method involving volitional activity of concentrating. Is it therefore possible to achieve a thought-less state through means other than the classical form of calm meditation?

Interesting information regarding removing thoughts of sensual desire, ill will and cruelty can be found in the *Dvedhāvitakka-sutta* (MN 19/i.114–118), where the Buddha recollects the period directly preceding his awakening. According to this text, such thoughts can be removed through a combination of three methods: the awareness of arising of an unskilful thought, active contemplation of its drawbacks and active thinking of wholesome thoughts, so as to replace a wrongful inclination (*nati*) of the mind with a righteous one. None of these methods are representative of classical calm meditation, and all of them may be implemented during everyday activities outside the meditative seat. If we are to take the early Buddhist texts at their word, then the actual practice in the sense of actively doing something is constituted by right endeavor or effort (*sammāvāyāma*), and not by right concentration or *jhānas*. It is in the description of right effort that we find the phrase: "he endeavors, undertakes effort, exerts the mind and strives" (*vāyamati vīriyaṃ ārabhati cittaṃ paggaṇhāti padahati*),[23] which suggests its active, volitionally directed character. The practice is to some extent connected with the sense faculty restraint (understood in the specifically early Buddhist sense not as insentience, but as evaluation and selection of stimuli which may potentially influence the practitioner) as part of a wider strategy for self-transformation. The fact that this practice, and

---

23 SN 45.8/v.9: *Idha, bhikkhave, bhikkhu anuppannānaṃ pāpakānaṃ akusalānaṃ dhammānaṃ anuppādāya chandaṃ janeti vāyamati vīriyaṃ ārabhati cittaṃ paggaṇhāti padahati.*

not meditation proper, bears the name of "right effort" is therefore very telling.

The *Sacitta-sutta* (AN 10.51/v.92–94) contains an interesting account of what may be considered the application of the right effort to combat mental defilements, which is relevant for our investigation. According to the text, a bhikkhu should often engage in "self-examination" (or reviewing/contemplation: *paccavekkhaṇā*) to check for the presence of various negative bodily and mental states. The sutta lists ten such flaws: being given to longing (or being covetous: *abhijjhālu*), given to ill will, overcome by dullness and drowsiness, restless, plagued by doubt, anger, defiled in mind, agitated in body, lazy, and being unconcentrated.[24] It is noteworthy that these flaws are not directly described as thoughts. However, each of these flaws can be seen as a root cause of a corresponding type of thought through which it manifests, and therefore eradication of these flaws would be tantamount to removal of the corresponding thoughts. According to the text, if through *paccavekkhaṇā* a bhikkhu discovers the presence of any of these flaws, he should "put forth extraordinary desire, effort, zeal, enthusiasm, indefatigability, mindfulness, and clear comprehension to abandon those same bad unwholesome qualities".[25]

This also suggests that in the Nikāyas, everyday practice which precedes meditation proper is not constituted by "naked awareness" or non-selective attention in the spirit of modern *vipassanā*, but by constant, active evaluation of potential influences one will be subjected to, by making choices, and if necessary, by conscious, active thinking of positive thoughts. At this stage, a bhikkhu is expected to often engage in active mental contemplations of various issues including the unsatisfactory character of experience and the negative and positive drawbacks of unskilful and skilful mental states respectively. For example, the *Pabbajitābhiṇha-sutta* (AN 10.48/v.77–78) lists ten topics that should be reflected upon (*paccavekkhitabba*) by a bhikkhu. To some extent these practices resemble the so-called analytic insight, as it was conceived of in a later tradition, with the difference being that they are not meant to produce any final liberating knowledge.

24 Translation by Bodhi (2012: 1402).

25 AN 10.51/v 93: *bhikkhunā tesaṃyeva pāpakānaṃ akusalānaṃ dhammānaṃ pahānāya adhimatto chando ca vāyāmo ca ussāho ca ussoḷhī ca appaṭivānī ca sati ca sampajaññañca karaṇīyaṃ*. Translation by Bodhi (2012: 1402).

The place for bare cognition seems to be reserved for the higher stages of meditation, such as the fourth *jhāna*. This is also because one cannot practise bare cognition by simply choosing to adopt such a cognitive attitude towards experience, due to the level of its conceptual and linguistic mediation. Garfield (2015: 210) emphasizes that even the supposedly fundamental and basic subjectivity characterizing our experience is "constructed by means of innumerable unconscious cognitive processes" and that these processes "lie below the level of introspectibility". Only through attenuation of these, can bare cognition become possible, and this seems to be reserved to higher meditative states.

However, this still does not answer the question of how exactly leading a virtuous life of right effort, right mindfulness and clear comprehension is conducive to removing the mechanisms responsible for production of unwholesome thoughts mentioned in the suttas we have analysed. Can one remove such thoughts without resorting to suppressing them by means of classical calm meditation? Can the movement of thought come to a rest through a special way of living? This idea seems so far removed from everything we have come to accept and take for granted regarding spiritual cultivation, that one is tempted to reject it immediately. Therefore, we should first consider whether such an idea is plausible on a psychological level. Since the Nikāyas do not explain this issue in detail, below I shall offer a hypothesis regarding the psychological mechanism by which this could occur.

What are the causes of mental movement? The significance of the urge-driven motivational system

In order to do this, we need to first consider the evolutionary role of thoughts and feelings connected with the negative states labelled by the Nikāyas as covetousness, dullness and drowsiness, restlessness, or laziness and in particular their role in motivating our behaviour. It is commonplace that the behaviour of ordinary people is not motivated in a fully rational way. By this I mean that quite often we do not act simply because we rationally know that we should behave in a certain way that agrees with our goals, beliefs and values. Instead, we need to be driven to act by a particular conscious feeling,[26] perception, thought

26 Cf. Solms (2021: 120), who claims that feelings/affects "regulate almost all our voluntary behaviour through their various inner spurs and spurts".

or urge[27] which can linger even for a long time in our awareness. To give an example, in our feeding behaviour there is a constant interplay of these two motivational systems. On the one hand, we may rationally know what to eat to sustain our health and provide energy for our activities, but on the other hand we are driven to eat by conscious urges connected with craving for the pleasure of eating particular foods. The latter motivational system can be considered an inheritance from our animal ancestors, who were to a large extent devoid of the capability to rationally plan their behaviours. Therefore, without being motivated by urges (which in the case of animals do not seem to have the verbal or conceptual components typical of humans) they simply would not eat at all. Similarly, animals would not know to avoid potentially dangerous situations if it were not for consciously felt fear or pain.

Theoretically, humans should be able to function efficiently just by relying on a rational motivational system. To give an example, we know what and when to eat to nourish ourselves or what situations to avoid in order not to die or hurt ourselves. In fact, the presence of the evolutionarily older motivational system in many ways hinders our efficient functioning and causes much of our suffering as it is clearly not adapted to the current conditions of human life. For example, our craving for pleasure of food motivates us to eat far too much for our welfare. This mechanism is a remnant of the times when food was scarce, and one would be motivated to eat as much as possible when the opportunity presented itself. In the conditions of a developed, stable society this only leads to a host of problems. To give another example: we often rationally know that we should not delay performing a particular act but rather should do it as soon as possible. However, we are prevented

27 It is difficult or perhaps even impossible to make a sharp distinction between these terms, as they seem to refer to different but complementary aspects of the same mental state. For the sake of convenience, I will mostly use the term "urges" to refer to conscious states which motivate us to a particular action and are connected with the desire for pleasure or aversion to discomfort. However, such urges possess emotional, perceptual and conceptual components. The notion of the interconnectedness of these states may have been expressed in the Nikāyas by formulations such as *yaṃ vedeti taṃ sañjānāti, yaṃ sañjānāti taṃ vitakketi, yaṃ vitakketi taṃ papañceti* (What one feels, that one perceives, what one perceives, that one thinks about, and what one thinks about, one complicates: MN 18/i.111–112) or *phuṭṭho, bhikkhave, vedeti, phuṭṭho ceteti, phuṭṭho sañjānāti* (contacted, o bhikkhus, one feels, contacted one wills, contacted one perceives: SN 35.93/iv.68), though these passages can also be interpreted in a way which emphasizes that these states are temporally distinct.

from doing so by the mechanism of procrastination which is driven by a conscious fear or aversion towards activities that need to be done but are perceived as unpleasant. Usually, we are at some moment finally able to overcome our procrastination, but it is not due to a rational decision. It is just that conscious fear of the potential results of not performing an action in question gradually grows until it overwhelms the aversion to that action, and we are forced to act. The feelings of boredom and the urges to occupy ourselves with various actions are also evolutionarily conditioned. A feeling of boredom motivates us not to remain inactive but to reach out for something new, or at least stimulate our various faculties, both mental and physical by undertaking various trivial activities as a distraction. Therefore, it is expected that people who get bored easily will be more evolutionary fit compared to those who can be simply satisfied with their current state.

We are driven to such a considerable extent by this older evolutionary mechanism, that many of our conscious states are feelings, thoughts and urges which motivate or demotivate us to perform particular actions. Ultimately, this mechanism is mediated by the conscious experiences of pleasure and discomfort. We are motivated to undertake certain actions because we associate them with pleasure and avoid others due to the discomfort or pain that they bring. In Buddhist terms this could be conceptualized as desire and aversion. The thoughts, feelings and urges which successfully motivate us to act are connected with a desire for pleasure, while the ones which make us avoid certain actions involve aversion to discomfort. Another example of irrationally motivated, urge-driven activities are the simple, repetitive and almost automatic actions known as fidgeting (e.g., playing with one's hands or small items). In this case it is not that one is driven into action by some prolonged conscious feeling; it is rather that restraining oneself from fidgeting causes mental discomfort. A similar case can be made for engaging in almost automatic speech patterns, such as small talk. It seems that in such cases, the habit of constantly giving in to particular urges reinforces them to such extent that they occur almost automatically, often without awareness of their initiation.

Let us now consider a hypothetical example of a person in whom this motivational system would be turned off and whose behaviour would be motivated by entirely rational decisions. Acting rationally does not require strong mediation of consciousness and does not entail the generation of a large number of feelings, thoughts and urges as they are not needed to drag and force us to a particular mode of action. We usually know very well what is a rational and proper way to act, at least in simple ordinary-life situations. As we have already noted in Chapter 2, the modules responsible for our intelligence operate in an unconscious way, while it is only their end results that emerge in the form of conscious thoughts. According to Carruthers' (2015) model, judgments, goals, action plans and beliefs constitute the so-called amodal attitudes,[28] which operate unconsciously, with conscious thoughts carrying the decisions which are their result.

Removing the urge-driven motivational system through a Buddhist way of life

But what does that all have to do with Buddhism? The way of life of a bhikkhu can be seen as a radical abandonment of the mode of behaviour that is motivated by conscious feelings, thoughts and urges connected with the pursuit of pleasure and avoidance of discomfort. Instead, the behaviour becomes entirely rational and rule-driven. The cultivation of virtue, sense restraint, mindfulness and clear comprehension can be conceptualized as various aspects of combating urge-driven behaviour and replacing it with rationally undertaken actions which conform to Buddhist ideals. Much of what is labelled *sīla* in the Nikāyas concerns abstaining from performing activities for the sake of pleasure. Food is to be eaten only for maintenance of the body; one needs to abstain from dancing, singing, music and theatrical shows and not engage in small talk. It is worth emphasizing that there is nothing ethically wrong in doing the abovementioned things for pleasure, so the point of abstaining from them is not about ethics, but rather about stopping engaging in activities that are motivated by the pursuit of pleasure.[29]

The practical path of Buddhism is also very much about abstaining from urge-motivated, seemingly semi-automatic activities and replacing them with consciously planned, deliberately performed actions which means acting according to what we have labelled the rational or

28 The term "amodal" refers to the fact that in contrast to the phenomenally conscious states these attitudes are not connected with any of the sense modalities, i.e., they are not visual, auditory etc.

29 Cf. Bronkhorst (2012: 182): "These practices do not promote 'Buddhist morality', and therefore a vision of society. Rather their aim is to calm body and mind".

rule-based motivation system.[30] In Buddhist terms this is conceptualized as acting with mindfulness (*sati*) and comprehension (*sampajañña*). Based on the textual evidence, it seems unlikely that mindfulness and comprehension at the initial, pre-meditative stages of the path are a sort of naked, or choiceless awareness which passively registers whatever is experienced at a given point like some recording device. Rather, they involve a strong proactive component, as one consciously undertakes the actions only after prior assessment of their accordance with the Dhamma and of the potential impact they will have on one's state of mind. One has to remember (i.e., have memory [*sati*]) not to follow urges, but to act according to Buddhist principles, and any act must be undertaken with comprehension (*sampajañña*) of what one is doing and how it relates to the Buddhist path.[31] It seems to me that the emphasis in this practice is more on preventing urge-driven acts than on just being aware without judgment of whatever we do. It needs to be emphasized that the Buddhist model of a renunciate life involves a great reduction and simplification of one's activities, thus significantly facilitating performing them in a fully conscious, deliberately planned way. Secondly, due to its rule-based character, this model greatly reduces a number of potentially problematic situations where one is faced with incommensurable alternatives and yet has to choose one. Such situations are unavoidable in the lives of ordinary people and generate additional mental movement.

What seems to be implied by this whole system of practice is that by stopping acting upon one's desires, aversions and urges one will start a gradual process of deconditioning oneself. Through years, the modules of the unconscious mind have learned that urges are a good way to change our behaviour, as we followed them almost automatically. Urges were connected to pleasure and discomfort. We conditioned ourselves into a pattern where following urges is associated with pleasure while abstaining from them brings discomfort. Through years of following the urges this pattern was greatly reinforced. This means

30 A somewhat parallel idea may be found in early Stoicism. The Stoics believed that one should not act motivated by emotions (gr. *pathos*): desire (gr. *epithumia*), pleasure (gr. *hēdonē*), fear (gr. *phobos*) and pain (gr. *lupē*). Instead, all actions should be undertaken under the guidance of reason (gr. *logos*). The personal ideal is that of dispassion (gr. *apatheia*). Cf. Reale (1985: 284–88).

31 This understanding of *sati* is close to Levman's (2017b), who emphasizes that the word "incorporates the meaning of 'memory' and 'remembrance' in much of its usage in both *suttas* and the commentary" (Levman 2017b: 122).

that our organism has learned that once it produces a particular urge, thought or emotion – the desired action follows. This has significant implications for meditation, as during idleness our consciousness will be bombarded by urges, thoughts and feelings as the organism perceives this situation as very uncomfortable and boring. However, the assumption behind the Buddhist system of practice is that this pattern can be broken. If the urges are not followed through, but instead one acts with rational consideration, then gradually the reason for the very existence of the urges will disappear. To refer to Bronkhorst's (2023) theory, if a conditioned stimulus is not met by a conditioned response, then this generates a mismatch and a possibility of a reconsolidation of an old, unbeneficial memory pattern. Gradually, one can recondition one's reactions, though this type of reconditioning does not seem to possess the final and irreversible character typical of the psychological transformation occurring in the fourth *jhāna*. It seems more like laying the ground for it by removing a significant source of mental movement during meditation without the need for actively suppressing it. If we were to conceptualize the practice of replacing the old urge-motivated system using Nikāya terms, we could say that it involves right effort, right mindfulness and right full comprehension. In order to stop urges, they must first be noted at the initial stage of their arising, so that the process of acting upon them is nipped in the bud. Then the initial urge may be replaced by a rational and deliberately performed action. The urges may best be noted if they occur against a background of some consciously undertaken, rationally driven activity, i.e., mindful and clearly comprehended action.[32] At the initial stages, such practice will require active effort.

Relevant in this context is the refrain contained in the *Kāyagatāsatisutta* (MN 119/iii.88–99)[33] which is repeated after the account of each

32 Cf. Bronkhorst (2012: 193): "[M]indfulness serves a double purpose. First of all, it limits all activity to conscious activity (in so far as this is possible). This prevents repressed urges from finding expression during these sessions even if the associated memory traces are activated. As a result these urges will give rise to feelings; this is the second function of mindfulness. Feelings and the state of body and mind in general are the object of attention during this exercise. Mindfulness, according to this understanding, permits practitioners to locate their repressed urges." It needs to be emphasized that I use the term "urges" in a slightly different way to Bronkhorst, in the sense of consciously feeling being compelled to do something.

33 For a thorough discussion of this text, see Kuan (2008: 81–103).

practice described in the text as a form of mindfulness connected with the body (*kāyagatāsati*), such as comprehending/knowing (*pajānāti*) that one's body is in a particular position or performing every act with clear comprehension (*sampajānakārī*). It states that for one who dwells vigilant (*appamatta*), ardent (*ātāpī*) and resolute (*pahitatta*), memories and intentions (*sarasaṅkappa*) connected with household life (*gehasita*) are abandoned. The text then directly states that due to their abandoning (*pahāna*), the mind steadies (*santiṭṭhati*), settles down (*sannisīdati*), is unified (*ekodi hoti*) and becomes concentrated (*samādhiyati*).[34] Let us note that when read directly, the text does not present concentration as a separate active and deliberately driven process but as a natural consequence of the absence of thoughts and memories connected with household lives. The latter need not be necessarily conceived of as merely mental images of one's family members or possessions but may correspond to the whole urge-driven system of motivation, which is a default system in ordinary people who lead household lives, and thus may be described as "connected with home" (*gehasita*). Urges are ultimately based on memories and may be conceived of as sorts of thoughts or intentions (*saṅkappa*).

Gradual abandonment of the urge-driven motivation system based on desire and aversion may also directly lead to the experience of the saintly feelings of pleasure (*sukha*) which according to the *Sāmaññaphala-sutta* are associated with virtue and sense restraint. One trivial explanation would explain this pleasure as arising due to a simple satisfaction from being successful in one's practice. However, it is also possible that the cause for the arising of pleasure is more fundamental. As we have already noted, according to the texts following the *Sāmaññaphala* pattern, it is during seated meditation prior to the attainment of the first *jhāna* that the awareness of the absence of the *nīvaraṇas* sets off a chain of mental and bodily states indirectly resulting in the feeling of *sukha*. All the *nīvaraṇas* can be understood exactly as types of urges, feelings and thoughts which motivate the behaviour of ordinary people. It may be the case that the removal of the hindrances through morality and sense restraint already reaches a sufficient level at the earlier stages of the path to generate a weaker, pre-jhānic form of *sukha* which is described in the *Sāmaññaphala* account. As I have suggested, being

34 MN 119/iii 89: *tassa evaṃ appamattassa ātāpino pahitattassa viharato ye gehasitā sarasaṅkappā te pahīyanti. tesaṃ pahānā ajjhattameva cittaṃ santiṭṭhati sannisīdati ekodi hoti samādhiyati.*

driven by urges and acting based on avoiding discomfort and pursuing pleasure is ultimately tiresome for the organism. Being freed from this burden may be perceived as a relief. The absence of urges connected with striving for more gross forms of pleasure may make one more sensitive to a subtler, but more fundamental form of pleasure stemming from just being in a relaxed state of the body. We have already noted Solms's (2021) suggestion that consciousness (which he pretty much identifies with feelings) arises in situations of uncertainty, to guide us through those situations, while the desired state of organism is that of no-consciousness (which does not entail mental and sensory inactivity). Hypothetically, a person whose life uncertainty would be reduced to a minimum and whose behaviour would be motivated in an entirely rational way would have relatively fewer conscious thoughts and urges. A life of an early Buddhist bhikkhu can certainly be conceived of as involving very little uncertainty in the sense of not knowing how to act in a particular situation. This, as we have hypothesized in Chapter 4, would entail staying to a much greater extent in a pleasant state of natural absorption, at least when idle.

A somewhat similar notion was proposed by the ancient philosophical school of the Epicureans[35] which held that the greatest pleasure results from the absence of pain. The mere sensation of being emancipated from pain and of relief from discomfort was considered a source of gratification. According to the Epicureans, a constant and subtle form of pleasure exists, which they labelled as "static" or "catastemic" and which is inherent to the body whose basic needs have been fulfilled and which is in a relative state of comfort and relaxation. However, according to Epicurus, this subtle pleasure is normally blunted by more intense "moving" pleasures connected with the process of satisfying desires. Since the latter pleasures have several drawbacks, they should be avoided in favour of catastemic pleasure. Thus, Epicurean hedonism paradoxically results in ascetism and self-moderation. Epicurus himself claimed that his body exalted in living delicately on bread and water and rejected the pleasures of luxury.[36]

The pleasure connected with the successful development of virtue and sense restraint spoken about in the Nikāyas might have been a similar type of pleasure. One final hypothesis, which should be seen as complementary to the abovementioned ones, would be that by eliminating

35 See Reale (1985: 163–72).

36 See Reale (1985: 170).

urges, one is removing much of the *saṅkhāras*, since they are connected with the conscious phenomenon of volition. Their removal also entails the elimination of most sources of bodily exertion and tension, thus generating a pleasant and relaxed state for the organism.

Above, I have offered a hypothesis regarding the mechanism by which the practices of morality, sense restraint, mindfulness and clear comprehension can facilitate the attainment of an altered, thought-less state of consciousness. I have suggested that this process could occur on two paths: by directly removing important sources of mental movement and indirectly, by generating pleasure which according to the already analysed Nikāya formulas contributes to concentration.

Social roots of verbal thinking and mental monologue

However, thoughts, feelings and urges connected with the pursuit of pleasure and avoidance of discomfort are not the only ones that a meditator needs to deal with. Probably the most common type of intruding thoughts during meditation is constituted by mental chatter, an internal monologue or rather a dialogue with an imaginary interlocutor. Such thoughts are clearly not of the same type as the ones analysed above. They do not directly motivate us to take any action, nor are they connected with the desire for pleasure or aversion to discomfort. Therefore, the methods discussed above would be only partially efficient for turning off the mechanism responsible for the arising of such thoughts. Can they therefore be stopped without resorting to meditative suppression? To even consider such a possibility, we need to first establish what mechanism is exactly responsible for generating this kind of mental dialogue. There has recently been some seminal research in the philosophy of mind and cognitive science, which can prove helpful in explaining this issue.

We already established in Chapter 2 that conscious thoughts through which we engage in mind wandering and internal monologue are not synonymous with thinking in the sense of processing data, solving cognitive problems and arriving at new ideas. The latter processes occur on a non-conscious level and it is their results that find their way to awareness in the form of conscious thoughts. However, bringing such insights to consciousness is not the only role of conscious thought, as we seem to constantly engage in mind wandering and internal monologue whenever we have nothing to do. Although this process of seemingly chaotic drifting and meandering from one thought to another might seem meaningless, current research in cognitive science points to its deeply adaptive value. An interesting hypothesis regarding this issue has been offered by Carruthers (2015: 171), who stated that:

> There are frequently lessons to be acquired from the past that were not learned at the time. Recalling those episodes, thereby making them globally available in working memory, can issue in novel inferences and affective reactions. ... By entertaining representations of various future actions in working memory, one can predict their likely consequences and respond affectively to them, thereby enabling one to plan.

As we have already noted, when the information is conscious it means that it is also globally available to all other modules throughout the cognitive system. These modules are responsible for processing information, creating solutions to problems, generating new ideas, as well as evaluation and formulation of sentences. However, they operate in relative isolation from one another. The only way in which the output of one module may become available to the other ones is when it becomes conscious, as consciousness is a sort of "global workspace" if we are to refer to Baars and Franklin's (2007: 958) theory. Let us consider a situation where we are asked a question regarding our knowledge in a situation when the potential consequences of our answer are socially important for us. Then, some module spontaneously processes the question and comes up with a straightforward answer which is simply based on our knowledge. To fully realize the functional significance of consciousness, let us imagine a hypothetical situation where there would not be any "global workspace" and the output of particular modules would never become available to the other modules. Then, any response to a question could only be semi-automatic and simply express our state of knowledge without considering the social consequences of our utterances. But in real life, before we break into speech, the answer may first take the form of a conscious thought. Since the main functional feature of consciousness lies in its global availability, this answer becomes available to other modules, including the ones responsible for social and emotional intelligence and for evaluating the potential social consequences of our answers. As Carruthers (2015: 164) points out: "... by providing a sentence that can be consciously perceived, one recruits all of the brain's circuits to evaluate it, and to compete with one another in offering suggestions about what should come next".

Consequently, the original spontaneous answer may be modified, and when we finally answer the question after deliberation, we do so in a way that will better suit our social interests. However, during real-life conversations there is usually very little time for efficient evaluation of our expressions and of their potential social impact. Therefore, in our free time we constantly rehearse past conversations or engage in imagined conversations with the people we know as if in anticipation of potential similar interactions in the future. As Carruthers (2015: 163) aptly observes, our "inner speech takes the form of an imagined conversation, or at least speech directed towards an imagined audience. Sometimes one rehearses (and thereby consciously evaluates) what one could say, or should say, or could have said to someone". In this way, when the time of actual conversation comes, we are able to communicate more efficiently and in a way that benefits our social standing. The other reason for this need for constant mental rehearsal may lie in the fact that linguistic capability has been acquired relatively recently by humans and efficient usage of language is still a difficulty for the brain. Constant rehearsal is needed to stimulate the relevant brain regions and thus prevent them from losing efficiency due to lack of stimulation.

In another relevant article *Why do humans reason? Arguments for an argumentative theory*, Hugo Mercier and Dan Sperber (2011: 57) make a sharp distinction between "inferential processes" which are unconscious and generate intuitive beliefs, and "reasoning" which is conscious and occurs at a conceptual level. Entertaining conscious, verbal thoughts is one of the forms of reasoning, though one can also reason aloud by talking to oneself or others. Mercier and Sperber (2011: 58) suggest that the primary function of reasoning, and by consequence also of conscious verbal thinking, is the production and evaluation of arguments for social communication, and not the pursuit of truth and knowledge. Contrary to prevalent, commonsense opinions, "reasoning falls short of delivering rational beliefs and rational decisions reliably, ... in a variety of cases it may even be detrimental to rationality" (Mercier and Sperber, 2011: 59) since it suffers from confirmation bias. Through reasoning, which most often takes the form of conscious verbal thinking, one can "devise and evaluate arguments intended to persuade" (Mercier and Sperber, 2011: 57).

What particularly matters for our study is that the real reasons for our internal monologue and mind wandering are connected with our way of life and our goals and interests. As long as we engage in social situations and are vitally interested in their results, the sources of thoughts will need to be active. As long as we believe that we have something to gain or lose due to our verbal interactions with other members of society, our minds will be constantly evaluating various possible courses of action, rehearsing potential verbal expressions with imaginary interlocutors and will be revisiting past events. Therefore, the major roots of conscious thinking lie in deeply engrained fundamental psychological mechanisms which make us interested in protecting our social welfare and safety. That is also why we greatly care about other people's opinion and about how we are perceived. Interestingly, the ancient Cynic philosophers, such as Diogenes and Crates, considered social norms and the connected feeling of shame to be one of the major sources of human misfortune. Therefore, their spiritual exercises would often aim at breaking down one's feelings of shame and concern about the way one is perceived by others.[37]

The understanding of these basic mechanisms seems to be implied in some of the Nikāya texts. According to the classification in the *Paṃsudhovaka-sutta* (AN 3.101/i.253–256),[38] after the removal of the medium (*majjhimasahagata*) defilements (*upakkilesa*)[39] one has to eradicate the so-called subtle (*sukhumasahagata*) defilements: thoughts of one's own clan (*ñātivitakka*), thoughts of one's own country (*janapadavitakka*) and thoughts about one's reputation or social standing (lit. thoughts connected with not being looked down upon or despised [*anavaññattipaṭisaṃyutta*]).[40] The thoughts classified as subtle defilements seem to be connected with the deeply ingrained mechanisms responsible for maintaining social identity and status that we have been considering above. They particularly concern preoccupation with the way we are perceived by others. Although they are labelled as thoughts, they should perhaps be seen as general tendencies which can give rise to more specific thoughts that are connected with them.

The awareness of such tendencies is also present in other texts of the Nikāyas which have been given relatively little attention so far. The *Bala-sutta* (AN 9.5/iv.363–365) contains a list of five fears (*bhaya*), among which one finds the fear of disrepute (*asilokabhaya*) and the fear

37 See White (2020: 239).

38 Cf. Bodhi (2012: 335–38) for a translation.

39 The gross defilements (*oḷārikā upakkilesā*) are not defined as thoughts, but as bodily, verbal and mental misconduct.

40 AN 3.101/i.255: *Tasmiṃ pahīne tasmiṃ byantīkate santi adhicittamanuyuttassa bhikkhuno sukhumasahagatā upakkilesā ñātivitakko janapadavitakko anavaññattipaṭisaṃyutto vitakko.*

of lacking confidence while in an assembly (*parisasārajjabhaya*). The *Vitakka-sutta* (Iti 80/72–73) of the *Itivuttaka* describes three unwholesome thoughts (*akusalavitakka*) which include the already familiar concept of thoughts connected with not wanting to be looked down upon (*anavaññattipaṭisaṃyutta*), the thoughts connected with gain, honour and fame (*lābhasakkārasilokapaṭisaṃyutta*) and quite interestingly, if not controversially, thoughts connected with sympathy for other people (*parānuddayatāpaṭisaṃyutta*). However, the last point is deeply justified from a psychological point of view. The majority of people usually not only care about their own safety, but also about the safety of certain others: their loved ones and their closest relatives. This in turn contributes to further intensification of conscious thinking. This point seems to be well-expressed by the *Paṭhamadārukkhandhopama-sutta* (SN 35.241/iv.179–181), which negatively evaluates a state where "someone lives in association with laypeople; he rejoices with them and sorrows with them, he is happy when they are happy and sad when they are sad, and he involves himself in their affairs and duties".[41] However brutal it may seem from the point of view of common beliefs and morality, having emotional attachment to other people is incompatible with the higher stages of the Buddhist path.

Even after their removal there still remain "thoughts connected with the Dhamma".[42] The *Paṃsudhovaka-sutta* attests that as long as they are present, one's meditation will not be peaceful, sublime and endowed with calm and oneness but will be held down by the restraint of *saṅkhāra*.

The radical life: An existential situation of an early Buddhist bhikkhu

Can these basic mechanisms be turned off, thus removing one of the most important sources of arising and movement of conscious thoughts? A case can be made that becoming a bhikkhu was originally meant to serve exactly that purpose. The commonly met idea that being a monk

41 SN 35.241/iv.180: *idha, bhikkhu, gihīhi saṃsaṭṭho viharati, sahanandī sahasokī, sukhitesu sukhito, dukkhitesu dukkhito, uppannesu kiccakaraṇīyesu attanā tesu yogaṃ āpajjati.* (trans. Bodhi 2000: 1242). The same line is contained in the *Hāliddikāni-sutta* (SN 22.3/iii 9–12).

42 AN 3.101/i.255: *Tasmiṃ pahīne tasmiṃ byantīkate athāparaṃ dhammavitakkāvasissanti.*

is about having a lot of time to devote oneself to meditation seems to miss some crucial points. It reflects the traditional paradigmatic view that formal seated meditation is the essence of Buddhist practice, something that can be cultivated and mastered in itself. However, the causes of this misunderstanding may have much to do with the fact that throughout the history of Buddhism, the lifestyle of monks was much different from that of the early Buddhist bhikkhus.

What was the existential situation of such a bhikkhu? In that period Buddhism was not yet an established and respected religion, being just one of the many *samaṇa* movements.[43] Becoming a bhikkhu was synonymous with renunciation of one's social status, family bonds, tradition and religion, essentially making one a social outcast. This crucial aspect of the bhikkhu's self-awareness is well-expressed in the *Samaṇasaññā-sutta* (AN 10.101/v.210–211) which advises the cultivation of three ascetic perceptions (*samaṇasañña*). Among them, one should cultivate the thought: "I have entered upon a classless condition" (*'vevaṇṇiyamhi ajjhupagato'ti*).[44] The same thought is included in the list of the things (*dhamma*) that should repeatedly be reflected upon (*paccavekkhitabba*) contained in the *Pabbajitābhiṇha-sutta* (AN 10.48/v.87–88).

Another absolutely key aspect which has not been emphasized enough is that by becoming a bhikkhu, one renounces fundamentally ingrained mechanisms of self-protection which make one preoccupied with preserving one's own safety. The already mentioned *Bala-sutta* mentions the fear regarding livelihood (*ājīvikabhaya*) as one of the major sources of anxiety one has to deal with. From the moment of renunciation, a bhikkhu is at the mercy of others, of the environment and of chance events.[45] This awareness is expressed by another of the contemplations suggested in an identical form in both the *Samaṇasaññā* and the *Pabbajitābhiṇha-sutta*, namely: "My life is dependent on others" (*'parapaṭibaddhā me jīvikā'ti*).[46]

---

43 I.e., homeless seekers of truth and liberation, rejecting the authority of Vedic tradition.

44 AN 10.101/v.210. Translation by Bodhi (2012: 1483). An identical formulation occurs in the *Pabbajitābhiṇha-sutta* (AN 10.48/v.87–88).

45 It is worth noticing that this aspect is especially well presented in Bodhidharma's *Erru sixing lun*, both in the account of the practice of following circumstances/conditions (*suiyuanxing* 隨緣行), and in the description of the practice of seeking nothing (*wusuoqiuxing* 無所求行) where it is said that one allows one's body to be transformed in accordance with destiny (*xingsuiyun-zhuan* 形隨運轉).

46 AN 10.48/v.87, AN 10.101/v.210. Translation by Bodhi (2012: 1398).

By leading a renunciate lifestyle, all major sources of responsibility become removed, and with them a major source of thought movement is gone. This also seems to be the real psychological motive behind the rule forbidding bhikkhus to handle money. Having no money makes one dependent on others regarding survival. Secondly, it cuts off an important source of thinking since one does not have to concern oneself with the ways of spending or saving one's money. All a bhikkhu can do is live day by day, not having anything to plan or look forward to. Paradoxically, it is psychologically plausible that such a lifestyle can bring happiness. In the Western world this was already discovered in the Hellenistic period by the Cynic philosophers, who considered a life concerned only with the barest necessities as the source of happiness. Crates, who disposed of all of his possessions in the name of the Cynic values, was reputed to say that the benefit that this philosophy gave him was the ability to be satisfied with "a quart of lupins and to care for nothing".[47] The *Sāmaññaphala-sutta* describes a bhikkhu as being content (*santuṭṭha*) when he uses his robe and his almsfood merely to protect his body and sustain himself. Such a bhikkhu is compared to a winged bird, which has just a pair of wings as his burden (*sapattabhāra*),[48] wherever it flies. This simile not only conveys a bhikkhu's contentment with having little possessions, but also a deep sense of freedom and a lack of constriction. It can therefore be seen as the fulfilment and realization of the initial insight that "the household life is a crowded dusty path" (*sambādho gharāvāso rajopatho*), while "going forth is like an open space" (*abbhokāso pabbajjā*) [49] which accompanied the decision to become a renunciate. This contentedness is also briefly mentioned in an earlier part of the text, where it is said that "having gone forth he dwells restrained in body, speech, and mind, content with the simplest food and shelter, 'delighting in solitude' (*abhirato paviveke*)".[50]

This type of happiness connected with a lack of possessions is also attested in the *Piṇḍa-sutta* (SN 4.18/i.113–114) which contains the following verse:

47 See Reale (1985: 32).

48 DN 2/i.71: *idha, mahārāja, bhikkhu santuṭṭho hoti kāyaparihārikena cīvarena, kucchiparihārikena piṇḍapātena. so yena yeneva pakkamati, samādāyeva pakkamati. seyyathāpi, mahārāja, pakkhī sakuṇo yena yeneva ḍeti, sapattabhārova ḍeti.*

49 DN 2/i.63: *sambādho gharāvāso rajopatho, abbhokāso pabbajjā.*

50 DN 2/i.61–62: *so evaṃ pabbajito samāno kāyena saṃvuto viharati, vācāya saṃvuto viharati, manasā saṃvuto viharati, ghāsacchādanaparamatāya santuṭṭho, abhirato paviveke.* Translation by Bodhi (2008: 27).

Happily (*susukhaṃ*) indeed we live,
We who own nothing at all.
We shall dwell feeding on rapture (*pītibhakkha*)
Like the devas of Streaming Radiance.[51]

In the *Araññа-sutta* (SN 1.10/i.4–5), a *devatā* (celestial being) asks about the cause of the serene complexion of those who live in the forest, who are peaceful, lead a holy life and only eat one meal a day (i.e., Buddhist bhikkhus).[52] The Buddha answers by stating that it is because "they do not sorrow over the past, nor do they hanker for the future, they maintain themselves with what is present".[53] In contrast, those that do worry about the past and long for the future are described as withering like a green reed that has been cut down.

The *Dhammacetiya-sutta* contains an account (MN 89/ii.121)[54] in which King Pasenadi describes the bhikkhus as being joyful and delighted (*haṭṭhapahaṭṭha*), elated and exultant (*udaggudagga*), plainly delighted (*abhiratarūpa*), with glad faculties (*pīṇindriya*), living at ease/ unbothered (*appossukka*), depending on what is given by others (*paradattavutta*) and "with minds like a wild deer" (*migabhūtena cetasā*). The latter epithet may suggest a free, unrestricted mode of wandering lifestyle similar to that of an animal to which it is compared. King Pasenadi concludes that these bhikkhus "have successively known lofty distinction of that Blessed One's teaching".[55] As we see, this account connects exultant feelings experienced by the bhikkhus with living at ease and unbothered, dependent on support from others and with "mind like a wild deer". This agrees with our hypothesis about a deep psychological link between exultant feelings experienced by a bhikkhu and his specific existential situation.[56]

51 SN 4.18/i.114: *'susukhaṃ vata jīvāma, yesaṃ no natthi kiñcanaṃ. pītibhakkhā bhavissāma, devā ābhassarā yathā'ti*. Translation by Bodhi (2000: 207–208).

52 This is yet another Nikāya account of a person's mental state manifesting itself through facial complexion.

53 SN 1.10/i.5: *atītaṃ nānusocanti, nappajappanti nāgataṃ. paccuppannena yāpenti ...* Translation by Bodhi (2000: 93).

54 Cf. translations of this fragment by Wynne (2022: 116) and Ñāṇamoli and Bodhi (1995: 730).

55 MN 89/ii.121: *'addhā ime āyasmanto tassa bhagavato sāsane uḷāraṃ pubbenāparaṃ visesaṃ jānanti.*

56 Wynne (2022: 116–17) sees the passage in the *Dhammacetiya-sutta* as an account of "living in a transformed manner", of "what the doctrine of liberation in life means in actual terms: living freely and naturally, with meditative flourishing alleviating the burdens of life". On such a reading, the exultant spiritual

Maintaining a very simple, regular order of the day also plays a crucial role in removing many of the sources of thought movement. There is no need to bother oneself with making plans, as everything is already settled. Even minute details, such as the suggestion that one sits down to experience *jhāna* after having eaten a meal, may be interpreted as having deep psychological significance. At this point of the day, a bhikkhu simply has nothing left to do and thus does not need to think, worry or plan anything. An additional factor may lie in the fact that having eaten a meal increases bodily relaxation, which as we have suggested may correspond to the tranquillization of the *saṅkhāras* and removal of striving and tensions. Having satisfied hunger, which is one of the most basic human needs, temporarily removes any potential thoughts connected with food. Sitting down to meditate after a meal would be considered a serious mistake according to the classical, quasi-yogic model of meditation. However, in the case of the type of meditation we are dealing with here, it can have very positive effects.

Another important role of thoughts is to remind us of the things that we should do or to suggest potential courses of action best suited to circumstances. In ordinary people, these types of thoughts are very rare in comparison with the types of thoughts we have already considered. In the case of bhikkhus, however, their life is so simple and regular that this mechanism is even more diminished. While there is indeed a place for such an activity of thoughts during the practice of right effort which fills much of the bhikkhu's life before meditation, when he sits down to meditate there is simply nothing of this sort to think about; all his activities for the day are done.

The psychological significance of right speech

Although it may perhaps appear surprising at first, right speech is another key element of everyday life that possesses fundamental consequences for the possibility of attaining a thought-less state. Its significance goes far beyond mere ethical aspects. According to the Nikāyas, a bhikkhu must abandon false speech and be a speaker of only that which is true (*saccavādī*).[57] A man who is a potential candidate for the

---

feelings would be resultant of liberation and not just of a particular mode of life as in our interpretation.

57 DN 1/i.4: *musāvādaṃ pahāya musāvādā paṭivirato hoti saccavādī saccasandho theto paccayiko avisaṃvādako lokassa.*

Buddha's teaching should be "honest and sincere, a man of rectitude" (*asaṭho amāyāvī ujujātiko*).[58]

Speaking according to one's own knowledge when asked may appear to be a simple thing, but it can bring revolutionary consequences. Ordinary people are usually forced to make all sorts of compromises, put on various social masks, and be very careful about what they say. Unconditional straightforwardness and speaking only truth would sooner or later put one in a conflict with society and endanger one's own social safety. This was already acknowledged by the ancient Cynics, as *parrhesia* (Greek word meaning unconditional sincerity in speech) went hand in hand with the denouncement of one's social status.[59] Therefore, as we have already noted, people are constantly rehearsing potential dialogues in their minds in preparation for real-life conversations which will have an impact on their lives. However, simply answering questions according to one's knowledge does not require any effort and comes about almost spontaneously. If a bhikkhu speaks in this way, then his need for mental rehearsing of imaginary conversations will gradually diminish, as there is nothing to be gained from it. Thus, an important source of mind wandering will become extinguished. It is also noteworthy that in both early Buddhist and Chan texts one finds a critical attitude towards debates, quarrels and views in general. As we have noted, according to Mercier and Sperber (2011), the main role of reasoning, and by extension verbal conscious thinking, is to prepare arguments intended to persuade others. But if one lives in such a way that there is no need to persuade anyone of anything, "without quarrelling with the world",[60] then there will also be no need for engaging in imaginary mental reasonings. The Nikāya texts generally advise limiting one's speech as much as possible without detriment to an efficient communication with other bhikkhus. The *Cūḷagosiṅga-sutta* presents bhikkhus as communicating using hand gestures (*hatthavikāra*), and only breaking into speech every fifth night to discuss the Dhamma.[61]

58 MN 80/ii.44: *etu viññū puriso asaṭho amāyāvī ujujātiko, ahamanusāsāmi ahaṃ dhammaṃ desemi*. Translation by Ñāṇamoli and Bodhi (1995: 664).

59 See Reale (1985: 23).

60 SN 22/iii.128: "I do not, bhikkhus, quarrel with the world" (*Nāhaṃ, bhikkhave, lokena vivadāmi*).

61 MN 31/i.207: *Sacassa hoti avisayhaṃ, hatthavikārena dutiyaṃ āmantetvā hatthavilaṅghakena upaṭṭhāpema, na tveva mayaṃ, bhante, tappaccayā vācaṃ bhindāma. Pañcāhikaṃ kho pana mayaṃ, bhante, sabbarattikaṃ dhammiyā kathāya sannisīdāma.*

If one restricts the usage of speech to such a bare minimum, and one's social position is no longer influenced by what one can say (because a bhikkhu has nothing to lose in this regard anyway), then the need for verbal, conscious thinking will gradually cease. It is therefore plausible on a psychological level that a particular lifestyle and mindset may put an end to the majority of thought movement, so there will be no need for its forceful suppression by classical methods of calm meditation.[62]

One could perhaps raise a point that this is an overly idealistic, naive and romantic description, and that very few monks in the history of Buddhism may have lived up to these ideals. The latter assessment is undoubtedly true. The majority of Buddhist practitioners were probably not able to experience intense, blissful spiritual feelings arising from a sanctified way of life described in the *Sāmaññaphala-sutta*. What could be the reasons for it? In order to answer that question, it is worthwhile to consider the fundamental change in the existential situation of monks that occurred throughout the history of Buddhism, and of Theravāda in particular.

The decline of a radical model of life and its reemergence in Chan Buddhism

Even during the time of the Buddha, only the leading disciples were depicted as leading this kind of holy life. Moreover, the conditions of the livelihood of bhikkhus were soon to undergo a drastic change. They were no longer solitary wanderers, but monastery dwellers living in large communities occupying permanent, fixed locations.[63] A social outcast from the times of the Buddha, was replaced by a respectable member of society with a high standing. Becoming a monk no longer meant forsaking one's old identity and a break up with one's old environment; on the contrary, one was adding a new social identity on top

62 Also see Bronkhorst (2012: 126, 127, 130, 164), who sees the main psychological role of renunciate life in minimizing social contact with others and complete disengagement from human society. This leads to a reduction of tension mobilized in anticipation of social contact which is essential for what he terms "complete cure".

63 See Wynne (2020a) for an interesting discussion of the emergence of various trends and directions of development within the early Buddhist Sangha in the fourth century bc. See also Stuart-Fox (1989) for a discussion of the change in bhikkhus' life conditions.

of the old one. In time, monks started to perform some of the traditional functions of priests, doctors and counsellors and became important members of society with duties to fulfil and responsibilities to uphold. Eventually some of them would wield political power. While originally being a bhikkhu meant living from day to day without any guarantees, becoming a monk would later turn out to be a major guarantee of social safety. It is therefore true that relatively very few monks have lived up to the lofty ideal presented in the Nikāyas. Likewise, very few bhikkhus throughout the history of Theravāda may have actually attained the *jhāna*s.

However, the spirit of a radical life was later to resurface in different Buddhist milieus. As Poceski (2007: 131–35) points out, it was definitely present in the Hongzhou school of the Tang period, as attested by the writings of Baizhang and Fenzhou Wuye 汾州無業 (760–821). Their portrayal of monastic life shows many similarities with the early Buddhist ideals. In the *Baizhang Huaihai chanshi guanglu*, Baizhang speaks about a monk who is free from any relations, as for him there is no sense of dearness or love (*wuqinwuai* 無親無愛). He uses a robe merely for protection from cold and sustains himself on unpolished rice.[64] In the *Zimen jingxun*, Fenzhou Wuye speaks about the monks of old, who lived as social recluses, "forgetting about human affairs" (*dawangrenshi* 大忘人世), and who "concealed their traces among rocks and thickets". Their radicality also manifested in refusing the summons from kings (*junwang* 君王) and the princes (*hou* 侯).[65] The Baotang school of Wuzhu was also renowned for its radicality regarding lifestyle. While their representatives rejected all formal rules and rituals, it did not lead to a loosening of lifestyle but to its radicalization. This is exemplified by the following statement of Wuzhu in the *Lidai fabao ji*:

> If you want to practice worship and recitation, then leave the mountains. On the plains there are gracious and easeful temple-quarters, and you are free to go. If you want to stay with me, you must utterly devote yourself to no-thought. If you can, then you are free to stay. If you cannot, then you must go down.[66]

---

64 X69, no. 1323, p. 8a12–13: 無親無愛。苦樂平懷。麤衣遮寒。糲食活命。See Poceski (2007: 131–32) for a translation.

65 T48, no. 2023, p. 1077a21–2: 大忘人世隱迹岩叢。君王命而不來。諸侯請而不赴。Translation by Poceski (2007: 132).

66 T51, no. 2075, p. 187a6–8: 若欲得禮念即出山。平下大有寬閑寺舍。任意出去。若欲得同住。一向無念。得即任住。不得即須下山去。Translation by Adamek (2007: 349).

Above, I have attempted to show that an elevated state of mind, characterized by the experience of saintly feelings and by the relative absence of thoughts, may be induced through a certain way of living and by maintaining a particular mindset. Thus, it would not require an active implementation of any meditative method. As we have seen, there is support for it on a textual level, and the idea is plausible from a psychological point of view. Accepting such a possibility would however entail a fundamental shift in the paradigm of meditation. It would no longer be an activity, a technique or a skill that can be mastered in itself,[67] but an extension and fruition of a specific lifestyle and mindset.[68] One must emphasize, however, that the model of life and practice that is presented here is extremely radical and very far from stereotypical views about the relation between morality and meditation, and particularly from those held in modern times. It needs to be said that classical works like the *Visuddhimagga*, which are representative of the mainstream paradigm, are to some degree to blame as they fail to explain the exact nature of the relation between *sīla* and meditation. In Buddhaghosa's treatise, relatively little place is devoted to the development of *sīla* in comparison to the accounts of the cultivation of concentration and wisdom.

---

67 By that, I do not mean that the monks did not spend the majority of their time in a seated, cross-legged position. They did, although again it does not mean that they were following any method that needed to be actively implemented. One should not conflate meditation as a deliberate performance of certain activities with spending time in a seated position. Of course, bhikkhus were spending a lot of time seated, because they had very little to do and such a situation was very conducive to the arising of an altered state of mind when several other conditions have been met. This will be explored in detail in the next chapters.

68 The idea that the four *jhānas* require no concentrative practices but are spiritual states of psychosomatic transformation which occur as a natural process dependent on a disciplined lifestyle and involving simplified cognition has also been suggested by Wynne (2018d) in one of his Oxford lectures.

Chapter 7

CALMING THE MIND THROUGH AWARENESS

While many sources of ordinary thinking may be extinguished due to living a specific way of life as described in the preceding chapter, it does not entail that all thoughts will disappear altogether of their own accord. According to the *Paṃsudhovaka-sutta*, after removal of the subtle defilements, there still remain (*avasissati*) thoughts of the dhamma (*dhammavitakka*) which prevent meditation from becoming truly spontaneous and non-constricted. The text of this sutta does not offer an explanation of any method or mechanism by which this process should occur but merely states that there comes a time (*samaya*) when the mind stills itself and settles down (*santiṭṭhati sannisīdati*) and enters a state of concentration that is not "held down by restraint of *saṅkhāra*" (*sasaṅkāraniggayhavāritagato*).[1] The exact nature of these "dhamma-thoughts" is unclear. It is not certain whether dhamma-thoughts represent active thinking of some Buddhist truths, or if their presence simply prevents spontaneous and natural concentration, thus entailing the necessity of employing *saṅkhāra*s for this task.

As we have noted, several Nikāya texts recommended active thinking of positive thoughts as part of the right effort and as an antidote to unwholesome thoughts connected with desire and aversion. According to the passage in the *Dvedhavitakka-sutta* (MN 19/i.115) this is meant to create a new, wholesome inclination (*nati*) of the mind (*cetas*). It needs to be emphasized that the Nikāyas propose a nuanced approach to the issue of employing active, deliberate mental effort. At the pre-jhānic levels of practice it is very much encouraged. According to the definition of right effort, one is even supposed to "generate desire"

1 AN 3.101/i.255: *Hoti so, bhikkhave, samayo yaṃ taṃ cittaṃ ajjhattaṃyeva santiṭṭhati sannisīdati ekodi hoti samādhiyati. So hoti samādhi santo paṇīto paṭippassaddhiladdho ekodibhāvādhigato na sasaṅkhāraniggayhavāritagato.*

(*chandaṃ janeti*), arouse energy, "exert the mind" (*cittaṃ paggaṇhāti*)[2] and strive (*padahati*) for the purpose of the arising of the wholesome states. Therefore, it can be said that in order to eventually cancel out desire and *saṅkhāras*, a practitioner resorts to the active generation of a particular type of desire and particular type of *saṅkhāras*, at least in the earlier stages of practice. However, the drawback is that these latter processes may become a problem at the higher levels of cultivation which are characterized by the tranquillization of *saṅkhāras* and absence of effort. It might be the case that the dhamma-thoughts that are said in the *Paṃsudhovaka-sutta* to hinder concentration are connected with such active processes. As we shall see later, it is also possible to offer alternate, but not necessarily mutually exclusive interpretations of the nature of the dhamma-thoughts.

Calming the mind through meditative awareness in the Nikāyas

Interesting hints regarding the removal of these type of thoughts may be found in the *Dvedhāvitakka-sutta* (MN19/i.114). We have already noted that this text provides a method for dealing with unwholesome thoughts by becoming aware of them, contemplating their drawbacks, and actively thinking wholesome thoughts. However, the Buddha recalls that before his awakening, "due to excessive thinking and examining" (*aticiraṃ anuvitakkayato anuvicārayato*) his body would get tired (*kilamati*) which in turn would lead to the mind being disturbed (*ūhaññati*), preventing its unification.[3] This formulation is yet another example of the Nikāya notion of the dependence of right concentration on a relaxed bodily state. While the order of the text is somewhat unclear at this point, it seems to suggest that the solution was to stop the practice of actively thinking wholesome thoughts and simply to be passively mindful of their presence: "(there are now) these *dhammas*" (*ete dhammā'ti*). The passive nature of this mindfulness is also suggested by an ensuing simile which compares this mode of practice to a shepherd sitting under

2 SN 45.8/v.9: *Idha, bhikkhave, bhikkhu anuppannānaṃ pāpakānaṃ akusalānaṃ dhammānaṃ anuppādāya chandaṃ janeti vāyamati vīriyaṃ ārabhati cittaṃ paggaṇhāti padahati*. Cf. Bodhi (2000: 1529) for a translation.

3 MN 19/i.116: *Api ca kho me aticiraṃ anuvitakkayato anuvicārayato kāyo kilameyya. Kāye kilante cittaṃ ūhaññeyya*. Cf. translation by Ñāṇamoli and Bodhi (1995: 208).

a tree who only needs to be maintaining mindfulness (*satikaraṇīya*) of his cows.[4] This is in contrast to the earlier mode of practice which was compared to a shepherd who would actively beat (*ākoṭeti*) and restrain (*sannivāreti*) his cows using a rod (*daṇḍa*).[5] This is then followed by the standard account of the four *jhāna*s and of awakening, which seems to suggest that the thoughts must have subsided. However, it is not stated explicitly that this passive awareness directly led to the settling down of excessive positive thoughts. What is emphasized is that dropping the active effort of thinking positive thoughts removes the obstacle in the form of bodily tiredness and disturbance of the mind which prevented concentration. But could the very awareness of mental states somehow contribute to their gradual tranquillization? This question is relevant for our investigation as such meditative awareness would meet the criteria of a right form of meditation in Nikāya and Chan texts, as it does not involve forceful concentrative suppression.

But by what mechanism could mere awareness of thoughts lead to their gradual calming down? The idea that awareness of the movement of thoughts may lead to calming the mind is generally not recognized by the classical paradigm of meditation. The methods for calming the mind are almost always connected with one-pointed concentration. As the focus on the meditation object strengthens, the latter is supposed to gradually fill up the whole consciousness pushing away everything else: thoughts, sounds and bodily sensations. Being aware of the movement of one's own thoughts would fall more under the heading of *vipassanā*, at least as how it is understood in the modern era, since it is similar in a way to mindfulness of sensations or bodily movements. However, as such, it would need to be assessed as incapable of leading to deeper *samādhi* and to an altered state of mind. What could be the exact mechanism by which being aware of the movements of thoughts could cause their calming?

The idea that awareness of one's own mental activity may lead to its gradual pacification is also present in a very interesting, although unclear, fragment contained in the *Vitakkasaṇṭhāna-sutta* (MN

4 MN 19/i.117: *Seyyathāpi, bhikkhave, gimhānaṃ pacchime māse sabbasassesu gāmantasambhatesu gopālako gāvo rakkheyya, tassa rukkhamūlagatassa vā abbhokāsagatassa vā satikaraṇīyameva hoti: 'etā gāvo'ti. Evamevaṃ kho, bhikkhave, satikaraṇīyameva ahosi: 'ete dhammā'ti.* Cf. translation by Ñāṇamoli and Bodhi (1995: 208).

5 MN 19/i.115: *So tā gāvo tato tato daṇḍena ākoṭeyya paṭikoṭeyya sannirundheyya sannivāreyya.* Cf. translation by Ñāṇamoli and Bodhi (1995: 209).

20/i.118–122). This text discusses five special measures or methods (*nimitta* – usually this term denotes a feature or a sign) to be used when the mind is troubled by the arising of unwholesome thoughts due to attending (*manasikaroti*) to some feature (*nimitta*). The first three methods consist of applying attention to some other wholesome feature (*nimitta*), reflecting (*upaparikkhati*) on the drawbacks of unwholesome thoughts, and forgetting and not giving attention to these thoughts (*asatiamanasikāra*). If the first three methods fail to calm the mind, the meditator is told that he should apply attention to what is expressed in Pali as *vitakkānaṃ vitakkasaṅkhārasaṇṭhānaṃ*. This problematic phrase is translated by Ñāṇamoli and Bodhi (1995: 212) as "stilling the thought-formation of those thoughts".[6] By using this method, unwholesome thoughts are expected to be abandoned (*pahīyati*) by the meditator and subside (*abbhatthaṃ gacchati*). Subsequently, the mind stills (*santiṭṭhati*) and settles down (*sannisīdati*), becoming concentrated (*samādhiyati*). While the mechanism by which this method works is not explicitly explained in detail, an interesting simile is provided as its illustration. It presents a man who would be walking (*gacchati*) quickly but would then consider: "Why am I walking fast? What if I walk slowly?"[7] which would indeed cause him to reduce his pace. Analogous considerations are said to lead to sitting and eventually lying down. The general principle of the whole process would therefore be that "he would substitute for each grosser posture one that was subtler".[8]

It is difficult to understand what exactly is meant by this method. Much depends on the degree to which the simile is a direct portrayal of its mechanism. The simile might just be a general depiction of the slowing down of the thoughts. However, it might also imply a mechanism of gradually replacing grosser thoughts with subtler ones, which would be psychologically plausible. A more direct interpretation could be that the simile represents the meditative process, where the very awareness of one's gross mental activity causes it to subside, revealing a more

6 According to Rhys Davids and Stede (2007: 671) one of the meanings of *saṇṭhāna* is "resting place" while the root *thā* has connotations of standing. The noun *saṇṭhāna* seems to come from the verb *santiṭṭhati* which may mean "to stand", "stand still" or "be put into order" (Rhys Davids and Stede 2007: 676). Therefore, the translation given by Ñāṇamoli and Bodhi seems probable.

7 MN 20/i.120: *'kiṃ nu kho ahaṃ sīghaṃ gacchāmi? yaṃnūnāhaṃ saṇikaṃ gaccheyyan'ti.*

8 MN 20/i.120: *puriso oḷārikaṃ oḷārikaṃ iriyāpathaṃ abhinivajjetvā sukhumaṃ sukhumaṃ iriyāpathaṃ kappeyya*. Translation by Ñāṇamoli and Bodhi (1995: 212).

subtle one, which can then itself undergo an analogous procedure. The most direct reading would be that a meditator should actively reflect upon one's thoughts in a manner similar to the one in which a man in a simile reflects on his postures. In conclusion, we may say that it seems possible that the text conveys the notion that merely being aware of one's mental movement may lead to its gradual calming down, though whether it takes the form of passive and non-conceptual awareness or active, conceptual contemplation is unclear.

Meditative awareness of mental activity in the East Mountain teachings

The idea that the dynamic, non-conceptual awareness of thoughts may lead to the pacification of the mind was quite prominent among early Chan authors and is present in several texts from the Tang period. The earliest mentions of this method may be found in the *Rudao anxin yao fangbian famen* attributed to Daoxin. The text states that at the time of sitting in meditation, one should become aware (*jue* 覺) of how the consciousness-mind (*shixin* 識心) starts to move (*chudong* 初動). It is said to be always moving (*yunyun* 運運) and fluctuating (*liuzhu* 流注). One's attention should follow its coming and going (*suiqilaiqu* 隨其來去), making all these movements known to the meditator (*jielingzhizhi* 皆令知之).[9]

Afterwards, there follows the fragment we already mentioned in Chapter 4, which compares this awareness with the way grass and trees do not distinguish between objects.[10] Its usage in the context of awareness of thoughts seems to suggest that this method succeeds in producing an altered and non-conceptual mode of awareness.

The same text contains another fragment which appears to deal with this type of practice. It states that at the time when there arises (*qi* 起) mental awareness (*jue* 覺) of a different object (*yijing* 異境), then one should contemplate (*guan* 觀) the point of its arising (*qichu* 起處), and it is said that it ultimately does not-arise (*bijingbuqi* 畢竟不起). Afterwards, the text advises to constantly contemplate (*guan* 觀) one's

9 T85, no. 2837, p. 1287b10–12: 坐時當覺。識心初動。運運流注。隨其來去。皆令知之。Cf. translations of this fragment by Chappell (1983: 110) and Van Schaik (2018: 157).

10 T85, no. 2837, p. 1287b12–13: 猶如草木無所別知之無知。乃名一切智。 Cf. translations by Chappell (1983: 110) and Van Schaik (2018: 157).

own clinging to objects (*panyuan* 攀緣),[11] thinking and examination (in the sense of *vitarka* and *vicāra*: *jueguan* 覺觀), deluded consciousness (*wangshi* 妄識), mentation (*sixiang* 思想) and various thoughts (*zanian* 雜念). Then, the scattered mind (*luanxin* 亂心) will not be aroused/activated (*buqi* 不起) and one will attain a coarse stability (*cuzhu* 麁住). If one can attain stabilization of the mind, and there will be no further conditional mentation (*yuanlü* 緣慮), one will be able accordingly (*suifen* 隨分) to be serene and concentrated (*jiding* 寂定) and end all afflictions (*fannao* 煩惱), while not creating new ones. This is said to be called liberation (*jietuo* 解脫).[12] While the translation of some of the terms in this passage is not absolutely certain, the general idea is that the awareness of various mental phenomena will gradually lead to stillness of the mind.

A very interesting and detailed account of meditative awareness of thoughts is provided in the *Xiuxin yao lun* attributed to Hongren. We have already focused on some of its aspects, namely the insistence on a gentle (*huanhuan* 緩緩), non-forceful mode of practice. The text advises to tranquilly and attentively (*wenshou* 穩熟) view (*kan* 看) and see how mind-consciousness (*xinshi* 心識) is always flowing (*liudong* 流動) like flowing water (*shuiliu* 水流), or dazzling sunlight (*yangyan* 陽炎), which sparkles (*yeye* 曄曄) and does not stop (*buzhu* 不住). One gently and naturally (*huanhuanruru* 緩緩如如) views the consciousness tranquilly (*wen* 穩) and attentively (*shou* 熟) until its fluctuations (*fanfu* 返覆) dissolve (*rongxiao* 融消) into peaceful and deep stability (*xuningshenzhu* 虛凝湛住). Ultimately, consciousness (*shi* 識) will cease by itself (*zimie* 自滅) like a gust of wind (*saran* 颯然). After the cessation of consciousness and of the body,[13] the mind will be peaceful (*xuning* 虛凝), simple (*danbo* 淡泊) and clear (*jiaojie* 皎潔). At this point the author concludes that he cannot describe this state further, which implies its ineffability and apophatic nature.[14]

---

11 Chappell (1983: 118) translates *panyuan* 攀緣 as "clinging to objectified phenomena"; Van Schaik (2018: 177) as "how objects are apprehended".

12 T85, no. 2837, p. 1289a2–6: 若心緣異境。覺起時即觀起處。畢竟不起。此心緣生時。不從十方來。去亦無所至。常觀攀緣。覺觀妄識。思想雜念。亂心不起。即得麁住。若得住心。更無緣慮。即隨分寂定。亦得隨分息諸煩惱。畢故不造新名。為解脫看。Cf. translations of this fragment by Chappell (1983: 118), McRae (1986: 141) and Van Schaik (2018: 177).

13 Perhaps in the sense of its first-person awareness.

14 McRae (1986: 427/十三): 穩熟看，即及見此心識流動猶如水流陽炎，曄曄不住。既見此識時，唯是不內不外。緩緩如如穩看熟即返覆融消，虛凝

As was the case with the *Rudao anxin yao fangbian famen*, the *Xiuxin yao lun* also advocates the idea that awareness of mental activity will ultimately lead to its gentle pacification up to the point of cessation of consciousness itself. This cessation, however, does not entail falling into insentience. As we have already noted, the text implies that consciousness (*shi* 識) and the mind (*xin* 心) are not synonymous, as the former can cease, while the latter remains. It is also noteworthy that viewing of mental activity is done in a simple, non-conceptual way and does not involve an active practice of analytical insight.

The account contained in the *Xiuxin yao lun* is unique in Chan meditative literature due to its detailed and vivid descriptions which suggest that it is based on actual meditative experience. It can be considered a rare example of a first-person "what it is like" phenomenological account of a meditative experience. This is also true to a slightly lesser extent with regard to the abovementioned fragments of the *Rudao anxin yao fangbian famen*. In later Tang-era Chan literature, such descriptions disappear and are replaced by apophatic and paradoxical statements. What is also remarkable is that like the earlier *Erru sixing lun*, both texts do not rely to a considerable extent on traditional meditative Buddhist terminology regarding the names of meditative stages and factors. This last feature can be said to characterize the majority of Chan literature from the Tang and Song period. Its independence from standard meditative terminology and its classifications can be interpreted in various ways. One can, for example, claim that the early Chan literature represents oversimplification or even dumbing down of sophisticated and difficult traditional Buddhist meditative ideas simply for the purpose of making them more easily available for the masses. Such a hypothesis is presented by Sharf (2014b: 945) in his article *Mindfulness and mindlessness in early Chan*. However, one can also consider the possibility that with time the traditional paradigm of meditation has become too theoretical and schematic, less psychologically plausible and more difficult to implement into practice. Therefore, some Chan authors may have felt that their meditative experiences did not conform to that model and thus rejected it altogether.

A very basic account of what seems to be awareness of mental activity may be found in the *Wuxin lun*. The questioner asks how he should

---

湛住。其此流動之識，颯然自滅。滅此識者，乃是滅十地菩薩眾中障惑。此識身等滅已，其心即虛凝淡泊皎潔然。吾更不能說其形狀。Cf. T48, no. 2011, p. 379a8–14. For a translation of this passage, see McRae (1986: 130–31).

practise (*xiuxing* 修行) with regard to the volitional activity within his mind (*xinzhongzuo* 心中作). As a response, he hears that one should be aware (*shangjue* 上覺) in regard to all affairs (*yuyiqieshi* 於一切事).[15]

Meditative awareness of thoughts in later Chan texts

The practice of meditative awareness of thoughts has occupied a particularly prominent place in the texts connected with the schools of Chan tracing their lineage to Huineng. As Bielefeldt (1988: 93–95) has pointed out, similar accounts of this practice can be found in the texts of Shenhui, Zongmi and Changlu Zongze 長蘆宗賾 (d.12th c.). Their far-reaching similarity may suggest that the historically earliest account by Shenhui had been a source for the later texts of Zongmi, which in turn may have influenced Changlu Zongze. Zongmi considered himself to be Shenhui's successor within the Heze lineage, so it seems plausible that he would come under his direct influence. In turn, Zongmi's texts proved to be very influential with later Chan authors, so it is possible that they could influence Changlu Zongze. Due to a lack of any earlier sources describing this type of meditative awareness of thoughts, one can consider Shenhui to be the originator of this meditative idea.

Shenhui's texts contain several relatively similar accounts of this practice. In the passage of the *Putidamo nanzong ding shifei lun*, we read that if in the mind there is arousing/activation of thought (*nianqi* 念起), then immediately (*jibian* 即便) one should become aware of it (*juezhao* 覺照).[16] When the arousing/activation of the mind has ceased (*qixinjimie* 起心既滅), the awareness [of it] will be gone by itself (*ziwang* 自亡). This, according to Shenhui, is no-thought (*wunian* 無念).[17]

A slightly different account of the same practice is found in the *Tanyu*, where it is juxtaposed to classical forms of calm meditation. The fragment reads:

> Friends, when you correctly employ the mind, if any deluded [thought] occurs and you think about things either near or far, you

15 T85, no. 2831, p. 1269c16–18: 問曰。今於心中作若為修行　答曰。但於一切事上覺了。Cf. translation by App (1995: 99).

16 McRae (2023: 117, 166) translates *juezhao* 覺照 as "shines the light of awareness".

17 B25, no. 142, pp. 90a11–91a1: 諸善知識，若在學地者，心若有念起，即便覺照。起心既滅，覺照自亡，即是無念。Cf. translations by Bielefeldt (1988: 93), and McRae (2023: 117–18).

> should not try to constrain it. Why? Because, if the putting forth of a thought is a sickness, the constraint of it is also a sickness. If any deluded [thought] occurs (*wangqi* 妄起), be aware of it (*jue* 覺). When awareness and delusion have both disappeared, this is the nonabiding mind (*wuzhuxin* 無住心) of the original nature (*benxing* 本性).[18]

In the *Wenda zazheng yi*, Shenhui seems to be describing the same psychological mechanism: if there is awareness of deluded thoughts (*juewangnian* 覺妄念), [this] awareness will by itself completely cease (*zijumie* 自俱滅).[19]

In Zongmi's *Chanyuan zhuquanji duxu* we find a similar account of the same practice. When the thought arises/activates (*nianqi* 念起), one should be aware (*jue* 覺) of it. In turn, this awareness will cease to exist (*wu* 無). The text then states that the wonderful gate of practice lies precisely at this place. Like Shenhui, Zongmi labels this practice as no-thought (*wunian* 無念).[20]

Although Changlu Zongze lived during the Song period, his account of meditative awareness of thoughts contained in a section of the *Chanyuan qinggui* 禪苑清規 (*Pure Regulations of the Chan Preserve*) known as the *Zuochan yi* 坐禪儀 (*Principles of seated meditation*)[21] deserves a brief mention. The passage reads:

> Do not think of any good or evil whatsoever. Whenever a thought occurs (*nianqi* 念起), be aware of it (*jue* 覺); as soon as you are aware of it, it will vanish (*shi* 失). If you remain for a long period forgetful (*wang* 忘) of objects (*yuan* 緣), you will naturally become unified (*zichengyipian* 自成一片).[22]

Meditative awareness of thoughts has also featured prominently in the teachings of Heshang Moheyan. Of all the Chan authors, he presents the most detailed accounts of this form of meditation. Unfortunately, due to the absence of the original Chinese text we have to rely on Tibetan

---

18 B25, no. 142, p. 31a8–11: 知識，非用心時，若有妄起，思憶遠近，不須攝來。何以故？去心既是病，攝來還是病，去來皆是病。經云，諸法無來去。法性遍一切處，故法無去來。若有妄起，即覺。覺滅即是本性無住心。Translation by Bielefeldt (1988: 93). Cf. translation by McRae (2023: 69).

19 B25, no. 143, p. 236a11: 若覺妄念者，覺妄自俱滅。Cf. translation by McRae (2023: 160).

20 T48, no. 2015, p. 403a5–6: 念起即覺。覺之即無。修行妙門唯在此也。Cf. translations by Broughton (2009: 123) and Bielefeldt (1988: 95).

21 Translation of both titles follows Bielefeldt (1986: 131).

22 X63, no. 1245, p. 545a10–11: 一切善惡都莫思量。念起即覺。覺之即失。久久忘緣。自成一片。Translation by Bielefeldt (1988: 80).

translations of his teachings. The following fragments have been translated by Gómez in *The direct and the gradual approaches of Zen Master Mahāyāna: Fragments of the teachings of Mo-ho-yen*:

> When he enters a state of deep contemplation he looks into his own mind. There being no-mind he does not engage in thought. If thoughts of discrimination arise, he should become aware of them.
>
> How should one practice this awareness? Whatever thoughts arise, one does not examine [to see] whether they have arisen or not, whether they exist or not, whether they are good or bad, afflicted or purified. He does not examine any dharma whatsoever (trans. Gómez 1983: 108).
>
> If after becoming aware of the thoughts one examines and pursues this awareness one is still a common man (trans. Gómez 1983: 112).
>
> If after becoming aware of the arising of deluded thoughts, one no longer examines or pursues this awareness, and every instant of thought is free, this is the highest contemplation (trans. Gómez 1983: 113).

Moheyan also describes progress in this type of meditation:

> After sitting [in this manner] for a long time, the mind will become tame, and one will realize that his awareness is also discriminating mind. How does this occur? It is comparable to becoming blemished by bodily actions, it is only on account of the blemish that one knows that one is blemished. In the same way, one has an awareness due to the blemished of the arising of thoughts. It is on account of this [arising] that we know that we have an awareness (trans. Gómez 1983: 109).
>
> To abide in no-mind by giving up all states of contemplation is in fact the only means of entering the contemplation of the Great vehicle (trans. Gómez 1983: 110).

Let us emphasize that meditative awareness of thoughts as described in Chan texts neither fits the characteristics of classical calm meditation, nor those of classical insight. Unlike the former, it is not practised by one-pointed concentration or focus and does not involve any suppression of negative states. On the other hand, it does not involve active analysis through the application of traditional Buddhist theoretical categories, which is the hallmark of classical insight. Many of the attacks directed against this type of meditation were due to the difficulty of classifying it either as a form of calm or insight, which resulted in its severe misinterpretations. Kamalaśila considered Moheyan's method to be a form of calm meditation and accused him of neglecting insight, the essential feature of Buddhism. However, Moheyan's method has also received diametrically opposite assessments. Gómez (1987: 111) writes:

> [I]n Wang-hsi's 'Record of the Council' Mo-ho-yen is not accused of overemphasizing serenity. On the contrary, he is asked how it could be that his school is called the Ch'an (*dhyāna*) school when its primary emphasis is on insight (*prajñā*), not serenity!

Moheyan replied that although his method of meditation involved abstaining from reflection, it was nonetheless the perfection of *prajñā*. This shows that at least for Moheyan himself, the meditative awareness of thoughts did not fit into the rigid taxonomy connected with the traditional paradigm of Buddhist meditation.

As a summary, we can say that the notion of calming the mind through passive and non-conceptual awareness of mental states was a prominent feature of early Chan texts. The idea that meditative awareness of mental activities can contribute to their pacification and lead to the attainment of concentration was also present in some Nikāya texts, though it was formulated very differently in comparison to the Chan scriptures.

Is meditative awareness of mental states an actively implemented meditative method?

The very idea of calming the mind through being aware of thoughts raises some very interesting interpretative problems which are relevant for the topic of this book. In earlier chapters we noted that any form of meditation which requires an act of intention and active implementation of any method through mental effort is a subject of criticism which is very explicit in Chan texts and seems to be implied in certain Nikāya texts. This criticism is grounded in a specific philosophy, which sees conscious acts of intention (*zuoyi*) and arousal of the mind (*qixin*) as a disturbance of the mind's original, fundamental layer. Initially, meditative awareness of thoughts certainly appears to be an intentionally implemented technique. After all, one receives an instruction or learns of a method to be aware of the movement of thoughts, and afterwards implements it by simply trying to be aware of mental activities. All this implies making acts of intention (*zuoyi*), using the mind (*jiangxin*) to watch the mind (*shixin* or *kanxin*) and activating the mind (*qixin*), if we are to refer to some of the explicitly criticized features of meditation in Chan writings.

The criticism of this approach to meditation is particularly prominent in Shenhui's writings and yet at the same time he is one of the strongest advocates of meditative awareness of thoughts which he defines as no-thought (*wunian* 無念). We have also already mentioned the fragment of the *Rudao anxin yao fangbian famen* which rejects all possible forms of meditation including watching the mind (*kanxin* 看心) and contemplation (*guanxing* 觀行),[23] claiming that the true method cannot be practised (lit. cannot be intentionally made or done: *wuzuo* 無作).[24] However, another passage of the same text advocates a form of meditation which appears to be a form of observing or contemplating the mind. What are we to make of these seeming discrepancies? While in case of the *Rudao anxin yao fangbian famen*, one can at least suspect the presence of input from different authors, this is not the case with Shenhui's texts. Are some Chan texts internally inconsistent? Did the Chan authors become carried away with their own rhetoric without fully realizing its consequences? This important problem has not escaped the attention of scholars. Thus, Gómez (1987: 83) aptly notes that "the practice of retired contemplation, of observing the mind, is after all a form of 'activity'".

Hoyu Ishida's paper *The problem of practice in Shen-hui's teaching of Sudden Enlightenment* contains several interesting remarks regarding apparent discrepancies and paradoxes inherent in Shenhui's texts. Ishida (1996: 5) acknowledges the fact that "if we 'try' to become aware of our true nature (it seems one has to try at some point), this very attempt becomes the practice that Shen-hui rejects as preventing us from actually seeing our true nature". However, as Ishida (1996: 8) points out, this is exactly what Shenhui tells us to do. The following statement by Ishida (1996: 8–9) captures the nature of this paradox:

> But if Shen-hui's awareness is a practice, the essential problem is not resolved. "Trying to become aware" of one's afflicted mind inevitably becomes a human endeavor, something like concentration before realization, which is what Shen-hui argued prevents one from becoming aware. Without some kind of gradual practice as a means, there is no place for practicers (*sic*) to begin.

23 T85, no. 2837, p. 1287b18–20.

24 T85, no. 2837, p. 1289a26–28.

Interestingly, Shenhui explicitly considers these issues in his texts. In the *Tanyu*, he claims that one needs to rely (*jie* 藉) on intentionally done (*youzuo* 有作) morality (*jie* 戒) and wisdom (*hui* 慧), in order to manifest (*xian* 顯) their non-intentionally done (*wuzuo* 無作) forms. However, the development of *sāmadhi* does not follow this two-level pattern, as its intentional practice cannot be cultivated.[25] As we have seen, the key mechanism of Shenhui's practice of *wunian* was that of *juezhao* 覺照 – meditative awareness, or as McRae (2023: 117) literally renders it, "shining the light of awareness". In the *Wenda zazheng yi*, Shenhui claims that he only "provisionally teaches" (*jiashuo* 假說) *juezhao*, and that once it ceases (*jimie* 既滅), birth and death (*shengsi*) will automatically disappear.[26]

Furthermore, as I will attempt to show below, meditative awareness of thoughts need not be obligatorily conceptualized as involving deliberate effort or intention. Let us start by making a distinction between an act of doing and an act of seeing. Doing is usually active in nature and requires an act of will or an effort in order to initiate a particular activity and to maintain it. Seeing, however, does not necessarily need to be a result of an act of will or of an intention. Let us imagine a situation where we idly sit in some place close to a street without having anything to do and without making any act or decision. If our eyes are open, we will be aware of the passing cars, regardless of whether we want to or not, as this act of seeing is entirely passive. The same is the case with the meditators who sit down with their legs crossed and without the intent to practise any particular method. Thoughts will naturally come into their consciousness and they will not be able to not be aware of them even if they wish to. Therefore, it is not obligatory to actively follow any instruction in order to become aware of one's own thoughts. When no instruction regarding the method of meditation is given, as is the case with the majority of early Buddhist and Chan texts, then after sitting down in a quiet and secluded place, meditators will unavoidably be confronted with the few of their activities and sensations that remain. This will involve becoming aware of breathing and sensations from the body, but mostly thoughts. Awareness of thoughts

25 B25, no. 142, p. 11a9–11: 要藉有作戒，有作慧，顯無作〔戒，無作〕慧。定則不然。若修有作定，即是人天因果，不與無上菩提相應。Cf. translation by McRae (2023: 50).

26 B25, no. 143, p. 237a5: 假說覺照。覺照既滅，生滅自無，即不生滅。Translation follows McRae (2023: 161, n. 218), with slight amendments.

will therefore occur by itself even if no explicit instruction or a method of meditation is given. It is therefore possible to read accounts such as those by Shenhui not as normative prescriptions or instructions for practice, but rather as descriptions of a particular psychological mechanism which occurs on its own. From a philological point of view, such a reading is possible, particularly considering the imprecise nature of Chinese language.[27] Although one's first natural impulse could be to read these accounts as instructions urging one to adopt a certain way of being aware, they just as well may be read as neutral descriptions, e.g.: "If when being aware, thought arises in the mind, then it will be immediately reflected in awareness. The arisen mind will cease. Then this reflective awareness will be gone by itself. This is no-thought."[28]

One can at this point raise a criticism that adopting the attitude of a passive observer of one's own thoughts is not something that comes naturally as it requires assuming an entirely new special perspective of which ordinary people are unaware. This very possibility usually needs to be directly pointed out by someone else. Does it not therefore imply that it is an instruction which needs to be implemented, thus meeting the criteria of the criticized forms of meditation in Chan texts? However, there are also situations when after having something pointed out, it does not have to be volitionally implemented at all. Let us consider a hypothetical situation when someone points out to us that spots on the wall of a certain building form a pattern resembling a shape of an animal. Even though we were not aware of this before, from that moment on we will always see the pattern due to being primed for it, regardless of our intention to see it or not, and it will no longer be possible to unsee it. The same mechanism may occur in the case of meditative awareness of thoughts. Once the possibility of adopting the perspective of an observer of one's own thoughts has been pointed out, one will no longer need to consciously try to be aware of them. It will happen naturally whenever one remembers it. Thus, mindfulness of mental activities as described above need not be conceptualized as a distinct, deliberately implemented practice but rather as an almost automatic mechanism which will occur in anyone who is not actively doing anything else while being mindful at the time.

---

27 Such a descriptive reading is actually offered by McRae (2023: 69, 160, 166) as opposed to a prescriptive reading by Bielefeldt (1988: 93).

28 B25, no. 142, pp. 90a11–91a1: 若在學地者，心若有念起，即便覺照。起心既滅，覺照自亡，即是無念。

Another implication is that a lack of direct explicit references to such a form of practice need not necessarily be read as confirmation of its total absence. This particularly concerns the Nikāya texts, which as we have seen contain relatively few detailed direct accounts of what may be considered mindfulness of thoughts. Any account of meditative states containing references to qualities such as mindfulness, clear comprehension, equanimity and perhaps discrimination of *dhammas* (*dhammavicaya*) could then be interpreted as implying awareness of mental activities. If after sitting down, one is not aware of the arising of one's mental states, then one cannot be said to be mindful or clearly comprehending at all. According to the *Sati-sutta* (SN 47.35/v.180–181), a bhikkhu is clearly comprehending (*sampajāna*), when feelings (*vedanā*), thoughts (*vitakka*) and perceptions (*saññā*) are known to him (*vidita*), as they arise, persist and subside.[29]

By what mechanism does meditative awareness of mental states lead to their pacification?

However, this still leaves the question of the exact mechanism by which this form of meditation leads to the calming of thoughts and concentration of mind, as the answer is certainly not obvious. A point could be made that if one is merely passively watching and not actively stopping thoughts, then their usual movement will simply continue uninterrupted. The only difference compared to an ordinary state of mind will be that the practitioner will become aware of it. But such a practice would fail to meet the criteria of right meditation in the Nikāya and Chan texts since they speak of the need for reaching a state of concentration characterized by an absence of thoughts. However, most accounts that we have analysed do connect this practice with attaining altered states of consciousness. Only Shenhui's and Zongmi's accounts could potentially be interpreted as not implying any significant meditative progress compared to the starting point of the practice.

One could perhaps argue that once the original thought and its awareness vanish, the mind will simply continue to be assailed by further thoughts without any lessening of their intensity. This would mean that the no-thought (*wunian*) they speak about would just refer to a very short moment of the absence of thought occurring once the

29 Cf. translation by Bodhi (2000: 1657).

original thought and its awareness vanish. Immediately afterwards, however, consciousness would simply continue to be flooded by further thoughts without any lessening of their intensity. Such a view would be in line with Sharf's (2014b: 952) hypothesis that Chan masters such as Shenhui "may have tendered a simplified practice accessible to laypersons that would circumvent the need for extended monastic training, for attainment of trance states, and for scriptural study". It is certainly possible. However, from the fact that Shenhui and Zongmi do not explicitly describe any deeply altered mental states resulting from their meditative instructions, it does not automatically follow that they did not imply their occurrence.

As we shall see in the next chapter, from the perspective of the paradigm we are trying to reconstruct, there may have been sound practical and psychological reasons for keeping silent about such states. Nonetheless, with the exception of the accounts by these two Chan authors, the other descriptions of the practice link it with significant meditative progress and attainment of altered states of the mind. This should be enough to take seriously the psychological possibility of simple awareness of mental activities leading by itself to their tranquillization. This conclusion is also supported by the occurrence of such practices in other contexts, both Buddhist and non-Buddhist. In the Indo-Tibetan Buddhist tradition, such practices are known as settling the mind into its original state. During such practice, one lets the mind remain at ease and "watches all manner of mental events arise and pass of their own accord, without intervention of any kind" (Wallace, 1999: 184). Similar practices are known in the Himalayan yoga tradition as evidenced by the following account by Swami Rama (Rama 2004: 101–102):

> During this exercise one makes an effort to consciously cut off each thought at the very moment of its appearance in the mind. One should keep a steady watch for each new thought as it is forming and stop it there. This will be quite difficult for the mind in the beginning. If the mind cannot be controlled, it should be allowed to flow. One relaxes completely and observes the mind's fantasies, its digressions, and its roaming here and there. As one's practice improves, the stream of ideas, rather than being cut short, will seem to arise even more rapidly. This is an indication that the practitioner is making significant progress and that his mind is becoming clearer and his observation sharper. This is the actual state of the mind's normal operation, but previously it had not been observed. A state of tranquility is reached when the thoughts seem to arise so fast that they are without

> number – the attempt to hinder thinking seems to have created more thoughts and more thinking. From this point on one should only act as an observer, letting the mind follow its own course. In this manner it will slow down on its own, and each mental process or operation can be inspected carefully and minutely. The ultimate result will be that the entire movement of the mind is brought under control. The mind may actually suspend itself for a moment. This moment of positive suspension in the mental processes is sufficient to make the aspirant realize his real self.

We have quoted this lengthy account in its entirety, as it is relevant to the issue we are considering. In some respects, it is more detailed than the Buddhist accounts we have been analysing, and it seems to be based on experience. Of course, Swami Rama describes the end result of this practice in accordance with the tenets of the philosophy and religion that he follows, but this is just an interpretation of what otherwise almost completely agrees with the Buddhist accounts. Most importantly, it supports the view that meditative awareness of mental activities can indeed lead to their pacification.

However, if this is the case, then this must occur through some psychological mechanism which is not obvious by itself. Therefore, we need to try to explain it. As we have already noted, the form of meditative awareness of mental activity that we are considering here fits neither the characteristics of the classical form of calm meditation nor those of insight.[30] In the case of traditional forms of calm, it is relatively easy to understand the mechanism by which they lead to the calming of thoughts as one's entire consciousness becomes occupied with a meditative object while all one's mental activity consists of one-pointedly concentrating on it. This simply leaves no place for awareness of any other mental phenomena or of any other mental activity, and by extension, thoughts cannot arise and intrude as they are pushed out. But this is not the case with meditative awareness of thoughts, as one is merely passively aware of one's own mental activities and they are not blocked or forcefully suppressed in any way. This raises the question of the possibility of some other psychological mechanism through which being aware of thoughts leads to their pacification.

In normal situations, thoughts arise unimpeded. We have already discussed the results of recent research from cognitive science which

30 However, the Indo-Tibetan Buddhist tradition classifies it as calm, simply due to its end result (Wallace 1999: 184). This was also evidenced by Kamalaśīla's criticism of Moheyan's method.

suggest that during mind-wandering we engage in imaginary dialogues or entertain various plans or possible future courses of action. Such thoughts are not entirely random, but have their own internal order, where one thought follows another because it is logically connected to it. The other form of mind-wandering has a more chaotic structure, where a certain experience stimulates a particular memory trace, causing the arising of thought associated with it. This thought usually gives rise to a whole series of additional thoughts through loose memory associations.

In order to explain how awareness of thoughts can stop this process, we must understand exactly what happens when one becomes aware of having a thought. Awareness of having a thought at a particular moment is in itself a form of mental phenomenon; it is a type of subtle thought. It is not necessarily a thought of verbal character, as it is not constituted by an act of silently telling oneself in one's mind: "I am just having a thought". It is a subtler form of awareness, but nonetheless a thought in the sense that it is a mental phenomenon of which we can become aware, it occurs at a particular moment in time and has its own content. It would then seem that when we become aware of a thought there are two thoughts at the same time: the original thought and its subtle awareness, or meta-thought. This seems to be in harmony with the assumption that awareness of thought is immediate and does not involve any delay. It appears to be a pretty common, intuitive view.

In the philosophy of mind, this view can be considered as a form of what is called the transparency thesis, the idea that the mind has transparent and immediate access to its own states or that the mental states are self-presenting (Siderits 2020). The latter view is also known as a reflexivity thesis: a notion that conscious cognition of an object or mental state is reflexively self-aware or self-intimating (Coseru 2020). The issue of self-reflexivity was a controversial topic and a subject of an important debate within Buddhist philosophy, with interesting arguments raised both by the proponents of the notion of self-reflexivity and by their opponents who were supporting the so-called opacity thesis, i.e., a view that mental states are not self-transparent but opaque. While the supporters of the former view used an example of a lamp which illuminates itself, the arguments in favour of the latter theory referred to the examples of a knife not being able to cut itself or of a fingertip being unable to point at itself (Funayama 2020).

In Chapters 3 and 4, we also considered some theories in the modern philosophy of mind which suggest that conscious introspection or metacognition (i.e., cognition of one's own mental states) does not have the privileged access to mental states that it was generally thought it did. It always involves a temporal delay, therefore when we are aware of something, the object of that awareness already belongs to the past. We have also considered Blackmore's (2017) highly counterintuitive view that most of the time we have no way of knowing what our conscious state is, and the very act of introspecting by asking the question "what am I conscious of now" carries with it a powerful distortion.

All this has significant implications for understanding the mechanism of meditative awareness of mental activities as according to the latter view, it should be impossible to become aware of a thought at the exact moment of its occurrence.

It is interesting to consider which of the competing philosophical views regarding access to one's own mental states is implied in the notion of meditative awareness of thoughts. Some interesting reflections on this issue are contained in the *Daofan qusheng xinjue* 道凡趣聖心決 (*Maxims for Leading Commoners to Sagehood*),[31] a unique but relatively obscure Dunhuang scripture connected with the Northern school. The text contains a statement that two minds cannot co-exist (*liangxinbubing* 兩心不並). At the time (*shi* 時) when one becomes aware (*jue* 覺) of the generation of [a certain state of] mind (*xinsheng* 心生), one is not aware (*bujue* 不覺) that [this state of] mind has already ceased (*xinyimie* 心已滅).[32] This statement could be interpreted as representing a strong stance against the self-reflexivity or transparency view.[33] This is reinforced by a later passage, which contains reference to the famous examples of a knife not being able to cut itself (*daobuzige* 刀不

31 Translation of the title follows Greene (2017).

32 Yamabe 2014: 280: 又來兩心不並. 覺心生時, 不覺心已滅. Cf. translations by McRae (1986: 216) and Yamabe (2014: 282).

33 It needs to be emphasized that it is very difficult to reach certainty regarding the intended meaning of some parts of this text, as they are not clear and are open to various interpretations. The reading of *jue* 覺 as "being aware" or "realizing" follows McRae's (1986) translation. Yamabe (2014) translates *juexin* 覺心 as "mind of enlightenment" which completely changes the meaning of the fragment, making it irrelevant for our investigation. In several aforementioned passages of Chan texts describing meditative awareness of thoughts, *jue* was used to express the notion of "becoming aware". Such was also the case with Shenhui's texts which were created in a relatively similar period to the *Daofan qusheng xinjue*. This may be an argument in favour of reading *juexin* as "awareness of mind" and not as "mind of enlightenment". See McRae (2023: 133, n. 24 and 160, n. 215) for a discussion of two different meanings of *bujue* 不覺 in Shenhui's texts: as "non-enlightenment" and "do not cognize".

自割) and a finger being unable to point at itself (*zhibuzizhi* 指不自指) which were used by the opponents of the self-reflexivity thesis.

The abovementioned fragment is significant in that it seems to convey a subtle psychological paradox which is extremely relevant to the problem we are dealing with. It implies that if one becomes aware of one's own state of mind or of a thought, it does not mean that one is aware of it exactly in the moment of its actual occurrence. That is because this awareness itself is a subtle state of mind or a meta-thought which has replaced the original thought of which it is aware. This logically follows from the thesis that the two states of mind cannot coexist. The original state of mind which has become the subject of awareness has at this point already passed and does not constitute the present state of mind as it has been replaced by another, subtler meta-state. The original state of mind or thought is now the content of the meta-state, or in other words the meta-state carries with it an awareness of the already passed state of mind.

This is quite significant for understanding how awareness of mental activities may lead to their pacification. Had the original thought not become the subject of awareness, it would have given rise to a whole cascade of new thoughts through the mechanism of loose memory associations, which is what happens in ordinary situations. But if the original thought has become replaced by the subtler meta-thought, then the original chain of thoughts gets broken up at this point. That is because this subtle meta-awareness of the original thought is in itself a thought, and due to the fact that two thoughts cannot coexist it cuts off the original thought which also prevents further, associated thoughts from arising. Thus, the chain of thoughts is stopped and cannot resume.

This interpretation harmonizes with the accounts of the meditative awareness of thoughts we have been considering. As we have noted, Shenhui and Zongmi have emphasized that the awareness of the original thought will disappear by itself (*zimie*), leaving one in a state of no-thought. In light of these considerations, the simile of watching passing cars to which we have referred in order to explain the passive nature of awareness of thoughts is truthful only to a certain degree. For it turns out that one cannot actually be mindful of thoughts in the way that one observes external moving objects; becoming aware of them exactly when they pass into the field of view, remain in it for a while and then disappear. It seems that one cannot self-reflectively become aware of having a thought at the very time of its presence. In this interpretation, the awareness of having a thought would in fact be merely a post-hoc mental reconstruction based on memory.

So far, we have been considering the mechanism by which awareness of mental states can lead to their cessation. It is also interesting to consider the mechanism of the very act of becoming aware of a thought from the perspective of cognitive science. Who is it that actually monitors the contents of consciousness and becomes aware? The commonsense answer would be that it is consciousness or the conscious self which becomes aware of thought, and that in fact "we" are that consciousness. However, in light of the developments we have discussed in Chapters 2 and 3, such a view must be considered naive and inadequate. According to these developments, phenomenal consciousness is considered to be entirely passive and all of its contents are resultant of the activity of various, often competing unconscious modules. Baars et al. (2021) postulate the existence of "unconscious onlooking systems viewing the conscious flow in the global workspace" and of "UN-conscious metacognition, where UN-conscious specialized processors monitor the conscious global workspace to interrupt the conscious flow, or otherwise intervene if the UN-conscious 'critic' detects a serious problem". Awareness of thoughts can certainly be considered a form of metacognition, as it is a form of cognition aimed at other mental states. If we look at awareness of thoughts in light of the above-mentioned theory, then this implies that during the practice, one of the unconscious modules monitors the content of consciousness. When it "detects a serious problem" which in this case is the presence of a thought, it proceeds to "interrupt the conscious flow" by producing a thought carrying the awareness of the previous thought, thus breaking up the stream of associations, which cannot be resumed afterwards.

Of course, as long as the potential sources of thinking are active, new thoughts will be produced and sent to consciousness with the potential to start a new chain. In such a case, mindfulness of thoughts would have very limited efficacy as, similarly to the Lernaean Hydra, in place of every chain of thoughts, a new one would emerge. Therefore, from the perspective of an ordinary, modern-day meditator it would be a highly inefficient practice that would fail to produce a prolonged altered state of consciousness. And this seems to be the case as evidenced by the relatively little popularity of such a practice amongst modern practitioners, especially in comparison with methods such as concentration on breathing or mantra meditation. However, the situation could look diametrically different for someone who would lead a radically transformed Buddhist life as described in a previous chapter. As we have suggested, such a person would cut off most of the roots of potential thinking. What would remain would be relatively few thoughts, such as those connected with the dhamma as described in the *Paṃsudhovaka-sutta.* Meditative awareness of mental activities as described in this chapter could potentially deal with these remaining thoughts, resulting in a deeply altered thought-less state. What is important is that such awareness meets the criteria of the right meditative state in both Nikāya and Chan texts, since it does not involve "being held down by the restraint of *saṅkhāras*", mental effort, arousal of the mind (*qixin*), acts of intention (*zuoyi*) or directing of the mind. Therefore, by extension, it does not obscure the natural potential of the mind, with its inherent capabilities for concentration and insight.

Chapter 8

BEYOND METHOD

The search and its cessation

In the previous chapters I often referred to the classification of thoughts contained in the *Paṃsudhovaka-sutta*. While I considered the possibility that the dhamma-thoughts (*dhammavitakka*) spoken about in the text are the remains of the wholesome thoughts that were actively generated through the practice of right effort, I also hinted at the possibility of different interpretations.

Both the metaphor of purifying gold and the idea of the hierarchy of defilements contained in the *Paṃsudhovaka-sutta* have almost direct parallels in Shenhui's texts. In the *Tanyu*, he distinguishes between the two forms of delusions of the mind (*wangxin* 妄心): coarse ones (*cuwang* 麁妄) and subtle ones (*xiwang* 細妄).[1] The former are constituted by craving (*tanai* 貪愛) for wealth, sensuality (*caise* 財色) with males and females, and gardens and residences. However, subtle delusions (*xiwang* 細妄) are produced by activating/arousing the mind (*qixin*) and grasping (*qu* 取) directed at awakening (*puti* 菩提), nirvana (*niepan* 涅槃), emptiness (*kong* 空), purity (*jing* 淨) and concentration (*ding* 定). As Shenhui puts it, "one hears about concentration, and arouses the mind and grasps concentration". However, all that one gets are merely "fetters of the dharma" (*fafu* 法縛) and views about the dharma (*fajian* 法見).

Shenhui's statement seems to touch upon a very important practical and psychological aspect of meditation. As long as one is vitally

1 B25, no. 142, p. 16a4–8: 知識諦聽，為說妄心。何者是妄心？仁者等今既來此間，貪愛財色男女等，及念園林屋宅，此是「麁妄」，應無此心。為有「細妄」，仁者不知。何者是「細妄」？心聞說菩提，起心取菩提。聞說涅槃，起心取涅槃。聞說空，起心取空。聞說淨，起心取淨。聞說定，起心取定。此皆是妄心，亦是法縛，亦是法見。For translations and discussions of this fragment, see Gómez (1987: 78–79) and McRae (2023: 54).

interested in the success of one's practice and becoming awakened or enlightened, it will be a source of an arousal of the mind: either in the form of efforts to concentrate and be aware, or in the form of constant self-evaluation of one's meditative progress. In this way, instead of pacifying the mind, one is only generating additional mental movement. This is especially problematic in the models which do not assume the possibility of actively suppressing the movement of thoughts by means of concentration-induced absorption.

Chan texts often refer to this fundamental psychological mechanism as seeking or searching (*qiu* 求). The negative evaluation of seeking is already present in Bodhidharma's *Erru sixing lun*, since one of the four practices is labelled as "seeking nothing" (*wusuoqiuxing* 無所求行). The concept becomes very prominent in the "subitist" schools of Chan tracing their lineage to Huineng. In the *Tanyu*, Shenhui describes arousing of the mind to "seek outside" (*waiqiu* 外求) as the devious search (*xieqiu* 邪求).[2]

As Poceski rightly points out, the awareness of "seeking" as a fundamental psychological mechanism that prevents one from finding oneself in an enlightened state was particularly strong in the texts of the Hongzhou school.[3] In the *Chuanxin fa yao*, Huangbo states that "sentient beings are attached to the characteristics (*zhuoxiang* 著相) and seek outside themselves (*waiqiu* 外求), but seeking it, they lose it (*shi* 失) even more".[4] In another fragment of the same text, he mentions "trainees these days" (*jinxuedaoren* 今學道人), who due to being unenlightened to the essence of the mind, generate mind on top of mind (*xinshangshengxin* 心上生心), seeking the Buddha (*qiufo* 求佛) outwardly.[5]

"Generating mind on top of mind" certainly refers to the process of arousal or activation (*qi* 起) leading to the arising of conscious thinking

2 B25, no. 142, p. 27a6: 起心外求者，即名邪求。Cf. translation by McRae (2023: 64), who renders 邪求 as "false seeking".

3 Poceski (2015b: 205) writes: "The view that the true Chan adept should not seeking (*sic*) anything, even the highest truth, is often expressed in the records of Mazu and other monks associated with the Hongzhou school. That is not, however, a uniquely Chan notion, as similar ideas can also be found in canonical literature, albeit presented in a somewhat different form. The basic idea is that all forms of seeking, including those that are subtle or spiritually inflected, presuppose some form of attachment".

4 T48, no. 2012A, p. 379c24: 但是眾生著相外求。求之轉失。Translation by McRae (2005: 13).

5 T48, no. 2012A, p. 380a14–15: 即心是佛。如今學道人。不悟此心體。便於心上生心。向外求佛。著相修行。For translation, see McRae (2005: 14).

and acts of will in addition to the basic, original layer of the mind. By trying to concentrate, attain purity or attain awakening, not only does one not pacify the already existing thoughts, but creates more of them. Paraphrasing the *Weimojie suo shuo jing* 維摩詰所說經 (*Vimalakīrti Sctipture*)[6] Mazu states in the *Zongjing lu* that those who seek the truth (lit. dharma: *fa* 法) should not seek anything (*yingwusuoqiu* 應無所求).[7] The *Baizhang Huaihai chanshi guanglu* contains a particularly interesting fragment, displaying deep awareness of fundamental paradoxes inherent to the process of seeking enlightenment. The fragment reads:

> The Buddha is a person who has nothing to seek. If there is seeking, then one is contradicting the principle (*liguai* 理乖). The principle is the principle of non-seeking; if one seeks it, one misses it. If one attaches to non-seeking (*zhuowuqiu* 著無求), then that becomes same as seeking; if one attaches to the unconditioned (*wuwei* 無為), then it becomes the conditioned (*youwei* 有為) again.[8]

In the *Tanyu*, graspings at various positive goals of the Buddhist path are said to be the most subtle delusions of the mind. As we have briefly noted, the structure of the passage in question parallels to a certain extent that of the *Paṃsudhovaka-sutta*. Could it therefore be that the dhamma-thoughts constituting the subtlest meditative obstacle in the Nikāya texts would be connected to a psychological mechanism similar to the one postulated in the Chan texts under the label of seeking?

Interestingly, the concept of seeking or searching (*esanā*) is explicitly present in the Nikāyas, though it does not have the prominence it possesses in Chan texts. It has also hardly drawn any attention from both the later commentators and modern scholars. The term *esanā* is encountered as part of a stock formula of the three searches which consists of the search for sensual pleasure (*kāmesanā*), the search for existence (*bhavesanā*) and the search for a holy life (*brahmacariyesanā*). For example, the *Esanā-sutta* (SN 45.161/v 54–55) states that the noble eightfold path is to be developed for the purpose of direct knowledge

---

6 Poceski (2015b: 205) writes: "The first sentence is a paraphrase of a sentence that appears in the Vimalakīrti Sctipture (*Weimojie suo shuo jing* 維摩詰所說經). In the scripture the sentence reads: 'If you seek the truth, in regard to all things you should not seek anything'. Similar statements also appear in other canonical sources."

7 T48, no. 2016, p. 418c6: 夫求法者。應無所求。Translation by Poceski (2015b: 205).

8 X69, no. 1323, p. 8a15–17: 佛是無求人求之理乖。理是無求理求之即失。若著無求復同於有求。若著無為復同於有為。Trans. Cheng Chien (1993: 104).

(*abhiññā*), full understanding (*pariññā*), utter destruction (*parikkhaya*) and abandoning (*pahāna*) of all the three searches.

The same pattern occurs in other texts of the *Saṃyutta Nikāya*, with the only difference being that the formula of the eightfold path is replaced by those of the seven factors of awakening (SN 46.111/v.136), the four establishments of mindfulness (SN 47.85/v.191) the four right strivings (SN 49.35/v.247) and other formulas constituting alternative but complementary conceptualizations of the positive elements of the Buddhist path to awakening. It is noteworthy that in this pattern, the three searches occupy a place that is usually reserved for unequivocally negative elements such as the influxes (*āsava*), floods (*ogha*) or fetters (*saṃyojana*). While such negative evaluation makes obvious sense regarding the first two of the searches, it is somewhat problematic regarding the third, i.e., the search for a holy life. After all, what could be wrong in searching for *brahmacariya*, as the latter is positively evaluated in the Nikāyas? The commentary to the *Saṃyutta Nikāya*, the *Sāratthapakāsinī*, seems to be puzzled by this feature and attempts to explain it away by stating that *brahmacariyesanā* is the search for a holy life consisting in a wrong view (*micchādiṭṭhi*).[9] However, nothing in the Nikāyas implies such a meaning.

One could consider an interpretation that the search for the holy life would be abandoned upon entering a Buddhist path, since this would be tantamount to the search discovering its goal and losing its purpose, as the practitioner would now know what the holy life is and would not need to search for it anymore. However, this is not the meaning implied by the formula as it clearly states that one must fully develop the Buddhist path (conceptualized in various ways) in order for the search for the holy life to be abandoned. Therefore, this implies that as long as the final awakening has not been reached, the search for the holy life continues, despite the practitioner being firmly on the Buddhist path. Another interpretation would be that when one reaches liberation, the search for holy life automatically loses its purpose, because it has succeeded. However, it seems peculiar that seeking understood in such a way would need to be emphasized or even articulated at all, as in this way one is merely stating the obvious. There are also several other Nikāya texts which contain a negative evaluation of searching. For example, the *Paṭhamāriyāvāsa-sutta* (AN 10.19/v.29) describes

9 Spk iii.174/iii.136: *brahmacariyesanāti micchādiṭṭhisaṅkhātassa brahmacariyassa esanā*. Also cf. Bodhi (2000: 1898).

the so-called ten abodes or dwellings of the noble ones (*ariyāvāsa*), the sixth of which is constituted by having totally renounced searching (*samavayasaṭṭhesana*).[10] The same description is present in the *Patilīna-sutta* (AN 4.38/ii.40–42) where it is said to be one of the characteristics of one who is drawn back[11] or withdrawn (*patilīna*). In both texts, renouncement of searching is accompanied by being in a state of tranquillization of bodily *saṅkhāra* (*passaddhakāyasaṅkhāra*), which is further defined as occurring in the fourth *jhāna*.

An unequivocally negative evaluation of all three searches is contained in the two *Esanā-sutta*s in the *Itivuttaka* (Iti 54–55/47–49). According to the first sutta, with the exhaustion (*khaya*) of the searches, a bhikkhu is satiated (*nicchāta*) and fully extinguished (*parinibbuta*). The second one states that with the destruction of the searches, the bhikkhu is said to be desireless or not longing for anything (*nirāsa*) and not confused (*akathaṃkathī*). According to what may be called the extended formula of dependent co-arising in the *Mahānidāna-sutta* (DN 15/ii.58), "acquisition is based on searching" (*pariyesanaṃ paṭicca lābho*) while the latter is based on craving (*taṇhā*). To sum things up, the contexts in which the term *esanā* occurs in the Nikāyas clearly point to its mostly negative role.[12]

Therefore, the most straightforward interpretation of the notions of the search for a holy life or of search in general would be that these terms refer to some sort of imperfection or an impediment on the path to awakening, even if only a very subtle one, which must be abandoned. Perhaps then, it referred to a similar psychological mechanism as the term *qiu* 求 in Chan texts? It might also be the case that the notion of dhamma-thoughts in the *Paṃsudhovaka-sutta* was meant to convey such meaning. Due to the concept of *esanā* not being presented with enough detail in the Nikāyas, we can only tentatively consider such a possibility.

Paradoxical aspects of meditation

Regardless of the intended meaning of the concept of *esanā*, the very idea that the desire to attain enlightenment or a thought-less state of

10 Translation of the term follows Bodhi (2012: 1359).

11 Translation of the term follows Bodhi (2012: 428).

12 One notable exception could be the concept of the noble search (*ariyapariyesanā*) as presented in the context of the *Pariyesanā-sutta* (AN 4.255/ii.247–248).

consciousness may at some stage of practice actually prove a hindrance seems to be plausible from a psychological point of view. This is particularly relevant in case of the paradigm of meditation present in early Chan and Nikāya texts, as it implies a passive nature of meditation and does not involve active suppression of negative factors. Therefore, the very presence of a strong desire for meditative success will lead to constant generation of thoughts connected with evaluation of one's meditative progress which cannot be suppressed in any way. For example, instead of simply being aware of the absence of thoughts, one may start thinking thoughts expressing satisfaction due to a temporary absence of thoughts at a given point. However, the very presence of such thoughts may in turn induce further thoughts of disappointment and self-criticism, since after all the goal of the practice was to stop thinking! Next, one may start thinking thoughts about practising better from that point on, and trying to be more mindful, but this again defeats the very purpose of the practice which is not to think thoughts.

However, even if one comes to understand this and makes a conscious decision to abandon that desire, one will still be in a similar trap. Deciding to abandon desire for meditative success because it prevents meditative success means that deep down one still desires meditative accomplishment. The very decision, volition and effort connected with an act of abandoning means that one will just be adding a new desire and a new effort on top of the old one. This in turn will just become a source of new thoughts connected with assessing whether the said desire has already disappeared or not.

This paradox is brilliantly acknowledged by Shenhui in the *Tanyu*. He claims that if one intentionally makes (*zuo* 作) the mind to not arise/activate (*xinbuqi* 心不起), then this is merely a "concentration of consciousness" (*shiding* 識定).[13] As long as the deeply rooted tendency to search for enlightenment or meditative success is still present, it will be a source of the movement of mind, which cannot be suppressed by the passive forms of meditation we are considering. As discussed in the previous chapter, by becoming aware of these thoughts one can probably temporarily break up their vicious cycle but as long as the tendency to search is present, this cycle will be restarted.

It therefore seems that at a certain level of progress both the active effort and desire for meditative success as well as a deliberate decision

13 B25, no. 142, p. 29a1: 若作心不起，是識定，亦名法見心自性定。Cf. translation by McRae (2023: 65).

to renounce it are equally hindering any actual breakthrough from happening. Perhaps it is this meditative paradox that is alluded to in the opening text of the *Saṃyutta Nikāya*, the *Oghataraṇa-sutta* (SN 1.1/i.1). In this short text, the Buddha is asked about the method that he used to cross (*tarati*) the torrent (*ogha*), and thus attain awakening since the latter is often symbolized by reaching the far shore. In response, the Buddha states that he was paradoxically able to cross the torrent without standing still (*appatiṭṭha*) but also without pushing forward (*anāyūha*).[14] He explains it further by saying that when he was standing, he drowned and that when he was pushing forward, he was carried by the waves (*nibbuyhati*). A similar interpretation may be attempted with respect to the passage in the *Ānanda-sutta* (AN 9.37/iv.426–428) which describes a state of concentration (*sāmadhi*) said to have final knowledge as its fruit (*aññāphala*).[15] This concentration is described as "neither leaning forward nor bent back" (*na cābhinato na cāpanato*). Interestingly, this *sāmadhi* is described as "not held down by restraint of *saṅkhāra*" (*na ca sasaṅkhāraniggayhavāritagato*), which is exactly the same epithet used with respect to the final stage of meditation in the *Paṃsudhovaka-sutta*. Like with many other enigmatic Nikāya fragments we cannot reach absolute certainty regarding the intended meaning of the passages in the *Oghataraṇa* and the *Ānanda-suttas*. However, their message makes relatively little sense in the context of the mainstream meditative model which hardly takes into account any paradoxical aspects of meditation and conceptualizes meditative progress in a relatively straightforward fashion.

Letting it be

A somewhat similar paradoxical message is contained in the already mentioned fragment of the *Rudao anxin yao fangbian famen* which denies all conceivable forms of meditation, including the most basic notions

14 SN 1.1/i.1: *'kathaṃ nu tvaṃ, mārisa, oghamatarī'ti? 'Appatiṭṭhaṃ khvāhaṃ, āvuso, anāyūhaṃ oghamatarin'ti. 'Yathākathaṃ pana tvaṃ, mārisa, appatiṭṭhaṃ anāyūhaṃ oghamatarī'ti? 'Yadāsvāhaṃ, āvuso, santiṭṭhāmi tadāssu saṃsīdāmi; yadāsvāhaṃ, āvuso, āyūhāmi tadāssu nibbuyhāmi. Evaṃ khvāhaṃ, āvuso, appatiṭṭhaṃ anāyūhaṃ oghamatarin'ti.* Cf. translation by Bodhi (2000: 89–90).

15 See Bodhi (2012: 1302) for a translation and Bodhi (2012: 1829, n. 1931) for a discussion of why *aññāphala* should be seen as a *bahubbīhi* compound and not a *tappurisa*. In the latter case, a translation of *aññāphala* would be "fruit of a final knowledge".

of making go (or causing to go: *lingqu* 令去) and making stay (*lingzhu* 令住).[16] Directly preceding this fragment, however, is a very important formulation which we have not yet given our full attention. It reads *zhirenyun* 直任運,[17] which McRae (1986: 143) translated as "just let it flow", while Van Schaik (2018: 158) as "just let it be", and Chappell (1983: 111) as "identification with the natural rhythms of things". Amongst the meanings given in the dictionaries for *renyun* 任運, one can find "naturally", "effortlessly", "that which is arisen spontaneously, and is not directly initiated 作 by one's present discrimination or volition"[18] or "to accomplish something by letting it occur naturally".[19] This meaning would coincide with the vision of Chan meditation we have been reconstructing so far. The term *renyun* also appears in another fragment of the *Rudao anxin yao fangbian famen*, where in response to a question about the method of contemplation (*guanxing* 觀行) Daoxin answers by stating that "the only thing you need to do is let it be" (*zhixurenyun* 直須任運).[20]

The term can also be found in other Chan texts. The *Dasheng kaixin xianxing dunwu zhenzong lun* contains a line: *renyunsanmei wendaoyude* 任運三昧溫道育德, which McRae translates as "consign yourself freely to *samādhi*, [so that you may] incubate the way (*dao* 道) and nurture virtue (*de* 德)".[21] *Renyun* can also be found in the fragment of the *Tiansheng guangdeng lu* attributed to Mazu, which reads 任運過時更有何事 *renyun guoshi geng you heshi*,[22] which Poceski (2015b: 207) translates as "allow things to follow their natural course. What else is there to do?".

In the *Chuanxin fa yao*, Huangbo identifies the state of being liberated with "sitting peacefully upright" (*anranduanzuo* 安然端坐), "letting

16 Van Schaik (2018: 158) translates it as "Don't try to get rid of it, Don't try to make it stay"; Chappell (1983: 110) as "Don't force anything to go. Don't force anything to stay".

17 T85, no. 2837, p. 1287b18–20: 信曰。亦不念佛。亦不捉心。亦不看心。亦不計心。亦不思惟。亦不觀行。亦不散亂。直任運。亦不令去。亦不令住。

18 Digital Dictionary of Buddhism, Copyright © 2010 Charles Muller, http://www.buddhism-dict.net/ddb/pcache/4eid(b4efb-904b).html.

19 NTI Reader, Copyright Fo Guang Shan 佛光山 2013–2019, https://ntireader.org/words/8002281.html.

20 T85, no. 2837, p. 1287c7–8: 問。臨時作若為觀行。信曰。直須任運。Translation by Van Schaik (2018: 159).

21 T85, no. 2835, p. 1278a22: 任運三昧溫道育德。Translation by McRae (2023: 20). Also cf. McRae (1987: 241).

22 X78, no. 1553, p. 448c17–18: 任運過時。更有何事。

things happen as they will" (*renyun*) and not restraining (*buju* 不拘).[23] This term also appears in Zongmi's account of the practices and views of the Hongzhou school found in his *Yuanjuejing dashu shiyi chao*. Broughton (2009: 185) translates the relevant fragment as:

> When you neither cut off (*buduan* 不斷) nor create (*buzao* 不造), but just give free rein to luck (*renyun* 任運) and exist in freedom (*zizai* 自在), then you are to be called a liberated person (*jietuo ren* 解脫人). You are also to be called a person who surpasses the measure (*guoliang ren* 過量人).[24]

While describing the views of the Hongzhou school, Zongmi also uses the term *renxin* 任心,[25] which Broughton (2009: 185) translates as "giving free rein to mind".

Due to its great significance, the term *renyun* deserves a more thorough analysis. To what psychological mechanism does it actually refer? In the earlier part of the book we analysed several fragments emphasizing the need for relaxation or "letting go" (*fang* 放) of the body during meditation. It seems, however, that the term *renyun* refers to a much more fundamental attitude and not merely to a form of bodily self-relaxation. Looking at it from an etymological perspective, *ren* 任 in this context can have the meaning of "letting", "allowing" or "giving free rein to". *Yun* 運, besides its most obvious connotations to motion and movement, can be rendered as "fate" or "luck". Therefore, *renyun* may also be translated as "giving free rein to fate", "letting fate [decide]" or "accepting destiny". Such a translation is an instant reminder of Bodhidharma's statement that "peacefully and spontaneously one's body follows the turns of fate (*yunzhuan* 運轉)".[26] It seems to express the same notion as the term *renyun*. How can one give free rein to fate? Perhaps, what seems to be implied here is an existential attitude of relinquishing all effort and strivings on one's own part and accepting whatever comes along. This also entails giving up any form of seeking for meditative success.

---

23 T48, no. 2012A, p. 384a17: 安然端坐任運不拘 。方名解脫。Translation follows McRae (2005: 42).

24 X09, no. 245, p. 534b21–22: 不斷不造。任運自在。名為解脫人。亦名過量人。

25 X09, no. 245, p. 534b23–24: 故云但任心即為修也。

26 X63, no. 1217, p. 1b13: 安心無為形隨運轉。McRae (1986: 104) translates it as "and accepts whatever happens to him" (lit. "[allows his] form to be transformed in accordance with fate").

As we have already noted, this should not be brought about by a conscious decision or be implemented as some sort of technique as this would be at odds with the essence of *renyun*. In previous chapters we hypothesized that in the paradigm we are considering, the emphasis shifts from meditation as a deliberately applied method to other important factors. In Chapter 6, for example, we considered the possibility that through living in a specific way one may eradicate most of the sources of mental movement. Although this in itself represents a radically different approach in comparison with the mainstream paradigm, the development of virtue can still be conceptualized as straightforwardly following or implementing certain rules or instructions. However, "letting it be" or renouncing searching is different in that regard, as it seemingly cannot be straightforwardly implemented through following any rules or instructions. Therefore, in the paradigm we are considering, in addition to straightforwardly practicable factors we would also need to distinguish the non-straightforwardly practicable ones. But since the latter factors cannot be straightforwardly implemented, does it mean that their occurrence should be seen as a completely chance, random event totally independent of the development of other factors?

The hidden logic of spiritual breakthrough

This is certainly not the case in the texts of the traditions we are considering. Many phenomena are not dependent on acts of will, and yet they possess their own regularity as their development follows particular patterns. One can readily think of examples such as the germination of a seed or the biological development of a young organism. We have already mentioned a simile contained in the *Vāsijaṭa-sutta* (SN 22.101/iii 152–155) and the *Sekha-sutta* (MN 53/i.353–359) which describes chicks that break from their shells simply when the necessary conditions are met, i.e., when they are properly covered, incubated and nurtured. According to the text, whether or not their mother wishes them to hatch is entirely irrelevant for their breaking out of the shells. Similarly, a bhikkhu "need not make such a wish" (*na evaṃ icchā uppajjeyya*) for his mind to be released from the influxes[27] as it depends on the develop-

27 SN 22.101/iii.154: *bhāvanānuyogaṃ anuyuttassa, bhikkhave, bhikkhuno viharato kiñcāpi na evaṃ icchā uppajjeyya –'aho vata me anupādāya āsavehi cittaṃ*

ment of the so-called *bodhipakkhiyadhammas*, i.e., various complementary sets of positive elements or qualities such as the noble eightfold path. The *Vāsijaṭa-sutta* continues with a very interesting simile[28] of a carpenter (*palagaṇḍa*) seeing his fingerprint on the handle of his adze or hatchet (*vāsijaṭa*), but not knowing how much of the handle has been worn (*khīṇa*) during a particular day. Only when it is completely worn out will he realize this. This is meant to symbolize the process of the destruction of the influxes, whose progress similarly cannot be traced in a quantifiable manner, but which becomes known to the practitioner only upon its success.

Another simile[29] likens this process to a sea ship (*nāvā*) whose rigging (*vettabandhana*) would first get damaged by sea water. After being hauled up on dry land it would continue to be attacked by the sun and wind, and finally by rain, eventually causing it to collapse (*paṭippassambhati*) and become rotten (*pūtika*). It needs to be said that the similes in the *Vāsijaṭa-sutta* do not explicitly convey the message that there are some elements of the path that cannot be practised at all. What they do convey is the implicit nature of the process leading to the elimination of the influxes in the sense that its progress cannot be traced in a quantifiable manner, and that this process is not consciously and volitionally controlled and driven in all of its stages. However, it is certainly not independent of the aspects of the Buddhist path which are practicable by implementing certain rules and instructions. It is just that this dependence is not simple and direct, but rather implicit. In other words, there is no simple overlap between the deliberate practice of various elements of the Buddhist path and between the reaching of some crucial stages of realization. The similes of chicks breaking-out from the eggs and of a ship's riggings coming apart under the impact of the elements imply that the process leading up to the breakthrough

---

vimucceyyā'ti, atha khvassa anupādāya āsavehi cittaṃ vimuccati. taṃ kissa hetu? 'bhāvitattā'tissa vacanīyaṃ. Cf. Bodhi (2000: 960) for a translation.

28 SN 22.101/iii.154: *seyyathāpi, bhikkhave, palagaṇḍassa vā palagaṇḍantevāsissa vā vāsijaṭe dissanteva aṅgulipadāni dissati aṅguṭṭhapadaṃ. no ca khvassa evaṃ ñāṇaṃ hoti – 'ettakaṃ vata me ajja vāsijaṭassa khīṇaṃ, ettakaṃ hiyyo, ettakaṃ pare'ti. atha khvassa khīṇe khīṇantveva ñāṇaṃ hoti*. For translation, see Bodhi (2000: 960–61).

29 SN 22.101/iii.155: *seyyathāpi, bhikkhave, sāmuddikāya nāvāya vettabandhanabaddhāya vassamāsāni udake pariyādāya hemantikena thalaṃ ukkhittāya vātātapaparetāni vettabandhanāni. tāni pāvusakena meghena abhippavuṭṭhāni appakasireneva paṭippassambhanti pūtikāni bhavanti*. For translation, see Bodhi (2000: 961).

certainly has its own regularity and is dependent on certain factors, but also that the breakthrough itself is not brought about by any deliberate act.

The notion that awakening leads to a fundamental and irreversible change of psychological functioning is one of the most basic tenets of Buddhism. However, given what we now know from modern philosophy of mind and cognitive science, this entails that such a change must be somehow implemented by unconscious mental processes. According to Baars (1997: 116), our intentions and expectations are to a considerable extent unconscious but steer our voluntary actions and conscious experiences. Carruthers (2015) argues that desires, judgments, beliefs and goals constitute the so-called "amodal attitudes" which operate in an unconscious way, while we merely become conscious of their end results.

Therefore, if awakening involves a fundamental change of intentions, beliefs and judgments, e.g., renouncing searching or "letting it be", then it ultimately must be correlated with a change in the biological structure of the brain responsible for these unconscious processes. Such biological changes are bound to have their own regularities and their own specific course which cannot be monitored from the first-person conscious perspective. Whether spiritual breakthrough will eventually occur may depend on the simultaneous coming together of various necessary conditions. The Nikāyas give the impression that in most cases this occurs in a relatively smooth, uncomplicated way. After the attainment of the fourth *jhāna*, one simply realizes that the mind is released and the influxes are exhausted. If this crucial transformative insight involved appeasement of searching, the standard account does not acknowledge it. However, this does not necessarily imply that the tranquillization of searching did not occur. In Chapter 2 we referred to Hassin's (2005) hypothesis that insights can occur not only in the absence of conscious awareness of the processes that lead to them, but also in the absence of the conscious awareness of the insights themselves. Therefore, one could only acknowledge that the search has ended after the transformative insight has occurred. This seems to be implied by the *Sāmaññaphala* account which states that after the fourth *jhāna* one realizes that the holy life has been lived and what was to be done has been done.[30]

30 DN 2/i.84: *vusitaṃ brahmacariyaṃ, kataṃ karaṇīyaṃ.*

Of course, based on just this fragment one can draw the conclusion that the ending of searching does not contribute in any way to the actual breakthrough as it is merely its direct result. However, there are Nikāya texts which suggest another course of events. As we have already suggested, in the case of the *Sāmaññaphala* account, it might be that the various factors responsible for awakening, including those that are not straightforwardly practicable, come together smoothly, simultaneously and unknowingly to the practitioner himself. At the higher stage of meditation there may occur some implicit insight through which the mind will understand that by actively searching for meditative success and enlightenment, one is inflicting suffering on oneself. This in turn will result in turning off this mechanism, just as a hand that touches a hot object, instantly draws away without any need for a conscious decision to do so. One can only hypothesize that maintaining mindfulness and clear comprehension of one's own mental processes in an equanimous way can contribute to this insight.

While according to the dominant strands in the modern philosophy of mind, the cognitive mechanisms that produce insights are unconscious, they usually work on data that was at least at some moment made globally available, i.e., conscious. To give an example, it is impossible for a person to solve some cognitive problem in an entirely unconscious way, from start to finish. Conscious occupation with a cognitive problem for a certain period of time is absolutely necessary to initiate the process which will eventually yield insight. Even if eureka moments of great scientists came in the midst of activities that were totally unconnected to the nature of the problem they solved, the whole process was originated by prolonged conscious thinking about the problem. Therefore, in order to break out from the vicious cycle of thinking one must first be fully aware of it. If through mindfulness and clear comprehension, one is continuously aware of how one's efforts to think and not to think, or to be aware of thinking, only fuel the mechanism of thought and create psychological discomfort, it may perhaps initiate a process leading to the abandoning of the whole mechanism. However, in some cases, such insight may not come easily which may result in spiritual stagnation where despite even the perfect implementation of Buddhist practice on the part of a practitioner, a breakthrough cannot be attained.

Can an existential crisis be conducive to a spiritual breakthrough?

Early Buddhist texts contain some very interesting accounts of sudden spectacular breakthroughs preceded by a long spiritual impasse. Two fascinating accounts of such occurrences are contained in the *Theragāthā* and the *Therīgāthā* of the *Khuddaka Nikāya*. In the first text (Thag 6.6/44), the Elder Sappadāsa recollects how despite twenty-five years of practice he had failed to obtain peace of mind (*cetosanti*) and mental unification (*cittassekagga*). Overcome by desperation, he finally decides to slice his veins with a razor. However, at that very moment comes a breakthrough. Thorough attention arises, danger becomes visible, and disenchantment is established. The text then reads: "Then, my mind was released, See the good nature of the Dhamma! Three knowledges have been attained, done is the teaching of the Buddha".[31]

In the *Therīgāthā* (Thig 5.3/132) we find a similar account by bhikkhuni Sīhā, who recounts how after seven years of practice she was still afflicted (*aṭṭita*) by sensual lust (*kāmarāga*), despite reaching a state of severe physical emaciation. Therefore, she decides to enter the forest to hang herself, rather than doing again what is lowly (*hīna*). The text reaches a dramatic climax:

> Having made a strong noose,
> and bound it to the branch of a tree.
> I put the noose over my neck
> then my mind was released.[32]

Another interesting account in a similar vein may be found in the *Cūḷavagga* portion of the *Khandhaka* in the Theravāda *Vinaya*. It is specifically contained in the *Pañcasatikakkhandhaka* (*The Chapter on the assembly of five hundred*: Kd 21/ii.284–293) which recounts the story of the so-called First Council. The text recounts how Ānanda was selected to be the reciter of the basket of discourses (i.e., the *Suttapiṭaka*) during the council. However, he felt inappropriate for that role, as out of all the attendants of the Council he was the only one to have not reached

31 Thag 6.6/44: *Tato cittaṃ vimucci me, passa dhammasudhammataṃ; Tisso vijjā anuppattā, kataṃ buddhassa sāsanan'ti*. Also cf. translation by Sujato: https://suttacentral.net/thag6.6/en/sujato.

32 Thig 5.3/132: *Daḷhapāsaṃ karitvāna, rukkhasākhāya bandhiya; Pakkhipiṃ pāsaṃ gīvāyaṃ, atha cittaṃ vimucci me'ti*. Also cf. translation by Sujato: https://suttacentral.net/thig5.3/en/sujato.

arahantship and was considered as one still in training (*sekkha*). Therefore, he decided to make one final effort hoping for a breakthrough. The text states:

> Having passed much of that night in mindfulness as to body (*kāyagatāya satiyā*), when the night was nearly spent, thinking: "I will lie down", he inclined his body, but (before) his head had touched the mattress and while his feet were free from the ground – in that interval his mind was freed (*cittaṃ vimucci*) from the cankers (*āsavehi*) with no residuum (for rebirth) remaining (*anupādāya*).[33]

All three accounts have a somewhat similar structure. They describe practitioners who very sincerely and diligently engage in Buddhist practice but fail to obtain the desired success. Paradoxically, the breakthrough comes only when they become resigned and give up their practice. At exactly that moment comes a release of mind and awakening. Let us note that in all the cases, release does not occur as a direct result of traditionally understood practice in the sense of a deliberate application of some method. The texts do not imply a notion of meditative progress as a steady and gradual accumulation of positive mental factors until they reach a certain threshold resulting in awakening. Furthermore, liberation from the influxes does not directly result from the practice of insight in the traditional sense.

It is worth emphasizing that the mainstream paradigm of meditation does not provide us with the means to understand the nature of the spiritual breakthrough undergone by the protagonists of the above three accounts. However, from the perspective of the paradigm we are trying to reconstruct, all three accounts make perfect sense. For all three protagonists, the breakthrough occurs only after they concede their defeat and give up on their practice. This is synonymous with giving up the search for meditative success, which as we have suggested, may represent the final obstacle standing in its way. This surrender also does not come about by means of a deliberate decision undertaken as a result of calculation and in hope of reaching enlightenment. Such a decision would imply that the search is still continuing on some fundamental level. The protagonists in all three accounts have genuinely given up and lost hope for any spiritual success. In the case

33 Kd 21/ii.285: *bahudeva rattiṃ kāyagatāya satiyā vītināmetvā rattiyā paccūsasamayaṃ 'nipajjissāmī'ti kāyaṃ āvajjesi. appattañca sīsaṃ bibbohanaṃ, bhūmito ca pādā muttā. etasmiṃ antare anupādāya āsavehi cittaṃ vimucci.* Translation by Horner (2001: 295–96).

of Sīhā and Sappadāsa this surrender is ultimate, while in the case of Ānanda it could be argued that it was temporary. It is a type of surrender which occurs to oneself as one just realizes at some moment that there is no more will to strive. The decision is taken on an unconscious level and simply manifests itself as a conscious feeling of resignation. The fact that the three protagonists attain a breakthrough only after giving up, indirectly implies that it was actually their striving that was preventing them from reaching it.

The accounts of Sappadāsa's and Sīhā's breakthroughs suggest that in order for the ultimate letting go of striving to occur, a very intense, existential crisis is needed in the case of some practitioners. The fundamental tendency of seeking may simply be too strong to be relinquished in any other way. In these two narratives, the crisis and internal conflict burning within the protagonists reach such intensity that they find themselves on the brink of death. It is only then that the surrender occurs, but ultimately the protagonists live on.

Sometimes, however, the spiritual breakthrough may coincide with actual death, as was the case with Venerable Godhika. According to the eponymous sutta (SN 4.23/i.120–122)[34] he was being diligent (*appamatta*), ardent (*ātāpī*) and resolute (*pahitatta*) and "touched a temporary release of the mind" (*sāmayikaṃ cetovimuttiṃ phusi*) six times, but each time he "fell away" (*parihāyi*) from it. Upon reaching this state for the seventh time, he decides to commit suicide, evidently in hope of preventing another setback. Despite Māra's temptation, he perseveres in his decision and eventually kills himself. Interestingly, the Buddha acknowledges that Godhika had attained final *nibbāna* (*parinibbuta*).

The most straightforward interpretation of this unusual account would be that by committing suicide, Godhika had simply prevented inevitable setback and died in a temporary state of being released in the mind, thus ensuring final nirvana. However, the attainment of merely temporary release from which one can fall back, can hardly be considered synonymous with arahantship according to the early Buddhist standards.[35] Therefore, another interpretation would be that it was only upon deciding to commit suicide that Godhika relinquished searching

34 See Bodhi (2000: 212–15) for a translation of this text.

35 In his interpretation of this account, Wynne (2022: 109–13) focuses on the unorthodox character of Godhika's meditative beliefs about the temporary release of the mind. He suggests that they may "reflect the presuppositions of the meditative tradition articulated in the early Upaniṣads and Mokṣadharma" about anticipating final *post-mortem* liberation through a meditative state.

and his mind attained ultimate and not merely temporary release. The Buddha praised Godhika afterwards by stating that such as him are not attached to life (lit. "do not wish to live": *nāvakaṅkhanti jīvitaṃ*). It seems that such a mental attitude is particularly conducive for ultimate relinquishment to occur, as it characterized not only Godhika but Sappadāsa and Sīhā as well. If someone has reached a state of being ready to die, it usually implies that such a person does not care about anything anymore. This may be synonymous with the dropping away of the most fundamental psychological mechanisms, such as those of self-preservation and searching for enlightenment. The *Aggadhamma-sutta* (AN 6.83/iii.433–434) lists being unconcerned (*anapekkha*) about one's body and life as one of the six qualities making a bhikkhu capable of realizing arahantship. In contrast, those that are concerned (*sāpekkha*) about their body and life are said to be unable to obtain that state.

Interestingly, the Buddha's own breakthrough as described in the Nikāyas may also be understood in line with the paradigm we are trying to reconstruct. This well-known account is contained in the three suttas of the *Majjhima Nikāya*: the *Mahāsaccaka-sutta* (MN 36/i.237–251), the *Saṅgarava-sutta* (MN 100/ii.209–213) and the *Bodhirājakumāra-sutta* (MN 85/ii.90–97). Regardless of whether this account is true in the historical sense, it implies certain ideas about the psychology of the process of awakening which are worth investigating. According to the narrative, after engaging in several radical yogic practices, and being almost at the brink of death due to severe emaciation, the Bodhisatta acknowledged his defeat, admitting: "Through that severe practice of austerities I had not attained any superhuman dhamma, not to even [speak] of noble knowledge and vision".[36]

The Buddha-to-be then asked himself a question: "would there be another path to awakening?"[37] Despite the relatively dry and formulaic style of the Nikāyas one can readily imagine the extent of desperation experienced by Gotama. The breakthrough comes with the recollection of the spontaneous experience of the first *jhāna* in his youth and with the subsequent realization that the path to awakening goes through that meditative state. What is important, however, is that immediately afterwards, the Bodhisatta realized the irrationality of fear of the pleasure connected with the first *jhāna* that was preventing him

36 MN 85/ii.94: *Na kho panāhaṃ imāya kaṭukāya dukkarakārikāya adhigacchāmi uttari manussadhammā alamariyañāṇadassanavisesaṃ.*

37 MN 85/ii.94: *siyā nu kho añño maggo bodhāyā'ti.*

from engaging in this practice. Subsequently, the fear dissipated, and Gotama could proclaim: "I am not afraid of that pleasure, which is apart from sensuality, apart from unskillful dhammas!"[38]

The Bodhisatta's fear of pleasure seemed to have been fuelled by a specific view, namely that pleasure is in itself unwholesome. Therefore, his attitude may be characterized as a form of grasping at views (*diṭṭhupādāna*) often described in the Nikāyas as one of the four kinds of grasping (e.g., SN 12.2/ii.3). In this set it is accompanied by grasping at rules and practices or rules and vows (*sīlabbatupādāna*),[39] which can also be an apt characteristic of Gotama's persistence in maintaining the radical yogic practices in spite of their inefficiency and harmfulness. While the Bodhisatta grasped at views and practices which seemed to be associated with a specific *samaṇa* group, the later Buddhists would be naturally inclined to grasp at the Dhamma. Therefore, the category of *dhammavitakka* described in the *Paṃsudhovaka-sutta* as the last meditative obstacle may have also included thoughts connected with grasping at views, rules and practices. This interpretation is not incompatible with the one that sees *dhammavitakka*s as connected with the mechanism of searching, as the latter may only be fuelled by having particular views about enlightenment or the nature of the path. Such understanding seems to be conveyed by the already mentioned *Esanā-sutta* of the *Itivuttaka* (Iti 55/48–49), which associates the three searches with clutching to truths (*saccaparāmāsa*) and with the accumulation (*samussaya*) of standpoints for views (*diṭṭhiṭṭhāna*). Conversely, when the searches are renounced (*paṭinissaṭṭha*), the standpoints for views are removed (*samūhata*).

Existential situation of a "finished person"

It appears that the view that pleasure is bad and that one needs to practise austerities (*dukkarakārika*) and painful strivings (*dukkhappadhāna*) was so strongly instilled in the mind of the future Buddha that its subsiding could occur only after acknowledging defeat and reaching the brink of death. The traditional interpretation would see this moment as merely an act of replacing the wrong view with the right one. Thus,

38 MN 85/ii.93: *'na kho ahaṃ tassa sukhassa bhāyāmi yaṃ taṃ sukhaṃ aññatreva kāmehi aññatra akusalehi dhammehī'ti.*

39 See Bodhi (2000: 726–27, n. 6), for a discussion of the meaning of this term.

subsequent Buddhist practitioners would be in a much better position than the Buddha himself, due to not having to repeat his mistakes and being able to straightaway enter upon the right path. But according to the paradigm we are considering, the Bodhisatta's struggles might actually have been conducive to reaching an existential situation of what we may call a "finished person", which in turn might have contributed to his spiritual breakthrough.[40]

In Chapter 6 we underlined the fact that according to the Nikāya ideal, a bhikkhu is a person in whom some of the most basic psychological mechanisms responsible for self-preservation have subsided. He has placed the responsiblity for his welfare in the hands of others, is a social outcast and lives from day to day without making any plans. The famous passage in the *Attadaṇḍa-sutta* (Snp 4.15/182–185) states that it is necessary to "dry up what pertains to the past" and "let there be nothing afterward".[41] In a similar vein, in the *Theranāmaka-sutta* (SN 21.10/ii.282–284), when redifining the notion of dwelling alone (*ekavihāra*), the Buddha proclaims that "what is in the past is abandoned" (*yaṃ atītaṃ taṃ pahīnaṃ*) and "what is in the future is relinquished" (*yaṃ anāgataṃ taṃ paṭinissaṭṭhaṃ*), while lust and desire (*chandarāga*) for present forms of existence are removed.[42]

While in Chapter 6, I emphasized how such a mental state could contribute to the removal of sources of mental movement during meditation, it should also be highly conducive to the abandoning of the fundamental attitude of seeking. As we noted, such an ideal was described in certain Chan texts, particularly those of the Hongzhou school. In that chapter we also briefly mentioned a passage of the *Baizhang Huaihai*

40 The quasi-yogic practices undertaken by the Bodhisatta before his spiritual breakthrough are described as strivings or exertions (*padhāna*), but the four *jhānas* are never labelled as such in the Nikāyas. This may reflect a substantial difference between these practices concerning the necessity of effort and active cultivation. As we have already noted, this understanding seems also to be implied by the *Sasaṅkhāra-sutta* (AN 4.169/ii.155–156), where the development of the four *jhānas* is described as leading to the attainment of *parinibbāna* without *saṅkhāra* (*asaṅkhāraparinibbāyī*). The lack of *saṅkhāra* could mean a lack of any volitional, deliberate and effortful practice.

41 Snp 4.15/184: *yaṃ pubbe taṃ visosehi, pacchā te māhu kiñcanaṃ*. Translation by Bodhi (2017: 316).

42 SN 21.10/ii.283: *idha, thera, yaṃ atītaṃ taṃ pahīnaṃ, yaṃ anāgataṃ taṃ paṭinissaṭṭhaṃ, paccuppannesu ca attabhāvapaṭilābhesu chandarāgo suppaṭivinīto*. Translation following Bodhi (2000: 721).

chanshi guanglu describing an ideal mindset of a Chan monk, which is now worth quoting in its entirety:

> Not thinking about fame and profit, robes and food, and not being greedy for any merit and blessings, he is not obstructed by anything in the world. With nothing dear, free from love, he can equally accept pain and pleasure. He uses a coarse robe to protect himself from the cold and simple food to support his body. Letting go, he is like a fool (*yu* 愚), like a deaf man (*long* 聾), like a dumb man (*ya* 啞). It is only then that one gains some understanding.[43]

In a way, the existential situation described above is that of a "finished person", for whom there is nothing left, at least regarding worldly pursuits. In general, the Tang-era Chan texts do not contain many descriptions of this kind. One notable exception is the following statement attributed to Mazu in the *Zutang ji* 祖堂集 (*Annals of the ancestral hall*),[44] which underlines the existential character of the ultimate letting go:

> Someone asked, "What is the essential purport of the Buddha's teaching?"
>
> Mazu said, "It is precisely the point (*chu* 處), at which you let go (*fang* 放) of your life (*shenming* 身命)".[45]

The earliest descriptions of this existential condition can be traced to Bodhidharma's account of the four "practices" (*xing* 行) in the *Erru sixing lun*. While I have already briefly commented on this fact, it is worthwhile in this context to emphasize again that this account does not actually describe any practices or methods in the sense of activities to perform. What it does describe is a specific mindset characterized by attitudes such as acceptance, coming to terms, and what is especially important in this context, the absence of seeking. Some interesting accounts that may be read as pertaining to the existential situation we are considering are also present in the Song-era literature. For example, the entry in the *Sengbao zhengxu zhuan* 僧寶正續傳 (*True continuation of the chronicles of the Saṃgha treasure*)[46] attributes the following statement to the Caodong master Chanti Weizhao 闡提惟照 (1084–1128):

---

43 X69, no. 1323, p. 8a11–13: 不念一切名聞利養衣食。不貪一切功德利益。不為世間諸法之所滯礙。無親無愛。苦樂平懷。麤衣遮寒。糲食活命。兀兀如愚。如聾如啞相似。稍有相應分。Translation by Poceski (2007: 131).

44 Translation of the title follows Sasaki (2009: 432).

45 B25, no. 144, p. 561b12–13: 問：「如何是佛法旨趣？」師云：「正是你放身命處。」Translation by Poceski (2015b: 226).

46 Translation of the title follows Schlütter (2008: 255).

> Now I only teach you to be like someone who has died the great death (*dasiren* 大死人). If you truly can be like someone who has died the great death, then why should you spend time on a lot of hard work [*gongfu* 工夫], like practicing Chan and studying the Way, or on bowing and burning incense? It is a lot of wasted effort (*feili* 費力).[47]

Like with so many Chan texts, it is not certain what was the intended meaning of the author. However, it is possible to read the phrase "someone who has died the great death" (*dasiren* 大死人) as referring to the existential condition we are considering.

I have suggested that some factors crucial for achieving spiritual breakthrough may not be straightforwardly developed by following a particular method. This also seems to be the case with attaining the mindset described above. It seems impossible to lay down a definite method that could lead one to becoming a finished person. There seems to be a process of maturation which prepares a person to be in a condition that is conducive for the breakthrough to occur, but it is not directly available to our introspection. One may perhaps suspect that continuously meeting life's experiences in their bare form without escaping into the refuge of pleasure seeking, beliefs or rituals may contribute to the process of developing such a mindset. However, whether one will develop such a mindset or not is probably related to several factors that are unique for a particular individual and cannot easily be conceptualized in a simple, almost quantifiable manner as accumulation and strengthening of certain positive factors or abandoning negative ones. For example, it will depend on the inherent intelligence and wisdom of an individual, their emotional characteristics and on the particular experiences they have encountered during their lives.

On the other hand, even sincere and diligent following of certain practical rules of Buddhism, such as those of right speech, right action or right mindfulness, may not in itself guarantee finding oneself in such a state if those other conditions are not met. It seems that one's experiences and personal development before entering on a Buddhist path are especially crucial in this regard. However, their role seems to be somewhat underappreciated in various mainstream conceptualizations of the Buddhist practice. The key insight which lays the foundation for potential spiritual achievement in the future takes place exactly at this

47 X79, no. 1561, p. 560a24–b2: 時寶峰只教你如大死人。你若真箇如大死人。有什麼閑工夫去。參禪學道。禮拜燒香。許多費力。Translation by Schlütter (2008: 165).

stage. It could be argued that this is when the understanding of the content of the four noble truths occurs, as evidenced by their placement in the form of the right view as the initial condition from which the other elements of the noble eightfold path arise.[48]

Taking into account the role of personal experiences and development before entering the Buddhist path may help to explain why the meditative progress in some cases is described as smooth, while in others we encounter stories of struggles and dramatic breakthroughs. It might be the case that at least in the times described in the Nikāyas, a decision to go forth would come as the result of an intense existential dilemma coinciding with a high level of personal development. As we have noted, becoming a bhikkhu virtually meant turning into a social outcast without any guarantees of survival. Therefore, a practitioner was to some extent already a "finished person" at the moment of becoming a renunciate, which was highly conducive to successful Buddhist training.

Psychological significance of going forth

Early Buddhist texts rarely explore in detail the existential crisis accompanying the decision to go forth. It seems that the schematic and relatively simple literary style of the Nikāyas was not yet well-developed enough to express such experiences. The *Raṭṭhapāla-sutta* (MN 82/ii.54–74) seems to be one of the notable exceptions to this rule. It tells the story of a young man of high social standing (*kulaputta* – lit. son of a clan) named Raṭṭhapāla. Hearing the Buddha preach his doctrine arouses in him a powerful longing to become a bhikkhu. However, Raṭṭhapāla's parents who love him dearly are vehemently opposed to their son's plans and categorically refuse to agree to his going forth. After initially failing to convince his parents, Raṭṭhapāla had reached such a level of determination that he laid down on the floor, emphatically proclaiming: "here will either be the death of me or going forth".[49] The text recounts that Raṭṭhapāla refused to eat any food or to change his position until his parents finally agreed to allow him to become a bhikkhu. Raṭṭhapāla's mindset fits the characteristics of a

48 E.g, in the *Vijjā-sutta* (AN 10.105/v.214). This is not meant to take away from the fact that someone on the end of the path understands the content of the Four Noble Truths in a much better way, as this is surely the case.

49 MN 82/ii.58: *idheva me maraṇaṃ bhavissati pabbajjā vā.*

"finished person" – someone whose existential crisis has reached the point of willing to die – but who lives on as a deeply changed individual. As with so many narratives in the Nikāyas, we cannot be certain whether this particular story was based on the life of an actual person named Raṭṭhapāla or is just a piece of early Buddhist propaganda. It might have also been created to provide some narrative context to the verses attributed to Raṭṭhapāla in the *Theragāthā* (Thag 16.4/769–793). Nonetheless, experiences similar to the ones described in this text may have been shared by many bhikkhus. If that was the case, then the often-repeated Nikāya statements about practitioners becoming arahants "in a short time" (*nacirasseva*) after going forth are perhaps not that implausible from a psychological point of view as they may appear to us now.

However, already in the period of the creation of the Nikāyas there was an awareness of the significant change of the renunciate way of living and of its negative impact on the soteriological efficacy of the Buddhist path. This is attested in the two important suttas of the *Kassapa-saṃyutta*, the *Tatiyaovāda-sutta* (SN 16.8/ii.208–209) and the *Saddhammappatirūpaka-sutta* (SN 16.13/ii.223–225).[50] In these texts, the Buddha and Kassapa reflect on the fact that bhikkhus are no longer forest-dwelling (*āraññika*), rag-wearing (*paṃsukūlika*) *samaṇa*s living in seclusion (*pavivitta*) and having few wishes (*appiccha*), but now live in close symbiosis with the lay people. However, despite the fact that in comparison to the earlier period there are more rules of training (*sikkhāpada*), the bhikkhus who are established (*saṇṭhahati*) in final knowledge (*aññā*: i.e., have realized the goal of Buddhism) are much fewer!

One could perhaps attempt to explain away such testimonies as resultant from factional polemics within the early Buddhist Saṅgha or from a natural psychological tendency to idealize the past and see the present as a state of decadence. However, from the perspective of the paradigm we are trying to reconstruct, it seems psychologically plausible that the change of conditions spoken about in the two suttas would negatively influence the soteriological efficacy of monastic livelihood. After a relatively brief early period, the conditions conducive for leading a radically uncompromising life, igniting an intense existential conflict and the ensuing breakthrough were simply not met throughout most of the history of Buddhism, barring a few notable exceptions. For how can

50 See Bodhi (2000: 670–71, 676–79) for translations of these two texts.

one reach this existential climax and stage of letting go if by becoming a monastic one merely cultivates the tradition of one's own nation or sect and maintains its social order, while the tenets of Buddhism are upheld only through religious faith and devotion? Consequently, the psychological situation of a Buddhist practitioner relatively quickly became similar to that of the followers of other religions. Those who become monastics out of respect and faith in the holy tradition of their nations may not be able to experience fundamental letting go and become "finished persons", no matter how many hours they spend concentrating on their breaths or being mindful of lifting and lowering of their feet. To use the categories from the *Paṃsudhovaka-sutta* (AN 3.101/i.253), they will not be able to abandon the thoughts of their homeland, clan and even more so the thoughts of the dhamma itself, as they will not be freed from grasping at views, rules and rituals. One cannot simply meditate one's way into this state.

The fact that various cases of "going forth" may substantially differ from one another, and that it may profoundly influence the very possibility of reaching awakening as a bhikkhu, has not been sufficiently recognized. This is hardly surprising, given the almost universal and unquestioning acceptance of the model according to which self-transformation is reached through a regular and diligent performance of necessary practices which results in an almost linear accumulation of positive factors. When a particular threshold of these accumulated positive factors is reached, it is synonymous with reaching a specific stage on the path to enlightenment. It seems to be a very simplified and psychologically implausible vision of the soteriological progress, the majority of which is accomplished through practising meditation. This vision has become especially prominent during the modern era. It pretty much identifies Buddhist practice with seated meditation and assumes that one can meditate one's own way to enlightenment, through a diligent and systematic practice of seated meditation by using the correct method.

However, according to the paradigm we are trying to reconstruct, one cannot simply meditate one's own way to enlightenment, since meditation is an extension and culmination of a particular way of life and mindset. Furthermore, the specific of the model we are considering lies in the fact that it acknowledges that there are certain essential factors which are not straightforwardly practicable. Some experiences must occur to a person, but they cannot be brought about by any method or conscious effort. It does not mean that they are chance events, as they depend on being at a particular stage of personal development, which is, however, not straightforward and follows its own tacit logic.

The type of relinquishment or "letting it be" that we are discussing here is a universal psychological phenomenon, and not something confined to Buddhism. It seems that this experience, at least to a certain extent, can be quite common. Although certainly not the ultimate form of relinquishment described in the Buddhist texts, it may give us a better understanding of its general mechanism. It usually occurs when we strive to achieve something or try to prevent something from occurring due to a fear of a particular outcome. We put effort into achieving the desired outcome, but the struggle itself is causing us suffering and draining our energy. The fight continues for as long as we cannot accept our defeat and let go of our striving. At some point, however, our resources become exhausted, our venues of escape are cut off and we reach a breaking point. We become so worn down by the whole process that we simply stop caring anymore. Then, the letting go occurs in us and we give up our struggle and resign ourselves to whatever outcome awaits us. Surprisingly, such letting go often provides a feeling of blissful release, as it turns out that the seemingly unwanted result to which we have become resigned is not actually that bad and that it was in fact our effort to prevent it that was causing our suffering. Such forms of letting go can also be observed in cases of people who after a long struggle come to terms with their impending demise.

Can letting go be facilitated?

It seems that within the Chan tradition there may have arisen an idea that such a climax can be induced, or at least augmented by special means. The so-called encounter dialogue (*jiyuan wenda* 機緣問答) texts often present Chan masters behaving in very unorthodox ways, such as uttering paradoxical and unresolvable statements or shouting at, and sometimes even physically beating their disciples. Some of these behaviours may be interpreted as devices intended to bring a disciple to a state of intense inner crisis, while others might have facilitated the subsequent breakthrough and letting go. The latter hypothesis has some psychological plausibility. Earlier, I suggested that the crucial transformative insight must be somehow correlated with a change in the brain. As the latter is a biological system, it might be influenced by physical means. A sudden shock, if properly timed, may, due to its physical impact on the nervous system, cause a shift of perspective or break-out from an impasse. Of course, it is certainly true that the vast majority of encounter dialogue stories were not based on any factual events and represent a fictional literary genre specific to the Song dynasty period.[51] Once the genre was established, it was very easy to fabricate further, entirely fictional stories with historical Chan figures as their protagonists. One can, however, consider the historical possibility of there being at least a few cases of such behaviour, which gave inspiration to the subsequent creation of such texts.

Finally, we have *huatou* 話頭, a technique that does not belong to the Tang period we are mostly dealing with but is relevant to our discussion. From the point of view of the mainstream paradigm, *huatou* appears to be just a peculiar form of a concentrative exercise, akin to concentrating on a mantra. However, we can also interpret it as a tool for inducing deep existential crisis that may result in a spiritual breakthrough. This is rightly noted by Yu, who describes Sheng Yen's approach towards this unique meditative practice:

> For Sheng Yen, a *huatou* is merely a tool. It is a critical phrase from a "public case" or *gong'an,* which is a record of an incident that usually involves a Chan awakening experience. Or, a *huatou* may stem from a real life situation. The point in meditating on a *huatou* or a *gong'an* is to generate an existential dilemma, a sense of wonderment, a yearning to resolve a question. The greater the sense of wonderment, or "doubt sensation", the greater the break through into awakening. In a state of unification, when the doubt suddenly shatters, all attachments are let go of and the "self" vanishes. With no attachments whatsoever, this is the Buddhist experience of things as they are, without the coloration of self-referentiality. (Yu, 2010: 18)

Viewed along these lines, *huatou* meditation appears to be representing the same paradigm as the one we have been tracing in the early Chan texts. However, whether all the aforementioned Chan devices actually worked in inducing a genuine existential crisis and facilitating a subsequent breakthrough is an entirely different issue, which will not be considered in this study. The Nikāyas do not contain even the slightest hints of using such approaches.

---

51 Schlütter (2012: 19) points out that some conversations in the Dunhuang version of the *Liuzu tanjing* already foreshadow later encounter dialogue.

Being ordinary

Instead of trying to induce an intense crisis and facilitate a subsequent breakthrough, several early Chan texts employed an entirely different strategy aimed at relinquishing seeking. This strategy involved undermining the very notion of seeking enlightenment or meditative success, by emphasizing that ultimately there is nothing to be gained. For example, in the *Tanyu*, Shenhui claims that "the fundamental essence is empty and serene, without a single thing (*yiwu* 一物) to be attained (*kede* 可得)".[52] In the *Dunwu rudao yaomen lun*, Dazhu declares that enlightenment (*wu* 悟) means becoming enlightened to the fact that there is nothing to be attained (*wusuode* 無所得).[53] According to the *Jueguan lun*, one is called a sage (*sheng* 聖) when one does not attain even a single dharma/truth (*yifabude* 一法不得).[54] In the *Chuanxin fa yao*, we find Huangbo's statement that "there is no singular truth (*fa* 法) to attain (*kede* 可得), nor is there a single practice (*xing* 行) to cultivate (*xiu* 修)".[55]

Such statements were not necessarily entirely pragmatic devices meant to trick practitioners into stopping seeking but were in harmony with some of the ideological tenets of the Chan school. We have already considered how the ideology of subitism stemming from the Tathāgatagarbha doctrine can lead to the rejection of the notion of any goal or any effort necessary to attain it. In Chapters 3 and 4, we discussed the apophatic teachings of the Chan school which implied that on the ultimate level of reality the distinctions between Buddhahood and one's ordinary state have no relevance. These concepts belong to the sphere of conventional truth which is not real in the ultimate and objective sense. Therefore, if the concepts of the Buddha and awakening do not represent the ultimate truth, then there is actually nothing to seek and nothing to gain in the positive sense.

---

52 B25, no. 142, p. 32a2–3: 本體空寂，無有一物可得，是名阿耨菩提。Translation by McRae (2023: 69).

53 X63, no. 1223, p. 18a10: 云何為頓悟。答。頓者。頓除妄念。悟者。悟無所得。Cf. translation by Blofeld (1962: 43).

54 B18, no. 101, pp. 693b15–694a1: 緣門問曰、夫言聖人者、當斷何法、當得何法、而云聖也。入理曰、一法不斷、一法不得、即為聖也。Translation by Tokiwa (1973: 6).

55 T48, no. 2012A, p. 381a3–4: 無一法可得。無一行可修。Translation by Poceski (2015a: 103).

Furthermore, in some texts associated with the Hongzhou school, one encounters statements about "being ordinary" (*pingchang* 平常) or about "the ordinary mind" (*pingchangxin* 平常心). This phrase goes back to a famous proclamation by Mazu that "the ordinary mind is the Way".[56] The ideal of being ordinary is particularly emphasized in the *Linji lu*, as evidenced by the following statement attributed to master Linji:

> Followers of the Way, as to buddhadharma, no effort (*yonggong* 用功) is necessary. You have only to be ordinary (*pingchang* 平常), with nothing to do (*wushi* 無事) – defecating, urinating, wearing clothes, eating food, and lying down when tired.[57]

In another fragment, Linji proclaims:

> He who has nothing to do is the noble one (*guiren* 貴人). Simply don't strive (*zaozuo* 造作)[58] – just be ordinary.[59]

Doing nothing

If the ordinary mind is the Way and there is nothing to attain nor any practice to cultivate, then there is no reason to care about meditation and its results anymore. Theoretically, a person with such an attitude will not be trapped in a vicious cycle of thoughts connected with the desire for meditative success. A good example of implementing this understanding to meditation practice can be found in the following statement by Read (2009: 13–14):

> I submit that meditation is this: the paradoxical act of not trying to do anything, not even trying to think more intensely, nor even trying not to think. How do you not do anything, not even think (or not

56 E.g., in the *Tiansheng guangdeng lu* at X78, no. 1553, p. 449c8: 平常心是道。This statement also occurs in the *Jingde chuandeng lu* 景德傳燈錄 (*Jingde-era Record of the transmission of the lamp*) at T51, no. 2076, p. 440a5. For a discussion of its meaning, see Poceski (2007: 183; 2015b: 302).

57 T47, no. 1985, p. 498a16–17: 道流！佛法無用功處。秖是平常無事。屙屎送尿、著衣喫飯、困來即臥。Translation by Sasaki (2009: 185).

58 The term *zaozuo* does not literally mean striving but carries with it the connotations of constructing something artificial. In Chan texts this usually also involves deliberately undertaken activities and is closely connected with terms such as *zuoyi* or *qixin*.

59 T47, no. 1985, p. 497c27–28: 無事是貴人，但莫造作，秖是平常。Translation by Sasaki (2009: 178).

> think)? Or, to put much the same question in other terms: how do you stop yourself from thinking, without acting and, in particular, without suppressing your thoughts? The answer surprisingly turns out to be: by giving up trying to stop yourself from thinking and by allowing yourself to think, if that's what happens.

Read rightly identifies some of the paradoxes connected with actively trying to induce a thought-less state; these are the same paradoxes we have been discussing in the earlier part of this chapter. The laissez-faire method suggested by Read looks deceivingly easy; after all, what could be easier than allowing oneself to think? However, upon closer scrutiny, some of its limitations become apparent. Firstly, if allowing oneself to think will result from a deliberate decision undertaken merely in order to stop thinking, then it is unlikely that it will bring about the expected result. As we have already discussed, this would imply that deep down one is still desiring the attainment of a thought-less state which will in turn result in the generation of thoughts. Therefore, if allowing oneself to freely think were to result in stopping thoughts, it would need to arise from genuinely stopping caring about meditative success.

Secondly, even if an ordinary person sits down and allows oneself to think freely, this will result in consciousness being constantly flooded with thoughts connected with urges and social demands which we have discussed in previous chapters. Such instruction could therefore potentially help only those practitioners who have already purified their minds through leading a radically transformed life, thus removing most of the sources of thinking. The seemingly easy solution of not doing anything paradoxically turns out to be exceptionally hard. This paradox is well-expressed in the passage of the *Jueguan lun*, in which Ruli says that doing something is easy (*youzuoyi* 有作易), but "not-doing" is difficult (*wuzuonan* 無作難).[60]

Some Chan authors were acutely aware of the problem of distinguishing an ordinary mind of the sage from that of an ordinary person in the common sense of the word. In the *Zhufang menren canwen yulu*,[61]

---

60 B18, no. 101, p. 705a7–10: 起心易、滅心難。是身易、非身難。有作易、無作難。故知玄功難會、妙理難合。不動即真、三聖希及。Cf. translation by McRae (1983: 214).

61 X63, no. 1224, p. 25b8–12: 有源律師來問。和尚修道還用功否。師曰用功。曰如何用功。師曰。飢來喫飯。困來即眠。曰。一切人總如是。同師用功否。師曰不同。曰何故不同。師曰。他喫飯時不肯喫飯。百種須索。睡時不肯睡。千般計校。所以不同也。律師杜口。Cf. translation by Blofeld (1962: 95–96).

a Vinaya (*lǜ* 律) Master, Yuan 源 asks Dazhu whether during cultivation (*xiudao* 修道) he makes effort (*yonggong* 用功). To this, Dazhu replies that his effort consists of eating when he is hungry (*jilaichifan* 飢來喫飯) and sleeping when he is tired (*kunlaijishui* 困來即眠). Upon hearing this, his interlocutor points out that all people in general behave like this and asks whether they make the same effort as the Chan master. Dazhu, however, points out a very important difference (*butong* 不同): while common people eat, they at the same time think about "one hundred kinds of necessities" (*baizhongxusuo* 百種須索), while during sleeping they are occupied with "thousand kinds of affairs" (*qianbanjijiao* 千般計校). This implies that a Chan master is fully engaged in all the activities he performs.

The *Jueguan lun* explicitly considers a question: "If there is no cutting-off nor attaining, then [how is the sage] different from the common man" (*yufanheyi* 與凡何異)? As a response, master Ruli explains that due to delusion (*wang* 妄) common people believe that they actually have something to cut-off (*yousuoduan* 有所斷) or to attain (*yousuode* 有所得).[62]

In light of these fragments, the notion of being ordinary cannot be seen as an affirmation of the mindset of ordinary people. Even though they may not be searching for enlightenment, their minds are stirred due to the demands of social life and because of the delusions they harbour. It is noteworthy in this context that Mazu's original statement in the *Tiansheng guangdeng lu* about the ordinary mind being the Way contains an important caveat; although the Way needs no cultivation (*buyongxiu* 不用修), one must prevent defilements (*wuran* 污染).[63] And as we discussed in Chapter 6, achieving this requires a complete transformation of one's mode of living, though it can be argued that this transformation is generally negative in nature and mostly involves abstention from certain activities and not actively doing something.

Therefore, the statements to the effect that there is nothing to attain, or that one should be ordinary, could be psychologically beneficial only with respect to seasoned Chan monks who have already purified their lifestyle due to living in perfect accordance with the Vinaya, but may have been caught up in a meditative impasse due to

62 B18, no. 101, p. 694a2–4: 問曰、若不斷不得、與凡何異。答曰、不同。何以故、一切凡夫妄有所斷、妄有所得。Translation follows Tokiwa (1973: 6).

63 X78, no. 1553, p. 449c7: 道不用修。但莫污染。Cf. translations by Poceski (2007: 183; 2015b: 301).

the mechanism involving active striving and desire for success which we have discussed.

Absence of a spiritual goal as a soteriological strategy

The absence of detailed descriptions of successive stages of meditative progress in Chan texts might have also been part of the same strategy. This absence needs to be distinguished from the lack of meditative instructions or techniques. These two features need not necessarily go hand in hand. The Nikāyas, for example, do not contain instructions for the attainment of the *jhānas*, but nonetheless contain an account of meditative progress in the form of the stock formula of the four *jhānas*. In early Chan, with the exception of the *Rudao anxin yao fangbian famen* and the *Xiuxin yao lun*, there are hardly any such accounts. We have already discussed scholarly hypotheses (e.g., McRae 2005) that such absence would stem from an ideological taboo. The other explanation would go in line with Sharf's (2014b) suggestion that Chan masters invented a simplified meditative technique in order to broaden its appeal. Therefore, there would be no meditative progress to describe as simply there was none to be accomplished by these simplified methods. However, abstention from discussing meditative progress could have potential psychological and practical value for preventing the mechanism of seeking in practitioners. The novices admitted to Chan monasteries would be made to live rigorously according to the Vinaya and to sit long hours in the meditative posture. However, they would not be given any specific instruction, nor told of any special purpose of their sitting. Instead, they would be instructed that this is just part of their natural order of the day. At the same time, they would receive teachings about having nothing to attain or being ordinary in order to vanquish any desire for meditative success that they could have. It seems that this was indeed the model of Chan monastic life, at least in the Hongzhou school.

The intent of such a strategy could be that if all the necessary conditions would be met, then the right meditation would spontaneously be born in monks during their daily sessions of sitting. The sources of thinking connected with urges and social demands would be dried out due to rigorously living according to the Vinaya. Following the rules of Vinaya would also ensure that maintaining mindfulness would become pretty much automatic at this point and thus, not require any active implementation during meditation. The tendency to seek would be nipped in the bud and never allowed to develop. Taking into account all that we considered in the previous chapters, it seems psychologically plausible that all these conditions would contribute to the arising of an altered state of mind characterized by absence of thoughts, and potentially leading to a life-transforming insight. Whether this was indeed the intent behind the Chan model of monastic life, and to what extent it succeeded, is impossible to verify. The obvious problem with such a model would lie in providing the necessary motivation for the effort to model one's life on the rules of the Vinaya without resorting to the aim of becoming enlightened.

The differences between Nikāya and early Chan approaches

The Nikāyas do not resort to the Chan strategies of denying that there is anything to attain or to cultivate, and of keeping silent about the stages of meditative progress. In contrast to the later Mahāyāna discourse, the emphasis in the early Buddhist texts was not really on reaching a state of future enlightenment, but rather on removing suffering which is an almost palpable feature of one's present state. In the famous Nikāya phrase, the Buddha says: "Formerly and also now, I make known just suffering and the cessation of suffering".[64] Wanting to be free from suffering when we are afflicted by it is an automatic, natural reaction and is not connected with construction of any ideal future goal. The soteriological process is therefore negative, and it could be argued that it is not accomplished by positively creating any quality, but rather by eradicating elements such as influxes, defilements or fetters. And since it is a major tenet of the Nikāya doctrine that suffering is ultimately self-inflicted due to deluded activities such as conceiving (*maññati*), constructing (*abhisaṅkharoti*) and complicating/proliferating (*papañceti*), therefore the eradication of defilements is not accomplished through their active removal, but merely by stopping those tendencies that have engendered them in the first place. Such an understanding would be in line with the already mentioned statement in the *Jueguan lun* to the effect that there is no cutting off or attaining.

64 E.g., SN 22.86/iii.119: *pubbe cāhaṃ, anurādha, etarahi ca dukkhañceva paññapemi, dukkhassa ca nirodhan'ti*. Translation by Bodhi (2000: 938).

The Nikāya presentation of the ultimate goal in the negative terms of absence of suffering, which in turn is tantamount to the stopping of our own deluded constructing activities, would be therefore much less conducive to generating the condition of seeking in a practitioner. The majority of Nikāya texts do not imply that the process of reaching awakening must involve struggles and dramatic breakthroughs as experienced by the likes of Sappadāsa, Sīhā or the Buddha himself.

It is worthwhile to again emphasize that the Nikāya ideal of the renunciate life differs significantly from the Chan monastic model. In the early Buddhist texts, we encounter much more emphasis on the pre-meditative way of life and find a comprehensive model of transforming oneself through practices such as right effort, right mindfulness or sense restraint. The Nikāyas do not give the impression that development of *sīla* may be simply reduced to maintaining the rules of *patimokkha*. It seems that the Nikāya model affords much more flexibility and creativity but also demands more personal responsibility as part of an individual approach towards transforming oneself. As attested in the already mentioned *Saddhammappatirūpaka-sutta* (SN 16.13/ii.223–225), in the earliest period after the Buddha's awakening there were hardly any rules, and yet a much greater number of bhikkhus were declaring final knowledge. The Chinese model of monastic life represented a sort of a compromise necessary to survive in an entirely different cultural and social environment to the Indian one in which Buddhism had originated. Therefore, it is possible that the ideal of the renunciate life laid out in the Nikāyas was soteriologically more efficacious than the Chan monastic model, and thus did not require special devices aimed at dissolving the tendency for searching for enlightenment.

When discussing differences between the way Nikāya and early Chan texts conceptualize meditation it is impossible not to consider the fact that the latter ones do not contain any scheme of stages of meditative progress similar to the account of the four *jhānas*. Does this difference not undermine the hypothesis of the presence of a similar paradigm of meditation in the texts of both traditions that is forwarded in this book?

One answer to this problem could be that within a general paradigm, there may function related but nonetheless different variants of meditation, just as different forms of insight meditation with different schemes of progress can be said to represent the more general traditional paradigm of insight meditation. On this account, the four *jhānas* and *zuochan* would be related and share some important features (like absence of active concentration on a meditation object and effortlessness) but would not exactly be the same practices with the same mechanism of progress.

However, this is not the only possible explanation. It might be the case that the same meditative process is described using different conceptual and terminological schemes. The fact that the schemes of meditative progress, such as that of the four *jhāna*s, must refer to private experiences and therefore rely on private language may mean that even if different practitioners independently attain an identical state, they will develop different terminologies and conceptual schemes to describe it. Such differences may also result from the focus on different aspects of the same meditative process. As we have already noted, it is generally assumed that the four *jhāna*s as presented in the *Visuddhimagga* are a practice known to non-Buddhists, and yet the exact account of the four *jhāna*s cannot be found in non-Buddhist texts, as they use their own specific terminology and classifications. This may also be the case with different texts of the same tradition. Texts such as the *Paṃsudhovaka-sutta*, the *Ānāpānassati-sutta* or some passages of the *Suttanipāta* seem to refer to the same form of early Buddhist meditation as the one described by the four *jhāna* scheme, but focus on its different aspects without using the same terminology or schemes of progress.

Therefore, it may also be possible that Nikāya and early Chan texts refer to the same type of meditation but describe it in terms specific to their respective traditions. A look at the early Chan texts shows not only the lack of a scheme similar to that of the the four *jhāna*s, but actually the absence of any common scheme of meditative progress at all. The general lack of descriptions of stages of meditative progress may have been motivated psychologically and intended to prevent the arising of various expectations, evaluations of one's state and comparisons, which all hinder the true progress of meditation. This would have also been in line with the Chan soteriological strategy of not-seeking and being ordinary that we have analysed in the preceding part of this chapter. It is also worth noting that pragmatically motivated abstention from describing in detail the stages of meditative progress, or even from recognizing that a disciple has reached a particular stage, has been a hallmark of some modern meditation teachers.[65]

65 E.g., of Ajaan Fuang, as described by his disciple Thanissaro in his aptly entitled essay "Jhana Not by the Numbers" (Thanissaro, 2005: 85–89).

In Chapter 7, I have noted that early Chan Buddhists rarely used traditional Buddhist terminology of meditative stages and mental factors in their texts. I have suggested that this may have been because they associated this terminology with the mainstream approach to meditation which they opposed. As we have seen in Chapter 1, the four *jhānas*/*dhyānas* (*sichan* 四禪 in Chinese) were by that time understood very differently than in the Nikāyas. Their scheme was a well-established element of the mainstream model described extensively in works such as Zhiyi's *Shi chan boluomi cidi famen*, and Chan Buddhists must have associated it with the classical form of calm meditation (*zhi* 止) practised by active one-pointed concentration on meditation objects, a practice they extensively criticized in their own texts. Therefore, it is only natural that they would be reluctant to use this scheme and associated terminology to describe their own specific form of meditation.

The universally stressed element in various Chan texts is that meditative progress should lead to absence of thoughts and gross mental activity, with many passages also focusing on reaching the stage of originally pure mind. Additionally, some accounts mention the arising of inner luminosity and clarity. There seems to be some correspondence of these features with the ones present in the account of the four *jhānas*, e.g., the disappearance of *vitakka* and *vicāra* after the first *jhāna*, or the stage of a very pure and clear, blemish-free mind reached after entering the fourth *jhāna*.

The most obvious difference between the Nikāya and Chan accounts lies in the strong emphasis that the *jhāna* account puts on the presence of positive affects (i.e., subjective affective states of positive valence) and their role in meditative progress, namely rapture (*pīti*), pleasure (*sukha*), and gladness (*pāmojja*); the latter appearing in the *Sāmaññaphala* description of overcoming the hindrances. Early Chan texts generally stay completely silent on this issue, neither affirming nor denying the presence of such states. Only Changlu Zongze's *Zuochan yi* from the early Song period mentions that at the higher stage of practice the meditator will be serene, clear and joyful (*jiranqingle* 寂然清樂) and that seated meditation is the dharma-gate of peace and joy (*anlefamen* 安樂法門).[66] Since as we have noted, Zongze's form of meditation was exactly the same practice as *wunian* described by Shenhui and Zongmi,

66 X63, no. 1245, p. 545a11–14: 竊謂坐禪乃安樂法門。而人多致疾者。蓋不善用心故也。若善得此意。則自然四大輕安。精神爽利。正念分明。法味資神。寂然清樂。Cf. translation by Bielefeldt (1988: 281–82).

it is possible that the latter form of meditation could also involve the arising of positive feelings.

It also needs to be considered that the account of the four *jhāna*s in its exact, detailed form present in the Nikāyas, and especially some of its features, may be an idiosyncratic reflection of a specific meditative experience of a particular person who authored this account. The *Sāmaññaphala* stock description of entering *jhāna* attaches great significance to the role of joy (*pāmojja*) and rapture (*pīti*) that arise as a positive reaction, almost that of a joyful surprise, to finding oneself in a state free from various mental hindrances (*nīvaraṇa*). Such a reaction makes especially strong sense in the case of initial attainments of *jhāna*, but not necessarily with regard to meditators who regularly stay in the higher *jhāna*s, or have perhaps even reached the final goal of practice and are permanently living in a state free from the hindrances. Why would they still need to always go through the clearly imperfect first *jhāna*? The ubiquity of this account in its strict, identical form including the first *jhāna* may simply stem from the repetitive, schematic nature of the Nikāya texts which resulted in an insertion of the four *jhāna* scheme whenever there was talk of meditative progress and the context allowed it.

As we have seen, the Chan ideal of being ordinary represented a way of being engaged in the world where every act and experience is pure and direct and does not involve the mediation of thoughts or of ideological constructs and contrived, effortful and deliberate acts. While the Nikāyas do not contain any explicit references to "being ordinary" it can be argued that at least some aspects of this idea are inherent in certain early Buddhist teachings. In Chapter 4, we considered a hypothesis that the *Māluṅkyaputta-sutta* (SN 35.95/iv.72–76) and the *Bāhiya-sutta* (Ud 1.10/6–9) may refer to pure cognition which coincides with the radical deconstruction of the most basic categories of our experience. However, these texts are also open to an alternative interpretation which emphasizes a different aspect of the Buddha's teaching. In both of these suttas, the Buddha offers a brief instruction that in the seen (*diṭṭha*) there should be merely the seen (*diṭṭhamatta*), in the heard (*suta*) merely the heard, in the sensed (or thought: *muta*) merely the sensed and in the cognized (*viññāta*) merely the cognized.[67] Initially, this

67 SN 35.95/iv.73: *Ettha ca te, mālukyaputta, diṭṭhasutamutaviññātabbesu dhammesu diṭṭhe diṭṭhamattaṃ bhavissati, sute sutamattaṃ bhavissati, mute mutamattaṃ bhavissati, viññāte viññātamattaṃ bhavissati.*

instruction appears deceivingly simple, as nothing seems to be easier than merely to see, hear, sense and cognize. Yet, the Buddha promises that it will lead to the end of suffering, the ultimate soteriological goal of Buddhism. The notion of "merely the seen in the seen" (and respectively heard, sensed and cognized) may be interpreted as implying that one does not think (*vitakketi*) about the seen, does not apperceive (*sañjānāti*) the seen,[68] does not conceive (*maññati*) of the seen, does not delight (*abhinandati*) in the seen, does not construct (*abhisaṅkharoti*) the seen and does not complicate and proliferate (*papañceti*) the seen. These verbs denote various ways in which the original pure and unmediated experience is conceptually and emotionally elaborated. Therefore, the ideal of merely the seen in the seen corresponds to some degree to the mode of the functioning of the Chan master as described by Dazhu or to the notion of being ordinary. Just seeing, hearing, sensing or cognizing without adding anything additional seems very easy, obvious or "ordinary" if we were to use the term present in Chan texts. But paradoxically, it is being ordinary and non-doing which is the hardest.

68 The *Paramaṭṭhaka-sutta* of the *Suttanipāta* (Snp 4.5/156–158) explicitly states that for a brahmin (i.e., a realized person), "not even a subtlest apperception is constructed with regard to what is seen, heard or thought" (*diṭṭhe va sute mute vā, pakappitā natthi aṇūpi saññā*). Cf. Wynne (2018a: 88), for a discussion of this passage in the context of the notion of bare cognition.

CONCLUSIONS

Our investigation has shown the presence of several important similarities and parallels in the way Nikāya and early Chan texts approach meditation. It would certainly be a gross oversimplification to say that all of the Nikāya and Chan texts that we have analysed contain exactly the same ideas, as there are sometimes significant differences even between individual texts belonging to each of these traditions. Nonetheless, it is possible to speak of a group of general ideas which are present to a various extent in several Nikāya and Chan texts and which form a specific paradigm or model of meditation. Many of these ideas are difficult or even not possible to harmonize with the historically dominant, mainstream model of meditation within Buddhism. Perhaps the most important results of this comparative study lie in showing the very possibility of an entirely different way of approaching various aspects of meditation in comparison to the mainstream model and in pointing out the latter's limitations as a vehicle for conceptualizing the nature of meditation and meditative progress. While throughout the book we have often characterized the meditative paradigm present in Nikāya and Chan texts by focusing on their differences with regard to the mainstream model, this paradigm is coherent and can stand in its own right. As we have only focused on particular features of both of the models, it is worthwhile here by way of a summary to provide their brief general description.

According to the mainstream paradigm, meditation is practised by a deliberate implementation of a certain technique. This usually involves activities requiring various amounts of mental effort such as concentrating, applying attention, analysing or contemplating. This paradigm implies a positive understanding of meditation as a form of activity or, in other words, of simply doing something.[1] Meditation is a skill which may be learned, and later mastered through systematic and ardent practice. Particular stages of meditation may require active implementation of techniques which are specific to a given stage. In this regard, meditation does not essentially differ from many other everyday activities. One can, for example, master a gymnastic movement or a musical instrument in a similar way. First, one receives a set of instructions from a person who has already mastered a particular technique and then systematically follows these instructions by repeatedly putting them into practice. Traditionally understood meditative practice follows a similar pattern. One first receives instructions from an experienced meditative teacher, and then repeatedly practises meditation in the way one was taught. Generally speaking, the mainstream paradigm recognizes only two main forms of meditation: calm and insight. The two are entirely distinct. One first practises calm, and then uses the strength of concentration developed through this form of meditation to practise insight. The mechanism by which concentration produces altered states of consciousness involves the suppression of mental defilements and hindrances by absorption into a meditative object.

Both meditative and soteriological progress are conceptualized in a relatively straightforward way as the strengthening and accumulation of positive factors, and the weakening and elimination of negative ones. Once the net sum of the positive factors reaches the necessary threshold, it results in a meditative attainment. All the elements of the path are straightforwardly practicable in the sense that the level of their development is a function of their active practice.

In this paradigm, the connection between morality and meditation is usually emphasized, but its exact psychological mechanism is not explained in detail. Furthermore, given the abovementioned characteristic of meditation as a technique or skill, it is difficult to understand why it could not be mastered regardless of one's moral level, as is the case with other techniques and skills.

The meditative paradigm present in the Nikāya and early Chan texts that we have analysed is in some respects the direct opposite of the mainstream one. Attainment of deeply altered states of mind through

1 Of course, in the case of calm meditation, active concentration is needed only at the initial stages, and after the process picks up the necessary strength and momentum, it results in a deep absorption in which mental activity comes to an end.

volitional activity and deliberate application of the mind is subject to negative evaluation as it results in an artificially fabricated, conditioned state.[2] Meditation in the sense of attaining altered states of mind does not consist in doing anything, but rather in "non-doing" or undoing. However, we must emphasize that "non-doing" is not another technique that may be learned and consciously implemented by an act or a decision. The understanding of meditation is therefore negative. Meditative progress coincides with the falling away of our various constructing activities which distort the original experience. A very strong and direct correlation exists between meditation and the pre-meditative way of life and state of mind. The actual practice in the sense of deliberate activity and striving takes place before meditation understood as an attainment of altered mental states. Meditation is an extension and culmination of leading a virtuous way of life and maintaining a specific mindset. Virtue consists of entirely transforming one's mode of behaviour through a lifestyle of radical self-discipline, so that it is no longer urge-driven but rational and rule-governed. This stage of practice involves conceptual reflection, active striving and effort directed at generating wholesome states and inculcating positive qualities of the mind. Crucial to meditative success is a mindset that involves uncompromising sincerity, living day-to-day without plans, and renunciation of psychological mechanisms of self-preservation and of care for social status. Maintaining such a lifestyle and mindset leads to gradual eradication of ordinary sources of mental movement and to the arising of blissful spiritual feelings. With the right conditions, intensification of these qualities naturally gives rise to a meditative altered state of mind. Maintaining awareness of one's feelings, thoughts and urges is an important factor of meditative success. It need not be considered a method in the sense of undertaking any new activity, as mindfulness and clear comprehension are at this point of practice already inculcated in the practitioner's mind to such a degree that they can be considered automatic. Importantly, this paradigm acknowledges the existence of paradoxical aspects of meditation. These include the fact that desire or seeking for meditative success and enlightenment are actually detrimental at higher stages of development.

2 It needs to be again emphasized that especially in the Nikāyas, at the earlier stages of the path, practices that involve active effort are very important. They, too, can be conceived of as forms of meditation but not in the sense of entering deeply altered states of mind.

These forms of seeking and desire must be relinquished or let go of, but this cannot result from a deliberate decision. Such letting go is, however, not a random or chance event, but follows its own logic which is often implicit and depends on the level of individual development which in turn reflects experiences and unique characteristics of a particular person. Therefore, this paradigm acknowledges the presence of crucial factors which may not be straightforwardly practicable in the sense of the lack of a direct and immediate correlation between active practice and their occurrence. What may facilitate the occurrence of the aforesaid relinquishment in certain individuals is finding oneself in an existential condition of having exhausted all means of striving to the point of accepting defeat. Conducive to this aim is the freedom from grasping at views and practices. This paradigm is based on a specific concept of the mind and vision of reality. It assumes the existence of a basic layer of the mind, which is capable of operating without the medium of conscious thoughts and is endowed with an inherent intelligence. This concept of the mind is the basis of the notion of a spontaneous and ineffable transformative insight which may occur in a deep meditative state of an absence of verbal thought.

According to this paradigm, human experience is strongly mediated and constructed by conceptual and linguistic factors. The notion of the world as we experience it is dependent on the particular mode of functioning of our cognitive apparatus. However, these mediating factors may be suspended in the highest meditative state. The state of a pure, unmediated condition is therefore tantamount to the deconstruction of the world of our experience. Its first-person content is not constituted by phenomenologically describable pure conscious experience but is entirely ineffable and may only be described apophatically. Due to the cessation of even the most basic categories and dichotomies characterizing our experience, it is also a paradoxical state of release from *saṃsāra* in this life. It needs to be emphasized that these philosophical notions are not characterized by simple opposition to the mainstream model in its entirety, as was the case with the remaining elements of the paradigm present in Nikāya and early Chan texts. They are definitely at odds with the vision of reality typical of classical Theravāda, but not with the views of certain antirealist strands of Mahāyāna.

It needs to be said that the two paradigms as presented above represent certain idealized extremes, which are nonetheless very useful for classifying and conceptualizing approaches to meditation present in particular Buddhist texts of specific traditions. Many of the texts that we have analysed cannot be said to perfectly correspond to one of these idealized models and do not exactly match all of their features or only match them to a certain extent. It would be too much of a simplification to merely speak about a mutually exclusive, simple dichotomy of either an affirmation of a method in a very strong sense or a total, paradoxical negation of any method. Rather, there is a wider spectrum of more nuanced positions situated close to each of these two idealized extremes. For example, even though the texts such as the *Visuddhimagga* or the early Chinese manuals of meditation conceptualize meditation as a deliberately undertaken activity, they cannot be said to represent the extreme position in the spectrum. This extreme position is in fact constituted by the modern stereotypical approach to meditation, where the latter is entirely reduced to a skill and virtually dissociated from the necessity of radical self-transformation through a disciplined lifestyle. Since meditation is a skill, it is possible to describe someone as knowing or not knowing how to meditate, just as one knows or does not know how to play a musical instrument. It needs to be said that in the case of the paradigm contained in Nikāya and Chan texts, such statements would not really be adequate for assessing the possibility of meditative success. Instead of asking if one knows how to meditate, it would be better to ask whether one approaches meditation having developed virtue, sense restraint, mindfulness, clear comprehension and contentedness, to almost directly quote the *Sāmaññaphala-sutta*.[3]

This modern model is at present so popular and widespread that the practice of Buddhism is virtually identified with the practice of meditation. Asking whether one practices Buddhism is virtually tantamount to asking whether one practises seated meditation. Another aspect of this approach lies in affording meditation complete causal efficacy regarding the process of self-transformation, as it is assumed that it is directly through meditation that one changes oneself. However, the extent of this change does not match the level of maximalism of Nikāya Buddhism and early Chan. Gone are the ideas of the fundamental transformation of a human being and of the ultimate eradication of suffering. The personal ideal of a holy sage living an authentic and uncompromising life is replaced by that of a meditation practitioner.

3 DN 2/i.71: *so iminā ca ariyena sīlakkhandhena samannāgato, iminā ca ariyena indriyasaṃvarena samannāgato, iminā ca ariyena satisampajaññena samannāgato, imāya ca ariyāya santuṭṭhiyā samannāgato, vivittaṃ senāsanaṃ bhajati.*

Not only does meditation not require radical change of lifestyle or finding oneself in a special existential condition; it is also dissociated from any belief system.

Ultimately, if meditation is an activity and a skill, then just like other activities and skills, it can be learnt and mastered in itself, regardless of other aspects of life. One just needs to devote a particular amount of time every day and lead a relatively healthy and regular lifestyle. It is truly difficult to point out a reason why people with a non-Buddhist worldview would have any trouble achieving success in such a form of meditation, provided they practise it diligently. There is nothing inherently Buddhist about focusing on the breath, a *kasiṇa* or on the movement of the abdomen. And indeed, during meditation retreats and courses it is often emphasized that following a different religion and having a different worldview is no obstacle to successful practice. No approach could be further from the one present in Nikāya and early Chan texts.

Compared to this approach, texts such as the *Visuddhimagga* still emphasize the link between meditation and a renunciate mode of life, though without explaining in detail its exact nature. Another relatively unorthodox feature of the *Visuddhimagga* is that it acknowledges the possibility of certain unusual forms of meditation, such as a spontaneous vision of certain *kasiṇa nimitta*s (e.g., of earth *kasiṇa nimitta* when looking at a freshly ploughed field) which is said to occur to certain practitioners based on their *kamma* from previous lives.

As to the paradigm that we have been tracing in the Nikāya and Chan texts, the extreme position of absolute denial of any form of meditative method, expressed through apophatic and paradoxical language, is limited to fragments of particular texts, such as the *Oghataraṇa* and the *Sandha-sutta*s, the selected passages of the *Rudao anxin yao fangbian famen*, the *Liuzu tanjing*, and the writings of the Niutou, Baotang and Hongzhou schools. Much more often we are dealing with what perhaps may be called a meditative method in a minimal sense. It usually involves undertaking some deliberate activities or implementation of certain mental patterns during the initial stage of meditation. Many of these activities are connected with adopting a proper meditative posture, an element that, as we have already seen, is often stressed in Chan texts. In the Nikāyas, this approach is exemplified in the texts following the *Sāmaññaphala* pattern, which explicitly speak about a meditator resorting to a secluded dwelling, sitting down, crossing the legs, holding the body erect, and setting up mindfulness before him (lit. "around the mouth or face": *parimukhaṃ*).[4]

The most elaborate Nikāya description of what may be considered a "minimal method" and represents the paradigm that we have been tracing, is probably found in the basic account of the mindfulness of breathing in the various *Ānāpānassati-suttas*.[5] The descriptions of the first two of the sixteen stages contain information that a bhikkhu knows (or understands: *pajānāti*) that his in-breaths and out-breaths are either long or short. It is worth emphasizing that although the descriptions of the remaining fourteen stages contain information that the meditator breathes in and out, they do not explicitly inform us that he knows that he is breathing. The descriptions of some of the stages (e.g., that one breathes experiencing rapture [*pītippaṭisaṃvedī*], one breathes experiencing pleasure [*sukhappaṭisaṃvedī*], and one breathes "unifying the mind" [*samādahaṃ cittaṃ*]) suggest that we are dealing with an alternative, but complementary description of the process which is described by the formula of the four *jhānas*.[6] Just as in the case of the latter, there are no explicit and detailed meditative instructions, particularly regarding the later stages.

In an attempt to fill this seeming gap, later treatises such as the *Visuddhimagga*[7] introduce new information which is absent in the Nikāya text. We learn that the meditators should first count the breaths, then follow them with their awareness and finally fix their attention on the tip of the nose or on the upper lip. When the subtle sensation connected with breath will start to fade, they should focus on the imagined sensation of breathing. This will lead to the appearance of the *nimitta* of breath which can have various forms and should become an object of concentration from now on. Nothing in the basic Nikāya formula itself suggests that this information was implied. Yet without

4 DN 2/i.71: *vivittaṃ senāsanaṃ bhajati araññaṃ rukkhamūlaṃ pabbataṃ kandaraṃ giriguhaṃ susānaṃ vanapatthaṃ abbhokāsaṃ palālapuñjaṃ. so pacchābhattaṃ piṇḍapātappaṭikkanto nisīdati pallaṅkaṃ ābhujitvā ujuṃ kāyaṃ paṇidhāya parimukhaṃ satiṃ upaṭṭhapetvā.*

5 These include the *Ānāpānassati-sutta* (MN 118/iii.78–88), and the twenty suttas of the *Ānāpāna-saṃyutta* (SN 54.1/v.311 – SN 54.20/v.341). The first tetrad of mindfulness of breathing is presented in the *Satipaṭṭhāna-suttas* (MN 10/i.55–63 and DN 22/ii.289–315) and the *Kāyagatāsati-sutta* (MN 119/iii.88–99).

6 This point has been made by Kuan (2008: 70–78). Also see Gethin (2020: 57–60) on the connection between the *jhānas* and the mindfulness of breathing.

7 Vism i.258–284/266–293/VIII.145–244.

it, the account does not fit the classical model of calm meditation, of which *ānāpānassati* is considered to be a form. Taken at face value, the lack of mention that a bhikkhu knows (*pajānāti*)[8] that he is breathing, suggests that breath is no longer the focus after the initial stages of meditation. Indeed, the text mentions that the meditator experiences the whole body (*sabbakāyappaṭisaṃvedī*), experiences mind-*saṅkhāra* (*cittasaṅkhārappaṭisaṃvedī*) or the mind itself (*cittappaṭisaṃvedī*).

The comparison between the *Visuddhimagga* and Nikāya accounts of *ānāpānassati*, allows us to highlight the differences between the approaches towards the method in the two paradigms of meditation we are considering. In Buddhaghosa's text, meditator must deliberately initiate and maintain various mental activities: counting breaths, following them with attention, focusing on the touch of breath on nose or lips, mentally imagining tactile sensation of breathing and concentrating on breath *nimitta*. Thus, the breath is in the very centre of focus throughout the whole meditative process. If we take Nikāya account at face value, then even if one starts with conscious awareness of breathing, as expressed by the usage of the verb *pajānāti*, it is no longer actively maintained at the later stages. This conscious awareness of breathing present at the initial stage of practice, could perhaps be interpreted as a minimal method, in the sense of involving deliberate, intentional

8 The fact that the verb *pajānāti* is used to describe awareness of breathing in the first two, but not the remaining stages of *ānāpānassati* may also carry additional, important meaning. It may be read as implying a reflective, conceptually mediated, introspectable and verbally expressible form of consciousness, which is not immediate. *Pajānāti* shares the same root and prefix (i.e., *pa* + √*ñā*) with words such as *paññā* and *paññatti*, which at least in the context of the *Mahānidāna-sutta* refer to conceptually mediated knowledge (in the expressions *paññattipatha* and *paññāvacara*). Thus, being aware of breathing in this way would be an imperfection of meditation which needs to be overcome, hence the absence of references to *pajānāti* in the description of the remaining fourteen stages. The mode of awareness of breathing described by the verb *pajānāti* would therefore fail to meet the criteria of bare, unmediated cognition as presented in the *Māluṅkyaputta-sutta* and the *Bāhiya-sutta*. Such an interpretation is in harmony with the remarks on the nature of absorption in Chapter 4, where I suggested that full absorption may be synonymous with the absence of introspectable, self-reflective consciousness. Those fully absorbed by their breathing process should not be able to reflectively know that they are breathing. This interpretation need not be seen as mutually exclusive with the one which reads *pajānāti* as referring to an act of deliberate meditative awareness, but rather as complementary to it and emphasizing an important additional aspect of mindfulness of breathing.

effort to be aware of one's breathing. In similar vein, the descriptions of successively experiencing the whole body, mind and mind-*saṅkhāra* could be read as implying that at the higher stages of practice, meditators make conscious, deliberate acts of will to direct their attention to these objects. However, these descriptions can also be interpreted differently. They need not be necessarily read in the sense of prescriptive instructions, telling the practitioners to be aware of their breathing, or of the states of their bodies and minds. The same can be said regarding the already mentioned phrase that a bhikkhu establishes mindfulness in front of him which is also present at the beginning of the *ānāpānassati* account. They can just as well be interpreted as descriptive in nature. If as we have considered, one sits down after having tranquillized much of the sources of mental movement through leading a disciplined virtuous lifestyle and maintaining a specific mindset, then what is left to be aware of? One's main activity is constituted by breathing, and the few remaining sensations, thoughts and urges connected with the body and the mind. At this point, the attitudes of mindfulness and comprehension have been so deeply inculcated by the training that they are pretty much automatic. One simply cannot but become aware of one's breathing, as well as of the bodily sensations and mental activities. This very awareness of the body and mind seems to contribute to a calming down of the urges, volitions and tensions connected with them respectively, as indicated by the statements that the meditator breathes "calming the body *saṅkhāra*" (*passambhayaṃ kāyasaṅkhāraṃ*) and "calming the mind *saṅkhāra*" (*passambhayaṃ cittasaṅkhāraṃ*).

It might be the case that *cittasaṅkhāra* is connected with the dhamma-thoughts mentioned in the *Paṃsudhovaka-sutta*, and represents one's striving for meditative success, and effort to concentrate or be more mindful, which as we have suggested are paradoxically detrimental to meditative progress. Read at face value, the account suggests a direct causal relationship between being aware of *cittasaṅkhāra* and its subsequent tranquillization. This may occur through the mechanism we have considered in Chapter 7 in connection with Chan texts on *wunian*, in which deliberately maintained form of awareness ultimately negates itself. If one tries to be aware of one's breathing but is not at that time aware of one's mental act of trying to be aware, then such a person cannot be said to be fully mindful or aware, as there remains an important element of mental activity of which one is not conscious. If, on the other hand, one becomes aware of one's own efforts to be aware of breathing, then this meta-awareness cuts off, at least temporarily, one's deliberate attempt to be aware, as these two mental states cannot simultaneously coexist. Thus, we could perhaps talk about a sort of a self-fuelling or self-propelling mechanism through which awareness intensifies itself and which does not require being driven by conscious mental effort, as the latter is negated during the higher stage of practice. Of course, the success of this type of meditation will to a great extent depend on the prior removal of hindrances which, as we have already discussed, results from maintaining a specific lifestyle and mindset.

Interpreted in this way, the mindfulness of breathing is in harmony with the paradigm we have been tracing in the Nikāya and Chan texts. As was the case with no-thought (*wunian*), even if one starts with a method in a minimal sense, it is eventually transcended and let go off at the higher stages of progress. We have also encountered this approach in the *Bhikkhunupassaya-sutta*, where intentionally directing the mind to an inspiring feature merely serves as temporary means to combat certain hindrances. The default mode of meditation seems to be that of non-directing (*appaṇidhāya*).

Throughout this book I have sometimes stressed that it is impossible to reach absolute and infallible certainty regarding the meaning intended by the authors of certain passages of Nikāya and Chan texts, due to the fact that they are not explicit, exhaustive and systematic enough. Let us suppose for the sake of argument that despite the abundant evidence to the contrary, Nikāya and Chan Buddhists were in fact practising meditation in the mainstream sense, counting breaths, focusing on mental *nimitta*s or recollecting the Buddha (*nianfo*), though somewhat perversely they have created texts that, when read directly, suggest the exact opposite. Would that make the considerations in this book meaningless and useless? I do not believe that to be the case. History knows of many instances when following wrong assumptions has led to valuable results, which would otherwise not be possible. By following up on the hypothesis of the absence of a meditative method, we have been able to identify several factors of the Buddhist path that are not strictly meditative, but greatly contribute to meditative success, and have proposed an explanation of the psychological mechanisms through which it occurs. Even in the unlikely case of meditation being practised in Nikāya Buddhism and early Chan in a mainstream way, these factors are still very important for understanding meditation and its progress. The historically dominant conceptualizations of meditation need to be considered limited and one-sided due to not taking these factors into account and instead focusing on various scholastic distinctions and classifications. Thus, the results of our investigation would still be relevant.

And finally, how can we explain the presence of the far-reaching similarities between Nikāya and Chan approaches to meditation? The notion of a direct, unbroken line of transmission between the Chan patriarchs and the Buddha himself, as contained in Chan texts, does not seem historically plausible. Nonetheless, it needs to be said that the teachings of Bodhidharma were significantly different from the dominant approach to meditation which was present in China in his era. Perhaps he was indeed a representative of some unique Indian tradition of which we unfortunately possess no knowledge whatsoever. However, it seems far more probable that Chan Buddhists have independently arrived at some ideas which were similar to the early Buddhist ones. Such a hypothesis is of course based on an assumption that it is possible for the thinkers or meditators to arrive at similar ideas without their direct transmission and in relatively different historical, social and cultural contexts. The possibility of Chan Buddhists arriving at ideas similar to early Buddhist ones is however based on the very idea of human nature. Ideas present in the Nikāyas and early Chan texts may have been similar, simply because they could have been a result of reflections on authentic experiences which were ultimately based on the actual functioning of the human mind. And as natural science tells us, the latter has not changed in the period which separates the time of creation of the Nikāyas from the Tang dynasty period in China.

The Chan discourse can be seen as a reemergence of certain ideas which have been neglected in the mainstream approach to meditation, and as a criticism of the latter's limitations. Of course, the Chan discourse could probably be considered guilty of its own specific excess and one-sidedness, particularly regarding its neglect of the forms of gradual practice. This resulted in certain difficulties and paradoxes with which the Chan authors struggled in their texts. However, in light of the considerations in this book, the view that Chan was merely a meta-discourse which had nothing new to offer regarding practical matters must be considered highly inadequate.

It is probably true that the paradigm present in Nikāya and early Chan texts did not have a particularly large influence on the history of Buddhism. The very fact that it is so different from mainstream Buddhist ideas implies that its impact was limited, and other interpretations of Buddhist teaching were ultimately more influential. However, the extent of historical influence is not the only criterion for assessing the value of philosophical ideas. Several great philosophers were ignored and forgotten, only to be rediscovered later.

Many of the Nikāya and early Chan ideas that we have considered in this book are original and impressive from a philosophical perspective and have no direct correspondents in the mainstream forms of Buddhism as well as in Western thought. Their relevance is not limited to their particular historical and cultural contexts, as the issues they touch upon are universally important. Therefore, they should be considered a very important contribution to human thought and deserve the utmost attention of anyone vitally interested in the questions of the nature of reality, personal identity, the meaning of life and self-realization.

BIBLIOGRAPHY

Primary sources

Pali texts

Aṅguttara Nikāya, Chaṭṭha Saṅgāyana Edition.
Dhammapada, Chaṭṭha Saṅgāyana Edition.
Dhammasaṅgaṇī, Chaṭṭha Saṅgāyana Edition.
Dīgha Nikāya, Chaṭṭha Saṅgāyana Edition.
Itivuttaka, Chaṭṭha Saṅgāyana Edition.
Khandhaka, Chaṭṭha Saṅgāyana Edition.
Khuddaka Nikāya, Chaṭṭha Saṅgāyana Edition.
Majjhima Nikāya, Chaṭṭha Saṅgāyana Edition.
Milindapañha, Chaṭṭha Saṅgāyana Edition.
Saṃyutta Nikāya, Chaṭṭha Saṅgāyana Edition.
Sāratthapakāsinī, Chaṭṭha Saṅgāyana Edition.
Suttanipāta, Chaṭṭha Saṅgāyana Edition.
Theragāthā, Chaṭṭha Saṅgāyana Edition.
Therīgāthā, Chaṭṭha Saṅgāyana Edition.
Udāna, Chaṭṭha Saṅgāyana Edition.
Visuddhimagga, Chaṭṭha Saṅgāyana Edition.

Chinese texts

Baizhang Huaihai chanshi guanglu 百丈懷海禪師廣錄, X69, no. 1323.
Chanyuan qinggui 禪苑清規, X63, no. 1245.
Chanyuan zhuquanji duxu 禪源諸詮集都序, T48, no. 2015.
Chuanxin fa yao 傳心法要, T48, no. 2012A.
Daofan qusheng xinjue 導凡趣聖心決, in Nobuyoshi Yamabe, "Yogācāra Influence on the Northern School of Chan Buddhism", in *Buddhist Meditative Traditions: Their Origin and Development*, edited by Kuo-pin Chuang, 280. Taipei: Shin Wen Feng, 2014.
Dasheng kaixin xianxing dunwu zhenzong lun 大乘開心顯性頓悟真宗論, T85, no. 2835.
Dasheng wusheng fangbian men 大乘無生方便門, T85, no. 2834.
Dunwu rudao yaomen lun 頓悟入道要門論, X63, no. 1223.

Erru sixing lun 二入四行論 (*Putidamo dashi lüebian dasheng rudao sixing guan* 菩提達磨大師略辨大乘入道四行觀), X63, no. 1217, p. 1a20–b24.
Fajie cidi chumen 法界次第初門, T46, no. 1925.
Jingde chuandeng lu, T51, no. 2076.
Jueguan lun 絕觀論, B18, no. 101.
Lengqie shizi ji 楞伽師資記, T85, no. 2837.
Liuzu tanjing 六祖壇經 (Full title: *Nanzong dunjiao zuishangsheng mohe boreboluomi jing, liuzu Huineng dashi yu shaozhou dafansi shi fa tanjing* 南宗頓教最上大乘摩訶般若波羅蜜經六祖惠能大師於韶州大梵寺施法壇經), T48, no. 2007.
Mazu Daoyi chanshi guanglu 馬祖道一禪師廣錄, X69, no. 1321.
Nanyang heshang dunjiao jietuo chanmen zhiliaoxing tanyu 南陽和上頓教解脱禪門直了性壇語, B25, no. 142, pp. 5a04–34a7.
Nanyang heshang wenda zazheng yi 南陽和尚問答雜徵義, B25, no. 143, pp. 213a06–238a9.
Putidamo nanzong dingshifei lun 菩提達磨南宗定是非論, B25, no. 142, pp. 42a02–52a5.
Rudao anxin yao fangbian famen 入道安心要方便法門, T85, no. 2837, pp. 1286c19–1289b10.
Sengbao zhengxu zhuan 僧寶正續傳, X79, no. 1561.
Shi chan boluomi cidi famen 釋禪波羅蜜次第法門, T46, no. 1916.
Tiansheng guangdeng lu 天聖廣燈錄, X78, no. 1553.
Xiuxi zhiguan zuochan fayao 修習止觀坐禪法要, T46, no. 1915.
Xiuxin yao lun 修心要論, in John R. McRae, *The Northern School and the Formation of Early Ch'an Buddhism*. Studies in East Asian Buddhism 3. Honolulu: University of Hawaii Press, 1986: 424–39.
Xu gao seng chuan 續高僧傳, T50, no. 2060.
Xuansha Shibei chanshi guanglu 玄沙師備禪師廣錄, X73, no. 1445.
Yuanjuejing dashu shiyi chao 圓覺經大疏釋義鈔, X09, no. 245.
Wuxin lun 無心論, T85, no. 2831.
Za ahanjing 雜阿含經, T02, no. 99.
Zhao lun 肇論, T45, no. 1858.
Zhenzhou Linji Huizhao chanshi yulu 鎮州臨濟慧照禪師語錄, T47, no. 1985.
Zhong ahanjing 中阿含經, T01, no. 26.
Zhufang menren canwen yulu 諸方門人參問語錄, X63, no. 1224.
Zimen jingxun 緇門警訓, T48, no. 2023.
Zongjing lu 宗鏡錄, T48, no. 2016.
Zuochan ming 坐禪名, T48, no. 2023, p. 1048b28–c21.

Secondary sources

Adamek, Wendi. 2007. *The Mystique of Transmission: On an Early Chan History and Its Contexts*. New York: Columbia University Press.
Adamek, Wendi. 2011. *The Teachings of Master Wuzhu: Zen and Religion of No-Religion.* New York: Columbia University Press.
Albahari, Miri. 2007. *Analytical Buddhism: The Two-tiered Illusion of Self.* New York: Palgrave Macmillan.

Allen, Micah, and Manos Tsakiris. 2019. "The body as first prior: Interoceptive predictive processing and the primacy of self-models", in *The Interoceptive Mind: From Homeostasis to Awareness*, edited by Manos Tsakiris and Helena De Preester, 27–45. Oxford: Oxford University Press.

Anālayo, Bhikkhu. 2009. "The Treatise on the Path to Liberation (解脫道論) and the Visuddhimagga", *Fuyan Buddhist Studies*, 4: 1–15.

Anālayo, Bhikkhu. 2010. *From Grasping to Emptiness: Excursions into the Thought-world of the Pāli Discourses*. Carmel: The Buddhist Association of the United States.

Anālayo, Bhikkhu. 2017a. "Nāma-rūpa", in *Buddhism and Jainism: Encyclopedia of Indian Religions*, edited by K.T.S. Sarao and Jeffrey D. Long, 802–804. Dordrecht: Springer.

Anālayo, Bhikkhu. 2017b. *Early Buddhist Meditation Studies*. Barre, MA: Barre Center for Buddhist Studies.

Anālayo, Bhikkhu. 2020. "A brief history of Buddhist absorption", *Mindfulness*, 11(3): 571–86. https://doi.org/10.1007/s12671-019-01268-7

App, Urs. 1995. "Treatise on No-Mind: A Chan text from Dunhuang", *The Eastern Buddhist. New Series*, 28(1): 70–107.

Arbel, Keren. 2017. *Early Buddhist Meditation: The Four Jhānas as the Actualization of Insight*. London: Routledge.

Attwood, Jayarava. 2022. "The cessation of sensory experience and *Prajñāpāramitā* philosophy", *International Journal of Buddhist Thought & Culture*, 32(1): 111–48. https://doi.org/10.16893/IJBTC.2022.06.32.1.111

Baars, Bernard. J. 1997. *In the Theatre of Consciousness: The Workspace of the Mind*. New York and Oxford: Oxford University Press.

Baars, Bernard J., and Stan Franklin. 2007. "An architectural model of conscious and unconscious brain functions: Global Workspace Theory and IDA", *Neural Networks*, 20: 955–61. https://doi.org/10.1016/j.neunet.2007.09.013

Baars, Bernard J., Natalie Geld, and Robert Kozma. 2021. "Global Workspace Theory (GWT) and prefrontal cortex: Recent developments", *Frontiers in Psychology*, 12 (10 November). https://doi.org/10.3389/fpsyg.2021.749868

Bagassi, Maria, and Laura Macchi. 2016. "The interpretative function and the emergence of unconscious analytic thought", in *Cognitive Unconscious and Human Rationality*, ed. Laura Macchi, Maria Bagassi, and Ricardo Viale, 43–76. Cambridge: The MIT Press.

Bapat, P.V. 1937. *Vimuttimagga and Visuddhimagga, a Comparative Study*. Poona: P. V. Bapat.

Bielefeldt, Carl. 1986. "Ch'ang-lu Tsung-tse's Tso-ch'an I and the 'secret' of Zen meditation", in *Traditions of Meditation in Chinese Buddhism*, edited by Peter Gregory, 129–61. Honolulu: University of Hawaii Press.

Bielefeldt, Carl. 1988. *Dōgen's Manuals of Zen Meditation*. Berkeley: University of California Press.

Blackmore, Susan. 2017. "Delusions of consciousness", in *Illusionism as a Theory of Consciousness*, edited by Keith Frankish, 64–79. Exeter: Imprint Academic.

Blofeld, John (trans.). 1962. *Zen Teaching of Instantaneous Awakening: being the teaching of the Zen Master Hui Hai, known as the Great Pearl*. London: Rider & Company.

Bodhi, Bhikkhu (trans.). 2000. *The Connected Discourses of the Buddha: A New Translation of the Saṃyutta Nikāya*. Boston: Wisdom Publications.

Bodhi, Bhikkhu (trans.). 2007. *The Great Discourse on Causation: The Mahānidāna-sutta and its Commentaries*. Kandy: Buddhist Publication Society.

Bodhi, Bhikkhu (trans.). 2012. *The Numerical Discourses of the Buddha: A Translation of the Aṅguttara Nikāya*. Boston: Wisdom Publications.

Bodhi, Bhikkhu (trans.). 2017. *The-suttanipāta: A Collection of Ancient Buddhist Texts. Translated from the Pāli Together with its Commentary Paramatthajotikā II, 'The Elucidator of the Supreme Meaning', and Excerpts from the Niddesa*. Boston: Wisdom Publications.

Brahm, Ajahn. 2006. *Mindfulness, Bliss, and Beyond: A Meditator's Handbook*. Boston: Wisdom Publications.

Braun, Erik. 2013. *The Birth of Insight: Meditation, Modern Buddhism, and the Burmese Monk Ledi Sayadaw*. Chicago and London: The University of Chicago Press.

Bronkhorst, Johannes. 1986. *The Two Traditions of Meditation in Ancient India*. Stuttgart: Franz Steiner Verlag Wiesbaden GmbH.

Bronkhorst, Johannes. 2007. *Greater Magadha: Studies in the Culture of Early India*, Leiden: Brill.

Bronkhorst, Johannes. 2012. *Absorption: Human Nature and Buddhist Liberation*. Paris: University Media.

Bronkhorst, Johannes. 2016. "Can religion be explained? The role of absorption in various religious phenomena", *Method and Theory in the Study of Religion*, 29(1): 1–30. https://doi.org/10.1163/15700682-12341375

Bronkhorst, Johannes. 2019. "What can we learn from Musīla and Nārada?", *The Indian International Journal of Buddhist Studies*, 20: 1–19.

Bronkhorst, Johannes. 2022. "Mystical experience", *Religions*, 13(7): 589 (1–20). https://doi.org/10.3390/rel13070589

Bronkhorst, Johannes. 2023. "The Buddhist noble truths: Are they true?", *Religions* 14(1): 82 (1–19). https://doi.org/10.3390/rel14010082

Broughton, Jeffrey L. 1999. *The Bodhidharma Anthology: The Earliest Records of Zen*. Berkeley: University of California Press.

Broughton, Jeffrey L. 2009. *Zongmi on Chan*. New York and Chichester: Columbia University Press.

Broughton, Jeffrey L., and Elise Yoko Watanabe. 2017. *The Letters of Chan Master Dahui Pujue*. New York: Oxford University Press.

Bucknell, Roderick S. 1993. "Reinterpreting the jhānas", *Journal of the International Association of Buddhist Studies*, 16(2): 375–409.

Bucknell, Roderick S. 2023. *Reconstructing Early Buddhism*. Cambridge and New York: Cambridge University Press.

Buonomano, Dean. 2017. *Your Brain is a Time Machine: The Neuroscience and Physics of Time*. New York and London: W. W. Norton and Company.

Carruthers, Peter. 2015. *The Centered Mind: What the Science of Working Memory Shows Us about the Nature of Human Thought*. Oxford: Oxford University Press.

Chappell, David. 1983. "The teachings of the fourth Ch'an Patriarch Tao-hsin (580–651)", in *Early Ch'an in China and Tibet*, Berkeley Buddhist Studies Series 5, edited by Lewis Lancaster and Whalen Lai, 89–129. Berkeley: University of California Press.

Cheng Chien, Bhikshu (Mario Poceski) (trans.). 1993. *Sun-Face Buddha: The Teachings of Ma-tsu and the Hung-chou School of Ch'an*. Berkeley: Asian Humanities Press.

Cleary, Thomas (trans). 1978. *Sayings and Doings of Pai-chang*. Los Angeles: Center Publications.

Collins, Steven. 1982. *Selfless Persons: Imagery and Thought in Theravāda Buddhism*. Cambridge: Cambridge University Press.

Cone, Margaret. 2001. *Dictionary of Pali. Part I a-kh*. Oxford: The Pali Text Society.

Cone, Margaret. 2010. *Dictionary of Pali. Part II g-n*. Bristol: The Pali Text Society.

Coseru, Christian. 2012. *Perceiving Reality: Consciousness, Intentionality and Cognition in Buddhist Philosophy*. New York: Oxford University Press.

Coseru, Christian. 2020. "Whose consciousness? Reflexivity and the problem of self-knowledge", in *Buddhist Philosophy of Consciousness: Tradition and Dialogue*, edited by Mark Siderits, Ching Keng, and John Spackman, 121–53. Leiden and Boston: Brill.

Costines, Cyril, Tilmann Lhündrup Borghardt, and Marc Wittmann. 2021. "The phenomenology of 'pure' consciousness as reported by an experienced meditator of the Tibetan Buddhist Karma Kagyu tradition. Analysis of interview content concerning different meditative states", *Philosophies*, 6(2): 50 (1–22). https://doi.org/10.3390/philosophies6020050

Crosby, Kate. 1999. "History versus modern myth: The Abhayagirivihāra, the *Vimuttimagga* and *Yogāvacara* meditation", *Journal of Indian Philosophy*, 27: 503–550.

Csikszentmihalyi, Mihaly. 1996. *Creativity*. New York: Harper Perennial.

Csikszentmihalyi, Mihaly. 2013. *Creativity: The Psychology of Discovery and Invention*. New York: Harper Perennial Modern Classics.

Damasio, Antonio. 1999. *The Feeling of What Happens: Body and Emotion in the Making of Consciousness*. New York: Harcourt Brace & Company.

Dambrun, Michaël. 2016. "When the dissolution of perceived body boundaries elicits happiness: The effect of selflessness induced by a body scan meditation", *Consciousness and Cognition*, 46: 89–98. https://doi.org/10.1016/j.concog.2016.09.013

Davis, Jake H. 2003. "From Burma to Barre", *Insight Journal*, 21: 9–14.

Davis, Jake H. 2004. *Strong Roots: Liberation Teachings of Mindfulness in North America*. Barre, MA: DHAMMA DANA Publications at the Barre Center for Buddhist Studies.

Davis, Jake H. 2016. "The scope for wisdom: Early Buddhism on reasons and persons", in *The Bloomsbury Research Handbook of Indian Ethics*, edited by Shyam Ranganathan, 127–54. London: Bloomsbury Academic.

Davis, Jake H., and David R. Vago. 2013. "Can enlightenment be traced to specific neural correlates, cognition or behavior? No, and (a qualified) yes", *Frontiers in Psychology*, 4: 870. https://doi.org/10.3389/fpsyg.2013.00870

Dietrich, Arne. 2003. "Functional neuroanatomy of altered states of consciousness: The transient hypofrontality hypothesis", *Consciousness and Cognition*, 12: 231–56. https://doi.org/10.1016/S1053-8100(02)00046-6

Dietrich, Arne. 2004. "Neurocognitive mechanisms underlying the experience of flow", *Consciousness and Cognition*, 13: 746–61. https://doi.org/10.1016/j.concog.2004.07.002

Dijksterhuis, Ap, Henk Aarts, and Pamela K. Smith. 2005. "The power of the subliminal: On subliminal persuasion and other potential applications", in *The*

New Unconscious, edited by Ran R. Hassin, James S. Uleman, and John A. Bargh, 77–106. New York: Oxford University Press.

Edkins, Joseph. 1890. *Chinese Buddhism: A Volume of Sketches, Historical, Descriptive, and Critical.* London: Kegan Paul, Trench, Trübner and Co.

Faure, Bernard. 1993. *Chan Insights and Oversights: An Epistemological Critique of the Chan Tradition.* Princeton: Princeton University Press.

Foulk, T. Griffith. 2021. *Record of the Transmission of Illumination: Volume 2. A Glossary of Terms, Sayings, and Names pertaining to Keizan's Denkōroku.* Honolulu: University of Hawai'i Press. https://doi.org/10.2307/j.ctv2crj1hm

Funayama, Toru. 2020. "The genesis of *Svasaṃvitti-saṃvitti* reconsidered", in *Buddhist Philosophy of Consciousness: Tradition and Dialogue*, edited by Mark Siderits, Ching Keng, and John Spackman, 209–224. Leiden and Boston: Brill.

Garfield, Jay L. 2015. *Engaging Buddhism*. New York: Oxford University Press.

Gethin, Rupert. 1986. "The five khandhas: Their treatment in the Nikāyas and early Abhidhamma", *Journal of Indian Philosophy*, 14(1): 35–53. https://doi.org/10.1007/BF00165825

Gethin, Rupert. 2001. *The Buddhist Path to Awakening*. Oxford: Oneworld Publications.

Gethin, Rupert. 2004. "On the practice of Buddhist meditation according to the Pāli Nikāyas and exegetical sources", *Buddhismus in Geschichte und Gegenwart*, 9: 201–221.

Gethin, Rupert. 2020. "Schemes of the Buddhist Path in the Nikāyas and Āgamas", in *Mārga: Paths to Liberation in South Asian Buddhist Traditions*, edited by Cristina Pecchia and Vincent Eltschinger, 5–77. Vienna: Austrian Academy of Sciences Press.

Glattfelder, James B. 2019. *Information–Consciousness–Reality: How a New Understanding of the Universe Can Help Answer Age-Old Questions of Existence.* Cham: Springer.

Gombrich, Richard F. 2004. "Religious experience in early Buddhism", in *Religion: Empirical Studies: A Collection to Mark the 50th Anniversary of the British Association for the Study of Religions*, edited by Steven J. Sutcliffe, 123–48. Aldershot: Ashgate.

Gombrich, Richard F. 2006. *How Buddhism Began: The Conditioned Genesis of the Early Teachings*. Second edition. London and New York: Routledge. First Edition, London: Athlone Press, 1996.

Gombrich, Richard F. 2009. *What the Buddha Thought*. London: Equinox Publishing.

Gómez, Luis O. 1976. "Proto-Mādhyamika in the Pāli canon", *Philosophy East and West*, 26(2): 137–65. http://www.doi.org/10.2307/1398186

Gómez, Luis O. 1983. "The direct and the gradual approaches of Zen Master Mahāyāna: Fragments of the teachings of Mo-ho-yen", in *Studies in Ch'an and Hua-Yen*, Kuroda Institute Studies in East Asian Buddhism 4, edited by Robert M. Gimello and Peter N. Gregory, 69–167. Honolulu: University of Hawaii Press.

Gómez, Luis O. 1987. "Purifying gold: The metaphor of effort and intuition in Buddhist thought and practice", in *Sudden and Gradual: Approaches to Enlightenment in Chinese Thought*, edited by Peter Gregory, 67–165. Honolulu: University of Hawaii Press.

Greene, Eric M. 2008. "Another look at Early Chan: Daoxuan, Bodhidharma, and the Three Levels movement", *T'oung Pao*, 94: 49–114. https://doi.org/10.1163/008254308X367022

Greene, Eric M. 2017. "The Dust Contemplation", *The Eastern Buddhist*, 48(2): 1–50.

Greene, Eric M. 2021. *Chan before Chan: Meditation, Repentance, and Visionary Experience in Chinese Buddhism.* Honolulu: University of Hawaii Press.

Gregory, Peter N. 2012. "The Platform Sūtra as the Sudden Teaching", in *Readings of the Platform Sūtra*, edited by Morten Schlütter and Stephen F. Teiser, 77–108. New York: Columbia University Press.

Griffiths, Paul. 1981. "Concentration or insight: The problematic of Theravāda Buddhist meditation-theory", *Journal of the American Academy of Religion*, 49(4): 605–624. https://doi.org/10.1093/jaarel/XLIX.4.605

Gunaratana, H. Mahathera. 1985. *The Path of Serenity and Insight: An Explanation of the Buddhist Jhānas.* Delhi: Motilal Banarsidass.

Hamilton, Sue. 1996. *Identity and Experience: The Constitution of the Human Being According to Early Buddhism.* London: Luzac Oriental.

Hamilton, Sue. 1999. "The 'external world': Its status and relevance in the Pali Nikayas", *Religion*, 29: 73–90. https://doi.org/10.1006/reli.1999.0166

Hamilton, Sue. 2000. *Early Buddhism: A New Approach.* Surrey: Curzon Press.

Harvey, Peter. 1995. *The Selfless Mind: Personality, Consciousness and Nirvana in Buddhism.* Surrey: Curzon Press.

Hassin, Ran. 2005. "Nonconscious control and implicit working memory", in *The New Unconscious*, edited by Ran Hassin, James S. Uleman, and John A. Bargh, 196–223. New York: Oxford University Press.

Heim, Maria. 2013. "Mind in Theravāda Buddhism", in *A Companion to Buddhist Philosophy*, edited by S.M. Emmanuel, 377–94. Malden: Wiley-Blackwell.

Hertrich, Ingo, Susanne Dietrich, and Hermann Ackermann. 2016. "The role of the supplementary motor area for speech and language processing", *Neuroscience and Biobehavioral Reviews*, 68: 602–610. https://doi.org/10.1016/j.neubiorev.2016.06.030

Hirakawa, Akira. 1990. *A History of Indian Buddhism: From Śākyamuni to Early Mahāyāna.* Honolulu: University of Hawaii Press.

Horner, I. B. (trans.). 2001. *The Book of the Discipline (Vinaya Piṭaka). Volume V (Cullavagga).* Oxford: The Pali Text Society.

Ishida, Hoyu. 1996. "The problem of practice in Shen-hui's teaching of Sudden Enlightenment", *Academic Reports of the University Center for Intercultural Education*, 1: 1–10. Hikone: The University of Shiga Prefecture.

Jammer, Max. 2002. *Einstein and Religion: Physics and Theology.* Princeton: Princeton University Press.

Jia, Jinhua. 2006. *The Hongzhou School of Chan Buddhism.* Albany: State University of New York Press.

Jianxun, Shi. 2022. *Mapping the Buddhist Path to Liberation: Diversity and Consistency Based on the Pāli Nikāyas and the Chinese Āgamas.* Singapore: Springer Nature Singapore.

Khalsa, Sahib S., and Justin S. Feinstein. 2019. "The somatic error hypothesis of anxiety", in *The Interoceptive Mind: From Homeostasis to Awareness*, edited by Manos Tsakiris and Helena De Preester, 144–64. Oxford: Oxford University Press.

King, Winston L. 1992. *Theravāda Meditation: The Buddhist Transformation of Yoga.* Delhi: Motilal Banarsidass.

Kornfield, Jack. 1996. *Living Dharma: Teachings of the Twelve Buddhist Masters.* Boston and London: Shambhala Publications.

Kuan, Tse-fu. 2008. *Mindfulness in Early Buddhism: New Approaches through Psychology and Textual Analysis of Pali, Chinese and Sanskrit Sources.* London: Routledge.

Laukkonen, Ruben E., and Heleen A. Slagter. 2021. "From many to (n)one: Meditation and the plasticity of the predictive mind", *Neuroscience & Biobehavioral Reviews*, 128: 199–217. https://doi.org/10.1016/j.neubiorev.2021.06.021

Laukkonen, Ruben E., Matthew D. Sacchet, Henk Barendregt, Kathryn J. Devaney, Avijit Chowdhury, and Heleen A. Slagter. 2023. "Cessations of consciousness in meditation: Advancing a scientific understanding of *nirodha samāpatti*", *Progress in Brain Research* 280: 61–87. https://doi.org/10.1016/bs.pbr.2022.12.007

Levman, Bryan Geoffrey. 2017a. "Language theory, phonology and etymology in Buddhism and their relationship to Brahmanism", *Buddhist Studies Review*, 34(1): 25–51. https://doi.org/10.1558/bsrv.31031

Levman, Bryan Geoffrey. 2017b. "Putting *smṛti* back into *sati* (Putting remembrance back into mindfulness)", *Journal of the Oxford Centre for Buddhist Studies*, 13: 121–49.

Libet, Benjamin. 2004. *Mind Time: The Temporal Factor in Consciousness.* Cambridge, MA and London: Harvard University Press.

Madl, Tamas, Bernard J. Baars, and Stan Franklin. 2011. "The timing of the cognitive cycle", *PLoS One* 6(4): e14803. https://doi.org/10.1371/journal.pone.0014803

Mahasi, Sayadaw. 1980. *Purpose of Practising Kammaṭṭhāna Meditation* (U. Min, trans.). Swe, Rangoon: Buddha Sāsanā Nuggaha Organization.

Marchetti, Giorgio. 2014. "Attention and working memory: Two basic mechanisms for constructing temporal experiences", *Frontiers in Psychology*, 5(880): 1–15. https://doi.org/10.3389/fpsyg.2014.00880

Mattes, Josef. 2022. "Positive psychology and philosophy-as-usual: An unhappy match?", *Philosophies* 7(3): 52. https://doi.org/10.3390/philosophies7030052

McRae, John R. 1983. "The Ox-head School of Chinese Ch'an Buddhism: From Early Ch'an to the Golden Age", in *Studies in Ch'an and Huayen*, Kuroda Institute Studies in East Asian Buddhism 4, edited by Robert M. Gimello and Peter N. Gregory, 169–252. Honolulu: University of Hawaii Press.

McRae, John R. 1986. *The Northern School and the Formation of Early Ch'an Buddhism.* Honolulu: University of Hawaii Press.

McRae, John R. 1987. "Shen-hui and the teaching of Sudden Enlightenment", in *Sudden and Gradual: Approaches to Enlightenment in Chinese Thought*, edited by Peter Gregory, 227–78. Honolulu: University of Hawaii Press.

McRae, John R. 2001. "Religion as revolution in Chinese historiography: Hu Shih (1891–1962) on Shen-hui (684–758)", *Cahiers d'Extrême-Asie*, 12: 59–102. https://doi.org/10.3406/asie.2001.1165

McRae, John R. 2003. *Seeing through Zen: Encounter, Genealogy, and Transformation in Chinese Chan Buddhism.* Berkeley: University of California Press.

McRae, John R. (trans.). 2005. "Essentials of the Transmission of Mind (Taishø Volume 48, Number 2012-A)", in *Zen Texts*, 1–42. Berkeley: Numata Center for Buddhist Translation and Research.

McRae, John R. 2023. *Zen Evangelist: Shenhui, Sudden Enlightenment, and the Southern School of Chan Buddhism.* Edited by James Robson, Robert H. Sharf, and Fedde De Vries. Honolulu: University of Hawaii Press.

Mercier, Hugo, and Dan Sperber. 2011. "Why do humans reason? Arguments for an argumentative theory", *Behavioral and Brain Sciences*, 34: 57–111. https://doi.org/10.1017/S0140525X10000968

Metzinger, Thomas. 2003. *Being No One: The Self-Model Theory of Subjectivity*. Cambridge, MA: MIT Press.

Metzinger, Thomas. 2009. *The Ego Tunnel: The Science of the Mind and the Myth of the Self*. New York: Basic Books.

Naccache, Lionel. 2018. "Why and how access consciousness can account for phenomenal consciousness", *Philosophical Transactions of the Royal Society B*. 373(1755). http://dx.doi.org/10.1098/rstb.2017.0357

Nagel, Thomas. 1974. "What is it like to be a bat?", *The Philosophical Review*, 83(4): 435–50. https://doi.org/10.2307/2183914

Ñāṇamoli, Bhikkhu. 2010. *The Path of Purification (Visuddhimagga) by Bhadantācariya Buddhaghosa*. Kandy: Buddhist Publication Society.

Nāṇamoli, Bhikkhu, and Bhikkhu Bodhi (trans.). 1995. *The Middle Length Discourses of the Buddha: A New Translation of the Majjhima Nikāya*. Boston: Wisdom Publications.

Ñāṇananda, Kaṭukurunde Bhikkhu. 2016. *Nibbāna – The Mind Stilled. Library Edition (Sermons 1-33)*. Sri Lanka: Kaṭukurunde Ñāṇananda Sadaham Senasun Bhāraya.

Nizamis, Khristos. 2012. "'*I*' without '*I am*': On the presence of subjectivity in early Buddhism, in the light of transcendental phenomenology", *Buddhist Studies Review*, 29(2): 175–250. https://doi.org/10.1558/bsrv.v29i2.175-250

Oakley, David A., and Peter W. Halligan. 2017. "Chasing the rainbow: The non-conscious nature of being", *Frontiers in Psychology* 8: 1–16. https://doi.org/10.3389/fpsyg.2017.01924

Poceski, Mario. 2007. *Ordinary Mind as the Way: The Hongzhou School and the Growth of Chan Buddhism*. Oxford: Oxford University Press.

Poceski, Mario. 2015a. "Conceptions and attitudes towards contemplative practice within the early traditions of Chan Buddhism", *Journal of Chinese Buddhist Studies*, 28: 67–116.

Poceski, Mario. 2015b. *The Records of Mazu and the Making of Classical Chan Literature*. New York: Oxford University Press.

Polak, Grzegorz. 2011. *Reexamining Jhāna: Towards a Critical Reconstruction of Early Buddhist Soteriology*. Lublin: Wydawnictwo UMCS.

Polak, Grzegorz. 2016. "How Was Liberating Insight Related to the Development of the Four Jhānas in Early Buddhism? A New Perspective through an Interdisciplinary Approach", *Journal of the Oxford Centre for Buddhist Studies*, 10: 85–112.

Polak, Grzegorz. 2022. "Does the not-Self (*anattā*) teaching in the Nikāyas presuppose the existence of a special type of consciousness?", *ARGUMENT: Biannual Philosophical Journal*, 12(1): 129–46.

Polak, Grzegorz. 2023a. "Can cessation be a cognitive state? Philosophical implications of the apophatic teachings of the early Buddhist Nikāyas", *Philosophy East and West*, 73(3): 740–61. https://doi.org/10.1353/pew.2023.a903371

Polak, Grzegorz. 2023b. "Who identifies with the aggregates? Philosophical implications of selected *khandha* passages in the Nikāyas", *Journal of Indian Philosophy*, 51: 663–85. https://doi.org/10.1007/s10781-023-09550-8

Polak, Grzegorz. 2023c. "The pleasure of not experiencing anything: Some reflections on consciousness in the context of the early Buddhist Nikāyas", *Religions*, 14(11): 1347 (1–25) https://doi.org/10.3390/rel14111347

Price, Huw. 1997. *Time's Arrow and Archimedes' Point: New Directions for the Physics of Time*. New York and Oxford: Oxford University Press.

Rahula, Walpola. 1980. "Psychology of Buddhist meditation", in *Indianisme et Bouddhisme: Mélanges offerts à Mgr Étienne Lamotte*, 267–79. Louvain-la-Neuve: Université Catholique de Louvain, Institut Orientaliste.

Rama, Swami. 2004. *Path of Fire and Light. Volume 1: Advanced Practices of Yoga.* Honesdale: Himalayan Institute Press.

Read, Rupert. 2009. "Wittgenstein and Zen Buddhism: One practice, no dogma", in *Pointing at the Moon: Buddhism, Logic, Analytic Philosophy*, edited by Mario D'Amato, Jay L. Garfield, and Tom J. F. Tillemans, 13–24. New York: Oxford University Press.

Reale, Giovanni. 1985. *A History of Ancient Philosophy III: The Systems of the Hellenistic Age*. Albany: State University of New York Press.

Reber, Arthur S. 1996. *Implicit Learning and Tacit Knowledge: An Essay on the Cognitive Unconscious.* New York and London: Oxford University Press.

Rhys Davids, Thomas W., and William Stede. 2007. *The Pali-English Dictionary.* Springfield, VA: Nataraj Books.

Robinson, Richard H. 1976. *Early Mādhyamika in India and China.* Delhi: Motilal Banarsidass.

Ronkin, Noa. 2005. *Early Buddhist Metaphysics: The Making of a Philosophical Tradition.* London and New York: RoutledgeCurzon.

Rose, Kenneth. 2016. *Yoga, Meditation, and Mysticism: Contemplative Universals and Meditative Landmarks.* London: Bloomsbury Academic.

Sapir, Edward. 1929. "The status of linguistics as a science", *Language*, 5(4): 207–214. https://doi.org/10.2307/409588

Sasaki, Ruth Fuller. 2009. *The Record of Linji.* Edited by Thomas Yuho Kirchner. Honolulu: University of Hawaii Press.

Schlütter, Morten. 2007. "Transmission and Enlightenment in Chan Buddhism seen through the Platform Sūtra (Liuzu tanjing 六祖壇經)", *Chung-Hwa Buddhist Journal*, 20: 379–410.

Schlütter, Morten. 2008. *How Zen Became Zen: The Dispute over Enlightenment and the Formation of Chan Buddhism in Song-Dynasty China.* Honolulu: University of Hawaii Press.

Schlütter, Morten. 2012. "Introduction: The Platform Sūtra, Buddhism, and Chinese religion", in *Readings of the Platform Sūtra*, edited by Morten Schlütter and Stephen F. Teiser, 1–24. New York: Columbia University Press.

Schmithausen, Lambert. 1981. "On some aspects of descriptions or theories of 'Liberating Insight' and 'Enlightenment' in early Buddhism", in *Studien zum Jainism und Buddhism*, edited by Klaus Bruhn and Albert Wezler, 199–250. Wiesbaden: Franz Steiner Verlag.

Sharf, Robert H. 1995. "Buddhist modernism and the rhetoric of meditative experience", *Numen*, 42(3): 228–83. https://doi.org/10.1163/1568527952598549

Sharf, Robert H. 2014a. "Is nirvāṇa the same as insentience? Chinese struggles with an Indian Buddhist ideal", in *India in the Chinese Imagination: Myth, Religion, and Thought*, edited by John Kieschnick and Meir Shahar, 141–70. Philadelphia: University of Pennsylvania Press.

Sharf, Robert H. 2014b. "Mindfulness and mindlessness in early Chan", *Philosophy East and West*, 64(4): 933–64. https://doi.org/10.1353/pew.2014.0074

Sharf, Robert H. 2015. "Is mindfulness Buddhist? (and why it matters)", *Transcultural Psychiatry*, 52(4): 470–84. https://doi.org/10.1177/1363461514557561

Sharf, Robert H. 2018. "Knowing blue: Early Buddhist accounts of non-conceptual sense perception", *Philosophy East and West* 68(3): 826–70. https://doi.org/10.1353/pew.2018.0075

Sheng Yen. 2001. *Hoofprint of the Ox: Principles of the Chan Buddhist Path as Taught by a Modern Chinese Master*. New York: Oxford University Press.

Sheng Yen. 2008. *The Method of No-Method*. Boston: Shambala Publications.

Shulman, Eviatar. 2008. "Early meanings of dependent-origination", *Journal of Indian Philosophy*, 36: 297–317. https://doi.org/10.1007/s10781-007-9030-8

Shulman, Eviatar. 2014. *Rethinking the Buddha: Early Buddhist Philosophy as Meditative Perception.* New York: Cambridge University Press.

Shulman, Eviatar. 2017. "Polyvalent philosophy and soteriology in early Buddhism", *Philosophy East and West*, 67(3): 864–86. https://doi.org/10.1353/pew.2017.0067

Shulman, Eviatar. 2021. *Visions of the Buddha: Creative Dimensions of Early Buddhist Scripture*. New York: Oxford University Press.

Siderits, Mark. 2011. "Buddhas as zombies: A Buddhist reduction of subjectivity", in *Self, No Self? Perspectives from Analytical, Phenomenological, and Indian Traditions*, edited by Mark Siderits, Evan Thompson, and Dan Zahavi, 308–331. Oxford: Oxford University Press.

Siderits, Mark. 2016. *Studies in Buddhist Philosophy*. Edited by Jan Westerhoff with the assistance of Christopher V. Jones. Oxford: Oxford University Press.

Siderits, Mark. 2020. "Self-knowledge and non-Self", in *Buddhist Philosophy of Consciousness: Tradition and Dialogue*, edited by Mark Siderits, Ching Keng, and John Spackman, 189–208. Leiden and Boston: Brill.

Smith, Douglass. 2015. "Was the Buddha an anti-realist?", *Journal of the Centre for Buddhist Studies*, 9: 143–78.

Solms, Mark. 2019. "The hard problem of consciousness and the free energy principle", *Frontiers in Psychology* 10: 2714 (1–16). https://doi.org/10.3389/fpsyg.2018.02714

Solms, Mark. 2021. *The Hidden Spring: A Journey to the Source of Consciousness*. London: Profile Books.

Soothill, William E., and Lewis Hodous. 2014. *A Dictionary of Chinese Buddhist Terms.* Abingdon and New York: Routledge. http://mahajana.net/texts/soothill-hodous.html

Stace, W.T. 1961. *Mysticism and Philosophy*. London: MacMillan & Co.

Stephane, Massoud, Mario Dzemidzic, and Gihyun Yoon. 2021. "Keeping the inner voice inside the head, a pilot fMRI study". *Brain and Behavior* 11: e02042. https://doi.org/10.1002/brb3.2042

Stuart, Daniel M. 2013. *Thinking about Cessation: The Pṛṣṭhapālasūtra of the Dīrghāgama in Context.* Vienna: Arbeitskreis für Tibetische und Buddhistische Studien, Universität Wien.

Stuart-Fox, Martin. 1989. "Jhāna and Buddhist scholasticism", *Journal of the International Association of Buddhist Studies*, 12(2): 79–110.

Sujato, Bhikkhu. 2012a. *A Swift Pair of Messengers: Calm with Insight in the Buddha's Words.* n.p.: Santipada.

Sujato, Bhikkhu. 2012b. *A History of Mindfulness: How Insight Worsted Tranquility in the Satipatthana sutta.* n.p.: Santipada.

Sujato, Bhikkhu, and Bhikkhu Brahmali. 2015. *The Authenticity of the Early Buddhist Texts.* Supplement to *Journal of the Oxford Centre for Buddhist Studies* vol. 5. https://ocbs.org/wp-content/uploads/2015/09/authenticity.pdf

Tartaglia, James. 2017. "What is at stake in illusionism?", in *Illusionism as a Theory of Consciousness*, edited by Keith Frankish, 294–317. Exeter: Imprint Academic.

Thanissaro, Bhikkhu (Geoffrey DeGraff). 2005. *Purity of Heart: Essays on the Buddhist Path.* Valley Center, CA: Metta Forest Monastery.

Thanissaro, Bhikkhu (Geoffrey DeGraff). 2012. *Right Mindfulness. Memory & Ardency on the Buddhist Path.* https://www.accesstoinsight.org/lib/authors/thanissaro/rightmindfulness.pdf

Tokiwa, Gishin. 1973. *A Dialogue on the Contemplation-Extinguished: Translated from the Chüeh-kuan lun, an Early Chineze Zen Text from Tun-huang.* Kyoto: Institute for Zen Studies.

Van Rullen, Rufin, and Christof Koch. 2003. "Is perception discrete or continuous?", *Trends in Cognitive Sciences*, 7(5): 207–213. https://doi.org/10.1016/S1364-6613(03)00095-0

Van Schaik, Sam. 2018. *The Spirit of Zen.* New Haven and London: Yale University Press.

Vetter, Tilmann. 1988. *The Ideas and Meditative Practices of Early Buddhism.* Leiden: Brill.

Wallace, B. Alan. 1999. "The Buddhist tradition of Samatha: Methods for refining and examining consciousness", *Journal of Consciousness Studies*, 6(2–3): 175–87.

Wallach, Wendell, Stan Franklin, and Colin Allen. 2010. "A conceptual and computational model of moral decision making in human and artificial agents", *Topics in Cognitive Science*, 2: 454–85. https://doi.org/10.1111/j.1756-8765.2010.01095.x

Wang, Huei-hsin (Wang, Ching-wei). 2001. "Zhiyi's interpretation of the concept 'dhyana' in His Shi Chan Boluomi Tsidi Famen". Dissertation, Department of East Asian Studies, The University of Arizona.

Warren, Jeff. 2013. "How understanding enlightenment could change science", *Psychology Tomorrow: Magazine*, 4. http://cecmeditate.com/inscapes4/

Wegner, Daniel. 2002. *The Illusion of Conscious Will.* Cambridge, MA: MIT Press.

Welter, Albert. 2008. *The Linji lu and the Creation of Chan Orthodoxy.* Oxford: Oxford University Press.

White, Stephen (trans.). 2020. *Diogenes Laertius: Lives of Eminent Philosophers. An Edited Translation.* Cambridge: Cambridge University Press.

Whorf, Benjamin Lee. 1940. "Science and linguistics", *MIT Technology Review*, 42: 229–31.

Wieger, Léon. 1927. *A History of the Religious Beliefs and Philosophical Opinions in China from the Beginning to the Present Time* (Edward Chalmers Werner, trans.). New York: Paragon Book Reprint Corp.

Wittgenstein, Ludwig. 2007. *Zettel.* Edited by G.E.M. Anscombe and G.H. von Wright. Translated by G.E.M Anscombe. Berkeley and Los Angeles: University of California Press.

Wittmann, Marc, and Karin Meissner. 2019. "The embodiment of time: How interoception shapes the perception of time", in *The Interoceptive Mind: From Homeostasis to Awareness*, edited by Manos Tsakiris and Helena De Preester, 63–79. Oxford: Oxford University Press.

Wolf, Chris. 2022. "The Three Similes: A comparative analysis of the Sanskrit and Pāli sources". Unpublished paper. https://www.academia.edu/51239392/The_Three_Similes_A_Comparative_Analysis_of_the_Sanskrit_and_P%C4%81li_Sources (accessed January 22, 2023).

Wynne, Alexander. 2007. *The Origin of Buddhist Meditation*. London and New York: Routledge.

Wynne, Alexander. 2009. "Early evidence for the 'no self' doctrine? A note on the second *anātman* teaching of the Second Sermon", *Thai International Journal for Buddhist Studies* 1: 59–79. (electronic version).

Wynne, Alexander. 2010. "The Ātman and its negation", *Journal of the International Association of Buddhist Studies*, 33(1–2): 103–171.

Wynne, Alexander. 2015a. *Buddhism: An Introduction*. London: IB Tauris.

Wynne, Alexander. 2015b. "Early Buddhist teaching as Proto-śūnyavāda", *Journal of the Centre for Buddhist Studies*, 9: 213–41.

Wynne, Alexander. 2018a. "Sariputta or Kaccāna? A preliminary study of two early Buddhist philosophies of mind and meditation", *Journal of the Oxford Centre for Buddhist Studies*, 14: 77–107.

Wynne, Alexander. 2018b. "Text-critical history is not exegesis: A response to Anālayo", *Journal of the Oxford Centre for Buddhist Studies*, 15: 78–105.

Wynne, Alexander. 2018c. *Early Buddhist Meditation: A Philosophical Investigation. 1. Conceptual Foundations: Sāriputta or Kaccāyana?* A talk given by Dr. Alex Wynne for the OCBS, January 29, 2018. https://soundcloud.com/user-715146666/early-buddhist-meditation-a-philosophical-investigation

Wynne, Alexander. 2018d. *Early Buddhist Meditation: A Philosophical Investigation. 4 – Jhāna*. A talk given by Dr. Alex Wynne for the OCBS on February 19, 2018. https://soundcloud.com/user-715146666/early-buddhist-meditation-a-philosophical-investigation-4

Wynne, Alexander. 2019a. "Did the Buddha exist?", *Journal of the Oxford Centre for Buddhist Studies*, 16: 98–148.

Wynne, Alexander. 2019b. "Further thoughts on the 'two path thesis'", *Journal of the Oxford Centre for Buddhist Studies*, 16: 149–62.

Wynne, Alexander. 2020a. "When the little Buddhas are no more: Vinaya transformation in the early 4th century BC", *Journal of the Oxford Centre for Buddhist Studies*, 18: 180–205.

Wynne, Alexander. 2022. "Suicide: An exploration of early Buddhist values", *Journal of the Oxford Centre for Buddhist Studies*, 22: 83–120.

Wynne, Alexander. 2023. *Meditation*. Lecture given on October 31, 2023 as part of Michaelmas DIRI Lecture Series 2023. https://www.youtube.com/watch?v=MrIJBTM-2Xo

Yamabe, Nobuyoshi. 2014. "Yogācāra influence on the Northern School of Chan Buddhism", in *Buddhist Meditative Traditions: Their Origin and Development*, edited by Kuo-pin Chuang, 249–314. Taipei: Shin Wen Feng.

Yampolsky, Philip (trans.). 1967. *The Platform Sutra of the Sixth Patriarch*. New York and London: Columbia University Press.

Yanagida, Seizan. 1983. *The Li-tai fa-pao chi and the Ch'an Doctrine of Sudden Awakening* (Carl Bielefeldt, trans.), in *Early Ch'an in China and Tibet*, edited by Whalen Lai and Lewis Lancaster, 13–49. Berkeley: Asian Humanities Press.

Yu, Jimmy. 2010. "A tentative exploration into the development of Master Sheng Yen's Chan teachings", *Chung-Hwa Buddhist Journal*, 23: 3–38.

Zahavi, Dan. 2005. *Subjectivity and Selfhood: Investigating the First-Person Perspective.* Cambridge, MA and London: The MIT Press.

INDEX

abhiññā (higher knowledge)/*abhijānāti* 107, 110, 150, 175, 322
Acinteyya-sutta 210, 217
Adamek, W. 49n, 117n
Āgamas 23–4, 72, 79–80, 130n, 136–7, 146n, 150n, 207, 249
agency 112, 114, 147, 153, 154
aggregates (*khandha*) 141, 143–9, 188, 196–7, 221
  as self, regarding 153–5, 194, 196
  in Chan texts 155–6
  non-*khandha* elements in a human being 143–4, 146–9, 188
Āḷāra Kālāma and Uddaka Rāmaputta 36, 78, 82, 83, 84, 206, 208–9
Anālayo, Bhikkhu 30n, 35n, 37n, 38–41, 61, 78, 94, 96, 163, 235n, 259n, 267n
Ānanda 161, 332–3, 334
Ānanda-sutta 75, 325
ānāpānassati (mindfulness of breathing) 33n, 190, 213, 258n, 362–5
antirealism 157–167, 220
  as opposed to naive realism and representationalism 145, 154
  in Chan texts 132–4
  in the Nikāyas 134–7
apophatic language 17, 24, 72, 101, 140, 199, 216, 225–7
apophatically described state transcending dichotomies in Chan texts 139–141, 207
Arbel, K. 2, 33n, 36n, 70, 92, 193n, 235n, 250
āruppa(s) (formless states) 36–41, 83, 199–205, 208–9
Aṭṭhakavagga 17, 139, 141, 166, 172, 175, 200, 248, 337, 355
Attwood, J. 204–5n
avyākata (undeclared questions) 219–20

Baars, B. J. 114, 179, 285, 317, 330
Baizhang Huaihai 15
  in the *Baizhang Huaihai chanshi guanglu* 53, 104, 133, 140–1, 155–6, 251–2, 295, 337–8
  in the *Tiansheng guangdeng lu* 52, 65, 170, 217, 226–7, 245, 272
Baotang school 13, 15, 52, 53n, 133, 156, 229, 295; *see also* Wuzhu
bare cognition 123, 130, 174–5, 275–6, 354–5, 363
Bhāra-sutta 144, 189
bhikkhu/bhikṣu, livelihood of
  decline of the Nikāya ideal of 294–6, 341–2
  features of, conducive for meditative progress in the Nikāyas 231–2, 280, 283, 287–94, 337
  re-emergence in Chan Buddhism 295–6
  significance of going forth 339–343
Bhikkhunupassaya-sutta 247–8, 258, 365
Bielefeldt, C. 8n, 54, 56, 105, 228–9
Blackmore, S. 180–1, 187, 193n
Bodhi, Bhikkhu 80n, 152n, 325n
Bodhidharma, in the *Erru sixing lun* 13, 100–101, 108–9, 140, 214, 272–3, 320, 327
Bodhisatta narrative 29, 36, 37, 40, 42–4, 78, 82–4, 335–7
bodily boundaries, as subjective and mentally constructed 147, 167, 184, 200–201, 203–4, 261
body ownership, sense of 153, 184, 190, 204, 261
bojjhaṅga(s) (factors of awakening) 30n, 33, 35n, 80, 249
Borghardt, T. L. 210–12, 215
Brahmajāla-sutta 78–9, 222–3
Brahmins/Brahminic ideas and practices 33–4, 35n, 43, 68, 77, 79–82, 120, 199, 206, 247
brain/neural basis of spiritual progress 126, 196, 198–9, 221, 262, 330, 343–4
Bronkhorst, J. 9n, 18n, 21, 33n, 68, 79, 80, 82n, 131n, 167, 170n, 201n, 216n, 222n, 260, 261, 279n
  on absorption and psychological transformation 94, 124, 126n,

127–31, 183, 186, 192–4, 199, 250, 258, 281n, 294n
Broughton, J. L. 243, 245n, 272n, 273n, 327
Bucknell, R. 2, 31n, 200n, 233, 235, 238n, 239, 266n
Buddhist texts
certainty regarding intended meaning, problem of 24–5, 39, 84, 125, 157, 205, 208, 243, 315, 325, 365
earliness, question of 22, 30n, 39
reading directly/at face value 8–10, 23, 40, 239
Buonomano, D. 159, 160, 178–9, 183–4

calm and insight, relation of
problems of 85–9
traditional 57, 62–3, 64, 66, 86–7, 106
various models in the Nikāyas 89–97
calm meditation, traditional form 3, 5, 19, 28–9, 34–5, 37, 43, 59–62, 253–4
as present in Chan texts 66–7
as a suppression of negative states 42–3, 49–50, 58, 70, 72, 74–6, 120, 190, 294, 299, 313
Carruthers, P. 112–13, 115, 145, 152, 182, 279, 285–6, 330
cataphatic, language 225–7
cessation
as direct cognition 172–6
as an extreme form of flow state 184–5, 191–2
in the Nikāyas, problem of 137–9, 171–6
mechanism of 172–5, 184–5, 198–9, 221
of perception and feeling (*saññāvedayitanirodha*) 36n, 139, 171, 173–4, 202–3, 205–9
short-term during daily life 185
two perspectives of describing 220–2
what is it like to be in a state of 209–15, 220
Cessations of consciousness in meditation... (Laukkonen et al.) 72n, 173n, 176n, 196, 197, 199
Cetanākaraṇīya-suttas 31, 90, 106, 255
citta/ceta(s) 42, 76, 107, 109–10, 129, 188, 221, 255, 333
and *viññāṇa* 149–53, 215, 221
during and after the fourth *jhāna* 90–91, 129, 150
vimutti (release of) *vimuccati/vimokkha* 76, 95, 107, 109, 149–50, 151, 328, 332–4
comparative study, rationale of
of Buddhism and Western philosophy 19–22
of Nikāya and Chan texts 7–10, 16–19
complementariness of different Nikāya formulas 31n, 33, 36n, 73, 190, 219, 249, 322, 329, 352, 362
concentration
as a deliberate act involving mental effort 58, 63, 68, 190, 233–4, 237–8, 247, 299, 313
developing naturally and not through a deliberate mental act 111, 247–8, 252–3, 255, 256–8, 263, 264, 282
consciousness; *see also* phenomenal consciousness; *shi* 識; *viññāṇa*
access consciousness 145, 176, 178, 182, 184–5, 194–5, 212n, 263
and the problem of identity 154–5, 194–5, 213–4, 317
and psychological time 181–8, 212–13
as discomfortable 188–9
connection with language and *saṃsāra* 162–7
discontinuity of 179–81, 186–7, 211, 215, 263
pure and self-less, possibility of experiencing 210–11, 359
role and reasons for arising of 112–15, 176–8, 191, 194, 285
constructivism, cultural 17–19, 21
Coseru, C. 21, 135, 314
Costines, C. 210–12, 215
Cūḷadukkhakkhandha-sutta 193, 261
Cūḷasakuludāyi-sutta 78–9, 81

Dambrun, M. 204n
Daofan qusheng xinjue 315–16
Daoxin 13, 16
in the *Rudao anxin yao fangbian famen* 65–7, 108, 118, 216, 244, 251–2, 271, 301–2, 308, 325–6
Dasheng kaixin xianxing dunwu zhenzong lun 132, 139, 242, 251, 326
Dasheng wusheng fangbian men 7–8, 67, 77, 101, 121, 169, 201, 251
Davis, J. H. 87n, 144n, 145, 172n, 185n
Dayi (Ehu Dayi), in the *Zuochan ming* 251
Dazhu Huihai
in the *Dunwu rudao yaomen lun* 170, 242, 271, 345
in the *Zhufang menren canwen yulu* 100, 347–8
defilements (*upakkilesa*) 75, 105, 110, 150, 257, 269, 287
ran 染 118, 170, 272, 348
Dhammapada 31, 90
Dietrich, A. 173, 182, 198–9
differences between Nikāya and early Chan approaches 131, 187, 244, 271, 350–4, 356
Dutiyasikkhattaya-sutta 149, 215
Dvedhāvitakka-sutta 78, 274, 297, 298–9

effort, right (*sammāvāyāma*) 274–5, 297–8
effortlessness, in Chan texts 250–3, 346, 348
existential
crisis, as conducive to spiritual breakthrough 332–6, 431–2
crisis, as induced through special techniques in Chan 343–4
situation of a bhikkhu 288–92
situation of a "finished person" 333–41

flow/absorption states 183–4, 186, 189, 191, 195, 199
Franklin, S. 114, 179, 235–6n, 285

Gaddulabaddha-suttas 144, 196
Garfield, J. 21, 181n, 186, 193n, 276
Gethin, R. 22, 29n, 30n, 33n, 36n, 80n, 81, 144n, 206n, 208n, 228, 230, 239, 266, 268, 362n
global accessibility/availability 129, 145, 152, 154, 157, 173, 184, 188, 207, 213, 235–6n, 285
global workspace, theory of consciousness 114–15, 177, 285
Godhika 334–5
Gombrich, R. F. 2, 22, 30n, 38–9, 91–2, 96, 134n, 135, 136n, 165–6, 197, 223, 226n, 249n
Gómez, L. O. 15, 17, 54, 59, 105–6, 307–8
Gopakamoggallāna-sutta 41, 44–5, 69
gradualism 14, 56, 57n, 105, 109, 229, 271
Greek philosophy, parallels with Buddhism 280, 283, 290, 293
Greene, E. 46, 49, 61–2, 66

Hamilton, S. 2n, 134n, 155, 144n, 166–7, 173n, 206, 219
Harvey, P. 2n, 214–5
Heze school 13, 105, 244, 304; *see also* Shenhui; Zongmi
Hinayanist meditation in the Chan discourse 46, 48, 58, 67, 77, 204
Hongren 13, 16, 77
in the *Xiuxin yao lun* 45, 52, 67, 101, 103–4, 108, 119, 155, 156, 216, 243, 252, 302–3
Hongzhou school 13, 15, 23, 49–50, 53, 217, 229, 244–5, 327, 337; *see also* Baizhang; Dayi; Dazhu; Huairang; Huangbo; Linji; Mazu
Huairang (Nanyue Huairang), in the *Zongjing lu* 140
Huangbo Xiyun, in the *Chuanxin fa yao* 49, 53, 105, 108, 141, 217, 245, 251, 320, 326–7, 345
Huineng 14, 46, 47
in the *Liuzu tanjing* 55–6, 65, 99, 109, 121, 155, 253

idealism, question of 133, 136
Indriyabhāvanā-sutta 33–35, 77
ineffability 216–20
influxes (*āsava*) 29, 40, 110, 122, 127, 129, 130, 150, 330, 333
insentience 33–36, 46, 77
problem of distinguishing from apophatically described state 116–20, 168–72, 178, 200, 207
insight meditation, traditional form 4, 5, 28, 30n, 60, 62–3, 86, 185
criticisms and problems 58–9, 85–9, 97n, 98, 125
insight/wisdom
formulas in the Nikāyas and their interpretations 95–98, 121–23, 125
coinciding with the absence of thoughts 102–5
content of 122, 123, 124
spontaneous 90, 103–8, 111
tacit 124, 125, 126, 129, 331
introspection, availability to 125, 146–7, 154, 157, 180, 181, 184, 186, 192, 193, 194, 213, 214, 215, 314, 339
Ishida, H. 308

Jains 19, 68, 78–80, 81
jhāna(s)
account of attaining in the Nikāyas 254–60
account of attaining in the *Visuddhimagga* 233–9, 253–4
and insight, various models in the Nikāyas 89–98
and insight/wisdom 31, 90, 125–6
and the removal of craving 126–7, 192–3
as a pre- or a non-Buddhist practice 28–9, 32, 60, 77–8
as a state of cognitive potency and not of insentience 91–5
breathless 41, 42–44
developing spontaneously/naturally 72, 254–60
differences between the *Visuddhimagga* and the Nikāya concept of 233–9, 253–7, 259
first, recollection by the Buddha 21, 37, 39–40, 259–60, 335
fourth 29, 35, 40, 41, 43, 52, 73, 74, 91, 92–5, 97, 125–6, 128, 129–30, 199, 209, 330
historically dominant view on 28–9
inconceivability of the range/object (*visaya*) of 210, 217
problem of 28–32
second 51, 79
third 34–5, 41, 79, 91–2, 209, 247–8

wrong 41, 44–5, 69–72
jhāyati (to meditate) 35n, 44–5, 69–70, 71–2
jiangxin 將心 (using the mind) 49, 58, 76, 85
Jianxun, Shi 93n, 255n
Jueguan lun 117, 120, 242, 345, 347, 348, 350

Kalahavivāda-sutta 139, 141, 172, 196, 200
Kāmaguṇa-sutta 137, 138, 141
Kantian, approach 142, 161,174, 201n, 202, 219
kāyagatāsati (mindfulness directed to the body) 94, 130, 262, 282, 333
Kim, Venerable (Wuxiang), in the *Lidai fabao ji* 245, 252
Kuan, Tse-fu 30n, 33n, 248, 362n

language 133, 136–7, 286
and phenomenal consciousness 162–7
brain regions, responsible for 262–3
limits of expressibility 134, 218–27
letting it be/letting go 328, 330, 333–4, 343–4
renyun 任運 66, 245, 326–8
Levman, B. G. 166, 280n
Libet, B. 113–14, 115, 147
Linji Yixuan, in the *Linji yulu* 47, 50–51, 346

Madhupiṇḍika-sutta 164, 166, 277n
Mahānidāna-sutta 162–65, 195, 323
Mahāparinibbāna-sutta 29, 36, 38–39, 231
Mahātaṇhāsaṅkhaya-sutta 94, 155
Māluṅkyaputta-sutta and *Bāhiya-sutta* 174–5, 354, 363
manuals of meditation, early Chinese 7, 8, 48–9, 61–2
Mattes, J. 183n
Mazu Daoyi 14, 15, 161
in the *Mazu Daoyi chanshi guanglu* 245
in the *Tiansheng guangdeng lu* 53, 65, 133, 139, 326, 346
in the *Zongjing lu* 64–5, 133–4, 245
in the *Zutang ji* 338
McRae, J. R. 8n, 13, 14, 15, 52, 56, 58n, 67, 101, 132n, 229, 243, 271, 349
meditation
as a deliberate activity involving mental effort 4, 5, 63, 68, 70, 76, 85, 111
as a skill in the sense of a set of activities to be learned and deliberately implemented 64, 70, 231, 232–3, 268, 296, 289, 357, 360–1
differences between right and wrong 54–59
forms criticized in Chan texts 8, 45–51, 64–6, 228–9, 246, 349
forms criticized in the Nikāyas 32–8, 42–5, 68–73
modern stereotypical approach to 360–1
prescriptive and descriptive accounts of 310, 363–4
meditative awareness of thoughts/mental activities
in Chan texts 301–7
in the Nikāyas 298–301
mechanism of pacification of thoughts 311–8
not as an actively implemented meditative method 307–11
Meissner, K. 261
memory 129, 130, 158, 182, 185, 211, 215, 282
and psychological time 179–86
traces 127, 128, 192–3, 211
Mercier, H. 115, 286, 293
metacognition 314–17
method of meditation, absence of detailed descriptions 3, 8, 228–30, 349
methodlessness of meditation 6, 10, 239–4
affirmation of, in Chan texts 241–6
affirmation of, in the Nikāyas 246–50
methodology, used in this book 3–25
Metzinger, T. 114, 153–4, 159, 178
mie 滅 (cessation/extinguishment) 46, 52, 84n, 103, 156, 302
mind
as inherently capable of concentration/insight, but obscured by negative mental factors 103–6, 108–9, 110–11, 246, 252–3, 256–7, 265, 318, 359
originally (*benlai*) pure (*qingjing*) in Chan texts 108–9, 120, 131, 155, 192
mindfulness as an active conceptual process 130, 275, 280, 297
Moheyan (Heshang Moheyan) 54, 133, 209, 305–7
motionlessness, significance in meditation 261–4
motivation of behaviour
rational and rule driven 277, 278–9
urge driven 276–84

nimitta (sign/feature) 60–1, 232–3, 238, 249–50, 300, 362, 365
Niutou (Oxhead) school 13, 15, 117–18, 120, 229; *see also Jueguan lun*; *Wuxin lun*
nīvaraṇa(s) (hindrances) 44, 70–71, 72–3
abandoning of 70, 72–3, 80, 255–7, 264, 265, 268–70, 282–3, 354
suppression in the *Visuddhimagga* 253–4
Nizamis, C. 214–5
Northern school (*beizong* 北宗) 13, 14, 15, 45, 47, 50, 132n, 271, 315

not-self (*anattā*) 147–8, 208, 214n
noumenal/objective reality 157–8, 160, 162, 224

Oghataraṇa-sutta, 247, 325, 361
ordinary mind (*pingchangxin* 平常心) 345, 347–8, 354–5

Pabhassara-sutta 109, 257, 265
pajānāti (to understand/know) 91, 122, 213, 362–3
Paṃsudhovaka-sutta 75, 110–11, 238, 257, 287–8, 297, 319, 336, 342
paññā (understanding/wisdom) 4, 162–3n, 164
paññatti (concept/designation) 135, 136, 137, 164, 167
papañca (proliferation)/*papañceti* 166, 200, 224, 350, 355
paradigm of meditation
    mainstream 5, 6, 59–64, 68, 230–31, 232–3, 233–4, 246, 303, 333, 342, 356
    unorthodox, found in Nikāya and Chan texts 5, 6, 25, 240, 246, 252, 296, 324, 342–3, 356, 357–9, 366–7
paradoxical aspects of meditation 319–20, 321, 323–5, 346–7
Pārāyanavagga 17, 139, 172, 176, 209, 212, 248
paṭiccasamuppāda (dependent origination) 197
phassa (contact)/*phuṭṭha* 139, 196, 277n
phenomenal consciousness/experience 143, 145, 146, 148, 151, 154
    as a distinct stream and inner space, problems of the concept 180–2, 212–3, 263
    as a distorted image of objective reality 154, 157–67, 178–9, 195–6
phenomenal self-model (PSM) 114n, 153–4
physicalism 145, 154
physics, modern 159–60, 163
pīti (rapture) 193, 254, 255–6, 258, 268, 353–4
pleasure 126n, 178, 183, 193, 261
    and the absence of consciousness 185–6, 191, 193
    as conducive for concentration 255–9, 353
    spiritual, arising due to a virtuous way of life 266–9, 282–4, 290–1
Poceski, M. 12n, 13, 15, 16, 48n, 50n, 217, 226n, 227n, 271, 272, 320
Polak, G. 2, 30n, 37n, 38n, 43n, 172–3, 205, 215n, 235n, 238n, 250n
predictive processing/coding 158, 172n, 176, 199
psychological transformation 124, 281
    mechanism of 126–31, 192–96

qixin 起心 (activation/arousal of the mind) 47, 52–3, 58, 65, 67, 85, 120, 121, 132–3, 139, 164, 173, 187, 191, 195, 307, 320
    non-activation (*buqi* 不起) 50, 52–3, 67, 100, 121, 139, 156, 187, 192, 323
qualitative phenomenal character/qualia 142–3, 150, 151, 159, 180, 195, 210, 212

Rama, Swami 43, 312–13
Raṭṭhapāla 340–1
Read, R. 346–7
reductionism, problem of 141, 143, 144
relaxation, significance during meditation 251–2, 259–60, 283, 292, 198
rhetoric, about meditation in the Buddhist texts 32, 55–6, 68, 80, 103, 118, 170, 229–30, 366
Rohitassa-sutta 135, 137
Rose, K. 17n
Rujing (Tiantong Rujing) 260
rūpa (shape/form/object) 139, 141, 145n, 146, 190, 196, 200

samaṇa 79, 81, 82, 199, 206, 247, 289, 336
Sāmaññaphala-sutta 7, 29, 78, 90, 129, 265–7, 290
Sāmaññaphala, pattern of the gradual path 29, 40, 73, 90, 97, 107, 248, 254–5, 257, 265–7, 282, 330–1, 354, 361–2
Samiddhilokapañhā-sutta 135, 136, 167
sampajañña (full comprehension)/*sampajāna* 34, 92, 267, 280, 282, 311
saṃsāra/birth and death (*shengsi* 生死) 132–3, 139, 140, 359
    dependence on language and phenomenal consciousness 162–7, 195, 202, 220–1
Sandha-sutta 44–5, 71–3, 172, 217–8, 222
sanjie 三界 (three Worlds) 133, 137, 167
saṅkhāra(s) 74, 189–91, 237, 284, 297–8, 300, 323, 325, 337n, 363–4
    abhisaṅkharoti / *abhisaṅkhata* 97, 111, 122, 139, 151–2n, 173, 190, 350, 355
saññā (perception)/*saññī(n)*/*sañjānāti* 135, 147, 164–6, 175, 196, 355
    cessation/absence of 137, 138–9, 175, 200, 250n
Sappadāsa 332, 335, 351
Sasaṅkhāra-sutta, 74, 97n, 190, 337n
sati/*sata* 34–5, 41, 92, 107, 130, 139, 176, 209, 279–82
satipaṭṭhāna(s) 33n, 36n, 80, 89, 247–9
Schlütter, M. 16, 55–6n, 344n
Schmithausen, L. 90
seeking/searching 328, 330–1, 333–4, 337, 345–50
    esanā 321–3, 336
    qiu 求 272–3, 320

Sekha-sutta 106, 328–9
self, illusion of 146–8, 153–5, 194
self-consciousness 184, 187, 210, 261
connection with *saṅkhāras* and tension 189–91
various levels of 183–4, 186
self-reflective, awareness 192, 199, 211, 213, 316, 363n
Sengzhao, in the *Zhaolun* 116–17
sense bases (*āyatana*) 142–3, 151, 218–19, 221
cessation of 138, 141, 143
sense faculties (*indriya*) 33–5, 142–3, 173, 221
senses, purified way of functioning 35–5, 94, 100, 117, 118, 121, 169, 173–4
sensory modalities, phenomenal and qualitative 142–3, 151, 161, 279n
Sharf, R. 54, 88, 103, 210, 229, 251n, 303, 312, 349
Sheng Yen 203–4, 244n, 344
Shenhui 14, 15, 54, 77, 139, 164, 209, 245, 272, 308, 312
in the *Putidamo nanzong ding shifei lun* 46–7, 304
in the *Tanyu* 47–8, 52, 58, 98–9, 100, 104, 109, 118, 253, 271, 304–5, 309, 319, 320, 323, 345
in the *Wenda zazheng yi* 47, 56, 58, 104, 109, 132, 156, 169, 226, 271, 305, 309
Shenxiu 14, 47
shi 識 (consciousness) 46, 52, 57n, 84n, 156, 217, 302–3, 324; *see also viññāṇa*
Shibei (Xuansha Shibei), in the *Xuansha Shibei chanshi guanglu* 49
Shulman, E. 2, 22, 36n, 43n, 91, 93, 124n, 135n, 144n, 147n, 171, 173n, 197, 206, 208n
Siderits, M. 21, 112, 114n, 135, 181n, 314
Sīhā 332, 335, 351
silent illumination (*mozhao* 默照) 102, 203–4
Solms, M. 112n, 158, 176–8, 186, 262, 263, 276n, 283
Song era Chan 13, 15, 16, 102, 260, 338–9, 344
Southern Chan 14, 15, 109, 244, 271
space and time, constructed nature of 159–61, 163, 178–9, 195–6, 219–20, 222–3
speech, significance for meditation 279, 292–4
Sperber, D. 115, 286, 293
spiritual breakthrough 327–44, 351
spiritual progress
factors of, not straightforwardly practicable 331, 333, 339–40, 342–3, 359
strivings (*padhāna*) 42–4, 76, 83–4, 205–6, 337n
Stuart-Fox, M. 235, 255, 294n
subitism 14, 55, 57n, 105, 109, 230, 244, 271, 320, 345
suicide 332–5
Sujato, Bhikkhu 11, 89

Tartaglia, J. 160–61
Tathāgata 137, 218–20, 222–25
teacher of meditation 4, 230–2
tension 126n, 128, 183, 186, 192–3
Thanissaro, Bhikkhu 83, 93–4
thoughts/mental movement; *see also vitakka*
connected with the dhamma (*dhammavitakka*) 110–11, 238, 288, 297, 318, 319, 321, 323, 336, 364
evolutionary and cognitive causes of 276–9, 284–7
social roots of 284–88
Tianzhu guo Putidamo chan shi lun 46
time, psychological 178–84, 191

Udayamāṇavapucchā 139, 172, 176, 212
uncertainty, tendency to minimize in cognition 177–8, 186, 263, 283
unconscious cognitive processes 112–15, 124, 131, 176–8, 276, 284, 330
Upakkilesa-sutta 78, 95, 232n
upekkhā (equanimity)/*upekkhaka/upekkhati* 34, 25, 41, 92, 95, 107, 129–30, 209

Vago, D. 172n, 185
Van Schaik, S. 66n, 244n, 252n, 272n, 273n, 302n, 326
vedayita (what is experienced/felt)/*vedanā* 94, 154, 188–9, 191–2, 194, 311
Vetter, T. 2, 259
Vinaya 93, 231, 232, 271n, 332–3, 348, 349–50
viññāṇa (consciousness) 91, 122, 155, 163; *see also citta*; consciousness; *shi* 識
cessation/stopping of/absence 139, 147, 150, 172, 176, 197, 215
special and luminous, that can exist after death 214–5, 224
virtuous and disciplined way of life 266–74, 279–84, 351
Visuddhimagga 7, 59–60, 86–7, 96, 98, 127, 208, 230, 233–9, 253–4, 296, 361
vitakka and *vicāra* 51, 233, 234–8, 254, 353
Vitakkasaṇṭhāna-sutta 77, 250n, 299–301

Wang, Huei-hsin (Wang Ching-wei) 235
wang 妄 (delusion/deluded) 65, 101, 109, 133, 214, 227, 245, 302, 348
wangnian 妄念 (deluded thought) 103, 104, 109, 305
wangxin 妄心 (deluded mind) 47, 85, 53, 132, 319

Warren, J. 172n, 185
Wegner, D. 114, 147
Weizhao (Chanti Weizhao), in the *Sengbao zhengxu zhuan* 338–9
will and deliberate decision, role in spiritual progress 325–6, 328, 330, 333–4, 347
wisdom (*hui* 慧/惠) in Chan texts 85, 99, 104, 155, 217
    and *sāmadhi* (*ding*), the union of 98–102, 121
Witmann, M. 210–12, 215, 261
Wittgenstein, L. 174n
world (*loka*) 134–6, 161–2
wunian 無念 (no-thought) 52, 118, 140, 156, 192, 209, 226, 245, 304–5, 353–4, 364
wuwei 無為 119, 187, 192, 216, 243, 273
Wuxin lun 23, 117–20, 303–4
wuxin 無心 (no-mind) 116–20, 187, 192
Wuye (Fenzhou Wuye), in the *Zimen jingxun* 295
Wuzhu, in the *Lidai fabao ji* 48, 52, 65, 118, 132–3, 137, 140, 164, 165, 216–7, 245, 252, 295
wuzuo 無作 (non-doing) 244, 308, 309, 347, 355
Wynne, A. 22, 23, 37n, 82n, 83n, 136, 206, 222n, 223, 291–2n, 294n, 296n, 334n
    on early Buddhist meditation 90, 92–3, 95, 122–3, 129, 130, 209, 239n, 250n, 296n, 355n
    on philosophical ideas of early Buddhism 136, 146, 147n, 148n, 165, 166, 197n, 218, 219, 220, 225

yogic practices 43, 74, 81, 83, 204–7, 292, 312, 335, 336, 337n
Yu, J. 344

zaozuo 造作 (fabrication) 58, 65, 74, 346
Zhiyi 7
    in the *Fajie cidi chumen* 63
    in the *Shi chan boluomi cidi famen* 234–5, 353
    in the *Xiuxi zhiguan zuochan fayao* 62
Zongmi (Guifeng Zongmi) 50n, 209, 245, 312
    in the *Chanyuan zhuquanji duxu* 50, 105, 108, 169, 228, 305
    in the *Yuanjuejing dashu shiyi chao* 133, 156, 397
Zongze (Changlu Zongze), in the *Zuochan yi* 305, 353
zuoyi 作意 (conscious act of intention/attention) 52, 58, 65, 74, 85, 139, 187, 191–2, 307

www.ingramcontent.com/pod-product-compliance
Lightning Source LLC
LaVergne TN
LVHW012233070225
803225LV00042B/1200
9781800504257